Out of Many

Out of Many

Fifth Edition

A History of the American People

TEACHING AND LEARNING CLASSROOM EDITION

VOLUME ONE

John Mack Faragher
YALE UNIVERSITY

Mari Jo Buhle
BROWN UNIVERSITY

Daniel Czitrom
MOUNT HOLYOKE COLLEGE

Susan H. Armitage
WASHINGTON STATE UNIVERSITY

PEARSON

Prentice
Hall

Upper Saddle River, New Jersey 07458

Library of Congress Cataloging-in-Publication Data

Out of many: a history of the American people / John Mack Faragher ... [et al.]. — Brief
  TLC 5th ed.
    p. cm.
  Includes bibliographical references and index.
  ISBN 0-13-601565-4 (combined volume) — ISBN 0-13-601567-0 (v. 1) — ISBN 0-13-601566-2 (v. 2)
  1. United States–History–Textbooks.   I. Faragher, John Mack, 1945–
E178.1.O935 2008
973—dc22   2008001076

> To Our Students,
> Our Sisters,
> And Our Brothers

AVP, Publisher: Charlyce Jones Owen
Executive Marketing Manager: Sue Westmoreland
Editorial Assistant: Maureen Diana
Marketing Assistant: Sarah Aswell
Operations Specialist: Maura Zaldivar
Media Editor: Mayda Bosco
Creative Design Director: Maria Lange
Interior Design: Ilze Lemesis
Cover Design: Blair Brown
AV Project Manager: Mirella Signoretto

Project Manager: Denise Brown
Full-Service Production and Composition: Fiorella Mari/Prepare
Director, Image Resource Center: Melinda Patelli
Manager, Rights and Permissions: Zina Arabia
Manager, Visual Research: Beth Brenzel
Manager, Cover Visual Research and Permissions: Karen Sanatar
Image Permission Coordinator: Michelina Viscusi
Printer/Binder: Quad/Graphics
Cover Printer: Phoenix Color

Credits and acknowledgments borrowed from other sources and reproduced, with permission, in this textbook appear on appropriate page within text (or on pages C1–C4).

Pearson Prentice Hall™ is a trademark of Pearson Education, Inc.
Pearson® is a registered trademark of Pearson plc
Prentice Hall® is a registered trademark of Pearson Education, Inc.

Pearson Education LTD.
Pearson Education Australia PTY, Limited
Pearson Education Singapore, Pte. Ltd
Pearson Education North Asia Ltd

Pearson Education, Canada, Ltd
Pearson Educación de Mexico, S.A. de C.V.
Pearson Education–Japan
Pearson Education Malaysia, Pte. Ltd

10 9 8 7 6 5 4

ISBN-10:   0-13-601567-0
ISBN-13:   978-0-13-601567-3

BRIEF CONTENTS

v

6 FROM EMPIRE TO INDEPENDENCE,
1750–1776   126

7 THE AMERICAN REVOLUTION,
1776–1786   154

8

THE NEW NATION, 1786–1800   180

Seeing History

9

AN EMPIRE FOR LIBERTY, 1790–1824   206

Seeing History

10

THE SOUTH AND SLAVERY, 1790s–1850s 238

Seeing History

11

THE GROWTH OF DEMOCRACY, 1824–1840 266

Seeing History

Interpreting the Past

21

URBAN AMERICA AND THE PROGRESSIVE ERA, 1900–1917 556

Seeing History

22

A GLOBAL POWER, 1901–1920 590

Seeing History

23

THE TWENTIES, 1920–1929   622

Seeing History

Interpreting the Past

24

THE GREAT DEPRESSION AND THE NEW DEAL, 1929–1940   660

29

WAR ABROAD, WAR AT HOME, 1965–1974   822

Seeing History

30

THE CONSERVATIVE ASCENDANCY, 1974–1991   854

Seeing History

MAPS

Denotes Interactive Map Exploration

CHARTS, GRAPHS & TABLES

SEEING HISTORY

INTERPRETING THE PAST

AMERICAN COMMUNITIES

OVERVIEW TABLES

Out of Many: A History of the American People, fifth edition, offers a distinctive and timely approach to American history, highlighting the experiences of diverse communities of Americans in the unfolding story of our country. The stories of these communities offer a way of examining the complex historical forces shaping people's lives at various moments in our past. The debates and conflicts surrounding the most momentous issues in our national life—independence, emerging democracy, slavery, westward settlement, imperial expansion, economic depression, war, technological change—were largely worked out in the context of local communities. Through communities we focus on the persistent tensions between everyday life and those larger decisions and events that continually reshape the circumstances of local life.

Each chapter opens with a description of a representative community. Some of these portraits feature American communities struggling with one another: African slaves and English masters on the rice plantations of colonial Georgia, or *Tejanos* and Americans during the Texas war of independence. Other chapters feature portraits of communities facing social change: the feminists of Seneca Falls, New York, in 1848, or the African Americans of Montgomery, Alabama, in 1955. As the story unfolds we find communities growing to include ever larger groups of Americans: the soldiers from every colony who forged the Continental Army into a patriotic national force at Valley Forge during the American Revolution, or the moviegoers who aspired to a collective dream of material prosperity and upward mobility during the 1920s.

Out of Many is also the only American history text with a truly continental perspective. With community vignettes from New England to the South, the Midwest to the far West, we encourage students to appreciate the great expanse of our nation. For example, a vignette of seventeenth-century Santa Fé, New Mexico, illustrates the founding of the first European settlements in the New World. We present territorial expansion into the American West from the viewpoint of the Mandan villagers of the upper Missouri River of North Dakota. A continental perspective drives home to students that American history has never been the preserve of any particular region.

Out of Many includes extensive coverage of our diverse heritage. Our country is appropriately known as "a nation of immigrants," and the history of immigration to America, from the seventeenth to the twenty-first centuries, is fully integrated into the text. There is sustained and close attention to our place in the world, with special emphasis on our relations with the nations of the Western Hemisphere, especially our near neighbors, Canada and Mexico.

In these ways *Out of Many* breaks new ground, but without compromising its coverage of the traditional turning points that we believe are critically important to an understanding of the American past. *Out of Many* also looks back in a new and comprehensive way—from the vantage point of the beginning of a new century and the end of the Cold War—at the salient events of the last fifty years and their impact on American communities. The community focus of *Out of Many* weaves the stories of the people and the nation into a single compelling narrative.

Out of Many, fifth edition, is completely updated with the most recent scholarship on the history of America and the United States. All the chapters have been extensively reviewed, revised, and rewritten. The final chapter details the tumultuous events of the new century, including a completely new section on the "war on terror," and concluding with the national election of 2004. Throughout the book the text and graphics are presented in a stunning new design. Moreover, this edition incorporates two important new features designed to bring history vividly alive for students: *Interpreting the Past*, featuring primary sources on a controversial provocative historical issue and *Seeing History*, carefully chosen images that show how visual sources can illuminate their understanding of American history.

SPECIAL FEATURES

With each edition of *Out of Many, Teaching and Learning Classroom Edition*, we have sought to strengthen its unique integration of the best of traditional American history with its innovative community-based focus and strong continental perspective and engage students through special features that encourage their exploration of the questions that historians seek to answer about the past. This new version is no exception. A wealth of special features and pedagogical aids reinforces our narrative and motivates students desire to understand and appreciate America's history. The special walkthrough on pages xxiii–xlii highlights these features.

COMMUNITY AND DIVERSITY

This special introductory essay begins students' journey into the narrative history that unfolds in *Out of Many*. The essay acquaints students with the major themes of the book and provides them with a framework for understanding American History. (pp. xliii–xlv)

SUPPLEMENTARY MATERIAL

Out of Many is supported by an extensive supplements package for instructors and students that gives flexibility to the process of teaching and learning. A full description of the supplements available with the text is provided on page xlii.

ACKNOWLEDGMENTS

In the years it has taken to bring *Out of Many* from idea to reality and to improve it in successive editions, we have often been reminded that although writing history sometimes feels like isolated work, it actually involves a collective effort. We want to thank the dozens of people whose efforts have made the publication of this book possible.

We wish to thank our many friends at Prentice Hall for their efforts in creating the fifth edition of *Out of Many*: Yolanda de Rooy, President; Charlyce Jones Owen, Publisher; Jeannine Cilotta and James Miller, Development Editors; Rochelle Diogenes, Editor-in-Chief, Development Sue Westmoreland, Executive Marketing Manager; Brandy Dawson, Director of Marketing; Mayda Bosco, Media Editor; Denise Brown, Production Liaison; Mary Carnis, Managing Editor; Blair Brown, Cover Designer; Fiorella Mari, Production Editor; and Donna Mulder, Copyeditor. We also thank John Reisbord for his editorial contributions to the fifth edition.

Although we share joint responsibility for the entire book, the chapters were individually authored: John Mack Faragher wrote chapters 1–8; Susan Armitage wrote chapters 9–16; Mari Jo Buhle wrote chapters 18–20, 25–26, 29; and Daniel Czitrom wrote chapters 17, 21–24, 27–28. (For this edition Buhle and Czitrom co-authored Chapters 30–31.)

Each of us depended on a great deal of support and assistance with the research and writing that went into this book. We want to thank: Kathryn Abbott, Nan Boyd, Krista Comer, Jennifer Cote, Crista DeLuzio, Keith Edgerton, Carol Frost, Jesse Hoffnung Garskof, Pailin Gaither, Jane Gerhard, Todd Gernes, Mark Krasovic, Melani McAlister, Cristi, Rebecca McKenna, and Mitchell, J. C. Mutchler, Keith Peterson, Alan Pinkham, Tricia Rose, Gina Rourke, Jessica Shubow, Gordon P. Utz Jr., Maura Young, Teresa Bill, Gill Frank, and Naoko Shibusawa.

Our families and close friends have been supportive and ever so patient over the many years we have devoted to this project. But we want especially to thank Paul Buhle, Meryl Fingrutd, Bob Greene, and Michele Hoffnung.

John Mack Faragher   John Mack Faragher is Arthur Unobskey Professor of American History and director of the Howard R. Lamar Center for the Study of Frontiers and Borders at Yale University. Born in Arizona and raised in southern California, he received his B.A. at the University of California, Riverside, and his Ph.D. at Yale University. He is the author of *Women and Men on the Overland Trail* (1979), *Sugar Creek: Life on the Illinois Prairie* (1986), *Daniel Boone: The Life and Legend of an American Pioneer* (1992), *The American West: A New Interpretive History* (2000), and *A Great and Noble Scheme: The Tragic Story of the Expulsion of the French Acadians from their American Homeland* (2005).

Daniel Czitrom   Daniel Czitrom is Professor of History at Mount Holyoke College. Born and raised in New York City, he received his B.A. from the State University of New York at Binghamton and his M.A. and Ph.D. from the University of Wisconsin, Madison. He is the author of *Media and the American Mind: From Morse to McLuhan* (1982), which won the First Books Award of the American Historical Association and has been translated into Spanish and Chinese. He is co-author of *Rediscovering Jacob Riis: Exposure Journalism and Photography in Turn of the Century New York* (2007). He has served as a historical consultant and featured on-camera commentator for several documentary film projects, including the PBS productions *New York: A Documentary Film; American Photography: A Century of Images;* and *The Great Transatlantic Cable.* He currently serves on the Executive Board of the Organization of American Historians.

Mari Jo Buhle   Mari Jo Buhle is William R. Kenan Jr. University Professor and Professor of American Civilization and History at Brown University, specializing in American women's history. She received her B.A. from the University of Illinois, Urbana–Champaign, and her Ph.D. from the University of Wisconsin, Madison. She is the author of *Women and American Socialism, 1870–1920* (1981) and *Feminism and Its Discontents: A Century of Struggle with Psychoanalysis* (1998). She is also coeditor of *Encyclopedia of the American Left,* second edition (1998). Professor Buhle held a fellowship (1991–1996) from the John D. and Catherine T. MacArthur Foundation.

Susan H. Armitage   Susan H. Armitage is Claudius O. and Mary R. Johnson Distinguished Professor of History at Washington State University. She earned her Ph.D. from the London School of Economics and Political Science. Among her many publications on western women's history are three coedited books, *The Women's West* (1987), *So Much To Be Done: Women on the Mining and Ranching Frontier* (1991), and *Writing the Range: Race, Class, and Culture in the Women's West* (1997). She currently serves as an editor of a series of books on women and American history for the University of Illinois Press.

Out of Many

Dear Reader,

Out of Many grew out of our years of experience teaching the American history survey course. When we were young professors, the old narrative of strict political history was in the process of being supplemented with a new narrative of social history. But the two remained mostly unconnected. New textbooks sequestered these two narratives in separate chapters. Isn't there a way, we wondered, to write a new, unified narrative of American history, in which political and social history might be combined? This was the inspiration behind *Out of Many*, one of the most successful American history textbooks of this generation. Organized around the theme of American communities, the text offers a single, engaging narrative of American social, economic, and political history.

We began working on this book twenty years ago. It has been a long and rewarding journey. We are proud to have been the first American history college text to put the diversity of America's peoples at the center of our historical experience. Our narrative weaves the distinct experiences and voices of northerners, southerners, and westerners, of African Americans, Latinos, and immigrants, of women and men, throughout each chapter. Coming ourselves from different backgrounds and from different regions of the country, we developed a continental approach to the American past, demonstrating how each region has been closely linked to the broader currents of global development. It is our hope that *Out of Many* will best help students understand the history that has produced the increasingly complex America of the twenty-first century.

Out of Many, you experience America's history...

Out of Many provides truly integrated coverage of American social and political history. The authors weave the everyday stories of individuals and communities and the major events of the nation's political history into a single compelling narrative that both enlightens and inspires students. This integrated approach to history offers students the best possible insight into the American experience.

The TLC Edition of *Out of Many* offers **an engaging visual presentation** to pique—and retain—student interest. The text is packed with **stunning visuals** including chapter openers that highlight key events in the chapter. **Chapter opening questions** provide an overview and guide to the important concepts students need to learn.

The TLC Edition of *Out of Many* includes **a variety of pedagogical tools** to help students organize and reinforce their learning.

AMERICAN COMMUNITIES
Expansion Touches Mandan Villages on the Upper Missouri

In mid-October 1804, news arrived at the Mandan Villages, prominently situated on bluffs overlooking the upper Missouri River, that an American military party led by Meriwether Lewis and William Clark was coming up the river. The principal chiefs, hoping for expanded trade and support against their enemies the Sioux, welcomed these first American visitors. As the expedition's three boats and forty-three men approached the village, Clark wrote, "great numbers on both sides flocked down to the bank to view us." That evening, the Mandans welcomed the Americans with an enthusiastic dance and gifts of food.

Lewis and Clark had been sent by President Thomas Jefferson to survey the Louisiana Purchase and to find an overland route to the Pacific Ocean. They were also instructed to inform the Indians that they now owed loyalty—and trade—to the American government. Meeting with the village chiefs, the Americans off...

ies, the party reached the Pacific Ocean at the mouth of the Columbia River, where they spent the winter. Overdue and feared lost, they returned in triumph to St. Louis in September 1806. Before long the Americans had established Fort Clark at the Mandan villages, giving American traders a base for challenging British dominance of the western fur trade. The permanent American presence brought increased contact, and with it much more disease. In 1837, a terrible smallpox epidemic carried away the vast majority of the Mandans, reducing the population to fewer than 150. Four Bears, a Mandan chief who had been a child at the time of the Lewis and Clark visit, spoke these last words to the remnants of his people:

"I have loved the whites," he declared. "I have lived with them ever since I was a boy." But in return for the kindness of the Mandans, the Americans had brought this plague. "I do not fear death, my friends," he said, "but to die with my face rotten, that even the wolves will shrink with horror at seeing me, and ...y to themselves, that is Four Bears, the friend of the whites. ...have deceived me," he pronounced with his last breath. ...always considered as brothers turned ou...

Out of Many is among the first texts to focus on the many ethnic and multicultural communities that have played a vital role in the evolution of the United States. Each chapter begins with an ***American Community*** feature that shows how the events discussed in the chapter affected a particular community. These snapshots of life add up to a well-rounded understanding of the American story.

Creating Celebrity

Seeing History

A common definition for "celebrity" is one who is famous for being famous. Although politics, the arts, science, and the military have produced famous people for centuries, the celebrity is a twentieth-century phenomenon, one closely linked to the emergence of modern forms of mass media. In the 1920s Hollywood's "star system," along with tabloid newspapers and the new profession of public relations, created the modern celebrity. Film producers were at first wary of identifying screen actors by name, but they soon discovered that promoting popular leading actors would boost the box office for their movies. The use of "close-ups" in movies and the fact that screen images were literally larger than life distinguished the images of film actors from, say, stage performers or opera singers.

WHAT VISUAL themes strike you as most powerful in the accompanying images? How do they compare to celebrity images of today? Why do you think male stars such as Valentino and Fairbanks were so often portrayed as exotic foreigners?

Fans identified with their favorites in contradictory ways. Stars like Charlie Chaplin and Mary Pickford were like royalty. Audiences were also curious about the stars' private lives. Film studios took advantage of this curiosity by carefully controlling the public im... releases, planted stories in newspapers, and ca... ...arances. By the 1920s film stars were essenti... ...ring enormous capital investment. ∎

New ***Seeing History*** features offer in-depth analysis of an image or series of images from a particular historical period. These visually engaging features help students to understand how various individuals and events have been depicted throughout American history and underscore the important role images and illustrations play in understanding and interpreting the past.

New to the Fifth Edition, ***Interpreting the Past*** features provide documents and images on a key event or topic to help students see how historians understand and interpret the past. A critical thinking question provides students with the opportunity to analyze how these historical records illuminate this event or topic.

Realities of Freedom

The Freedmen's Bureau established in 1865 by Congress provided freedmen with clothing, temporary shelter, food, and series of freedmen's schools across the South. Southern response was to fall into the use of terror to deter blacks from becoming economically independent using the agencies of groups like the Ku Klux Klan. Sharecropping, tenant farming, and peonage were insidious economic arrangements that placed whites and blacks in a form of economic slavery to large land holders in the South of the post-Civil War era.

FOLLOWING EMANCIPATION, what economic and social opportunities existed for African Americans in the United States? How did these opportunities change the lives of freedmen after the official end to slavery?

The story of African Americans after the end of slavery is complex and varied. Some blacks attempted to seek out better places to establish their new lives while others remained in the security of the only home they had known as slaves. ∎

Interpreting the Past

AN ACT TO ESTABLISH A BUREAU FOR THE RELIEF OF FREEDMEN AND REFUGEES, 1865

BE IT enacted, That there is hereby established in the War Department, to continue during the present war of rebellion, and for one year thereafter, a bureau of refugees, freedmen, and abandoned lands, to which shall be committed, as hereinafter provided, the supervision and management of all abandoned lands, and the control of all subjects relating to refugees and freedmen from rebel states, or from any district of country within the territory embraced in the operations of the army, under such rules and regulations as may be prescribed by the head of the bureau and approved by the President. The said bureau shall be under the management and control of a commissioner to be appointed by the President, by and with the advice and consent of the Senate... ∎

◄ African-American family working together in the cotton fields.

WHEN WE WORKED ON SHARES, WE COULDN'T MAKE NOTHING

AFTER SLAVERY we had to get in before night too. If you didn't, Ku Klux would drive you in. They would come and visit you anyway. . . . When he got you good and scared he would drive on away. They would whip you if they would catch you out in the night time. . . .

I've forgot who it is that that told us that we was free. Somebody come and told us we're free now. I done forgot who it was.

After freedom, we worked on shares a while. Then we rented. When we worked on shares, we couldn't make nothing, just overalls and something to eat. Half went to the other man and you would destroy your half if you weren't careful. A man that didn't know how to count would always lose. He might lose anyhow. They didn't give no itemized statement. No, you just had to take their word. They never give you no details. They just say you owe so much. No matter how good account you kept, you had to go by their account and now, Brother, I'm tellin' you the truth about this. It's been that way for a long time. You had to take the white man's word on note, and everything. Anything you

A Share croppers and their families were evicted from the plantation they were working after being convicted of engaging in a conspiracy to retain their homes. This picture was taken just after the evictions before the families were moved into a tent colony.

wanted, you could git if you were a good hand. You could git anything you wanted as long as you worked. If you didn't make no money, that's all right; they would advance you more. But you better not leave him, you better not try to leave and get caught. They'd keep you in debt. . . . Anything that kept you a slave because he was always right and you were always wrong. . . . ∎

SHARE CROPPER CONTRACT, 1882

To every one applying to rent land upon shares, the following conditions must be read, and agreed to.

To every 30 or 35 acres, I agree to furnish the team, plow, and farming implements, except cotton planters, and I do not agree to furnish a cart to every cropper. The croppers are to have half of the cotton, corn and fodder (and peas and pumpkins and potatoes if any are planted. . . .

Croppers are to have no part or interest in the cotton seed raised from the crop planted and worked by them. No vine crops of any description, that is, no watermelons, muskmelons,...squashes or anything of that kind, except peas and pumpkins, and potatoes, are to be planted in the cotton or corn. All must work under my direction. All plantation work to be done by the croppers. . . .

For every mule or horse furnished by me there must be 1000 good sized rails...hauled, and the fence repaired as far as they will go, the fence to be torn down and put up from the bottom if I so direct. All croppers to haul rails and work on fence whenever I may order. Rails to be split when I may say. . . .

Each cropper must keep in good repair all bridges in his crop or over ditches that he has to clean out and when a bridge needs repairing that is outside of all their crops, then any one that I call on must repair it. . . .

No cropper to work off the plantation when there is any work to be done on the land he has rented, or when his work is needed by me or other croppers. Trees to be cut down on Orchard, House field & Evanson fences, leaving such as I may designate. . . . . ∎

*O*ut *of* Many, you experience America's history...

Out of Many's Teaching and Learning Classroom (TLC) Edition offers an engaging visual design and numerous tools that help students learn and review the material.

---

864   CHAPTER 30   THE CONSERVATIVE ASCENDANCY, 1974–1991

QUICK REVIEW

Hostages

* November 4, 1979: Iranian fundamentalists seized U.S. embassy in Tehran.
* Fifty-two Americans held hostage for 444 days.
* Crisis doomed the Carter presidency.

WHAT EXPLAINS the rise of the New Right in the 1980s?

myhistorylab

Review Summary

QUICK REVIEW

The Conservative Critique

* Free markets work better than government programs.
* Government intervention does more harm than good.
* Government assistance saps the initiative of the poor.

leaving eight Americans dead, their burned corpses displayed by the enraged Iranians. Short of an all-out ...
death, Carter had used ...
The political and ...
secretary of state in six ...
the president. The price ...
he had proclaimed cen...
violated his own huma...
mark on American fore...

THE NEW RI...

The failures in U...
played a large ...
resentment."

NEOCONSERVATIS...

By the mid-1970s, a new...
scape: neoconservatism...
been liberal Democrats...
tling social movement...
Deal–style liberalism an...
to repeal affirmative a...
enacted during the Joh...
was, however, foreign po...
neoconservatives called...
Neoconservatives ...
dation for the rightwar...
donors, they established...
shaping discussions. T...
neoconservatives and p...

THE RELIGIOUS R...

Evangelical Protestants, ...
the backbone of the n...
neoconservative positio...
they provided the politi...
the margins to the cen...

WHAT MAJOR groups made up the Southern Republicans?

myhistorylab

Review Summary

Union League Republican party organizations in Northern cities that became an important organizing device among freedmen in Southern cities after 1865.

Carpetbaggers Northern transplants to the South, many of whom were Union soldiers who stayed in the South after the war.

...ican political activi...
out the South.
Begun during the wa...
club, the Union League now be...
Union League chapters brought togethe...
Freedmen's Bureau agents to demand the vote and ...
tion against African Americans. It brought out African American voters, ...
freedmen in the rights and duties of citizenship, and promoted Republican candidates. Not surprisingly, newly enfranchised freedmen voted Republican and formed the core of the Republican Party in the South. For most ordinary African Americans, politics was inseparable from economic issues, especially the land question. Grassroots political organizations frequently intervened in local disputes with planters over the terms of labor contracts. African American political groups closely followed the congressional debates over Reconstruction policy and agitated for land confiscation and distribution. Perhaps most important, politics was the only arena where black and white Southerners might engage each other on an equal basis.

SOUTHERN POLITICS AND SOCIETY

By the summer of 1868, when the South had returned to the Union, the majority of Republicans believed the task of Reconstruction to be finished. Ultimately, they put their faith in a political solution to the problems facing the vanquished South. Most Republican congressmen were moderates, conceiving Reconstruction in limited terms. They rejected radical calls for confiscation and redistribution of land, as well as permanent military rule of the South. The Reconstruction Acts of 1867 and 1868 laid out the requirements for the readmission of southern states, along with the procedures for forming and electing new governments.

Yet over the next decade, the political structure created in the southern states proved too restricted and fragile to sustain itself. To most southern whites, the active participation of African Americans in politics seemed extremely dangerous. Federal troops were needed to protect Republican governments and their supporters from violent opposition. Congressional action to monitor southern elections and protect black voting rights became routine. Despite initial successes, southern Republicanism proved an unstable coalition of often conflicting elements, unable to sustain effective power for very long. By 1877, Democrats had regained political control of all the former Confederate states.

SOUTHERN REPUBLICANS

Three major groups composed the fledgling Republican coalition in the postwar South. African American voters made up a large majority of southern Republicans throughout the Reconstruction era. Yet African Americans outnumbered whites in only three southern states; Republicans would have to attract white support to win elections and sustain power.

A second group consisted of white Northerners, derisively called "**carpetbaggers**" by native white Southerners. Most were veterans of the Union army who stayed in the South after the war. Others included Freedmen's Bureau agents and businessmen who had invested capital in cotton plantations and other enterprises. Although they made up a tiny percentage of the population, carpetbaggers played

---

Critical thinking questions from the chapter opener are repeated in the margins at each major section of the chapter to promote critical reading. **Quick reviews** help students review selected topics as they go through the chapter.

A running glossary provides definitions for key terms and concepts, which are then listed at the end of the chapter for review.

...through an engaging learner-centered format.

OVERVIEW | Currents of Progressivism

	Key Figures	Issues
Local Communities	Jane Addams, Lillian Wald, Florence Kelley, Frederic C. Howe, Samuel Jones	• Improving health, education, welfare in urban immigrant neighborhoods • Child labor, eight-hour day • Celebrating immigrant cultures • Reforming urban politics • Municipal ownership/regulation of utilities
State	Robert M. La Follette, Hiram Johnson, Al Smith	• Limiting power of railroads, other corporations • Improving civil service • Direct democracy • Applying academic scholarship to human needs
National	James K. Vardaman, Hoke Smith, Theodore Roosevelt, Woodrow Wilson	• Disfranchisement of African Americans • Trust-busting • Conservation and western development • National regulation of corporate and financial excesses • Reform of national banking
Intellectual/Cultural	Jacob Riis, Lincoln Steffens, Ida Tarbell, Upton Sinclair, S. S. McClure	• Muckraking
	John Dewey, Louis Brandeis, Edwin A. Ross	• Education reform • Sociological jurisprudence • Empowering "ethical elite"

myhistorylab

Overview: *Currents of Progressivism*

She offered Henry Street as a meeting place to the National Negro Conference in 1909, out of which emerged the National Association for the Advancement of Colored People.

Social reformer Florence Kelley helped direct the support of the settl... behind groundbreaking state and federal lab...

Overview tables help students review key points of complex topics and issues. References to the **Myhistorylab** website and the **Primary Source CDROM** are included in the margins throughout the chapters to alert students to documents, activities, and additional content related to topics in the chapters.

Map Explorations are selected maps that can be explored interactively on the Web and MyHistoryLab. **Critical thinking questions** help to strengthen map analysis skills and geographic literacy.

THE CONSERVATIVE ASCENDANCY, 1974–1991 **CHAPTER 30** 859

depressed Northeast to boost the region's population (see Map 30.2).

The Sunbelt witnessed a dramatic turnaround in demographic and economic trends. Southern cities reversed the century-long trend of out-migration among African Americans. The Southwest and West changed yet more dramatically. California became the nation's most populous state; Texas moved to third, behind New York. Former farms and deserts were turned almost overnight into huge metropolitan areas ringed by new automobile-dependent suburbs. Phoenix grew from 664,000 in 1960 to 1,509,000 in 1980, Las Vegas from 127,000 to 463,000.

Much Sunbelt wealth tended to be temporary or sharply cyclical, producing a boom-and-bust economy. Income was also distributed unevenly. Older Hispanic populations made only modest gains, while recent Mexican immigrants and Indian peoples suffered from a combination of low wages and poor public services. The Sunbelt states directed their tax and federal dollars to strengthening police forces, building roads or sanitation systems for the expanding suburbs, and creating budget surpluses.

The "Snowbelt" (or "Rustbelt") states, longtime centers of voting strength for the Democratic Party, meanwhile suffered severe population losses accompanying the sharp decline of industry.

New York City offered a spectacular example of decline. A fiscal crisis in 1975 forced Democratic Mayor Abraham Beame to choose between wage freezes for public employees and devastating cuts and layoffs. Eventually, with the municipal government teetering on the brink of bankruptcy, he chose both. In respon... ...backs in mass transit and the deteriorati... ...r of the middle class fled.

  MAP EXPLORATION

To explore an interactive version of this map, go to http://www.prenhall.com/faraghertic/map30.2

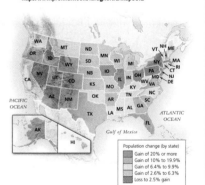

MAP 30.2
Population Shifts, 1970–80 Industrial decline in the Northeast coincided with an economic boom in the Sunbelt, encouraging millions of Americans to head for warmer climates and better jobs.

HOW WERE the changes in population between 1970 and 1980 reflected in the American economy?

OUT OF MANY **xxxvii**

*O*ut *of* Many, you experience America's history…

Every new copy of *Out of Many* includes the *Primary Source: Documents in U.S. History* CD-ROM. This versatile resource offers 400 primary source documents—in accessible PDF format—and over 350 images and maps. It also provides a number of features that help students work with documents, including headnotes, focus questions, highlighting and note-taking tools, and a glossary of terms for certain documents.

Primary Source
Documents in U.S. History

View Tutorial | Help | Exit

| Chapter | Theme | Author | Timeline | Recent Documents |

▶ **Chapter 1: A CONTINENT OF VILLAGES TO 1500**

▶ **Chapter 2: WHEN WORLDS COLLIDE 1492-1590**

▶ **Chapter 3: PLANTING COLONIES IN NORTH AMERICA 1588-1701**

▶ **Chapter 4: SLAVERY AND EMPIRE 1441-1770**

▶ **Chapter 5: THE CULTURES OF COLONIAL NORTH AMERICA 1700-1780**

▶ **Chapter 6: FROM EMPIRE TO INDEPENDENCE 1750-1776**

▶ **Chapter 7: THE AMERICAN REVOLUTION 1776-1786**

▶ **Chapter 8: THE NEW NATION 1786-1800**

▶ **Chapter 9: AN AGRARIAN REPUBLIC 1790-1824**

▶ **Chapter 10: THE SOUTH AND SLAVERY 1790s-1850s**

▶ **Chapter 11: THE GROWTH OF DEMOCRACY 1824-1840**

▶ **Chapter 12: INDUSTRY AND THE NORTH 1790s-1840s**

▶ **Chapter 13: COMING TO TERMS WITH THE NEW AGE 1820s-1850s**

▶ **Chapter 14: THE TERRITORIAL EXPANSION OF THE UNITED STATES 1830s-1850s**

An **easy navigation function** allows students to search for documents by chapter, theme, author, or timeline.

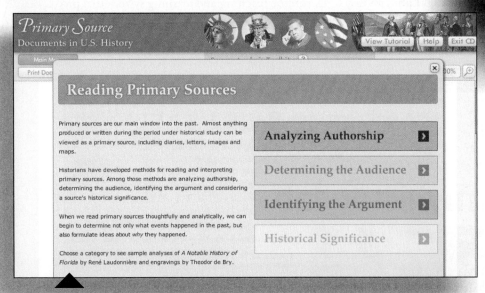

Reading Primary Sources

Primary sources are our main window into the past. Almost anything produced or written during the period under historical study can be viewed as a primary source, including diaries, letters, images and maps.

Historians have developed methods for reading and interpreting primary sources. Among those methods are analyzing authorship, determining the audience, identifying the argument and considering a source's historical significance.

When we read primary sources thoughtfully and analytically, we can begin to determine not only what events happened in the past, but also formulate ideas about *why* they happened.

Choose a category to see sample analyses of *A Notable History of Florida* by René Laudonnière and engravings by Theodor de Bry.

Analyzing Authorship

Determining the Audience

Identifying the Argument

Historical Significance

An **interactive tutorial** offers strategies for reading, analyzing, and writing about various types of documents.

An accessible *Source Analysis Toolkit* helps students easily utilize reading, analyzing, and writing tools.

MyHistoryLab is an easy to use online teaching and learning system that provides helpful tools to both students and instructors. In addition to numerous instructor and student resources, it includes a complete e-book version of *Out of Many*, making an interactive online text available to students.

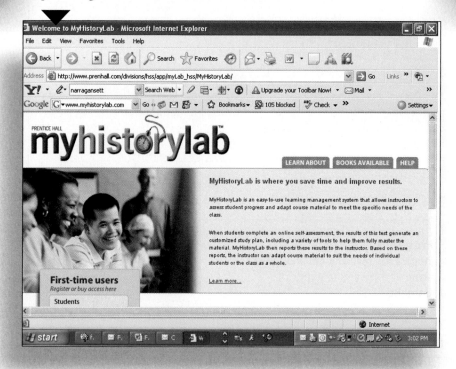

For students

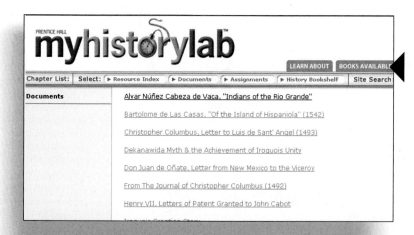

MyHistoryLab is packed with **readings that expand upon the material** found in the text. These include over 300 primary source documents with questions for analysis as well as classic works such as Thomas Paine's *Common Sense*.

...with online resources available through MyHistoryLab.

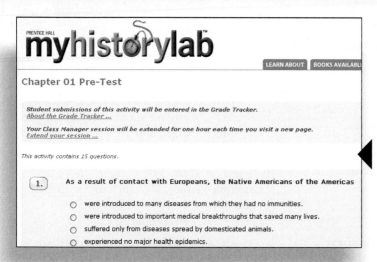

MyHistoryLab offers students various **review and assessment tools** in one convenient on-line platform. Self-study quizzes with targeted feedback help students assess their progress. A study guide, PowerPoint™ presentations, and key terms flashcards help students master the material in preparation for exams.

MyHistoryLab interactive activities and exercises let students explore materials from the text in an engaging fashion. MyHistoryLab brings U.S. history to life via *Exploring America* interactive learning activities, map explorations, animation, and audio and video clips.

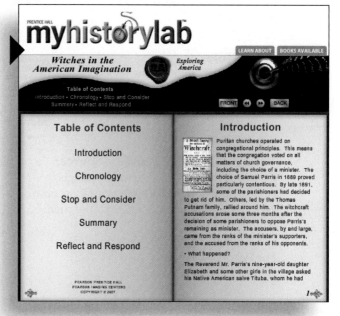

For instructors

MyHistoryLab is a one-stop collection of instructional material for teaching from *Out of Many*, including the instructor's manual, the test item file, images, maps, charts, and graphs from the text, video and audio clips, and PowerPoint™ lecture presentations. In addition, MyHistoryLab provides instructor access to all student resources.

For more information, contact your local Pearson sales representative or visit www.myhistorylab.com and click Prentice Hall.

Out of Many, you experience America's history... ...with tools for instructors and students.

Prentice Hall is proud to offer a number of supplementary resources that help students and instructors get the most from *Out of Many*.

For students

- A robust **Study Guide** provides practice tests, essay questions, chronologies, an expanded map skills section, and *Interpreting the Past* activities for each chapter.
  For **Volume I**: 978-0-13-602836-9
  For **Volume II**: 978-0-13-602835-2

- A full-color **Atlas of United States History** offers maps and charts depicting crucial times and events in U.S. History. An index lists historically important places, areas, events, and geographical features.
  978-0-13-603349-3

- **VangoNotes** downloadable audio study guides are ideal for both concept review and exam preparation. The content includes *Big Ideas* overviews, practice tests, audio flashcards of key terms, and *Rapid Review* quick drill sessions.
  www.vangonotes.com

- The print version of **Primary Source: Documents in U.S. History** presents a collection of more than 300 primary source documents that directly relate to the themes and content of the text.
  For **Volumes I**: 978-0-13-605198-5
  For **Volume II**: 978-0-13-605199-2

For instructors

- The **Instructor's Resource Manual** contains everything instructors need for developing and preparing lecture presentations, including chapter outlines and overviews, lecture topics, discussion questions, and information about audio-visual resources. It also includes a new section on teaching American history.
  ISBN: 978-0-13-606049-9

- An **Instructor's Resource CD-ROM** includes all of the instructor supplements, multimedia resources, images, and art from the text.
  ISBN: 978-0-13-606052-9

- The **Test Item File** contains more than 3,000 multiple-choice, identification, matching, and essay questions.
  ISBN: 978-0-13-606051-2

- **Test Generator**—a computerized test management program available for Windows and Macintosh environments—allows instructors to design their own exams by selecting items from the Test Item File. Instructors may download the Test Gen from the Pearson Instructor Resource Center.
  www.prenhall.com/irc

- The **Transparencies Set** offers over 150 full-color transparency acetates of all the maps, charts, and graphs in the text for easy classroom presentation.
  978-0-13-602839-0

- A customized **Retrieving the American Past reader** may be created to accompany *Out of Many*. Instructors can select from a database of 300 primary source documents on key topics in American history to create a reader ideally suited to their course.
  http://www.pearsoncustom.com/database/rtap.html

- The two-volume **American Stories: Biographies in United States History, Third Edition** presents sixty-two biographies of key figures in American history with introductions, pre-reading questions, suggested readings, and a special prologue about the role of biography in the study of American history.
  For **Volumes I**: 978-0-13-182654-0
  For **Volume II**: 978-0-13-182653-3

- The Prentice Hall **Package a Penguin program** provides instructors an opportunity to receive significant discounts on Penguin American history titles when ordered with *Out of Many*.

One of the most characteristic features of our country is its astounding variety. The American people include the descendants of native Indians, colonial Europeans of British, French, and Spanish background, Africans, and migrants from virtually every country and continent. Indeed, at the beginning of the new century the United States is absorbing a flood of immigrants from Latin America and Asia that rivals the great tide of people from eastern and southern Europe one hundred years before. The struggle to meld a single nation out of our many far-flung communities is what much of American history is all about. That is the story told in this book.

Every human society is made up of communities. A community is a set of relationships linking men, women, and their families to a coherent social whole that is more than the sum of its parts. In a community people develop the capacity for unified action. In a community people learn, often through trial and error, how to transform and adapt to their environment. The sentiment that binds the members of a community together is the mother of group consciousness and ethnic identity. In the making of history, communities are far more important than even the greatest of leaders, for the community is the institution most capable of passing a distinctive historical tradition to future generations.

Communities bind people together in multiple ways. They can be as small as local neighborhoods, in which people maintain face-to-face relations, or as large as the nation itself. This book examines American history from the perspective of community life—an ever-widening frame that has included larger and larger groups of Americans.

Networks of kinship and friendship, and connections across generations and among families, establish the bonds essential to community life. Shared feelings about values and history establish the basis for common identity. In communities, people find the power to act collectively in their own interest. But American communities frequently took shape as a result of serious conflicts among groups, and within communities there was often significant fighting among competing groups or classes. Thus the term *community*, as we use it here, includes conflict and discord as well as harmony and agreement.

For decades Americans have complained about the "loss of community." But community has not disappeared—it has been continuously reinvented. Until the late eighteenth century, community was defined

Harvey Dinnerstein, *Underground, Together* 1996, oil on canvas, 90" × 107".

Photograph courtesy of Gerold Wunderlich & Co., New York, NY.

COMMUNITY & DIVERSITY

xliii

primarily by space and local geography. But in the nineteenth century communities were reshaped by new and powerful historical forces such as the marketplace, industrialization, the corporation, mass immigration, mass media, and the growth of the nation-state. In the twentieth century, Americans struggled to balance commitments to multiple communities. These were defined not simply by local spatial arrangements, but by categories as varied as race and ethnicity, occupation, political affiliation, and consumer preference. The "American Communities" vignettes that open each chapter reflect these transformations.

The title for our book was suggested by the Latin phrase selected by John Adams, Benjamin Franklin, and Thomas Jefferson for the Great Seal of the United States: *E Pluribus Unum*—"Out of Many Comes Unity." These men understood that unity could not be imposed by a powerful central authority but had to develop out of mutual respect among Americans of different backgrounds. The revolutionary leadership expressed the hope that such respect could grow on the basis of a remarkable proposition: "We hold these truths to be self-evident, that all men are created equal; that they are endowed by their Creator with certain unalienable rights; that among these are life, liberty, and the pursuit of happiness." The na-

tional government of the United States would preserve local and state authority but would guarantee individual rights. The nation would be strengthened by guarantees of difference.

"Out of Many" comes strength. That is the promise of America and the premise of this book. The underlying dialectic of American history, we believe, is that as a people we must locate our national unity in the celebration of the differences that exist among us; these differences can be our strength, as long as we affirm the promise of the Declaration. Protecting the "right to be different," in other words, is absolutely fundamental to the continued existence of democracy, and that right is best protected by the existence of strong and vital communities. We are bound together as a nation by the ideal of local and cultural differences protected by our common commitment to the values of the American Revolution.

Our history demonstrates that the promise has always been problematic. Centrifugal forces have been powerful in the American past, and at times the country seemed about to fracture into its component parts. Our transformation from a collection of groups and regions into a nation was marked by painful and often violent struggles.

Our most influential leaders have also sometimes suffered a crisis of faith in the American project of "liberty

Thomas Satterwhite Noble, *Last Sale of Slaves on the Courthouse Steps*, 1860, oil on canvas, Missouri Historical Society.

COMMUNITY & DIVERSITY **xlv**

and justice for all." Thomas Jefferson not only believed in the inferiority of African Americans but feared that immigrants from outside the Anglo-American tradition might "warp and bias" the development of the nation "and render it a heterogeneous, incoherent, distracted mass." We have not always lived up to the American promise and there is a dark side to our history. It took the bloodiest war in American history to secure the human rights of African Americans, and the struggle for full equality for all our citizens has yet to be won.

The process by which diverse communities have come to share a set of common American values is one of the most fundamental aspects of our history. It did not occur, however, because of compulsory Americanization programs, but because of free public education, popular participation in democratic politics, and the impact of popular culture. Contemporary America does have a common culture: We share a commitment to freedom of thought and expression, we join in the aspirations to own our own homes and send our children to college, we laugh at the same television programs or video clips on You Tube.

To a degree that too few Americans appreciate, this common culture resulted from a complicated process of mutual discovery that took place when different ethnic and regional groups encountered one another.

The American educator John Dewey recognized this diversity early in the last century. "The genuine American, the typical American, is himself a hyphenated character," he declared, "international and interracial in his make-up." It was up to all Americans, Dewey argued, "is to see to it that the hyphen connects instead of separates." We, the authors of *Out of Many*, endorse Dewey's perspective. "Creation comes from the impact of diversity," the American philosopher Horace Kallen wrote about the same time. We also endorse Kallen's vision of the American promise: "A democracy of nationalities, cooperating voluntarily and autonomously through common institutions, . . . a multiplicity in a unity, an orchestration of mankind." And now, let the music begin.

Out of Many

Native Americans build thatch houses beside a massive pyramid in "Community Life at Cahokia" by Michael Hampshire.

10

A CONTINENT OF VILLAGES

TO 1500

WHAT EVENTS led to the migration of Asian peoples into North America?

IN WHAT ways did native communities adapt to the distinct regions of North America?

WHAT WERE the consequences of the development of farming for native communities?

WHAT IMPORTANT differences were there between Indian societies in the Southwest, South, and Northeast on the eve of colonization?

AMERICAN COMMUNITIES
Cahokia: Thirteenth-Century Life on the Mississippi

AS THE SUN ROSE OVER THE RICH FLOODPLAIN, THE PEOPLE OF THE riverbank city set about their daily tasks. Some went to shops where they manufactured tools, crafted pottery, worked metal, or fashioned ornamental jewelry—goods destined to be exchanged in the far corners of the continent. Others left their densely populated neighborhoods for the outlying countryside, where in the summer heat they worked the seemingly endless fields that fed the city. From almost any point people could see the great temple that rose from the city center—the place where priests in splendid costumes acted out public rituals.

The Indian residents of this thirteenth-century city lived and worked on the east banks of the Mississippi River, across from present-day St. Louis, a place known today as **Cahokia**. In the thirteenth century, Cahokia was an urban cluster of twenty or thirty thousand people. Its farm fields were abundant with corn, beans, and squash. The temple, a huge earthwork pyramid, covered fifteen acres at its base and rose as high as a ten-story building. On top were the sacred quarters of priests and chiefs.

By the fourteenth century Cahokia had been abandoned, but its great central temple mound and dozens of smaller ones in the surrounding area, as well as hundreds of other large mounds throughout the Mississippi Valley, remained to puzzle the colonists and settlers who came in the eighteenth and nineteenth centuries.

The Europeans and Americans who explored and excavated those mounds were convinced they were the ruins of a vanished civilization, not the work of Indians. They were wrong. The ancestors of contemporary Native Americans constructed massive earthworks in the Mississippi Valley. The vast urban complex of Cahokia, which at its height stretched six miles along the Mississippi River, flourished from the tenth to the fourteenth centuries. Its residents were not nomadic hunters but farmers, participants in a complex agricultural culture archaeologists term "Mississippian." Hundreds of acres of crops fed the people of Cahokia, the largest urban community north of the Aztec civilization of central Mexico. Mississippian farmers constructed ingenious raised plots of land on which they heaped compost in wide ridges for improved drainage and protection against unseasonable frosts. To their square houses of wood and mud they attached pens in which they kept flocks of domesticated turkeys and small herds of young deer, slaughtered for meat, feathers, and hide. Cahokia stood at the center of a long-distance trading system that linked it to other Indian communities over a vast area. Copper came from Lake Superior, mica from the southern Appalachians, conch shells from the Atlantic coast. Cahokia's specialized artisans were renowned for the manufacture of high-quality flint hoes, which were exported throughout the Mississippi Valley.

Archaeological evidence suggests that Cahokia was a city-state supported by tribute and taxation. Like the awe-inspiring public works of other early urban societies in other parts of the world, most notably the pyramids of ancient Egypt and the acropolis of Athens, the great temple mound of Cahokia was intended to showcase the city's wealth and power. The mounds and other colossal public works at Cahokia were the monuments of a society ruled by a class of elite leaders. From their residences atop the mound, priests and chiefs looked down on their subjects both literally and figuratively.

The 1848 Smithsonian report on Cahokia reflected the stereotypical American view that all Indian people were hunters. It is a view that persists. But the long history of North America before European colonization reveals that the native inhabitants developed a great variety of societies. Beginning as migrant hunting and gathering bands, they found ways to fine-tune their subsistence strategies to fit environmental possibilities and limitations. Communities in the highlands of Mexico invented systems of farming that spread to all the regions where cultivation was possible. Not only the Aztecs of Mexico and the Mayans of Central America but also communities in the Southwest and the Mississippi Valley constructed densely settled urban civilizations. North America before colonization was, as historian Howard R. Lamar phrases it, "a continent of villages," a land spread with thousands of communities. The wonders and mystery of the lost city of Cahokia are but one aspect of the little-understood history of the Indians of the Americas.

Cahokia

Cahokia   One of the largest urban centers created by Mississippian peoples, containing 30,000 residents in 1250.

THE FIRST AMERICAN SETTLERS

" Why do you call us Indians?" a Massachusetts native complained to Puritan missionary John Eliot in 1646. Christopher Columbus, who mistook the Taino people of the Caribbean for the people of the East Indies, called them "**Indios**." Within a short time this Spanish word had passed into English as "Indians" and was commonly used to refer to all the native peoples of the Americas. Today anthropologists sometimes employ the term "Amerindians," and others use "Native Americans." But in the United States most of the descendants of the original inhabitants refer to themselves as "Indian people."

WHO ARE THE INDIAN PEOPLE?

At the time of their first contacts with Europeans at the beginning of the sixteenth century, the inhabitants of the Western Hemisphere represented over 2,000 separate cultures, spoke several hundred different languages, and made their livings in scores of different environments. No single physical type characterized all the peoples of the Americas. Indeed, it was only when Europeans had compared Indian peoples with natives of other continents, such as Africans, that they seemed similar enough to be classified as a group.

Once Europeans realized that the Americas were in fact a "New World," rather than part of the Asian continent, a debate began over how people might have moved there from Europe and Asia, where (according to the Judeo-Christian Bible) God had created the first man and woman. In 1590, the Spanish Jesuit missionary Joseph de Acosta reasoned that because Old World animals were present in the Americas, they must have crossed by a land bridge that could have been used by humans as well.

MIGRATION FROM ASIA

Acosta was the first to propose the Asian migration hypothesis that is widely accepted today. Analysis of the genetic drift of Siberian and American Indian populations suggests that migrants to North America began leaving Asia approximately 30,000 years ago (see Map 1.1).

The migration was possible because during the last Ice Age, from 70,000 to 10,000 years ago, huge glaciers locked up massive volumes of water, and sea levels were as much as 300 feet lower than they are today. Asia and North America, now separated by the Bering Straits, were joined by a huge subcontinent of ice-free, treeless grassland, which geologists have named **Beringia**.

A forensic artist reconstructed this bust from the skull of "Kennewick Man," whose skeletal remains were discovered along the Columbia River in 1996. Scientific testing suggested that the remains were more than nine thousand years old.

WHAT EVENTS led to the migration of Asian peoples into North America?

myhistory**lab**

Review Summary

1–11
Jose de Acosta, *A Spanish Priest Speculates on the Origins of the Indians*

IMAGE KEY

for pages xlviii–1

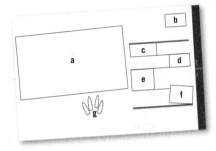

a. Native Americans build thatch houses beside a massive pyramid in "Community Life at Cahokia" by Michael Hampshire.
b. A hut from the coastal Algonquian village of Secoton.
c. In July 1585 John White visited the coastal Algonquian village of Secoton where he painted this composite scene.
d. Projectile point embedded in the rib bones of a long-extinct North American species of bison.
e. The ruins of the Anasazis' Pueblo Bonito in Chaco Canyon, northern New Mexico.
f. "The New Queen Being Taken to the King," engraved from a drawing by an early French colonist of a hierarchical community of Florida.
g. Clovis points used to make spears.

1–1
Marco Polo Recounts His Travels Through Asia

Indios   Name first used by Christopher Columbus for the Taino people of the Caribbean.

Beringia   A subcontinent bridging Asia and North America, named after the Bering Straits.

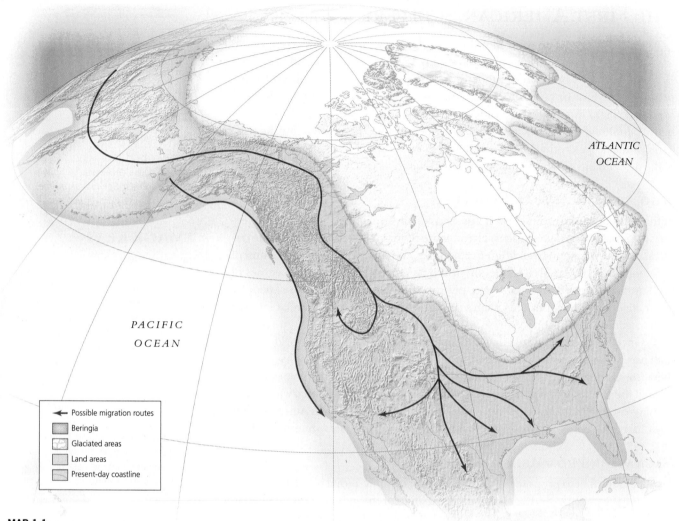

MAP 1.1

Migration Routes from Asia to America   During the Ice Age, Asia and North America were joined where the Bering Straits are today, forming a migration route for hunting peoples. These migrants began making their way to the heartland of the continent as much as 30,000 years ago.

WHAT GEOGRAPHICAL features shaped the dispersal of Asian migrants throughout the Americas?

QUICK REVIEW

The Earliest Americans

♦ Paleo-Indians were resourceful hunters.

♦ During the Archaic period Indians adapted to regional environments.

♦ Farming began near the end of the Archaic Period.

Athapascan   A people that began to settle the forests in the northwestern area of North America around 5000 BCE.

Access to lands to the south, however, was blocked by huge ice sheets covering much of what is today Canada. How did the migrants get through those 2,000 miles of deep ice? The standard hypothesis is that with the warming of the climate and the end of the Ice Age, about 13,000 BCE (Before the Common Era), glacial melting created an ice-free corridor—an original "Pan-American Highway"—along the eastern front range of the Rocky Mountains. Using this thoroughfare, the hunters of big game reached the Great Plains as early as 11,000 BCE.

Recently, however, new archaeological finds along the Pacific coast of North and South America have complicated this hypothesis. Radiocarbon analysis of remains discovered at several newly excavated human sites suggested dates of 12,000 BCE or earlier. A number of archaeologists believe that the people who founded these settlements moved south in boats along a coastal route—an ancient "Pacific Coast Highway."

There were two later migrations into North America. About 5000 BCE the **Athapascan** people moved across Beringia and began to settle the forests in the northwestern area of the continent. Eventually groups of Athapascan speakers, the ancestors of the Navajos and Apaches, migrated across the Great Plains to the Southwest. A third and final migration began about 3000 BCE, long after Beringia had disappeared under rising seas, when a maritime hunting people crossed the Bering Straits in small boats.

THE CLOVIS CULTURE:
THE FIRST ENVIRONMENTAL ADAPTATION

The tools found at the earliest North American archaeological sites, crude stone or bone choppers and scrapers, are similar to artifacts from the same period found in Europe or Asia. About 11,000 years ago, however, ancient Americans developed a much more sophisticated style of making fluted blades and lance points, a tradition named "Clovis," after the location of the initial discovery near Clovis, New Mexico, in 1926. In the years since, archaeologists have unearthed Clovis stone tools at sites throughout the continent all dating within 1,000 or 2,000 years of one another, suggesting that the Clovis technology spread quickly throughout the continent.

These Clovis points are typical of thousands that archaeologists have found at sites all over the continent, dating from a period about 12,000 years ago. When inserted in a spear shaft, these three- to six-inch fluted points made effective weapons for hunting mammoth and other big game. The ancient craftsmen who made these points often took advantage of the unique qualities of the stone they were working to enhance their aesthetic beauty.

The global warming trend that ended the Ice Age dramatically altered the North American climate. About 15,000 years ago the giant continental glaciers began to melt and the northern latitudes were colonized by plants, animals, and humans. Meltwater created the lake and river systems of today and raised the level of the surrounding seas.

NEW WAYS OF LIVING ON THE LAND

These huge transformations produced new patterns of wind, rainfall, and temperature, reshaping the ecology of the entire continent and gradually producing the distinct North American regions of today (see Map 1.2). The great integrating force of a single continental climate faded, and with its passing the continental Clovis culture fragmented into a number of different regional patterns.

The retreat of the glaciers led to new ways of finding food: hunting in the Arctic, foraging in the arid deserts, fishing along the coasts, hunting and gathering in the forests. These developments took place roughly 10,000 to 2,500 years ago, during what archaeologists call the Archaic period (corresponding to the Mesolithic period in the archaeological chronology of Eurasia).

Hunting Traditions   One of the most important effects of this massive climatic shift was the stress it placed on the big-game animals best suited to an Ice Age environment. The archaeological record documents the extinction of thirty-two classes of large New World mammals. Changing climatic conditions lowered the reproduction and survival rates of these large mammals, forcing hunting bands to intensify their hunting.

As the other large-mammal populations declined, hunters on the Great Plains concentrated on the herds of American bison (known more familiarly as buffalo). To hunt these animals, people needed a new weapon. In archaeological sites dating from about 10,000 years ago, a new style of tool is found mingled with animal remains. This technology, named "Folsom" (for the site of the first major find near Folsom, New Mexico) was a refinement of Clovis that featured more delicate but deadlier spear points. Hunters probably hurled the lances to which

QUICK REVIEW

The Clovis Tradition
- Emerged around 10,000 BCE.
- A new and powerful style of tool making.
- Clovis artifacts found throughout North and Central America.

QUICK REVIEW

Hunting the Bison
- Climate shift resulted in the extinction of many large New World animals.
- As other large-mammal populations declined, hunters concentrated on bison herds.
- The growing complexity of Indian communities was reflected in bison hunting strategies.

these points were attached with wooden spear-throwers, attaining far greater momentum than possible using their arms alone.

These archaeological finds suggest the growing complexity of early Indian communities. Hunters frequently stampeded herds of bison into canyon traps or over cliffs. Such tasks required a sophisticated division of labor among dozens of men and women and the cooperation of a number of communities. Taking food in such great quantities also suggests a knowledge of basic preservation techniques.

MAP EXPLORATION

To explore an interactive version of this map, go to **http://www.prenhall.com/faraghertlc/map1.2**

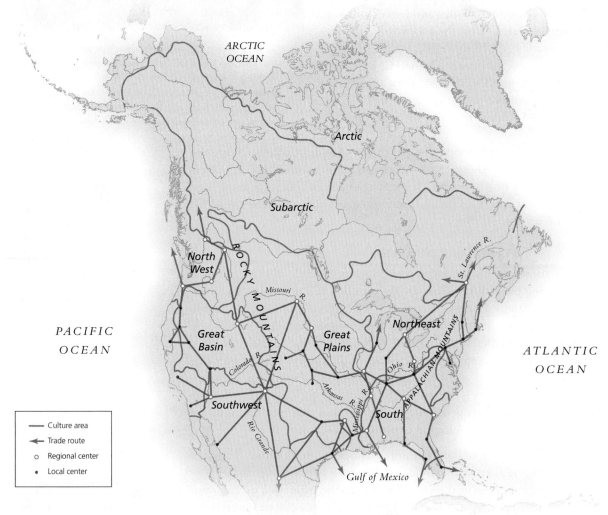

MAP 1.2

Native North American Culture Areas and Trade Networks, ca. 1400 CE   By considering the ways in which Indian peoples developed distinct cultures and adapted to their environments, anthropologists developed the concept of "culture areas." Just as regions shaped the lifeways and history of Indian peoples, after the coming of the Europeans they nurtured the development of regional American cultures. And by determining the origin of artifacts found at ancient sites, historians have devised a conjectural map of Indian trade networks. Among large regional centers and smaller local ones, trade connected Indian peoples of many different communities and regions.

HOW DID the environment influence the relationship between trade and culture?

Desert Culture In the Great Basin, the warming trend created a desert where once there had been enormous inland seas. Here Indian people developed what anthropologists call "**Desert culture**," a way of life based on the pursuit of small game and the intensified foraging of plant foods. Small communities of desert foragers migrated seasonally within a small range.

Archaeologists today find the artifacts of desert foragers in the caves and rock shelters in which they lived. In addition to stone tools, there are objects of wood, hide, and fiber, wonderfully preserved for thousands of years in the dry climate. Desert culture persisted into the nineteenth century among modern Shoshone and Ute communities.

The innovative practices of Desert culture gradually spread from the Great Basin to the Great Plains and the Southwest, where foraging for plant foods began to supplement hunting. About 6,000 years ago, these techniques were carried to California, where, in the natural abundance of the valleys and coasts, communities developed economies capable of supporting some of the densest populations and the first permanently settled villages in North America. Another dynamic center developed along the coast of the Pacific Northwest, where Indian communities developed a way of life based on the abundance of fish and sea mammals. Densely populated and permanently settled communities developed there as well.

Forest Efficiency There were similar trends east of the Mississippi. In the centuries prior to colonization and settlement by Europeans, the whole of eastern North America was a vast forest. Communities of native people achieved a comfortable and secure life by developing a sophisticated knowledge of the rich and diverse available resources, a principle anthropologists term "**forest efficiency**."

When, in 1927, archaeologists at Folsom, New Mexico, uncovered this dramatic example of a projectile point embedded in the ribs of a long-extinct species of bison, it was the first proof that Indians had been in North America for many thousands of years.

Courtesy of the Denver Museum of Nature and Science.

Desert culture A way of life based on hunting small game and the foraging of plant foods.

Forest Efficiency Creation of a comfortable life through the development of a sophisticated knowledge of available resources.

Archaeological sites in the East suggest that during the late **Archaic period**, community populations grew and settlements became increasingly permanent, providing convincing evidence of the practicality of forest efficiency.

THE DEVELOPMENT OF FARMING

At the end of the Stone Age, communities in different regions of the world independently created systems of farming, each based on a unique staple crop: rice in Southeast Asia, wheat in the Middle East, potatoes in the Andean highlands of South America, and maize (what Americans call "corn") in Mexico. The dynamic center of this development in North America was in the highlands of Mexico, from which the new technology spread north and east.

ORIGINS IN MEXICO

Archaeological evidence suggests that plant cultivation in the highlands of central Mexico began about 5,000 years ago. Ancient Mexicans developed crops that responded well to human care and produced larger quantities of food in a limited space than did plants growing in the wild. Maize was particularly productive.

As farming became increasingly important, it radically reshaped social life. Where a foraging society might require 100 square miles to support 100 people, a farming society required only a single square mile. Farming provided not only the incentive for larger families (more workers for the fields) but also the means to feed them. People became less mobile, built more substantial residences near their crops, and developed more effective means of storage. Villages grew into towns and eventually into large, densely settled communities like Cahokia. Autumn harvests had to be stored during winter months, and the storage and distribution of food had to be managed. The division of labor increased with the appearance of specialists like toolmakers, craft workers, administrators, priests, and rulers.

By 1000 BCE urban communities governed by permanent bureaucracies had begun to form in **Mesoamerica**, the region stretching from central Mexico to Central America. By the beginning of the first millennium CE (Common Era), highly productive farming was supporting complex urban civilizations in the Valley of Mexico (the location of present-day Mexico City), the Yucatan Peninsula, and other parts of Mesoamerica. Like many of the ancient civilizations of Asia and the Mediterranean, these Mesoamerican civilizations were characterized by the concentration of wealth and power in the hands of an elite class of priests and rulers, the construction of impressive temples and other public structures, and the development of systems of mathematics and astronomy and several forms of hieroglyphic writing. These civilizations also engaged in warfare between states and practiced ritual human sacrifice.

The great city of Teotihuacan in the Valley of Mexico, which emerged about 100 BCE, had a population of as many as 200,000 at the height of its power around 500 CE. Teotihuacan's elite class of religious and political leaders controlled an elaborate state-sponsored trading system that stretched from

IN WHAT ways did native communities adapt to the distinct regions of North America?

myhistorylab
Review Summary

Mesoamerican maize cultivation, as illustrated by an Aztec artist for the *Florentine Codex*, a book prepared a few years after the Spanish conquest. The peoples of Mesoamerica developed a greater variety of cultivated crops than those found in any other region in the world, and their agricultural productivity helped sustain one of the world's great civilizations.

Image #1739-3, courtesy the Library, American Museum of Natural History.

Archaic period The period roughly 10,000 to 2,500 years ago marked by the retreat of glaciers.

Mesoamerica The region stretching from central Mexico to Central America.

present-day Arizona to Central America and may have included coastal shipping connections with the civilizations of Peru.

Teotihuacan began to decline in the sixth century, and by the eighth century it was mostly abandoned. A new empire, that of the Toltecs, dominated central Mexico from the tenth to the twelfth centuries. By the fourteenth century a people known as the **Aztecs**, migrants from the north, had settled in the Valley of Mexico and begun a dramatic expansion into a formidable imperial power (see Chapter 2).

The Mayan peoples of the Yucatan Peninsula developed a group of competing city-states that flourished from about 300 BCE until 900 CE. Their achievements included advanced writing and calendar systems and a sophisticated knowledge of mathematics.

INCREASING SOCIAL COMPLEXITY

In a few areas, farming truly did result in a revolutionary change in Indian communities, producing urban civilizations like those in Mesoamerica or on the banks of the Mississippi at Cahokia. It is likely that among the first social transformations was the development of significantly more elaborate systems of kinship. Greater population density prompted families to group themselves into clans, and separate clans gradually became responsible for different social, political, or ritual functions. Clans may have been an important mechanism for binding together the people of several communities into larger social units based on ethnic, linguistic, and territorial unity. These "tribes" were headed by leaders or chiefs from honored clans, often advised by councils of elders.

Chiefs' primary functions were the supervision of the economy, the collection and storage of the harvest, and the distribution of food to the clans. Differences in wealth, though small by the standards of modern societies, might develop between the families of a farming tribe. These inequalities were kept in check by redistribution according to principles of sharing similar to those operating in foraging communities. Nowhere in North America did Indian cultures develop a concept of the private ownership of land or other resources, which were usually considered the common resource of the people and were worked collectively.

Indian communities practiced a rather strict division of labor according to gender. In foraging communities, hunting was generally men's work, while the gathering of food and the maintenance of home-base camps were the responsibility of women. The development of farming may have challenged that pattern. Where hunting remained an important activity, women took responsibility for the growing of crops. But in areas like Mexico, where communities were almost totally dependent on cultivated crops for their survival, both men and women worked the fields.

In most North American Indian farming communities, women and men belonged to separate social groupings, each with its own rituals and lore. Membership in these gender societies was one of the most important elements of a person's identity. Marriage ties, on the other hand, were relatively weak, and in most Indian communities divorce was a simple matter: the couple separated without a great deal of ceremony, and the children almost always remained with the mother.

Farming communities were far more complex than foraging communities, but they were also less stable. Growing populations demanded increasingly large surpluses of food, and this need often led to social conflict and warfare. Moreover, farming systems were especially vulnerable to changes in climate, such as drought, as well as to crises of their own making, such as soil depletion or erosion.

The creation of man and woman depicted on a pot (dated about 1000 CE) from the ancient villages of the Mimbres River of southwestern New Mexico, the area of Mogollon culture. Mimbres pottery is renowned for its spirited artistry. Such artifacts were usually intended as grave goods to honor the dead.

Mimbres black on white bowl, with painted representations of man and woman under a blanket. Grant County, New Mexico. Diam. 26.7 cm. Courtesy National Museum of the American Indian, Smithsonian Institution, 24/3198.

QUICK REVIEW

Indian Agrarian Society

- Families grouped themselves in clans which, in turn, were grouped in tribes.
- Chiefs supervised economic activities.
- No concept of private ownership of land.
- Strict division of labor according to gender.

Aztecs   A warrior people who dominated the Valley of Mexico from 1100–1521.

THE RESISTED REVOLUTION

Some scholars describe the transition to farming as a revolution. Their argument is that farming offered such obvious advantages that communities rushed to adopt it. But there is very little evidence to support the notion that farming was a clearly superior way of life. Anthropologists have demonstrated that farmers work considerably longer and harder than do foragers. Moreover, farmers depend on a relatively narrow selection of plants and animals for food and are vulnerable to famine. Foragers experience periods of want, but they have a much higher probability of securing food under stressful conditions. Finally, compared to foragers, farmers experienced degenerative conditions of the spine (probably the result of hard labor), a threefold increase in iron-deficiency anemia, and twice the amount of tooth decay and loss.

Moreover, ignorance of cultivation was never the reason communities failed to take up farming. All foraging cultures understand a great deal about plant reproduction. When gathering wild rice, the Menominee Indians of the northern forests of Wisconsin purposely allowed some of it to fall back into the water to ensure a crop for the next season. Paiutes of the Great Basin systematically irrigated stands of their favorite wild food sources. Cultures in different regions assessed the relative advantages and disadvantages of adopting farming. In California and the Pacific Northwest, acorn gathering or salmon fishing made the cultivation of food crops seem a waste of time. In the Great Basin, there were attempts to farm but without much success. Before the invention of modern irrigation systems, which require sophisticated engineering, only the Archaic Desert culture could prevail in this harsh environment.

FARMING IN EARLY NORTH AMERICA

WHAT WERE the consequences of the development of farming for native communities?

myhistorylab
Review Summary

Maize farming spread north from Mexico into the area now part of the United States in the first millenuim BCE. Over time maize was adapted to a range of climates and its cultivation spread to all the temperate regions.

FARMERS OF THE SOUTHWEST

Farming communities began to emerge in the arid Southwest during the first millennium BCE. Among the first to develop a settled farming way of life was a culture known to archaeologists as Mogollon. These people farmed maize, beans, squash, and constructed ingenious food storage pits in permanent village sites along what is today the southern Arizona–New Mexico border.

During the same centuries, a culture known as Hohokam ("those who are gone," in the language of the modern tribes of the region) flourished in the region along the floodplain of the Salt and Gila Rivers in southern Arizona. The Hohokam, who lived in farming villages, built and maintained the first irrigation system in America north of Mexico, channeling river water through five hundred miles of canals to water desert fields of maize, beans, squash, tobacco, and cotton.

THE ANASAZIS

The best-known ancient farming culture of the Southwest is the Anasazi, which developed around the first century CE in the Four Corners area, where the states of Arizona, New Mexico, Utah, and Colorado meet on the great plateau of the Colorado River. Around 750 CE, possibly in response to population pressure and an

Cliff Palace, at Mesa Verde National Park in southwest Colorado, was created 900 years ago when the Anasazis left the mesa tops and moved into more secure and inaccessible cliff dwellings. Facing southwest, the building gained heat from the rays of the low afternoon sun in winter, and overhanging rock protected the structure from rain, snow, and the hot midday summer sun. The numerous round kivas, each covered with a flat roof originally, suggest that Cliff Palace may have had a ceremonial importance.

increasingly dry climate, the residents of communities there began shifting from pit-house villages to densely populated, multistoried apartment complexes that the Spanish invaders called "pueblos." These farmers grew high-yield varieties of maize in terraced fields irrigated by canals flowing from mountain catchment basins. To supplement this vegetable diet, they hunted animals for their meat, using the bow and arrow that first appeared in the region in the sixth century.

The Anasazis faced a major challenge in the thirteenth and fourteenth centuries. The arid climate became even drier, and growing populations had to redouble their efforts to improve food production, building increasingly complex irrigation canals, dams, and terraced fields. A devastating drought resulted in repeated crop failures and eventual famine. The ecological crisis was heightened by the arrival in the fourteenth century of Athapascan migrants, ancestors of the Navajos and the Apaches. Athapascans raided Anasazi farming communities, taking food, goods, and possibly slaves. Gradually Anasazi communities abandoned the Four Corners area altogether, most resettling along the Rio Grande, joining with local residents to form the Pueblo communities that were living there when the Spanish arrived.

FARMERS OF THE EASTERN WOODLANDS

Archaeologists date the beginning of the farming culture of eastern North America, known as Woodland culture, from the first appearances of pottery in the region about 3,000 years ago. Woodland culture was based on a sophisticated way of life that combined gathering and hunting with the cultivation of a few local crops. Woodland people began cultivating maize during the first millennium CE, but even before that they had begun to adopt an increasingly settled existence and a more complex social organization, evidenced by complex earthen constructions.

Mound building was also a characteristic activity of the peoples living in the Ohio Valley during this period. The people of a culture known as Adena lived in semipermanent villages and constructed large burial mounds during the first millennium BCE. They were succeeded by a culture called Hopewell, which honored the dead with even larger and more elaborate burial mounds.

The Great Serpent Mound in southern Ohio, the shape of an uncoiling snake more than 1,300 feet long, is the largest effigy earthwork in the world. Monumental public works like these suggest the high degree of social organization of the Mississippian people.

MISSISSIPPIAN SOCIETY

The Hopewell culture collapsed in the fifth century CE, perhaps as a result of an ecological crisis brought on by shifting climate patterns. Over the next several centuries, however, a number of important technological innovations were introduced in the East. The bow and arrow, developed first on the Great Plains, appeared east of the Mississippi in about the seventh century, greatly increasing the efficiency of hunting. At about the same time maize farming spread widely through the East. Indian farmers developed a new variety (known today as Northern Flint) that matured in a short enough time to make it suitable for cultivation in temperate northern latitudes. A shift from digging sticks to flint hoes also took place about this time, further increasing the productive potential of maize farming.

On the basis of these innovations, a powerful new culture known as Mississippian arose in the seventh or eighth century CE. The peoples of Mississippian culture were master maize farmers living in permanent community sites along the floodplains of the Mississippi Valley. Cahokia was the largest and most spectacular, with its monumental temple mounds, its residential neighborhoods, and its surrounding farmlands. But there were dozens of other urban communities, each with thousands of residents. Archaeologists have excavated sites on the Arkansas River near Spiro, Oklahoma; on the Black Warrior River at Moundville, Alabama; at Hiawassee Island on the Tennessee River; and along the Etowah and Okmulgee Rivers in Georgia. The Great Serpent Mound, the largest effigy earthwork in the world, was constructed by Mississippian peoples in southern Ohio.

This bottle in the shape of a nursing mother (dated about 1300 BCE) was found at a Mississippian site. Historians can only speculate about the thoughts and feelings of the Mississippians, but such works of art are testimonials to the universal human emotion of maternal affection.

"Nursing Mother Effigy Bottle." From the Whelpley Collection at the St. Louis Science Center. Photograph © 1985 the Detroit Institute of Arts.

THE POLITICS OF WARFARE AND VIOLENCE

These centers, linked by the vast river transportation system of the Mississippi River and its many tributaries, became the earliest city-states north of Mexico, hierarchical chiefdoms that extended political control over the farmers of the surrounding countryside (see Map 1.3 for an illustration of

MAP EXPLORATION

To explore an interactive version of this map, go to **http://www.prenhall.com/faraghertlc/map1.3**

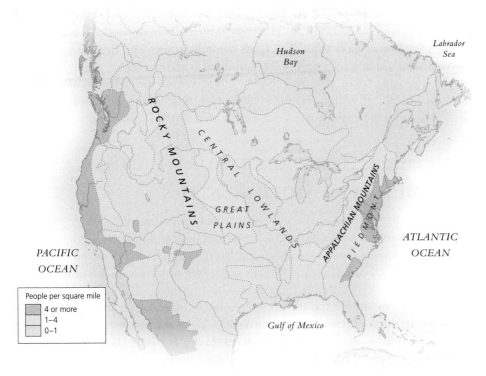

MAP 1.3

Population Density of Indian Societies in the Fifteenth Century   Based on what is called the "carrying capacity" of different subsistence strategies—the population density they could support—historical demographers have mapped the hypothetical population density of Indian societies in the fifteenth century, before the era of European colonization. Populations were densest in farming societies or in coastal areas with marine resources and sparsest in extreme environments like the Great Basin.

WHY WERE some regions more populated than others?

trade networks). With continued population growth, these cities engaged in vigorous and probably violent competition for the limited space along the rivers. It may have been the need for more orderly ways of allocating territories that stimulated the evolution of political hierarchies. The tasks of preventing local conflict, storing large food surpluses, and redistributing foodstuffs from farmers to artisans and elites required a leadership class with the power to command. Mound building and the use of tribute labor in the construction of other public works testified to the power of chiefs, who lived in sumptuous quarters atop the mounds.

Mississippian culture reached its height between the eleventh and thirteenth centuries CE, the same period in which the Anasazi culture constructed its desert cities. Both groups adapted to their own environment the technology that was spreading northward from Mexico. Both developed impressive artistic traditions, and their feats of engineering reflect the beginnings of science and technology. They were complex societies characterized by urbanism, social stratification, craft specialization, and regional trade—except for the absence of a writing system, all the traits of European civilization.

Warfare among Indian peoples certainly predated the colonial era. Organized violence was probably rare among hunting bands, which could seldom manage more than a small raid against an enemy. Certain hunting peoples, though, such as the southward-moving Athapascans, must have engaged in systematic raiding of settled farming communities. Warfare was also common among farming confederacies fighting to gain additional lands for cultivation. The first Europeans to arrive in the southeastern part of the continent described highly organized combat among large tribal armies. The bow and arrow was a deadly weapon of war, and the practice of scalping seems to have originated among warring tribes, who believed one could capture a warrior's spirit by taking his scalp lock.

Cultural Regions of North America on the Eve of Colonization

An appreciation of the ways human cultures adapted to geography and climate is fundamental to an understanding of American history, for just as regions shaped the development of Indian cultures in the centuries before the arrival of Europeans, so they continued to influence the character of American life in the centuries thereafter.

In order to understand the impact of regions on Indian cultures, anthropologists divide North America into several distinct "culture areas" within which groups shared a significant number of cultural traits: Arctic, Subarctic, Great Basin, Great Plains, California, Northwest, Plateau, Southwest, South, and Northeast.

The Population of Indian America

Determining the size of early human population is a tricky business, and estimates vary greatly, but there seems to be general agreement among historical demographers that the population of the North American continent (excluding Mesoamerica) numbered between 5 and 10 million at the time of the first European voyages of discovery. Millions more lived in the complex societies of Mexico and Central America (estimates run from 5 to 25 million). The population of the Western Hemisphere as a whole may have numbered 50 million or more, the same order of magnitude as Europe's population at the time.

Demographers may disagree about numbers but agree that population varied tremendously by cultural region. The largest populations of the continent were concentrated in the farming regions of the Southwest, South, and Northeast. These were the areas in which European explorers, conquerors, and colonists concentrated their first efforts, and they deserve more detailed examination (see Map 1.4).

The Southwest

The single overwhelming fact of life in the Southwest is aridity. Summer rains average only ten to twenty inches annually, and on much of the dry desert cultivation is impossible. A number of rivers, however, flow out of the pine-covered mountain plateaus, making possible irrigation farming along their courses.

On the eve of European colonization, Indian farmers in the Southwest had been cultivating their fields for nearly 3,000 years. In the floodplain of the Gila and Salt Rivers lived the Pimas and Tohono O'Odhams, descendants of the ancient Hohokam culture, and along the Colorado River, even on the floor of the Grand

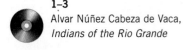

An Early European Image of Native Americans

From the very beginning of Europeans' contact with native American peoples, they depicted Indians as savages rather than as peoples with complex cultures. This woodcut by German artist Johann Froschauer was included in a 1505 German edition of Amerigo Vespucci's account of his voyage to the New World in 1499 and is among the very first images of Native Americans published. The image is a complete fantasy, lacking any ethnographic authenticity. Indians gather for a feast on the beach. The caption in the original publication read, in part: "The people are naked, handsome, brown, well-shaped in body. ... No one has anything, but all things are in common. And the men have as wives those who please them, be they mothers, sisters, or friends; therein they make no distinction. They also fight with each other; and they eat each other, even those who are slain, and hang the flesh of them in the smoke." A cannibalized body is being devoured. A couple is kissing. Women display their breasts. The image sent a powerful message: that some of the strongest taboos of Europeans—nakedness, sexual promiscuity, and cannibalism—were practiced by the people of the New World. It is an unrelentingly negative picture. The arrival of European vessels in the background of the image suggests that all this was about to change. Images like these continued to dominate the depiction of Indians for the next four hundred years, and were used as justifications for conquest. ■

> **HOW ARE** European stereotypes of savage people conveyed visually in this image?

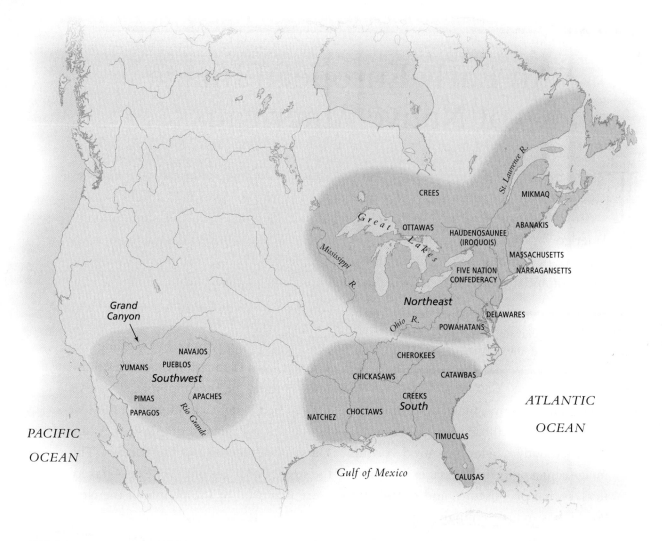

MAP 1.4

Indian Groups in the Areas of First Contact The Southwest was populated by desert farmers like the Pimas, Tohono O'Odhams, Yumans, and Pueblos, as well as by nomadic hunters and raiders like the Apaches and Navajos. On the eve of colonization, the Indian societies of the South shared many traits of the complex Mississippian farming culture. The Indians of the Northeast were mostly village peoples.

HOW DID the lack of rain shape the lives of the Indians of the Southwest?

Canyon, the Yuman peoples worked small irrigated fields. In their oasis communities, desert farmers cultivated corn, beans, squash, sunflowers, and cotton, which they traded throughout the Southwest. Often described as individualists, desert farmers lived in dispersed settlements that the Spanish called **rancherias**, their dwellings separated by as much as a mile. That way, say the Pimas, people avoid getting on each other's nerves. Rancherias were governed by councils of adult men whose decisions required unanimous consent, although a headman was chosen to manage the irrigation works.

East of the Grand Canyon lived the Pueblo peoples. Although speaking several languages, the Pueblos had a great deal in common, most notably their commitment to communal village life. A strict communal code of behavior that regulated personal conduct was enforced by a maze of matrilineal clans and secret religious societies; unique combinations of these clans and societies formed the governing systems of different Pueblo villages. Seasonal public ceremonies in the

Rancherias Dispersed settlements of Indian farmers in the Southwest.

"The New Queen Being Taken to the King," engraved by Theodor de Bry in the sixteenth century from a drawing by Jacques le Moyne, an early French colonist of Florida. The communities of Florida were hierarchical, with classes and hereditary chiefs, some of whom were women. Here, le Moyne depicted a "queen" being carried on an ornamental litter by men of rank.

Neg. No. 324281, Photographed by Rota, Engraving by de Bry. American Museum of Natural History Library.

village squares included singing and chanting, dancing, colorful impersonations of the ancestral spirits called *kachinas,* and the comic antics of clowns who mocked in slapstick style those who did not conform to the communal ideal.

The Pueblos inhabit the oldest continuously occupied towns in the United States. The village of Oraibi, Arizona, dates from the twelfth century, when the Hopis ("peaceful ones") founded it in the isolated central mesas of the Colorado Plateau. Using dry-farming methods and drought-resistant plants, the Hopis produced rich harvests of corn and squash amid shifting sand dunes. On a mesa top about fifty miles southwest of present-day Albuquerque, New Mexico, Anasazi immigrants from Mesa Verde built Acoma, the "sky city," in the late thirteenth century. The Pueblo peoples established approximately seventy other villages over the next two centuries; fifty of these were still in existence in the seventeenth century when the Spanish founded Santa Fé, and two dozen survive today, including the large Indian towns of Laguna, Isleta, Santo Domingo, Jémez, San Felipe, and Taos.

The Athapascans, more recent immigrants to the Southwest, also lived in the arid deserts and mountains. They hunted and foraged, traded meat and medicinal herbs with farmers, and often raided and plundered these same villages and rancherias. One group of Athapascans, the Apaches, continued to maintain

QUICK REVIEW

The South
- Mild, moist climate ideal for farming.
- Indian peoples of the South farmed, fished, and hunted.
- Peoples of the South shared agricultural festivals.

OVERVIEW | Origins of Some Indian Tribal Names

Cherokee	A corruption of the Choctaw *chiluk-ki*, meaning "cave people," an allusion to the many caves in the Cherokee homeland in the highlands of present-day Georgia. The Cherokees called themselves *Ani-Yun-Wiya*, or "real people."
Cheyenne	From the Sioux *Sha-hiyena*, "people of strange speech." The Cheyennes of the Northern Plains called themselves *Dzi-tsistas*, meaning "our people."
Hopi	A shortening of the name the Hopis of northern Arizona use for themselves, *Hópitu*, which means "peaceful ones."
Mohawk	From the Algonquian *Mohawaúuck*, meaning "man-eaters." The Mohawks of the upper Hudson Valley in New York called themselves *Kaniengehaga*, "people of the place of the flint."
Pawnee	From the Pawnee term *paríki*, which describes a distinctive style of dressing the hair with paint and fat to make it stand erect like a horn. The Pawnees, whose homeland was the Platte River valley in present-day Nebraska, called themselves *Chahiksichahiks*, "men of men."

Overview: *Origins of Some Indian Tribal Names*

their nomadic ways. But another group, known as the Navajos, gradually adopted the farming and handicraft skills of their Pueblo neighbors.

THE SOUTH

The South enjoys a mild, moist climate with short winters and long summers, ideal for farming. From the Atlantic and Gulf Coasts, a broad fertile plain extends inland to the Piedmont, a plateau separating the coastal plains from the Appalachian Mountains. The upper courses of the waterways originating in the Appalachian highlands offered ample rich bottom land for farming. The extensive forests, mostly of yellow pine, offered abundant animal resources. In the sixteenth century, large populations of Indian peoples farmed this rich land, fishing or hunting local fauna to supplement their diets. They lived in communities ranging from villages of twenty or so dwellings to large towns of a thousand or more inhabitants (see Map 1.4).

Mississippian cultural patterns continued among many of the peoples of the South. Along the waterways, many farming towns were organized into chiefdoms. Because most of these groups were decimated by disease in the first years of colonization, they are poorly documented. Archaeologists have excavated sites on the east bank of the Mississippi, in what is now Arkansas, inhabited by the Caddo people. The evidence suggests that in the fifteenth century they lived in complex ranked communities, built monumental temple mounds, and counted a population of more than 200,000. There is historical evidence about the Natchez, who survived into the eighteenth century before being defeated and dispersed in a war with the French. They too lived on the Mississippi, on the opposite bank from the Caddos, where they farmed the rich floodplains. The Natchez were also a ranked society, with a small group of nobility ruling over the majority. Persistent territorial conflict with other confederacies elevated warriors to an honored status. Public torture and human sacrifice of enemies were common.

These chiefdoms were rather unstable. Under the pressure of climate change, population growth, and warfare, many were weakened and others collapsed. As a result, thousands of people left behind the grand mounds and earthworks and migrated to the woodlands and hill country, where they took up hunting and foraging, returning to the tried and true methods of "forest efficiency." They formed communities and banded together in confederacies, which were less centralized and more egalitarian than the Mississippian chiefdoms and would prove considerably more resilient to conquest.

Among the most prominent of these new ethnic groups were a people in present-day Mississippi and Alabama who came to be known as the Choctaws. Another group in western Tennessee became known as the Chickasaws, and another people in Georgia later became known as the Creeks. On the mountain plateaus lived the Cherokees, the single largest confederacy, which included more than sixty towns. For these groups, farming was somewhat less important, hunting somewhat more so. There were no ruling classes or kings, and leaders included women as well as men. Women controlled household and village life and were influential in the matrilineal clans that linked communities together. Councils of elderly men governed the confederacies but were joined by clan matrons for annual meetings at the central council house.

THE NORTHEAST

The Northeast, the colder sector of the eastern woodlands, has a varied geography of coastal plains and mountain highlands, great rivers, lakes, and valleys. In the first millennium CE, farming became the main support of the Indian economy in those places where the growing season was long enough to bring a crop of corn to maturity. In such areas of the Northeast, along the coasts and in the river valleys, Indian populations were large and dense (see Map 1.4).

The Iroquois of present-day Ontario and upstate New York have lived in the Northeast for at least 4,500 years and were among the first northeastern peoples to adopt cultivation.

Population growth and the resulting intensification of farming in Iroquoia stimulated the development of chiefdoms there as it did elsewhere. By the eleventh century, several centers of population, each in a separate watershed, had coalesced from east to west across upstate New York. These were the five Iroquois chiefdoms or nations: the Mohawks, Oneidas, Onondagas, Cayugas, and Senecas. Oral histories collected from Iroquois speakers during the nineteenth century remember this as an era of persistent violence, possibly the consequence of conflicts over territory.

To control this violence, the five nations established a confederacy. The Iroquois called their confederacy Haudenosaunee, meaning "people of the longhouse." Each nation, they said, occupied a separate hearth but acknowledged a common mother. As in the longhouse, women played important roles in the confederacy, choosing male leaders who would represent their lineages and chiefdom on the Iroquois council. The confederacy suppressed violence among its members but did not hesitate to encourage war against neighboring Iroquoian speakers, such as the Hurons or the Eries, who constructed defensive confederacies of their own at about the same time.

The other major language group of the Northeast was Algonquian, whose speakers divided among at least fifty distinct cultures. The Algonquian peoples

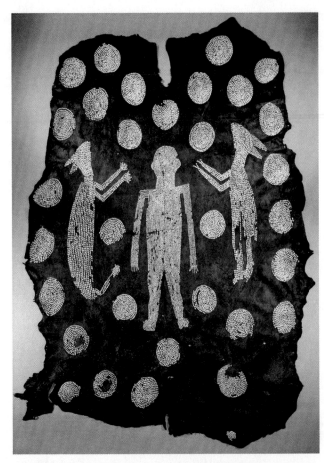

This deerskin cape, embroidered with shells by an Indian craftsman, is thought to be the chief's mantle that Powhatan, leader of a confederacy of Algonquian villages in the Chesapeake region, gave to an English captain as part of an exchange of presents in 1608. The animal effigies are suggestive of the complex of religious beliefs centering on the relationship of hunters to their prey.

Ashmolean Museum, Oxford, England, U.K.

QUICK REVIEW

The Northeast
- Varied geography of plains, mountains, rivers, lakes, and valleys.
- The Iroquois have lived in the region for 4,500 years.
- Population growth and intensification of farming led to the development of chiefdoms.

1–10
Thomas Harriot, *The Algonquian Peoples of the Atlantic Coast*

CHRONOLOGY

30,000 BCE	First humans populate Beringia	**1000 BCE**	First urban communities in Mexico
13,000 BCE	Global warming trend begins	**200 BCE–400 CE**	Hopewell culture flourishes
12,500 BCE	Monte Verde site in southern Chile flourishes	**650**	Bow and arrow, flint hoes, and Northern Flint corn in the Northeast
10,000 BCE	Clovis technology	**775–1150**	Hohokam culture flourishes
9000 BCE	Extinction of big-game animals	**1000**	Tobacco in use throughout North America
8000 BCE	Beginning of the Archaic period		
7000 BCE	First cultivation of plants in the Mexican highlands	**1142**	Founding of Haudenosaunee Confederacy
5000 BCE	Athapascan migration to America begins	**1150**	Founding of Hopi village of Oraibi, oldest continuously occupied town in the United States
4000 BCE	First settled communities along the Pacific coast	**1200**	High point of Mississippian and Anasazi cultures
3000 BCE	Inuit, Yupik, and Aleut migrations begin		
1500–1000 BCE	Maize and other Mexican crops introduced into the Southwest	**1276**	Severe drought begins in the Southwest
		1300	Arrival of Athapascans in the Southwest

north of the Great Lakes and in northern New England were hunters and foragers, organized into bands with loose ethnic affiliations. Several of these peoples, including the Míkmaq, Crees, Montagnais, and Ojibwas (also known as the Chippewas), were the first to become involved in the fur trade with European newcomers. Among the Algonquians of the Atlantic coast from present-day Massachusetts south to Virginia, as well as among those in the Ohio Valley, farming led to the development of settlements as densely populated as those of the Iroquois.

In contrast to the Iroquois, most Algonquian peoples were patrilineal. In general, they lived in less extensive dwellings and in smaller villages, often without palisade fortifications. Although Algonquian communities were relatively autonomous, they began to form confederacies during the fifteenth and sixteenth

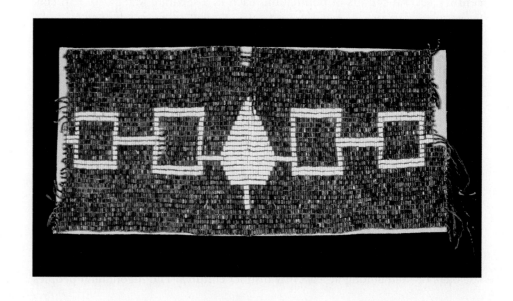

The Hiawatha wampum belt of the Haudenosaunee or Iroquois Five Nation Confederacy is exquisitely constructed of nearly seven thousand purple and white drilled shell beads, woven together with buckskin thongs and hemp thread. It is a ceremonial artifact, a symbol of the unity of the five Iroquois nations. With the central tree or heart pointed up, the first two squares on the right represent the Mohawk and Oneida, the tree stands for the Onondaga, where the council met, and the third and fourth squares for the Cayuga and Seneca nations. The belt itself dates from the early eighteenth century, but the design is thought to have originated with the Confederacy itself, perhaps in the twelfth century CE.

centuries. Among these groupings were those of the Massachusetts, Narragansetts, and Pequots of New England; the peoples of the Delaware Valley and Chesapeake Bay on the mid-Atlantic coast; and the Shawnees, Miamis, Kickapoos, and Potawatomis of the Ohio Valley.

CONCLUSION

Over the thousands of years that elapsed between the initial settlement of North America and the arrival of Europeans at the end of the fifteenth century, Indian peoples developed dozens of distinctive cultures, each fine-tuned to the geographic and climatic possibilities and limitations of their environments. In the northern forests, they hunted game and perfected the art of processing furs and hides. Along the coasts and rivers they harvested the abundant runs of fish and learned to navigate the waters with sleek and graceful boats. In the arid Southwest, they mastered irrigation farming and made the deserts bloom, while in the humid Southeast, they mastered the large-scale production of crops that sustained large cities with sophisticated political systems. The ruins of the ancient city of Cahokia provide dramatic evidence that North America was not the "virgin" continent Europeans proclaimed it to be. Indians had transformed the natural world, making it into a human landscape.

REVIEW QUESTIONS

1. List the evidence for the hypothesis that the Americas were settled by migrants from Asia.

2. Discuss the impact of environmental change and human hunting on the big-game populations of North America.

3. Review the principal regions of the North American continent and the human adaptations that made social life possible in each of them.

4. Define the concept of "forest efficiency." How does it help to illuminate the major development of the Archaic period?

5. Why did the development of farming lead to increasing social complexity? Discuss the reasons why organized political activity began in farming societies.

6. What were the hunting and agrarian traditions? In what ways did the religious beliefs of Indian peoples reflect their environmental adaptations?

7. What factors led to the organization of the Iroquois Five Nation Confederacy?

KEY TERMS

Archaic period (p. 8)   **Desert culture** (p. 7)
Athapascan (p. 4)   **Forest Efficiency** (p. 7)
Aztecs (p. 9)   **Indios** (p. 3)
Beringia (p. 3)   **Mesoamerica** (p. 8)
Cahokia (p. 2)   **Rancherias** (p. 16)

RECOMMENDED READING

Colin G. Calloway, *One Vast Winter Count: The Native American West Before Lewis and Clark* (2003). A masterful synthesis that emphasizes the continuities between the precolonial and colonial history of North America.

Sally Kitt Chappell, *Cahokia: Mirror of the Cosmos* (2002). An engaging, comprehensive, and thoughtful account of America's most impressive ancient monument.

Tom D. Dillehay, *The Settling of the Americas: A New Prehistory* (2000). A summary of the most recent archaeological findings, suggesting a much earlier migration to the Americas. For the newest discoveries, see recent issues and websites of *National Geographic* and *Scientific American.*

Patricia Galloway, *Choctaw Genesis, 1500–1700* (1995). A path-breaking work that uses both archaeological and written evidence to tie together the precolonial and colonial periods of a tribal people of the South.

Alvin M. Josephy Jr., ed., *America in 1492* (1992). Important essays by leading scholars of the North American Indian experience. Includes beautiful illustrations and maps as well as an excellent bibliography.

Alice Beck Kehoe, *America Before the European Invasions* (2002). A major new synthesis of the history of North America in the centuries before 1492.

Charles C. Mann, *1491: New Revelations of the Americas Before Columbus* (2005). A popular and engaging journalistic account of the increasing recognition among historians "that the Western Hemisphere played a role in the human story just as interesting and important as that of the Eastern Hemisphere."

Stephen Plog, *Ancient Peoples of the American Southwest* (1998). Covers the shift to agriculture with a focus on both the costs and the benefits. An accessible text with wonderful photographs.

Robert Silverberg, *Mound Builders of Ancient America: The Archaeology of a Myth* (1968). A history of opinion and theory about the mound builders.

William C. Sturtevant, general editor, *Handbook of North American Indians*, 20 vols. proposed (1978–). The most comprehensive collection of the best current scholarship. When completed the series will include a volume for each of the culture regions of North America, plus volumes on origins, Indian-white relations, languages, and art; a biographical dictionary; and a general index.

David Hurst Thomas, *Skull Wars: Kennewick Man, Archaeology, and the Battle for Native American Identity* (2000). A page-turner that details the controversy over the discovery of "Kennewick Man" and changing ideas about ancient North American history.

Russell Thornton, *American Indian Holocaust and Survival: A Population History since 1492* (1987). The best introduction to the historical demography of North America. Provides a judicious review of all the evidence in a field of considerable controversy.

For study resources for this chapter, go to **www.myhistorylab.com** and choose *Out of Many, Teaching and Learning Classroom Edition.* You will find a wealth of study and review material for this chapter, including pretests and posttests, customized study plan, key-term review flash cards, interactive map and document activities, and documents for analysis.

Our lord and king it is true that the strange people have come to the shores of the great sea . . .
—Miguel Leon-Portilla

The French, under the command of Jean Ribault, discover the River of May (St Johns River) in Florida on 1 May 1562: colored engraving, 1591, by Theodor de Bry after a now lost drawing by Jacques Le Moyne de Morgues. The Granger Collection.

2

WHEN WORLDS COLLIDE
1492–1590

HOW DID social change in Europe contribute to European expansion overseas?

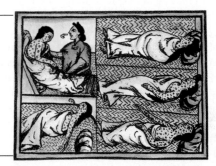

WHAT FACTORS contributed to the defeat of the Aztecs and Incas by European forces?

WHAT IMPORTANT differences were there between Spanish, English, and French patterns of colonization?

AMERICAN COMMUNITIES

The English at Roanoke

IN LATE AUGUST 1590 GOVERNOR JOHN WHITE RETURNED TO Roanoke Island, the first English community established in America. He had left three years before, sailing home to appeal for additional support. He was extremely anxious about the fate of the colonists, including his daughter, son-in-law, and granddaughter Virginia Dare, the first English child born in the New World. Rowing ashore, he found the colonists' houses "taken down," their possessions "spoiled and scattered about." Looking around for some sign of hope, White noticed a word carved on a nearby tree trunk: "CROATOAN," the name of a friendly Indian village some fifty miles south. White had left instructions that in the event of trouble the colonists were to leave the sign of a cross, and not finding one he reassured himself that his people awaited him at Croatoan. He returned to his vessel, anxious to rescue them.

In 1584 Sir Walter Raleigh sponsored a small group of adventurers who first landed on the island the Indians called Roanoke. The men found the coastal region densely populated by a "very handsome and goodly people" and were "entertained with all love and kindness" by a local chief named Wingina. To Wingina, the English were potential allies in his struggle to extend authority over more villages, and he granted the men permission to plan a large English settlement. He even sent two of his leading men, Manteo and Wanchese, back to England to help prepare the enterprise.

When the Englishmen returned in 1585, the two Indians offered Wingina conflicting reports. Manteo argued that English technology made these men powerful allies. But Wanchese told of the disturbing inequalities he had seen among the English and warned his chief of the potential brutality of these men. He rightly suspected their intentions, for Raleigh's plans were based on the expectation of exploiting the Indians. Raleigh hoped for profits from a lucrative trade in furs, a flourishing plantation agriculture, or the possibility of gold and silver mines. In each case the Indians were to supply the labor.

After building a rough fort on the island, the English requested supplies from Wingina. With the harvest in the storage pits, fish running in the streams, and fat game in the woods, the chief did the hospitable thing. But as fall turned to winter and the stores diminished, he grew weary of their persistent

demands. In the spring Wingina ran out of patience. Before the Indians could act, however, the Englishmen caught wind of the rising hostility and in a surprise attack in May 1586 they killed several leaders, including Wingina. Leaving his head on a stake, they fled back to England.

John White and Thomas Harriot, who had spent their time exploring the physical and human world of the coast and recording their findings in notes and sketches, were appalled by the turn of events. White proposed a new plan for a colony of genuine settlers, families who would attempt to live in harmony with the natives.

In 1587, with Raleigh's financial support, John White returned to Virginia as governor of a new colony of 117 men, women, and children. They were supposed to land on Chesapeake Bay after checking on the situation at Roanoke. But the captain, eager to get on with the profitable activity of plundering Spanish shipping, insisted on dropping the colonists there. White found himself among Indians who had already been completely alienated. Within a month, one of the colonists had been shot full of arrows. White's counterattack only increased the Indians' resolve to expel the intruders. The colonists begged White to sail home in their only seaworthy vessel to ask Raleigh for additional support. He left reluctantly, never to return.

Blinded by their desire for immediate rewards, the colonists wasted the opportunity presented by the natives' initial welcome. But the Roanoke story also says something about the importance of community in the first attempts at colonization. Bits of evidence suggest that the so-called lost colonists lived out the rest of their lives as residents of Indian villages. Virginia Dare and other English children may have been adopted by Indian families, grown up and taken Indian spouses, in the process creating the first mixed community of English and Indians in North America.

European colonists came to the Americas for a variety of reasons, but high on their list of priorities were plunder and profit. The invasion of America often included terrible violence, as well as frequent possibilities for accommodation and cooperation between natives and newcomers. The invasion also introduced mortal epidemic diseases that devastated native communities. The encounter of communities at Roanoke was, in numerous ways, a template for New World colonization.

THE EXPANSION OF EUROPE

The connection between Europe and America established by Columbus' 1492 voyage had earthshaking consequences. Within a generation, the exchanges of peoples, crops, animals, and germs had transformed the world. The key to understanding these remarkable events is the transformation of Europe during the several centuries preceding the voyage of Columbus.

WESTERN EUROPE BEFORE COLUMBUS

Western Europe was an agricultural society: Most Europeans lived in family households clustered in farming villages. Farming and raising livestock had been practiced in Europe for thousands of years, but during the late Middle Ages there were great advances in technology. Water mills, iron plows, improved devices for harnessing ox and horse power, and systems of crop rotation greatly increased productivity. From the eleventh to the fourteenth centuries the quantity of land under cultivation in western Europe more than doubled. During the same period the population nearly tripled.

Europe was divided into hundreds of small territories, each ruled by a family of lords that held a monopoly of wealth and power. Lords commanded labor service from peasants and tribute in the form of crops. They were the main beneficiaries of medieval economic expansion, accumulating great estates and building imposing castles.

Western Europe was officially Christian, united under the authority of the Roman Catholic Church, whose complex organization spanned thousands of local communities with a hierarchy that extended from parish priests to the pope in Rome. The Catholic Church was one of the most powerful landowners in Europe. It insisted on its dogmas and actively persecuted heretics, nonbelievers, and devotees of older "pagan" religions. The Church provided legitimacy for the relationship of lord and peasant, counseling the poor and downtrodden to place their hopes in heavenly rewards.

For the great majority of Europeans, living conditions were harsh. Most rural people survived on bread and porridge, supplemented with seasonal vegetables and an occasional piece of meat or fish. Infectious diseases abounded and famines periodically ravaged the countryside. In the fourteenth century, for example, a series of crop failures resulted in widespread starvation and death. This episode prepared the way for the so-called Black Death, a widespread epidemic of bubonic plague that swept in from Asia and wiped out a third of Europe's population between 1347 and 1353.

Strengthened by the technological developments of the Middle Ages, Europe's agricultural economy quickly recovered. By 1500 the population had rebounded to its former high of 65 million.

THE MERCHANT CLASS AND THE RENAISSANCE

The economic growth of the late Middle Ages was accompanied by the expansion of commerce. Commercial expansion stimulated the growth of markets and towns. The heart of this dynamic European commercialism lay in the city-states of Italy.

During the late Middle Ages, the cities of Venice, Genoa, and Pisa launched armed commercial fleets that seized control of Mediterranean trade. The merchants of these cities became the principal outfitters of the Crusades, a series of great military expeditions promoted by the Catholic Church to recover Palestine from

HOW DID social change in Europe contribute to European expansion overseas?

Review Summary

IMAGE KEY

for pages 24–25

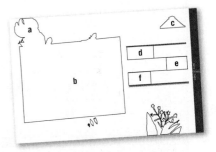

a. An illustration of a banana blossom.
b. The French, under the command of Jean Ribault, discover St Johns River in Florida on May 1, 1562.
c. Pyramid of Kukulcan at Chichen Itza.
d. Peter Minuet purchases Manhattan island from the local Native Americans.
e. Aztec Indians, with smallpox contracted from the Spaniards, ministered to by a medicine man.
f. John White finding no trace of the colony of Roanoke on his return to Virginia in 1590.

QUICK REVIEW

European Society
♦ European states were hierarchical.
♦ Most Europeans were peasant farmers.
♦ European society was patriarchal.

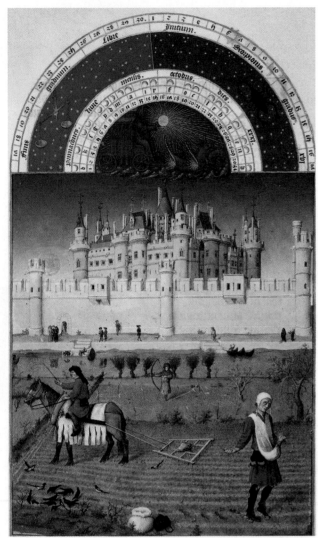

A French peasant labors in the field before a spectacular castle in a page taken from the illuminated manuscript *Tres Riches Heures*, made in the fifteenth century for the duc de Berry. In 1580 the essayist Montaigne talked with several American Indians at the French court who "noticed among us some men gorged to the full with things of every sort while their other halves were beggars at their doors, emaciated with hunger and poverty" and "found it strange that these poverty-stricken halves should suffer such injustice, and that they did not take the others by the throat or set fire to their houses."

Renaissance The intellectual and artistic flowering in Europe during the fourteenth, fifteenth, and sixteenth centuries sparked by a revival of interest in classical antiquity.

the Muslims. With the conquest of Jerusalem at the end of the eleventh century, the silk and spice trades of Asia were delivered into the hands of Italian merchants. Asian civilization also supplied a number of technical innovations that further propelled European economic growth.

Contact with Muslim civilization provided access to important ancient texts, long lost in Europe but preserved in the great libraries of Alexandria (Egypt) and Baghdad (Iraq). The revived interest in classical antiquity triggered a period of intellectual and artistic flowering from the fourteenth to sixteenth centuries that later generations called the **Renaissance**.

❧ The Renaissance celebrated human possibility. "The nature of all other beings is limited," wrote the Italian intellectual Pico della Mirandola in 1486; "but you, constrained by no limits, in accordance with your own free will, shall ordain for yourself the limits of your nature." This human-centered perspective was part of what became known as humanism, in which human life on earth took precedence over the afterlife of the soul. This outlook was a critical component of the inquisitive and acquisitive spirit that motivated the exploration of the Americas.❧

THE NEW MONARCHIES

The Renaissance began amid the ruins of the plague. Famine and disease led to violence, as groups battled for their share of a shrinking economy. A series of peasant rebellions culminated in the great English Peasants' Revolt of 1381. Warfare among the nobility weakened and greatly reduced the power of the landed classes, and the Catholic Church was seriously destabilized by an internal struggle between French and Italian factions.

❧ It was during this period of social and political chaos that the monarchs of western Europe began to replace the lords as the new centers of power. They built their legitimacy by promising internal order as they unified their realms (see Map 2.1). In many cases, the new monarchs found support among the increasingly wealthy merchants, who in return sought lucrative royal contracts and trading monopolies. This alliance between commerce and political power was another important development that prepared the way for European expansion. ❧

THE PORTUGUESE VOYAGES

Portugal, a narrow land along the western coast of the Iberian Peninsula with a long tradition of seafaring, became the first of the new Renaissance kingdoms to send out explorers on voyages to distant lands. Lisbon, the principal port on the sea route between the Mediterranean and northwestern Europe, was a bustling, cosmopolitan city with large enclaves of Italian merchants. By 1385 the local merchant community had grown powerful enough to place João I, their favorite, on the throne. João had ambitious plans to establish a Portuguese trading empire.

A central figure in this development was the king's son, Prince Henry, known to later generations as "the Navigator." Prince Henry established an academy of

MAP EXPLORATION

To explore an interactive version of this map, go to **http://www.prenhall.com/faraghertlc/map2.1**

MAP 2.1

Western Europe in the Fifteenth Century   By the middle of the century, the monarchs of western Europe had begun to build royal bureaucracies and standing armies and navies. These states sponsored the voyages that inaugurated the era of European colonization.

WHY WERE some European states better positioned for colonizing than others?

eminent geographers, instrument makers, shipbuilders, and seamen at his institute on the southwestern tip of Portugal at Sagres Point. By the mid-fifteenth century, as a result of their efforts, most educated Europeans knew the earth was round. Studying the seafaring traditions of Asia and the Muslim world, the learned men of Sagres Point incorporated them into the design of a new ship called the *caravel*, faster and better-handling than any ship previously known in Europe. They promoted the use of Arab instruments for astronomical calculation. With such innovations, Europeans became the masters of the world's seas, a supremacy that would continue until the twentieth century.

The Portuguese explored the Atlantic coast of northwestern Africa for direct access to the lucrative gold and slave trades of that continent. The Portuguese eventually built strategic trading forts along the coasts of Africa, India, Indonesia, and China, the first and longest-lasting outposts of European world colonization, and gained control of much of the Asian spice trade. Most important for the history of the Americas, the Portuguese established the Atlantic slave trade. (For a full discussion of slavery, see Chapter 4.)

QUICK REVIEW

Portuguese Explorations

- Prince Henry the Navigator played a key role in sponsoring exploration.
- Technological innovations made longer sea voyages possible.
- The Portuguese explored the Atlantic coast of Africa seeking direct access to gold and slaves.

The astrolabe, an instrument used for determining the precise position of heavenly bodies, was introduced into early modern Europe by the Arabs. This is one of the earliest examples, an intricately engraved brass astrolabe produced by a master craftsman in Syria in the thirteenth century.

© National Maritime Museum Picture Library, London, England. Neg. #E5555-3.

1–2

Christopher Columbus, *Letter to Ferdinand and Isabella of Spain* (1494)

Reconquista   The long struggle (ending in 1492) during which Spanish Christians reconquered the Iberian peninsula from Muslim occupiers.

COLUMBUS REACHES THE AMERICAS

In 1476, Christopher Columbus, a young Genoan sailor, joined his brother in Lisbon, where he became a seafaring merchant for Italian traders. He developed the simple idea of opening a new route to the Indies by sailing west across the Atlantic Ocean, known at that time as the "Western Sea." Such a venture would require royal backing, but when he approached the various monarchs of Europe with his idea, their advisers laughed at his geographic ignorance, pointing out that his calculation of the distance to Asia was much too short. They were right, Columbus was wrong. But it turned out to be an error of monumental good fortune.

Columbus finally sold his plan to the monarchs of Castile and Aragon, Isabel and Ferdinand. These two had just completed the **Reconquista**, a centuries-long struggle between Catholics and Muslims that ended Muslim rule in Spain. The Catholic monarchs of Spain were eager for new lands to conquer, and observing the successful Portuguese push to the south along the west coast of Africa, they became interested in opening lucrative trade routes of their own to the Indies.

Columbus' mission was more than commercial. One of his prime goals was to "occupy" the islands he found, establishing title for Spain by the right of occupancy. Like the adventurers who later established the first English colony at Roanoke, Columbus' objectives were starkly imperial.

Columbus' three vessels reached the Bahamas in October 1492. But Columbus believed he was in the Indies, somewhere near the Asian mainland. He explored the northern island coasts of Cuba and Hispaniola before heading home, fortuitously catching the westerly winds that blow from the American coast toward Europe north of the tropics.

Leading Columbus' triumphal procession to the royal court were half a dozen Taíno Indians, taken by force from their homes, and dressed for the occasion in bright feathers with ornaments of gold. "Should your majesties command it," Columbus told the monarchs, "all the inhabitants could be made slaves." Moreover, he reported, "there are many spices and great mines of gold and of other metals." In fact, none of the Eastern spices familiar to Europeans grew in the Caribbean and there were only small quantities of alluvial gold in the riverbeds of the islands. But the sight of the gold ornaments worn by the Taínos infected Columbus with gold fever. He reported that he had left a small force behind in a rough fort on the northern coast of Hispaniola to explore for gold—the first European foothold in the Americas.

The enthusiastic monarchs financed a return convoy of seventeen vessels and 1,500 men that sailed in late 1493 to begin the systematic colonization of the islands. But returning to Hispaniola, Columbus found his fort in ruins and his men all killed by the Taínos. Columbus directed his men to attack and destroy the nearby Taíno villages, enslaving the inhabitants and demanding tribute in gold.

Columbus' voyages were a disaster for the Taínos. The combined effects of warfare, famine, and demoralization resulted in the collapse of their society. By the 1520s they had been effectively eliminated as a people. As the native population fell, the colony plunged into depression. As early as 1500 the Spanish monarchs had grown so dissatisfied that they ordered Columbus arrested and sent back to Spain in irons.

Columbus bids farewell to the monarchs Isabel and Ferdinand at the port of Palos in August 1492, illustrated in a copperplate engraving published in 1594 by Theodore de Bry of Frankfort. While armed men are ferried out to the vessels, three accountants in a room directly above the monarchs count out the gold to fund the journey.

Columbus made two additional voyages to the Caribbean, both characterized by the same obsessive searching for gold and violent raiding for slaves. He died in Spain in 1506, still convinced he had opened a new way to Asia. This belief persisted among many Europeans well into the sixteenth century.

THE SPANISH IN THE AMERICAS

The Spanish had created a huge and wealthy empire in the Americas. In theory, all law and policy for the empire came from Spain; in practice, the isolation of the settlements led to a good deal of local autonomy. The Spanish created a caste system, in which a small minority of settlers and their offspring controlled the lives and labor of millions of Indian and African workers. But it was also a society in which colonists, Indians, and Africans mixed to form a new people.

THE INVASION OF AMERICA

The first stages of the Spanish invasion of America included frightful violence. Columbus and his successors established an institution known as the *encomienda,* in which Indians were compelled to labor in the service of Spanish lords. Faced with labor shortages, slavers raided the Bahamas and soon depopulated them of native people. The depletion of gold on Hispaniola led to the invasion of the islands of Puerto Rico and Jamaica in 1508, then Cuba in 1511. Meanwhile, rumors of wealthy native societies to the west led to scores of probing expeditions (see Map 2.2). The Spanish invasion of Central America began in 1511, and two years later Vasco Núñez de Balboa crossed the Isthmus of Panama to the Pacific Ocean. In 1517, Spaniards landed on the coast of Mexico, and within a year they made contact with the Aztec empire.

WHAT FACTORS contributed to the defeat of the Aztecs and Incas by European forces?

myhistorylab
Review Summary

myhistorylab
Exploring America: *Exploitation of the Americas*

MAP EXPLORATION

To explore an interactive version of this map, go to **http://www.prenhall.com/faragherltc/map2.2**

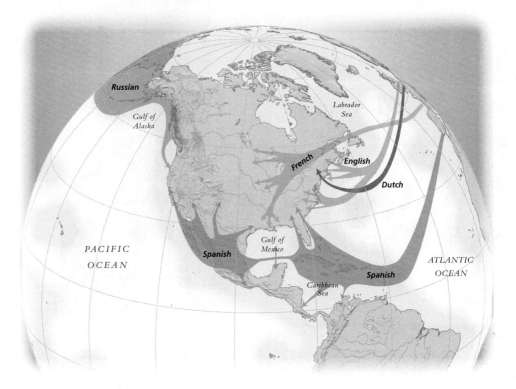

MAP 2.2

The Invasion of America   In the sixteenth century, the Spanish first invaded the Caribbean and used it to stage their successive wars of conquest in North and South America. In the seventeenth century, the French, English, and Dutch invaded the Atlantic coast. The Russians, sailing across the northern Pacific, mounted the last of the colonial invasions in the eighteenth century.

WHAT IMPORTANT differences were there among the Spanish, French, and English approaches to conquest and settlement of the Americas?

Hernán Cortés, a veteran of the conquest of Cuba, landed on the Mexican coast in 1519 with armed troops. Within two years he overthrew the Aztec empire, a spectacular military accomplishment that has no parallel in the annals of conquest. Cortés skillfully exploited the resentment of the many peoples who lived under Aztec domination, forging Spanish–Indian alliances that became a model for the subsequent European colonization of the Americas. The Aztecs were militarily powerful. They succeeded in driving the Spaniards from Tenochtitlán, then put up a bitter and prolonged defense when Cortés returned with tens of thousands of Indian allies to besiege the capital. In the meantime, however, the Aztecs suffered a devastating epidemic of smallpox that killed thousands and undermined their ability to resist. In the aftermath of conquest, the Spanish plundered Aztec society, providing the Catholic monarchs with wealth beyond their wildest imagining.

THE DESTRUCTION OF THE INDIES

The Indian peoples of the Americas resisted Spanish conquest with determination, but most proved a poor match for mounted warriors with steel swords. The record of the conquest includes many brave Indian leaders and thousands of martyrs.

1–12

An Aztec Remembers the Conquest of Mexico a Quarter Century Afterwards (1550)

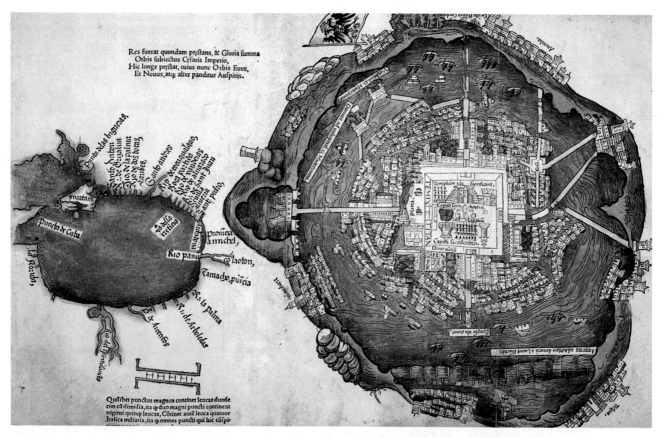

This map of Tenochtitlán, published in 1524 and attributed to the celebrated engraver Albrecht Dürer, shows the city before its destruction, with the principal Aztec temples in the main square, causeways connecting the city to the mainland, and an acqueduct supplying fresh water. The information on this map must have come from Aztec sources, as did much of the intelligence Cortés relied on for the Spanish conquest.

Some Europeans protested the horrors of the conquest. In 1511 the Catholic priest Antonio de Montesinos condemned the violence in a sermon delivered to colonists on Hispaniola. In the congregation was Bartolomé de las Casas, a man who had participated in the plunder of Cuba. Renouncing his own wealth, las Casas entered the priesthood and dedicated his life to the protection of the Indians. Long before the world recognized the concept of universal human rights, las Casas was proclaiming that "the entire human race is one," earning him a reputation as one of the towering moral figures in the early history of the Americas.

In his brilliant history of the conquest, *The Destruction of the Indies* (1542), las Casas blamed the Spanish for cruelties resulting in millions of Indian deaths—in effect he accused them of genocide. Translated into several languages and widely circulated throughout Europe, las Casas's book was cynically used by other European colonial powers to condemn Spain, thereby covering up their own dismal colonial practices.

1–13
Bartolomé de Las Casas, *The Devastation of the Indies* (1565)

THE VIRGIN SOIL EPIDEMICS

Las Casas was incorrect, however, in attributing most of these Indian deaths to warfare. The primary cause of the drastic reduction in native populations was epidemic disease—influenza, plague, smallpox, measles, typhus. Although preconquest America was by no means disease free, there were no diseases of epidemic potential. Indian peoples lacked the antibodies necessary to protect them from

This drawing of victims of the smallpox epidemic that struck the Aztec capital of Tenochtitlán in 1520 is taken from the *Florentine Codex*, a postconquest history written and illustrated by Aztec scribes. "There came amongst us a great sickness, a general plague," reads the account, "killing vast numbers of people. It covered many all over with sores: on the face, on the head, on the chest, everywhere. . . . The sores were so terrible that the victims could not lie face down, nor on their backs, nor move from one side to the other. And when they tried to move even a little, they cried out in agony."

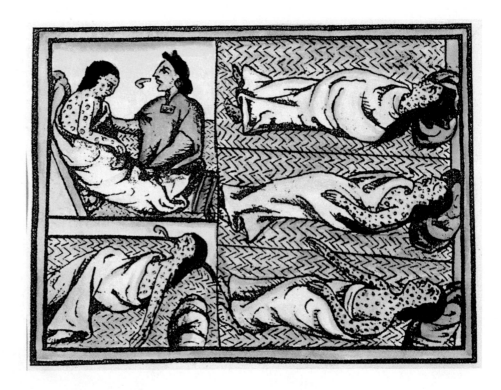

European germs and viruses. Such devastating outbreaks of disease, striking for the first time against a completely unprotected population, are known as "virgin soil epidemics." Smallpox made its first appearance in America in 1518, exploding in an epidemic so virulent that, in the words of an early Spanish historian, "it left Hispaniola, Puerto Rico, Jamaica, and Cuba desolated of Indians." The epidemic hit Mexico in 1520, destroying the Aztecs and preparing the way for their conquest, then spreading along the Indian trade network. In 1524 it strategically weakened the Inca civilization of the Andes eight years before their empire was conquered by Francisco Pizarro. Disease was the secret weapon of the Spanish, and it helps explain their extraordinary success in the conquest.

Warfare, famine, lower birthrates, and epidemic disease knocked the native population of the Americas into a downward spiral that was not reversed until the twentieth century (see Figure 2.1). By that time native population had fallen by more than 90 percent. It was the greatest demographic disaster in world history.

QUICK REVIEW

Causes of Indian Population Decline
- Disease
- Warfare
- Famine
- Declining birthrates

Figure 2.1

North America's Indian and Colonial Populations in the Seventeenth and Eighteenth Centuries

The primary factor in the decimation of native peoples was epidemic disease, brought to the New World from the Old. In the eighteenth century, the colonial population overtook North America's Indian populations.

Historical Statistics of the United States (Washington, DC: Government Printing Office, 1976), 8, 1168; Russell Thornton, *American Indian Holocaust and Survival* (Norman: University of Oklahoma Press, 1987), 32.

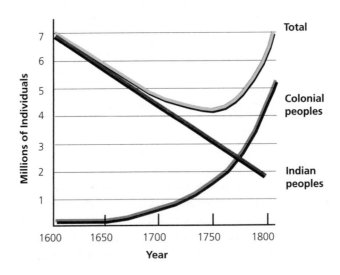

THE COLUMBIAN EXCHANGE

1–19
Jose de Acosta, *The Columbian Exchange* (1590)

The passage of diseases between the Old and New Worlds was one part of the large-scale exchange of people, animals, plants, and goods—what the historian Alfred Crosby terms "the Columbian Exchange"—that marks the beginning of the modern era of world history (see Map 2.3). The most obvious exchange was the vast influx into Europe of the precious metals plundered from the Aztec and Incan empires of the New World. Most of this golden booty was melted down, destroying forever thousands of priceless native artifacts. Silver from mines the Spanish discovered and operated with Indian labor in Mexico and Peru tripled the amount of silver coin circulating in Europe between 1500 and 1550, then tripled it again before 1600. The result of so much new coin in circulation was runaway inflation, which stimulated commerce and raised profits but lowered the standard of living for most people.

Of even greater long-term importance were the New World crops brought to Europe. Maize (Indian corn), the staff of life for most native North Americans, became a staple crop in Mediterranean countries, the dominant feed for livestock elsewhere in Europe, and the primary provision for the slave ships of Africa. Potatoes provided the margin between famine and subsistence for the peasant peoples of northern Europe and Ireland.

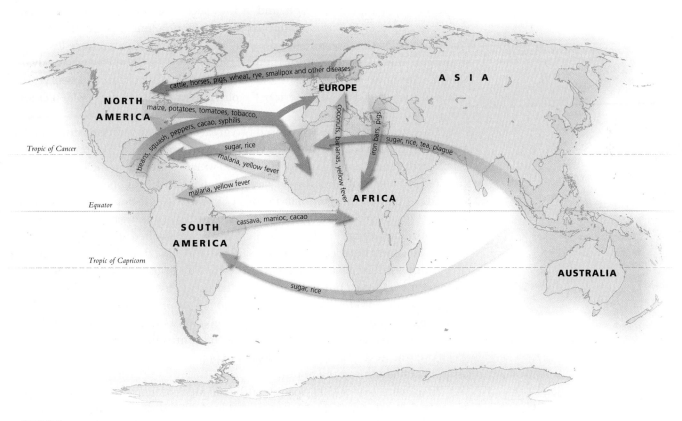

MAP 2.3

The Columbian Exchange Europeans voyaging between Europe, Africa, Asia, and the Americas in the fifteenth and sixteenth centuries began a vast intercontinental movement of plants, animals, and diseases that shaped the course of modern history.

THE COLUMBIAN EXCHANGE marked the beginning of the modern era of world history. What developments and events contributed to this? What were its advantages and disadvantages?

Although the Spanish failed to locate valuable spices such as black pepper or cloves in the New World, new tropical crops more than compensated. Tobacco, first introduced to Europe about 1550 as a cure for disease, was soon in wide use as a stimulant. American vanilla and chocolate both became highly valued. American cotton proved far superior to Asian varieties for the production of cheap textiles. Each of these native plants—along with tropical transplants from the Old World to America, with sugar, rice, and coffee being the most important—supplied the basis for important new industries and markets that altered the course of world history.

Columbus introduced domesticated animals into Hispaniola and Cuba, and livestock were later transported to Mexico. The movement of Spanish settlement northward through Mexico was greatly aided by an advancing wave of livestock, for grazing animals did serious damage to native fields and forests. Horses, used by Spanish stockmen to tend their cattle, also spread northward. In the seventeenth century, horses reached the Great Plains of North America, where they eventually transformed the lives of the nomadic hunting Indians (see Chapter 5).

THE SPANISH IN NORTH AMERICA

Ponce de León, governor of Puerto Rico, was the first Spanish conquistador to attempt to extend the Spanish conquest to North America (see Map 2.4). In search of slaves, he made his first landing on the mainland coast, which he named Florida, in 1513. Warriors from the powerful Indian chiefdoms there beat back this and several other attempts at invasion, and in 1521 succeeded in killing Ponce. Seven years later, another Spanish attempt to colonize Florida, under the command of Pánfilo de Narváez, also ended in disaster. Most of Narváez's men were lost in a shipwreck, but a small group of them survived. One of these castaways, Alvar Núñez Cabeza de Vaca, published an account of his adventures in which he repeated rumors of a North American empire known as Cíbola, with golden cities "larger than the city of Mexico."

1–3
Alvar Núñez Cabeza de Vaca, *Indians of the Rio Grande* (1528-1536)

Cabeza de Vaca's report inspired two great Spanish expeditions into North America. The first was mounted in Cuba by Hernán de Soto, a veteran of the conquest of Peru. Landing in Florida in 1539 with over 700 men, de Soto pushed hundreds of miles through the heavily populated South, commandeering food and slaves from the Mississippian towns in his path. But de Soto failed to locate another Aztec empire. Moving westward, his expedition was twice mauled by powerful native armies and reduced by half. When he reached the Mississippi, he was met by a great flotilla of 200 vessels said to have come down river from a great city to the west. The Spaniards crossed the river and pushed westward through present-day Arkansas, but failing to find the great city, returned to the Mississippi. There de Soto fell sick and died. Some 300 dispirited survivors eventually made it back to Mexico on rafts. The native peoples of the South had successfully turned back Spanish invasion. But de Soto had introduced epidemic disease, which over the next several years drastically depopulated and undermined the Mississippian chiefdoms of the South.

In the same year of 1539, Spanish officials in Mexico launched a second attempt to conquer North America, this one aimed at the Southwest. Francisco Vásquez de Coronado led 300 mounted men and infantry and 800 Indian porters north along well-marked Indian trading paths, passing through the settlements of Piman Indians near the present border of the United States and Mexico and finally reaching the Pueblo villages along the Rio Grande. Coronado sent out expeditions in all directions in search of the legendary golden cities of Cíbola. He led his army as far north as the Great Plains, where they observed great herds of "shaggy cows"

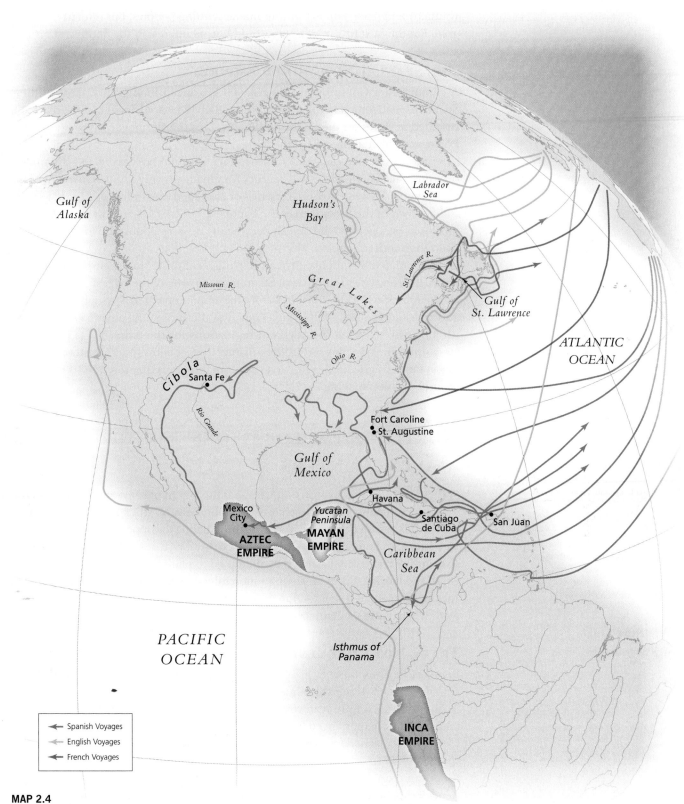

MAP 2.4

European Exploration, 1492–1591 By the mid-sixteenth century, Europeans had explored most of the Atlantic coast of North America and penetrated into the interior in the disastrous expeditions of de Soto and Coronado.

WHAT WERE the reasons behind the different experiences of the French, Spanish, and English explorations?

(buffalo) and made contact with nomadic hunting peoples, but returned without gold. For the next fifty years Spain would lose all interest in the Southwest.

THE SPANISH NEW WORLD EMPIRE

A century after Columbus, some 250,000 European immigrants, most of them Spaniards, had settled in the Americas. Another 125,000 Africans had been forcibly resettled as slaves on the Spanish plantations of the Caribbean, as well as on the Portuguese plantations of Brazil.

Spanish women came to America as early as Columbus' second expedition, but over the course of the sixteenth century they made up only about 10 percent of the immigrants. Most male colonists married or cohabited with Indian or African women. Indians died by the thousands in the conquest, but Indian genes were passed on in mixed-ancestry people who quickly became the majority population in the mainland Spanish American empire.

Populated by Indians, Africans, Spanish colonists, and their hybrid descendants, the New World colonies of Spain made up one of the largest and most powerful empires in world history. In theory the empire operated as a highly centralized and bureaucratic system. But the Council of the Indies, the advisers of the Spanish king who made all the laws and regulations for the empire, was located far away in Spain. What looked in the abstract like a centrally administered empire was in fact a fragmented collection of colonial regions that tolerated a great deal of local decision making.

NORTHERN EXPLORATIONS AND ENCOUNTERS

WHAT IMPORTANT differences were there between Spanish, English, and French patterns of colonization?

myhistorylab
Review Summary

When the Spanish empire was at the height of its power in the sixteenth century, the merchants and monarchs of other European seafaring states began looking across the Atlantic for opportunities of their own (see Map 2.4). France was first to sponsor expeditions to the New World in the early sixteenth century. The French first attempted to plant settlements on the coasts of Brazil and Florida, but Spanish opposition forced them to concentrate on the North Atlantic. England did not develop its own plans to colonize North America until the second half of the sixteenth century.

TRADE NOT CONQUEST: FISH AND FURS

Long before France and England made attempts to found colonies, however, European fishermen were exploiting the coastal North American waters of the North Atlantic. The first European voyages of exploration in the North Atlantic used the talents of these experienced European sailors and fishermen. Giovanni Caboto (or John Cabot) reached Labrador in 1497, but the English did little to follow up on his voyage. In 1524, Giovanni da Verrazano, sailing for the French, explored the North American coast. Encouraged by his report, the French crown commissioned experienced captain Jacques Cartier to locate a "Northwest Passage" to the Indies. In a series of voyages undertaken in 1534, 1535, and 1541, Cartier failed to locate such a passage but became the first European to explore the St. Lawrence River, which led to the Great Lakes, and provided easy access to the Ohio and Mississippi rivers. Cartier's exploration established France's imperial claim to the lands of Canada and provided the French with an incomparable geographic advantage over other colonial powers.

The French and other northern Europeans thus discovered the Indian people of the northern woodlands, and the Indians in turn discovered them. Contacts here were quite different than those of the tropics, based on commerce rather than conquest. The natives immediately appreciated the usefulness of textiles, glass, copper, and ironware. For his part, Cartier was interested in the fur coats of the Indians.

The fur trade would continue to play an important role in the Atlantic economy for the next three centuries. The trade also had familiar negative consequences. European epidemic disease soon followed in the wake of the traders, and violent warfare broke out between tribes over access to hunting grounds. Moreover, as European-manufactured goods, such as metal knives, kettles, and firearms, became essential to their way of life, Indians grew dependent upon European suppliers.

By the end of the sixteenth century over a thousand European ships were trading for furs each year along the northern Atlantic coast. The village of Tadoussac on the St. Lawrence, where a wide bay offered Europeans safe anchorage, became the customary place for a late summer trading fair. Within a few years the French would attempt to monopolize the northern trade by planting colonies along the coast and on the St. Lawrence. The first French colonies in North America, however, were planted farther south by a group of French Protestant religious dissenters known as the **Huguenots**.

THE PROTESTANT REFORMATION AND THE FIRST FRENCH COLONIES

The **Protestant Reformation**—the religious revolt against the Roman Catholic Church—began in 1517 when German priest Martin Luther publicized his differences with Rome. Luther declared that eternal salvation was a gift from God and not related to works or service to the Catholic Church. One of Luther's most prominent converts was Jean Chauvin (known to English speakers as John Calvin), a young theology student in Paris. In 1533, as the persecution of **Protestants** intensified, Calvin fled France, eventually taking up residence in Geneva, Switzerland, where civic leaders had renounced the Catholic Church and expelled the city's bishop. Working with those leaders, Calvin established a Protestant theocracy in Geneva. His systematic writings and teachings concerning theology, liturgy, ritual, and church government proved highly influential among Protestants. His followers in France, known as Huguenots, largely came from the urban middle class but also included a portion of the nobility, those opposed to the central authority of the Catholic monarch. In 1560 the French crown successfully defeated a plot among powerful Huguenots to seize royal power, inaugurating nearly forty years of violent religious conflict in France.

The first French colonies developed as attempts to establish a religious refuge in the New World for Huguenots. In 1562 French naval officer Jean Ribault and a group of 150 Huguenots from Normandy landed on Parris Island, near present-day Beaufort, South Carolina, and began construction of a fort and crude mud huts. In 1564, Ribault and his followers established a second Huguenot colony, Fort Caroline, on the St. Johns River of Florida, south of present-day Jacksonville.

The Spanish were alarmed by these moves. They had shown little interest themselves in colonizing Florida but worried about protecting their convoys, riding home to Spain on the offshore Gulf Stream, loaded with gold and silver. Not only was Fort Caroline manned by Frenchmen but also by Protestants— mortal enemies of the Catholic monarchs of Spain. In 1565 King Philip II of Spain sent Don Pedro Menéndez de Avilés, captain general of the Indies, to

1–4

Jacques Cartier, *First Contact with the Indians* (1534)

QUICK REVIEW

The Fur Trade

◆ Fur traders were critical to New France's success.

◆ New France ruled by royal appointees.

◆ *Coureurs de bois*: independent fur traders living among the Indians.

Huguenots French Protestant religious dissenters who planted the first French colonies in North America.

Protestant Reformation Martin Luther's challenge to the Catholic Church, initiated in 1517, calling for a return to what he understood to be the purer practices and beliefs of the early church.

Protestants All European supporters of religious reform under Charles V's Holy Roman Empire.

This watercolor of Jacques Le Moyne, painted in 1564, depicts the friendly relations between the Timucuas of coastal Florida and the colonists of the short-lived French colony of Fort Caroline. The Timucuas hoped that the French would help defend them against the Spanish, who plundered the coast in pursuit of Indian slaves.

Jacques Le Moyne, "Rene de Loudonniere and Chief Athore," 1564. Gouache and metallic pigments on vellum. Print Collection, The New York Public Library, New York. The New York Public Library/Art Resource, NY.

1–8
Pedro Menéndez de Avilés,
The Founding of St. Augustine
(1565)

crush the Huguenots, which he did. To prevent further French incursions the Spanish built massive Castillo San Marcos (still standing) and established a garrison at St. Augustine, which has the distinction of being the oldest continuously occupied European city in North America.

SOCIAL CHANGE IN SIXTEENTH-CENTURY ENGLAND

The English movement across the Atlantic, like the French, was tied to social change at home. Perhaps most important were changes in the economy. As prices for goods rose steeply—the result of New World inflation—English landlords, their rents fixed by custom, sought ways to increase their incomes. Seeking profits in the woolen trade, many converted the common pasturage used by tenants into grazing land for sheep, dislocating large numbers of farmers.

Sixteenth-century England also became deeply involved in the Protestant Reformation. At first King Henry VIII of England (reigned 1509–47) supported the Catholic Church and opposed the Protestants. But when the pope refused to grant Henry an annulment of his marriage to Catherine of Aragon, daughter of Ferdinand and Isabel of Spain, the king took up the cause of reform. In 1534, he declared himself head of a separate Church of England. He later took over the English estates of the Catholic Church and utilized their revenues in the construction of a powerful English state system, including a standing army and navy. Working through Parliament, Henry carefully enlisted the support of the merchants and landed gentry for his program. By 1547, when Henry died, he had forged a solid alliance between the English monarchy and the wealthy merchant class.

A Watercolor from the First Algonquian–English Encounter

Some of the first accurate images of the native inhabitants of North America were produced by the artist John White during his stay in 1685 at the first English colony in North America, at Roanoke Island on North Carolina's Outer Banks.

IN WHAT ways does this image document John White's powers of observation?

Two years later White would become governor of the famous "Lost Colony." This image of an Indian mother and daughter illustrates the care White brought to the task of recording as fully as possible the Indians' way of life. The woman wears an apron-skirt of fringed deerskin, its borders edged with white beads, and a woven beadwork necklace. The body decorations on her face and upper arms are tattooed. One of her arms rests in a sling, an unusual posture, something quite unique to this culture. In the other hand she holds an empty gourd container for carrying water. The little girl holds an English wooden doll, a gift from White, and it seems to greatly please her. In the written account that accompanied White's images, Thomas Harriot wrote that all the Indian girls "are greatly delighted with puppetts and babes which were brought out of England" as gifts of exchange. Historic images bear close observation, for it is often small details like this one that are most revealing. ■

Henry was succeeded by his young and sickly son Edward VI (reigned 1547–53), who soon died. Next in succession was Edward's Catholic half-sister Mary (reigned 1553–58), who persecuted and martyred hundreds of English Protestants and married Philip II of Spain, self-declared defender of the Catholic faith. With Mary's premature death, however, her Protestant half-sister Elizabeth I (reigned 1558–1603) reversed course, tolerating a variety of perspectives within the English church. Spain's monarch, Mary's widower, head of the most powerful empire in the world, vowed to overthrow Elizabeth.

Fearing Spanish subversion on the neighboring Catholic island of Ireland, Elizabeth urged enterprising supporters such as Walter Raleigh and his half-brother Humphrey Gilbert to subdue the Irish Catholics and settle homeless English families on their land. During the 1560s, Raleigh, Humphrey, and many other commanders invaded the island and viciously attacked the Irish, forcing them to retreat beyond a frontier line of English settlement along the coast. The English considered the Irish an inferior race, and the notion that civilized people could not mix with such "savages" was an assumption English colonists would carry with them to the Americas.

EARLY ENGLISH EFFORTS IN THE AMERICAS

England's first ventures in the New World were made against the backdrop of its conflict with Spain. In 1562, John Hawkins violated Spanish regulations by transporting a load of African slaves to the Caribbean, bringing back valuable tropical goods. (For a full discussion of the slave trade, see Chapter 4.) The Spanish attacked Hawkins on another of his voyages in 1567, an event English privateers such as Francis Drake used as an excuse for launching a series of devastating and lucrative raids against Spanish New World ports and fleets.

A consensus soon developed among Elizabeth's closest advisers that the time had come to enter the competition for American colonies, and Elizabeth autho-

The Armada Portrait of Elizabeth I, painted by an unknown artist in 1648. The queen places her hand on the globe, symbolizing the rising seapower of England. Through the open windows, we see the battle against the Spanish Armada in 1588 and the destruction of the Spanish ships in a providential storm, interpreted by the queen as an act of divine intervention.

"Elizabeth I", Armada portrait, c. 1588 (oil on panel) by English School (C16th) Private Collection/The Bridgeman Art Library, London/New York.

CHRONOLOGY

1000	Norse settlement at L'Anse aux Meadows
1347–53	Black Death in Europe
1381	English Peasants' Revolt
1488	Bartolomeu Días sails around the African continent
1492	Christopher Columbus first arrives in the Caribbean
1494	Treaty of Tordesillas
1497	John Cabot explores Newfoundland
1500	High point of the Renaissance
1508	Spanish invade Puerto Rico
1513	Juan Ponce de León lands in Florida
1514	Bartolomé de las Casas begins preaching against the conquest
1516	Smallpox introduced to the New World
1517	Martin Luther breaks with the Roman Catholic Church
1519	Hernán Cortés lands in Mexico
1534	Jacques Cartier first explores the St. Lawrence River
1539–40	Hernán de Soto and Francisco Vásquez de Coronado expeditions
1550	Tobacco introduced to Europe
1552	Bartolomé de las Casas's *Destruction of the Indies* published
1558	Elizabeth I of England begins her reign
1562	Huguenot colony planted along the mid-Atlantic coast
1565	St. Augustine founded
1583	Humphrey Gilbert attempts to plant a colony in Newfoundland
1584–87	Walter Raleigh's colony on Roanoke Island
1588	English defeat the Spanish Armada
1590	John White returns to find Roanoke colony abandoned

rized several private attempts at exploration and colonization. In the late 1570s, Martin Frobisher conducted three voyages of exploration in the North Atlantic. Next Gilbert and Raleigh, fresh from the Irish wars, planned the first true colonizing ventures. In 1583 Gilbert sailed with a flotilla of ships from Plymouth and landed at St. John's Bay, Newfoundland. He encountered fishermen from several other nations but nevertheless claimed the territory for his queen. But Gilbert's ship was lost on the return voyage.

Following his brother's death, Raleigh moved to establish a colony to the south, in the more hospitable climate of the mid-Atlantic coast. The Roanoke enterprise of 1584–87 seemed far more promising than Gilbert's, but it too failed. In contrast to the French, who concentrated on commerce, the English attempted to dominate and conquer the natives, drawing on their Irish experience.

Philip II was outraged at the English incursions into territory reserved by the pope for Catholics. He committed himself to smashing England. In 1588, he sent a fleet of 130 ships carrying 30,000 men to invade the British Isles. Countered by captains such as Drake and Hawkins, who commanded smaller and more maneuverable ships, and frustrated by an ill-timed storm that the English chose to interpret as an act of divine intervention, the Spanish Armada foundered. The Spanish monopoly of the New World had been broken in the English Channel.

CONCLUSION

The era of European colonization in the Americas opened with Columbus' voyage in 1492. The subsequent Spanish invasion of America had catastrophic consequences for the Indian peoples of the Caribbean, Mesoamerica, and beyond. Wars of conquest and dispossession, and especially the introduction of epidemic disease, took an enormous toll in human life. Civilizations collapsed and whole cultures disappeared. Amidst this destruction, the Spanish succeeded in constructing the world's most powerful empire through the use of forced labor. Enormous wealth flowed across the Atlantic to Spain.

Inspired by the Spanish success, the French and the English sought to plant colonies on the coast of North America in the second half of the century, but neither succeeded in establishing lasting communities. Meanwhile, a very different kind of colonial encounter, one based on commerce rather than conquest, was taking place along the coasts of northeastern North America. Early in the next century the French would turn this development to their advantage.

The English would move in a different direction. The colony of Roanoke in the land the English called Virginia failed because of the imperial assumptions and the brutal behavior of the first colonists toward the native residents. The experience might have suggested the importance and necessity of "discreet dealing" with native peoples. But instead the English would put their Irish experience to use, pioneering an altogether new kind of American colonialism.

REVIEW QUESTIONS

1. Discuss the roles played by the rising merchant class, the new monarchies, Renaissance humanism, and the Reformation in the development of European colonialism.

2. Define a "frontier of inclusion." In what ways does this description apply to the Spanish empire in the Americas?

3. Make a list of the major exchanges that took place between the Old World and the New World in the centuries following the European invasion of America. Discuss some of the effects these exchanges had on the course of modern history.

4. In what ways did colonial contact in the Northeast differ from contacts in the Caribbean and Mexico?

5. In what ways might the English experience in Ireland have shaped expectations about American colonization?

KEY TERMS

Flashcard Review

Huguenots (p. 39)	**Reconquista** (p. 30)
Protestant Reformation (p. 39)	**Renaissance** (p. 28)
Protestants (p. 39)	

RECOMMENDED READING

David Noble Cook, *Born to Die: Disease and New World Conquest, 1492–1650* (1998). A synthetic history of the impact of disease, including Indian and European views.

Alfred W. Crosby Jr., *The Columbian Exchange: Biological and Cultural Consequences of 1492* (1972). Pathbreaking account of the intersection of the biospheres of the Old and New Worlds.

Kathleen Deagan and José María Cruxent, *Columbus's Outpost Among the Taínos: Spain and America at La Isabela, 1493–1498* (2002). An archaeological and historical account of the first European outpost in the New World.

Richard Flint, *Great Cruelties Have Been Reported: The 1544 Investigation of the Coronado Expedition* (2001). Testimony regarding the treatment of Indians and subsequent human rights debates in Spain.

Lewis Hanke, *The Spanish Struggle for Justice in the Conquest of America* (1949). The classic account of las Casas's attempts to rectify the wrongs committed by the Spanish against the Indians.

Charles M. Hudson, *Knights of Spain, Warriors of the Sun: Hernando de Soto and the South's Ancient Chiefdoms* (1997). A very readable history of the de Soto expedition, told from the viewpoint of the Indians.

Henry Kamen, *Spain's Road to Empire: The Making of a World Power, 1492–1763* (2002). A fascinating account arguing that it was not Spain that made the empire but rather the empire that made Spain.

John T. McGrath, *The French in Early Florida: In the Eye of the Hurricane* (2000). A meticulously researched history of the French Huguenot colony in Florida.

Samuel Eliot Morison, *The European Discovery of America: The Northern Voyages, A.D. 500–1600* (1971) and *The Southern Voyages, A.D. 1492–1616* (1974). The most detailed treatment of all the important European explorations of the Americas.

Karen Vieira Powers, *Women in the Crucible of Conquest: The Gendered Genesis of Spanish American Society, 1500–1600* (2005). This new interpretation of the conquest demonstrates the ways native women adapted to the new order imposed upon them.

Matthew Restall, *Seven Myths of the Spanish Conquest* (2003). A concise and refreshing new perspective on Spain's intrusion into the New World.

David Beers Quinn, *Set Fair for Roanoke: Voyages and Colonies, 1584–1606* (1985). The story of Roanoke—the Indian village, the English settlement, and the Lost Colony.

Carl Ortwin Sauer, *Sixteenth Century North America: The Land and the People as Seen by the Europeans* (1971). A classic source for the explorations of the continent, providing abundant descriptions of the Indians.

Hugh Thomas, *Conquest: Montezuma, Cortés, and the Fall of Old Mexico* (1993). A fascinating account, written by a master of historical style, that incorporates the Aztec view as well as the words of the conquerors.

Gustavo Verdesio, *Forgotten Conquests: Rereading New World History from the Margins* (2001). An argument that the old master historical narrative represents only one of many possible histories and a suggestion for finding the colonial subjects who did not produce documents.

For study resources for this chapter, go to **www.myhistorylab.com** and choose *Out of Many, Teaching and Learning Classroom Edition.* You will find a wealth of study and review material for this chapter, including pretests and posttests, customized study plan, key-term review flash cards, interactive map and document activities, and documents for analysis.

These seventeen ships . . . made a long, a troublesome, and costly voyage . . . with contrary winds after they set sail, and so scattered with mist and tempests that few of them arrived together . . .
—Thomas Dudley, March 28, 1631

New Mexico. Pueblos de Taos.

3

PLANTING COLONIES IN NORTH AMERICA
1588–1701

HOW DID conditions in New Spain and New France differ from Virginia and New England?

HOW DID tobacco change the nature of English colonization in Virginia?

WHAT WERE the social and political values of Puritanism and how did religious dissent shape the history of the New England colonies?

WHAT ROLE did the crown play in the founding of English colonies after 1660?

WHAT LED to violent conflict between Indians and colonists?

AMERICAN COMMUNITIES

Communities and Diversity in Seventeenth-Century Santa Fé

IT WAS A HOT AUGUST DAY IN 1680 WHEN THE FRANTIC MESSENGERS rode into the small mission outpost of El Paso with the news that the Pueblo Indians to the north had risen in revolt. The corpses of more than 400 Spanish colonists lay bleeding in the dust. Two thousand survivors huddled inside the Palace of Governors in Santa Fé, surrounded by 3,000 angry warriors. The Pueblo leaders had sent two crosses into the palace—white for surrender, red for death. Which would the colonists choose?

Spanish colonists had been in New Mexico for a century. Franciscan priests from Mexico came first, in the 1580s, followed by a military expedition in search of precious metals. In 1609, colonial authorities founded La Villa Real de la Santa Fé de San Francisco soon known simply as Santa Fé. The Pueblos were to be converted to Christianity, subjected to the authority of the king of Spain, and forced to labor for the Hispanic colonists. The Pueblos at first resisted, but in the face of Spanish armed might, they were forced to give in.

Colonization took a tremendous toll on them. Epidemic disease, striking in successive waves, claimed thousands of lives. Taxes, tribute, and labor service left Pueblo storehouses empty, and starving times came much more frequently. Nomadic Apache neighbors, mounted on stolen Spanish horses, raided their villages with increasing frequency. From 1610 to 1680 the Pueblo population plummeted by two-thirds to fewer than 20,000 people.

A devastating drought in the 1670s seemed a sign of final and complete collapse. Over the decades thousands of Pueblos had accepted Christianity, but in the face of disaster there was a revival of their traditional religious rituals. Outraged Franciscan missionaries invaded the underground *kivas*, destroyed sacred Indian artifacts, and publicly humiliated holy men. In 1675 the Spanish governor rounded up religious leaders from many villages, publicly executed three of them, and whipped the others. One of those men, Popé of San Juan Pueblo, vowed to overthrow the regime. During the next several years he and other rebel leaders organized a conspiracy among more than twenty Pueblo communities.

In response to the Pueblo demand of surrender, the besieged colonists were defiant, sending back the red cross. Three days later, with supplies running out, they counterattacked, winning just enough time to allow for the evacuation of the capital. Harassed by the Pueblos, they made their way south to El Paso, "the poor women and children on foot and unshod,"

in the words of one account, and "of such a hue that they looked like dead people." The Pueblos ransacked the missions, desecrating the holy furnishings and leaving the mutilated bodies of priests lying upon the altars. They transformed the governor's chapel into a traditional *kiva*, his palace into a communal dwelling.

Santa Fé became the capital of a Pueblo confederacy led by Popé. He forced Christian Indians "to plunge into the rivers" to wash away the taint of baptism and ordered the destruction of everything Spanish. Getting rid of Jesus was one thing, but the rest was harder. Horses and sheep, fruit trees and wheat, new tools and new crafts—these things the Pueblos found useful. They also found that they missed the support of the Spanish in their struggle against the Apaches. With chaos mounting, Popé was deposed in 1690.

In 1692, a Spanish force under Governor Diego de Vargas returned to New Mexico in an attempt to reestablish the colonial regime. Some communities welcomed him while others resisted. In 1696 there was another attempt at revolt, but Vargas crushed it with overwhelming force. The Spanish succeeded in their reconquest, but they seemed to have learned something in the process. They began to practice greater restraint, which enabled the Pueblos to accept their authority. As long as Pueblos dutifully observed Catholic rituals in the missionary chapels, missionaries looked the other way when the people also resorted to their *kivas* and their old faith. Royal officials promised the inviolability of Pueblo title to their lands, and Pueblos in turn swore loyalty to the Spanish monarch. Pueblos turned out for service on colonial lands, while colonists abandoned the system of forced labor. New Mexico remained a colony under the authority of the Spanish. But in the aftermath of the Pueblo Revolt, the governing principle was accommodation.

Thus did the Spanish in New Mexico and elsewhere seek to include native peoples as subjects of the king and communicants of the Church. Because the French developed a commercial empire, they too came to rely on a policy of native inclusion. In New England, Virginia, and Carolina, however, where English settlers developed agricultural colonies, the policy was one of exclusion. Indians were pushed to the periphery. These differences help explain the very different histories of the three principal colonial empires in North America.

Santa Fé

THE SPANISH, THE FRENCH, AND THE DUTCH IN NORTH AMERICA

At the beginning of the seventeenth century the Spanish controlled the only colonial outposts on the North American mainland, a series of forts along the Florida coast to protect the Gulf Stream sea-lanes used by the convoys carrying wealth from their New World colonies to Spain. During the first two decades of the new century, however, the Spanish, French, Dutch, and English were all drawn into planting far more substantial colonies in North America.

NEW MEXICO

After the 1539 expedition of Francisco Vásquez de Coronado failed to turn up vast Indian empires to conquer in the northern Mexican deserts, Spanish interest in the Southwest faded. The densely settled farming communities of the Pueblos did offer a harvest of converts for Christianity, however, and by the 1580s Franciscan missionaries were at work there. Soon rumors drifted back to Mexico City of rich mines along the Rio Grande. In 1598, Juan de Oñate financed an expedition made up of Indians and *mestizos* (people of mixed Indian and European ancestry) with the purpose of mining both gold and souls.

Moving north into the upper Rio Grande Valley, Oñate encountered varying degrees of resistance. He lay siege at Acoma, set high atop a great outcropping of desert rock. Indian warriors killed dozens of Spaniards with their arrows, and women and children bombarded them with stones. But in the end, the attackers succeeded in climbing the rock walls and laying waste to the town, killing 800 men, women, and children. All surviving warriors had one of their feet severed, and more than 500 people were enslaved. In 1606 Spanish authorities in Mexico recalled Oñate for his failure to locate the fabled gold mines. The Church, however, convinced the Spanish monarchy to subsidize New Mexico as a special missionary colony. In 1609, a new governor founded the capital of Santa Fé, and from this base the Franciscan missionaries penetrated all the surrounding Indian villages (see Map 3.1).

IMAGE KEY

for pages 46–47

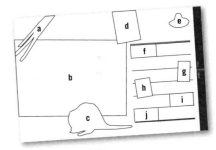

a. Several sugarcane stems. Sugar was an important New World crop.

b. New Mexico. Pueblos de Taos.

c. Beavers were a plentiful source of clothing and income for their pelts.

d. Matoaka, or Pocahontas (c. 1595–1617), the daughter of Native American Chief Powhatan, after her conversion to Christianity and marriage to settler John Rolfe under the new name Rebecca.

e. A tattered historical beaver hat from 1620.

f. New Amsterdam traders bargaining with each other.

g. An illustration of a tobacco plant.

h. John Winthrop (1588–1649), governor of the Massachusetts Bay Colony.

i. Ships sail into the port of New Amsterdam (New York).

j. Colonists square off against Indians in a detail of a 17th century map of new England.

Acoma Pueblo, the "sky city," was founded in the thirteenth century and is one of the oldest continuously inhabited sites in the United States. In 1598, Juan de Oñate attacked and laid waste to the pueblo, killing some 800 inhabitants and enslaving another 500.

2–2
Samuel de Champlain, *Journal of Samuel de Champlain* (1609)

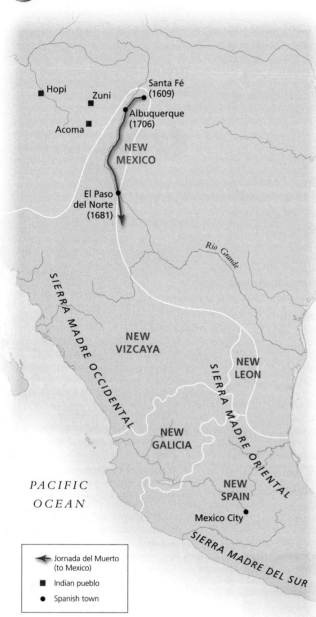

MAP 3.1
New Mexico in the Seventeenth Century By the end of the seventeenth century, New Mexico numbered 3,000 colonial settlers in several towns, surrounded by an estimated 50,000 Pueblo Indians living in some fifty farming villages.

WHAT ROLE did church officials play in the government of New Mexico?

Coureurs de bois French for "woods runner," an independent fur trader in New France.

The colonial economy of New Mexico, based on small-scale agriculture and sheep raising, was never very prosperous. Very few newcomers came from Mexico. Population growth was almost entirely the result of marriages between colonial men and Indian women. By 1700 this northernmost outpost of the Spanish empire in America contained some 3,000 *mestizos* in a few towns along the Rio Grande, surrounded by an estimated 50,000 Pueblos in some fifty villages. New Mexico was a "frontier of inclusion."

NEW FRANCE

In the early seventeenth century the French devised a strategy to monopolize the northern fur trade. In 1608 Samuel de Champlain, acting as the agent of a royal monopoly, founded the settlement of Quebec on the St. Lawrence River at a site where he could intercept the traffic in furs. He forged an alliance with the Huron Indians, who controlled access to the rich fur grounds of the Great Lakes, and in 1609 and 1610 joined them in making war on their traditional enemies, the Five Nation Iroquois Confederacy. Champlain sent agents and traders to live among native peoples, where they learned native languages and customs, and directed the flow of furs to Quebec.

Thousands of Frenchmen went to New France as *engagés* ("hired men") in the fur trade or the fishery, but nine out of ten returned to France when the term of their service ended. The French might have populated their American empire with thousands of willing Huguenot religious dissenters, but the state resolved that New France would be exclusively Catholic. As a result, the population grew very slowly, reaching a total of only 15,000 colonists by 1700.

Rather than facing the Atlantic, the communities of Canada tended to look westward toward the continental interior. It was typical for the sons of habitants to take to the woods, working as independent traders or **coureurs de bois**, paid agents of the fur companies. Most eventually returned to their home communities, but others married Indian women and raised mixed-ancestry families in distant Indian villages. French traders were living on the Great Lakes as early as the 1620s, and both missionaries and traders were exploring the upper Mississippi River by the 1670s. In 1681–82, fur-trade commandant Robert Sieur de La Salle navigated the mighty river to its mouth on the Gulf of Mexico and claimed its entire watershed for France (see Map 3.2).

Thus, the French, like the Spanish, established a frontier of inclusion in North America. But in other ways the two colonial systems were quite different. The Spanish program was the conquest of native peoples and their exploitation as a labor force in mining, farming, or livestock raising. The French, on the other hand, lacking sufficient manpower to bully, dispossess, or enslave native peoples, sought to build an empire

This drawing by Samuel de Champlain shows how Huron men funneled deer into enclosures, where they could be trapped and easily killed.

3–3

James Marquette, *Early French Explorations of the Mississippi River* (1673)

through alliance and commerce with independent Indian nations. There were also important differences between Spanish and French missionary efforts. Unlike Franciscans in seventeenth-century Santa Fé, who insisted that natives must accept European cultural norms as part of their conversion, Jesuit missionaries in New France learned native languages and attempted to understand native customs, in an effort to introduce Christianity as a part of the existing Indian way of life.

NEW NETHERLAND

The United Provinces of the Netherlands, commonly known as Holland, was only a fraction of the size of France, but in the sixteenth century it became the center of Europe's economic transformation. Amsterdam became the site of the world's first stock exchange and investment banks. Dutch investors built the largest commercial fleet in Europe and captured the lucrative Baltic and North Sea trade in fish, lumber, iron, and grain. It was said that the North Sea was Holland's "America."

Soon, however, the Dutch were establishing trading outposts in America itself. Early in the seventeenth century the United Netherlands organized two great monopolies, the Dutch East India Company and the Dutch West India Company, combining naval military might and commercial strength in campaigns to seize the maritime trade of Asia and the Atlantic. The Dutch first established themselves in North America with the explorations of Henry Hudson in 1609, and within a few years had founded settlements on the Hudson River at the head of oceangoing navigation, a place they called Fort Orange (today's Albany), and at New Amsterdam on Manhattan Island, which guards the entrance to the river. In the 1640s the Dutch also succeeded in overwhelming a small colony of Swedes planted by a Swedish company on the lower Delaware River in 1637, incorporating that region as well into their sphere of influence (see Map 3.2).

MAP 3.2

New France in the Seventeenth Century   By the late seventeenth century, French settlements were spread from the town of Port Royal in Acadia to the post and mission at Sault Ste. Marie on the Great Lakes.

HOW DID French settlements differ from their English counterparts?

2–8

A Jesuit Priest Describes New Amsterdam (1642)

HOW DID tobacco change the nature of English colonization in Virginia?

myhistorylab

Review Summary

myhistorylab

Exploring America: *Jamestown*

Beaver Wars Series of bloody conflicts, occurring between 1640s and 1680s, during which the Iroquois fought the French for control of the fur trade in the east and the Great Lakes region.

Virginia Company A group of London investors who sent ships to Chesapeake Bay in 1607.

Powhatan Confederacy A village of communities of the Chesapeake united under Chief Wahunsonacook, who was called King Powhatan by the colonists.

Seeking to match French success in the fur trade, the Dutch West India Company negotiated a commercial alliance with the Five Nation Iroquois Confederacy. Access to Dutch products, including metal tools and firearms, greatly augmented the power of the Iroquois, and they soon launched a campaign to make themselves into the strategic middlemen of the fur trade. Beginning in the 1640s the Iroquois conducted a series of military expeditions against their northern, western, and southern neighbors, known as the **Beaver Wars**. They attacked and dispersed the Hurons, who had long controlled the flow of furs from the Great Lakes to their French allies.

THE CHESAPEAKE: VIRGINIA AND MARYLAND

England first attempted to plant colonies in North America during the 1580s in Newfoundland and at Roanoke Island in present-day North Carolina (see Chapter 2). Both attempts were dramatic failures. England's war with Spain (1588–1604) suspended further efforts, but thereafter the English once again turned to the Americas.

JAMESTOWN AND THE POWHATAN CONFEDERACY

In 1607, a group of London investors known as the **Virginia Company** sent a small convoy of vessels to Chesapeake Bay, where a hundred men built a fort they named Jamestown in honor of King James I (reigned 1603–1625). It was destined to become the first permanent English settlement in North America.

The Chesapeake was already home to an estimated 14,000 Indian inhabitants. The village communities of the Chesapeake were united in a politically sophisticated union known as the **Powhatan Confederacy**, led by a powerful chief named Wahunsonacook, whom the Jamestown colonists called "King Powhatan." Powhatan's feelings about Europeans were mixed. He knew they could mean trou-

This illustration, taken from Samuel de Champlain's 1613 account of the founding of New France, depicts him joining the Huron attack on the Iroquois in 1609. The French and their Huron allies controlled access to the great fur grounds of the West. The Iroquois then formed an alliance of their own with the Dutch, who had founded a trading colony on the Hudson River. The palm trees in the background of this drawing suggest that it was not executed by an eyewitness, but rather by an illustrator more familiar with South American scenes.

John Smith's Cartoon History of His Adventures in Virginia

This elaborate illustration, executed by English engraver Robert Vaughan, accompanied John Smith's 1624 account of his years at the English settlement of Jamestown, from 1606 to 1609. It constitutes an early kind of cartoon history. Smith knew how to spin a tale, and these illustrations depict some of the most important turns in his story. A map of "Ould Virginia" (bottom center) is surrounded by vignettes depicting Smith's adventures, including his seizure by the Powhatans (top left), his capture of notable leaders (top right and bottom left), and his rescue from execution by Pocahontas (bottom right). The images told a story of conflict and violence. Much more was to come. One interesting detail is the immense size of the chiefs compared to Smith. The costume, hairstyles, and body decorations of the Indians were taken directly from the images produced by English artist and colonial governor John White. ∎

WHAT MESSAGE do you think Smith and Vaughan were trying to send with this complex illustration?

John Smith, *The General History of Virginia* (1624) from Beinecke Rare Book and Manuscript Library, Yale University.

ble. In 1571, Spanish missionaries had attempted to plant a colony on the Chesapeake shore, but after they interfered with the practice of native religion they were violently expelled. Still, Powhatan was eager to forge an alliance with these people from across the sea to obtain access to supplies of metal tools and weapons. He allowed the English colonists to build their outpost at Jamestown.

The Jamestown colonists had come to find gold and a passage to the Indies, and failing at both they spent their time gambling and drinking. They survived only because of Powhatan's help. But as more colonists arrived from England and demands for food multiplied, Powhatan had second thoughts. He now realized, he declared to Smith, that the English had come "not for trade, but to invade my people and possess my country." During the terrible winter of 1609–10 more than 400 colonists starved and a number resorted to cannibalism. Of the 500 colonists at Jamestown in the fall, only 60 remained alive by the spring.

Determined to prevail, the Virginia Company sent out a large additional force of men, women, and livestock, committing itself to a protracted war against native men, women, and children. The grim fighting persisted until 1613, when the English captured one of Powhatan's favorite daughters, Matoaka, a girl of about fifteen whom the colonists knew by her nickname, Pocahontas. Eager for the return of his child, and worn down by violence and disease, the next year Powhatan accepted a treaty of peace. The peace was sealed by the marriage of Pocahontas, who converted to Christianity, to John Rolfe, one of the leading colonists. For a brief moment it seemed the English too might move in the direction of a society of inclusion.

In 1617 Rolfe traveled with his wife and son to England, where they were greeted as a new American noble line. But Pocahontas fell ill and died there. Crushed by the news, Powhatan abdicated in favor of his brother Opechancanough before dying of despair. Economic and social developments, however, were already pushing Virginia in the direction of a frontier of exclusion.

TOBACCO, EXPANSION, AND WARFARE

Tobacco had been introduced to the English by Francis Drake in the 1580s, and by the 1610s a craze for smoking had created strong demand for the product. Pocahontas's husband John Rolfe developed a mild hybrid variety, and soon the first commercial shipments of cured Virginia leaf reached England. Tobacco provided the Virginia Company with the first returns on its investment.

Questions of land and labor would dominate the history of colonial Virginia. Tobacco cultivation required a great deal of hand labor, and it quickly exhausted the soil. The Virginia Company instituted a program of "headright grants," awards of large plantations to wealthy colonists who agreed to transport workers from England at their own cost. Because thousands of English families were being thrown off the land (see Chapter 2), many were attracted to Virginia. Thus, English colonization took a different turn from the Spanish, who mostly sent male colonists. Moreover, the English concentration on plantation agriculture contrasted with the French emphasis on trade. With little need to incorporate Indians into the colony as workers or marriage partners, the English pushed natives out. Virginia became a "frontier of exclusion."

Pressed for additional lands on which to grow tobacco, Chief Opechancanough decided on an assault that would expel the English for good. He encouraged a cultural revival under the guidance of a native shaman named Nemattanew, who instructed his followers to reject the English and their ways. This was the first of many Indian resistance movements led jointly by strong political and religious figures. Opechancanough's uprising, which began on Good Friday, March 22, 1622, completely surprised the English, claiming the lives of 347 colonists, nearly a third of Virginia's colonial population. Yet the colony managed to hang on. The attack stretched into a ten-year war of attrition with horrors committed by both sides.

In this eighteenth-century engraving used to promote the sale of tobacco, slaves pack tobacco leaves into "hogsheads" for shipment to England, overseen by a Virginia planter and his clerk. Note the incorporation of the Indian motif.

The Powhatans finally sued for peace in 1632. In the meantime, however, the war had bankrupted the Virginia Company. In 1624 England converted Virginia into a royal colony with civil authorities appointed by the crown, although property-owning colonists continued to elect representatives to the colony's **House of Burgesses**, created in 1619 in an attempt to encourage immigration.

In 1644 Opechancanough organized a final desperate revolt in which more than 500 colonists were killed. But the next year the Virginians crushed the Powhatans, capturing and executing their leader. A formal treaty granted the Indians a number of small reserved territories. By 1670 the Indian population had fallen to just 2,000, overwhelmed by the 40,000 English colonists.

MARYLAND

In 1632, King Charles I (reigned 1625–49) granted 10 million acres at the northern end of Chesapeake Bay to the Calvert family, important Catholic supporters of the English monarchy. The Calverts named their colony Maryland. Two features distinguished Maryland from Virginia. First, it was a "proprietary" colony in which the Calvert family held the sole power to appoint civil officers and was sole owner of all the land. Second, the Calvert family encouraged settlement by Catholics, a persecuted minority in seventeenth-century England. In fact, Maryland became the only English colony in North America with a substantial Catholic minority.

Yet Maryland quickly became much like neighboring Virginia. The tobacco plantation economy created pressures for labor and land. In 1640, the colony adopted the system of headright grants previously developed in Virginia, and settlements of independent planters quickly spread out on both sides of Chesapeake Bay.

COMMUNITY LIFE IN THE CHESAPEAKE

At least three-quarters of the English migrants to the Chesapeake came as **indentured servants**. In exchange for the cost of their transportation to the New World, men and women contracted to labor for a master for a fixed term. Most were young, unskilled males, who served for two to seven years, but some were skilled craftsmen, unmarried women, or even orphan children. African slaves were first

House of Burgesses The legislature of colonial Virginia. First organized in 1619, it was the first institution of representative government in the English colonies.

Indentured Servants Individuals who contracted to serve a master for a period of four to seven years in return for payment of the servant's passage to America.

introduced to the Chesapeake in 1619, but slaves were more expensive than servants, and as late as 1680 they made up less than 7 percent of the population. In the hard-driving economy of the Chesapeake, however, masters treated servants as cruelly as they treated slaves.

Many indentured servants who survived their terms and were able to raise the price of passage quickly returned to England. Those who remained became eligible for "freedom dues"—clothing, tools, a gun, or a spinning wheel to help them get started on their own. They often headed west in the hope of cutting a farm from the forest.

Because most emigrants were men, whether free or indentured, free unmarried women often married as soon as they arrived in the Chesapeake, and widows remarried quickly, sometimes within days. Their scarcity provided women with certain advantages. Shrewd widows bargained for a remarriage agreement that gave them a larger share of the estate than what was set by common law. So notable was the concentration of wealth in the hands of these widows that one historian has suggested early Virginia was a "matriarchy." But because of high mortality rates, family size was smaller and kinship bonds—one of the most important components of community—were weaker than in England.

Prosperous planters, investing everything in tobacco production, lived in rough wooden dwellings. On the western edge of the settlements, freed servants lived with their families in shacks, huts, even caves. Colonists spread across the countryside in search of new tobacco lands, creating dispersed settlements with hardly any towns. Before 1650 there were few community institutions such as schools and churches.

Nevertheless, the Chesapeake was a growing region. By the end of the seventeenth century the combined population of the Maryland and Virginia colonies was nearly 90,000. In contrast to the colonists of New France, who were developing a distinctive identity because of their connections with native peoples, the English residents of the Chesapeake maintained close emotional ties to the mother country.

THE NEW ENGLAND COLONIES

Both in climate and in geography, the northern coast of North America was far different from the Chesapeake. "Merchantable commodities" such as tobacco could not be produced there, and thus it was far less favored for investment and settlement. Instead, the region became a haven for Protestant dissenters from England, who gave the colonies of the north a distinctive character of their own (see Map 3.3).

PURITANISM

Most English men and women continued to practice a Christianity little different from traditional Catholicism. But the English followers of John Calvin, known as **Puritans** because they wished to purify and reform the English church from within, grew increasingly influential during the last years of Elizabeth's reign at the end of the sixteenth century. The Calvinist emphasis on enterprise meant that **Puritanism** appealed to merchants, entrepreneurs, and commercial farmers, those most responsible for the rapid economic and social transformation of England. Yet the Puritans were also the most vocal critics of the disruptive effects of that change, condemning the decline of the traditional rural community and the growing number of "idle and masterless men" produced by the enclosure of common lands. They argued for reviving communities by placing reformed Christian congregations at their core to monitor the behavior of individuals.

James I abandoned Queen Elizabeth's policy of religious tolerance. His persecution of the Puritans, however, merely stiffened their resolve and turned them toward open political opposition. James's son and successor, Charles I (reigned 1625–49), was heavily criticized by the increasingly vocal Puritan minority for marrying a French Roman Catholic princess and supporting "High Church" policies, emphasizing the authority of the clerical hierarchy and traditional forms of worship. In 1629, determined to rule without these troublesome opponents, Charles dismissed Parliament and launched a campaign of repression against the Puritans. This political turmoil provided the context for the migration of thousands of English Protestants to New England.

PLYMOUTH COLONY

The first English colony in New England was founded by a group of religious dissenters known to later generations as the **Pilgrims**. At the time they were called **Separatists** because they believed the English church was so corrupt they had to establish independent congregations. One group moved to Holland in 1609, but fearful that tolerant and secular Dutch society was seducing their children, they decided on emigration to North America. Backed by the Virginia Company of London and led by tradesman William Bradford, 102 people sailed from England on the *Mayflower* in September 1620.

The little group, mostly families but including a substantial number of single men hired by the investors, arrived in Massachusetts Bay at the site of the former Indian village of Pawtuxet, which the English renamed Plymouth. Soon the hired men began to grumble about being excluded from decision making, and to reassure them Bradford drafted an agreement by which all the male members of the expedition did "covenant and combine together into a civil body politic." The **Mayflower Compact** was the first document of self-government in North America.

Weakened by scurvy and malnutrition, nearly half the colonists perished over the first winter. Like the earlier settlers of Roanoke and Jamestown, however, they were rescued by Indians. Massasoit, the *sachem* or chief of the Pokanokets, offered the newcomers food and advice in return for an alliance against his enemies, the Narragansets. It was the familiar pattern of Indians attempting to incorporate European colonists into their own world.

The Pilgrims supported themselves by farming, but like all colonies Plymouth needed a source of revenue, in their case in order to pay off their English investors. The foundation of their commercial economy was the cod fishery in the rich coastal banks of the Atlantic. With this revenue the Pilgrims were able to establish a self-sufficient community.

MAP EXPLORATION

To explore an interactive version of this map, go to
http://www.prenhall.com/faraghertlc/map3.3

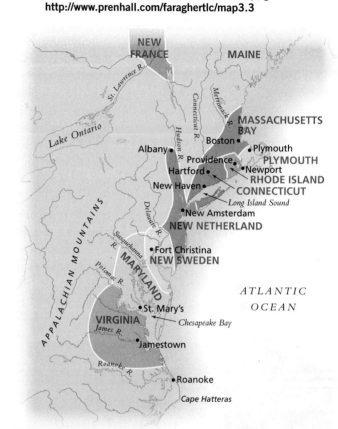

MAP 3.3

European Colonies of the Atlantic Coast, 1607–39   Virginia, on Chesapeake Bay, was the first English colony in North America, but by the mid-seventeenth century, Virginia was joined by settlements of Scandinavians on the Delaware River and Dutch on the Hudson River, as well as English religious dissenters in New England.

HOW MANY European nations had established colonies on the Atlantic coast by the middle of the seventeenth century?

Pilgrims   Settlers of Plymouth Colony, who viewed themselves as spiritual wanderers.

Separatists   Members of an offshoot branch of Puritanism. Separatists believed that the Church of England was too corrupt to be reformed and hence were convinced they must "separate" from it to save their souls.

Mayflower Compact   The first document of self-government in North America.

QUICK REVIEW

Mayflower Compact

◆ Mayflower Compact signed in 1620.

◆ Established self-government in North America.

◆ Pilgrim leaders urged all adult males to sign the compact.

2–5

John Winthrop, *A Modell of Christian Charity* (1630)

Massachusetts Bay Company A group of wealthy Puritans who were granted a royal charter in 1629 to settle in Massachusetts Bay.

Governor John Winthrop, ca. 1640, a portrait by an unknown artist. Winthrop was first elected governor of Massachusetts Bay Colony in 1629, then was voted out of office and reelected a total of twelve times.

THE MASSACHUSETTS BAY COLONY

In England, the political climate of the late 1620s convinced growing numbers of influential Puritans that the only way to protect their congregations was by emigration. In 1629 a royal charter was granted to a group of wealthy Puritans who called their enterprise the **Massachusetts Bay Company**, and an advance force of 200 settlers left for the fishing settlement of Naumkeag on Massachusetts Bay, which they renamed Salem.

The colonists hoped to establish what John Winthrop, their leader and first governor, called "a city on a hill," a New England model of reform for old England. In this they differed from the Pilgrims, who never considered returning. Between 1629 and 1643 some 20,000 individuals relocated to Massachusetts, establishing the port town of Boston and ringing it with towns. By the 1640s their settlements had spread seventy-five miles west to the Connecticut River Valley.

Taking advantage of a loophole in their charter, in 1629 Puritan leaders transferred company operations from England to Massachusetts, and within a few years had transformed the company into a civil government. The original charter established a General Court composed of a governor and his deputy, a board of magistrates (or advisers), and the members of the corporation, known as freemen. In 1632, Governor Winthrop and his advisers declared that all the male heads of households in Massachusetts, who were also church members, were freemen. Two years later, the freemen secured their right to select delegates to represent the towns in drafting the laws of the colony. These delegates and the magistrates later became the colony's two legislative houses. Thus, the procedures of a joint-stock company provided the origins for democratic suffrage and the bicameral division of legislative authority in America.

DISSENT AND NEW COMMUNITIES

Doctrinal disagreements among the Puritans often led to the establishment of new colonies. In 1636 Thomas Hooker, minister of the congregation at Cambridge, after objecting to the Massachusetts policy of restricting male suffrage to church members, led his followers west to the Connecticut River, where they founded the town of Hartford. The same year Roger Williams, the minister at Salem, was banished from Massachusetts for advocating religious tolerance. With a group of his followers, Williams emigrated to the country surrounding Narraganset Bay.

In 1637 religious controversy produced another schism. Anne Hutchinson, the brilliant and outspoken wife of a Puritan merchant, criticized a number of Boston ministers. Their concentration on good works, she argued, led people to believe they could earn their way to heaven. Hutchinson was called before the General Court, and in an extraordinary hearing was reprimanded, excommunicated, and banished. She and a group of followers relocated to the Williams colony on Narraganset Bay.

To protect the dissenters in his settlement from Puritan interference, Williams won royal charters in 1644 and 1663 establishing the independent colony of Rhode Island, with guarantees of self-government and complete religious liberty.

INDIANS AND PURITANS

The Indian communities of southern New England discovered soon after the arrival of the Pilgrims and the Puritans that these colonists were quite different from the French and Dutch traders who had preceded them. Although the fur trade was an important part of the economy of Plymouth and Massachusetts, the principal concern of the colonists was the acquisition of Indian land for their growing settlements.

Like the Jamestown colonists, most Puritans believed they had the right to take what they considered "unused" lands, that is, lands not used in the English way. Potential conflicts among settlers over title, however, made it necessary to obtain original deeds from Indians, and the English used a variety of tactics to pressure leaders into signing "quitclaims," relinquishing all claim to specified properties. Meanwhile epidemic disease continued to devastate Indian villages. Disorganized and demoralized, many coastal native communities not only gave up their lands but also placed themselves under the protection of the English. By the late 1630s only a few tribes in southern New England retained the power to challenge Puritan expansion. The Pequots, who lived along the shores of Long Island Sound near the mouth of the Connecticut River, were one of the most powerful. Allies of the Dutch, the Pequots controlled the production of wampum, woven belts of seashells used as a medium of exchange in the Indian trade. In 1637, Puritan leaders pressured the Pequots' traditional enemies, the Narragansets of present-day Rhode Island, to join them in waging war on the Pequots. Narragansett warriors and English troops attacked the main Pequot village, burning the houses and killing most of their slumbering residents.

THE ECONOMY: NEW ENGLAND MERCHANTS

In England, the dispute between King Charles I and the Puritans in Parliament escalated into armed conflict in 1642. Several years of revolutionary confrontation finally led to Charles's arrest, his execution in 1649, and the creation of an English Commonwealth, headed by the Puritan military leader Oliver Cromwell. Because the Puritans were on the victorious side in the English civil war, they no longer had the same incentive to migrate to New England. A number of colonists returned to England.

New England's economy had depended on the sale of supplies and land to arriving immigrants, but this market collapsed as the migration tailed off. Puritan merchants turned to the flourishing fishery, shipping cod (in addition to lumber and farm products) to the West Indies, where they bartered for sugar, molasses and rum. By midcentury New England had constructed a commercial fleet of more than 300 vessels, and by the end of the century Boston had become the third largest English commercial center in the Atlantic (after London and Bristol). The development of a diversified economy provided New England with important long-term strength and offered a striking contrast with the specialized fur-trade economy of New France.

COMMUNITY AND FAMILY IN NEW ENGLAND

Pilgrims and Puritans stressed the importance of well-ordered communities. Settlers typically clustered their dwellings in a central village, near the meetinghouse that served as both church and civic center. Clustered settlements and strong communities distinguished New England from the dispersed and weak communities of the Chesapeake.

2–7
The Trial of Anne Hutchinson (1638)

2–6
John Mason, *The Taking of the Fort at Mystic* (1637)

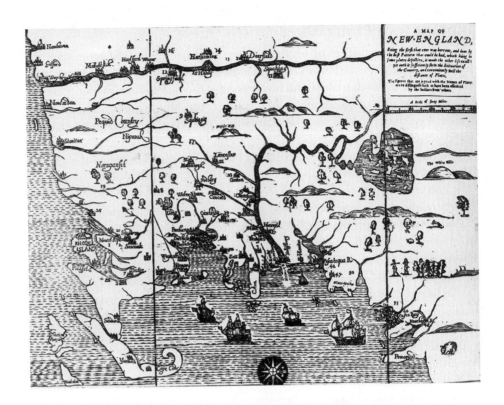

The first map printed in the English colonies, this view of New England was published in Boston in 1677. With north oriented to the right, it looks west from Massachusetts Bay, the two vertical black lines indicating the approximate boundaries of the Commonwealth of Massachusetts. The territory west of Rhode Island is noted as an Indian stronghold, the homelands of the Narraganset, Pequot, and Nipmuck peoples.

The ideal Puritan family was also well ordered. Parents often participated in the choice of mates for their offspring, and children typically married in the order of their births, younger children waiting until arrangements had been made for their elder siblings. Another source of New England's strength was the impressive Puritan education system. In 1647 the Massachusetts General Court required that towns with 50 families or more support a public school; those with 100 families were to establish a grammar school instructing students in Latin, knowledge of which was required for admission to Harvard College, founded in 1636. The Puritan colony of Connecticut enacted similar requirements. By the mid-seventeenth century, New England men boasted the highest rates of literacy in North America and much of Europe. Because girls were excluded from grammar schools, however, women's literacy remained relatively low.

The Puritans were not "puritanical" in the modern sense of the word. Although they treated adultery as a capital crime, they celebrated sexual expression within marriage. Courting couples were encouraged to engage in "petting," and married couples were expected to enjoy sexual relations.

THE POSITION OF WOMEN

Families were supposed to operate as "little commonwealths," with everyone working cooperatively. The domestic economy required the combined efforts of husband and wife. Men were generally responsible for fieldwork, women for the work of the household, garden, henhouse, and dairy.

Still, the cultural ideal was the subordination of women to men. Married women could not make contracts, own property, vote, or hold office. A typical woman, marrying in her early twenties and surviving through her forties, could expect to bear eight children and devote herself to husband and family. Aside from abstinence, there was no form of birth control. Wives who failed to have

myhistorylab

Exploring America: *Witches in the American Imagination*

children, or widows who were economically independent, aroused significant suspicion among their neighbors.

THE SALEM WITCH TRIALS

The cultural mistrust of women came to the surface most notably in periodic witchcraft scares. During the seventeenth century, according to one historian, 342 New England women were accused by their neighbors of witchcraft. The majority of the accused were unmarried, or childless, or widowed, or had reputations in their communities for assertiveness and independence. In the vast majority of cases, the charges were dismissed by authorities as baseless. In the infamous 1692 case of Salem, Massachusetts, however, the whole community was thrown into a panic of accusations when a group of girls claimed that they had been bewitched by a number of old women. Before the colonial governor finally called a halt to the persecutions in 1693, twenty people had been tried, condemned, and executed.

The Salem witchcraft scare may have reflected social tensions that found their outlet through an attack on people perceived as outsiders. Salem was a booming commercial port, but while some residents were prospering, others were not. Most of the victims came from the commercial eastern end of town, the majority of their accusers from the economically stagnant western side. Most of the accused also came from Anglican, Quaker, or Baptist families. Finally, a majority of the victims were old women, suspect because they lived alone, without the guidance of men. The Salem witchcraft crisis exposed the dark side of Puritan thinking about women.

THE PROPRIETARY COLONIES

Oliver Cromwell died in 1658 and two years later Parliament, anxious for stability, restored the Stuart monarchy, placing on the throne Charles II (reigned 1660–85), eldest son of the deposed king. Charles took an active interest in North America, establishing several new proprietary colonies on the model of Maryland (see Map 3.4).

THE CAROLINAS

Charles II issued the first of his charters in 1663, establishing a new colony called Carolina, which stretched along the Atlantic coast from Virginia south to the northern limits of Spanish Florida. Virginians had already begun moving into the vicinity of Albermarle Sound in the northern part of this territory, and in 1664 the Carolina proprietors appointed a governor and created a popularly elected assembly. By 1700 North Carolina, as it became known, included 11,000 small farmers and large tobacco planters.

Settlement farther south began in 1670 with the founding of coastal Charles Town (renamed Charleston in

WHAT ROLE did the crown play in the founding of English colonies after 1660?

myhistorylab
Review Summary

MAP EXPLORATION

To explore an interactive version of this map, go to
http://www.prenhall.com/faraghertlc/map3.4

MAP 3.4
The Proprietary Colonies   After the restoration of the Stuart monarchy in 1660, King Charles II of England created the new proprietary colonies of Carolina, New York, Pennsylvania, and New Jersey. New Hampshire was set off as a royal colony in 1680, and in 1704, the lower counties of Pennsylvania became the colony of Delaware.

EXAMINE THE processes underlying the founding of the Proprietary Colonies. How had the political landscape changed since 1639?

The earliest known view of New Amsterdam, published in 1651. Indian traders are shown arriving with their goods in a dugout canoe of distinctive design known to have been produced by the native people of Long Island Sound. Twenty-five years after its founding, the Dutch settlement still occupies only the lower tip of Manhattan Island.

Fort New Amsterdam, New York, 1651. Engraving. Collection of The New-York Historical Society, 77354d.

1783). Most South Carolina settlers came from the sugar colony of Barbados, a Caribbean colony founded by the English in 1627. They lent a distinctly West Indian character to the colony. By 1700 South Carolina's population was more than 6,000, including some 3,000 enslaved Africans. (For a complete discussion of slavery see Chapter 4.)

NEW YORK AND NEW JERSEY

Charles also coveted the lucrative Dutch colony of New Netherland. In 1651, Parliament passed a Trade and Navigation Act that barred Dutch vessels from English colonial possessions. This led to an inconclusive naval war between the two nations from 1652 to 1654. Ten years later the two powers clashed once again, this time along the West African coast, leading to a second Anglo-Dutch war. In September 1664 a small English fleet sailed into Manhattan harbor and forced the surrender of New Amsterdam without firing a shot. When the war ended with an inconclusive peace in 1667, the English were left in possession. Holland briefly regained control during a third and final conflict from 1672 to 1674, but the English won the war and won possession of the colony in the peace negotiations. This final war bankrupted the Dutch West India Company and marked the ascension of the English to dominance in the Atlantic, although Holland remained supreme in the Baltic and the East Indies.

Charles II issued a proprietary charter granting the former Dutch colony to his brother James, the Duke of York, renaming it New York in his honor. Ethnically and linguistically diversified, and accommodating a wide range of religious sects, New York society was the most heterogeneous in North America. In 1665, the communities of the Delaware Valley were split off as the **proprietary colony** of New Jersey.

Proprietary colony A colony created when the English monarch granted a huge tract of land to an individual or group of individuals, who became "lords proprietor."

Quakers Members of the Society of Friends, a radical religious group that arose in the mid-seventeenth century. Quakers rejected formal theology, focusing instead on the Holy Spirit that dwelt within them.

THE FOUNDING OF PENNSYLVANIA

In 1676, the proprietary rights to the western portion of New Jersey were sold to a group of English religious dissenters, including William Penn. A member of the Society of Friends (known popularly as the **Quakers**), Penn intended to

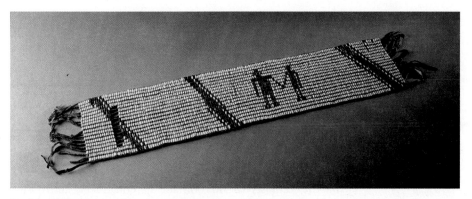

The Delawares presented William Penn with this wampum belt after the Shackamaxon Treaty of 1682. In friendship, a Quaker in distinctive hat clasps the hand of an Indian. The diagonal stripes on either side of the figures represent the "open paths" between the English and the Delawares. Wampum belts like this one, made from strings of white and purple shell beads, were used to commemorate treaties throughout the colonial period, and were the most widely accepted form of money in the northeastern colonies during the seventeenth century.

make the colony a haven for religious toleration and pacifism. In 1681, to settle a large debt he owed William Penn's father, King Charles issued to his son a proprietary grant to a huge territory west of the Delaware River.

Penn wanted this colony to be a "holy experiment." In his first **Frame of Government**, drafted in 1682, he included guarantees of religious freedom, civil liberties, and elected representation. He also attempted to deal fairly with the native peoples, refusing to permit colonization to begin until settlement rights were negotiated and lands purchased. Although relations between Pennsylvania and Indian peoples later soured, during Penn's lifetime his reputation for fair dealing led a number of native groups to resettle in the Quaker colony.

During the first two decades of Pennsylvania's settlement, nearly 20,000 settlers spread agricultural communities from the banks of the Delaware to the fertile interior valleys. In 1704 Penn approved the creation of a separate colony called Delaware for the governance of the counties near the mouth of the river formerly controlled first by the Swedes and then the Dutch.

Conflict and War

Pennsylvania's ability to maintain peaceful relations with the Indians proved the great exception. The last quarter of the seventeenth century became a time of great violence throughout the colonial regions of the continent, mostly because of the expansion of European settlement (see Map 3.5). Much of this warfare was between colonists and Indians, but intertribal warfare and intercolonial rivalry greatly contributed to the violence.

King Philip's War

In New England, nearly forty years of peace followed the **Pequot War** of 1637. Natives and colonists lived in close, if tense, contact. Some two thousand native converts eventually relocated to Christian communities known as "praying towns." But there remained several independent tribes, including the Pokanokets, the

3-6
William Penn, *Charter of Privileges* (1701)

QUICK REVIEW

Pennsylvania

♦ Territory west of the Delaware River granted to William Penn in 1681.

♦ Penn supervised the establishment of Philadelphia in 1682.

♦ Penn, a Quaker, saw the colony as a "holy experiment."

WHAT LED to violent conflict between Indians and colonists?

Review Summary

Frame of Government   William Penn's constitution for Pennsylvania which included a provision allowing for religious freedom.

Pequot War   Conflict between English settlers and Pequot Indians over control of land and trade in eastern Connecticut.

MAP 3.5
Spread of Settlement: British Colonies, 1650–1700   The spread of settlement in the English colonies in the late seventeenth century created the conditions for a number of violent conflicts, including King Philip's War, Bacon's Rebellion, and King William's War

WHAT FACTORS were behind the spread of British settlement in the second half of the seventeenth century?

3–4
Edward Randolph, *King Philip's War* (1685)

King Philip's War   Conflict in New England (1675–1676) between Wampanoags, Narragansetts, and other Indian peoples against English settlers; sparked by English encroachments on native lands.

Covenant Chain   An alliance between the Iroquois Confederacy and the colony of New York which sought to establish Iroquois dominance over all other tribes.

Narragansets, and the Abenakis of northern New England. The extraordinary expansion of the colonial population, and the increasing hunger for land, created inexorable pressures for expansion into their territories.

The Pokanokets, whose homeland lay between Rhode Island and Plymouth, were led by the sachem Metacom, whom the English called King Philip. Metacom had been raised among English colonists and educated in their schools. He operated on the assumption that his people had a future in the English colonial world but was gradually forced to conclude that the colonists had no room for the Pokanokets. In 1671 the colonial authorities of Plymouth pressured Metacom into granting them sovereign authority over his homeland. This humiliation convinced him that he had to break the half-century alliance with Plymouth and take up armed resistance. The Puritan colonies, meanwhile, prepared for a war of conquest.

What became known as **King Philip's War** came in the spring of 1675, and at first things went well for the Indians. They forced the abandonment of English settlements on the Connecticut River and torched towns less than twenty miles from Boston. By the beginning of 1676, however, their campaign was collapsing. A combined colonial army defeated a large Indian force in a battle known as the Great Swamp Fight in Narraganset country. Metacom led his men and fled west to the border with New York where he appealed for support from the Iroquois. But instead of helping, the Iroquois attacked forcing Metacom back to Pokanoket territory, where colonists annihilated his army in August 1676. Metacom was quartered, his severed head mounted on a pike at Plymouth.

In attacking the Pequots, the Iroquois were motivated by interests of their own. Extending the role they had played in the Dutch trading system, they now cast themselves as powerful intermediaries between other tribes and the English. In a series of negotiations conducted at Albany in 1677, the Iroquois Confederacy and the colony of New York created an alliance known as the **Covenant Chain**. It envisioned Iroquois dominance over all other tribes, thus putting New York in an economically and politically dominant position among the other colonies.

An estimated 4,000 natives and 2,000 colonists died during the war, and dozens of native and colonial towns lay in ruins. Fearing attack from Indians close at hand, colonists also destroyed most of the Indian praying towns, killing many of the Christian residents. Calculated in the number of lives lost, King Philip's War was the most destructive Indian–colonist conflict in early American history.

BACON'S REBELLION AND SOUTHERN CONFLICTS

While King Philip's War raged in New England, another English–Indian confrontation took shape in the Chesapeake and mutated into civil war. The basic cause of the conflict was the old problem of land and labor. By the 1670s Indian communities residing on the frontier of the colony were under assault by colonists in search of new tobacco lands. The insatiable hunger came not only from established planters with lands reaching exhaustion but also from former servants who

Colonial officials in South Carolina seemed to be paying attention. They encouraged Indians allied with the colony—Yamasees, Creeks, Cherokees, and Chickasaws—to wage war on tribes affiliated with rival colonial powers, including the mission Indians of Spanish Florida, the Choctaw allies of the French, and the Tuscaroras, trading partners of the Virginians. In addition to opening new lands for settlement, the brutal fighting resulted in the capture of many thousands of Indians who were sold into slavery. These wars continued into the first quarter of the eighteenth century.

THE GLORIOUS REVOLUTION IN AMERICA

Dynastic change in England was another factor in the violence in North America. After Charles II died in 1685, his brother and successor, James II (reigned 1685–88), began a concerted effort to strengthen royal control over the colonies. The king's ministers believed colonial assemblies had grown too powerful and independent and were determined to rein them in. The New York assembly, considered particularly troublesome, was abolished and all power placed in the hands of the colony's royal governor. In the other colonies governors challenged the authority of assemblies. The king annulled the charter governments of New England, New York, and New Jersey and combined them into a single supercolony known as the Dominion of New England. Edmund Andros, appointed royal governor, imposed Anglican forms of worship in Puritan areas and overthrew longstanding traditions of local autonomy.

James ruled England in the same imperious style. He was a practicing Catholic, and his appointment of Catholics to high positions of state added to rising discontent and protest. The last straw was the birth of a royal son in 1688. Fearing the establishment of a Catholic dynasty, Parliamentary leaders deposed James and replaced him with his Protestant daughter Mary, who was married to William of Orange, hereditary head of state of the Netherlands. When the army refused to prevent William and Mary from landing in England, James fled to France. The relatively nonviolent "Glorious Revolution," as it came to be known, included a Bill of Rights, issued by the new monarchs at the insistence of Parliament, in which they promised to respect traditional civil liberties, to summon and consult with Parliament annually, and to enforce and administer its legislation. These were significant concessions with profound implications for the future of English politics. In essence, England had become a "constitutional monarchy."

In North America, news of the Glorious Revolution sparked a series of colonial rebellions against the authorities set in place by King James. In the spring of 1689, Governor Andros was attacked by a Boston mob. He escaped their wrath but was arrested and deported. The Boston uprising inspired another in New York led by merchant Jacob Leisler that included many prominent Dutch residents. They seized control of the city and called for the formation of a new legislature. In Maryland, rumors of a Catholic plot led to the overthrow of the proprietary rule of the Calvert family by an insurgent group calling itself the Protestant Association.

The new regime in London carefully measured its response to these uprisings. When Jacob Leisler attempted to prevent the landing of the king's troops in New York, he was arrested, tried, and executed. But William and Mary also consented to the breakup of the Dominion of New England and the termination of proprietary rule in Maryland. All the affected colonies quickly revived their assemblies and returned to their tradition of self-government. The monarchs strengthened royal authority, however, by decreeing that henceforth Massachusetts, New York, and Maryland would be royal colonies.

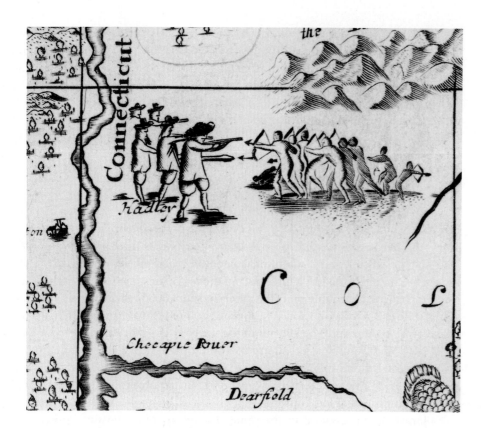

had served out their indentures. Governor William Berkeley, in office since the 1640s, ruled in alliance with the big planters, who feared landless freemen even more than they did Indians. In 1670 the Burgesses had enacted legislation restricting the suffrage to property owners; nevertheless every man still had to pay taxes. Smoldering class antagonism thus added to the volatile mix. When in 1675 the governor declined to send the militia against the Indians, colonists under the leadership of wealthy backcountry planter Nathaniel Bacon embarked on unauthorized raids resulting in the indiscriminate murder of many natives, including those allied with the colony. Bacon became a hero to former servants, and although Berkeley fumed, he ordered the first elections in many years in an attempt to appease the people.

But Berkeley's move backfired when Bacon went further, demanding the death or removal of all Indians from the colony as well as an end to the rule of aristocratic "grandees" and "parasites." Berkeley fled across the Chesapeake, Bacon seized control, and his volunteer force burned Jamestown to the ground. Soon thereafter, however, the rebel leader came down with dysentery. He died and the rebellion collapsed. Berkeley returned, reestablished control, and ordered the execution of Bacon's lieutenants.

This brief but violent clash signaled a developing conflict between backcountry districts and more established coastal regions where the "Indian problem" had long since been settled. Backcountry men in the Albermarle region of North Carolina staged a similar revolt in 1677, an episode known as **Culpeper's Rebellion**. They overthrew the established government and held power for two years before the proprietors reestablished authority. These rebellions revealed the power of class antagonism. But they also suggested that the Indians could play the role of convenient scapegoats.

QUICK REVIEW

King Philip's War
- King Philip's War broke out in 1675.
- Conflict between Wampanoags and settlers led to war.
- Thousands of settlers and Indians died in the fighting.

3–2
Nathaniel Bacon's Challenge to William Berkeley and the Governor's Response

Culpeper's Rebellion   The overthrow of the established government in the Albermarle region of North Carolina by backcountry men in 1677.

CHRONOLOGY

1598	Juan de Oñate leads Spanish into New Mexico	**1675**	King Philip's War
1607	English found Jamestown		Bacon's Rebellion
1608	French found Quebec	**1680**	Pueblo Revolt
1609	Spanish found Santa Fé	**1681–82**	Robert Sieur de La Salle explores the Misissippi
1620	Pilgrim emigration	**1688**	The Glorious Revolution
1622	Indian uprising in Virginia	**1689**	King William's War
1625	Jesuit missionaries arrive in New France	**1696**	Spanish reconquest of the Pueblos completed
1629	Puritans begin settlement of Massachusetts Bay	**1701**	English impose royal governments on all colonies but Massachusetts, Connecticut, and Pennsylvania
1637	Pequot War		
1649	Charles I executed		
1660	Stuart monarchy restored, Charles II becomes king		

KING WILLIAM'S WAR

The year 1689 also marked the beginning of nearly seventy-five years of armed conflict between English and French forces for control of the North American interior. The competition in the colonies was part of a larger conflict between England and France over the European balance of power. Armed conflict in what is known as the War of the Grand Alliance began in Europe in 1688 and spread to the colonies, where it was known as **King William's War** (for the new king of England). The inconclusive war ended in 1697 with an equally inconclusive peace. War between England and France would resume only five years later.

The persistent violence of the last quarter of the seventeenth century greatly concerned English authorities, who began to fear the loss of their North American possessions by outside attack or internal disorder. In 1701 the English Board of Trade converted the remaining charter and proprietary colonies into royal ones. Eventually William Penn succeeded in regaining private control of Pennsylvania, and Rhode Island and Connecticut won reinstatement of their charter governments. But the most lasting result of this quarter-century of turmoil was the tightening of English control over its North American colonies.

King William's War   The first of a series of colonial struggles between England and France, these conflicts occur principally on the frontiers of northern New England and New York between 1689 and 1697.

CONCLUSION

At the beginning of the seventeenth century, the European presence north of Mexico was extremely limited: Spanish bases in Florida, a few Franciscan missions among the Pueblos, and fishermen along the North Atlantic coast. By 1700 the human landscape of the Southwest, the South, and the Northeast had been transformed. More than a quarter million migrants from the Old World had come to North America, the great majority of them to the English colonies. Indian societies had been disrupted, depopulated, and in some cases destroyed. The violence that flared during the last quarter of the seventeenth century was a measure of the cost of empire. Indian people resisted colonial rule in New Mexico, New England, and the Chesapeake.

Like King Philip's War and Bacon's Rebellion, the Pueblo Revolt was an episode of great violence and destruction. Yet it resulted in a long period of accommodation between the Pueblos and the Spanish colonists. The English colonists, however, took a different lesson from the violent conflicts in their colonies. They renewed their commitment to establishing communities of exclusion with ominous implications for the future of relations between colonists and natives.

REVIEW QUESTIONS

1. Using examples drawn from this chapter, discuss the differences between colonizing "frontiers of inclusion" and "exclusion."

2. What factors turned England's Chesapeake colony of Virginia from stark failure to brilliant success?

3. Discuss the role of religious dissent in the founding of the first New England colonies and in stimulating the creation of others.

4. Compare and contrast William Penn's policy with respect to Indian tribes with the policies of other English settlers, in the Chesapeake and New England, and with the policies of the Spanish, the French, and the Dutch.

5. What were the principal causes of colonial violence and warfare of the late seventeenth century?

KEY TERMS

Flashcard Review

Beaver Wars (p. 52)
Coureurs de bois (p. 50)
Covenant Chain (p. 64)
Culpeper's Rebellion (p. 65)
Frame of Government (p. 63)
House of Burgesses (p. 55)
Indentured Servants (p. 55)
King Philip's War (p. 64)
King William's War (p. 67)
Massachusetts Bay Company (p. 58)

Mayflower Compact (p. 57)
Pequot War (p. 63)
Pilgrims (p. 57)
Powhatan Confederacy (p. 52)
Proprietary colony (p. 62)
Puritans (p. 56)
Puritanism (p. 56)
Quakers (p. 62)
Separatists (p. 57)
Virginia Company (p. 52)

RECOMMENDED READING

James Axtell, *The European and the Indian: Essays in the Ethnohistory of Colonial America* (1981). A readable introduction to the dynamics of mutual discovery between natives and colonizers.

Leslie Choquette, *Frenchmen into Peasants: Modernity and Tradition in the Peopling of French Canada* (1997). A history of French immigrants to North America, based on a comprehensive database of hundreds of individuals. The most detailed study of French colonization.

James Horn, *A Land as God Made It: Jamestown and the Birth of America* (2005). Near the 400th anniversary of Jamestown's founding, a new history that includes important archaeological evidence.

Andrew L. Knaut, *The Pueblo Revolt of 1680* (1995). The most complete and sophisticated account of the revolt.

Edmund S. Morgan, *American Slavery, American Freedom* (1975). A classic interpretation of early Virginia, arguing that early American ideas of freedom
for some were based on the reality of slavery for many.

Diana Newton, *Papists, Protestants, and Puritans, 1559–1714* (1998). The best
survey of religious change during the Protestant Reformation with a focus
on the turmoil in England.

Daniel K. Richter, *Facing East from Indian Country: A Native History of Early America* (2001). Colonial history from the point of view of the Indians. Includes
remarkable biographical chapters on Pocahontas and Metacom.

Nicholas A. Robins, *Native Insurgencies and the Genocidal Impulse in the Americas*
(2005). A comparative study of several native insurgencies on the Spanish
frontier, prominently featuring the Pueblo Revolt.

Helen C. Rountree, *Pocahontas, Powhatan, Opechancanough: Three Indian Lives
Changed by Jamestown* (2005). The leading authority on the Indians of eastern Virginia tells the story of colonization from the native perspective.

Susan Sleeper-Smith, *Native Women and French Men: Rethinking Cultural Encounter in the Western Great Lakes* (2001). A study of Indian women who
married French traders and became cultural intermediaries.

David J. Weber, *The Spanish Frontier in North America* (1992). A powerful
overview that includes comprehensive histories of New Mexico and
Florida.

Democratic Roots in New England Soil

The Puritans of New England were less than democratic in both beliefs and goals. Contrary to popular myth, they did not migrate to the New World to establish religious freedom. They were seeking to establish a religious utopia to serve as what Governor John Winthrop called a "light upon a hill" for the world to emulate. They forbid the establishment of other religious doctrine, especially the Quakers and Roman Catholic faith. In Puritan communities nonconformist behavior was looked upon with deep suspicion, especially if it was religious in nature.

However, the Puritans unknowingly planted the seeds for the very democracy that they viewed as an abomination of the purity of God's social order. In the Mayflower Compact, Puritan separatists agreed to a governmental covenant that allowed for majority rule and later established the idea of the town meeting. The charter of the Massachusetts Bay Colony provided for the elections of governors, colonial legislatures, and a General Court. Puritan customs forbid church ministers from serving in public office, an early version of separation of Church and State. Most important of all, the Puritans required that all church members be able to read and interpret the Bible. This emphasis upon the individual and his right to interpret the Bible, within certain doctrinal limits, without the intercession of a priest or minister would lead to political consequences.

A hundred years later, the political seeds they planted would bear democratic fruit. ■

WHY COULD New England society move from a firm condemnation of democracy to embracing the basic ideals that would lead to the Declaration of Independence and the Constitution of 1787?

▲The Signing of the *Mayflower Compact* a painting by E. Percy Moran shows the historic ceremonial signing on November 21, 1620 below the deck of the Mayflower.

MAYFLOWER COMPACT, 1620

IN THE NAME OF GOD, AMEN. We, whose names are underwritten, the Loyal Subjects of our dread Sovereign Lord King James, by the Grace of God, of Great Britain, France, and Ireland, King, Defender of the Faith, &c. Having undertaken for the Glory of God, and Advancement of the Christian Faith, and the Honour of our King and Country, a Voyage to plant the first Colony in the northern Parts of Virginia; Do by these Presents, solemnly and mutually, in the Presence of God and one another, covenant and combine ourselves together into a civil Body Politick, for our better Ordering and Preservation, and Furtherance of the Ends aforesaid: And by Virtue hereof do enact, constitute, and frame, such just and equal Laws, Ordinances, Acts, Constitutions, and Officers, from time to time, as shall be thought most meet and convenient for the general Good of the Colony; unto which we promise all due Submission and Obedience. IN WITNESS whereof we have hereunto subscribed our names at Cape-Cod the eleventh of November, in the Reign of our Sovereign Lord King James, of England, France, and Ireland, the eighteenth, and of Scotland the fifty-fourth, Anno Domini; 1620.■

JOHN WINTHROP, *ON LIBERTY* (1645)

THERE IS a twofold liberty, natural (I mean as our nature is now corrupt) and civil or federal. The first is common to man with beasts and other creatures. By this, man, as he stands in relation to man simply, hath liberty to do what he lists; it is a liberty to evil as well as to good. This liberty is incompatible and inconsistent with authority and cannot endure the least restraint of the most just authority. The exercise and maintaining of this liberty makes men grow more evil and in time to be worse than brute beasts: omnes sumus licentia deteriores. This is that great enemy of truth and peace, that wild beast, which all of the ordinances of God are bent against, to restrain and subdue it. The other kind of liberty I call civil or federal; it may also be termed moral, in reference to the covenant between God and man, in the moral law, and the politic covenants and constitutions amongst men themselves. This liberty is the proper end and object of authority and cannot subsist without it; and it is a liberty to that only which is good, just, and honest. This liberty you are to stand for, with the hazard (not only of your goods, but) of your lives, if need be. Whatsoever crosseth this is not authority but a distemper thereof.... If you will be satisfied to enjoy such civil and lawful liberties, such as Christ allows you, then will you quietly and cheerfully submit unto that authority which is set over you, in all the administrations of it, for your good. ■

FUNDAMENTAL ORDERS OF CONNECTICUT (1639)

It is Ordered, sentenced, and decreed, that there shall be yearly two General Assemblies or Courts, the one the second Thursday in April, the other the second Thursday in September following; the first shall be called the Court of Election, wherein shall be yearly chosen from time to time, so many Magistrates and other public Officers as shall be found requisite: Whereof one to be chosen Governor for the year ensuing and until another be chosen, and no other Magistrate to be chosen for more than one year: provided always there be six chosen besides the Governor, which being chosen and sworn according to an Oath recorded for that purpose, shall have the power to administer justice according to the Laws here established....

It is Ordered, sentenced, and decreed, that the election of the aforesaid Magistrates shall be in this manner: every person present and qualified for choice shall bring in (to the person deputed to receive them) one single paper with the name of him written in it whom he desires to have Governor, and that he that hath the greatest number of papers shall be Governor for that year. And the rest of the Magistrates or public officers to be chosen in this manner: the Secretary for the time being shall first read the names of all that are to be put to choice and then shall severally nominate them distinctly, and every one that would have the person nominated to be chosen shall bring in one single paper written upon, and he that would not have him chosen shall bring in a blank; and every one that hath more written papers than blanks shall be a Magistrate for that year....

It is Ordered, sentenced, and decreed, that no person be chosen Governor above once in two years, and that the Governor be always a member of some approved Congregation....■

JOHN ADAMS, CO-AUTHOR OF THE DECLARATION OF INDEPENDENCE, 1776
"WE HOLD THESE TRUTHS TO BE SELF-EVIDENT, THAT ALL MEN ARE CREATED EQUAL, THAT THEY ARE ENDOWED BY THEIR CREATOR WITH CERTAIN UNALIENABLE RIGHTS, THAT AMONG THESE ARE LIFE, LIBERTY AND THE PURSUIT OF HAPPINESS.–THAT TO SECURE THESE RIGHTS, GOVERNMENTS ARE INSTITUTED AMONG MEN, DERIVING THEIR JUST POWERS FROM THE CONSENT OF THE GOVERNED,..."

FUNDAMENTAL AGREEMENT, OR ORIGINAL CONSTITUTION OF THE COLONY OF NEW HAVEN (1639)

Query II. WHEREAS there was a covenant solemnly made by the whole assembly of free planters of this plantation, the first day of extraordinary humiliation, which we had after we came together, that as in matters that concern the gathering and ordering of a church, so likewise in all public officers which concern civil order, as choice of magistrates and officers, making and repealing laws, dividing allotments of inheritance, and all things of like nature, we would all of us be ordered by those rules which the scripture holds forth to US; this covenant was called a plantation covenant, to distinguish it from a church covenant. which could not at that time be made a church not being then gathered, but was deferred till a church might be gathered, according to GOD. It was demanded whether all the free planters do hold themselves bound by that covenant, in all businesses of that nature which are expressed in the covenant, to submit themselves to be ordered by the rules held forth in the scripture....■

The wooden Old Ship Meeting House in Hingham, Massachusetts hosted the annual town meeting where Puritans voted and openly debated town policy.

The first object that saluted my eyes when I arrived on the coast was the sea, and a slave ship, which was then riding at anchor, and waiting for its cargo.

—*from* The Interesting Life of Olaudah Equiano

Slaves on the deck of the captured ship "Wildfire."

4

SLAVERY AND EMPIRE
1441–1770

HOW DID the modern system of slavery develop?

WHAT IS the history of the slave trade and the Middle Passage?

HOW DID slavery in the North differ from slavery in the South?

HOW DID African slaves attempt to preserve African culture in America?

HOW DID slavery fuel the economic development of Europe in the seventeenth and eighteenth centuries?

HOW DID slavery shape southern colonial society?

AMERICAN COMMUNITIES
Rebellion in Stono, South Carolina

ON SUNDAY MORNING, SEPTEMBER 9, 1739, WHILE MOST PLANTER families were attending church, a group of twenty slaves gathered on the banks of the Stono River, twenty miles south of Charles Town, South Carolina. Led by an Angolan known in some accounts as Jemmy, in others as Cato, the slaves made their way to Hutchinson's general store in the hamlet of Stono Bridge. They killed the two storekeepers, ransacked the place, and arming themselves with firearms and ammunition, set off on the road headed southwest for Florida, where the Spanish governor had issued a proclamation promising freedom for all runaway British slaves. They made no attempt to hide themselves but marched boldly to the beat of drummers and shouts of "Liberty!" The commotion drew the attention of curious slaves from the numerous rice plantations scattered across the swampy countryside, and dozens joined the marchers, women and children as well as men. They plundered and burned the homes of planters and pursued and killed every white person they encountered along the way, with the exception of an innkeeper, who was spared when several rebels spoke up in his defense, saying he had been kind to his slaves.

Word of the rebellion quickly spread throughout the planter community, and soon a heavily armed and mounted posse was hot on the rebels' trail. Late in the afternoon, near the crossing of the Edisto River, the posse overtook them. The rebel band, grown to nearly a hundred strong, had halted in a field where, in the words of the report, they "set to dancing, singing, and beating drums to draw more Negroes to them." Bottles of rum were passed and there was a good deal of drinking. Quietly the planters surrounded the field, then opened fire. Most of the slaves scattered, although according to the report the group of original conspirators "behaved boldly," forming themselves into a body and returning several volleys with the stolen firearms. But they were outmanned and outgunned, and at least two dozen slaves were killed. According to another account, the posse "cutt off their heads and set them up at every mile post" along the road leading back to Charles Town. Over the next few weeks the remaining fugitives were tracked down and killed by Indian allies of the South Carolina colony. A total of forty-five or fifty African Americans died. Thus

ended the Stono Rebellion, the most violent slave uprising of the colonial period.

That slaves would rise up with the odds so stacked against them was a sign of their desperation. Most of these men and women were West Africans who had endured the shock of enslavement. On the rice plantations of low-country South Carolina, they suffered from overwork, poor diet, minimal clothing, and inadequate housing. Colonial laws permitted masters to discipline and punish harshly and indiscriminately. Slaves were whipped, confined in irons, mutilated, sold away, even murdered.

That slaves would rise up was also a sign of their community. The Stono Rebellion required the kind of careful organization possible only with the social trust and confidence built by community ties. Plantation slaves married, raised children, and constructed kinship networks. They passed on African names and traditions and created new ones. Many of the slaves of coastal South Carolina came from the central African rice coast, from Angola or the Kingdom of the Kongo, where men not only knew about the cultivation of rice but also shared a military tradition and knew how to handle firearms.

Community is also what enables a people to remember their history, to pass tales down the generations. In the 1930s, nearly two hundred years after the uprising at Stono, George Cato, great-great-grandson of the leader of the Stono Rebellion, had stories to tell. "As it come down to me, I thinks de first Cato take a darin' chance on losin' his life, not so much for his own benefit as it was to help others." He and the other rebels died in their attempt to free themselves, and not only did slavery continue, but also it grew even harsher and more oppressive as planters sought to stamp out the merest possibility of revolt. Yet the slaves' cry of "Liberty!" had not been in vain. Although in the twentieth century most white Americans had never heard of the Stono Rebellion, stories of the rebels' bravery and daring continued to inspire the local African American community. "I sho' does come from dat old stock who had de misfortune to be slaves," said Cato, who had been born into slavery himself. But the rebels "decided to be men," he declared, "and I's right proud of it."

Stono, SC

THE BEGINNINGS OF AFRICAN SLAVERY

Household slaves had been a part of the Mediterranean world since ancient times. In the fifteenth century, merchants did a booming business in the sale of captive Slavs—the word "slave" derives from "Slav"—as well as Muslims and Africans. Many Europeans were disturbed, however, by the moral implications of enslaving other Europeans, and in the early fifteenth century the pope excommunicated a number of merchants engaged in selling Christians. But the same penalty did not apply to selling Africans and Muslims.

One of the goals of Portuguese expansion in the fifteenth century was to gain access to the lucrative West African trade in gold, ivory, textiles, and slaves previously dominated by the Moors of northern Africa. The first African slaves to arrive in Lisbon had been kidnapped by a Portuguese captain in 1441. But European traders found it more efficient to leave the dirty work of taking captives to Africans who were willing to exchange slaves for European commodities. By the mid-fifteenth century, the Portuguese were shipping a thousand or more slaves each year from Africa. Most of them were sent to labor on the sugar plantations on the Portuguese island colony of Madeira, off the coast of northern Africa.

SUGAR AND SLAVERY

Sugar and slaves had gone together since Italian merchants of the fourteenth century set up the first modern sugar plantations on islands in the Mediterranean. Columbus introduced sugar to Hispaniola on his second voyage, and plantations were soon in operation there. Because the Indian population had been devastated by warfare and disease, colonists imported African slaves as laborers. Meanwhile, the Portuguese, aided by Dutch financiers, created a center of sugar production in their Brazilian colony that became a model for the efficient and brutal exploitation of African labor.

HOW DID the modern system of slavery develop?

myhistorylab
Review Summary

IMAGE KEY
for pages 72–73

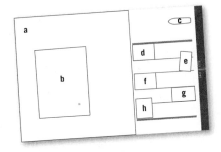

a. White Hills map by John Foster, 1677, woodcut. America's first map.

b. Slaves on the deck of the captured ship "Wildfire."

c. Model of the slave ship *Brookes*, showing plan view of slave positions.

d. William Clark's *Ten Views Found in the Island of Antigua* shows slaves working on a plantation.

e. "To be sold, a cargo of ninety-four prime, healthy Negroes."

f. The London Coffee House near the docks of Philadelphia was the site of many slave auctions in the mid-eighteenth century.

g. The Old Plantation, showing slaves at work.

h. Goods from the American colonies being unloaded from eighteenth-century ships on London's Old Custom House Quay.

This image of Mansa Musa (1312–37), the ruler of the Muslim kingdom of Mali in West Africa, is taken from the *Catalan Atlas*, a magnificent map presented to the king of France in 1381 by his cousin, the king of Aragon. In the words of the Catalan inscription, Musa was "the richest, the most noble lord in all this region on account of the abundance of gold that is gathered in his land." He holds what was thought to be the world's largest gold nugget. Under Musa's reign, Timbuktu became a capital of world renown.

Skilled at finance and commerce, the Dutch greatly expanded the European market for sugar, converting it from a luxury item for the rich to a staple for ordinary people. Once the demand for sugar and its profitability had been demonstrated, England and France began seeking West Indian sugar colonies of their own. They began by seizing islands of the Lesser Antilles, constructing plantations, and importing slaves. By the 1640s, English Barbados and French Martinique had become highly profitable sugar colonies. In 1655 the English seized the island of Jamaica from the Spanish, and by 1670 the French had established effective control over the western portion of Hispaniola, which they renamed Saint Domingue (present-day Haiti) when they acquired it by treaty. By then, Caribbean sugar and slavery had become the centerpiece of the European colonial system.

WEST AFRICANS

The men and women whose labor made these tropical colonies so profitable came from the long-established societies and local communities of West Africa. In the sixteenth century more than a hundred different peoples lived along the coast of West Africa, from Cape Verde south to Angola. Farming sustained large populations and thriving networks of commerce. There were a number of lesser states and kingdoms along the coast, and it was with these that the Portuguese first bargained for Africans who could be sold as slaves.

Varieties of household slavery were common in West African societies, although slaves there were often treated more as members of the family than as mere possessions. They were allowed to marry, and their children were born free. When African merchants sold the first slaves to the Portuguese, they may have thought that European slavery would be similar.

African slaves operate a sugar mill on the Spanish island colony of Hispaniola, illustated in a copperplate engraving published by Theodore de Bry in 1595. Columbus introduced sugar on his second voyage and plantations were soon in operation. Because the native population was devastated by warfare and disease, colonists imported African slaves as laborers.

THE AFRICAN SLAVE TRADE

The movement of Africans across the Atlantic to the Americas was the largest forced migration in world history (see Map 4.1). Africans made up the largest group of people to come to the Americas before the nineteenth century, outnumbering European immigrants by a ratio of six to one. The Atlantic slave trade, which began with the Portuguese in the fifteenth century and did not end in the United States until 1807 (and continued elsewhere in the Americas until the 1870s), is a brutal chapter in the making of America.

WHAT IS the history of the slave trade and the Middle Passage?

myhistorylab
Review Summary

 MAP EXPLORATION

To explore an interactive version of this map, go to **http://www.prenhall.com/faraghertlc/map4.1**

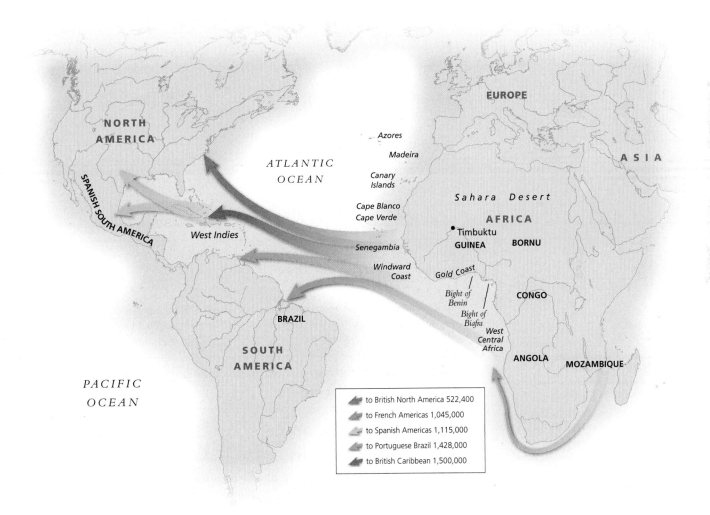

MAP 4.1
The African Slave Trade   The enslaved men, women, and children transported to the Americas came from West Africa, the majority from the lower Niger River (called the Slave Coast) and the region of the Congo and Angola.

HOW AND why were the people of Africa enslaved and brought to America?

MAP 4.2

Slave Colonies of the Seventeenth and Eighteenth Centuries   By the eighteenth century, the system of slavery had created societies with large African populations throughout the Caribbean and along the southern coast of North America.

HOW DID the sugar boom contribute to the importation of large numbers of Africans to the Americas?

A GLOBAL ENTERPRISE

Scholars estimate that 10 to 12 million Africans arrived in the Americas during the four-century history of the trade. Seventy-six percent arrived from 1701 to 1810, the peak period of colonial demand for labor, when tens of thousands were shipped from Africa each year. Of this vast multitude, about half were delivered to Dutch, French, or British sugar plantations in the Caribbean, a third to Portuguese Brazil, and a tenth to Spanish America (see Map 4.2). A much smaller proportion, about one in twenty, a total of approximately 600,000 individuals, were transported to the British colonies of North America. With the exception of the 1750s, when the British colonies were engulfed by the **Seven Years' War**, the slave trade continued to rise in importance in the decades before the Revolution (see Figure 4.1).

QUICK REVIEW

Demography of Slavery

- 10 to 12 million Africans brought to the Americas over the course of four hundred years.

- Almost twice as many men as women were enslaved.

- Most Africans captured and transported to the Americas were between the ages of fifteen and thirty.

Seven Years' War   War fought in Europe, North America, and India between 1756 and 1753, pitting France and its allies against Great Britain and its allies.

All the nations of Western Europe participated in the slave trade. Dutch slavers began challenging Portuguese control of the trade at the end of the sixteenth century, and during the sugar boom of the seventeenth century Holland was the most prominent slave-trading nation. The English entered the trade at the same time. As a result, the number of slaves shipped to North America skyrocketed. The Dutch and Portuguese, however, continued to play important roles, alongside slave traders from France, Sweden, and several German duchies.

The European presence in Africa generally was confined to coastal outposts. As the volume of slave trading expanded, the forts of trading companies gave way to the smaller coastal posts of independent traders who set up operations with the cooperation of local headmen or chiefs. This informal manner of trading offered opportunities for small operators, such as the slave traders of New England. Many great American fortunes were built from profits in the slave trade.

The slave trade was a collaboration between European or American and African traders. Dependent on the favor of local rulers, many colonial slave traders lived permanently in coastal forts and married African women, reinforcing their commercial ties with family relations. In many areas their mixed-ancestry offspring became prominent players in the slave trade. Continuing the practice of the Portuguese, the grim business of slave raiding was left to the Africans themselves.

THE SHOCK OF ENSLAVEMENT

Most Africans were enslaved through warfare. Sometimes large armies launched massive attacks, burning whole towns and taking hundreds of prisoners. More common were smaller raids in which a group of armed men attacked at nightfall, seized everyone within reach, then escaped with their captives. Enslavement was an unparalleled shock. Venture Smith, an African born in Guinea in 1729, was eight years old when he was captured. After many years in North American slavery, he still vividly recalled the attack on his village, the torture and murder of his father, and the long march of his people to the coast.

On the coast, European traders and African raiders assembled their captives. Prisoners waited in dark dungeons or in open pens called "barracoons." To lessen the possibility of collective resistance, traders split up families and ethnic groups. Captains carefully inspected each man and woman, and those selected for transport were branded on the back or buttocks with the mark of the buyer. Olaudah Equiano remembered that he and his fellow captives became convinced that they "had got into a world of bad spirits" and were about to be eaten by cannibals.

THE MIDDLE PASSAGE

In the eighteenth century, English sailors christened the voyage of slave vessels across the Atlantic as the "**Middle Passage**," the middle part of a trading triangle from England to Africa, to America, and back to England. From coastal forts and barracoons, crews rowed small groups of slaves out to the waiting transports and packed them into shelves below deck only six feet long by two and a half feet high. People were forced to sleep "spoon fashion," and the tossing of the ship knocked them about so violently that the skin over their elbows sometimes was worn to the bone from scraping on the planks.

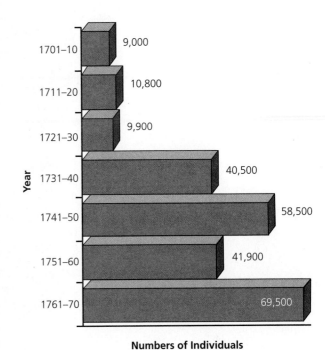

Figure 4.1 Estimated Number of Africans Imported to British North America, 1701–70
These official British statistics include only slaves imported legally and, consequently, undercount the total number who arrived on American shores. But the trend over time is clear. With the exception of the 1750s, when the British colonies were engulfed by the Seven Years' War, the slave trade continued to rise in importance in the decades before the Revolution.

R. C. Simmons, *The American Colonies: From Settlement to Independence* (London: Longman, 1976), 186.

Middle Passage   The voyage between West Africa and the New World slave colonies.

A group of slaves being led from the interior to the West African coast by two traders, from Rene Geoffroy de Villeneuve, *l' Afrique* (1814).

Portrait of Olaudah Equiano, by an unknown English artist, ca. 1780. Captured in Nigeria in 1756 when he was eleven years old, Equiano was transported to America and was eventually purchased by an English sea captain. After ten years as a slave, he succeeded in buying his own freedom and dedicated himself to the antislavery cause. His book, *The Interesting Narrative of the Life of Olaudah Equiano* (1789), was published in numerous editions, translated into several languages, and became the prototype for dozens of other slave narratives in the nineteenth century.

Royal Albert Memorial Museum, Exeter, Devon, UK/Bridgeman Art Library.

Their holds filled with human cargo, the transports headed up the African coast to Cape Verde where they caught the trade winds blowing toward America. A favorable voyage from Senegambia to Barbados might be accomplished in as little as three weeks, but a ship from Guinea or Angola, becalmed in the doldrums or driven back by storms, might take as much as three months.

Most voyages were marked by a daily routine. In the morning the crew opened the hatch and brought the captives on deck, attaching their leg irons to a great chain running the length of the bulwarks. After a breakfast of beans the crew commanded men and women to jump up and down, a bizarre session of exercise known as "dancing the slave." A day spent chained on deck was concluded by a second bland meal and then the stowing away. Down in the hold, the groans of the dying, the shrieks of women and children, and the suffocating heat and stench were, in the words of Olaudah Equiano, "a scene of horror almost inconceivable"

Among the worst of the horrors was the absence of adequate sanitation. Crews were supposed to swab the holds daily, but so sickening was the task that it was rarely performed, and Africans were left to wallow in their own wastes. According to Atlantic sailors, they could "smell a slaver five miles down wind." Many captives sickened and died in these conditions. Others contracted dysentery, known as the "flux." Frequent shipboard epidemics of smallpox, measles, and yellow fever added to the misery. The dying continued even as the ships anchored at their destinations. Historians estimate that one in every six Africans perished during the Middle Passage.

The unwilling voyagers offered plenty of resistance. As long as ships were still within sight of the African coast, hope remained alive and the danger of revolt was great. Once on the open sea, however, the captives' resistance took more desperate form. Equiano witnessed several Africans jump overboard and drown, "and I believe many more would very soon have done the same if they had not been prevented by the ship's crew."

Slaves below deck on a Spanish slaver, a sketch made when the vessel was captured by a British warship in the early nineteenth century. Slaves were "stowed so close, that they were not allowed above a foot and a half for each in breadth," wrote one observer. The close quarters and unsanitary conditions created a stench so bad that Atlantic sailors said you could "smell a slaver five miles down wind."

As the vessels approached their destination, crews prepared the human cargo for market. All but the most rebellious were freed from their chains and allowed to wash themselves and move about the deck. Buyers painstakingly examined the Africans, who once again suffered the indignity of probing eyes and poking fingers. In ports such as Charles Town in South Carolina, sales were generally made by auction or by a cruel method known as the scramble: with prices fixed in advance the Africans were driven into a corral, and on cue the buyers would rush in among them, grabbing their pick. The noise, clamor, and eagerness of the buyers, Equiano remembered, renewed all their apprehensions. "In this manner, without scruple, are relations and friends separated, most of them never to see each other again."

POLITICAL AND ECONOMIC EFFECTS ON AFRICA

Africa began the sixteenth century with genuine independence. But as surely as Europe and America grew stronger as a result of the transport of Africans, so Africa grew weaker by their loss. For every individual taken captive, at least another died in the chronic slave raiding. Death and destruction spread deep into the African interior. Coastal slave-trading kingdoms drew slaves from central Africa. Many of the new states became little more than machines for supplying captives to European traders, and a "gun-slave cycle" pushed them into a destructive arms race with each other. Soldiers captured in these wars were themselves enslaved.

More serious still was the long-term stagnation of the West African economy. Labor was drawn away from productive activities while imported consumer goods stifled local manufacturing. African traders were expert at driving a hard bargain for slaves, but even when they appeared to get the best of the exchange, the ultimate advantage lay with the

Africans herded from a slave ship to a corral where they were to be sold by the cruel method known as "the scramble," buyers rushing in and grabbing their pick. This image was featured in an antislavery narrative published in 1796.

Europeans, who received wealth-producing workers in return for mere consumer goods. This political, economic, and cultural demoralization prepared the way for the European conquest of Africa in the nineteenth century.

THE DEVELOPMENT OF NORTH AMERICAN SLAVE SOCIETIES

HOW DID slavery in the North differ from slavery in the South?

myhistorylab

Review Summary

2–12
Robert Beverly, *A Virginian Describes the Difference between Servants and Slaves* (1722)

New World slavery was nearly two centuries old before it became an important system of labor in North America. There were slaves in all the British colonies of the seventeenth century, but as late as 1700 slaves accounted for less than 12 percent of the colonial population. During the eighteenth century, however, slavery expanded greatly, and by 1770 there were 460,000 Africans and African Americans in British North America, making up more than 20 percent of the population (see Figure 4.2).

SLAVERY COMES TO NORTH AMERICA

The first Africans arrived in Virginia in 1619 when a Dutch slave trader exchanged "20 and odd Negars" for badly needed provisions with planter John Rolfe, the widower of Pocahontas and pioneering Virginia tobacco planter. But because slaves generally cost twice as much as indentured servants yet had the same appallingly short life expectancy, they proved to have little economic benefit for planters. Consequently, seventeenth-century Chesapeake planters employed far more indentured servants than slaves. Servants and the small number of slaves worked together, ate and slept in common quarters, and often developed intimate relationships. The Chesapeake was what one historian has termed a "society with slaves," a society in which slavery was one form of labor among several.

Under these circumstances the status of black Virginians could be ambiguous. Seventeenth-century Virginia records document Africans acquiring farms, servants, and slaves of their own. Many slaves were Christians, and it raised traditional legal and moral doubts about whether co-religionists could be enslaved. Moreover, sexual relations among Africans, Indians, and Europeans produced a sizable group of free people of mixed ancestry known as mulattoes. It was only later that dark skin came automatically to mean slavery, segregation, and the absence of the rights of freemen.

During the last quarter of the seventeenth century, however, the Chesapeake became a "slave society," a place where slavery was the dominant form of labor. Among several developments, perhaps most important was the sharp decline in the number of indentured servants migrating to the Chesapeake. The incentive had been the availability of land after the term of service, but by midcentury most of the arable land had fallen into the hands of the planter elite. Bacon's and Culpeper's rebellions (see Chapter 3) offered examples of the violent potential of the land crisis. They also suggested how much serious trouble servants and former servants could make for planters. After Bacon's Rebellion, English immigrants turned away from the Chesapeake to colonies such as Pennsylvania, where there was more land and, thus, more opportunity.

The British Royal African Company, which began to import slaves directly to North America in the 1670s, was more than happy

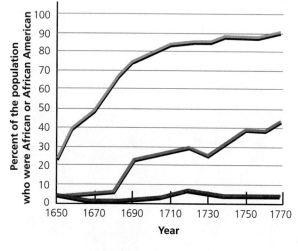

Figure 4.2 Africans as a Percentage of Total Population of the British Colonies, 1650–1770
Although the proportion of Africans and African Americans was never as high in the South as in the Caribbean, the ethnic structure of the South diverged radically from that of the North during the eighteenth century.

Robert W. Fogel and Stanley L. Engerman, *Time on the Cross* (Boston: Little, Brown, 1974), 21.

to supply planters' need for labor. Slaves were expensive, but planters expected to keep them in the fields for longer hours, with fewer days off, and hopefully with less risk of an uprising. By 1700 there were 5,000 slaves in Virginia, and more than 22 percent of the Chesapeake population was of African descent.

Slavery had no English legal precedent, no laws or traditions allowing for life-time enslavement or for making that status inheritable. So as the proportions of slaves in the colonial population gradually rose, colonists wrote slavery into law, a process best observed in the case of Virginia. In 1662 the planter assembly declared that henceforth children would be "bond or free only according to the condition of the mother." Five years later they passed a law that Christian baptism could no longer alter conditions of servitude. Thus, two important avenues to freedom were closed. The colony then gave masters the right to administer life-threatening violence, declaring in 1669 that the death of a slave during punishment "shall not be accounted felony." Such rules accumulated piecemeal until 1705, when Virginia gathered them into a comprehensive slave code that became a model for other colonies.

Thus, slavery was institutionalized just as the Atlantic slave trade reached flood tide in the eighteenth century. In the single decade of 1701 to 1710 more Africans were imported into North America than during the entire previous century. The English colonies were primed for an unprecedented growth of plantation slavery.

THE TOBACCO COLONIES

During the eighteenth century the European demand for tobacco increased more than tenfold, and it was supplied largely by increased production in the Chesapeake region. Tobacco was far and away the single most important commodity produced in eighteenth-century North America, accounting for more than a quarter of the value of all colonial exports.

The expansion of tobacco production could not have taken place without a corresponding growth in the size of the slave labor force. Unlike sugar, tobacco did not require large plantations and could be produced successfully on small farms. But the crop demanded a great deal of hand labor and close attention. As tobacco production expanded, slaveholding became widespread. By 1770 more than a quarter million slaves labored in the colonies of the Upper South (Maryland, Virginia, and North Carolina), and because of the exploding market for tobacco, their numbers expanded at about double the rate of the general population. From 1700 to 1770, an estimated 80,000 Africans were imported into the tobacco region. But natural increase was even more important. In the Caribbean and Brazil, where profits from sugar were extremely high, many planters literally worked their slaves to death, replenishing them with a constant stream of new arrivals from Africa. In the Chesapeake, however, significantly lower profits led tobacco planters to pay more attention to the health of their labor force, establishing work routines that were not as deadly. Moreover, food supplies were more plentiful in North America and slaves better fed, making them more resistant to disease. As a consequence, by the 1730s the slave population of the Chesapeake had become the first in the Western Hemisphere to achieve self-sustained growth. By the 1750s, about 80 percent of Chesapeake slaves were "country-born."

THE LOWER SOUTH

South Carolina was a slave society from the beginning. The most valuable part of the early Carolina economy was the Indian slave trade. Practicing a strategy of divide and conquer, using Indian tribes to fight one another, Carolinians established a trade in Indian captives during the 1670s. By the early eighteenth century more

2–3
William Waller Hening, *The Statutes at Large; Being a Collection of All the Laws of Virginia, from the First Session of the Legislature in the Year 1619*

QUICK REVIEW

Growth of Slavery

♦ Slavery grew rapidly in the South.

♦ The use of slaves made economic sense on tobacco and rice plantations.

♦ Northern slaves worked as servants, craftsmen, and day laborers.

Residence and Slave Quarters of Mulberry Plantation, by Thomas Coram, ca. 1770. The slave quarters are on the left in this painting of a rice plantation near Charleston, South Carolina. The steep roofs of the slave cabins, an African architectural feature introduced in America by slave builders, kept living quarters cool by allowing the heat to rise and dissipate in the rafters.

Thomas Coram, "View of Mulberry Street, House and Street." Oil on paper, 10 × 17.6 cm. Gibbes Museum of Art/Carolina Art Association. 68.18.01.

than 12,000 mission Indians from Florida had been captured and sold into slavery and thousands more killed or dispersed.

In the early eighteenth century, however, planter preference turned toward African rather than Indian slaves. Rice production had become the most dynamic sector of the South Carolina economy, and their experience in agriculture made West Africans much better rice workers. Another important crop was added to the mix in the 1740s when a young South Carolina woman named Elizabeth Lucas Pinckney successfully adapted West Indian indigo to the low-country climate. The indigo plant, native to India, produced a deep blue dye important in textile manufacture. Rice grew in the lowlands, but indigo could be cultivated on high ground, and with different seasonal growing patterns, planters were able to harmonize their production. Rice and indigo became two of the most valuable commodities exported from the mainland colonies of North America. The boom in these two crops depended on the growth of African slavery. Before the international slave trade to the United States was ended in 1808, at least 100,000 slaves landed in South Carolina.

By the 1740s many of these arriving Africans were being taken to Georgia, a colony created by an act of the English Parliament in 1732. Its leader, James Edward Oglethorpe, hoped to establish a buffer against Spanish invasion from Florida and make the colony a haven for poor British farmers who could sell their products in the markets of South Carolina. Under Oglethorpe's influence, Parliament agreed to prohibit slavery in Georgia. But soon Georgia's coastal regions were being colonized by South Carolina rice planters with their slaves. By the time Oglethorpe and Georgia's trustees opened their colony to slavery in 1752, the Georgia coast had already become an extension of the Carolina low-country slave system.

By 1770 nearly 90,000 African Americans made up about 80 percent of the coastal population of South Carolina and Georgia. The African American communities of the Lower South had achieved self-sustained growth by the middle of the eighteenth century, a generation later than those in the Chesapeake.

SLAVERY IN THE SPANISH COLONIES

Slavery was basic to the Spanish colonial labor system, yet doubts about the enslavement of Africans were raised by both church and crown. The papacy denounced slavery as a violation of Christian principles. But the institution remained intact,

QUICK REVIEW

Slavery in the Lower South

- Indian slavery prominent in early Carolina economy.
- Boom in rice and indigo production depended on African slaves.
- 1770: African Americans make up 80 percent of population of South Carolina and Georgia coast.

and later in the eighteenth century, when sugar production expanded in Cuba, the slave system there turned as brutal as any in the history of the Americas.

In New Mexico, the Spanish depended on Indian slavery. In the sixteenth century the colonial governor sent Indian slaves to the mines of Mexico. The enslavement of Indians was one of the causes of the **Pueblo Revolt** (see Chapter 3). In the aftermath of the revolt the Spanish became much more cautious in their treatment of the Pueblos, who were officially considered Catholics. But they participated in a robust trade in captured and enslaved "infidel Indians," mostly nomadic people from the Great Plains, employing them as house servants and fieldworkers.

SLAVERY IN FRENCH LOUISIANA

Slavery was also important in Louisiana, the colony founded by the French in the lower Mississippi Valley. In the early eighteenth century, French colonists established settlements and forts at Biloxi and Mobile on the Gulf of Mexico and in 1718 laid out the city of New Orleans on the lower Mississippi River. The French Company of the Indies imported some 6,000 African slaves, and planters invested in tobacco and indigo plantations along the river banks north of the city. This was the country of the Natchez Indians, who greatly resented the French intrusion. In 1729 the Natchez joined forces with rebellious slaves in an armed uprising. The Natchez Rebellion claimed the lives of more than 200 French settlers, 10 percent of the population. An alliance of slaves and Indians was the greatest of all planter fears. The French colonial militia put down the rebellion with brutal force, crushing and dispersing the Natchez people in the process.

Bitter memories of the Natchez Rebellion kept the Louisiana French from committing themselves totally to slavery. In 1750 African slaves amounted to less than a third of the colonial population of 10,000. It was not until the end of the century that the colony of Louisiana became an important North American slave society.

SLAVERY IN THE NORTH

Slavery was a fundamental, acceptable, thoroughly American institution. None of the northern colonies could be characterized as slave societies, but slavery was an important form of labor in a number of localities. During the eighteenth century

Pueblo Revolt Rebellion in 1680 of Pueblo Indians in New Mexico against their Spanish overlords.

London Coffee House.

The London Coffee House, near the docks of Philadelphia, was the center of the city's business and political life in the mid-eighteenth century. Sea captains and merchants congregated here to do business, and as this contemporary print illustrates (in the detail on the far right), it was the site of many slave auctions. Slavery was a vital part of the economy of northern cities.

John F. Watson, "Annals of Philadelphia," being a collection of memoirs, anecdotes, and incidents of Philadelphia. The London Coffee House. The Library Company of Philadelphia.

it grew increasingly significant in the commercial farming regions of southeast Pennsylvania, central New Jersey, and Long Island, areas where slaves made up about 10 percent of rural residents. In Rhode Island—a center of the slave trade—large gangs of slaves were used in cattle and dairy operations, and the proportion of slaves in the population of Narragansett County reached nearly a third.

Slavery was common in all northern port cities, including Boston. Slave ownership was nearly universal among the wealthy and ordinary among craftsmen and professionals. By 1750 slaves along with small populations of free blacks made up 15 to 20 percent of the residents of Boston, New York City, and Philadelphia.

The Quakers of Pennsylvania and New Jersey, many of whom kept slaves, were the first colonists to voice antislavery sentiment. In 1715, John Hepburn of New Jersey published the first North American critique of slavery, but his was a lonely voice. By midcentury, however, there was a significant antislavery movement among the Quakers.

2–13
John Woolman, *An Early Abolitionist Speaks Out Against Slavery*, (1757)

HOW DID African slaves attempt to preserve African culture in America?

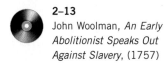

Review Summary

AFRICAN TO AFRICAN AMERICAN

Men and women from dozens of ethnic groups, representing many different languages, religions, and customs, were transported across the Atlantic without any of their cultural possessions. In America they were subjected to the control of masters intent on maximizing their work and minimizing their liberty. Yet African Americans carved out lives of their own with a degree of independence. Their African heritage was not erased; it provided them with a fundamental outlook, the basis for a common identity.

The majority of Africans transported to North America arrived during the eighteenth century. They joined a rapidly growing population of country-born slaves or "creoles" (from the Spanish *criollo* and Portuguese *creole,* meaning "born" or "raised"), a term first used by slaves in Brazil to distinguish their children, born in the New World, from newly arrived Africans. The perspective of creoles was shaped by their having grown up under slavery, and that perspective helped them to determine which elements of African culture they would incorporate into the emerging culture of the African American community. That community was formed out of the relationship between creoles and Africans, and between slaves and their European masters.

THE DAILY LIFE OF SLAVES

Slaves did the work that made the plantation colonies so profitable. As an agricultural people, Africans, both women and men, were accustomed to the routines of field labor. Most slaves were field hands, and even domestic servants labored in the fields when necessary. Masters provided their workers with rude clothing, sufficient in the summer but nearly always inadequate in the winter.

On small plantations and farms, typical in the tobacco country of the Chesapeake, Africans might work side by side with their owners and, depending on the character of the master, might enjoy a standard of living not too different from that of other family members. The work was more demanding and living conditions far worse on the great rice and indigo plantations of the Lower South, where slaves usually lived separately from the master in their own quarters. But large plantations, with large numbers of slaves, created a concentration of population that made for more resilient African American communities. It was one of the profound ironies of American slavery: life was much harder on the great plantations, but slaves had more opportunity for some autonomy.

FAMILIES AND COMMUNITIES

The family was the most important institution for the development of community and culture, but **slave codes** did not provide for legal slave marriages: that would have contradicted the master's freedom to dispose of his property as he saw fit. Planters commonly separated families by sale or bequest, dividing husbands from wives and even separating mothers from children. Charles Ball was a mere boy in Virginia when his family was separated by sale. "Oh, master, do not take me from my child!" his mother cried. But her new owner gave her two or three heavy blows on the shoulders with a rawhide whip, "snatched me from her arms, and seizing her by one arm, dragged her back towards the place of sale." Ball never saw her again. Later, after he had grown and married, his master sold him to a rice planter in Georgia. "My heart died away within me," Ball remembered vividly. "I felt incapable of weeping or speaking, and in my despair I laughed loudly." On his journey south he dreamed his wife and children were "beseeching and imploring my master on their knees." He never saw them again.

Despite the odds against them, however, slaves in both the Chesapeake and the Lower South created the families that were essential for the development of African American culture. On large plantations throughout the southern colonies, travelers found Africans living in family households. In the Lower South, where there were greater concentrations of slaves on the great rice plantations, husbands and wives often lived together in the slave quarters. On the smaller plantations of the Upper South, men frequently married women from neighboring farms, and with the permission of both owners visited their families in the evenings or on Sundays.

Emotional ties to particular places, connections between the generations, and relations of kinship and friendship linking neighboring plantations and farms were the foundation stones of African American community life. Kinship was especially important. African American parents encouraged their children to use family terms in addressing unrelated persons: "auntie" or "uncle" became a respectful way of addressing older men and women, "brother" and "sister" affectionate terms for agemates. This may have been one of the first devices enslaved Africans used to humanize the world of slavery.

AFRICAN AMERICAN CULTURE

The eighteenth century was the formative period in the development of the African American community, for it was then that the high birthrate and the growing numbers of country-born provided the necessary stability for the evolution of culture. During this period, men and women from dozens of African ethnic groups molded themselves into a new people. Distinctive patterns in music and dance, religion, and oral tradition illustrate the resilience of the human spirit under bondage as well as the successful struggle of African Americans to create a spiritually sustaining culture of their own.

Eighteenth-century masters were reluctant to allow their slaves to become Christians, fearing that baptism would open the way to claims of freedom or give Africans dangerous notions of universal brotherhood and equality with masters. Large numbers of African Americans were not converted to Christianity until the **Great Awakening**, which swept across the South just before the American Revolution (see Chapter 5).

Mum Bett, also known as Elizabeth Freeman, was born into slavery in a Massachusetts household about 1742. As a young woman she was subjected to the violent abuse of her mistress, who struck her with a hot shovel, leaving an indelible scar. Fleeing her owner, Mum Bett enlisted the aid of antislavery lawyer Thomas Sedgwick, who helped win her freedom in 1772. This miniature was painted by Sedgwick's daughter Susan in 1811.

2–9
James Oglethorpe, *The Colonial Records of the State of Georgia* (1739)

QUICK REVIEW

Slave Society

- Traces of African culture remained in slave society.
- Labor consumed most of slave's time.
- Kinship played a key role in solidifying African American communities.

Slave codes A series of laws passed mainly in the Southern colonies in the late seventeenth and early eighteenth centuries to defend the status of slaves and codify the denial of basic civil rights to them.

Great Awakening Tremendous religious revival in colonial America striking first in the Middle Colonies and New England in the 1740s and then spreading to the southern colonies.

One crucial area of religious practice concerned the rituals of death and burial. African Americans generally believed that the spirits of their dead would return to Africa. The burial ceremony was often held at night to keep it secret from masters, who objected to the continuation of African traditions. The deceased was laid out, and around the body men and women would move counterclockwise in a slow dance step while singing ancestral songs. The pace gradually increased, finally reaching a frenzied but joyful conclusion. As slaves from different backgrounds joined together in the circle, they were beginning the process of cultural unification.

Music and dance may have formed the foundation of African American culture, coming even before a common language. Many Africans were accomplished players of stringed instruments and drums, and their style featured improvisation and rhythmic complexity, elements that would become prominent in African American music. In America, slaves re-created African instruments such as the banjo, and mastered the art of the European violin and guitar.

One of the most important developments of the eighteenth century was the invention of an African American language. An English traveler during the 1770s complained he could not understand Virginia slaves, who spoke "a mixed dialect between the Guinea and English." But such a language made it possible for country-born and "saltwater" Africans to communicate. The two most important dialects were Gullah and Geechee, named after two of the African peoples most prominent in the Carolina and Georgia low country, the Golas and Gizzis of the African Windward Coast. These creole languages were a transitional phenomenon, gradually giving way to distinctive forms of black English, although in certain isolated areas, such as the sea islands of the Carolinas and Georgia, they persisted into the twentieth century.

The Africanization of the South

The African American community often looked to recently arrived Africans for religious leadership and medical magic. Throughout the South, many whites had as much faith in slave conjurers and herb doctors as the slaves themselves did, and slaves won fame for their healing powers. This was one of many ways in which white and black Southerners came to share a common culture. Acculturation was by no means a one-way street; English men and women in the South were also being Africanized.

Slaves worked in the kitchens of their masters and thus introduced an African style of cooking into colonial diets already transformed by the addition of Indian crops. African American culinary arts are responsible for such southern culinary specialties as barbecue, fried chicken, black-eyed peas, and collard greens. And the liberal African use of red pepper, sesame seeds, and other sharp flavors established the southern preference for highly spiced foods.

Mutual acculturation was also evident in many aspects of material culture. Southern basket weaving used Indian techniques and African designs. Woodcarving often featured African motifs. African architectural designs featuring high, peaked roofs (to drain off the heat) and broad, shady porches gradually became part of a distinctive southern style.

Even more important were less tangible aspects of culture. Slave mothers nursed white children as well as their own. As one English observer wrote, "each child has its [black] Momma, whose gestures and accent it will necessarily copy, for children, we all know, are imitative beings." In this way many Africanisms passed into the English language of the South. Some linguists have argued that the southern "drawl," evident among both black and white speakers, derived from the incorporation of African intonations of words and syllables.

A Musical Celebration in the Slave Quarters

This anonymous watercolor, discovered in South Carolina, dates from the last quarter of the eighteenth century. It offers a wonderfully detailed depiction of Africans or African Americans gathered together in the slave quarters celebrating with music. This is clearly a community celebration, involving several families. Seated on the right, two men play instruments that suggest continuity with the African heritage. One plucks on something that looks like a banjo, and indeed, the banjo can be traced back to West Africa. "The instrument proper to them," Thomas Jefferson wrote of his slaves, "is the *banjar,* which they brought hither from Africa." The other man plays a drum that resembles the gudugudu, a small wooden kettledrum from Nigeria played with two long thin rawhide sticks. The dancing man with the carved stick may indicate that this is a wedding ceremony that involves jumping the broom, an African custom for newly married couples. One planter's description of a slave dance seems to fit this scene: the men leading the women in "a slow shuffling gait, edging along by some unseen exertion of the feet, from one side to the other—sometimes courtesying down and remaining in that posture while the edging motion from one side to the other continued." The women, he wrote, "always carried a handkerchief held at arm's length, which was waved in a graceful motion to and fro as she moved." The painting is a tribute to the celebration of life amidst adversity. ■

WHY DO you think the plantation master is omitted from this painting?

Seeing History

Abby Aldrich Rockefeller Folk Art Museum, Colonial Williamsburg Foundation, VA.

Fugitive slaves flee through the swamps in Thomas Moran's *The Slave Hunt* (1862). Many slaves ran away from their masters, and colonial newspapers included notices urging readers to be on the lookout for them. Some fled in groups or collected together in isolated communities called "maroon" colonies, located in inaccessible swamps and woods.

Thomas Moran (American, 1837–1926), Slave Hunt, Dismal Swamp, Virginia, 1862. Gift of Laura A. Clubb, 1947.8.44. © 2007 The Philbrook Museum of Art, Inc., Tulsa, Oklahoma.

VIOLENCE AND RESISTANCE

Slavery was made possible by the threat and reality of violence. The only way to make slaves work, Virginia planter Robert "King" Carter instructed his overseer, was "to make them stand in fear." Even the most cultured plantation owners thought nothing about floggings of fifty or seventy-five lashes. Some masters were downright sadistic, stabbing, burning, maiming, mutilating, raping, and even castrating their slaves.

Yet African Americans demonstrated a resisting spirit. In their day-to-day existence they often refused to cooperate: they malingered, they mistreated animals and broke tools, they wantonly destroyed the master's property. Flight was another option. An analysis of hundreds of eighteenth-century advertisements for runaways concludes that 80 percent were young men in their twenties, suggesting that most runaways were unattached males.

Runaways sometimes collected together in isolated and hidden communities called "maroons," from the Spanish word *cimarron*, meaning "wild and untamed." Slaves who escaped from South Carolina or Georgia into Spanish Florida created maroon communities among the Creek Indians there. These mixed African and Indian peoples came to call themselves "Seminoles," a name deriving from their pronunciation of "cimarron."

The most direct form of resistance was revolt. The first notable slave uprising of the colonial era occurred in New York City in 1712. Taking an oath of secrecy, twenty-three Africans vowed revenge for what they called the "hard usage" of their masters. They armed themselves, killed nine colonists, and burned several buildings before being surrounded by the militia. Six of the conspirators committed suicide rather than surrender. Thirteen were hanged, another was starved to death in chains, another broken on the wheel, and three more burned at the stake.

A series of small rebellions and rumors of large ones in 1720s' Virginia culminated in the Chesapeake Rebellion of 1730, the largest slave uprising of the colonial period. Several hundred slaves assembled in Norfolk and Princess Anne counties where they chose commanders for their "insurrection." More than three hundred escaped en masse. Hunted down by Indians hired by the colony, their

QUICK REVIEW

Resistance to Slavery

- Refusal to cooperate or destruction of property.
- Running away and establishing fugitive communities.
- Revolting.

community was soon destroyed. Twenty-nine leaders were executed and the rest were returned to their masters.

In the Lower South, where slaves were a majority of the population, there were isolated but violent uprisings in 1704, 1720, and 1730. In 1738 a series of revolts broke out in South Carolina and Georgia. These prepared the way for the **Stono Rebellion** of 1739 (see Introduction), the most violent slave rebellion of the colonial period. In the aftermath of Stono several similar uprisings were quickly crushed by planters. Attributing these revolts to the influence of newly arrived Africans, colonial officials shut down the slave trade through Charles Town for the next ten years.

Wherever masters held slaves, fears of uprisings persisted. But compared with such slave colonies as Jamaica, Guiana, or Brazil, there were relatively few revolts in North America. The conditions favoring revolt (large African majorities, brutal exploitation with correspondingly low survival rates, little acculturation, and geographic isolation) prevailed only in some areas of the Lower South. Indeed, the very success of African Americans in British North America at establishing families, communities, and a culture of their own inevitably made them less likely to take the risks that rebellions required.

SLAVERY AND THE ECONOMICS OF EMPIRE

The British slave colonies—the sugar plantations of the West Indies, the tobacco plantations of the Chesapeake, and the rice and indigo plantations of the Lower South—accounted for 95 percent of exports from the Americas to Great Britain from 1714 to the eve of the American Revolution. Moreover, there was the prime economic importance of the slave trade itself, which one eighteenth-century economist described as the "foundation" of the British economy, "the mainspring of the machine which sets every wheel in motion." The labor of African slaves was largely responsible for the economic success of the British Empire in the Americas. New World slavery contributed enormously to the growth and development of the Old World economy. During the eighteenth century slavery was the most dynamic force in the Atlantic economy, responsible for the capital formation that made possible the beginnings of the industrial economy.

SLAVERY: FOUNDATION OF THE BRITISH ECONOMY

Slavery contributed to the economic development of Great Britain in three principal ways. First, it generated enormous profits. Profits derived from the triangular trade in slaves, plantation products, and manufactured goods (see Map 4.3) furnished from 21 to 35 percent of Great Britain's fixed capital formation in the eighteenth century. This capital funded the first modern banks and insurance companies and, through loans and investments, found its way into a wide range of economic activities. Merchant capitalists were prominent investors in the expansion of the merchant marine, the improvement of harbors, and the construction of canals.

Second, slave colonies in the Caribbean supplied 69 percent of the raw cotton for British textile mills, the earliest sector of industrial development. The insatiable demand for cotton would eventually lead to the development of the cotton gin and the rise of cotton plantations in the United States (see Chapter 11).

Third, slavery provided an enormous stimulus to the growth of manufacturing by creating a huge colonial market for exports. From 1700 to 1740, the growth in American and African demand for manufactured goods accounted for nearly 70 percent of the expansion of British exports.

The multiplier effects of these activities are best seen in the growth of English ports such as Liverpool and Bristol. There the African and American trades provided

Stono Rebellion   One of the largest and most violent slave uprisings during the Colonial Period that occurred in Stono, South Carolina.

HOW DID slavery fuel the economic development of Europe in the seventeenth and eighteenth centuries?

myhistorylab
Review Summary

QUICK REVIEW

British Trade Policy

- All trade in empire to be conducted in English or colonial ships.
- Channeling of colonial trade through England or another English colony.
- Subsidization of English goods offered for sale in the colonies.
- Colonists prohibited from large-scale manufacture of certain products.

MAP EXPLORATION
To explore an interactive version of this map, go to **http://www.prenhall.com/faraghertlc/map4.3**

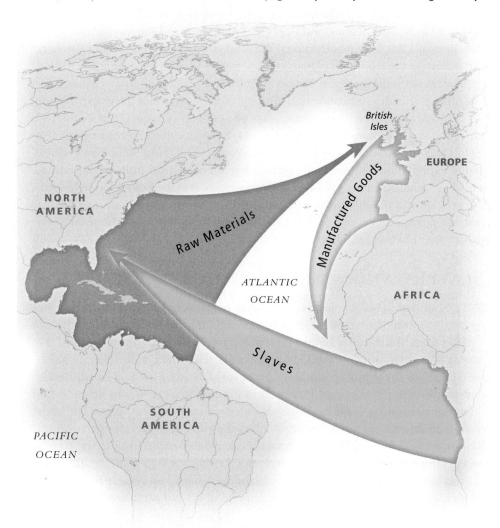

MAP 4.3

Triangular Trade Across the Atlantic   The pattern of commerce among Europe, Africa, and the Americas became known as the "triangular trade." Sailors called the voyage of slave ships from Africa to America the "Middle Passage" because it formed the crucial middle section of this trading triangle.

HOW WERE Europe, Africa, and America linked together by commerce?

employment for ships' crews, dockmen, construction workers, traders, shopkeepers, lawyers, clerks, factory workers, and officials of all ranks down to the humblest employees of the custom house. It was said of Bristol that "there is not a brick in the city but what is cemented with the blood of a slave." In the countryside surrounding Liverpool and elsewhere, capital acquired through slavery was invested in the new industrial methods of producing cotton textiles, the beginning of the Industrial Revolution.

THE POLITICS OF MERCANTILISM

Imperial officials argued that colonies existed solely for the benefit of the mother country. What they principally had in mind was the great wealth produced by slavery. To ensure that this wealth benefited their own nation-state, imperialists cre-

The New England artist John Greenwood painted this amusing view of New England sea captains in Surinam in 1757. By the early eighteenth century, New England merchant traders like these had become important participants in the traffic in slaves and sugar to and from the West Indies. Northern ports thus became important pivots in the expanding commercial network linking slave plantations with Atlantic markets.

John Greenwood, "Sea Captains Carousing in Surinam," 1758. Oil on bed ticking, 95.9 × 191.1 cm. Saint Louis Art Museum, Museum Purchase.

ated a system of regulations that became known as "**mercantilism**." The essence of mercantilist policy was the political control of the economy by the state. The British monarchy and Parliament established a uniform national monetary system, regulated wages, subsidized agriculture and manufacturing, and protected themselves from foreign competition by erecting tariff barriers. Britain also sought to organize and control colonial trade to the maximum advantage of its own shippers, merchants, manufacturers, and bureaucrats.

The mercantilists viewed the economy as a "zero-sum game," in which total economic gains were equal to total losses. The essence of the competition between states, the mercantilists argued, was the struggle to acquire and hoard the fixed amount of wealth that existed in the world. The nation that accumulated the largest treasure of gold and silver would be the most powerful.

BRITISH COLONIAL REGULATION

The Spanish monarchy created the Casa de Contratación, the first state trading monopoly, to manage the commerce of its empire in the sixteenth century. It was widely emulated by other powers. The Dutch East Indies Company, the French Company of the Indies, the English East India Company, the Hudson's Bay Company, and the Royal African Company were all state-sponsored trading monopolies.

English manufacturers complained that the nation's trading monopolies too frequently carried foreign (particularly Dutch) products to colonial markets, ignoring English domestic industry. Parliament reacted by passing a series of Navigation Acts between 1651 and 1696, creating the legal and institutional structure of Britain's eighteenth-century colonial system. The acts defined the colonies as both suppliers of raw materials and as markets for English manufactured goods. Merchants from

Mercantilism Economic system whereby the government intervenes in the economy for the purpose of increasing national wealth.

other nations were forbidden from doing business in the English colonies, and colonial commodities were required to be transported in English vessels.

The regulations specified a list of "enumerated commodities" that could be shipped to England only. Those included the products of the southern slave colonies (sugar, molasses, rum, tobacco, rice, and indigo), those of the northern Indian trade (furs, pelts, and skins), and those essential for supplying the shipping industry (pine masts, tar, pitch, resin, and turpentine). The bulk of these products was not destined for English consumption but was exported elsewhere at great profit.

England also placed limitations on colonial enterprises that might compete with those at home. A series of enactments—including the Wool Act of 1699, the Hat Act of 1732, and the Iron Act of 1750—forbade the manufacture of those products in the colonies. Moreover, colonial assemblies were forbidden to impose tariffs on English imports as a way to protect colonial industries. Banking was disallowed, local coinage prohibited, and the export of coin from England forbidden.

Robert Walpole, prime minister of the king's government from 1721 to 1742, argued that it made little sense to tamper with such a prosperous system. Walpole pursued a policy later characterized as "salutory neglect." Any colonial rules and regulations deemed contrary to good business practice were simply ignored and not enforced. Between 1700 and 1760 the quantity of goods exported from the colonies to the mother country rose 165 percent, while imports from Britain to North America increased by more than 400 percent. In part because of the lax enforcement, but mostly because the system operated to the profit of colonial merchants, colonists complained very little about the operation of the mercantilist system before the 1760s. It seemed that everyone was getting rich off the labor of slaves.

WARS FOR EMPIRE

During the 1720s and 1730s, Prime Minister Walpole steered Great Britain away from war with other mercantilist powers. Earlier in the century, a war pitting Great Britain against Spain and France (known as the War of the Spanish Succession in Europe, **Queen Anne's War** in America) had ended in a significant British victory and in the Peace of Utrecht in 1713 Britain gained a good deal. France was forced to cede Acadia, Newfoundland, and Hudson Bay to Great Britain in exchange for guarantees of security for the French-speaking residents of those provinces. Spain was forced to open its American ports to British traders, who were also granted the exclusive right to supply slaves to the Spanish colonies.

For more than fifteen years Walpole prevailed over militant factions in the House of Commons that demanded complete elimination of Spanish competition in the Americas. But in 1739, at their urging, a one-eared sea captain by the name of Robert Jenkins testified about the indignities suffered by British merchant sailors at the hands of Spanish authorities in Caribbean ports. In a dramatic flourish, Jenkins produced a dried and withered ear, which he claimed the Spanish had cut from his head. The public outrage that followed forced Walpole to agree to a war of Caribbean conquest known as the War of Jenkins's Ear. "They now ring the bells," Walpole declared, "but they will soon wring their hands."

Walpole was right. The British underestimated Spanish strength and the troops were ravaged by yellow fever and other diseases. The only success of the war for the British came when the Georgia militia blocked a Spanish invasion from Florida in 1742. The war ended with no territorial gains on either side.

The war with Spain merged into a war with France that began in 1744. Known as **King George's War** in America (the War of the Austrian Succession in Europe), it began with a French invasion of their former colony of Acadia, which the British had renamed Nova Scotia. Indian and Canadian raids again devastated the border

Queen Anne's War American phase (1702–1713) of Europe's War of the Spanish Succession.

King George's War The third Anglo-French war in North America (1744–1748), part of the European conflict known as the War of the Austrian Succession.

OVERVIEW | The Colonial Wars

1689–97	King William's War	France and England battle on the northern frontiers of New England and New York.
1702–13	Queen Anne's War	England fights France and Spain in the Caribbean and on the northern frontier of New France. Part of the European conflict known as the War of the Spanish Succession.
1739–43	War of Jenkins's Ear	Great Britain versus Spain in the Caribbean and Georgia. Part of the European conflict known as the War of the Austrian Succession.
1744–48	King George's War	Great Britain and France fight in Acadia and Nova Scotia; the second American round of the War of the Austrian Succession.
1754–63	French and Indian War	Last of the great colonial wars pitting Great Britain against France and Spain. Known in Europe as the Seven Years' War.

towns of New England and New York, and hundreds of British subjects were killed or captured. New England forces attacked and conquered the great French fortress at Louisbourg. But Great Britain fared less well in the European fighting, and the war ended in stalemate with the return of all territory.

THE COLONIAL ECONOMY

Despite the resumption of warfare, the colonial economy continued to operate to the great benefit of planters, merchants, and white colonists in general. Southern slave owners made healthy profits on the sale of their commodities. They enjoyed a protected market in which competing goods from outside the empire were heavily taxed. Planters found themselves with steadily increasing purchasing power. Pennsylvania, New York, and New England, and increasingly the Chesapeake as well, produced grain, flour, meat, and dairy products. None of these was included in the list of **enumerated goods** and could be sold freely abroad. Most of this trade was carried in New England ships.

The greatest benefits for the port cities of the North came from their commercial relationship to the slave colonies (see Figure 4.3). In addition to entering the slave trade itself, New England merchants began to make inroads into the export trade of the West Indian colonies. It was in the Caribbean that northern merchants most blatantly ignored mercantilist laws. In violation of Spanish, French, and Dutch regulations prohibiting foreign trade, New Englanders traded foodstuffs for sugar in foreign colonies. By 1750, more than sixty distilleries in Massachusetts were exporting more than 2 million gallons of rum, most of it produced from molasses obtained illegally. Because the restrictive rules and regulations enacted by Britain for its colonies were not enforced, the merchants and manufacturers of the port cities of the North prospered.

By the mid-eighteenth century, the Chesapeake and Lower South regions were major exporters of tobacco, rice, and indigo to Europe, and the middle colonies were major exporters of grain. The carrying trade in the products of slave labor made it possible for the northern and middle colonies to earn the income necessary to purchase British imports despite the lack

myhistorylab

Overview: *The Colonial Wars*

Enumerated goods   Items produced in the colonies and enumerated in acts of Parliament that could be legally shipped from the colony of origin only to specified locations.

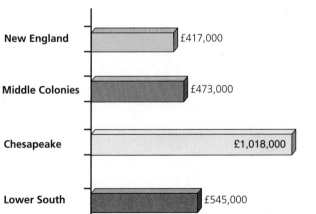

New England	£417,000
Middle Colonies	£473,000
Chesapeake	£1,018,000
Lower South	£545,000

Figure 4.3 Value of Colonial Exports by Region, Annual Average, 1768–72
With tobacco, rice, grain, and indigo, the Chesapeake and Lower South accounted for nearly two-thirds of colonial exports in the late eighteenth century.

James F. Shepherd and Gary M. Walton, *Shipping, Maritime Trade and the Economic Development of Colonial America* (Cambridge: Cambridge University Press, 1972), 211–27.

of valuable products from their own regions. Gradually, the commercial economies of the Northeast and the South were becoming integrated. Like London, Liverpool, and Bristol—though on a smaller scale—the port cities of the North became pivots in the expanding trade network linking slave plantations with Atlantic markets. This trade provided northern merchants with the capital that financed commercial growth and development in their cities and the surrounding countryside. Slavery thus contributed to the growth of a score of northern port cities, forming an indirect but essential part of their economies.

SLAVERY, PROSPERITY, AND FREEDOM

The prosperity of the eighteenth-century plantation economy thus improved the living conditions for the residents of northern cities as well as for a large segment of the white population of the South, providing them with the opportunity for a kind of freedom unknown in the previous century. The price of this prosperity and freedom, however, was the enslavement and exploitation of millions of Africans and African Americans. Freedom for white men based on the enslavement of black people is one of the most glaring contradictions in American history.

THE SOCIAL STRUCTURE OF THE SLAVE COLONIES

Slavery produced a highly stratified class society. At the summit of power stood an elite of wealthy planters who held more than half the cultivated land and over 60 percent of the wealth. Although there was no formal colonial aristocracy—no royal recognition of social rank—the landed elite of the slave colonies sought to present itself as one.

The typical wealthy Virginia planter of the eighteenth century lived in a Tidewater county; owned several thousand acres of prime farmland and more than a hundred slaves; resided in a luxurious plantation mansion, built perhaps in the fashionable Georgian style; and had an estate valued at more than £10,000. Elected to the House of Burgesses and forming the group from which the magistrates and counselors of the colony were chosen, these "first families of Virginia" were a self-perpetuating governing class.

A similar elite ruled the Lower South, although wealthy landowners spent little time on their plantations. They lived instead in fashionable Charles Town, where they made up a close-knit group who controlled the colonial government.

A considerable distance separated this elite from typical southern landowners. About half the adult white males were small planters and farmers. But while the gap between rich and middling colonists grew larger during the eighteenth century, the prosperity of the plantation economy created generally favorable conditions for the landowning class as a whole. Slave ownership, for example, became widespread among this group during the eighteenth century. In Virginia at midcentury, 45 percent of heads of household held one to four slaves and even poorer farmers kept one or two.

Despite the prosperity that accompanied slavery, however, a substantial number of white colonists owned no land or slaves at all. Some rented land or worked as tenant farmers, some hired out as overseers or farm workers, and still others were indentured servants. Throughout the plantation region, landless men constituted about 40 percent of the population. A New England visitor found a "much greater disparity between the rich and poor in Virginia" than at home.

WHITE SKIN PRIVILEGE

But all the white colonists of eighteenth-century North America shared the privileged status of their color. In the early seventeenth century, there had been more diversity in views about race. As slavery became increasingly important, however, Vir-

ginia officials took considerable care to create legal distinctions between the status of colonists and that of Africans. Beginning in 1670, free Africans were prohibited from owning Christian servants. Ten years later, another law declared that any African, free or slave, who struck a Christian would receive thirty lashes on his bare back. One of the most important measures was designed to suppress intimate interracial contacts between white servants and enslaved Africans. A 1691 act "for prevention of that abominable mixture and spurious issue which hereafter may encrease in this dominion" established severe penalties for interracial sexual relationships. Such penalties were rarely applied to masters who had sexual relations with their slave women. Because by law the children of slave mothers were born into bondage, many plantations included light-skinned slaves who were the masters' kin.

RUN away from the subscriber in *Albemarle*, a Mulatto slave called *Sandy*, about 35 years of age, his stature is rather low, inclining to corpulence, and his complexion light; he is a shoemaker by trade, in which he uses his left hand principally, can do coarse carpenters work, and is something of a horse jockey; he is greatly addicted to drink, and when drunk is insolent and disorderly, in his conversation he swears much, and in his behaviour is artful and knavish. He took with him a white horse, much scarred with traces, of which it is expected he will endeavour to dispose; he also carried his shoemakers tools, and will probably endeavour to get employment that way. Whoever conveys the said slave to me, in *Albemarle*, shall have 40 s. reward, if taken up within the county, 4 l. if elsewhere within the colony, and 10 l. if in any other colony, from

THOMAS JEFFERSON.

Thomas Jefferson placed this advertisement in the *Virginia Gazette* on September 14, 1769. Americans need to seriously consider the historical relationship between the prosperity and freedom of white people and the oppression and exploitation of Africans and African Americans.

Relationships between free whites and enslaved blacks produced a large mixed-ancestry group known as mulattoes. The majority of them were slaves; a minority, the children of European women and African men, were free. According to a Maryland census of 1755, more than 60 percent of the mulattoes of that colony were slaves. But mulattoes also made up three-quarters of the small free African American population. This group, numbering about four thousand in the 1770s, was denied the right to vote, to hold office, or to testify in court—all on the basis of racial background. Denied the status of citizenship enjoyed by even the poorest white men, free blacks were an outcast group who raised the status of white colonials by contrast. Racial distinctions were a constant reminder of the freedom of white colonists and the debasement of all blacks, slave or free.

Racism set up a wall of contempt between colonists and African Americans.

2–11
William H. Browne, *Maryland Addresses the Status of Slaves* (1664)

Conclusion

During the eighteenth century, nearly half a million Africans were kidnapped from their homes, marched to the African coast, and packed into ships for up to three months before arriving in British North America. They provided the labor that made colonialism profitable. Southern planters, northern merchants, and especially British traders and capitalists benefited greatly from the commerce in slave-produced crops, and that prosperity filtered down to affect many of the colonists of British North America. Slavery was fundamental to the operation of the British empire in North America. Mercantilism was a system designed to channel colonial wealth produced by slaves to the nation-state, but as long as profits were high, the British tended to wink at colonists' violations of mercantilist regulations.

African Americans helped to build the greatest accumulation of capital Europe had ever seen, receiving nothing in return but blood, sweat, and tears. It is little wonder that slaves resisted, by malingering, by fleeing, by rising up in rebellion, as did the slaves of the Stono River. Yet that rebellion itself was a sign that despite enormous hardship and suffering, African Americans were forming new communities, rebuilding families, restructuring language, and reforming

CHRONOLOGY

1441	African slaves first brought to Portugal
1619	First Africans brought to Virginia
1655	English seize Jamaica
1662	Virginia law makes slavery hereditary
1672	Royal African Company organized
1691	Virginia prohibits interracial sexual contact
1698	Britain opens the slave trade to all its merchants
1699	Spanish declare Florida a refuge for escaped slaves
1702	South Carolinians burn St. Augustine
1705	Virginia Slave Code established
1706	French and Spanish navies bombard Charles Town
1710	English capture Port Royal in Acadia

1712	Slave uprising in New York City
1713	Peace of Utrecht
1721–48	Robert Walpole leads British cabinet
1729	Natchez Rebellion in French Louisiana
1739	Stono Rebellion in South Carolina
1739–43	War of Jenkins's Ear
1741	Africans executed in New York for conspiracy
1744–48	King George's War
1752	Georgia officially opened to slavery
1770s	Peak period of the English colonies' slave trade
1808	Importation of slaves into the United States ends

culture. African American culture added important components of African knowledge and experience to colonial agriculture, art, music, and cuisine. The African Americans of the English colonies lived better lives than the slaves worked to death on Caribbean sugar plantations but lives of misery compared with the men they were forced to serve.

REVIEW QUESTIONS

1. Trace the development of the system of slavery and discuss the way it became entrenched in the Americas.

2. Describe the effects of the slave trade both on enslaved Africans and on the economic and political life of Africa.

3. Describe the process of acculturation involved in becoming an African American. In what ways did slaves "Africanize" the South?

4. Explain the connection between the institution of slavery and the building of a commercial empire.

5. In what ways did colonial policy encourage the growth of racism?

KEY TERMS

Flashcard Review

Enumerated goods (p. 95)
Great Awakening (p. 87)
King George's War (p. 94)
Mercantilism (p. 93)
Middle Passage (p. 79)

Pueblo Revolt (p. 85)
Queen Anne's War (p. 94)
Seven Years' War (p. 78)
Slave codes (p. 87)
Stono Rebellion (p. 91)

RECOMMENDED READING

Ira Berlin, *Many Thousands Gone: The First Two Centuries of Slavery in North America* (1998). A history of colonial slavery with attention to the differences between the regions of the Chesapeake, the Lower South, Louisiana, and the North. Emphasizes the distinction between slave societies and societies with slaves.

Andrew Burstein, *Jefferson's Secrets: Death and Desire at Monticello* (2005). An examination of the last decade of Jefferson's life, as he looks back on political struggles, slavery, and personal relationships.

Michael Craton, *Sinews of Empire: A Short History of British Slavery* (1974). An introduction to the British mercantilist system that emphasizes the importance of slavery. Includes a comparison of the mainland colonies with the Caribbean.

Winthrop D. Jordan, *White over Black: American Attitudes Toward the Negro, 1550–1812* (1968). Remains the best and most comprehensive history of racial attitudes. A searching examination of British and American literature, folklore, and history.

Herbert S. Klein, *The Atlantic Slave Trade* (1999). A new and important synthesis of the most recent studies of the slave trade, covering the social and cultural effects of the trade, especially for Africans.

Philip D. Morgan, *Slave Counterpoint: Black Culture in the Eighteenth-Century Chesapeake and Lowcountry* (1998). A comprehensive and detailed examination of cultural forms and ways of life in the two regions that leaves hardly a stone unturned.

Anthony S. Parent Jr., *Foul Means: The Formation of a Slave Society in Virginia, 1660–1740* (2003). A vivid and disturbing portrayal of colonial Virginia's patriarchal and violent character. An analysis of the apparatus of oppression from the planters' seizure of land to the efforts to keep poor whites and slaves apart.

Walter Rodney, *How Europe Underdeveloped Africa* (1974). This highly influential book traces the relationship between Europe and Africa from the fifteenth to the twentieth centuries, and demonstrates how Europe's industrialization became Africa's impoverishment.

Mechal Sobel, *The World They Made Together: Black and White Values in Eighteenth-Century Virginia* (1987). Demonstrates the ways in which both Africans and Europeans shaped the formation of American values, perceptions, and identities.

Lucia Stanton, *Some Free Day: The African-American Families of Monticello* (2001). The stories of six enslaved families who lived and worked for Jefferson at Monticello.

Ian K. Steele, *Warpaths: Invasions of North America* (1994). A new synthesis of the colonial wars from the sixteenth to the eighteenth centuries that places Indians as well as empires at the center of the action.

Henry Wiencek, *Imperfect God: George Washington, His Slaves, and the Creation of America* (2003). The story of Washington as planter and slave master, a man tormented by the contradictions.

For study resources for this chapter, go to **www.myhistorylab.com** and choose *Out of Many, Teaching and Learning Classroom Edition.* You will find a wealth of study and review material for this chapter, including pretests and posttests, customized study plan, key-term review flash cards, interactive map and document activities, and documents for analysis.

*Mr. Lawrence, Be pleased to send me
a geenteel sute of Cloaths made of superfine
broad Cloth handsomely chosen...*
—George Washington, April, 26, 1763

George Whitefield preaches an outdoor sermon to a crowd
of worshippers.

5

THE CULTURES OF COLONIAL NORTH AMERICA
1700–1780

HOW DID Indian America adapt to the new conditions created by colonization?

HOW DID the structure of colonial society differ from European social structure?

TO WHAT extent did North America participate in the Enlightenment?

AMERICAN COMMUNITIES
The Revival of Religion and Community in Northampton

JONATHAN EDWARDS, MINISTER OF THE PURITAN CHURCH IN Northampton, a rural town on the Connecticut River in western Massachusetts, rose before his congregation and began to preach. His words were frightening: "God will crush you under his feet without mercy, He will crush out your blood and make it fly, and it shall be sprinkled on His garments." Such torments would continue for "millions of millions of ages," and there could be no hope of relief from hell's fires. The people needed to "have their hearts touched," Edwards believed, and he was gratified by their response to his sermon.

"Before the sermon was done," one Northampton parishioner later recalled, "there was a great moaning and crying through the whole house—What shall I do to be saved?—I am going to Hell!—Oh what shall I do for Christ?" Religious fervor swept through the community, and church membership increased. A few years later an even greater revival known as the Great Awakening swept through all the colonies and plunged Northampton into turmoil once again. Important underlying issues prepared the ground for these religious revivals. They reflected the tensions that had arisen in the maturing communities of the colonies in which frontier opportunity was giving way to class inequity.

Founded in 1654 on the site of an Algonquin village, Northampton had grown from the original fifty households to more than 200 by the time of the 1734 revival. The last of the community's land had been parceled out to its residents. With the French and their Indian allies barring movement northward, and the colony of New York to the west, there was little opportunity for young men. Few could afford to buy land at the high market prices, so they had to rely on gifts or bequests from their fathers. Meanwhile, a small elite of well-to-do families, known as the "River Gods," controlled a disproportionately large share of local real estate. From their ranks came the majority of the officials of local and county government, as well as the ministers and elders of the Puritan congregations.

By the time Edwards became pastor in 1729, the authority and influence of the church had declined greatly from the heyday of Puritan power in the seventeenth century. In those early days, church and community had been one, but as Northampton's leaders devoted their energies to the pursuit of wealth, the fires of religious enthusiasm dimmed. The Northampton community, Edwards believed, had been divided into "two parties," the rich and the envious.

Many of the town's young people faced a bleak future. The farm household was the most important economic unit, and the tight supply of real estate meant that most couples were forced to postpone marriage until they were in their late twenties. Restless young people of both sexes began to meet together at nightly "frolics," and pastor Edwards issued a warning about the "growth of uncleanness that has been in the land."

This group became Edwards's special constituency. It was the same everywhere throughout the British colonies. Young people in their early twenties played the most important role in the movement to restore religious enthusiasm. Reversing a long-standing tendency for women to be more active in the church, young men predominated among the reborn. Edwards and other revival preachers called for a return to the Calvinist traditions of the Puritan faith, criticizing what they saw as the growing materialism, joining the rising generation in questioning the order of the world into which they had been born.

The revival of religion that shook communities throughout the British colonies in the mid-eighteenth century was one of the first unifying events in American history. Thousands of people experienced conversion, new sects and churches sprang up, and old ones split into opposing factions. In the town of South Hadley, near Northampton, the congregation voted to dismiss their minister, who lacked the emotional fire they desired in a preacher. When he refused to vacate his pulpit they pulled him down, roughed him up, and threw him out the church door. According to one minister: "Multitudes were seriously, soberly, and solemnly out of their wits."

The disaffection of young people with the social and economic conditions of the mid-eighteenth century created the conditions for the Great Awakening, but the revival remained a religious event. The social order in Northampton was challenged, but it remained intact. The "River Gods" had always been uncomfortable with the message Edwards preached, and when the fervor died down, as it inevitably did, they succeeded in voting him out. The turmoil in Northampton subsided, yet the tensions remained.

Northampton, MA

NORTH AMERICAN REGIONS

American history too often is written as if only the British colonists really mattered. It is an error residents of the British colonies could not afford to make. Most critically, there was Indian America. In the mid-eighteenth century Indian peoples retained their majority in North America (see Table 5.1). From the fringes of colonial societies to the native heart of the continent, thousands of native communities, despite being deeply affected by the spread of colonial cultures, remained firmly in control of their homelands.

Neither could British colonists afford to ignore their colonial competitors. North and west of the English-speaking enclaves along the Atlantic coast, French-speaking communities were clustered along the St. Lawrence and scattered down the Mississippi to the Gulf of Mexico. South and west, isolated Spanish-speaking communities of the northern Spanish borderlands stretched from Florida to Texas and on to California (see Map 5.1).

INDIAN AMERICA

After two centuries of European colonization, Indian peoples had adapted and changed. They incorporated firearms and metal tools and learned to build their homes of logs. They participated enthusiastically in the fur trade. But in the process they became dependent on European commerce.

MAP 5.1

Regions in Eighteenth-Century North America   By the middle of the eighteenth century, European colonists had established a number of distinctive colonial regions in North America. The northern periphery of New Spain, stretched from Baja California to eastern Texas, then jumped to the settlements on the northern end of the Florida peninsula. New France was like a great crescent, extending from the plantation communities along the Mississippi near New Orleans to the French colonial communities along the St. Lawrence.

WHAT STEPS did Spain take to reinforce and expand its holdings in North America in the eighteenth century?

HOW DID Indian America adapt to the new conditions created by colonization?

myhistorylab
Review Summary

IMAGE KEY
for pages 100–101

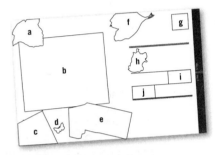

a. A brown patterned neckcloth.
b. George Whitefield preaches an outdoor sermon to a crowd of worshippers.
c. A small pile of muscovado sugar.
d. A mounted moth.
e. A half-loom width of oyster silk damask of the 18th century.
f. Dried tobacco leaves.
g. A merchant ship.
h. A Jesuit missionary baptizing an Indian in New France.
i. A hand-colored woodcut of a settler's log cabin in the Blue Ridge Mountains (Appalachians).
j. George Whitefield extends his hands over kneeling worshippers while wearing black ministerial robes in a 1770 painting by John Wallaston.

TABLE 5.1

Population of North America in 1750

Region	Population
New France	70,000
New England	400,000
New York	100,000
Pennsylvania	230,000
Chesapeake	390,000
Lower South	100,000
Backcountry	100,000
Northern New Spain	20,000
Indian America	1,500,000
TOTAL	2,910,000

Exploring America: *America and the Horse*

A portrait of the Delaware chief Tishcohan by Gustavus Hesselius, painted in 1732. In his purse of chipmunk hide is a clay pipe, a common item of the Indian trade. Tishcohan was one of the Delaware leaders forced by Pennsylvania authorities into signing a fraudulent land deal that reversed that colony's history of fair dealing with Indians over land. He moved west to the Ohio River as settlers poured into his former homeland.

Gustavus Hesselius, "Tishcohan," Native American Portrait, 1735. Courtesy of the Historical Society of Pennsylvania Collection, Atwater Kent Museum of Philadelphia.

Yet Indian peoples continued to assert a proud independence and demonstrated considerable skill in playing off colonial powers one against the other. In 1701 the Iroquois, allies of the British, signed a treaty of neutrality with the French. Exploiting the vulnerabilities of these two powers, the Iroquois Confederacy became a major power broker during the first half of the eighteenth century. In the Lower South native peoples found similar room to maneuver between the competing interests of Britain, France, and Spain.

But native leaders confronted enormous difficulties. In the eastern portion of the continent the preeminent concern was the tremendous growth of the population in the British colonies and especially the movement of settlers westward. In the 1730s and 1740s Pennsylvania abandoned its tradition of fair dealing and perpetrated a series of fraudulent seizures of western lands from the Delawares. It was a disturbing sign of things to come.

Meanwhile, Indian communities continued to suffer from long-term population decline as the result of epidemic Old World diseases. Historical demographers estimate that from a high of 7 to 10 million north of Mexico in 1500, the native population had fallen to around a million by 1800. Population loss did not affect all Indian tribes equally, however. Native peoples with a century or more of colonial contact and interaction had lost 50 percent or more of their numbers, but most Indian societies in the interior had yet to be struck by the epidemics.

Other changes offered opportunity. By the early eighteenth century, Indians on the southern fringe of the Great Plains had acquired horses from Spanish colonists in New Mexico (see Map 5.2). Horses enabled Indian hunters to exploit the buffalo herds much more efficiently. Great numbers of Indian peoples moved onto the plains during the eighteenth century, pulled by this new way of life and pushed by colonial invasions and disruptions radiating southwest from Canada and north from the Spanish borderlands. The invention of nomadic Plains Indian culture was another of the dramatic cultural innovations of the eighteenth century.

THE SPANISH BORDERLANDS

In the mid-eighteenth century the region now known as the Sunbelt formed the periphery of the largest and most prosperous European colony on the North American continent, the viceroyalty of New Spain, with a population of approximately 1 million Spanish-speaking inhabitants and 2 million Indians. Mexico City, the administrative capital of New Spain, was the most sophisticated city in the Western Hemisphere. New Spain's northern provinces of Florida, Texas, New Mexico, and California, however, were far removed from this sophistication. Officials who oversaw these colonies thought of them as buffer zones, protecting New Spain from the expanding empires of Spain's rivals. Compared to the dynamic changes going on in the English colonies, society in the Spanish borderland was relatively static.

In Florida, the oldest of the European colonies in North America, fierce fighting with the British and their Indian allies had reduced the Spanish presence to little more than the forts of St. Augustine on the Atlantic and Pensacola on the Gulf of Mexico, each surrounded by small colonized territories populated with the families of Spanish troops. In their weakened condition, the Spanish had no choice but to establish cooperative relations with the Creek and Seminole Indians who dominated the region, as well as hundreds of African American runaways who fled to Florida.

Nearly 2,000 miles to the west, New Mexico was similarly isolated from the mainstream of New Spain. In 1750 New Mexico included some 20,000 Pueblo Indians (their numbers greatly reduced by disease) and perhaps 10,000 mestizo colonists. The prosperity of these colonists, who supported themselves with subsistence agriculture, was severely limited by a restrictive colonial economic policy that required them to exchange their wool, pottery, and buffalo hides for imported goods at unfavorable rates. But unlike the population of Florida, that of colonial New Mexico was gradually expanding, as settlers left the original colonial outposts along the upper Rio Grande to follow the valleys and streams leading north and east.

Concerned about the expansion of other colonial empires, the Spanish founded several new northern outposts in the eighteenth century. French activity in the Mississippi Valley prompted authorities to establish a number of military posts or presidios on the fringes of Louisiana and in 1716 to begin the construction of a string of Franciscan missions among the Indian peoples of Texas. By 1750 the settlement of San Antonio had become the center of a developing frontier province known as Tejas (Texas). New colonial outposts were also founded west of New Mexico in what is today southern Arizona. In the 1690s, Jesuit missionaries built missions among the desert Indians of the lower Colorado River and Gila River Valleys and introduced cattle herding.

In 1769, acting on rumors of Russian expansion in the north Pacific (for a discussion of Russian America, see Chapter 9), officials in Mexico City ordered Gaspar de Portolá, governor of what is today Baja California, to establish a Spanish presence along the Pacific coast to the north. With Portolá were Franciscan missionaries

MAP EXPLORATION
To explore an interactive version of this map, go to
http://www.prenhall.com/faraghertlc/map5.2

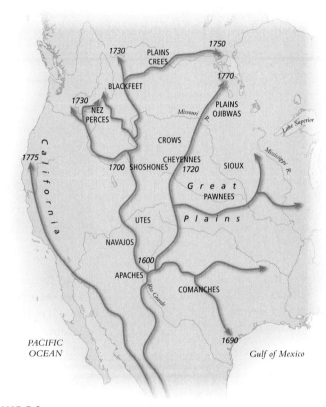

MAP 5.2

Growing Use of the Horse by Plains Indians   In the seventeenth and eighteenth centuries, Spanish settlers introduced horses into their New Mexican colony. The horse offered the Indian peoples of the Great Plains the opportunity to create a distinctive hunting and warrior culture.

HOW DID the spread of the horse transform Indian lifestyles?

A mounted Soldado de Cuera (Leather-Coated Soldier), a watercolor by Ramón de Murillo, c. 1803. Thick leather coats offered protection from Indian arrows for the cavalry posted to the northern frontiers of eighteenth-century New Spain.

led by Junípero Serra, president of the missions in Baja. At the harbor of San Diego their company, composed of some 200 men, founded the first mission and presidio in present-day California. Over the next fifty years the number of California settlements grew to include twenty-one missions and a half-dozen presidios and pueblos (towns).

The Spanish plan for California called for converting the natives to Catholicism, subjecting them to the rule of the crown, and putting them to work raising the subsistence necessary for a small civil and military establishment that would hold the province against colonial rivals. The first contacts between Franciscans and natives were not encouraging, but numerous native families were attracted by offerings of food and clothing, by new tools and crafts, and by fascination with the spiritual power of the newcomers. Gradually the Spanish built a flourishing local economy based on irrigated farming and livestock raising.

Indians were not forced to join the missions, but once they did so they were not permitted to leave. The Franciscan missionaries resorted to cruel and sometimes violent means of controlling their Indian subjects, including shackles, solitary confinement, and whipping posts. Resistance developed early. In 1775, the natives at San Diego rose up and killed several priests, and over the years several other missions experienced similar revolts. But Spanish soldiers suppressed the uprisings. Another form of protest was flight. Soldiers hunted the runaways down and brought many back. Aggressive tribes in the hills and deserts, however, often proved even more threatening than the Spanish, so many Indians remained at the missions despite the harsh discipline. Overwork, inadequate nutrition, overcrowding, poor sanitation, and epidemic disease contributed to death rates that exceeded birthrates. During the period of the mission system, the native population of coastal California fell by 74 percent.

Throughout the Spanish borderlands the Catholic Church played a dominant role in community life. The object of colonization, one colonial promoter wrote in 1584, was "enlarging the glorious gospel of Christ, and leading the infinite multitudes of these simple people that are in error into the right and per-

QUICK REVIEW

Spanish Colonies

- Mexico City was the capital of New Spain.
- Conflict with Indians and the British reduced the Spanish presence in Florida.
- New Mexico was isolated from the mainstream of New Spain.

The Church of San Xavier del Bac, constructed in the late eighteenth century, is located a few miles south of the city of Tucson, where Jesuit Father Eusebio Kino founded a mission among the Pima Indians in 1700. Known as the White Dove of the Desert, it is acclaimed as the most striking example of Spanish colonial architecture in the United States.

fect way of salvation." Although these were the words of the English imperialist Richard Hakluyt, they could as easily have come from a Jesuit missionary in New France or the Spanish padres Kino or Serra. There was no tradition of religious dissent.

THE FRENCH CRESCENT

In France, as in Spain, church and state were closely interwoven. During the seventeenth century the chief ministers to the French monarchy, Cardinal Richelieu and his successor Cardinal Mazarin, laid out a fundamentally Catholic imperial policy, and under their guidance colonists constructed a second Catholic empire in North America. In 1674 church and state collaborated in establishing the bishopric of Quebec, which founded local seminaries, oversaw the appointment and review of priests, and laid the foundation of the resolutely Catholic culture of New France. Jesuit missionaries, meanwhile, continued to carry Catholicism deep into the continent.

The French sent few colonists to New France, but by natural increase the population rose from less than 15,000 in 1700 to more than 70,000 by 1750. The French used their trade and alliance network to establish colonies, military posts, and settlements that extended in a great crescent from the mouth of the St. Lawrence River southwest through the Great Lakes, then down the Mississippi River to the Gulf of Mexico (see Map 5.3). The great port and fortress of Louisbourg on Ile Royale (Cape Breton Island) was built to guard the northern approach to New France. The southern approach was protected by French troops at the port of New Orleans in Louisiana. Between these two points, the French laid a thin colonial veneer. By the middle of the century, the French were ascending the Missouri and Arkansas Rivers, placing missionaries and traders in Indian communities on the fringe of the Great Plains.

At the heart of the French empire in North America were the communities of farmers or habitants that stretched along the banks of the St. Lawrence between the provincial capital of Quebec and the fur trade center of Montreal. There were

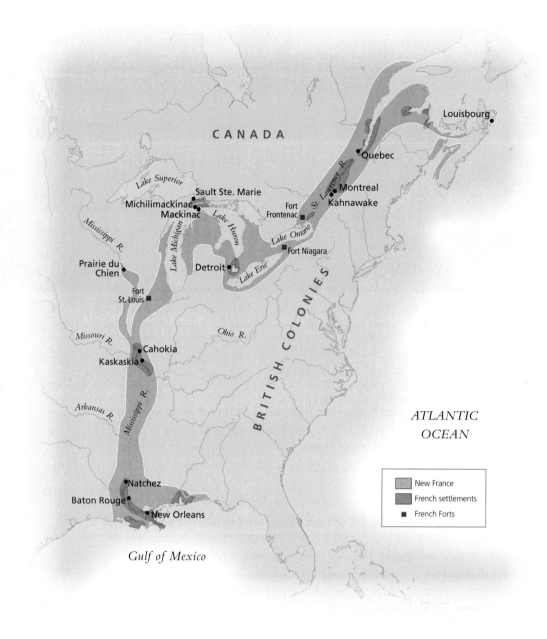

MAP 5.3

The French Crescent The French empire in North America was based on a series of alliances and trade relations with Indian nations linking a great crescent of colonies, settlements, and outposts that extended from the mouth of the St. Lawrence River to the Gulf of Mexico.

WHAT GEOGRAPHIC rationale might have been behind French decisions to convert native peoples to Catholic Christianity?

also farming communities in the Illinois country, supplying wheat to sugar plantations in Louisiana. By the 1750s, those plantations, extending along the Mississippi from Natchez and Baton Rouge to New Orleans, had become the most profitable French enterprise in North America.

Among the most distinctive French stamps on the North American landscape were the "long lots" stretching back from the rivers, providing each settler a share of good bottomland to farm and frontage on the waterways, the "interstate highway system" of the French Crescent. Long lots were laid out along the Mississippi River in Louisiana and Illinois and at the strategic passages of the Great Lakes. Detroit, the most important of those, was a stockaded town with a military garrison, a small administrative center, several stores, a Catholic church, and 100 households of *métis* (French for mestizo) families. Farmers worked the land along the Detroit River, not far from communities inhabited by several thousand Indians from the Ottawa, Potawatomi, and Huron tribes.

Communities of this sort, combining both European and native American elements, were in the tradition of the inclusive frontier. Detroit had much of the character of a mixed community. Family and kinship were cast in the Indian pattern, yet the people focused their activities on commerce and overwhelmingly identified themselves as Catholics.

NEW ENGLAND

Just as New Spain and New France had their official church, so too did the inhabitants of New England. Rather than the centralized authority of the Catholic hierarchy, however, communities in New England (except Rhode Island) were governed by Puritan congregations. Adult male church members constituted the freemen of the town, so there was very little distinction between religious and secular authority. At the town meeting the freemen chose their minister, voted on his salary, and elected local men to offices ranging from town clerk to animal warden.

The Puritan tradition was a curious mix of freedom and repression. Although local communities had considerable autonomy, they were tightly bound by the religious restrictions. The Puritans had not come to America to create a society where religion could be freely practiced but in order to establish their own version of the "right and perfect way." Puritan authorities banned and exiled Anglicans, Baptists, Quakers, and other dissidents. Between 1659 and 1661 four Quakers were executed for proselytizing.

Soon after the last of these executions King Charles II, newly placed on the throne, ordered a stop to religious persecution in Massachusetts. Several years later Roger Williams, whose Rhode Island colony had no established religion, made one of the first formal arguments for religious toleration. The new climate of opinion was best expressed by English political philosopher John Locke in "A Letter Concerning Tolerance," written in 1689. Churches were voluntary societies, Locke argued, and could gain genuine converts only through persuasion. The state, he asserted, had no legitimate concern with religious belief. That same year Parliament passed **The Act of Toleration**, granting religious freedom to Protestant dissenters (but not to Catholics). It was at first resisted by New England Puritans, but in 1700, under pressure from English authorities, Massachusetts and Connecticut reluctantly permitted other Protestant denominations to meet openly.

By then New Englanders were less concerned with religious conformity than with the problem of land. As population grew, groups of residents left established towns, "hiving off" to form new congregations and towns elsewhere. By the 1730s, Puritan communities had taken up most of the available land of Massachusetts, Connecticut, and Rhode Island, leaving only a few isolated reservations for small

The persistence of French colonial long lots in the pattern of modern landholding is clear in this enhanced satellite photograph of the Mississippi River near New Orleans. Long lots, the characteristic form of property holding in New France, were designed to offer as many settlers as possible a share of good bottomland as well as a frontage on the waterways, which served as the basic transportation network.

The Act of Toleration   Act passed in 1661 by King Charles II ordering a stop to religious persecution in Massachusetts.

This view of the Philadelphia waterfront, painted about 1720, conveys the impression of a city firmly anchored to maritime commerce. The long narrow canvas was probably intended for display over the mantel of a public room.

Peter Cooper, "The South East Prospect of the City of Philadelphia," ca. 1720. The Library Company of Philadelphia.

communities of Pequots, Narragansets, and Wampanoagas. New England had reached the limit of its land supply.

THE MIDDLE COLONIES

New York featured one of the most ethnically diverse populations on the continent. At midcentury, society along the lower Hudson River, including the counties in northern New Jersey, was a veritable mosaic of ethnic communities. African Americans, both slave and free, constituted more than 15 percent of the population of the lower Hudson. Puritan, Baptist, Quaker, and Catholic congregations worshiped without legal hindrance, and in New York City, several hundred Jewish families built North America's first synagogue in 1730.

Although New York City grew by leaps and bounds in the eighteenth century, the colony as a whole was less attractive to immigrants than neighboring Pennsylvania. The region along the Delaware River—encompassing not only Pennsylvania but New Jersey, Delaware, and the northern portion of Maryland—grew more dramatically than any other in North America during the eighteenth century. Immigration played the dominant role in achieving the astonishing annual growth rate of nearly 4 percent. With access to some of the best farmland in North America, farmers and merchants were soon exporting abundant produce through the prosperous port at Philadelphia.

The Quakers quickly became a minority, but unlike the Puritans they were generally comfortable with religious and ethnic pluralism. This was a perspective well suited to the ethnically and religiously diverse population of the colony. Most German immigrants were Lutherans or Calvinists, most North Britons were Presbyterians, and there were plenty of Anglicans and Baptists as well.

The institutions of government were another pillar of community organization. Colonial officials appointed justices of the peace who provided judicial authority for the countryside. Property-owning farmers chose their own local officials. Country communities were bound together by kinship bonds as well as economic relations between neighbors. These communities were more loosely bound than those of New England. Because land was sold in individual lots rather than in communal parcels, farmers tended to disperse themselves over the open countryside. Villages gradually developed at crossroads and ferries but with little forethought or planning.

THE BACKCOUNTRY

By 1750 Pennsylvania's exploding population had pushed beyond the first range of the Appalachian highlands (see Map 5.4). Settlers moved southwest, through western Maryland and down the valley of the Shenandoah River into western Virginia (see Seeing History).

A Plan of an American New Cleared Farm

Patrick Campbell, a Scottish gentleman traveler, included this plate in the account of his tour of the American backcountry, published in 1793. The illustration provides a composite view of the raw frontier farms he visited, entirely typical of the eighteenth century. Note the way the pioneers hacked out their farms from the forest, leaving stumps standing in the fields. See how they fenced their fields to keep out livestock, which were allowed to forage freely. The engraving illustrates four different types of fencing: plain log (marked 4), worm fence made of split poles (5), post-and-rail (6), and Virginia rail fence of crossed stakes (7). The use of wood from the abundant forest was an essential economic strategy. Campbell was notably free of the prejudice of many British visitors to the frontier, but he could not disguise his scorn of pioneer cabins, which he described as "miserable little hovels covered with bark." He included one of them in the engraving (14), one of the first illustrations of a log cabin to appear in print. Also notable here are the Indian canoes, one poled by a man, the other paddled by two women with what Campbell's note mistakenly labels a "Babose." Campbell made the entire trip with his own hunting dog, seen in the front of the canoe on the left. Note also the wonderful little "Indian dog" (15). ■

HOW DOES the presence of Indians in this image contradict the popular view of frontier life?

Patrick Campbell, *Travels in the Interior Inhabited Parts of North America* (1793).

MAP EXPLORATION

To explore an interactive version of this map, go to
http://www.prenhall.com/faraghertlc/map5.4

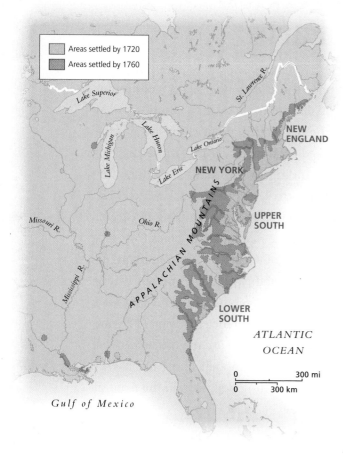

Areas settled by 1720
Areas settled by 1760

MAP 5.4

Spread of Settlement: Movement into the Backcountry, 1720–60
The spread of settlement from 1720 to 1760 shows the movement of
population into the backcountry during the midcentury.

HOW DID the movement into the backcountry affect the
relations among colonists, Indians, and English authorities?

The movement into the Pennsylvania and Virginia backcountry that began during the 1720s was the first of the great
pioneer treks that would take white pioneers into the continental interior. Many, perhaps most, of these pioneers held
no legal title to the lands they occupied. They simply hacked
out and defended squatter's claims from native proprietors
and all other comers. To the Delawares and Shawnees, who
had been pushed into the interior, or the Cherokees, who
occupied the Appalachian highlands to the south, these settlers presented a new and deadly threat. Rising fears and
resentments over this expanding population triggered much
eighteenth-century violence.

THE SOUTH

The Chesapeake and the Lower South were triracial societies,
with intermingled communities of white colonists and black
slaves, along with substantial Indian communities living on the
fringes of colonial settlement. Much of the population growth
of the region resulted from the forced migration of enslaved
Africans, who by 1750 made up 40 percent of the population.
Specializing in rice, tobacco, and other commercial crops, these
colonies were overwhelmingly rural. Farms and plantations were
dispersed across the countryside, and villages or towns were few.

English authorities established the Church of England as
the state religion in the Chesapeake colonies. Residents paid
taxes to support the church and were required to attend services. No other churches were allowed into Virginia or Maryland (despite its founding by Catholics) and dissenters were
excluded or exiled. Yet the Anglican establishment was inter-
nally weak. It maintained neither a colonial bishop nor local
institutions for training clergy.

Along the rice coast, the dominant social institution
was the large plantation. Transforming the tangle of woods
and swamps along the region's rivers into an ordered pattern
of dams, dikes, and flooded fields required heavy capital
investment. Consequently, only men of means could undertake rice cultivation. By midcentury established rice plantations typically were dominated by a large main house,
generally located on a spot of high ground overlooking the fields. Nearby, but a
world apart, were the slave quarters, rough wooden cabins lining two sides of a
muddy pathway near the outbuildings and barns.

Because tobacco, unlike rice, could be grown profitably in small plots, the
Chesapeake included a greater variety of farmers and a correspondingly diverse landscape. The poorest farmers lived in wooden cabins little better than the shacks of the
slaves. More prosperous farm families lived with two or three slaves in houses that nevertheless were considerably smaller than the substantial homes of New England.

Compared to the Lower South, where there was almost no community life
outside the plantation, the Chesapeake boasted well-developed neighborhoods constructed from kinship networks and economic connections. The most important
community institution was the county court, which held both executive and judicial
power. The gentleman justices of the county, appointed by the governor, included

the heads of the elite planter families. These men in turn selected the grand jury, composed of substantial freeholders. One of the most significant bonding forces in this free white population was a growing sense of racial solidarity in response to the increasing proportion of African slaves dispersed throughout the neighborhoods.

SOCIAL AND POLITICAL PATTERNS

Despite important similarities among the colonial regions of North America, during the eighteenth century the trajectory of the British colonies began to diverge sharply from that of the French and Spanish. Immigration, economic growth, and provincial political struggles all pushed British colonists in a radically new direction.

HOW DID the structure of colonial society differ from European social structure?

THE PERSISTENCE OF TRADITIONAL CULTURE IN THE NEW WORLD

In each of the regional North American societies, family and kinship, the church, and the local community were the most significant factors in everyday life. Everywhere colonists tended to live much as people had lived in European homeland communities at the time the colonies were settled. The residents of New Mexico, Quebec, and New England continued to be attached to the religious passions of the seventeenth century long after their mother countries had put those religious controversies aside in favor of imperial geopolitics. Nostalgia for Europe helped to fix a conservative colonial attitude toward culture.

myhistorylab
Review Summary

These were oral cultures, depending on the transmission of information by the spoken rather than the printed word, on the passage of traditions through oral story and song. North American colonial folk cultures, traditional and suspicious of change, preserved an essentially medieval worldview. The rhythms of life were regulated by the hours of sunlight and the seasons of the year. People rose with the sun and went to bed soon after sundown. The demands of the season determined their working routines. They farmed with simple tools, and drought, flood, or pestilence might quickly sweep away their efforts. Experience told them that the natural world imposed limitations within which men and women had to learn to live.

These were also communal cultures. In Québec, villagers worked side by side to repair the roads. In New Mexico they collectively maintained the irrigation ditches. In New England they gathered in town meetings to decide the dates when common fields were to be plowed, sowed, and harvested. Houses offered little privacy, with families often sleeping together in the same chamber, sitting together on benches rather than in chairs, and taking their supper from a common bowl or trencher. For most North American colonists of the mid-eighteenth century, the community was more important than the individual.

Most colonists continued the traditional European occupation of working the land. The majority of North American farmers grew crops and raised livestock for their own needs or for local barter, and communities were largely self-sufficient. Most farmers attempted to produce small surpluses as well, which they sold to pay their taxes and buy some manufactured goods. But rather than specializing in the production of one or two crops for sale, most farmers diversified production in order to remain as independent of the market as possible. The primary goal was ownership of land and the assurance that children and descendants would be able to settle on lands nearby.

Colonial cities, by contrast, were centers of commerce. Artisans and craftsmen worked at their trades full time, organizing themselves according to the European craft system. A young man who wished to pursue a trade served several

3–15
Peter Kalm, *A Swedish Visitor Tells about Philadelphia* (1748)

A spinner and carpenter from *The Book of Trades*, an eighteenth-century British survey of the crafts practiced in colonial America. In colonial cities, artisans organized themselves into the traditional European craft system with apprentices, journeymen, and masters. There were few opportunities for the employment of women outside the household, but women sometimes earned income by establishing sidelines as midwives or spinners.

years as an apprentice, working in exchange for learning the skills and secrets of the craft. After completing his apprenticeship, the young craftsman sought employment in a shop, often necessitating his migration to some other area, thus becoming a "journeyman." Most craftsmen remained at the journeyman level for the whole of their careers. But by building a good name and carefully saving, a journeyman hoped to become a master craftsman, opening his own shop and employing journeymen and apprentices of his own. As in farming, the ultimate goal was independence.

There were few opportunities for women outside the household. By law, husbands held managerial rights over family property, but widows received support in the form of a one-third lifetime interest, known as "dower," in a deceased husband's real estate (the rest of the estate being divided among the heirs). And in certain occupations, such as printing (which had a tradition of employing women), widows succeeded their husbands in business. As a result, some colonial women played active roles in eighteenth-century journalism.

QUICK REVIEW

Key Aspects of Early Colonial Culture

♦ Family and kinship.

♦ Church and religion.

♦ Local community.

THE FRONTIER HERITAGE

The colonial societies of eighteenth-century North America also shared a set of assumptions originating in their common frontier heritage. European colonists came from Old World societies in which land was scarce and monopolized by property-owning elites. They settled in a continent where, for the most part, land was abundant and cheap. The widespread and general expectation of property ownership was the most important cultural distinction between North America and Europe.

This expectation led to rising popular demands in all the colonial regions of the continent that land be taken from the Indian inhabitants and opened to colonial settlement. The majority of colonists—whether British, Spanish, or French—endorsed the violence directed against Indian peoples as an essential aspect of colonial life. This attitude was as true of inclusive as exclusive societies, with the difference that in the former, native peoples were incorporated into colonial society, while in the latter, tribes were pushed from the frontier.

American historians once tied the existence of this "free land" directly to the development of democracy. But the frontier heritage encouraged the popular acceptance of forced labor, a system that was anything but democratic. When asked how to achieve a good living, a woman of eighteenth-century South Carolina offered the following advice: "get a few slaves and beat them well to make them work hard." Labor was the key to prosperity, and it was in short supply throughout the colonies. In a land where free men and women could work for themselves on their own plot of ground, there was little incentive to work for wages. The use of forced labor was one of the few ways a landowner could secure an agricultural workforce.

More than half the immigrants to eighteenth-century British America arrived as indentured servants. Agents paid for the Atlantic crossing of poor immigrants in exchange for several years of service in America. But at the conclusion of their indentures, eighteenth-century servants enjoyed considerably more opportunity than their seventeenth-century counterparts, probably because of the rise in overall prosperity in the British colonies.

POPULATION GROWTH AND IMMIGRATION

All the colonial regions of North America experienced unprecedented growth in the eighteenth century. "Our people must at least be doubled every twenty years," Benjamin Franklin wrote in a remarkable 1751 essay on population, and he was nearly right. In 1700, there were 290,000 colonists north of Mexico; fifty years later they had grown to approximately 1.3 million, an average annual growth rate of about 3 percent. Preindustrial societies typically grew at rates of less than 1 percent per year.

High fertility and low mortality played important roles. Colonial women typically bore seven or more children during their childbearing years. And blessed with an abundance of food, colonists enjoyed generally good health and relatively low mortality.

But the British colonies grew far more rapidly than those of France or Spain (see Figure 5.1). It was immigration that made the difference. Fearful of depleting their population at home, the Spanish severely limited the migration of their own subjects and absolutely forbade the immigration of foreigners. Dedicated to keeping their colonies exclusively Catholic, the French ignored

 5–1
Benjamin Franklin, *Observations Concerning the Increase of Mankind, Peopling of Countries, &c.* (1751)

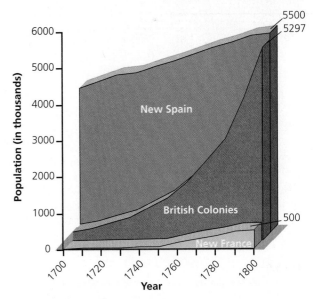

Figure 5.1 Estimated Total Population of New Spain, New France, and the British North American Colonies, 1700–1780
Although the populations of all three North American colonial empires grew in the eighteenth century, the explosive growth of the British colonies was unmatched.

Historical Statistics of the United States (Washington, DC: Government Printing Office, 1976), 1168.

Engagés Catholic immigrants to New France.

Encomienda In the Spanish colonies, the grant to a Spanish settler of a certain number of Indian subjects, who would pay him tribute in goods and labor.

3–7
William Byrd II, *Diary—An American Gentleman* (1709)

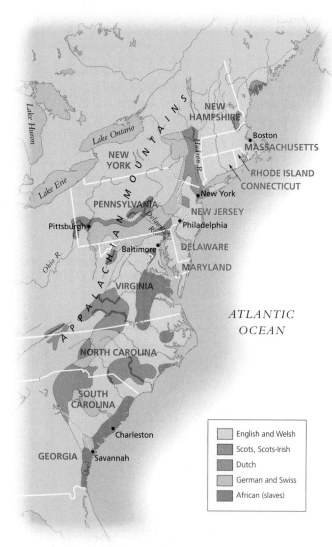

MAP 5.5

Ethnic Groups in Eighteenth-Century British North America The first federal census, taken in 1790, revealed remarkable ethnic diversity. New England was filled with people from the British Isles, but the rest of the colonies were a patchwork. Most states had at least three different ethnic groups within their borders.

IN WHAT areas were Scots and Scots-Irish most heavily concentrated? Why?

the desire of Protestant Huguenots to emigrate, instead sending thousands of Catholic **engagés** to Canada, most of whom returned, discouraged by the climate and the lack of commercial opportunity. But the English dispatched an estimated 400,000 of their own countrymen to populate their North American colonies during the seventeenth and eighteenth centuries. Moreover, the British were the only colonial power to encourage the immigration of foreign nationals.

Trans-Atlantic migration made for colonies characterized by extraordinary ethnic diversity (see Map 5.5 and Figure 5.2). First there were the Africans, the largest group to come to North America in the colonial period, larger even than the English. Forced relocation brought an estimated 600,000 to the colonies before the official end of the slave trade to the United States in 1807. Then there was the massive emigration from the northern British Isles. Squeezed by economic hardship, an estimated 150,000 Highland Scots and Protestant Irish from the Ulster region of northern Ireland (known as the "Scots-Irish") emigrated in the eighteenth century. German speakers were next in importance, at least 125,000 of them settling in the colonies. It is worth noting once again that a majority of these immigrants to British North America came as bonded servants or slaves.

SOCIAL CLASS

In New France, landowning seigneurs (lords) claimed privileges similar to those enjoyed by their aristocratic counterparts at home; the Spanish system of **encomienda** and the great manors created by the Dutch and continued by the English along the Hudson River also represented attempts to transplant European feudalism to North America. But because settlers in most areas had relatively free access to land, these monopolies proved difficult or impossible to maintain. North American society was not aristocratic in the European fashion, but neither was it without social hierarchy.

In New Spain the official criterion for status was racial purity. *Españoles* (Spaniards), also known as *gente de razon* (literally, "people of reason"), occupied the top rung of the social ladder, with mestizos, mulattoes, and others on descending levels, with Indians and African slaves at the bottom. In the isolated northern borderlands, however, such distinctions tended to blur, with castas (persons of mixed background) enjoying considerably more opportunity. Mestizos who acquired land might suddenly be reclassified as españoles. Even so, Spanish and French colonial societies were cut in the style of the Old World, with its hereditary ranks and titles.

In the British colonies the upper class was made up of large landowners, merchants, and prosperous professionals. Despite the lack of titles, wealthy planters and merchants of the British colonies lived far more extravagantly than the seigneurs of New France or the dons of the Spanish borderlands. What separated the culture of class in the British colonies from that of New France or New Mexico was not so much the material conditions of life as the prevailing attitude toward social rank. In the Catholic cultures, the upper class attempted to obscure its origins, claiming descent from European nobility. But British North America celebrated social mobility. The class system was remarkably open, and the entrance of newly successful planters, commercial farmers, and merchants into the upper ranks was not only possible but also common.

There was also a large and impoverished lower class in the British colonies. Slaves, bound servants, and poor laboring families made up 40 percent or more of the population. For them the standard of living did not rise above bare subsistence. American slaves stood apart from the gains in the standard of living enjoyed by immigrants from Europe. Their lives in America had been degraded beyond measure from the conditions that had prevailed in their native lands.

The feature of the class system most often commented on by eighteenth-century observers was not the character or composition of the lower ranks, but rather the size and strength of the middle class, a rank entirely absent in the colonies of France and Spain. More than half the population of the British colonies, and nearly 70 percent of all white settlers, might have been so classified. Most were landowning farmers of small to moderate means, but the group also included artisans, craftsmen, and small shopkeepers. Households solidly in the center of this broad ranking enjoyed a standard of living higher than that of the great majority of people in England and Europe.

ECONOMIC GROWTH AND ECONOMIC INEQUALITY

One of the most important differences among North American colonial regions in the eighteenth century was the economic stagnation of New France and New Spain compared with the impressive economic growth of the British colonies. Weighed down by royal bureaucracies and regulations, the communities of the French Crescent and New Spain never evidenced much prosperity. In eighteenth-century British North America, by contrast, per capita production grew at an annual rate of 0.5 percent. As economic growth increased the size of the economic pie, most middle- and upper-class British Americans began to enjoy improved living conditions. Improving standards of living and open access to land encouraged British colonists to see theirs as a society where hard work and savings could translate into prosperity.

At the same time, economic growth produced increasing social inequality. In the commercial cities, for example, prosperity was accompanied by a concentration of assets in the hands of wealthy families. The general standard of living may have been rising, but the rich were getting richer and the poor poorer. The greatest concentrations of wealth occurred in the cities and in regions dominated by commercial farming, whether slave or free, while the greatest economic equality was found in areas of self-sufficient farming.

Another eighteenth-century trend, however, stymied upward economic mobility in the countryside. As population grew and as generations succeeded one another in older settlements, all the available land eventually was taken up. Under the pressure of increased demand, land prices rose beyond the reach of families of modest means. And as a family's land was divided among the heirs of the second and third generations, parcels became ever smaller and more intensively

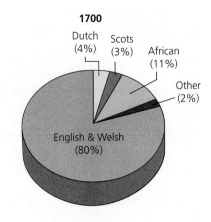

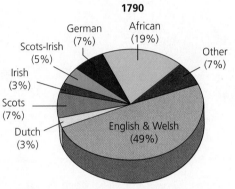

Figure 5.2 The Ancestry of the British Colonial Population

The legacy of eighteenth-century immigration to the British colonies was a population of unprecedented ethnic diversity.

Thomas L. Purvis, "The European Ancestry of the United States Population," *William and Mary Quarterly* 61 (1984): 85–101.

QUICK REVIEW

Poverty in the Colonies

◆ Gap between rich and poor widened in the eighteenth century.

◆ Most cities had workhouses or shelters.

◆ Much smaller percentage of population depended on public assistance in the colonies than in England.

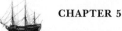

Español con India
Mestizo.

Mestizo con Española
Castizo.

Castizo con Española
Español.

Español con Mora
Mulato.

5

6

Mulato con Española
Morisco.

Morisco con Española
Chino.

7

Chino con India
Salta atras.

Salta atras con Mulata
Lobo.

An eighteenth-century genre painting from New Spain showing various racial *castas*, the result of ethnic mixing.

farmed. Eventually, the soil was exhausted. There were increases in the number of landless poor, as well as the disturbing appearance of what were called the "strolling poor," homeless people who traveled from town to town looking for work or simply a handout.

COLONIAL POLITICS

The administration of the Spanish and French colonies was highly centralized. Although local communities had informal independence, these highly bureaucratized and centralized governments left little room for the development of vigorous traditions of self-government.

The situation in the British colonies was quite different. During the early eighteenth century the British government of Prime Minister Robert Walpole assumed that a decentralized administration would best accomplish the nation's economic goals. With the exception of Connecticut and Rhode Island, both of which retained their charters and continued to choose their own governors, the colonies were administered by royally appointed governors. But taxation and spending continued to be controlled by elected assemblies. The right to vote was restricted to men with property. Yet the proportion of adult white males who qualified approached 50 percent in the British colonies, considerably higher in New England, considerably lower in some southern jurisdictions.

That did not mean that the colonies were democratic. The basic principle of order in eighteenth-century British culture was the ideal of deference to natural hierarchy. The common metaphor for civil order was the well-ordered family, in which children were strictly governed by their parents, wives by their husbands. Members of subordinate groups, such as women, non-English immigrants, African American slaves, servants, and Indians, were not allowed to vote or hold public office. Moreover, for the most part, the men who did vote nearly always chose wealthy landowners, planters, or merchants to serve as their leaders. Consequently, provincial assemblies were controlled by colonial elites.

Yet over the century there was an important trend toward stronger institutions of representative government. By midcentury most colonial assemblies in British North America had achieved considerable power over provincial affairs, sharing authority with governors. They collected local revenues and allocated funds for government programs, asserted the right to audit the accounts of public officers, and in some cases even acquired the power to approve the appointment of provincial officials. Because the assemblies controlled the finances of government—the "purse strings"—most royal governors were unable to resist this trend.

The royal governors who were most successful at realizing their agendas were those who became adept at playing one provincial faction off against another. All this had the important effect of schooling the colonial elite in the art of politics—not democratic politics, but the politics of patronage, coalition-building, and behind-the-scenes intrigue. This would have important implications for the development of American institutions.

THE CULTURAL TRANSFORMATION OF BRITISH NORTH AMERICA

Inspired by the sixteenth- and seventeenth-century revolution in scientific thought represented by giants such as Copernicus, Galileo, Descartes, and Newton, intellectuals in Europe and Great Britain became advocates for the power of human reason rather than spiritual revelation or mystical illumination as the sole way of discovering natural law. They sought to establish an authoritative canon of logic, ethics, and aesthetics, as well as political philosophy.

The Catholic Church banned the works of hundreds of rationalist thinkers whose opinions were considered threats to the authority of faith. In New Spain and New France colonial officials worked diligently to suppress such challenging ideas and writings. Cultural censorship in the French and Spanish colonies was effective because literacy was confined to a tiny minority of elite men. In the British colonies, by contrast, literacy was widespread. British colonial officials made little attempt at cultural censorship, and as a result these new ideas sparked a cultural transformation in eighteenth-century British North America.

THE ENLIGHTENMENT CHALLENGE

The **Enlightenment** is a simple label for a complex movement encompassing many different thinkers with many different ideas. But Enlightenment writers shared some things in common. They were optimistic about the ability of the rational human mind to discover the natural laws that were thought to govern the physical world and human affairs. Coupled with their commitment to reason was their belief in progress.

Such thinking was most attractive to the British colonial elite, families experiencing rising prosperity. This group had good reason to believe in progress. They sent their sons to colonial colleges, the focal point for the dissemination of Enlightenment ideas. The curricula of these colleges, modeled on those of Oxford and Cambridge in England, were designed to train ministers, but gradually each institution changed to curricula influenced by Enlightenment thinking.

The tastes of ordinary readers ran to traditional rather than Enlightenment fare. By the mid-eighteenth century there were more than twenty newspapers in the British colonies. These papers did not employ reporters but instead depended on official government announcements, travelers' and correspondents' reports, and articles reprinted from other sources. Most literate people had access to them, and they were often read aloud in local taverns, making their information available to all within hearing.

The best-selling book of the colonial era, not surprisingly, was the Bible. But in second place was a unique American literary form, the captivity narrative. The genre originated with the appearance of *The Sovereignty and Goodness of God* (1682), Mary Rowlandson's tale of her captivity among Indians during King Philip's War.

Another popular literary genre was the **almanac**, a combination calendar, astrological guide, sourcebook of medical advice, and farming tips that largely reflected the concerns of traditional folk culture.

A mixture of traditional and Enlightenment views characterized the thinking of many colonial intellectuals. Boston minister Cotton Mather offers a good example. A conservative defender of the old order, Mather wrote of the existence of witches and supported the executions during the Salem witchcraft crisis (see Chapter 3). Yet he

TO WHAT extent did North America participate in the Enlightenment?

myhistorylab
Review Summary

3–8
Manners and Etiquette in the Eighteenth Century (1748)

4–1
John Peter Zenger and the Responsibility of the Press (1734)

3–5
Cotton Mather, *Memorable Providences, Relating to Witchcrafts and Possessions* (1689)

Enlightenment Intellectual movement stressing the importance of reason and the existence of discoverable natural laws.

Almanac A combination calendar, astrological guide, and sourcebook of medical advice and farming tips.

was also a member of the Royal Society (Great Britain's national academy of science), a defender of the Copernican sun-centered model of the universe, and an early supporter of inoculation against smallpox.

A DECLINE IN RELIGIOUS DEVOTION

As Enlightenment thinking gradually gained in popularity, religious commitment seemed to decline. In the South, by the 1730s, only one adult in fifteen was affiliated with a church. The Anglican establishment in the Chesapeake and the Lower South was institutionally feeble, its ministers uninspiring, and many families "unchurched."

Puritan churches in New England also suffered declining membership and falling attendance. By the second decade of the eighteenth century only one in five New Englanders belonged to an established congregation. And among the churched, an increasing number began to question the **Calvinist theology of election**, the belief that salvation was the result of God's sovereign decree, that only a small number of men and women would be the recipients of God's grace. Many turned instead to the view that people had a natural ability to accept God's grace by developing their faith and doing good works. It became a force at Harvard and Yale in the first quarter of the eighteenth century, and soon a generation of ministers with more liberal ideas were taking positions in New England churches. Their ideas appealed to the same men and women attracted to Enlightenment thinking, those experiencing rising prosperity and social improvement. Among ordinary people in the countryside, however, especially among those in communities with narrowing opportunities, there was a good deal of opposition to these unorthodox ideas.

THE GREAT AWAKENING

The first stirrings of a movement challenging the rationalist approach to religion occurred during the 1730s, most notably in the revival sparked by Rev. Jonathan Edwards in the community of Northampton. Similar revivals soon broke out in other New England communities, as well as among German Lutherans and Scots-Irish Presbyterians in Pennsylvania. Not all the revivalists were Calvinists. Some promoted a theology that emphasized human choice. But the common thread was a complaint of "spiritual coldness," of ministers whose sermons read like rational dissertations. People clamored for preaching that was more emotional.

These local revivals became an intercolonial phenomenon thanks to the preaching of George Whitefield, an evangelical Anglican minister from England, who in 1738 made the first of several tours of the colonies. By all accounts, his preaching had a powerful effect. Even Benjamin Franklin, a religious skeptic, wrote of the "extraordinary influence of his oratory" after attending an outdoor service in Philadelphia where 30,000 people crowded the streets to hear him preach. Whitefield began as Edwards did, chastising his listeners as "half animals and half devils," but he parted company from Edwards by leaving them with the hope that God would be responsive to their desire for salvation. Whitefield avoided sectarian differences. "God help us to forget party names and become Christians in deed and truth," he declared.

This widespread colonial revival of religion, which later generations called the **Great Awakening**, was an American version of the second phase of the Protestant Reformation (see Chapter 2). Religious leaders condemned the lax-

3–16
Jonathan Edwards, *A Puritan Preacher Admonishes His Flocks* (1741)

myhistorylab

Exploring America: *The Great Awakening*

QUICK REVIEW

The Great Awakening

- Opposition to rationalist approach to religion grew in the 1730s.
- Jonathan Edwards focused his attention on inspiring young people.
- Movement spread throughout the colonies.

Calvinist theology of election   Belief that salvation was the result of God's sovereign decree and that few people would receive God's grace.

Great Awakening   North American religious revival in the middle of the eighteenth century.

ity, decadence, and bureaucracy of established Protestantism and sought to reinvigorate it with renewed piety and purity. People undergoing the economic and social stresses of the age, unsure about their ability to find land, marry, and participate in the promise of a growing economy—like those in Northampton—found relief in religious enthusiasm.

Among Presbyterians, open conflict broke out between the revivalists and the old guard, and in some regions the church hierarchy divided into separate organizations. In New England, where these factions were known as the **New Lights** and the **Old Lights**, the two sides accused each other of heresy. New Lights railed against liberal theology as a "rationalist heresy" and called for a revival of Calvinism. Old Lights condemned emotional enthusiasm as a "lawless heresy," the belief in a personal and direct relationship with God outside the order of the church. Itinerant preachers appeared in the countryside, stirring up trouble. Many congregations split into feuding factions, and ministers found themselves challenged by their newly awakened parishioners. Never had there been such turmoil in New England churches.

The revivals began somewhat later in the South, first developing in the mid-1740s, reaching full impact in the 1760s. They affected not only white Southerners but also for the first time introduced many slaves to Christianity. Baptist churches of the South in the era of the American Revolution included members of both races and featured spontaneous preaching by slaves as well as masters. In the nineteenth century white and black Christians would go their separate ways, but the joint experience of the eighteenth-century Awakening shaped the religious cultures of both groups.

Many other "unchurched" colonists were brought back to Protestantism by revivalism. But a careful examination of statistics suggests that the proportion of church members in the general population did not increase during the middle decades of the century. While the number of churches more than doubled from 1740 to 1780, the colonial population grew even faster, increasing threefold. The greatest impact was on families already associated with congregations. Before the Awakening, attendance at church had been mostly an adult affair, but throughout the colonies the revival of religion had its deepest effects on young people, who flocked to church in greater numbers than ever before. For years the number of people experiencing conversion had been steadily falling but now full membership surged. Church membership previously had been concentrated among women, leading Cotton Mather, for one, to speculate that perhaps women were indeed more godly. But men were particularly affected by the revival of religion, and their attendance and membership rose.

George Whitefield (who, contemporaries noted, was cross-eyed) enjoyed a remarkable career as a powerful preacher on both sides of the Atlantic. This portrait shows him preaching indoors to a rapt audience. During his tour of the colonies, Whitefield reportedly had a similar effect on crowds of thousands who gathered outdoors to hear his sermons.

John Wollaston, "George Whitefield" ca. 1770. By courtesy of the National Portrait Gallery, London.

New Lights People who experienced conversion during the revivals of the Great Awakening.

Old Lights Religious faction that condemned emotional enthusiasm as part of the heresy of believing in a personal and direct relationship with God outside the order of the church.

THE POLITICS OF REVIVALISM

Revivalism appealed most of all to groups that felt bypassed by the economic and cultural development of the British colonies during the first half of the eighteenth century. The New Lights tended to draw their greatest strength from small farmers and less prosperous craftsmen. Many members of the upper class and the comfortable "middling sort" viewed the excesses of revivalism as indications of anarchy, and they became even more committed to rational religion.

Revivalism sometimes had political implications. In Connecticut, for example, Old Lights politicized the religious dispute by passing a series of laws in the General Assembly designed to suppress revivalism. In one town, revivalists refused to pay taxes supporting the established church and were jailed. Judges sympathetic to New Light views were thrown off the bench, and others were denied their elected seats in the assembly. The arrogance of these actions was met with popular outrage: by the 1760s the Connecticut New Lights had organized themselves politically and, in what amounted to a political rebellion, succeeded in turning the Old Lights out of office. New Light politicians would provide the leadership for the American Revolution in Connecticut.

Such direct connections between religion and politics were rare. There can be little doubt, however, that for many people revivalism offered the first opportunity to participate actively in public debate and public action that affected the direction of their lives. Choices about religious styles, ministers, and doctrine were thrown open for public discourse, and ordinary people began to believe that their

Baptism by Full Immersion in the Schuylkill River of Pennsylvania, an engraving by Henry Dawkins illustrating events in the history of American Baptists, was published in Philadelphia in 1770. With calls for renewed piety and purity, the Great Awakening reinvigorated American Protestantism. The Baptists preached an egalitarian message, and their congregations in the South often included both white and black Protestants.

Henry Dawkins, "Baptismal Ceremony Beside the Schuykill." Engraving, 1770. John Carter Brown Library at Brown University.

CHRONOLOGY

1636	Harvard College founded	1732	Franklin begins publishing *Poor Richard's Almanac*
1674	Bishopric of Quebec established	1738	George Whitefield first tours the colonies
1680s	William Penn begins recruiting settlers from the European continent	1740s	Great Awakening gets under way in the Northeast
1682	Mary Rowlandson's *The Sovereignty and Goodness of God*	1740	Parliament passes a naturalization law for the colonies
1689	Toleration Act passed by Parliament	1746	College of New Jersey (Princeton University) founded
1690s	Beginnings of Jesuit missions in Arizona	1760s	Great Awakening achieves full impact in the South
1693	College of William and Mary founded	1769	Spanish colonization of California begins
1700s	Plains Indians begin adoption of the horse	1775	Indian revolt at San Diego
1701	Yale College founded; Iroquois sign treaty of neutrality with France	1781	Los Angeles founded
1716	Spanish begin construction of Texas missions		

opinions actually counted for something. Underlying the debate over these issues were insecurities about warfare, economic growth, and the development of colonial society. Revivalism empowered ordinary people to question their leaders, an experience that would prove critical in the political struggles to come.

CONCLUSION

By the middle of the eighteenth century a number of distinct colonial regions had emerged in North America, all of them with rising populations demanding that more land be seized from the Indians. Some colonies attempted to ensure homogeneity, whereas others embraced diversity. Within the British colonies, New England in particular seemed bound to the past, whereas the middle colonies and the backcountry pointed the way toward pluralism and expansion. These developments placed them in direct competition with the expansionist plans of the French and at odds with Indian peoples committed to the defense of their homelands.

The economic development of the British colonies introduced new social and cultural tensions that led to the Great Awakening, a massive revival of religion that was the first transcolonial event in American history. Beginning in small communities like Northampton, Massachusetts, the revivals affected thousands of people, leading to a renewal of religious passions. Rather than resuscitating old traditions, however, the Awakening seemed to point people toward a more active role in their own political futures. Those transformations added to the differences between the British colonies, on the one hand, and New Spain and the French Crescent on the other.

REVIEW QUESTIONS

1. What were the principal colonial regions of North America? Discuss their similarities and their differences. Contrast the development of their political systems.

2. Why did the Spanish and the French close their colonies to immigration? Why did the British open their colonies? How do you explain the ethnic homogeneity of New England and the ethnic pluralism of New York and Pennsylvania?

3. What were the principal trends in the history of Indian America in the eighteenth century?

4. Discuss the development of class differences in the Spanish, French, and British colonies in the eighteenth century.

5. Discuss the effects of the Great Awakening on the subsequent history of the British colonies.

myhistorylab

Flashcard Review

KEY TERMS

The Act of Toleration (p. 109)
Almanac (p. 119)
Calvinist theology of election (p. 120)
Encomienda (p. 116)
Engagés (p. 116)

Enlightenment (p. 119)
Great Awakening (p. 120)
New Lights (p. 121)
Old Lights (p. 121)

RECOMMENDED READING

Jon Butler, *Becoming America: The Revolution Before 1776* (2000). A history that emphasizes the diversity, economic prosperity, participatory politics, and religious pluralism of the eighteenth-century British colonies.

Edward Countryman, *Americans: A Collision of Histories* (1996). An important synthesis that includes the many peoples and cultures of North America.

W. J. Eccles, *The Canadian Frontier, 1534–1760* (1983). An introduction to the history of French America by a leading scholar of colonial Canada.

David Hackett Fischer, *Albion's Seed: Four British Folkways in America* (1990). An engaging history with fascinating details on the regions of New England, Pennsylvania, Virginia, and the backcountry.

Jack P. Greene, *Pursuits of Happiness: The Social Development of Early Modern British Colonies and the Formation of American Culture* (1986). A distillation of a tremendous amount of historical material on community life in British North America.

Frank Lambert, *Inventing the "Great Awakening"* (1999). Argues that the revivialists themselves created the idea of the Great Awakening to further their evangelical work.

Jackson Turner Main, *The Social Structure of Revolutionary America* (1965). A classic study of colonial social structure, with statistics, tables, and enlightening interpretations.

George Marsden, *Jonathan Edwards: A Life* (2005). A new and comprehensive biography that emphasizes Edwards's work as both a pastor and an intellectual.

Martha McCollough, *Three Nations, One Place: A Comparative Ethnohistory of Social Change Among the Comanches and Hasinais During Spain's Colonial Era, 1689–1821* (2004). A detailed study of change and innovation among native peoples of the Great Plains during the eighteenth century.

Lucy Eldersveld Murphy, *A Gathering of Rivers: Indians, Métis, and Mining in the Western Great Lakes, 1737–1832* (2000). Demonstrates the success of Indian communities in adapting to colonialism through the diversification of their economies, intermarriage, and constructing multiethnic communities.

James A. Sandos, *Converting California: Indians and Franciscans in the Missions* (2004). A balanced treatment of missionaries and natives in eighteenth- and nineteenth-century California.

David J. Weber, *The Spanish Frontier in North America* (1992). A magnificent treatment of the entire Spanish borderlands from Florida to California. Includes important chapters on colonial government and social life.

Marianne S. Wokeck, *Trade in Strangers: The Beginning of Mass Migration to North America* (1999). The first important study of immigration in the eighteenth century, arguing that these migrations served as models for European mass migration of the next century.

My dear Jack, All the Provinces [are] arming and Training in the same Manner, for they are all determined to die or be Free . . .

—Eliza Farmer, June 28, 1775

Chaplain Jacob Duche' leading the first prayer in the First Continental Congress at Carpenter's Hall, Philadelphia, September 1774.

6

FROM EMPIRE TO INDEPENDENCE
1750–1776

WHAT WERE the most important weaknesses of the British Empire in North America at the outset of the Seven Years' War?

WHAT FACTORS led to the growth of American nationalism in the 1760s?

HOW DID political and economic problems in Britain contribute to unrest in the colonies?

WHAT STEPS did Britain take to punish Massachusetts for the colonists' acts of resistance?

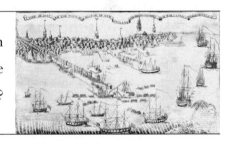

WHO MADE up the second Continental Congress and why was it formed?

AMERICAN COMMUNITIES

The First Continental Congress Begins to Shape a National Political Community

THE OPENING MINUTES OF THE FIRST CONTINENTAL CONGRESS, HELD in Philadelphia in September 1774, did not bode well. One of the delegates moved that the session open with prayer, but others objected. "We were so divided in religious sentiments," wrote John Adams, a representative from Massachusetts, "that we could not join in the same act of worship." Was the Congress to be stymied, here at the very beginning, by the things separating them? Putting aside their religious differences, the delegates agreed to a prayer by a local clergyman, who took as his text the Thirty-fifth Psalm: "Plead my cause, O Lord, with them that strive with me; fight against them that fight against me."

This incident highlighted the most important task confronting the First Continental Congress—strengthening their common cause without compromising their local identities. The delegates, noted Adams, were like "ambassadors from a dozen belligerent powers of Europe." They represented distinct colonies with traditions and histories as different as those of separate countries. Moreover, these lawyers, merchants, and planters, leaders in their respective colonies, were strangers to one another.

Britain's North American colonies enjoyed considerable prosperity during the first half of the eighteenth century. But in 1765—in the aftermath of the great war for empire during which Great Britain soundly defeated France and forced the cession of the French North American colonies—the British government began to apply new trade restrictions and levy new taxes, inspiring resistance among the colonists. By the opening session of the First Continental Congress peaceful protest had escalated into violent riot, and in an attempt to force the colonists to acknowledge the power of Parliament to make laws binding them "in all cases whatsoever," the British had proclaimed a series of repressive measures. In this atmosphere of crisis, the colonial assemblies (with the exception of Georgia's) elected delegates for a "Continental Congress" to map out a coordinated response.

Despite their differences, during seven weeks of deliberations, the delegates succeeded in forging an agreement on the principles and policies they would follow in this, the most serious crisis in the history of the British North American colonies. These were the first tentative steps toward the creation of an American national political community. Communities are not simply local but can also be regional, national, even international. In a town or village, feelings of association come from daily, face-to-face contacts, but for larger groups those connections must be deliberately constructed. In their final declaration the delegates pledged to "firmly agree and associate, under the sacred ties of virtue, honor and love of our country." They asked their countrymen to remember "the poorer sort" among them during the time of trouble they knew was coming. They demanded that patriotic Americans "break off all dealings" with those refusing to act, thus drawing a distinction between "insiders" and "outsiders," one of the essential first steps in the construction of community identity.

Patrick Henry, a Virginia delegate strongly committed to American independence, was exuberant by the time the Congress adjourned in late October. "The distinctions between Virginians, Pennsylvanians, New Yorkers, and New Englanders, are no more," he declared. "I am not a Virginian, but an American." He was exaggerating the unity. It remained a work in progress. Local, provincial, and regional differences would continue to clash. But Henry voiced an important truth.

In its attempt to force the colonists to pay a share of the costs of empire through taxation, Great Britain had sparked a revolt of both elite and ordinary colonists. The road to a shared community of interest among British colonists that distinguished them from the mother country had been marked by milestones with legendary names: the Stamp Act, the Boston Massacre, the Tea Party, the Intolerable Acts. The violent events that would follow the First Continental Congress—the first clash at Lexington and Concord, the siege of Boston, the Battle of Bunker Hill—would lead to a second session of the Congress. Reluctantly at first, then enthusiastically, the delegates would move toward independence. The difficult months and years of warfare would sorely test the imagined community of the united colonies, and the differences among them would frequently threaten to abort the nation being born. But the sessions of the First Continental Congress marked the moment when Americans first began the struggle to overcome local differences in pursuit of national goals.

Philadelphia

THE SEVEN YEARS' WAR IN AMERICA

Leaders of the British colonies made an early attempt at cooperation in 1754, when representatives from New England, New York, Pennsylvania, and Maryland met to consider a joint approach to military challenges from the French and their Indian allies. Even as the delegates met, fighting between French Canadians and Virginians began near the headwaters of the Ohio River in the Appalachian Mountains, the first shots in a great global war for empire pitting Great Britain (and Prussia) against the combined might of France, Spain, and Austria.

THE ALBANY CONFERENCE OF 1754

The British Board of Trade convened the 1754 meeting in the New York town of Albany on the Hudson River. They wanted the colonies to consider a collective response to the continuing conflict with New France and the Indians of the interior. High on the agenda was the negotiation of a settlement with the leaders of the Iroquois Confederacy, who had grown impatient with colonial land grabbing. But as the negotiations began, behind the scenes real estate developers were bribing minor Iroquois chiefs, affixing their signatures on a "deed" for an enormous tract of land in Pennsylvania, and turning the meeting into a vehicle for the very abuses the British sought to correct. Angered by these manipulations, the official Iroquois delegation walked out of the conference, refusing all offers to join a British alliance.

The **Albany Conference** did adopt a "**Plan of Union**" put forward by Benjamin Franklin, a delegate from Pennsylvania. Franklin, whom the British had appointed Postmaster General of the North American colonies, was especially sensitive to the need for cooperation. His proposal would have placed Indian affairs, western settlement, and other items of mutual interest under the authority of a grand council composed of representatives elected by the colonial assemblies and led by a British-appointed president. All the colonies rejected the Albany Plan of Union, fearful of losing their autonomy. The absence of cooperation among the colonies would prove one of the greatest weaknesses during the subsequent war with the French.

FRANCE VS. BRITAIN IN AMERICA

There were three violent flash points in the conflict between Great Britain and France for control of North America. First was the northern Atlantic coast, the ragged boundary between New France and New England. To protect the ocean approach to their colonial heartland, the French constructed the port and fortress of Louisbourg on Cape Breton Island. In 1749 the British established a large naval facility at Halifax in Nova Scotia, but worried about the loyalty of the 18,000 French-speaking Acadians of the province.

The second flash point was the border region between New France and New York, extending from Niagara Falls to Lake Champlain, where Canadians and New Yorkers were rivals for the lucrative Indian trade. The French, who found it difficult to compete against superior English goods, resorted instead to military might, garrisoning fortifications on Lake George and at Niagara. In this zone the strategic advantage was held by the Iroquois Confederacy.

Third was the Ohio country, the trans-Appalachian region bisected by the Ohio River. This rich country was a prime target of British land speculators and backcountry settlers, whom the French feared would overrun their isolated outposts and threaten their entire Mississippi trading empire. To reinforce their claim, in 1749 the French sent a heavily armed force down the Ohio River to ward off the British, and in 1752 they attempted to expel all British traders from the region.

WHAT WERE the most important weaknesses of the British Empire in North America at the outset of the Seven Years' War?

myhistorylab
Review Summary

IMAGE KEY
for pages 126–127

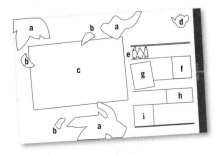

a. Green tea and dried tea leaves.
b. Flank and breast feathers.
c. Chaplain Jacob Duche' leading the first prayer in the First Continental Congress at Carpenter's Hall, Philadelphia, September 1774.
d. A "No Stamp Act" teapot.
e. Three Imrie/Risley by Wilson 1750s 77mm diorama figures, Roger Ranger with two soldiers, French and Indian War, on a diorama base.
f. Propaganda of 1765 against the Stamp Act that was emblazoned on teapots.
g. American colonists force feed hot tea to an English tax collector after tar and feathering the agent under a Liberty Tree in colonial Boston.
h. Colored engraving, published by Paul Revere, shows British troops disembarking from a ship in Boston in 1768.
i. The Declaration of Independence.

Albany Conference A 1754 meeting, held in Albany, NY, between the British and leaders of the Iroquois Confederacy.

Plan of Union Plan put forward by Benjamin Franklin in 1754 calling for an intercolonial union to manage defense and Indian affairs. The plan was rejected by participants at the Albany Congress.

French Canadian troops then began in 1753 the construction of a line of forts running south from Lake Erie to the headwaters of the Ohio River. In a direct challenge to the French claims in the West, the British government issued a royal charter for more than 200,000 acres to the Ohio Company, organized by London and Virginia investors.

The Indian peoples of the Ohio country had interests of their own. In addition to native inhabitants, the region had become a refuge for Indian peoples who had fled the Northeast. Most of the Indians of the Ohio country opposed British expansion and were anxious to make the Appalachians into a wall of protection. Meanwhile the Iroquois Confederacy continued the game of playing the British against the French. In the South the Creeks (and to a lesser extent the Cherokees and Choctaws) attempted to carve out a similar balancing role for themselves among the British in the Lower South, the French in Louisiana, and the Spanish in Florida. These Indian confederacies saw it as in their interest to perpetuate the existing colonial stalemate. Their position would be greatly undermined by an overwhelming victory for either side.

FRONTIER WARFARE

As the delegates to the Albany Conference conducted their business they received news of the first clash with the French. Colonel George Washington, a young militia officer sent by the governor of Virginia to expel the French from the upper Ohio, had been forced to surrender his troops to a French Canadian force. The French now commanded the interior country from Fort Duquesne, at the "Forks of the Ohio," the junction of the Allegheny and Monongahela Rivers.

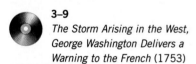

3–9
The Storm Arising in the West, George Washington Delivers a Warning to the French (1753)

Taking up the challenge, in 1755 the British launched an effort to strike the French in all three zones. An army of New England militiamen succeeded in capturing two important French forts on the border of Nova Scotia. Elsewhere the British campaigns failed. In northern New York a large colonial force was repulsed by the French. And on July 9, 1755, 1,500 British troops were ambushed and destroyed by a much smaller force of 600 confederated Indian fighters supported by a mere 30 French Canadians. It was the worst military defeat of a British army during the eighteenth century.

Full-scale warfare between Great Britain (supported by Prussia) and France (supported by Spain) began the next year in 1756. It was truly a global war, fought in Europe, Asia, and America, and known to history as the Seven Years' War (or the **French and Indian War** in America) (see Map 6.1). The first two years were a near catastrophe for Great Britain. Indians pounded backcountry settlements, killed thousands of settlers, and raided deep into the coastal colonies, throwing British colonists into panic. French Canadians captured British forts in northern New York. The lack of colonial cooperation greatly hampered the British attempt to mount a counterattack. When British commanders tried to exert direct control over provincial troops, they succeeded only in angering local authorities.

THE CONQUEST OF CANADA

In 1757 William Pitt, an enthusiastic advocate of British expansion, became prime minister of Great Britain. Believing that the global war could be won in North America, he subsidized Prussian allies to fight the war in Europe, reserving his own forces for naval and colonial operations. Pitt committed himself to the conquest of Canada and the final elimination of French competition in North America. Promising that the war would be fought "at His Majesty's expense," Pitt secured colonial cooperation with a massive infusion of British currency and credit.

French and Indian War The last of the Anglo-French colonial wars (1754–1763) and the first in which fighting began in North America. The war ended with France's defeat. Also known as the **Seven Years' War.**

MAP EXPLORATION

To explore an interactive version of this map, go to **http://www.prenhall.com/faraghertlc/map6.1**

MAP 6.1

The War for Empire in North America, 1754–1763   The Seven Years' War in America was fought in three principal areas: Nova Scotia and what was then Acadia, the frontier between New France and New York, and the upper Ohio River.

HOW DID the Indian trade affect the war? Which military defeats dealt the worst blows to the French?

The British were also effective at attracting Indian support. In 1758 officials promised the Iroquois and the Ohio Indians that the crown would "agree upon clear and fixed boundaries between our settlements and their hunting grounds, so that each party may know their own and be a mutual protection to each other of their respective possessions."

Thus did Pitt succeed in reversing the course of the war. Regular and provincial forces captured the fortress of Louisbourg in July 1758, setting the stage for the invasion of New France. A month later a force of New Englanders captured the strategic French fort of Oswego on Lake Ontario, thereby preventing the Canadians from resupplying their western posts. Encouraged by British promises,

The death of General James Wolfe, at the conclusion of the battle in which the British captured Quebec in 1759, became the subject of American artist Benjamin West's most famous painting, which was exhibited to tremendous acclaim in London in 1770.

Benjamin West (1738–1820), "The Death of General Wolfe," 1770. Oil on canvas, 152.6 × 214.5 cm. Transfer from the Canadian War Memorials, 1921 (Gift of the 2nd Duke of Westminster, Eaton Hall, Cheshire, 1918). National Gallery of Canada, Ottawa, Ontario.

Treaty of Paris The formal end to British hostilities against France and Spain in February 1763.

numerous Indian tribes deserted the French, forcing them to abandon Fort Duquesne, which the British occupied and renamed Fort Pitt (today's Pittsburgh) in honor of the prime minister. The last of the French forts in northern New York fell in 1759. In the South, regular and provincial British troops crushed the Cherokees and opened negotiations with the Creeks and Choctaws.

British forces now converged on French Canada. In 1759 colonial and British troops, acting on General James Wolfe's order to "burn and lay waste the country," plundered farms along the St. Lawrence and shelled the city of Quebec. The British army prevailed and Quebec fell. The next year another British force moved up the Hudson and conquered Montreal. Its fall marked the end of the French empire in America.

In the final two years of the war the British swept French ships from the seas, conquered the Spanish colony of Cuba, captured the Spanish Philippines, and achieved dominance in India. In the 1763 **Treaty of Paris**, France lost all its possessions on the North American mainland, ceding to Great Britain all its claims east of the Mississippi, with the exception of New Orleans, which was passed to Spain, along with other French claims to the trans-Mississippi region. In exchange for the return of its Caribbean and Pacific colonies, Spain ceded Florida to Britain. Three centuries of European imperial rivalry in eastern North America ended with complete victory for the British Empire (see Map 6.2).

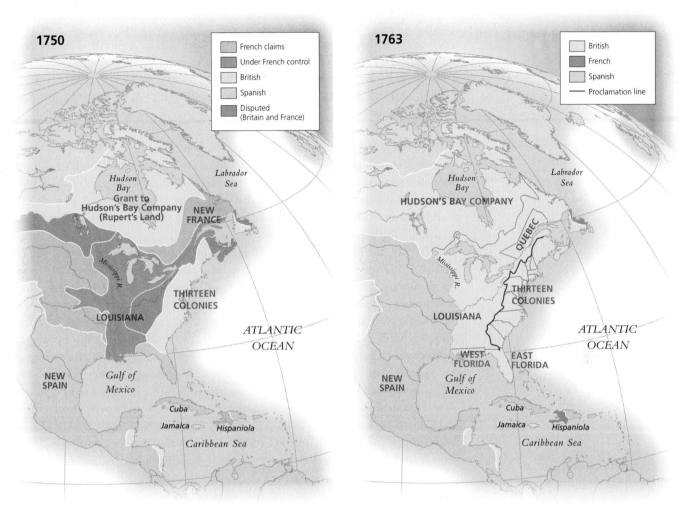

MAP 6.2
European Claims in North America, 1750 and 1763   As a result of the British victory in the Seven Years' War, the map of colonial claims in North America was fundamentally transformed.

HOW DID the balance of power in North America change between 1750 and 1763?

THE STRUGGLE FOR THE WEST

The Ohio Indians were shocked when told of the French cession. "The French had no right to give away [our] country," they responded. They were "never conquered by any nation." A new set of British policies soon shocked them even more. The French and the British had long used gift-giving as a way of gaining favor with Indians. Spanish officials who replaced the French in Louisiana continued that old policy. But in one of his first official acts, General Jeffery Amherst, British military governor of the western region, banned presents to Indian chiefs and tribes, demanding that they learn to live without "charity." Not only were Indians angered by Amherst's reversal of custom, but they were also frustrated by his refusal to supply them with the ammunition they needed for hunting. Many were left destitute.

In this climate, hundreds of Ohio Indians became disciples of an Indian visionary named Neolin ("The Enlightened One"), known to the English as the Delaware Prophet. The core of Neolin's teaching was that Indians had been corrupted by European ways and needed to purify themselves by returning to their traditions and

Royal Proclamation of 1763 Royal proclamation declaring the trans-Appalachian region to be "Indian Country."

3–10
The Closing of the Frontier
(1763)

preparing for a holy war. In the spring of 1763 a confederacy of tribes inspired by Neolin's ideas laid plans for a coordinated attack on British frontier posts. The principal leader of this resistance was the Ottawa chief Pontiac, renowned as an orator and political leader. In May 1763 Pontiac's confederacy simultaneously attacked all British forts in the West, destroying eight but failing to take the key posts of Niagara, Detroit, and Pitt. Pontiac and his followers fought on for another year, but most Indians sued for peace.

They were encouraged by the announcement of the British **Royal Proclamation of 1763**, which declared the trans-Appalachian region to be "Indian Country." Specific authorization from the crown would be required for any purchase of these protected Indian lands. British colonists had expected that the removal of the French threat would allow them to move into the West. They were outraged that the British would award territory to mortal enemies who during the war had slaughtered more than 4,000 settlers.

In fact, the British proved unable and ultimately unwilling to prevent the westward migration that was to be a dynamic part of the colonization of British North America. Within a few years of the war, New Englanders by the thousands were moving into the northern Green Mountain district, known as Vermont. In the middle colonies, New York settlers pushed ever closer to the homeland of the Iroquois, while others settled within the protective radius of Fort Pitt in western Pennsylvania. Hunters, stock herders, and farmers crossed over the first range of the Appalachians in Virginia and North Carolina, planting pioneer communities in what are now the states of West Virginia and Tennessee. In response to demands by settlers and speculators, British authorities were soon pressing the Iroquois and Cherokees for cessions of land in Indian Country. No longer able to play off rival colonial powers, Indians were reduced to a choice between compliance and resistance. Weakened by the recent war, they chose to sign away lands.

The individual colonies were even more aggressive. Locked in a dispute with Pennsylvania about jurisdiction in the Ohio country, in 1773 Virginia governor John Murray, Earl of Dunmore, sent a force to occupy Fort Pitt. In 1774, in an attempt to gain legitimacy for his dispute with Pennsylvania, Dunmore provoked

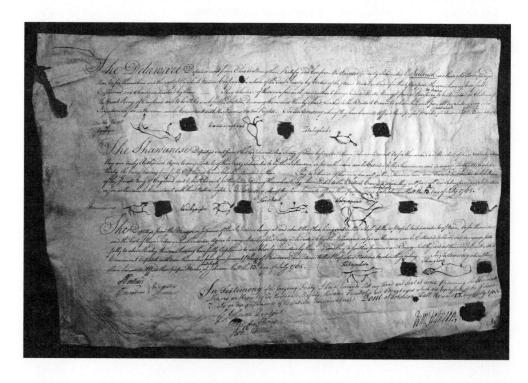

A treaty between the Delaware, Shawnee, and Mingo (western Iroquois) Indians and Great Britain, July 13, 1765, at the conclusion of the Indian uprising. The Indian chiefs signed with pictographs symbolizing their clans, each notarized with an official wax seal.

a frontier war with the Shawnees. After dealing them a humiliating defeat, Dunmore forced them to cede the upper Ohio River Valley to Virginia. The continuing struggle for the West would be an important issue in the coming Revolutionary struggle.

The Emergence of American Nationalism

No colonial power of the mid-eighteenth century could match Britain in projecting imperial power over the face of the globe. During the years following its victory in the Seven Years' War, Britain turned confidently to the reorganization of its North American empire. The new colonial policy plunged British authorities into a new and ultimately more threatening conflict with the colonists, who had begun to develop a sense of a separate identity.

An American Identity

Despite the anger of frontier settlers over the Proclamation of 1763, the conclusion of the Seven Years' War left most colonists proud of their place in the British Empire. But many people had begun to note important contrasts between themselves and the mother country. The arrival of thousands of British troops raised the problem of where to house them. British commanders demanded they be quartered in private homes. British subjects at home were protected against such demands by an act of Parliament, but that protection had expressly not been extended to the colonies.

Americans who were thrown into contact with regular British troops were shocked by their profanity, lewdness, and violence. They were equally shocked by the swift and terrible punishment inflicted by aristocratic officers to keep those men in line. A Massachusetts militiaman wrote of witnessing the punishment of two soldiers sentenced to eight hundred lashes apiece. Men who had witnessed such scenes found it easy to believe in the threat of British "slavery."

Colonial forces, by contrast, were composed of volunteer companies. Militia officers were moderate in the administration of punishment, knowing they had to maintain the enthusiasm of their troops. Discipline thus fell considerably below the standards to which British officers were accustomed. Many Americans believed the British ignored the important role they had played in the Seven Years' War. The mutual scorn and suspicion were sometimes expressed in name-calling. Regular soldiers derisively called New Englanders "Yankees," while colonists heckled the red-coated British as "lobsters." During the war many colonists began to view themselves as distinct from the British.

The Seven Years' War also strengthened a sense of intercolonial identity among the colonists. Farm boys who never before had ventured outside the communities of their birth fought in distant regions with men like themselves from other colonies. Such experiences reinforced a developing nationalist perspective and sense of national community. From 1735 to 1775, while trade with Great Britain doubled, commerce among the colonies quadrupled. People and ideas moved along with goods. The first stagecoach lines linking seaboard cities began operation in the 1750s. Spurred by Postmaster Benjamin Franklin, many colonies built or improved post roads for transporting the mails.

The Press, Politics, and Republicanism

One of the most important means of intercolonial communication was the weekly newspaper. Newspapers became a lively means of public discourse, and by 1760 more than twenty weekly papers were being published in the British colonies.

WHAT FACTORS led to the growth of American nationalism in the 1760s?

myhistorylab
Review Summary

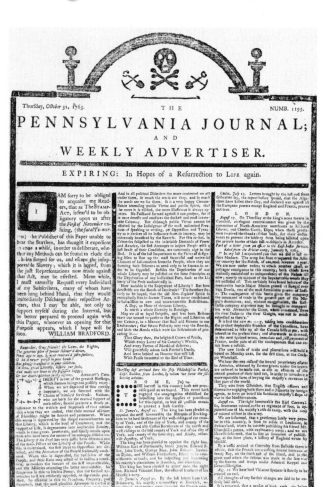

A protest against the Stamp Act from newspaper editor William Bradford, publisher of *The Pennsylvania Journal and Weekly Advertiser*. Bradford decorated his masthead with skull and crossbones, reproduced a satiric version of "the fatal Stamp," also with skull and crossbones, and included the note, "The TIMES are Dreadful, Dismal, Doleful, Dolorous, and Dollar-less." The text below is an open letter from Bradford to his readers.

The papers carried an increasing amount of colonial news. From the 1730s to the 1770s intercolonial coverage in the colonial press increased sixfold. Editors began to look at events from what they called a "continental" perspective. The trend accelerated during the Seven Years' War, when communities demanded news of the distant places where their men were fighting. The war promoted a new spirit of nationalism and a wider notion of community. Editors began using the term "American" to denote the common identity of British colonists. It was an early sign of the political community the delegates began to construct at the First Continental Congress.

Colonial editors frequently reprinted writings by British authors, poems by Alexander Pope, satiric essays by Jonathan Swift, and political philosophy by John Locke. They frequently reprinted essays by British republicans, who warned of the growing threat to liberty posed by the unchecked exercise of government power. Some essayists suggested that a conspiracy existed among European monarchs, aristocrats, and Catholics to quash liberty and reinstitute tyranny. These ideas came to define a political consensus in the British colonies, a point of view called "**republicanism**."

Republicanism asserted that state power, by its very nature, was antithetical to liberty and, consequently, must be limited. The authority of rulers should be conditional rather than absolute, and the people had the inherent right to draw up their own form of government and to withdraw their support if it did not fulfill their expectations. The best guarantee of good government was the broad distribution of power to the people, who could not only select their own leaders but also vote them out of office. Republican government depended on the virtue of the people, on their willingness to make the stability and justice of the political community their first priority. But that kind of virtue was possible only for an "independent" population that controlled its own affairs.

This was a political theory that fit well with the circumstances of American life, with its wide base of property ownership, its tradition of representative assemblies, and its history of struggle with royal authority. Contrast the assumptions of republicans with those of British monarchists, who argued that the good society was one in which a strong state, controlled by a hereditary elite, kept a vicious and unruly people in line.

Republicanism A complex, changing body of ideas, values, and assumptions that influenced American political behavior during the eighteenth and nineteenth centuries.

Sugar Act Law passed in 1764 to raise revenue in the American colonies. It lowered the duty from 6 pence to 3 pence per gallon on foreign molasses imported into the colonies and increased the restrictions on colonial commerce.

 ## THE SUGAR AND STAMP ACTS

The emerging sense of American political identity was soon tested by British measures designed to raise revenues in the colonies. To quell Indian uprisings and stifle discontent among the French and Spanish populations of Quebec and Florida, the British kept 10,000 regular troops stationed in North America at the conclusion of the war. The cost of maintaining this force added to the enormous debt run up during the fighting. In 1764 Prime Minister George Grenville decided to obtain the needed revenue from America, and Parliament passed a measure known as the **Sugar Act**, which placed a tariff on sugar imported into the colonies.

Anticipating that American importers would attempt to avoid the duty by smuggling, Parliament broadened the jurisdiction of the vice-admiralty court at

Halifax, which had jurisdiction over customs cases. Courts of vice-admiralty were hated and feared because they neither provided for trial by jury nor acted on the presumption of innocence. Both merchants and artisans viewed the Sugar Act as a threat to their livelihoods, and there were public protests in many port towns. Boston was especially vocal. The town meeting proposed a boycott of certain English imports, and the tactic of nonimportation soon spread to other port towns.

James Otis, a brilliant Massachusetts lawyer, became one of the first Americans to give voice to these protests, striking a number of themes that were repeated many times over the next fifteen years. Every man, Otis declared in rhetoric lifted directly from the Great Awakening, "was an independent sovereign, subject to no law but the law written on his heart and revealed to him by his Maker." No government, he argued in the tradition of the radical **Whigs**, could rightfully deprive a man of the right "to his life, his liberty, and his property." His most memorable phrase would echo for the next decade: "Taxation without representation is tyranny."

THE STAMP ACT CRISIS

Wasn't it only fair, Prime Minister Grenville responded, that the colonists help pay the costs of the empire? And what better way to do so than by taxation? Although colonial assemblies had raised taxes during the war, colonial tax rates remained significantly lower than rates in the mother country. Ignoring American protests, in early 1765 Grenville pushed through a considerably more sweeping revenue measure known as the **Stamp Act**. This legislation required the purchase of specially embossed paper for all newspapers, legal documents, licenses, insurance policies, ship's papers, even dice and playing cards. It affected nearly every colonial resident in one way or another.

The American reaction to the Stamp Act during the summer and autumn of 1765 created a crisis of unprecedented proportions. The stamped paper had to be purchased with hard money, and it came during a period of economic stagnation. Many colonists complained of being "miserably burdened and oppressed with taxes." But constitutional objections had more importance over the long term. Although colonial male property owners elected their own assemblies, they could not vote in British elections and had no representatives in Parliament. The British government argued that colonists were still subject to the acts of Parliament because of what they termed "**virtual representation**." As one British conservative put it, the colonists were "represented in Parliament in the same manner as those inhabitants of Britain are who have not voices in elections," such as women, children, and servants.

Americans did not take well to the comparison. Just such constitutional issues were emphasized in the Virginia Stamp Act Resolutions, written by Patrick Henry, a passionate young backcountry lawyer and member of the House of Burgesses. Although his colleagues rejected the most radical of Henry's resolutions, all of them were reprinted in the colonial press. By the end of 1765 the assemblies of eight other colonies had approved similar measures denouncing the Stamp Act and proclaiming their support of "no taxation without representation."

The most violent protests took place in Boston. The city's elite had prospered over the previous decade, but conditions for workers and the poor had worsened. Unemployment, inflation, and high taxes greatly increased the level of poverty during the depression following the Seven Years' War. Ordinary Bostonians were resentful. Their discontent was channeled by Samuel Adams, the son of a brewer, who became a powerful local politician. Adams was a leader of the anti-British alliance spanning Boston's social classes. In the late summer of 1765 he and his associates organized a protest of Boston workingmen.

5–2
James Otis, *The Rights of the British Colonies Asserted and Proved* (1763)

Exploring America: *The Stamp Act*

4–3
Benjamin Franklin, *Testimony Against the Stamp Act* (1766)

4–4
John Dickinson, *Letters from a Farmer in Pennsylvania* (1767)

Whigs The name used by advocates of colonial resistance to British measures during the 1760s and 1770s.

Stamp Act Law passed by Parliament in 1765 to raise revenue in America by requiring taxed, stamped paper for legal documents, publications, and playing cards.

Virtual representation The notion that parliamentary members represented the interests of the nation as a whole, not those of the particular district that elected them.

Samuel Adams, a second cousin of John Adams, was a leader of the Boston radicals and an organizer of the Sons of Liberty. The artist of this portrait, John Singleton Copley, was known for setting his subjects in the midst of everyday objects; here he portrays Adams in a middle-class suit with the charter guaranteeing the liberties of Boston's freemen.

John Singleton Copley (1738–1815), "Samuel Adams," ca. 1772. Oil on canvas, 49 1/2 × 39 1/2 in. (125.7 cm × 100.3 cm). Deposited by the City of Boston, 30.76c. Courtesy, Museum of Fine Arts, Boston. Reproduced with permission. © 2000 Museum of Fine Arts, Boston. All Rights Reserved.

On August 14 a large crowd assembled near Boston Common, and in an old elm, known as the "Liberty Tree," strung up effigies of several British officials, including Boston's stamp distributor, Andrew Oliver. The restless crowd then invaded and vandalized Oliver's office as well as his home. Soon thereafter, Oliver resigned his commission. Several days later another mob broke into the mansion of Thomas Hutchinson, lieutenant governor of the colony. During the fall and winter, urban crowds protested in port towns from Halifax in the north to Savannah in the south (see Map 6.3). Growing alarmed at the rising potential for violence, merchants, lawyers, and respectable craftsmen seized control of the resistance movement. Calling themselves the **Sons of Liberty**, these leaders encouraged more moderate forms of protest, such as circulating petitions and publishing pamphlets. Always they emphasized limited political goals. There were few repetitions of mob attacks, but by the end of 1765 almost all the stamp distributors had resigned or fled, making it impossible for Britain to enforce the Stamp Act. Pressured by British merchants, worried over the effects of the growing **nonimportation movement** among the colonists, in March 1766 Parliament repealed the Stamp Act and reduced the duties under the Sugar Act. This news was greeted with celebrations throughout the American colonies.

Overlooked in the mood of optimism, however, was the fact that repeal was coupled with what was termed a "**Declaratory Act**," in which Parliament affirmed its full authority to make laws binding the colonies "in all cases whatsoever." The Declaratory Act signaled that the conflict between the mother country and the colonies had not been resolved but merely postponed.

HOW DID political and economic problems in Britiain contribute to unrest in the colonies?

myhistorylab

Review Summary

Sons of Liberty Secret organizations in the colonies formed to oppose the Stamp Act.

Nonimportation movement A tactical means of putting economic pressure on Britain by refusing to buy its exports to the colonies.

Declaratory Act Law passed in 1776 to accompany repeal of the Stamp Act that stated that Parliament had the authority to legislate for the colonies "in all cases whatsoever."

"SAVE YOUR MONEY AND SAVE YOUR COUNTRY"

Colonial resistance to the Stamp Act was stronger in urban than in rural communities, stronger among merchants, craftsmen, and planters than among farmers and frontiersmen. When Parliament next moved to impose its will, as it had promised to do in the Declaratory Act, the American opposition again adopted the tactic of nonimportation. But this time resistance spread from the cities and towns into the countryside. As the editor of the *Boston Gazette* phrased the issue, "Save your money and you save your country." It became the slogan of the movement.

THE TOWNSHEND REVENUE ACTS

The foremost problem facing the new British government in the mid-1760s was the national debt. Britain suffered massive unemployment, riots over high prices, and tax protests. Fearing opposition at home more than the protest in the colonies, in June 1767 Charles Townshend, Chancellor of the Exchequer, proposed a new series of **Revenue Acts** placing tariffs on the importation of commodities such as lead, glass, paint, paper, and tea into the colonies.

The most influential colonial response came in a series of articles by wealthy Philadelphia lawyer John Dickinson, which were reprinted in nearly every colonial newspaper. Posing as a humble farmer, Dickinson argued that Parliament had no constitutional authority to tax goods in order to raise revenue in America. Other Americans warned that the Revenue Acts were part of a British conspiracy to suppress American liberties. Their fears were reinforced by stringent enforcement.

In response some colonists argued for violent resistance. But it was Dickinson's essays that had the greatest effect on the public debate, not only because of their convincing arguments but also because of their mild and reasonable tone. "Let us behave like dutiful children," Dickinson urged, "who have received unmerited blows from a beloved parent." No sentiment for independence yet existed in the British colonies.

AN EARLY POLITICAL BOYCOTT

In October 1767 the Boston town meeting revived the tactic of nonimportation, drawing up a long list of British products to boycott. Over the next few months other port cities, including Providence, Newport, and New York, set up nonimportation campaigns of their own. Artisans took to the streets in towns and cities throughout the colonies to force merchants to stop importing British goods. Coercion was very much a part of the movement, and occasionally there was violence.

Protestors formed "nonimportation associations," pledging to curtail luxuries and stimulate local industry. These aims had great appeal in small towns and rural districts, which previously had been uninvolved in the anti-British struggle. In 1768 and 1769 colonial newspapers paid a great deal of attention to women's support for the boycott. "The industry and frugality of American ladies," wrote the editor of the *Boston Evening Post*, "are contributing to bring about the political salvation of a whole continent."

Nonimportation was greatly strengthened in May 1769 when the Virginia House of Burgesses enacted the first provincial legislation banning the importation of goods enumerated in the Townshend Acts. Over the next few months all the colonies but New Hampshire enacted similar legislation. Because of these efforts, the value of colonial imports from Britain declined by 41 percent.

THE MASSACHUSETTS CIRCULAR LETTER

Boston and Massachusetts were at the center of the agitation over the Townshend Revenue Acts. In February 1768 the Massachusetts House of Representatives approved a letter addressed to the speakers of the other colonial assemblies. The letter denounced the Revenue Acts, attacked the British plan to make royal officials independent of colonial assemblies, and urged the colonies to find a way to "harmonize with each other." Massachusetts governor Francis Bernard condemned the document for stirring up rebellion and dissolved the legislature. In Britain, Lord Hillsborough, secretary of state for the colonies, ordered each royal governor in America to dissolve his colony's assembly if it should endorse the letter. Before this

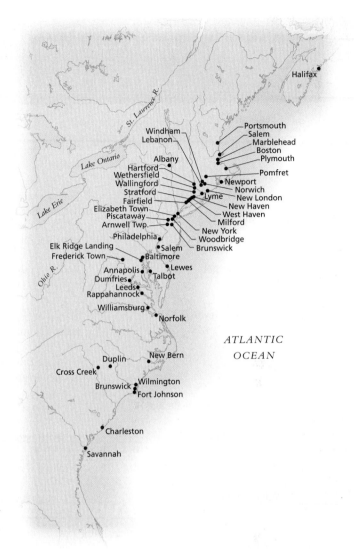

MAP 6.3
Demonstrations Against the Stamp Act, 1765 Popular demonstrations against the Stamp Act forced the resignation of British tax officials.

WHAT GROUPS in British North America were most opposed to the Stamp Act?

Townshend Revenue Acts Act of Parliament, passed in 1767, imposing duties on colonial tea, lead, paint, paper, and glass.

QUICK REVIEW

Resistance

♦ Response to the Sugar Act divided.

♦ 1764: New York and Boston merchants launch nonimportation movement.

♦ Response to Stamp Act overwhelming and intense.

OVERVIEW | Eleven British Measures that Led to Revolution

Year	Legislation	
1764	**Sugar Act**	Placed prohibitive duty on imported sugar; provided for greater regulation of American shipping to suppress smuggling
1765	**Stamp Act**	Required the purchase of specially embossed paper for newspapers, legal documents, licenses, insurance policies, ships' papers, and playing cards; struck at printers, lawyers, tavern owners, and other influential colonists. Repealed in 1766
1766	**Declaratory Act**	Asserted the authority of Parliament to make laws binding the colonies "in all cases whatsoever"
1767	**Townshend Revenue Acts**	Placed import duties, collectible before goods entered colonial markets, on many commodities including lead, glass, paper, and tea. Repealed in 1770
1773	**Tea Act**	Gave the British East India Company a monopoly on all tea imports to America, hitting at American merchants
1774	**Coercive or Intolerable Acts**	
	Boston Port Bill	Closed Boston Harbor
	Massachusetts Government Act	Annulled the Massachusetts colonial charter
	Administration of Justice Act	Protected British officials from colonial courts by sending them home for trial if arrested
	Quartering Act	Legalized the housing of British troops in private homes
	Quebec Act	Created a highly centralized government for Canada

myhistorylab

Overview: *Eleven British Measures that Led to Revolution*

4–6
The Boston "Massacre" or Victims of Circumstance (1770)

demand reached America, the assemblies of New Hampshire, New Jersey, and Connecticut had commended Massachusetts. Virginia, moreover, had issued a circular letter encouraging a "hearty union" among the colonies and urging common action against the British measures that "have an immediate tendency to enslave us."

Throughout this crisis there were rumors and threats of mob rule in Boston. Fearful of insurrection, on October 1, 1768, the British occupied Boston with infantry and artillery regiments. This action added greatly to the growing tensions.

THE BOSTON MASSACRE

British troops stationed in the colonies were the object of scorn and hostility over the next two years. There were regular conflicts between soldiers and radicals in New York City, often focusing on protests organized by the Sons of Liberty. In Boston Sam Adams played up each and every rumor of soldiers harassing women, picking fights with men, or simply taunting residents with versions of "Yankee Doodle." There were a number of violent confrontations.

A persistent source of conflict was the competition between troops and townsmen over jobs. Soldiers were permitted to work when they were off-duty, thus competing with poor day laborers. In early March 1770 a British soldier walked into a Boston rope-walk in search of a job. "You can clean my shit-house," the owner told him. The soldier returned later with his friends and a small riot resulted. Over the next few days sporadic fighting between soldiers and townsmen continued. Finally, on the evening of March 5, 1770, a crowd at the Customs House began taunting a guard, calling him a "damned rascally scoundrel lobster" and worse. A captain and a company of seven soldiers went to his rescue, only to be pelted with snowballs and stones. Suddenly someone shouted "Fire!" and the frightened soldiers shot indiscriminately into the crowd. Five men fell dead and six more were wounded, two dying later. The soldiers escaped to their barracks, but a mob numbering in the hundreds rampaged through the streets demanding vengeance.

What became known as "the **Boston Massacre**" was soon infamous throughout the colonies. For many colonists the incident was a disturbing reminder of the extent to which relations with the mother country had deteriorated. During the next two years many people found themselves pulling back from the brink.

The growth of American resistance was slowed as well by the news that Parliament had repealed most of the Revenue Acts on March 5—the same day as the Boston Massacre. In the climate of apprehension and confusion, there were few celebrations of the repeal, and the non-importation associations almost immediately collapsed. The parliamentary retreat on the question of duties, like the earlier repeal of the Stamp Act, was accompanied by a face-saving measure—retention of the tax on tea.

In Paul Revere's version of the Boston Massacre, issued three weeks after the incident, the British fire an organized volley into a defenseless crowd. Revere's print—which he plagiarized from another Boston engraver—may have been inaccurate, but it was enormously effective propaganda. It hung in so many Patriot homes that the judge hearing the murder trial of these British soldiers warned the jury not to be swayed by "the prints exhibited in our houses."

FROM RESISTANCE TO REBELLION

There was a lull in the American controversy during the early 1770s, but the situation turned violent once more in 1773, when Parliament again infuriated the Americans. This time it was an ill-advised tax on tea, and it propelled the colonists onto a swift track from resistance to outright rebellion.

COMMITTEES OF CORRESPONDENCE

In June 1772, Governor Hutchinson of Massachusetts inaugurated another controversy by announcing that henceforth his salary and those of other royally appointed officials would be paid by the crown. In effect this made the executive and judiciary branches of the colony's government independent of control by elected representatives. In October, the Boston town meeting appointed a committee of correspondence to communicate with other communities regarding this challenge.

WHAT STEPS did Britain take to punish Massachusetts for the colonists' acts of resistance?

myhistorylab
Review Summary

Boston Massacre   After months of increasing friction between townspeople and the British troops stationed in the city, on March 5, 1770, British troops fired on American civilians in Boston.

In March 1773 the Virginia House of Burgesses appointed a standing committee of correspondence. The Virginia committee served as a model for the other colonies, and within a year all but Pennsylvania (where conservatives were in control of the legislature) had created committees of their own. The committees of correspondence became the principal channel for sharing information, shaping public opinion, and building cooperation among the colonies before the opening meeting of the First Continental Congress in 1774.

The information most damaging to British influence came from the radicals in Boston. In June 1773 the Boston committee circulated a set of confidential letters from Governor Hutchinson to the ministry in Britain. The letters revealed Hutchinson's call for "an abridgment of what are called English liberties" in the colonies. "I wish to see some further restraint of liberty," he had written, "rather than the connection with the parent state should be broken." This statement seemed to be the "smoking gun" of the conspiracy theory, and it created a torrent of anger against the British and their officials in the colonies.

THE BOSTON TEA PARTY

4–7
John Andrews, *Letter Regarding the Boston Tea Party* (1773)

4–12
Jonathan Boucher, *An Anglican Preacher Denounces the American Rebels* (1775)

It was in this context that the colonists received the news that Parliament had passed the **Tea Act**. Colonists were major consumers of tea, typically drinking from five to ten cups a day. But because of the Townshend duties the market for tea had collapsed. The British East India Company, the sole agent of British power in India, was on the brink of bankruptcy. Parliament would not allow it to fail and devised a scheme to offer tea to Americans at prices that would tempt even the most patriotic drinker. The radicals argued that this was merely a device to make palatable the payment of unconstitutional taxes and further evidence of the British effort to seduce and corrupt the colonists.

In October 1773 a mass meeting in Philadelphia denounced anyone importing the tea as "an enemy of his country." A group calling itself "the Committee for Tarring and Feathering" published a poster, plastered all over the city, asking if the captains of ships carrying the tea might like "ten gallons of liquid tar decanted on your pate—with the feathers of a dozen wild geese laid over that to enliven your appearance." The Philadelphia consignees resigned in terror. Similar protests in New York City forced resignations there as well. The town meeting in Boston soon passed resolutions patterned on those of Philadelphia.

The first of three tea ships arrived in Boston Harbor late in November. Mass meetings in Old South Church, including many country people drawn to the scene of the crisis, resolved to keep the tea from being unloaded. On the evening of December 16, 1773, a disciplined group of fifty or sixty men, including farmers, artisans, merchants, professionals, and apprentices, marched to the wharf. Dressed as Indians and cheered on by Boston's citizens, they boarded the ships and dumped into the harbor some forty-five tons of tea, valued at £18,000. Boston's was the first tea party, and other incidents of property destruction soon followed. But it was the initial action in Boston that infuriated the British. The government became convinced that something had to be done about the rebellious colony of Massachusetts. Strong measures were required, King George III (reigned 1760–1820) wrote to Lord North, for "we are now to dispute whether we have, or have not, any authority in that country."

THE INTOLERABLE ACTS

During the spring of 1774 an angry Parliament passed a series of acts—officially called the **Coercive Acts** but known by Americans as the **Intolerable Acts**—calculated to punish the colony of Massachusetts and strengthen the British

Tea Act   Act of Parliament that permitted the East India Company to sell through agents in America without paying the duty customarily collected in Britain, thus reducing the retail price.

Boston Tea Party   Incident that occurred on December 16, 1773, in which Bostonians, disguised as Indians, destroyed £18,000 worth of tea belonging to the British East India Company in order to prevent payment of the duty on it.

Coercive Acts   Legislation passed by Parliament in 1774; included the Boston Port Act, the Massachusetts Government Act, the Administration of Justice Act, and the Quartering Act of 1774.

Intolerable Acts   American term for the Coercive Acts and the Quebec Act.

The Bostonians Paying the Excise-Man, or Tarring and Feathering

Political cartoons played an important role in the public controversy leading to the American Revolution. This print, published in London in 1774 and sold on the streets for a few pennies, depicts the violent attack of a Boston mob on customs commissioner John Malcolm several weeks after the "Tea Party." Malcolm, an ardent Loyalist, had been the frequent target of protests. That night a mob dragged Malcolm from his house and covered him with tar and feathers, a ritual of public humiliation. Hot tar produced painful blistering of the skin, and the effort to remove it made the condition worse. The feathers made the victim into an object of ridicule. Hauled to the Liberty Tree in Boston Common, Malcolm was threatened with hanging if he did not apologize and renounce his commission. When he did he was allowed to return home. The pro-Loyalist print includes a number of telling details. Malcolm is attacked by a group that includes a leather-aproned artisan. A broadside announcing the Stamp Act is posted upside down on the Liberty Tree. A hangman's noose dangles from a branch. The Boston Tea Party takes place in the background. In the foreground is a tar bucket and a pole topped by a "liberty cap," a symbol of freedom adopted by American protesters (and later an icon of the French Revolution). These details were intended to mock the Americans. But when the print found its way to North America it was embraced by Patriots and became an enduring American favorite. In the nineteenth century it was reprinted as a celebration of the righteous violence of the Revolution. ■

HOW COULD this image, intended to ridicule and shame the American patriots, have been embraced and celebrated by them?

Philip Dawe, "The BOSTONIANS Paying the EXCISE-MAN, or TARRING & FEATHERING" (1774).

MAP EXPLORATION
To explore an interactive version of this map, go to
http://www.prenhall.com/faraghertlc/map6.4

MAP 6.4
The Quebec Act of 1774 With the Quebec Act, Britain created a centralized colonial government for Canada.

HOW DID the boundaries set by the Quebec Act of 1774 contribute to rising tensions between the colonists and imperial authorities?

QUICK REVIEW

The Intolerable Acts

◆ Boston Port Bill.
◆ Massachusetts Government Act.
◆ Administration of Justice Act.
◆ Quartering Act.
◆ Quebec Act.

Quartering Act Acts of Parliament requiring colonial legislatures to provide supplies and quarters for the troops stationed in America.

Quebec Act Law passed by Parliament in 1774 that provided an appointed government for Canada, enlarged the boundaries of Quebec, and confirmed the privileges of the Catholic Church.

hand. The Boston Port Bill prohibited the loading or unloading of ships in any part of Boston Harbor until the town fully compensated the East India Company and the customs service for the destroyed tea. The Massachusetts Government Act annulled the colonial charter. Town meetings, an important institution of the resistance movement, were prohibited from convening more than once a year except with the approval of the governor, who was placed in control of their agendas. With these acts, the British terminated the long history of self-rule by communities in the colony of Massachusetts.

Additional measures affected the other colonies and encouraged them to see themselves in league with suffering Massachusetts. The Administration of Justice Act protected British officials from colonial courts, thereby encouraging them to pursue the work of suppression. Those accused of committing capital crimes while putting down riots or collecting revenue were now to be sent to England for trial. The **Quartering Act** legalized the housing of troops at public expense not only in taverns and abandoned buildings but also in occupied dwellings and private homes.

Finally, in the **Quebec Act**, the British authorized a permanent government for the territory taken from France during the Seven Years' War: a strictly antirepublican government with an appointed council (see Map 6.4). To the American colonists it seemed a frightening preview of what imperial authorities had in store for them, and it confirmed the contention of the committees of correspondence that there was a British plot to destroy American liberty.

THE FIRST CONTINENTAL CONGRESS

It was amid this crisis that town meetings and colonial assemblies alike chose representatives for the **First Continental Congress**. The delegates who arrived in Philadelphia in September 1774 included the most important leaders of the American cause. Cousins Samuel and John Adams from Massachusetts were joined by Patrick Henry and George Washington of Virginia and Christopher Gadsden of South Carolina. Many of the delegates were conservatives, including John Dickinson and Joseph Galloway of Philadelphia, and John Jay and James Duane from New York. With the exception of Gadsden, a hothead who proposed an attack on British forces in Boston, the delegates wished to avoid war and favored a policy of economic coercion.

After one of their first debates, the delegates passed a Declaration and Resolves, in which they asserted that all the colonists sprang from a common tradition and enjoyed rights guaranteed "by the immutable laws of nature, the principles of the English constitution, and the several charters or compacts" of their provinces. Thirteen acts of Parliament, passed since 1763, were declared in violation of these rights. Until these acts were repealed, the delegates pledged, they would impose a set of sanctions against the British. These would include not only the nonimportation and nonconsumption of British goods but also a prohibition on the export of colonial commodities to Britain or its other colonies.

To enforce these sanctions, the Continental Congress urged that "a committee be chosen in every county, city, and town, by those who are qualified to vote for representatives in the legislature, whose business it shall be attentively to observe the conduct of all persons." Known as the committees of observation and safety, these groups took over the functions of local government throughout the colonies. By dissolving the colonial legislatures, royal governors had unwittingly aided the work of these committees. Throughout most of the colonies the committees formed a bridge between the old colonial administrations and the revolutionary governments organized over the next few years. Committees began to link localities together in the cause of a wider American community.

LEXINGTON AND CONCORD

On September 1, 1774, General Thomas Gage sent troops to seize stores of gunpowder and arms from several storehouses on the outskirts of Boston. In response, the Massachusetts House of Representatives, calling itself the Provincial Congress, created a committee of safety empowered to call up the militia. On October 15 the committee authorized the creation of special units, to be known as "minutemen," who stood ready to be called at a moment's notice. The armed militia of the towns and communities surrounding Boston faced the British army, quartered in the city. The stalemate continued throughout the fall and winter.

British monarch George III believed the time for war had come. "The New England Governments are in a State of Rebellion," he wrote privately, "blows must decide whether they are to be subject to this Country or independent." In Virginia, at almost the same moment, Patrick Henry predicted that hostilities soon would begin. Three weeks later, on April 14, 1775, General Gage received instructions to immediately strike against the Massachusetts militia.

On the evening of April 18, Gage ordered 700 troops to Concord, some miles outside Boston, to take possession of the armory there. Learning of the operation, the Boston committee dispatched two men, Paul Revere and William Dawes, to alert the militia of the countryside. By the time the British forces had reached Lexington, midway to their destination, some seventy armed minutemen had assembled on the green in the center of town, but they were disorganized and confused. In the fact of what appeared overwhelming force, the Americans began to withdraw with their arms. No order to fire was given, but suddenly shots rang out. Eight Americans were killed, ten wounded.

The British marched on to Concord where they burned a small quantity of supplies and cut down a liberty pole. Meanwhile, news of the skirmish at Lexington had spread throughout the country, and the militia companies from communities from miles around converged on the town. At Concord bridge they encountered the enemy and opened fire. Three soldiers were killed, the first British casualties. Seeing that their men were greatly outnumbered by Massachusetts militia, British officers immediately ordered a return to Boston, but at many points along the way they were subjected to withering fire

First Continental Congress Meeting of delegates from most of the colonies held in 1774 in response to the Coercive Acts.

QUICK REVIEW

Congressional Response to the Intolerable Acts

- All agreed that Acts were unconstitutional.
- A minority prepared to go to war with Britain.
- Most delegates thought of the interests of their own colony first.

 5–7
Joseph Warren, *Account of the Battle of Lexington* (1775)

 5–3
William Legge, *The Crisis Comes to a Head* (1775)

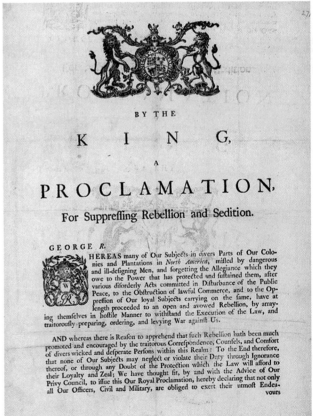

Ignoring the Olive Branch Petition from the Continental Congress, on August 23, 1775, King George III issued this Proclamation, declaring that the colonies stood in open rebellion to his authority and were subject to severe penalty, as was any British subject who failed to report the knowledge of rebellion or conspiracy. This document literally transformed loyal subjects into traitorous rebels.

(see Map 6.5). The engagement forecast what would be a central problem for the British: they would be forced to fight an armed population defending their own communities against outsiders.

DECIDING FOR INDEPENDENCE

WHO MADE up the second Continental Congress and why was it formed?

Review Summary

"We send you momentous intelligence," read the letter reporting the violence received by the committee of correspondence in Charleston, South Carolina, on May 8, 1775. Throughout the colonies community militia companies mobilized for war. At Boston, thousands of militiamen besieged the city, leaving the British no escape but by sea. The siege would last for nearly a year. Meanwhile, delegates from twelve colonies converged again on Philadelphia.

THE SECOND CONTINENTAL CONGRESS

The Second Continental Congress, which opened on May 10, 1775, included representatives from twelve of the British colonies on the mainland of North America. Few conservatives or Loyalists were among them. Georgia, unrepresented at the First Continental Congress, remained absent at the opening of the Second. But in 1775 the political balance in Georgia shifted in favor of the radicals, and by the end of the summer the colony had delegates in Philadelphia.

On May 15 the representatives resolved to put the colonies in a state of defense but were divided on how best to do it. They lacked the power and the funds to raise and supply an army. John Adams made the winning proposal that they simply designate as a Continental Army the militia forces besieging Boston. In order to emphasize their national aspirations, they decided to select a man from the South to command these New England forces. On June 15 Jefferson and Adams nominated George Washington to be commander-in-chief, and he was elected by acclaim. Washington served without salary. On June 22, in a highly significant move, the Congress voted to finance the army with an issue of $2 million in bills of credit, backed by the good faith of the "Confederated Colonies." Thus began the long and complicated process of financing the Revolution.

During the early summer of 1775 the Congress began to move cautiously toward independence. Few would admit, even to themselves, that this was their goal. Before the Second Continental Congress adjourned at the beginning of August, the delegates appointed commissioners to negotiate with the Indian nations in an attempt to keep them out of the conflict.

QUICK REVIEW

The Second Continental Congress

- Opened on May 10, 1775.
- May 15: Congress resolved to put the colonies in a state of defense.
- June 15: George Washington nominated to be commander-in-chief.

CANADA AND THE SPANISH BORDERLANDS

How did the rest of North America react to the coming conflict? The Continental Congress made contact with leaders of all the British colonies. In one of their first acts, delegates called on "the oppressed inhabitants of Canada" to join in the struggle for "common liberty." When the Canadians failed to respond positively and immediately, the Congress reversed itself and voted to authorize a military expedition against Quebec to eliminate any possibility of a British invasion from that quarter, thus killing any chance of the Canadians joining the anti-British cause. This set a course toward the development of the separate nations of the United States and Canada.

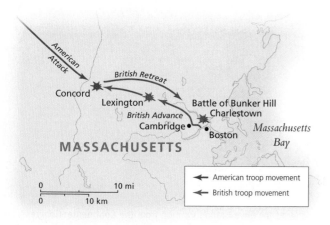

MAP 6.5
The First Engagements of the Revolution   The first military engagements of the American Revolution took place in the spring of 1775 in the countryside surrounding Boston.

In the British island colonies, there was at first considerable sympathy for the American struggle. The island colonies, however, would remain aloof from the imperial crisis, largely because the colonists there were dependent on a British military presence to guard against slave revolts. Things at first seemed more promising in Nova Scotia (not then a part of Canada), where many New Englanders had relocated after the expulsion of the Acadians. The British naval stronghold at Halifax, however, secured the province for the empire. Large contingents of British troops also kept Florida (which Britain had divided into two colonies, East and West Florida) solidly in the empire.

In Cuba, some 3,000 exiled Spanish Floridians, who had fled there in 1763 rather than live under British rule, now clamored for Spain to take advantage of the situation and retake their homeland. Many of them were active supporters of American independence.

In 1775 Spain publicly declared itself neutral but secretly searched for an opportunity to support the Americans. One presented itself in the late spring of 1776 when a contingent of Americans arrived in Spanish New Orleans via the Mississippi River bearing a proposal from patriot forces in Virginia. Would the Spanish be willing to quietly sell guns, ammunition, and other provisions to the Americans in New Orleans and allow them to be shipped by way of the Mississippi and Ohio Rivers? If the Spanish could be cooperative, the Americans might agree to a Spanish "protectorate" of the Floridas. The Spanish government eventually approved the plan, turning Havana and New Orleans into important supply centers for the Americans.

FIGHTING IN THE NORTH AND SOUTH

Violent conflict took place between British forces and American rebels in both the northern and southern colonies in 1775 and early 1776. On the evening of May 10, 1775, a small force of armed New Englanders jointly commanded by Ethan Allen of Vermont and Benedict Arnold of Connecticut surprised the

5–6
Petition of "A Grate Number of Blackes of the Province" to Governor Thomas Gage and the Members of the Massachusetts General Court (1774)

British garrison at Fort Ticonderoga on Lake Champlain. With great effort, the Americans hauled the fort's cannon overland to be used in the siege of Boston.

At Boston, the British reinforced Gage's forces, and by the middle of June had approximately 6,500 soldiers in the city. They were besieged by more than 10,000 New England militia. Fearing a move by Gage to occupy the heights south of town, the Americans made a countermove, occupying the Charlestown peninsula on the north. Gage decided on a frontal assault to dislodge them. In bloody fighting at Breed's and Bunker Hill, the British overran the Americans, killing 140 men, but not before suffering over a thousand casualties of their own, including 226 dead. The fierce patriotic reaction in England to this enormous loss ended any possibility of a last-minute reconciliation. In August 1775 King George issued a royal proclamation declaring the colonists in "open and avowed rebellion."

In June Congress assembled an expeditionary force against Canada. One thousand Americans moved north up the Hudson River corridor, and in November General Richard Montgomery forced the capitulation of Montreal. In the meantime Colonel Benedict Arnold set out from Massachusetts with another American army and, after a torturous march through the forests and mountains of Maine, joined Montgomery outside the walls of Quebec. But the American assault failed to take the city. Although Arnold held his position, the American siege was broken the following spring by British reinforcements. By the summer of 1776 the Americans had been forced back from Canada.

Elsewhere there were successes. In the South local militia rose against the Loyalist forces of Virginia's Governor Dunmore, who alienated the planter class by promising freedom to any slave who would fight with the British. After Dunmore was decisively defeated, he retreated to British naval vessels and shelled the city of Norfolk, nearly obliterating it. The next month the North Carolina rebel militia crushed a Loyalist force at the Battle of Moore's Creek Bridge near Wilmington, ending British plans for an invasion there. The British elected to attack Charleston, but an American force turned back the assault. It would be more than two years before the British would try to invade the South again. At Boston, Washington installed the captured British artillery on the heights south of town, placing the city and harbor within cannon range. The British had little choice but to evacuate. In March 1776 they sailed out of Boston Harbor heading northeast to Halifax, accompanied by at least a thousand American Loyalists.

No Turning Back

Hopes of reconciliation died with the mounting casualties. The Second Continental Congress, which was rapidly assuming the role of a general government for all the colonies (increasingly called states), reconvened in Philadelphia in September 1775, where the delegates received the royal proclamation that they were in open rebellion. Although the Congress continued to disclaim any intention of denying the sovereignty of the king, it now moved to organize an American navy. It declared British vessels open to capture and authorized privateering. The Congress took further steps toward independence when it authorized contacts with foreign powers through its agents in Europe. In the spring of 1776 France joined Spain in approving the shipping of supplies to the rebellious provinces. The Continental Congress then declared colonial ports open to the trade of all nations but Britain.

But the emotional ties to Great Britain proved difficult to break. Help arrived in January 1776 in the form of *Common Sense* written by Thomas Paine,

The Connecticut artist John Trumbull painted *The Battle of Bunker Hill* in 1785, the first of a series that earned him the informal title of "the Painter of the Revolution." Trumbull was careful to research the details of his paintings but composed them in the grand style of historical romance. In the early nineteenth century, he repainted this work and three other Revolutionary scenes for the rotunda of the Capitol in Washington, DC.

a radical Englishman recently arrived in Philadelphia. For years Americans had defended their actions by wrapping themselves in the mantle of British tradition. But Paine argued that the British system rested on "the base remains of two ancient tyrannies," aristocracy and monarchy, neither of which was appropriate for America. *Common Sense* was the single most important piece of writing during the Revolutionary era. It reshaped popular thinking and put independence squarely on the agenda.

In April, the North Carolina convention, operating as the revolutionary substitute for the old colonial assembly, became the first to empower its delegates to the Continental Congress to vote for independence. News that the British were recruiting a force of German mercenaries to use against the Americans provided an additional push toward what now began to seem inevitable. In May the Congress voted to recommend that the individual states move as quickly as possible toward the adoption of state constitutions. In the preamble to this statement John Adams wrote that "the exercise of every kind of authority under the said crown should be totally suppressed." This sent a strong signal that the delegates were on the verge of approving a momentous declaration.

THE DECLARATION OF INDEPENDENCE

On June 7, 1776, Richard Henry Lee of Virginia offered the first motion for independence. After some debate, a vote was postponed until July, but a committee composed of John Adams, Thomas Jefferson, Benjamin Franklin, Roger Sherman of Connecticut, and Robert Livingston of New York was asked to prepare

5–8
Thomas Jefferson, *"Original Rough Draught" of the Declaration of Independence* (1776)

5–11
The Declaration of Independence (1776)

The Manner in Which the American Colonies Declared Themselves INDEPENDENT of the King of ENGLAND, a 1783 English print. Understanding that the coming struggle would require the steady support of ordinary people, in the Declaration of Independence, the upper-class men of the Continental Congress asserted the right of popular revolution and the great principle of human equality.

5–9
Abigail Adams and John Adams, Letters on the Rights of Women in an Independent Republic (1776)

a draft declaration of American independence. The committee assigned the writing to Jefferson.

The intervening time allowed the delegates to debate and receive instructions from their state conventions. By the end of the month all the states but New York had authorized a vote for independence. When the question came up for debate again on July 1, a large majority supported independence. The final vote, taken on July 2, was twelve in favor of independence, none against, with New York abstaining. The delegates then turned to the declaration itself and made a number of changes in Jefferson's draft, striking out, for example, a long passage condemning slavery. In this and a number of other ways the final version was more cautious than the draft, but it was still a stirring document.

The central section of the Declaration reiterated the "long train of abuses and usurpations" on the part of George III that had led the Americans to their drastic course. But it was the first section that expressed the highest ideals of the delegates:

We hold these truths to be self-evident, that all men are created equal, that they are endowed by their creator with certain unalienable rights, that among these are life, liberty, and the pursuit of happiness. That to secure these rights, governments are instituted among men, deriving their just powers from the consent of the governed. That whenever any form of government becomes destructive of these ends, it is the right of the people to alter or to abolish it, and to institute a new government, laying its foundation on such principles, and organizing its powers in such form, as to them shall seem most likely to effect their safety and happiness.

There was very little debate in the Continental Congress about this extraordinary statement. The unanimity was the result of the widespread influence of Enlightenment and republican thought. Notably, there was no recourse to biblical authority. The delegates, mostly men of wealth and position, realized that the coming struggle for independence would require the steady support of ordinary people, and thus they asserted this great principle of equality and the right of revolution. The idea of equality would inspire the poor as well as the wealthy, women as well as men, blacks as well as whites.

By voting for independence, the delegates were not only proclaiming a belief in their newly conceived national community, but they were also committing treason against their king and empire. They would be condemned as traitors, hunted as criminals, and might stand on the scaffold in payment for their sentiments. On July 4, 1776, the Declaration of Independence was adopted without dissent.

CHRONOLOGY

1713	France cedes Acadia to Britain
1745	New Englanders capture Louisbourg
1749	French send an expeditionary force down the Ohio River
1753	French begin building forts from Lake Erie to the Ohio
1754	Albany Conference
1755	British General Edward Braddock defeated by a combined force of French and Indians
	Britain expels Acadians from Nova Scotia
1756	Seven Years' War begins in Europe
1757	William Pitt becomes prime minister
1758	Louisbourg captured by the British for the second time
1759	British capture Quebec
1763	Treaty of Paris
	Pontiac's uprising
	Proclamation of 1763 creates "Indian Country"
	Paxton Boys massacre

1764	Sugar Act
1765	Stamp Act and Stamp Act Congress
1766	Declaratory Act
1767	Townshend Revenue Acts
1768	Treaties of Hard Labor and Fort Stanwix
1770	Boston Massacre
1772	First Committee of Correspondence organized in Boston
1773	Tea Act
	Boston Tea Party
1774	Intolerable Acts
	First Continental Congress
	Dunmore's War
1775	Fighting begins at Lexington and Concord
	Second Continental Congress
1776	Americans invade Canada
	Thomas Paine's *Common Sense*
	Declaration of Independence

CONCLUSION

Great Britain emerged from the Seven Years' War as the dominant power in North America. Yet despite its attempts at strict regulation and determination of the course of events in its colonies, it faced consistent resistance. The British underestimated the political consensus that existed among the colonists about the importance of republican government. They also underestimated the ability of the colonists to inform one another, to work together, to build the bonds of national community cutting across boundaries of ethnicity, region, and economic condition. Through newspapers, pamphlets, committees of correspondence, community organizations, and group protest, the colonists discovered the concerns they shared, and in so doing fostered a new American identity. Without that identity it would have been difficult for them to consent to the treasonous act of declaring independence, especially when the independence they sought was from an international power that dominated much of the globe.

REVIEW QUESTIONS

1. How did overwhelming British success in the Seven Years' War lead to an imperial crisis in British North America?

2. Outline the changes in British policy toward the colonies from 1750 to 1776.

3. Trace the developing sense of an American national community over this same period.

4. What were the principal events leading to the beginning of armed conflict at Lexington and Concord?

5. How were the ideals of American republicanism expressed in the Declaration of Independence?

myhistorylab

Flashcard Review

KEY TERMS

Albany Conference (p. 129)	**Quebec Act** (p. 144)
Boston Massacre (p. 141)	**Republicanism** (p. 136)
Boston Tea Party (p. 142)	**Royal Proclamation of 1763** (p. 134)
Coercive Acts (p. 142)	**Sons of Liberty** (p. 138)
Declaratory Act (p. 138)	**Stamp Act** (p. 137)
First Continental Congress (p. 145)	**Sugar Act** (p. 136)
French and Indian War (p. 130)	**Tea Act** (p. 142)
Intolerable Acts (p. 142)	**Townshend Revenue Acts** (p. 139)
Nonimportation movement (p. 138)	**Treaty of Paris** (p. 132)
Plan of Union (p. 129)	**Virtual representation** (p. 137)
Quartering Act (p. 144)	**Whigs** (p. 137)

RECOMMENDED READING

Benedict Anderson, *Imagined Communities: Reflections on the Origin and Spread of Nationalism*, rev. ed. (1991). An argument that the essential first act of national consciousness is the effort to create a community that encompasses more than just local individuals and groups.

Fred Anderson, *The Crucible of War: The Seven Years' War and the Fate of Empire in British North America, 1754–1766* (2000). A new and powerful history of the war, arguing that it created a "hollow British empire."

Bernard Bailyn, *The Ideological Origins of the American Revolution* (1967). This classic argument emphasizes the role of ideas in the advent of the Revolution. Includes an analysis of American views of the imperial crisis.

Gregory Evans Dowd, *War Under Heaven: Pontiac, the Indian Nations, and the British Empire* (2002). Artfully crafted and gracefully written, this book restores Pontiac as a preeminent figure in the uprisings that bore his name.

Eric Foner, *Tom Paine and Revolutionary America* (1976). Combines a biography of Paine with a community study of the Revolution in Philadelphia and Pennsylvania.

Pauline Maier, *American Scripture: Making the Declaration of Independence* (1997). The deep background of this foundation of American democracy.

Richard L. Merritt, *Symbols of American Community, 1735–1775* (1966). A study of colonial newspapers that provides evidence for a rising sense of national community. The French and Indian War emerges as the key period for the growth of nationalist sentiment.

Gary B. Nash, *The Unknown American Revolution: The Unruly Birth of Democracy and the Struggle to Create America* (2005). A noted social historian focuses on the revolution's lesser-known freedom fighters.

Ray Raphael, *First American Revolution: Before Lexington and Concord* (2002). A vivid account of the turbulent days in Massachusetts from the time the province received word of the Massachusetts Government Act in August 1774 until the fighting broke out at Lexington and Concord the following April.

These are the times that try men's souls. . .
—Thomas Paine

UNITE OR DIE

The surrender of Lord Cornwallis at Yorktown on October 19, 1781, led to the British decision to withdraw from the war. Cornwallis, who claimed to be ill, absented himself from the ceremony and is not in the picture. Washington, who is astride the horse under the American flag, designated General Benjamin Lincoln (on the white horse in the center) as the one to accept the submission of a subordinate British officer. John Trumbull, who painted The Battle of Bunker Hill and some three hundred other scenes from the Revolutionary War, finished this painting while he was in London about fifteen years after the events depicted. A large copy of the work now hangs in the rotunda of the United States Capitol in Washington, D.C. Source: Surrender of Lord Cornwallis at Yorktown, by John Trumbull (American, 1756-1843). Oil on canvas, 20 7/8 × 30 5/8 in.

7

THE AMERICAN REVOLUTION
1776–1786

WHAT STRATEGIES and tactics did American forces employ in the war for independence?

WHAT CONCERNS were reflected in the terms of the Articles of Confederation?

HOW DID political debate in America change in the years after 1774?

AMERICAN COMMUNITIES

A National Community Evolves at Valley Forge

A DRUM ROLL ANNOUNCED THE DAWN OF A COLD JANUARY MORNING IN 1778. Along a two-mile line of rude log cabins, doors slowly opened and the ragged men of the Continental Army stepped out onto the frozen ground of Valley Forge. The reek of unwashed bodies and foul straw filled the air. "No bread, no soldier!" The chant began as a barely audible murmur, then was picked up by men all along the line. "No bread, no soldier! No bread, no soldier!" At last the chanting grew so loud it could be heard at General Washington's headquarters, a mile away. The 11,000 men of the American army were surviving on little more than "firecake," a mixture of flour and water baked hard before the fire. Two thousand men were without shoes; others were without blankets and had to sit up all night about the fires to keep from freezing. Washington fired off an appeal to the Continental Congress for supplies. "Three or four days of bad weather," he wrote, "would prove our destruction."

The hard winter at Valley Forge became a national symbol of endurance. After suffering a series of shattering defeats at the hands of a British force nearly twice their number, the soldiers of the Continental Army straggled into winter headquarters in this valley, some twenty miles northwest of Philadelphia, only to find themselves at the mercy of indifferent local suppliers. Congress refused to pay the exorbitant rates demanded by contractors for food and clothing. Local farmers preferred to deal with the British, who paid in pounds sterling rather than depreciated Continental currency.

The 11,000 men of the Continental Army were divided into sixteen brigades composed of regiments from the individual states. Many were drawn from the ranks of the poor and disadvantaged. They included landless tenant farmers, indentured servants, and nearly a thousand African Americans, both slave and free. A majority of the men came from rural districts or small towns. Some 2,500 men died that winter. The women encamped at Valley Forge—an estimated 700 wives, lovers, laundresses, cooks, and prostitutes—were kept busy nursing the sick and burying the dead. "What then is to become of this army?" Washington worried in December.

Yet the army that marched out of Valley Forge five months later was considerably stronger for its experience there. The men of the Continental Army spent the late winter and spring drilling under the strict discipline of Friedrich Wilhelm Augustus von Steuben, a Prussian officer who came to America to volunteer for the American cause. But most important were the bonds forged among the men. In their small cabins they "shared with each other their hardships, dangers, and sufferings," wrote Private Joseph Plumb Martin, "sympathized with each other in trouble and sickness, assisted in bearing each other's burdens, [and] endeavored to conceal each other's faults." In short, he concluded, the men fashioned "a band of brotherhood" among themselves. On May Day they celebrated the end of winter and the coming of spring by raising maypoles before the cabins of each state regiment. Led by a sergeant decked out as King Tammany, the great Delaware chief of American folklore, and accompanied by thirteen honor guards representing each of the states, the men paraded through the rough streets of camp, pausing at each maypole to dance together. It was a ritual of their new sense of national community.

To some American Patriots—as the supporters of the Revolution called themselves—the European-style Continental Army betrayed the revolutionary ideals of the citizen-soldier and the autonomy of local communities. Washington argued strongly, however, that the Revolution could not be won without a national army insulated from politics and able to withstand shifts in the popular mood. Moreover, during the critical period of the nation's founding, the Continental Army acted as a popular democratic force, counterbalancing the conservatism of the new republic's elite leadership. The national spirit built at places like Valley Forge sustained the fighting men through years of war and provided momentum for the long process of forging a national political system out of the persistent localism of American politics. The soldiers of the Continental Army were among the first of their countrymen to think of themselves as Americans.

The Revolutionary years were characterized by warfare not only between armed American and British forces but also between Patriots and Loyalists, settlers and Indians, masters and slaves. Jealous of their autonomy, the individual colonies shaped a weak central government that just barely managed to keep them unified. Battered and bruised by British armies, the Continental Army pulled off an unexpected and remarkable victory against a large British force in upper New York State that led to financial support from Holland and a military alliance with France that in the end proved to be a decisive element in winning American independence. The glue that held Americans together during this long struggle was the sense of national community that emerged in places like Valley Forge during the winter of 1777.

THE WAR FOR INDEPENDENCE

At the beginning of the Revolution, the British had the world's best-equipped and most disciplined army, as well as a navy that was unopposed in American waters. But this overwhelming force encouraged them to greatly underestimate the American capacity to fight. The British also misperceived the sources of the conflict. Seeing the rebellion as the work of a small group of disgruntled conspirators, they defined their objective as defeating this Patriot opposition. They believed that in the wake of a military victory they could easily reassert political control. But the geography of eastern North America offered no single vital center whose conquest would end the war. When the British succeeded in defeating the **Patriots** in one area, resistance would spring up in another. The key factor in the outcome of the war for independence was popular support for the American cause.

THE PATRIOT FORCES

Most American men of fighting age had to face the call to arms. From a population of approximately 350,000 eligible men, more than 200,000 saw action. More than 100,000 served in the **Continental Army** under Washington's command, the rest in militia companies.

These militias—armed bodies of men drawn from local communities—proved important in the defense of their own areas, for they had homes as well as local reputations to protect. But the Revolution was not won by citizen-soldiers who traded plows for guns or backcountry riflemen who picked off Redcoats from behind trees. Because men preferred to serve with their neighbors in local companies rather than subject themselves to the discipline of the regular service, the states failed to meet their quotas for regiments in the Continental Army. Indeed, in the face of battle, militia companies demonstrated appalling rates of desertion.

The final victory resulted primarily from the steady struggle of the Continental Army. The American Revolution had little in common with modern national liberation movements in which armed populations engage in guerrilla warfare. Washington and his officers wanted a force that could directly engage the British, and from the beginning of the war, he argued that victory could be won only with a full commitment to

Jean Baptiste Antoine de Verger, a French officer serving with the Continental Army, made these watercolors of American soldiers during the Revolution. Some 200,000 men saw action, including at least 5,000 African Americans; more than half of these troops served with the Continental Army.

WHAT STRATEGIES and tactics did American forces employ in the war for independence?

myhistory**lab**
Review Summary

IMAGE KEY
for pages 154–155

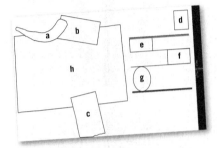

a. An 18th-century powder horn decorated with a map.
b. An engraving printed by Benjamin Franklin in 1754 urging the colonies to unite.
c. The 1783 Treaty of Paris that ended the American Revolution and recognized the independence of the United States.
d. A drum belonging to William Diamond (Lexington Historical Society) and a fife said to have been played at the Lexington fight early in the morning of April 19, 1775.
e. A painting by a French army officer showing the diversity of American soldiers.
f. Benjamin West's painting of the American commissioners who negotiated the Peace of Paris.
g. Mather Brown's sensitive portrait of Thomas Jefferson is the earliest known likeness of him.
h. The *Surrender of Lord Cornwallis at Yorktown* on October 19, 1781, a painting by John Trumbull.

Patriots British colonists who favored independence from Britain.

Continental Army The regular or professional army authorized by the Second Continental Congress and commanded by General George Washington during the Revolutionary War.

a truly national army. His views conflicted with popular fears of a standing army. Would they not be defeating their own purpose, many wondered, by adopting the corrupt institutions of their British enemies? Led by such views, Congress initially refused to invoke a draft or mandate army enlistments exceeding one year.

The failings of the militias in the early battles of the war, however, sobered Congress, and it responded with greatly enlarged state quotas for the army and terms of service that extended for the duration. To spur enlistment, Congress offered bounties, regular wages, and promises of free land after victory. By the spring of 1777, Washington's army had grown to nearly 9,000 men.

The New England militia companies that made up the original core of the Continental Army included small numbers of African Americans. But in late 1775, under pressure from Southern delegates, the Continental Congress barred blacks from the army. After an appeal from Washington, African Americans already serving were allowed to remain, but new enlistments were forbidden. The northern states continued to recruit African Americans. As the war spread to the South, slaves responded enthusiastically to a British promise of liberty for those who would fight for the crown. Thousands of slaves enlisted. In response, Maryland, Virginia, and North Carolina grudgingly allowed free persons of color and even slaves into their armed forces. By war's end, at least 5,000 African Americans had served in Patriot militias or the Continental Army, and in the Upper South some slaves won their freedom through military service. In the Lower South, however, where the numerical superiority of slaves inspired fears of rebellion among whites, there was no similar movement.

The Continental Army played an important political role during the war. At a time when Americans identified most strongly with their local communities or their states, the Continental Army evolved into a powerful force for nationalist sentiment. Over 100,000 men from every state served in the Continental Army, contributing mightily to the unity of purpose—the formation of a national political community—that was essential to the process of nation making.

THE TOLL OF WAR

The best estimate is that 25,324 American men died in the fighting, approximately 6,800 from wounds suffered in battle, most of the rest from the effects of disease. But since these numbers include only the major battles, the total death toll must have been considerably higher. The Continental Army experienced the heaviest casualty rates, losses in some regiments approaching 40 percent. Indeed, the casualty rate overall was higher than in any other American conflict except the Civil War. In New England and the mid-Atlantic states the war claimed few civilian lives, for it was confined largely to direct engagements between armies. In the South and backcountry, however, where Patriot and Loyalist militias waged violent and often vicious campaigns, there were many noncombatant casualties. There are no overall statistics for Loyalist casualties, but British forces suffered at least 10,000 killed or wounded in the major battles of the war.

THE LOYALISTS

Not all Americans were Patriots. Many were confused by the conflict and waited for a clear turn in the tide of the struggle before

A Patriot mob torments Loyalists in this print published during the Revolution. One favorite punishment was the "grand Tory ride," in which a crowd hauled the victim through the streets astride a fence rail. In another, men were stripped to "buff and breeches" and their naked flesh coated liberally with heated tar and feathers.

The TORY'S Day of JUDGMENT.

declaring their allegiance. Between a fifth and a third of the population, somewhere between a half a million and a million people, remained loyal to the British crown. They called themselves **Loyalists** but were known to Patriots as **Tories**, the popular name for the conservative party in England, traditionally supporters of the king's authority over that of Parliament.

A large proportion of the Loyalists were relatively recent migrants to the colonies, born in England, Scotland, or Ireland. Others, such as royal officeholders or Anglican clergymen, were dependent on the British government for their salaries. Many Loyalists were men of conservative temperament, fearful of political or social upheaval. The Loyalists included ethnic minorities who had been persecuted by the dominant majority, such as the Highland Scots of the Carolinas and western New York, or southern tenant farmers who had Patriot landlords. Loyalists were particularly strong in some colonies. They were nearly a majority in New York and were so numerous in Pennsylvania that an officer of the Continental Army described that colony as "the enemy's country." In Georgia, Loyalists made up such a large majority that the colony would probably have abandoned the revolutionary movement had the British not surrendered at Yorktown in 1781.

Patriots passed state treason acts that prohibited speaking or writing against the Revolution. They also punished Loyalists by issuing bills of attainder, a legal process (later made illegal by the United States **Constitution**) by means of which Loyalists were deprived of civil rights and property. In some areas, notably New York, South Carolina, Massachusetts, and Pennsylvania, Loyalists faced mob violence.

The British strategy for suppressing the Revolution depended on mobilizing the Loyalists, as many as 50,000 of whom took up arms for Great Britain. Many joined Loyalist militias or engaged in irregular warfare, especially in the Lower South.

As many as 80,000 Loyalists fled the country during and after the Revolution. Although the British government compensated many Loyalists for their losses when their property was confiscated by the states and sold at auction, most were unhappy exiles. "I earnestly wish to spend the remainder of my days in America," William Pepperell, formerly of Maine, wrote from London in 1778. "I love the country. I love the people." Despite their disagreement with the Patriots on essential political questions, they remained Americans, and they mourned the loss of their country.

WOMEN AND THE WAR

As men marched off to war, thousands of women assumed the management of farms and businesses. Abigail Adams ran the Adams family's farm at Quincy for years, reporting on operations in frequent letters to her husband John, letters that included commentary on the American struggle for independence and the political structure of the new republic. Some women participated even more directly in Patriot politics. Mercy Otis Warren, sister of the Massachusetts leader James Otis, turned her home into a center of Patriot political activity and published a series of satires supporting the American cause and scorning the Loyalists. Thousands of women volunteered to support the war effort by working as seamstresses, nurses, even spies.

Loyalists British colonists who opposed independence from Britain.

Tories A derisive term applied to Loyalists in America who supported the king and Parliament just before and during the American Revolution.

Constitution The written document providing for a new central government of the United States.

John Singleton Copley's portrait of Mercy Otis Warren captured her at the age of thirty-six, in 1765. During the Revolution, her home in Boston was a center of Patriot political activity.

John Singleton Copley (American, 1738–1815), "Mrs. James Warren (Mercy Otis)," ca.1763. Oil on canvas. 49 5/8 × 39 1/2 in. (126 × 100.3 cm). Bequest of Winslow Warren. Courtesy, Museum of Fine Arts, Boston (31.212). Reproduced with permission.
© 2000 Museum of Fine Arts, Boston. All Rights Reserved.

Thousands of women also traveled with the armies of both sides. Some camp followers were prostitutes, but most were wives, nurses, cooks, and laundresses.

These women not only shared the hardships of the soldiers, but also they were on the battlefields bringing water, food, and supplies to the front lines under withering cannon and musket fire and nursing the wounded and dying. The Continental Congress and state legislatures awarded pensions to numerous women wounded in battle. According to one estimate, several hundred women dressed themselves as men and enlisted.

THE CAMPAIGN FOR NEW YORK AND NEW JERSEY

During the winter of 1775–76, the British developed a strategic plan for the war. From his base at Halifax, Sir William Howe would take his army to New York City, which the British navy would protect. From there Howe was to drive north along the Hudson, while another British army marched south from Canada. The two armies would converge at Albany, cutting New England off from the rest of the colonies, then turn eastward. Washington, in command of Patriot forces at Boston, shifted his forces southward toward New York in the spring of 1776.

In early July, as Congress adopted the Declaration of Independence, the British began their operation by landing 32,000 troops on Staten Island. The Patriots set up fortified positions across the harbor in Brooklyn. In late August the British attacked, inflicting heavy casualties. The Battle of Long Island ended in disaster for the Patriots, and they were forced to withdraw across the East River to Manhattan.

The British then offered Congress an opportunity to negotiate, and on September 6, Benjamin Franklin, John Adams, and Edward Rutledge sat down on Staten Island with General Howe and his brother, Admiral Richard Howe. But the meeting broke up when the Howes demanded repeal of the Declaration of Independence, setting the stage for another round of fighting. By November, the Americans were fleeing south across New Jersey in a frantic attempt to avoid the British under General Charles Cornwallis (see Map 7.1).

With morale desperately low, whole militia companies deserted. American resistance seemed to be collapsing, and Washington was pessimistic. "Our Troops will not do their duty," he wrote painfully to Congress as he crossed the Delaware River into Pennsylvania. But rather than fall back farther, which would surely have meant the dissolution of his entire force, he decided to risk a counterattack. On Christmas night 1776, Washington led 2,400 troops back across the Delaware, and the next morning defeated the Hessian forces in a surprise attack on their headquarters at Trenton, New Jersey. The Americans inflicted further heavy losses on the British at Princeton, then drove them all the way back to the environs of New York City.

These victories had little strategic importance, but they salvaged American morale. As Washington settled into winter headquarters at Morristown, he realized he had to pursue a defensive strategy, avoiding direct confrontations with the British while checking their advances and hurting them wherever possible. The most important thing would be the survival of the Continental Army.

MAP 7.1
Campaign for New York and New Jersey, 1775–77

HOW DID American victories at Trenton and Princeton help turn the tide of the war?

THE NORTHERN CAMPAIGNS OF 1777

The fighting with American forces prevented Howe from moving north up the Hudson River, and the British advance southward from Canada was stalled by American resistance at Lake Champlain. In 1777, however, the British decided to replay their strategy. From Canada they dispatched General John Burgoyne with nearly 8,000 British and allied German troops. Howe was to move his force from New York, first taking the city of Philadelphia, the seat of the Continental Congress, and then moving north to meet Burgoyne (see Map 7.2).

Fort Ticonderoga fell to Burgoyne on July 6, but by August the general found himself bogged down and harassed by Patriot militias in the rough country south of Lake George. After several defeats in September at the hands of an American army commanded by General Horatio Gates, Burgoyne retreated to Saratoga. There he was surrounded by a considerably larger force of Americans, and on October 19 he surrendered his army. It would be the biggest British defeat until Yorktown, decisive because it forced the nations of Europe to recognize that the Americans had a fighting chance to win their Revolution.

The Americans were less successful against Howe. A force of 15,000 British troops left New York in July and landed a month later at the northern end of Chesapeake Bay. In September, at Brandywine Creek outside Philadelphia, the British outflanked the Americans, inflicting heavy casualties and forcing a retreat. Ten days later they routed the Americans a second time. This cleared the way for the British occupation of Philadelphia.

After this campaign, the Continentals headed into winter quarters at Valley Forge, the bitterness of their defeats muted somewhat by news of Burgoyne's surrender at Saratoga. The British had possession of Philadelphia, the most important city in North America, but it would prove of little strategic value to them. The Continental Congress continued to function, so the unified effort suffered little disruption. At the end of two years of fighting, despite numerous military victories, the British strategy for suppressing the Revolution had been a failure.

A GLOBAL CONFLICT

During these two years of fighting, the Americans were sustained by loans from France and Spain, traditional enemies of Great Britain. Both saw an opportunity to win back North American territories lost as a result of the Seven Years' War. Seeking more support, the Continental Congress sent a diplomatic delegation to Paris headed by Benjamin Franklin.

MAP 7.2
Northern Campaigns, 1777–78

WHAT WAS the significance of the Battle of Saratoga?

The American victory at Saratoga, and the fear that Great Britain might enter into negotiations with the revolutionaries, persuaded the French to recognize American independence in December 1777. Neither country was to conclude peace with the British "without the formal consent of the other." The treaty was to take effect "should war break out" between France and Great Britain. The alliance was sealed when fighting between the two traditional enemies began in June. Americans also found much support in the Netherlands. Although officially allied with Great Britain, the Dutch maintained a position of neutrality and opened secret negotiations with the Americans for a treaty of trade and friendship. Clandestine trade through the Dutch island of St. Eustatius in the Caribbean helped sustain the Patriot cause. In 1779 the British shelled the Dutch colony and the next year declared war on the Netherlands. The Dutch became the second European nation to recognize the United States and its financiers became the most important source of loans for the new nation.

Spain had entered the war in 1779. As early as 1775 Spanish officials in New Orleans were providing substantial ammunition and provisions for American forts in the West, including supplies of beef from herds of cattle driven to New Orleans by vaqueros (cowboys) from Texas. The viceroy of New Spain levied a special tax to pay for these supplies, and borderland colonists in Sonora, Texas, New Mexico, and California contributed their share. But unlike France and the Netherlands, the Spanish refused to establish a formal alliance with the United States.

Thus, the Spanish pursued an independent strategy against the British, seizing the weakly defended Mississippi River towns of Natchez and Baton Rouge in 1779, and winning the important Gulf ports of Mobile in 1780 and Pensacola in 1781. The victory at Pensacola was achieved with the help of several companies of Florida exiles, many of them African Americans.

With France and Spain now in the war, the British rethought their military strategy. Considering their West Indies sugar colonies at risk, they shipped 5,000 troops from New York to the Caribbean, where they succeeded in beating back a French attack. Fearing the arrival of the French fleet along the North American coast, the new British commander in America, General Henry Clinton, evacuated Philadelphia in June 1778. Washington's Continentals, fresh out of Valley Forge, went in hot pursuit. In the Battle of Monmouth, fought in stifling New Jersey heat on June 28, the British blunted the American drive and succeeded in making an orderly retreat to New York City. After a failed American-French joint campaign against the British at Newport, Rhode Island, Washington decided on a defensive strategy. Although the Americans enjoyed several small successes in the Northeast over the next two years, the war there went into a stalemate.

INDIAN PEOPLES AND THE REVOLUTION IN THE WEST

At the beginning of the conflict, both sides looked for Indian support. Most important was the stance of the Iroquois Confederacy, long one of the most potent political forces in colonial North America. A delegation from Congress told the Iroquois that the conflict was a "family quarrel" and urged them to keep out of it. British agents, on the other hand, pressed the Iroquois to unite against the Americans. Many Indian leaders were reluctant to get involved: "We are unwilling to join on either side of such a contest," declared one Oneida chief. "Let us Indians be all of one mind, and live with one another, and you white people settle your own disputes between yourselves."

Joseph Brant, the brilliant chief of the Mohawks who sided with Great Britain during the Revolution, in a 1786 painting by the American artist Gilbert Stuart. After the Treaty of Paris, Brant led a large faction of Iroquois people north into British Canada, where they established a separate Iroquois Confederacy.

Ultimately, however, the British proved persuasive. It became clear to Indians that a Patriot victory would mean the extension of American settlements into their homelands. Native peoples fought in the Revolution for some of the same reasons Patriots did—for political independence, cultural integrity, and the protection of their land and property—but Indian fears of American expansion led them to oppose the Patriot rhetoric of natural rights and the equality of all men. Almost all the tribes that engaged in the fighting did so on the side of the British.

In the summer of 1776 a large number of Cherokees, led by the warrior chief Dragging Canoe (Tsiyu-Gunsini), attacked dozens of American settlements. It required hard fighting before Patriot militia companies managed to drive the Cherokees into the mountains. Although the Cherokees eventually made an official peace, sporadic violence between Patriots and Indians continued along the southern frontier.

Among the Iroquois of New York, the Mohawk leader Joseph Brant (Thayendanegea) succeeded in bringing most Iroquois warriors into the British camp, although he was opposed by the chiefs of the Oneidas and Tuscaroras, who supported the Patriots. In 1777 and 1778, Iroquois and Loyalist forces raided the northern frontiers of New York and Pennsylvania. In retaliation an American army invaded the Iroquois homelands in 1779. Supported by Oneida and Tuscarora warriors, the Americans destroyed dozens of western villages and thousands of acres of crops. For the first time since the birth of their confederacy centuries before, the Iroquois were fighting each other (see Map 7.3).

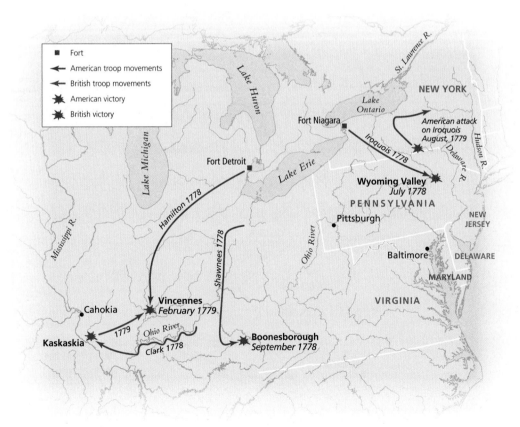

MAP 7.3
Fighting in the West, 1778–79

WHAT ROLE did Indian peoples play in the fighting in the West?

Across the mountains, the Ohio Indians formed an effective alliance under the British at Detroit, and in 1777 and 1778 they sent warriors south against pioneer communities in western Virginia and Kentucky that had been founded in defiance of the Proclamation of 1763. Virginian George Rogers Clark countered by organizing an expedition of Kentucky militia against the old French settlements in the Illinois country, which were controlled by the British. They succeeded in taking the British post at Kaskaskia in the summer of 1778, and in early 1779, in a daring winter raid on Vincennes, they captured Colonel Henry Hamilton, British commander in the West.

But Clark lacked the strength to attack the strategic British garrison at Detroit. Coordinating his Iroquois forces with those in Ohio, Brant mounted a new set of offensives that cast a shadow over Clark's successes. The war in the West would not end with the conclusion of hostilities in the East. With barely a pause, the fighting in the trans-Appalachian West between Americans and Indians would continue for another two decades.

THE WAR IN THE SOUTH

The most important fighting of the Revolution took place in the South (see Map 7.4). General Clinton regained the initiative for Britain in December 1778 by sending a force from New York against Georgia, the weakest of the colonies. The British

MAP 7.4
Fighting in the South, 1778–81

WHAT ROLE did African American slaves play in the fighting in the South?

In 1845 Artist William Ranney depicted a famous moment during the Battle of Cowpens that took place in January 1781. Lieutenant Colonel William Washington, leader of the Patriot cavalry and a relative of George Washington, was attacked by a squadron of British dragoons. As Washington was about to be cut down, he was saved by his servant William Ball, who fired a pistol that wounded the attacker. Nothing more is known about Ball, but he was one of a number of African Americans who fought on the Patriot side in the battle.

William Ranney, "The Battle of Cowpens." Oil on canvas. Photo by Sam Holland. Courtesy South Carolina State House.

crushed the Patriot militia at Savannah and began to organize the Loyalists in an effort to reclaim the colony. Encouraged by their success in Georgia, the British decided to apply the lessons learned there throughout the South. This involved a fundamental change from a strategy of military conquest to one of pacification. Territory would be retaken step by step, then handed over to Loyalists who would reassert the crown's authority.

In October 1779 Clinton evacuated Rhode Island, the last British stronghold in New England, and proceeded with 8,000 troops for a campaign against Charleston. Outflanking the American defenders, he forced the surrender of more than 5,000 troops in May. It was the most significant American defeat of the war. Patriot resistance collapsed in the Lower South, and American fortunes were suddenly at their lowest ebb since the beginning of the war.

 5–10
William Dobein James, *The Rise of Partisan Warfare in the South* (1778)

The southern campaign was marked by vicious fighting between partisan militias of Patriots and Loyalists. The violence peaked in September 1780 with Cornwallis's invasion of North Carolina, where the Patriots were stronger and better organized. There the British found their southern strategy untenable: plundering towns and farms in order to feed the army in the interior had the effect of producing angry support for the Patriots.

Into 1781 the Continentals and Patriot militias waged what General Greene called a fugitive war of hit and run against the British. Finally in the summer of 1781, deciding he would not be able to hold the Carolinas as long as Virginia remained a base of support and supply for the Americans, Cornwallis led his army north. After marauding through the Virginia countryside, he reached the Chesapeake where he expected reinforcements from New York. The British withdrawal from North Carolina allowed Greene to reestablish Patriot control of the Lower South.

THE YORKTOWN SURRENDER

While the British raged through the South, the stalemate continued in the Northeast. In the summer of 1780, taking advantage of the British evacuation of Rhode Island, the French landed 5,000 troops at Newport under the command of General Jean Baptiste Donatien de Vimeur, comte de Rochambeau. But it was not until the spring of 1781 that Rochambeau risked joining his force to Washington's Continentals north of New York City. In August Washington learned that the French Caribbean fleet was headed for the Chesapeake. If he and Rochambeau could move their troops south, they might lock up Cornwallis in his camp at Yorktown. Leaving a small force behind as a decoy, they marched their 16,000 men overland to the Virginia shore in little more than a month.

The maneuver was a complete success. The French and Americans surrounded and besieged the British encampment. French and American heavy artillery hammered the British unmercifully until the middle of October. After the failure of a planned retreat across the York River, Cornwallis opened negotiations for the surrender of his army. Two days later, on October 19, 1781, between lines of victorious American and French soldiers, the British troops came out from their trenches to surrender (see Seeing History). Everyone was aware that it was an event of incalculable importance, but few guessed it was the end of the war. The British still controlled New York.

In London a month later Lord North received the news "as he would have taken a ball in the breast," the colonial secretary reported. "Oh God!" North moaned, "it is all over!" The American Revolution had turned into war with France and Spain, and British fortunes were at low ebb in India, the West Indies, Florida, and the Mediterranean. The cost of the war was enormous, and there was little support for it among either the British public or the members of Parliament. George III wished to press on, but North submitted his resignation, and in March 1782 the king was forced to offer the office of prime minister to Charles Watson-Wentworth, Lord Rockingham, who long had favored granting the Americans their independence.

THE UNITED STATES IN CONGRESS ASSEMBLED

The motion for independence, offered to the Continental Congress by Richard Henry Lee on June 7, 1776, called for a confederation of the states. The Articles of Confederation, the first written constitution of the United States, created a national government of sharply limited powers. This arrangement reflected the concerns of people fighting to free themselves from a coercive central government. But the weak Confederation government had a difficult time forging the unity and assembling the resources necessary to fight the war and win the peace.

THE ARTICLES OF CONFEDERATION

The debate over confederation that took place in the Continental Congress during 1776 made it clear that delegates favoring a loose union of autonomous states outnumbered those who wanted a strong central government. A consensus finally emerged in 1777, and the "**Articles of Confederation**" were formally adopted by the Continental Congress in November and sent to the states for ratification. The Articles created a national assembly, called the Congress, in which each state had a single vote. Delegates, selected annually in a manner determined by the individual state legislatures, could serve no more than three years out of six. A presiding president, elected annually by Congress, was eligible to hold office no more than

---

QUICK REVIEW

Yorktown

- American and French forces surround British encampment.
- British General Cornwallis forced to surrender his army.
- Defeat forced the British to accept American independence.

WHAT CONCERNS were reflected in the terms of the Articles of Confederation?

myhistorylab
Review Summary

Articles of Confederation Written document setting up the loose confederation of states that comprised the first national government of the United States.

The Surrender of Lord Cornwallis

American artist John Trumbull displayed a preliminary version of *Surrender of Lord Cornwallis* in 1797 along with three other history paintings of the Revolution, including his depiction of the signing of the Declaration of Independence, the surrender of General Burgoyne at Saratoga, and the resignation of General Washington from his military commission at the war's conclusion. Young Trumbull had been an officer in the Continental Army and served for a time as Washington's aide-de-camp, but he had not been at Yorktown. By that time he was in London studying with the American expatriate artist Benjamin West. This painting was done in the heroic style of nationalist art popular at the time in Great Britain and Europe. Trumbull was at pains to get the details right. He visited Yorktown to sketch the landscape and traveled across the United States and France to capture the likenesses of the senior American and French officers, including Washington and Rochambeau, shown lining the two sides, colors flying, as the British troops file by. But Trumbull was criticized by the public for getting one detail appallingly wrong. He depicted Cornwallis on horseback in the center, when in fact the British commander was not present at the ceremony but was sulking in his tent. Trumbull corrected his error by changing the color of the central figure's uniform from red to blue, thereby turning Cornwallis into General Benjamin Lincoln, who is seen reaching for the sword in the possession of the British second-in-command, General Charles O'Hara. In 1817 the Senate commissioned Trumbull to repaint his Revolutionary scenes for placement in the Rotunda of the Capitol. ■

IN WHAT ways does Trumbull create a heroic painting by the arrangement of his subjects?

one year out of three. Votes would be decided by a simple majority of the states, except for major questions, which would require the agreement of nine states.

Congress was granted national authority in the conduct of foreign affairs, matters of war and peace, and maintenance of the armed forces. It could raise loans, issue bills of credit, establish a coinage, and regulate trade with Indian peoples, and it was to be the final authority in jurisdictional disputes between states. It was charged with establishing a national postal system as well as a common standard of weights and measures. Lacking the power to tax citizens directly, however, the national government was to apportion its financial burdens among the states according to the extent of their surveyed land. The Articles explicitly guaranteed the sovereignty of the individual states, reserving to them all powers not expressly delegated to Congress. Ratification or amendment required the agreement of all thirteen states. The Articles of Confederation thus created a national government of specific yet sharply circumscribed powers.

The legislatures of twelve states soon voted in favor of the Articles, but final ratification was held up for more than three years by the state of Maryland. Representing the interests of states without claims to lands west of the Appalachians, Maryland demanded that states cede to Congress their western claims, the new nation's most valuable resource, for "the good of the whole" (see Map 7.5). It was 1781 before Virginia, the state with the largest western claims, broke the logjam by agreeing to the cession. Maryland then ratified the Articles of Confederation, and in March they took effect.

MAP 7.5

State Claims to Western Lands The ratification of the Articles of Confederation in 1781 awaited settlement of the western claims of eight states. Vermont, claimed by New Hampshire and New York, was not made a state until 1791, after disputes were settled the previous year. The territory north of the Ohio River was claimed in whole or in part by Virginia, New York, Connecticut, and Massachusetts. All of them had ceded their claims by 1786, except for Connecticut, which had claimed an area just south of Lake Erie, known as the Western Reserve; Connecticut ceded this land in 1800. The territory south of the Ohio was claimed by Virginia, North Carolina, South Carolina, and Georgia; in 1802, the latter became the last state to cede its claims.

WHAT WAS the reason for the delay in ratifying the Articles of Confederation?

FINANCING THE WAR

Lacking the authority to levy direct taxes, Congress financed the Revolution through grants and loans from friendly foreign powers and by issuing paper currency. The total foreign subsidy by the end of the war approached $9 million, but this was not enough to back the circulating Continental currency that Congress authorized, the face value of which amounted to $200 million. In an attempt to retire this currency, Congress called on the states to raise taxes, payable in Continental dollars. But most of the states were unwilling to do this. In fact, most had resorted to printing currency of their own, estimated at a face value of another $200 million by war's end. The result of this expansion in the money supply was the rapid depreciation of Continental currency. By the time Robert Morris, one of the wealthiest merchants in the country, became secretary of finance in May 1781, Continental currency had ceased to circulate. In the jargon of the day, things of no value were "not worth a Continental." Yet the paper currency had funded a revolution.

Morris was able to turn things around. He persuaded Congress to charter a "Bank of North America" located in Philadelphia, the first private commercial bank in the United States. Into its vaults he deposited large quantities of gold and silver coin and bills of exchange obtained through loans from Holland and France. He then issued new paper currency backed by this treasure. Once he established confidence in the bank, Morris was able to supply the Continental Army through private contracts. He also began making interest payments on the debt, which in 1783 was estimated at $30 million.

NEGOTIATING INDEPENDENCE

Peace talks between the United States and Great Britain opened in July 1782, when Benjamin Franklin sat down with the British emissary in Paris. Congress had issued its first set of war aims in 1779. The fundamental demand was recognition of American independence and withdrawal of British forces. American negotiators were instructed to press for the largest territorial limits possible, as well as guarantees of American rights to fish North Atlantic waters. As for its French ally, Congress instructed the commissioners to be guided by friendly advice, but also by "knowledge of our interests, and by your own discretion, in which we repose the fullest confidence." The French were not happy with this, and partly as a result of French pressure, in June 1781 Congress issued a new set of instructions. The commissioners were to settle merely for a grant of independence and withdrawal of troops and to be subject to the guidance and control of the French in the negotiations.

Ben Franklin, John Jay, and John Adams, the peace commissioners in Paris, were well aware of French attempts to manipulate the outcome of negotiations and place limits on American power. In violation of both Congressional instructions and treaty obligations to France, they signed a preliminary treaty with Britain in November 1782 without consulting the French. In the treaty, Britain acknowledged the United States as "free, sovereign & independent" and agreed to withdraw its troops from all forts within American territory "with all convenient speed." The American commissioners pressed the British for Canada but settled for western territorial boundaries extending to the Mississippi (see Map 7.6) with unencumbered navigation of the river.

The Continental Congress printed currency to finance the Revolution. Because of widespread counterfeiting, engravers attempted to incorporate complex designs, like the unique vein structure in the leaf on this eighteen-pence note. In case that wasn't enough, the engraver of this note also included the warning: "To counterfeit is Death."

QUICK REVIEW

Peace of Paris

- Signed September 3, 1783.
- United States got virtually everything it sought at peace talks.
- Treaty addressed important economic issues, but said nothing about slavery.

MAP EXPLORATION

To explore an interactive version of this map, go to **http://www.prenhall.com/faraghertlc/map7.6**

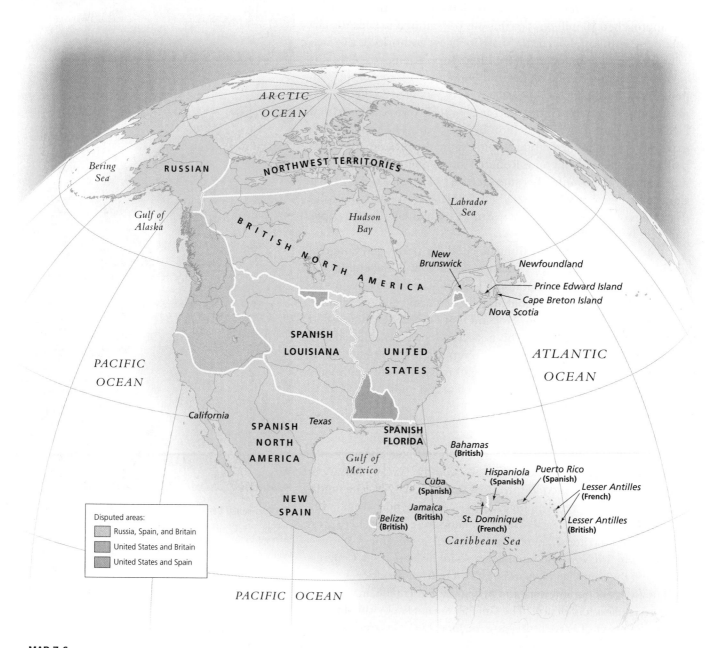

MAP 7.6

North America After the Treaty of Paris, 1783 The map of European and American claims to North America was radically altered by the results of the American Revolution.

HOW DID the Treaty of Paris alter the balance of power in North America?

The British guaranteed Americans "the right to take fish" in the waters of the North Atlantic. Britain received American promises that Congress would erect "no lawful impediments" to the recovery of debts, end the confiscation of Loyalist property, and attempt to persuade the states to fairly compensate Loyalist exiles. All in all, it was an astounding coup for the Americans.

The preliminary treaty confronted France with an accomplished fact. When French diplomats criticized the American commissioners, they responded by hinting that resistance to the treaty provisions could result in a British–American alliance. Thereupon France quickly made an agreement of its own with the British.

Spain did not participate in the negotiations with the Americans. But having waged a successful campaign against the British on the Mississippi and the Gulf Coast, its government issued a claim of sovereignty over much of the trans-Appalachian territory granted to the United States by Great Britain. Spain arranged a separate peace with Great Britain, in which it won the return of Florida. The final Treaty of Paris—actually a series of separate agreements among the United States, Great Britain, France, and Spain—was signed at Versailles on September 3, 1783.

American artist Benjamin West never completed his painting of the "American Commissioners of the Preliminary Peace Negotiations with Great Britain, 1783–1785," but he left this "cartoon" or study. It features portraits of (left to right) John Jay, John Adams, Henry Laurens, Benjamin Franklin, and William Temple Franklin, who served as secretary for his grandfather. West intended to include the British commissioners, but the death of one and the uncooperative attitude of the other aborted the project.

Benjamin West, 1783 "American Commissioners of Preliminary Negotiations". Courtesy, Winterthur Museum.

THE CRISIS OF DEMOBILIZATION

In 1778 Continental officers had won from Congress a promise of life pensions at half pay in exchange for enlistment for the duration of the war. By 1783, however, Congress had still not made any specific provisions for officers' pensions. With peace at hand, the officers began to fear that the army would be disbanded before the problem was resolved, and they would lose whatever power they had to pressure Congress. In January 1783, a group of prominent senior officers petitioned Congress, demanding that pensions be converted to a bonus equal to five years of full pay. "Any further experiments on their patience," they warned, "may have fatal effects." Despite the barely veiled threat of military intervention, Congress rejected their petition.

With the backing of congressional nationalists, a group of army officers associated with General Horatio Gates circulated a letter arguing for direct military intervention and calling an extraordinary meeting of the officer corps at Newburgh. But General Washington, on whom the officers counted for support, criticized the meeting as "disorderly" and called an official meeting of his own. There was enormous tension as the officers assembled on March 15, 1783. Washington strode into the room and mounted the platform. Turning his back in disdain on Gates, he delivered an address from memory condemning the circular letter. After he left, the officers adopted resolutions rejecting intervention, and a week later, on Washington's urging, Congress converted the promised pensions to bonuses.

Washington's role in this crisis was one of his greatest contributions to the nation. At stake was nothing less than the possibility of a military coup at the very moment of victory. The American Revolution was the first of many successful colonial revolutions, and in hindsight it is clear that postindependence military rule was a common outcome in many of them. In December 1783 Washington resigned his commission as general of the army despite calls for him to remain. There is little doubt he could have assumed the role of an American dictator. Instead, by his actions and example, the principle of military subordination to civil authority was firmly established.

As for the common soldiers, they wanted simply to be discharged. In May 1783, Congress voted the soldiers three months' pay as a bonus and instructed Washington to begin dismissing them. By the beginning of 1784, the Continental Army had shrunk to no more than a few hundred men.

6–3
George Washington, *The Newburgh Address* (1783)

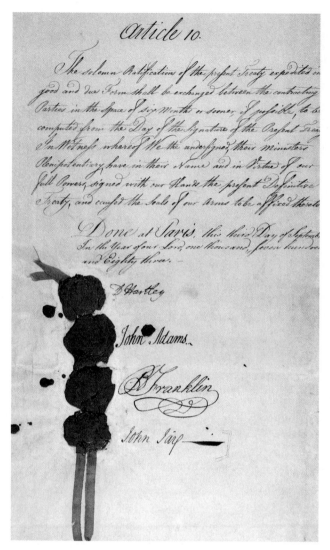

The last page of the Treaty of Paris, signed in Paris on September 3, 1783, by David Hartley for Great Britain, and for the United States by John Adams, Benjamin Franklin, and John Jay.

5–12
Congress Decides What to Do with the Western Lands (1785)

Land Ordinance of 1785   Act passed by Congress under the Articles of Confederation that created the grid system of surveys by which all subsequent public land was made available for sale.

Northwest Ordinance of 1787
Legislation that prohibited slavery in the Northwest Territories and provided the model for the incorporation of future territories into the union as co-equal states.

THE PROBLEM OF THE WEST

Even during the Revolution thousands of Americans migrated westward, and after the war settlers poured over the mountains and down the Ohio River. Thousands of Americans pressed against the Indian country north of the Ohio River, and destructive violence continued along the frontier. British troops continued to occupy posts in the Great Lakes region and encouraged Indian attacks on vulnerable settlements. Spain refused to accept the territorial settlement of the Treaty of Paris and closed the port of New Orleans to Americans, effectively blockading the Mississippi River. Westerners who saw that route as their primary access to markets were outraged.

John Jay, appointed secretary for foreign affairs by the Confederation Congress in 1784, attempted to negotiate with the British for their complete withdrawal but was told that was not possible until all outstanding debts from before the war were settled. Jay also negotiated with the Spanish for guarantees of territorial sovereignty and commercial relations, but they insisted that the Americans relinquish free navigation of the Mississippi. Congress would approve no treaty under those conditions, and some frustrated Westerners considered leaving the Confederation. In the West, local community interest continued to override the fragile development of national community sentiment.

In 1784, Congress took up the problem of extending national authority over the West. Legislation was drafted, principally by Thomas Jefferson, providing "Government for the Western Territory." The legislation proposed a remarkably republican colonial policy. The western public domain would be divided into states, fully the equals of the original thirteen, with Congressional guarantees of self-government and republican institutions. Once the population of a territory numbered 20,000, the residents could call a convention and establish a constitution and government of their own choosing. And once the population grew to equal that of the smallest of the original thirteen states, the territory could petition for statehood, provided it agreed to remain forever a member of the Confederation. Congress accepted these proposals but rejected by a vote of seven to six Jefferson's clause forever prohibiting slavery in the West.

Passed the following year, the **Land Ordinance of 1785** provided for the survey and sale of western lands. The settlement of Kentucky had been characterized by a chaos of overlapping surveys and land claims, a problem the Land Ordinance was designed to solve by creating an ordered system of survey, dividing the land into townships composed of thirty-six sections of one square mile (640 acres) each. Jefferson argued that land ought to be given away to actual settlers. But, eager to establish a revenue base for the government, Congress provided for the auction of public lands for not less than one dollar per acre.

In the treaties of Fort Stanwix in 1784 and Fort McIntosh in 1785, congressional commissioners forced the Iroquois and a number of Ohio tribes, respectively, to cede portions of their territory in what is now eastern Ohio. These treaties were not the result of negotiation but intimidation. The commissioners dictated the terms by seizing hostages and forcing compliance. Surveyors were immediately sent west to divide up the land. The first surveyed lands did not come onto the market until the fall of 1788, and in the meantime Congress, desperate for revenue, sold a tract of more than 1.5

MAP EXPLORATION

To explore an interactive version of this map, go to **http://www.prenhall.com/faraghertlc/map7.7**

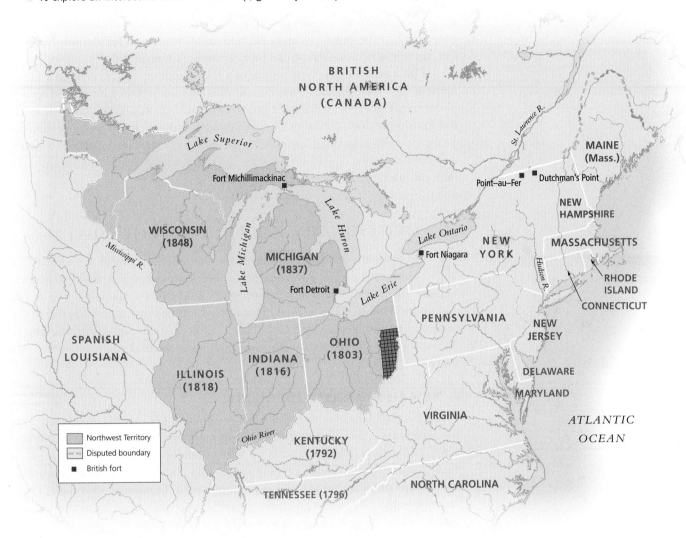

MAP 7.7
The Northwest Territory and the Land Survey System of the United States　The Land Ordinance of 1785 created an ordered system of survey, dividing the land into townships and sections.

IN WHAT ways did the Northwest Ordinance affect the admission of new states into the Union? What were the consequences for western lands?

million acres to the Ohio Company, a new consortium of land speculators, for a million dollars. Thousands of Westerners chose not to wait for the official opening of the public lands north of the Ohio River but simply settled illegally by making squatters' claims. In 1785 Congress raised troops and evicted many of them, but once the troops departed the squatters returned. The persistence of this problem convinced many congressmen to revise Jefferson's democratic territorial plan.

In the **Northwest Ordinance of 1787**, Congress established a system of government for the territory north of the Ohio (see Map 7.7). Three to five states were to be carved from the giant

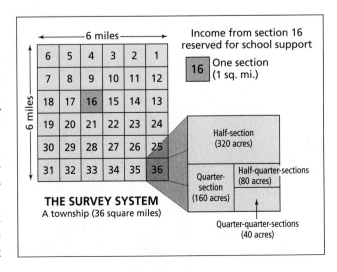

THE SURVEY SYSTEM
A township (36 square miles)

Northwest Territory. Slavery was prohibited. But the initial guarantee of self-government in Jefferson's plan was replaced by a congressionally appointed governor and court of judges. Once the free white male population of the territory had grown to 5,000, these citizens would be permitted to choose an assembly, but the governor had the power of absolute veto on all territorial legislation. National interest would be imposed on the local western communities.

The creation of the land system of the United States was the major achievement of the Confederation government. But there were other important accomplishments. Under the Articles of Confederation, Congress led the country through the Revolution and its commissioners negotiated the terms of a comprehensive peace treaty. And by organizing the departments of war, foreign affairs, finance, and the post office, the Confederation government created the beginnings of a national bureaucracy.

REVOLUTIONARY POLITICS IN THE STATES

HOW DID political debate in America change in the years after 1774?

myhistorylab
Review Summary

Despite the accomplishments of the Confederation, most Americans were focused on the governments of their own states. The national government was distant and had relatively little effect on people's lives. Social and political identity was located in local communities and states rather than the American nation. People spoke of "these United States," emphasizing the plural. The states were the setting for the most important political struggles of the Confederation period.

A NEW DEMOCRATIC IDEOLOGY

The political mobilization that took place in 1774 and 1775 greatly broadened political participation. Mass meetings in which ordinary people expressed their opinions, voted, and gained political experience were common not only in the cities but in small towns and rural communities as well. During these years a greater proportion of the population began to participate in elections. Compared with the colonial assemblies, the new state legislatures included more men from rural and western districts—farmers and artisans as well as lawyers, merchants, and large landowners.

This transformation was accompanied by a dramatic shift in the content of political debate. During the colonial period, when only the upper classes were truly engaged in the political process, the principal argument followed the lines of the traditional Tory and Whig divide in Great Britain. The Tory position, taken by colonial officials, was that colonial governments were simply convenient instruments of royal prerogative, serving at the king's pleasure. The Whig position, adopted by colonial elites who sought to preserve and increase their own power, emphasized the need for a government balancing the power of a governor with an upper house and an assembly. As a result of the Revolution, the Tory position lost all legitimacy and the Whig position was challenged by farmers, artisans, and ordinary people armed with a new and radical democratic ideology. The spectrum of politics shifted to the left.

THE FIRST STATE CONSTITUTIONS

One of the first post-Revolution debates focused on an appropriate governmental structure for the new states. The thinking of democrats was indicated by the title of a New England pamphlet of 1776: *The People the Best Governors*. Power, this anonymous author argued, should be vested in a single, popularly elected assembly. The people, in the words of this pamphlet, "best know their wants and necessities, and therefore are best able to govern themselves." The ideal form of government, according to

QUICK REVIEW

The New Politics

- Ordinary people gained political experience during the Revolution.
- New state legislatures included more men from rural and western districts.
- Political spectrum shifted left.

democrats, was the community or town meeting, in which the people set their own tax rates, created a militia, controlled their own schools and churches, and regulated the local economy. State government was necessary only for coordination among communities.

Conservative Americans took up the Whig argument of the need for balanced government. The "unthinking many," wrote a conservative pamphleteer, should be checked by a strong executive and an upper house. Both of these would be insulated from popular control by property qualifications and long terms in office. The greatest danger, according to conservatives, was the possibility of majority tyranny, which might lead to the violation of property rights and dictatorship.

Fourteen states—the original thirteen plus Vermont, an independent republic from 1777 until 1791—adopted constitutions between 1776 and 1780. Each of those political charters was shaped by the debate between radicals and conservatives, democrats and Whigs, and reflected a particular political alignment. Pennsylvania was the first state to adopt a radically democratic constitution, with a unicameral assembly elected annually by all free male taxpayers. North Carolina, Georgia, and Vermont followed the Pennsylvania model. Indeed, Vermont went even further and became the first state to adopt universal manhood suffrage. At the other extreme, South Carolina and Maryland created a conservative set of institutions designed to keep citizens and rulers as far apart as possible. The other states adopted constitutional systems somewhere in the middle.

DECLARATIONS OF RIGHTS

One of the most important innovations of the state constitutions were the guarantees of rights patterned on the Virginia "Declaration of Rights" of June 1776. Written by George Mason—a wealthy planter, democrat, and brilliant political philosopher—the Virginia declaration set a distinct tone in its very first article: "That all men are by nature equally free and independent, and have certain inherent rights, namely, the enjoyment of life and liberty, with the means of acquiring and possessing property and pursuing and obtaining happiness and safety." The fifteen articles of the Virginia Declaration declared, among other things, that sovereignty resided in the people, that government was the servant of the people, and that the people had the "right to reform, alter, or abolish" that government. There were guarantees of due process and trial by jury in criminal prosecutions, as well as prohibitions against excessive bail and "cruel and unusual punishment." Freedom of the press was guaranteed as "one of the great bulwarks of liberty," and the people were assured of "the free exercise of religion, according to the dictates of conscience."

Eight state constitutions included a general declaration of rights similar to the first article of the Virginia declaration; others incorporated specific guarantees. A number of states proclaimed the right of the people to engage in free speech and free assembly, to instruct their representatives, and to petition for the redress of grievances—rights either inadvertently or deliberately omitted from Virginia's declaration. These declarations were important precedents for the **Bill of Rights**, the first ten amendments to the federal Constitution of 1789. Indeed, George Mason of Virginia would be the leader of the democrats who insisted that the Constitution stipulate such rights.

THE SPIRIT OF REFORM

The political upheaval of the Revolution raised the possibility of other reforms in American society. The New Jersey constitution of 1776 granted the vote to "all inhabitants of this colony, of full age, who are worth fifty pounds . . . and have resided within the county . . . for twelve months," thus enfranchising women as well

5–13
Territorial Governments are Established by Congress (1787)

6–1
Constitution of Pennsylvania (1776)

6–2
John Adams, *A Declaration of the Rights of the Inhabitants of the Commonwealth of Massachusetts* (1780)

Bill of Rights A written summary of inalienable rights and liberties.

By giving the vote to "all free inhabitants," the 1776 constitution of New Jersey enfranchised women as well as men who met the property requirements. The number of women voters eventually led to male protests. Wrote one: "What tho' we read, in days of yore, / The woman's occupation / Was to direct the wheel and loom, / Not to direct the nation." In 1807, a new state law explicitly limited the right of franchise to "free white male citizens."

as men. Because married women could own no property in their own names, only single women voted in New Jersey, but large numbers of them participated in elections and spoke out on political issues. There were male protests of this "irregular" situation, and in 1807 the legislature passed a law explicitly limiting the right to vote to "free white male citizens."

The New Jersey controversy was something of an anomaly, yet women's participation in the Revolution wrought subtle but important changes. In the aftermath of the Revolution, there was evidence of increasing sympathy in the courts for women's property rights and fairer treatment of women's petitions for divorce. And the postwar years witnessed an increase in opportunities for women seeking an education. From a strictly legal and political point of view, the Revolution may have done little to change women's role in society, but it did seem to help change expectations.

The most steadfast reformer of the day was Thomas Jefferson, who after completing work on the Declaration of Independence returned to Virginia to take a seat in its House of Delegates. In 1776 he introduced a bill in the Virginia legislature abolishing entail (restriction of inheritance to particular heirs in order that landed property remain undivided) and primogeniture (the inheritance of all the family property by the firstborn son), legal customs long in effect in aristocratic England that Jefferson believed had no place in a republican society. Jefferson's reform of inheritance law passed and had a dramatic effect. By 1798, every state had followed Virginia's lead.

Jefferson's other notable success was his **Bill for Establishing Religious Freedom**. He considered it one of his greatest accomplishments. At the beginning of the Revolution, there were established churches—denominations officially supported and funded by the government—in nine of the thirteen colonies. Many Anglican clergymen harbored Loyalist sympathies, and as part of an anti-Loyalist backlash, New York, Maryland, the Carolinas, and Georgia had little difficulty passing acts that disestablished the Anglican Church. In Virginia, however, many planters viewed Anglicanism as a bulwark against Baptist and Methodist democratic thinkers, resulting in bitter and protracted opposition to Jefferson's bill. It did not pass until 1786.

Jefferson proposed several more reforms of Virginia law, all of which failed to pass. He would have created a system of public education, revised the penal code to restrict capital punishment to the crimes of murder and treason, and established the gradual emancipation of slaves by law. On the whole, Jefferson and the Revolutionary generation were more successful at raising questions than at accomplishing reforms. The problems of penal reform, public education, and slavery remained for later generations of Americans to resolve.

AFRICAN AMERICANS AND THE REVOLUTION

For most African Americans there was little to celebrate, for the American victory guaranteed the continuation of slavery as an institution. Few people were surprised when thousands of black fighters and their families departed with the Loyalists and the British at the end of the war, settling in the West Indies, Canada, and Africa. Most of

Bill for Establishing Religious Freedom A bill authored by Thomas Jefferson establishing religious freedom in Virginia.

these refugees were fugitive slaves rather than committed Loyalists. In Virginia alone, some 30,000 slaves fled during the Revolution.

There was an obvious contradiction in waging a war for liberty while continuing to support the institution of slavery. "How is it," English critic and essayist Samuel Johnson asked pointedly in 1775, "that we hear the loudest yelps for liberty among the drivers of Negroes?" The contradiction was not lost on Washington, who during the Revolution began to agonize over the morality of slavery. He was not alone. Revolutionary idealism, in combination with a shift away from tobacco farming, weakened the commitment of many Chesapeake planters to the slave system. After the Revolution, a sizable number of Virginians granted freedom to their slaves, and there was a small but important movement to encourage gradual emancipation by convincing masters to free their slaves in their wills.

George Washington was one of them, making a will that not only freed several hundred slaves upon his death but also included an elaborate plan for apprenticeship and tenancy for the able-bodied, and lodging and pensions for the aged. Planters in the Lower South, however, heavily dependent as they were on slave labor, resisted the growing calls for an end to slavery. Between 1776 and 1786 all the states but South Carolina and Georgia prohibited or heavily taxed the international slave trade, and this issue became an important point of conflict at the **Constitutional Convention** in 1787 (see Chapter 8).

Perhaps the most important result of this development was the growth of the free African American population. From a few thousand in 1750, their number grew to more than 200,000 by the end of the century. The increase was most notable in the Upper South. Largely excluded from the institutions of white Americans, the African American community now had enough strength to establish schools, churches, and other institutions of its own. At first, this development was opposed by whites. In Williamsburg, Virginia, for instance, the leader of a black congregation was seized and whipped when he attempted to gain recognition from the Baptist Association. But by the 1790s the Williamsburg African Church had grown to over 500 members, and the Baptist Association reluctantly recognized it. The incorporation of the word "African" in the names of churches, schools, and mutual benefit societies reflected the pride African Americans took in their heritage.

In the North, slavery was first abolished in the state constitution of Vermont in 1777, in Massachusetts in 1780, and New Hampshire in 1784. Pennsylvania, Connecticut, and Rhode Island adopted systems of gradual emancipation during these years, freeing the children of slaves at birth. By 1804, every northern state had provided for abolition or gradual emancipation, although as late as 1810, 30,000 African Americans remained enslaved in the North.

During the era of the Revolution, a small group of African American writers rose to prominence. Benjamin Banneker, born free in Maryland, where he received an education, became one of the most accomplished mathematicians and astronomers of late eighteenth-century America. In the 1790s, he published a popular almanac that both white and black Americans consulted. Jupiter Hammon, a New York slave, took up contemporary issues in his poems and essays, one of the most important of which was his "Address to the Negroes of the State of New York," published in 1787. But the most famous African American writer was Phyllis Wheatley, who came to public attention when her *Poems on Various Subjects, Religious and Moral* appeared in London in 1773, while she was still serving as a domestic slave in Boston. Kidnapped in Africa as a young girl and converted to Christianity during the Great Awakening, Wheatley wrote poems combining piety with a concern

This portrait of the African American poet Phyllis Wheatley was included in the collection of her work published in London in 1773, when she was only twenty years old. Kidnapped in Africa when a girl, then purchased off the Boston docks, she was more like a daughter than a slave to the Wheatley family. She later married and lived as a free woman of color before her untimely death in 1784.

QUICK REVIEW

African Americans and the Revolution

- Revolutionary principles sparked some to challenge slavery.
- More than 50,000 slaves gained freedom as result of the war.
- By 1800 free black population reached 100,000.

Constitutional Convention
Convention of delegates from the colonies that first met to organize resistance to the Intolerable Acts.

CHRONOLOGY

1775	Lord Dunmore, royal governor of Virginia, appeals to slaves to support Britain
1776	July: Declaration of Independence
	August: Battle of Long Island initiates retreat of Continental Army
	September: British land on Manhattan Island
	December: George Washington counterattacks at Trenton
1777	Slavery abolished in Vermont
	September: British General William Howe captures Philadelphia
	October: British General John Burgoyne surrenders at Saratoga
	November: Continentals settle into winter quarters at Valley Forge
	December: France recognizes American independence
1778	June: France enters the war
	June: Battle of Monmouth hastens British retreat to New York
	July: George Rogers Clark captures Kaskaskia
	December: British capture Savannah
1779	Spain enters the war
1780	February: British land at Charleston
	July: French land at Newport
	September: British General Charles Cornwallis invades North Carolina
1781	March: Articles of Confederation ratified
	May: Robert Morris appointed secretary of finance
	October: Cornwallis surrenders at Yorktown
1782	Peace talks begin
1783	March: Washington mediates issue of officer pensions
	September: Treaty of Paris signed
	November: British evacuate New York
1784	Treaty of Fort Stanwix
	Postwar depression begins
1785	Land Ordinance of 1785
	Treaty of Fort McIntosh
1786	Jefferson's Bill for Establishing Religious Freedom

for her people. Writing to the Mohegan Indian minister Samuel Occom in 1774, Wheatley penned a line that not only applied to African Americans but also to all Americans struggling to be free. "In every human breast God has implanted a principle, which we call love of freedom; it is impatient of oppression, and pants for deliverance. The same principle lives in us."

CONCLUSION

The Revolution was a tumultuous era, marked by violent conflict between Patriots and Loyalists, masters and slaves, settlers and Indian peoples. The advocates of independence emerged successfully, largely because of their ability to pull together and consolidate their identification with the national community. Fearful of the power of central authority, however, Americans created a relatively weak national government. People identified strongly with their local and state communities, and these governments became the site for most of the struggles over political direction that characterized the Revolution and its immediate aftermath. But not all problems, it turned out, could be solved locally. Within a very few years, the nation would sink into a serious economic depression that sorely tested the resources of local communities. By the mid-1780s, many American nationalists were paraphrasing the question Washington had asked at Valley Forge in 1777: "What then is to become of this nation?"

REVIEW QUESTIONS

1. Assess the relative strengths of the Patriots and the Loyalists in the American Revolution.

2. What roles did Indian peoples and African Americans play in the Revolution?

3. Describe the structure of the Articles of Confederation. What were its strengths and weaknesses?

4. How did the Revolution affect politics within the states?

5. What was the effect of the Revolution on African Americans?

KEY TERMS

Articles of Confederation (p. 166)
Bill for Establishing Religious
    Freedom (p. 176)
Bill of Rights (p. 175)
Constitution (p. 159)
Continental Army (p. 157)

Constitutional Convention (p. 177)
Land Ordinance of 1785 (p. 172)
Loyalists (p. 159)
Northwest Ordinance of 1787 (p. 172)
Patriots (p. 157)
Tories (p. 159)

myhistorylab
Flashcard Review

RECOMMENDED READING

Carol Berkin, *Revolutionary Mothers: Women in the Struggle for America's Independence* (2005). Uses a topical and biographical approach to introduce to general readers women's experiences during the Revolution.

Merrill Jensen, *The New Nation: A History of the United States during the Confederation, 1781–1789* (1950). Still the standard work on the 1780s.

Max M. Mintz, *Seeds of Empire: The American Revolutionary Conquest of the Iroquois* (1999). The Revolution as a war for the control of Iroquois lands in upstate New York.

John W. Pulis, *Moving On: Black Loyalists in the Afro-Atlantic World* (1999). Essays on their military role and especially on their communities in Canada, Great Britain, and Africa. In each place, they remained second-class citizens.

Charles Royster, *A Revolutionary People at War* (1979). A pathbreaking study of the Continental Army and popular attitudes toward it. Emphasizes the important role played by the officer corps and the enlisted men in the formation of the first nationalist constituency.

Henry Wiencek, *Imperfect God: George Washington, His Slaves, and the Creation of America* (2003). An award-winning study of Washington's changing attitude toward slavery.

*Here individuals of all nations
are melted into a new race of men,
whose labours and posterity will one day
cause great changes in the world.*
—Hector St. John Crèvecoeur

Congress voting on the issue of independence.

8

THE NEW NATION
1786–1800

WHAT WERE the tensions and conflicts between local and national authorities in the decades after the American Revolution?

GENERAL GEORGE WASHINGTON
Reviewing the Western army at Fort Cumberland the 18th of October

HOW DID Americans differ in their views of the new Constitution, and how were those differences reflected in the struggle to achieve ratification?

WHAT WERE the essential structures of national government under the Constitution?

HOW DID American political parties first begin?

WHAT WERE the first stirrings of an authentic American national culture?

AMERICAN COMMUNITIES
A Rural Massachusetts Community Rises in Defense of Liberty

SEVERAL HUNDRED FARMERS FROM THE TOWN OF PELHAM AND SCORES of other rural communities in western Massachusetts converged on the courthouse in Northampton, the county seat, before sunrise on Tuesday, August 29, 1786. They arrived in military formation, fifes playing and drums beating, armed with muskets, broadswords, and cudgels, the men's tricorner hats festooned with sprigs of evergreen, symbols of freedom frequently worn by Yankee soldiers during the war for independence, which had concluded only four years before. At least a third of the men and virtually all their officers were veterans. The country was in the midst of an economic depression that had hit farm communities particularly hard. Two-thirds of the men who marched on Northampton had been sued for debt, and many had spent time in debtor's prison. Dozens of rural towns petitioned the state government for relief, but not only did the merchant-dominated legislature reject their pleas, but also it raised the property tax in order to pay off the enormous debt the state had accumulated during the Revolution. The new tax was considerably more oppressive than any levied by the British and was considered even more odious, since the revenue would go to a small group of wealthy eastern Massachusetts creditors, to whom the debt was owed.

The farmers decided to take matters into their own hands. When outsiders threatened a man's property, they argued, the community had the right, indeed the duty, to rise up in defense. During the Revolution, armed men had marched on the courts, shutting down the operation of government, and now they were doing it again. The judges of the Northampton court had no choice but to shut down, and that success led to similar actions in many other Massachusetts counties.

This uprising quickly became known as Shays' Rebellion, named for Daniel Shays, a decorated Revolutionary officer and one of the leaders from the town of Pelham. Although rebellion was most widespread in the state of Massachusetts, similar disorders occurred in the country districts of New Hampshire, Vermont, Pennsylvania, Maryland, and Virginia. Conservatives around the country were thrown into panic.

Washington and other conservative leaders saw Shays' Rebellion as a class conflict pitting poor against rich, debtor against creditor. Yet the residents of Pelham and other rural towns acted in common, without regard to rank or property. Big farmers and small farmers alike marched on the county court. They came from tight-knit communities, bound together by family and kinship. Whether well-to-do or poor, they considered themselves "husbandmen," and they directed their protest against "outsiders," the urban residents of Boston and other coastal towns. "I am a man that gets his living by hard labor," one rebel announced, "and I think that husbandry is as honest a calling as any in the world." The country would be a lot better off, he concluded, "if there were less white shirts and more black frocks."

The crisis in Massachusetts ended when a militia force raised by the "white shirts" in the eastern part of the state, and financed by the great merchants, marched west and crushed the Shaysites in January 1787. Daniel Shays fled the state and never returned. Fifteen of the leaders were tried and sentenced to death. Two were hanged before the remainder were pardoned, and some four thousand other farmers temporarily lost their right to vote, to sit on juries, or to hold office. Yet many of them considered their rebellion a success. The next year Massachusetts voters rejected the old governor and elected a new legislature, which passed a moratorium on debts and cut taxes to only 10 percent of what they had been.

The most important consequence of Shays' Rebellion, however, was its effect on conservative nationalists unhappy with the distribution of power between the states and national governments under the Articles of Confederation. The uprising "wrought prodigious changes in the minds of men respecting the powers of government," noted Henry Knox. "Everybody says they must be strengthened and that unless this shall be effected, there is no security for liberty and property." Popular participation had been a necessity during the Revolution. But now the time had come, he declared, "to clip the wings of a mad democracy."

The economic and political crisis of the 1780s would lead to the Constitutional Convention and a new charter for a national state. It would be enthusiastically supported by many, passionately opposed by many others. Its ratification would bring a new and stronger government to power, headed by the leaders of the Revolution. Before the end of the century, that government would lay the groundwork for the longest-lived democratic republic in the world.

Pelham

5–14
Daniel Gray, *Massachusetts Farmers Take Up Arms in Revolt Against Taxes*, 1786

THE CRISIS OF THE 1780S

The depression of the mid-1780s and the political protests it generated were instrumental in the development of strong nationalist sentiment among elite circles. In the aftermath of Shays' Rebellion, these sentiments coalesced into a powerful political movement dedicated to strengthening the national government.

THE ECONOMIC CRISIS

The economic crisis that produced Shays' Rebellion had its origins in the Revolution. The shortage of goods resulting from the British blockade, the demand for supplies by the army and the militias, and the flood of paper currency issued by the Confederation Congress and the states combined to create the worst inflation in American history (see Figure 8.1). Most of this paper money ended up in the hands of merchants who had paid only a fraction of its face value.

After the war ended, inflation gave way to depression. Political revolution could not alter economic realities: the independent United States continued to be a supplier of raw materials and an importer of manufactured products, and Great Britain remained the country's most important trading partner. In 1784, British merchants began dumping goods in the American market, offering easy terms of credit. But the production of exportable goods had been drastically reduced by the fighting, and thus the trade deficit with Britain for the period 1784–86 rose to approximately £5 million (see Figure 8.2). The deficit acted like a magnet, drawing hard currency from American accounts, leaving the country with little silver or gold coin in circulation. Commercial banks insisted on the repayment of old loans and refused to issue new ones. By the end of 1784, the country had fallen into the grip of economic depression, and within two years, prices had fallen by 25 percent.

The depression struck while the nation was attempting to dig out from the huge mountain of debt incurred during the Revolution. Creditors were owed more than $75 million by national and state governments. Not allowed to raise taxes on its own, the Confederation Congress requisitioned the states for the funds necessary for debt repayment. The states in turn taxed their residents. At a time when there was almost no money in circulation, ordinary Americans feared being crushed by the burden of private debt and public taxes. The economic problem became a political problem.

WHAT WERE the tensions and conflicts between local and national authorities in the decades after the American Revolution?

myhistorylab
Review Summary

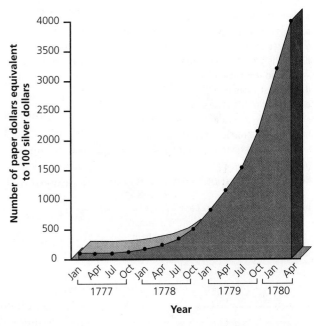

Figure 8.1 Postwar Inflation, 1777–80: The Depreciation of Continental Currency
The flood of Continental currency issued by Congress, and the shortage of goods resulting from the British blockade, combined to create the worst inflation Americans have ever experienced. Things of no value were said to be "not worth a Continental."

John McCusker, "How Much Is That in Real Money?" *Proceedings of the American Antiquarian Society*, N.S. 102 (1992): 297–359.

 6–6
Shays' Rebellion: Letters of Generals William Shepard and Benjamin Lincoln to Governor James Bowdoin of Massachusetts (1787)

Figure 8.2 The Trade Deficit with Great Britain
The American trade deficit with Great Britain rose dramatically with the conclusion of the Revolution.

Historical Statistics of the United States (Washington, DC: Government Printing Office, 1976), 1176.

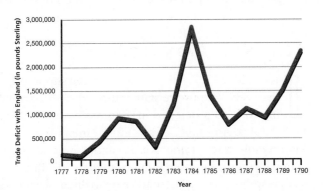

IMAGE KEY
for pages 180–181

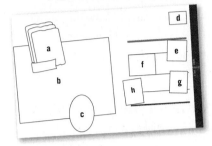

a. The Articles of Confederation.
b. Congress voting on the issue of independence.
c. Phyllis Wheatley, an acclaimed African American poet.
d. The first Stars and Stripes, 1777.
e. The Bill of Rights–the first ten amendments to the U.S. Constitution.
f. A 1794 painting of President George Washington reviewing troops at Fort Cumberland.
g. John Adams in a framed painting by John Trumbull.
h. A 1792 cartoon from *Lady's Magazine* shows allegorical figure of "Columbia" receiving a petition for the "Rights of Woman."

Annapolis Convention   Conference of state delegates at Annapolis, Maryland, that issued a call in September 1786 for a convention to meet at Philadelphia to consider fundamental changes.

HOW DID Americans differ in their views of the new Constitution, and how were those differences reflected in the struggle to achieve ratification?

Review Summary

STATE REMEDIES

In the states, radicals called for regulation of the economy. Farmers and debtors pressed their state governments for legal tender laws, which required creditors to accept a state's paper currency at face value (rather than depreciated market value) for all debts public and private. Despite the opposition of creditors, seven states enacted such laws. For the most part, these were modest programs that worked rather well, caused little depreciation, and did not result in the problems creditors feared.

It was the plan of the state of Rhode Island, however, that received most of the attention. A rural political party campaigning under the slogan "To Relieve the Distressed" captured the legislature in 1786 and enacted a radical currency law. The supply of paper money issued in relation to the population was much greater under this program than in any other state. The law declared the currency legal tender for all debts. If creditors refused to accept it, debtors were allowed to satisfy their obligations by depositing the currency with a county judge, who would then advertise the debt as paid.

Some states erected high tariff barriers to curb imports and protect domestic industries. But foreign shippers found it easy to avoid these duties simply by unloading their cargo in states without tariffs and distributing the goods by overland transport. To be effective, commercial regulations had to be national. Local sentiment had to give way to the unity of a national community.

TOWARD A NEW NATIONAL GOVERNMENT

In 1786 the legislature of Virginia invited all the states to appoint delegates to a convention where they might consider political remedies for the economic crisis. The meeting, held in Annapolis, Maryland, in September was sparsely attended (only twelve delegates from five states), but the men shared their alarm over the rebellion that was simultaneously taking place in Massachusetts, and the possibility of others like it. Convinced of the absolute necessity of strengthening the national government, the **Annapolis Convention** passed a resolution requesting that the Confederation Congress call on all the states to send delegates to a national convention that they might "render the constitution of the federal government adequate to the exigencies of the union." A few weeks later, with some reluctance, the Congress voted to endorse a convention, to be held in Philadelphia in May 1787, "for the sole and express purpose of revising the Articles of Confederation."

Conservatives had in mind more than simply a revision of the Articles, however. They looked forward to a considerably strengthened national government. Believing that the consolidation of power in a strong central government would better serve their interests as merchants, bankers, and planters, the conservatives hid their motives behind the call for revision of the Articles.

THE NEW CONSTITUTION

In late May 1787, a few weeks after the suppression of Shays' Rebellion, fifty-five men from twelve states (the radical government of Rhode Island refusing to send a delegation) assembled at the Pennsylvania State House in Philadelphia. A number of prominent men were missing. Thomas Jefferson and John Adams were serving as ambassadors in Europe, and Patrick Henry of backcountry Virginia declared that he "smelt a rat." But most of America's best-known leaders were present. There were no ordinary farmers or artisans and, of course, no women, African Americans, or Indians. The Constitution was framed by white men who represented America's social and economic elite.

These men were patriots, however, and committed to republicanism: that government must rest on the consent of the governed, and that the authority of rulers must be conditional on popular support. But they were not democrats. They believed that the country already suffered from too much democracy. They feared that ordinary people, if given ready access to power, would enact policies against the interests of the privileged classes and, thus, the nation as a whole. The specter of Shays' Rebellion hung over the proceedings.

THE CONSTITUTIONAL CONVENTION

On their first day of work, the delegates agreed to vote by states, as was the procedure of Congress. They chose Washington to chair the meeting. Although the sessions were closed to the public, James Madison, a young, conservative Virginian with a profound knowledge of history and political philosophy, took voluminous daily minutes that provide the best record of the proceedings. Madison and his fellow Virginians had drafted what became known as the **Virginia Plan**. Presented to the convention shortly after it convened, their plan set the agenda for the convention.

George Washington presides over a session of the Constitutional Convention meeting in Philadelphia's State House (now known as Independence Hall) in an engraving of 1799.

The Virginia Plan proposed scrapping the Articles of Confederation in favor of a "consolidated government" with the power to tax and to enforce its laws directly rather than through the states. The Virginia Plan would have reduced the states to little more than administrative institutions, something like counties. There would be a bicameral national legislature with all seats apportioned by population; members of the House of Representatives would be elected by popular vote, but members of the Senate chosen indirectly by state legislators, insulating them from democratic pressure. The Senate would lead, controlling foreign affairs and the appointment of officials. An appointed chief executive and a national judiciary would together form a Council of Revision having the power to veto both national and state legislation.

The main opposition to the Virginia Plan came from the delegates of the small states who feared being swallowed up by the large ones. After two weeks of debate, William Paterson of New Jersey introduced an alternative, a set of "purely federal" principles that became known as the **New Jersey Plan**. This plan also proposed increasing the powers of the central government but retained the single-house Congress of the Confederation government in which the states were equally represented. After much debate and a series of votes that split the convention down the middle, the delegates finally agreed to what has been called the **Great Compromise**. Representation would be proportional to population in the House, with equal representation to each of the states in the Senate. The compromise allowed for the creation of a strong national government while still providing an important role for the states.

Part of this Great Compromise was a second fundamental agreement between North and South. Southern delegates wanted protections for slavery. They wanted provision for the mandatory return of fugitive southern slaves from the free northern states. To boost their power in Congress, they wanted slaves counted for the purpose of determining a state's proportional representation but excluded from

6–8
James Madison, *The "Distracting Question" in Philadelphia* (1787)

Virginia Plan Proposal calling for a national legislature in which the states would be represented according to population.

New Jersey Plan Proposal of the New Jersey delegation for a strengthened national government in which all states would have an equal representation in a unicameral legislature.

Great Compromise Plan proposed at the 1787 Constitutional Convention for creating a national bicameral legislature in which all states would be equally represented in the Senate and proportionally represented in the House.

7–5
Alexander Hamilton, *Opposing Visions for the New Nation* (1791)

QUICK REVIEW

Central Government Under the Constitution

◆ More powerful than Congress under the Articles of Confederation.

◆ Establishment of strong single person executive.

◆ Establishment of the Supreme Court.

◆ Expanded economic powers for Congress.

---

myhistory lab

Exploring America: *Ratifying the Constitution*

6–17
The Constitution of the United States of America (1789)

Federalists Supporters of the Constitution who favored its ratification.

Anti-Federalists Opponents of the Constitution in the debate over its ratification.

---

the apportioning of taxes. Northern delegates, who wanted a central government with the power to regulate commerce, agreed to count five slaves as the equivalent of three free men—the so-called "three-fifths rule"—in exchange for southern support for a "commerce clause," providing the federal government with the power to regulate commerce with foreign nations, among the several states, and with Indian tribes. Furthermore, representatives from South Carolina and Georgia demanded protection for the slave trade, and after bitter debate the delegates also agreed to include a provision preventing any federal restriction on the importation of slaves for twenty years.

The word "slave" appeared nowhere in the text. Instead the drafters employed phrases such as "persons held to labor." But these provisions amounted to national guarantees for southern slavery. Although a minority of delegates were opposed to slavery and regretted having to give in on this issue, they agreed with Madison, who wrote that "great as the evil is, a dismemberment of the union would be worse."

There was still much to decide regarding the other branches of government. Madison's Council of Revision was scratched in favor of a strong federal judiciary with the implicit power to declare unconstitutional acts of Congress. There were demands for a powerful chief executive, and Alexander Hamilton made the antirepublican proposal that the executive should be appointed for life, raising fears that the office might prove to be, in the words of Edmund Randolph of Virginia, "the fetus of monarchy." But there was considerable support for a president with veto power to check the legislature. To keep the president independent, the delegates decided he should be elected rather than appointed by the Congress, as was the procedure under the Articles of Confederation. But fearing that ordinary voters would never "be sufficiently informed" to select wisely, they insulated the process from popular choice by creating the electoral college. Voters in the states would not actually vote for president. Rather, each state would select a slate of "electors" equal in number to the state's total representation in the House and Senate. Following the general election, the electors in each state would meet to cast their ballots and elect the president.

The delegates voted their approval on September 17, 1787, and transmitted the document to the Confederation Congress, agreeing that it would become operative after ratification by nine states. A number of congressmen were outraged that the convention had exceeded its charge of simply modifying the Articles, but Congress agreed to issue a call for a special ratifying convention in each of the states.

RATIFYING THE NEW CONSTITUTION

The supporters of the new Constitution immediately adopted the name Federalists to describe themselves. In this, as in much of the subsequent process of ratification, the Federalists (or nationalists) grabbed the initiative, and their opponents had to content themselves with the negative label Anti-Federalists (see Map 8.1). The critics of the Constitution were by no means a unified group. But most believed it granted far too much power to the central government, weakening the autonomy of local communities and states.

The argument between **Federalists** and **Anti-Federalists** played out in dozens of essays published in the popular press in 1787 and early 1788. It is doubtful, however, whether any of them made much of a difference in the voting to select delegates for the state ratification conventions. The alignment of forces generally followed the lines laid down during the fights over economic issues in the years since the Revolution.

An agrarian-localist versus commercial-cosmopolitan alignment characterized most of the states. The most critical convention took place in Massachusetts in early 1788. Five states—Delaware, Pennsylvania, New Jersey, Georgia, and Connecticut—had already voted to ratify, but the states with the strongest Anti-Federalist movements had yet to convene. If the Constitution lost in Massachusetts, its fate would be in great danger.

At the Massachusetts convention, the opponents of ratification—which included supporters of Shays' Rebellion—enjoyed a small majority. But several important Anti-Federalist leaders, including Governor John Hancock and Revolutionary leader Samuel Adams, were swayed by the enthusiastic support for the Constitution among Boston's townspeople, whose livelihoods were tied to the commercial economy. On February 16, the convention voted narrowly in favor of ratification. To no one's surprise, Rhode Island rejected the Constitution in March, but Maryland and South Carolina approved it in April and May. On June 21, 1788, New Hampshire became the ninth state to ratify. The Constitution was now the law of the land.

New York, Virginia, and North Carolina were left with the decision of whether to join the new Union. Anti-Federalist support was strong in these states. North Carolina voted to reject. (It would reconsider and join the next year, followed by a still reluctant Rhode Island in 1790.) In New York the delegates were moved to vote their support by a threat from New York City to secede from the state and join the Union separately if the state convention failed to ratify. The Virginia convention was almost evenly divided, but promises to amend the Constitution to protect the people from the potential abuses of the federal government persuaded enough delegates to produce a victory for the Constitution. The promise of such a "Bill of Rights" was important in the ratification vote of five of the states.

MAP EXPLORATION

To explore an interactive version of this map, go to
http://www.prenhall.com/faraghertlc/map8.1

MAP 8.1

The Ratification of the Constitution, 1787–90   The distribution of the vote for the ratification of the Constitution demonstrated its wide support in sections of the country linked to the commercial economy and its disapproval in more remote and backcountry sections. (Note that Maine remained a part of Massachusetts until admitted as a separate state in 1820.)

WHY DID some regions support the Constitution and others did not?

THE BILL OF RIGHTS

The Constitutional Convention had considered a bill of rights patterned on the declarations of rights included in several state constitutions but then rejected it as superfluous. Anti-Federalist delegates in numerous state ratification conventions, however, had proposed a grab bag of over 200 potential amendments protecting the rights of the people against the power of the central government. In June 1789, James Madison, elected to the first Congress as a representative from Virginia, set about transforming these proposed amendments into a coherent series of proposals. Congress approved twelve and sent them to the states, and ten survived the ratification process to become the **Bill of Rights** in 1791.

The First Amendment prohibited Congress from establishing an official religion and provided for the freedom of assembly. It also ensured freedom of speech, a free press, and the right of petition. The other amendments guaranteed the right to bear arms, to limit the government's power to quarter troops in private homes, and to restrain the government from unreasonable searches or seizures; they guaranteed the traditional legal rights under the common law, including the prohibition of double

7–1
James Madison Defends the Constitution (1788)

7–2
William Maclay, *"For the Independent Gazetteer"* (1790)

Bill of Rights   The first ten amendments to the Constitution.

A cartoon published in July 1788, when New York became the eleventh state to ratify the Constitution. After initially voting to reject, North Carolina soon reconsidered, but radical and still reluctant Rhode Island did not join the Union until 1790.

The Federal Edifice "On the Erection of the Eleventh Pillar," caricature from the "Massachusetts Central," August 2, 1788. Neg. #33959. Collection of The New York Historical Society.

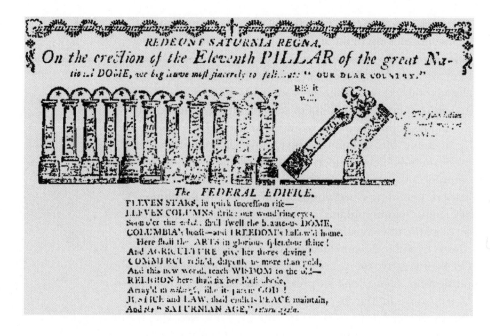

jeopardy, the right not to be compelled to testify against oneself, and due process of law before life, liberty, or property could be taken away. Finally, the unenumerated rights of the people were protected, and the powers not delegated to the federal government were reserved to the states.

The first ten amendments to the Constitution have been a restraining influence on the growth of government power over American citizens. Their provisions have become an admired aspect of the American political tradition throughout the world. The Constitution was authored by the Federalists, but the Bill of Rights is the most important legal legacy of the Anti-Federalists.

THE FIRST FEDERAL ADMINISTRATION

Ratification of the Constitution was followed in the fall of 1788 by the first federal elections for Congress and the presidency, and in the spring of 1789 the new federal government assumed power. The first years under the new federal Constitution were especially important for the future because they shaped the structure of the American nation-state in ways that would be enormously significant for later generations.

THE WASHINGTON PRESIDENCY

Although he dressed in plain American broadcloth at his inauguration and claimed to be content with a plain republican title, Washington was anything but a man of the people. By nature reserved and solemn, he chose to ride about town in a grand carriage drawn by six horses and attended by uniformed liverymen. In the tradition of British royalty, he delivered his addresses personally to Congress and received from both houses an official reply. On the other hand, Washington worked hard to adhere to the letter of the Constitution, refusing, for example, to use the veto power except where he thought Congress had acted unconstitutionally and personally seeking the "advice and consent" of the Senate.

Congress quickly moved to establish departments to run the affairs of state, and Washington soon appointed Thomas Jefferson as secretary of state, Alexander Hamilton as secretary of the treasury, Henry Knox as secretary of war (continuing in the position he held under the Confederation government), and

---

QUICK REVIEW

Amendments to the Constitution

◆ First eight amendments concerned with individual rights.

◆ Guarantees of religious freedom, freedom of expression, protection against arbitrary legal proceedings.

◆ Powers not granted to the national government retained by the people and the states.

WHAT WERE the essential structures of national government under the Constitution?

Review Summary

 6–4
Henry Knox, *Letter to George Washington* (1786)

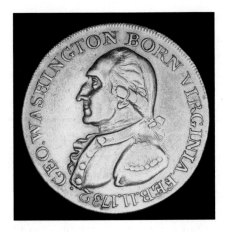 

Two coins from the first decade of the federal republic illustrate political controversies of the period. The Washington cent was proposed by Treasury Secretary Alexander Hamilton in 1792, in the hope of enhancing popular respect for the new government by having the president's bust impressed on coins in the manner of European kings. But after long debate, Congress defeated the plan, the opponents claiming it smacked of monarchy. The Liberty coin, issued by the Mint of the United States in 1795, when under the authority of Secretary of State Thomas Jefferson, features Liberty wearing a liberty cap and bearing a marked resemblance to the French Revolutionary icon Marianne.

Edmund Randolph as attorney general. The president consulted each of these men regularly and during his first term met with them as a group to discuss matters of policy. By the end of Washington's presidency the secretaries had coalesced in what came to be known as the cabinet, an institution that has survived to the present despite the absence of constitutional authority. Washington understood the importance of national unity, and in his style of leadership, his consultations, and his appointments he sought to achieve a balance of conflicting political perspectives and sectional interests. His intentions would be sorely tested during the eight years of his administration.

THE FEDERAL JUDICIARY

The most important piece of legislation to emerge from the first session of Congress was the **Judiciary Act of 1789**, implementing the judicial clause of the Constitution, which empowered Congress to set the number of justices on the Supreme Court and create a system of federal courts. The act established a High Court of six justices (increased to nine in 1869) and established circuit and district federal courts. Strong nationalists argued for a powerful federal legal system that would provide a uniform code of civil and criminal justice throughout the country. But the localists in Congress, intent on preserving local community autonomy, successfully fought to retain the various bodies of law that had developed in the states. The act gave federal courts limited original jurisdiction, restricting them mostly to appeals from state courts. But it established the principle of federal **judicial review** of state legislation, despite the silence of the Constitution on this point.

Washington appointed and the Senate confirmed the six Supreme Court justices, including John Jay, who became Chief Justice. During the Court's first decade it heard relatively few cases yet managed to raise considerable political controversy. In *Chisholm* v. *Georgia* (1793) the Court ruled in favor of two South Carolina residents suing the State of Georgia for the recovery of confiscated property, thus supporting the Constitution's grant of federal jurisdiction over disputes "between a state and citizens of another state." Many localists believed the ruling threatened the integrity of the states, and in response, they proposed an Eleventh Amendment to the Constitution, protecting states against suits by citizens of another state. It was ratified in 1798. The Supreme Court nevertheless established itself as the final authority on questions of law when it invalidated a Virginia statute in *Ware* v. *Hylton* (1796) and upheld the constitutionality of an act of Congress in *Hylton* v. *United States* (1796).

Judiciary Act of 1789 Act of Congress that implemented the judiciary clause of the Constitution by establishing the Supreme Court and a system of lower federal courts.

Judicial review A power implied in the Constitution that gives federal courts the right to review and determine the constitutionality of acts passed by Congress and state legislatures.

Alexander Hamilton (ca. 1804) by John
Trumbull. Although Hamilton's fiscal
program was controversial, it restored
the financial health of the United
States.

HAMILTON'S FISCAL PROGRAM

Fiscal and economic affairs were important in the new government. Lacking revenue and facing the massive national
debt run up during the Revolution, the government took
power in a condition of virtual bankruptcy.

Treasury Secretary Hamilton took on the task of reorganizing the nation's finances. In 1790 he submitted a
"Report on the Public Credit," recommending the federal
"redemption" at full value of the national debt owed to foreign and domestic creditors, as well as the "assumption" of the
obligations accumulated by the states during the previous fifteen years. Congress readily agreed to settle the $11 million
owed to foreign creditors but balked at the redemption of
the domestic debt of $42 million and the assumption of the
state debts of another $25 million. Hamilton proposed issu-
ing new interest-bearing government bonds that would be
exchanged for the full face value of all the notes, warrants,
and securities the government had distributed during
the Revolution.

Thousands of veterans had been rewarded for their service with warrants for land or money, but as they waited for
Congress to mark out the territory or provide the funding,
many had been forced by necessity to sell to speculators at
deep discounts. Hamilton's proposal, his colleague James Madison objected,
would result in windfall profits for speculators and create a permanent federal
debt. Hamilton did not dispute these claims but instead argued that they were
good things. The creation of a federal debt by the issue of securities would give
the government the ability to finance national projects or provide for national
defense in the event of war, and the possession of those securities in the hands of
a wealthy class of citizens would offer a guarantee for the government's stability.
There was even greater congressional opposition to Hamilton's proposal for the
assumption of state debts. Some states (mostly in the South) had already arranged
to pay off their debts, whereas others (mostly in the North) had not, so the plan
seemed to reward the insolvent and punish the thrifty. Congress remained deadlocked on these issues for six months, until congressmen from Pennsylvania and
Virginia arranged a compromise that facilitated the eventual passage of Hamilton's credit program.

Hamilton now proposed a second component of his fiscal program, the
establishment of a Bank of the United States. The bank, a public corporation
funded by private capital, would serve as the depository of government funds
and the fiscal agent of the Treasury. Congress narrowly approved it, but Madison's
opposition raised doubts in the president's mind about the constitutionality of
the measure, and Washington solicited the opinion of his cabinet. Here for the
first time were articulated the classic interpretations of constitutional authority.
Jefferson took a "strict constructionist" position, arguing that the powers of the
federal government must be limited to those specifically enumerated in the Constitution. This position came closest to the basic agreement of the men who had
drafted the document. Hamilton, on the other hand, reasoned that the Constitution "implied" the power to use whatever means were "necessary and proper"
to carry out its enumerated powers, the "loose constructionist" position. Persuaded by Hamilton's opinion, Washington signed the bill, and the bank went into
operation in 1791.

The final component of Hamilton's fiscal program, outlined in his famous "Report on Manufactures," was an ambitious plan, involving the use of government securities as investment capital for "infant industries" and high protective tariffs to encourage the development of an industrial economy. Congressmen from farming areas, whose previous objections to Hamilton's preference for the "monied interests" had not prevailed, were finally able to frustrate him on this last proposal. Hamilton's views, they argued, would limit them to roles exactly like those they had played within the British empire and would amount to exchanging British for Boston and New York masters. Of equal importance, the plan failed to inspire the enthusiasm of American capitalists, who continued to be more interested in investments in shipping or in land speculation than in industrial production.

Many of Hamilton's specific proposals for increased tariff protection, however, became part of the revision of duties that took place in 1792. Moreover, his fiscal program as a whole dramatically restored the financial health of the United States.

The Federalist political coalition, forged during the ratification of the Constitution, was sorely strained by these debates over fiscal policy. By the middle of 1792 Jefferson—representing southern agrarians—and Hamilton—speaking for northern capitalists—were locked in a full-scale feud within the administration. Hamilton conducted himself more like a prime minister than a cabinet secretary, greatly offending Jefferson, who considered himself the president's heir apparent. But the dispute went deeper than a mere conflict of personalities. Hamilton stated the difference clearly when he wrote that "one side appears to believe that there is a serious plot to overturn the State governments, and substitute a monarchy to the present republican system," while "the other side firmly believes that there is a serious plot to overturn the general government and elevate the separate powers of the States upon its ruins."

Distressed by these political disputes, Washington considered retiring at the end of his first term, but both factions encouraged him to remain in office to bridge their differences. The factions did contest the vice presidency. In December 1792 Washington was reelected by unanimous vote in the electoral college, but incumbent Vice President John Adams was only narrowly returned to office. It was an indication of things to come.

AMERICAN FOREIGN POLICY

The conflict between Hamilton and Jefferson grew even more bitter over the issue of American foreign policy. The commanding event of the Atlantic world during the 1790s was the French Revolution, which broke out in 1789. Most Americans enthusiastically welcomed the fall of the French monarchy. But with the inauguration of the Reign of Terror in 1793, which claimed the lives of hundreds of aristocrats and politicians upon the guillotine, American conservatives began to voice their opposition. The execution of King Louis XVI in January 1793 and the outbreak of war between revolutionary France and monarchical Great Britain a few weeks later firmly divided American opinion.

Most at issue was whether the Franco-American alliance of 1778 required the United States to support France in its war with Britain. All of Washington's cabinet agreed on the importance of American neutrality. With France and Britain

Little Turtle, a war chief of the Miami tribe of the Ohio Valley, led a large pan-Indian army to victory over the Americans in 1790 and 1791. After his forces were defeated at the Battle of Fallen Timbers in 1794, he became a friend of the United States. This lithograph is a copy of an oil portrait, which no longer survives, by the artist Gilbert Stuart.

Little Turtle, or Mich-i-kin-i-qua, Miami War Chief, Conqueror of Harmar and St. Clair. Lithograph made from a portrait painted in 1797 by Gilbert Stuart. Indiana Historical Society Library (negative no. C2584).

 6–13
Thomas Jefferson, *The Secretary of State and the Secretary of the Treasury Battle about the Constitution* (1791)

QUICK REVIEW

Hamilton's Reports

◆ Plan to address Revolutionary War debt.

◆ Proposal to charter a national bank.

◆ Recommendation for government to promote industry.

prowling for each other's vessels on the high seas, the vast colonial trade of Europe was delivered up to neutral powers, the United States prominent among them. Jefferson believed it highly unlikely that the French would call upon the Americans to honor the 1778 treaty and that the administration should simply wait and see. But Hamilton argued that so great was the danger of American involvement in the war that Washington should immediately declare the treaty "temporarily and provisionally suspended."

These disagreements revealed two contrasting perspectives on the course the United States should chart in international waters. Hamilton and the nationalists believed in the necessity of an accommodation with Great Britain, the most important trading partner of the United States and the world's greatest naval power. Jefferson, Madison, and their supporters, on the other hand, looked for more international independence, less connection with the British, and thus closer relations with Britain's traditional rival, France. They pinned their hopes for the future on American western expansion.

The debate in the United States grew hotter with the arrival in early 1793 of French ambassador Edmond Genêt. Knowing he must act before "Citizen" Genêt (as the ambassador was popularly known) compromised American sovereignty and involved the United States in a war with Britain, Washington issued a proclamation of neutrality on April 22, 1793. In it he assured the world that the United States intended to pursue "a conduct friendly and impartial towards the belligerent powers," while continuing to do business with all sides.

Hamilton's supporters applauded the president, but Jefferson's friends were outraged. Throughout the country, activists sympathetic to France organized Democratic Societies, political clubs modeled after the Sons of Liberty. Society members corresponded with each other, campaigned on behalf of candidates, and lobbied with congressmen.

Citizen Genêt miscalculated, however, alienating even his supporters, when he demanded that Washington call Congress into special session to debate neutrality. Jefferson, previously a confidant of the ambassador, now denounced Genêt as "hot-headed" and "indecent towards the President." But his words came too late to save his reputation with Washington, and at the end of 1793 Jefferson left the administration.

THE UNITED STATES AND THE INDIAN PEOPLES

One of the most pressing problems of the Washington presidency concerned the West. The American attempt to treat western Indian tribes as conquered peoples after the Revolution had resulted only in further violence and warfare. In the Northwest Ordinance of 1787 (see Chapter 7), the Confederation Congress abandoned that course for a new approach. "The utmost good faith shall always be observed towards the Indians," the ordinance read. "Their lands and property shall never be taken from them without their consent." Yet the ordinance was premised on the survey and sale to American settlers of Indian land north of the Ohio River and the creation of new state governments. The ordinance pointed in wildly contradictory directions.

The new federal government continued to pursue this inconsistent policy. In 1790 Congress passed the **Intercourse Act**, the basic law by which the United States would "regulate trade and intercourse with the Indian tribes." The act declared public treaties between the United States and the Indian nations the only legal means of obtaining Indian land. Treaty making, thus, became the procedure for establishing and maintaining relations with Indian nations. To eliminate the abuses of unscrupulous traders, the act also created a federal licensing

---

Intercourse Act Passed in 1790, this law regulated trade and intercourse with the Indian tribes and declared public treaties between the United States and Indian nations the only means of obtaining Indian lands.

system, and subsequent legislation authorized the creation of subsidized trading houses, or "factories," where Indians could obtain manufactured goods at reasonable prices. These provisions indicated the best intentions of the Washington administration.

On the other hand, one of the federal government's highest priorities was the acquisition of western Indian land to support a growing population of farmers (see Map 8.2). The federal government, in fact, was unable to control the flood of settlers coming down the Ohio River. In defense of their homelands, villages of Shawnees, Delawares, and other Indian peoples confederated with the Miamis under their war chief Little Turtle. In the fall of 1790 Little Turtle lured federal forces led by General Josiah Harmar into the confederacy's stronghold in Ohio and badly mauled them. In November 1791 the confederation inflicted an even more disastrous defeat on a large American force. More than 900 Americans were killed or wounded, making this the worst defeat of an army by Indians in North American history (see Seeing History).

SPANISH FLORIDA AND BRITISH CANADA

The position of the United States in the West was made even more precarious by the hostility of Spain and Great Britain, which controlled the adjoining territories. Under the dynamic leadership of King Carlos III and his able ministers, Spain introduced liberal reforms to revitalize the rule-bound bureaucracy of its American empire. As a result the economy of New Spain grew rapidly in the 1780s. Moreover, Spain had reasserted itself in North America, acquiring the French claims to Louisiana before the end of the Seven Years' War, expanding into California, seizing the Gulf Coast during the American Revolution, and regaining Florida from Britain in the Treaty of Paris in 1783. Spain claimed for itself much of the territory that today makes up the states of Tennessee, Alabama, and Mississippi and pursued a policy designed to block the continued expansion of the young republic (see Map 8.3).

Spain's anti-American policy in the West had several facets. Controlling both sides of the lower Mississippi, the Spanish closed the river to American shipping, making it impossible for western American farmers to market their crops through the port of New Orleans. They also sought to create a barrier to American settlement by promoting immigration to Louisiana and Florida. They succeeded in attracting several thousand Acadians, whom the British had deported from Nova Scotia during the Seven Years' War. Reassembling their distinctive communities in the bayou country of Louisiana, these tough emigrants became known as the Cajuns.

But otherwise, the Spanish had little success with immigration and relied mostly on creating a barrier of pro-Spanish Indian nations in the lower Mississippi Valley.

North of the Ohio River, the situation was much the same. Thousands of Loyalists had fled the United States in the aftermath of the Revolution and settled

MAP EXPLORATION

To explore an interactive version of this map, go to **http://www.prenhall.com/faraghertlc/map8.2**

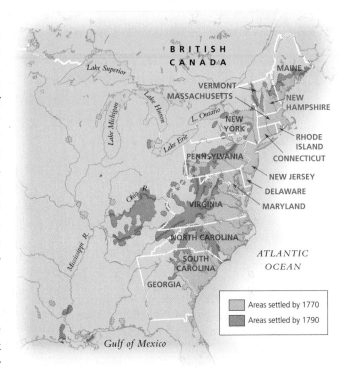

MAP 8.2

Spread of Settlement: The Backcountry Expands, 1770–90 From 1770 to 1790, American settlement moved across the Appalachians for the first time. The Ohio Valley became the focus of bitter warfare between Indians and settlers.

WHY DID tensions between Indians and settlers increase during this period?

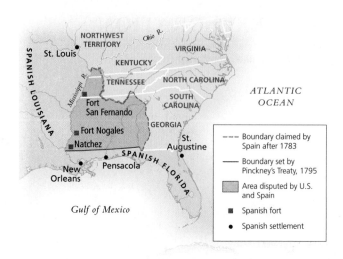

MAP 8.3

Spanish Claims to American Territory, 1783–95   Before 1795, the Spanish claimed the American territory of the Old Southwest and barred Americans from access to the port of New Orleans, effectively closing the Mississippi River. This dispute was settled by Pinckney's Treaty in 1795.

WHAT WERE the terms of Pinckney's Treaty?

7–7
Backcountry Turmoil Puts the New Government to the Test (1794)

Whiskey Rebellion   Armed uprising in 1794 by farmers in western Pennsylvania who attempted to prevent the collection of the excise tax on whiskey.

Treaty of Greenville   Treaty of 1795 in which Native Americans in the Old Northwest were forced to cede most of the present state of Ohio to the United States.

north of lakes Ontario and Erie. They were understandably hostile to the new republic. In 1791 the British Parliament passed the Canada Act, creating the province of Upper Canada (later renamed Ontario) and granting the Loyalists limited self-government. To protect this province, British troops remained at a number of posts within American territory, such as Detroit, where they supplied arms to the Indian nations, in hopes of creating a buffer to American expansion.

THE CRISES OF 1794

These conditions laid the groundwork for the gravest crisis of Washington's presidency in 1794. In the West, the inability of the federal government to subdue the Indians, eliminate the British from the northern fur trade, or arrange with the Spanish for unencumbered use of the Mississippi River stirred frontiersmen to loud protest. Secret agents for Great Britain and Spain sought to entice American settlers to quit the Union and join themselves to Canada or Florida. In the Atlantic, Great Britain declared a blockade of France and its colonies in the West Indies, and by early 1794 the Royal Navy had confiscated the cargoes of more than 250 American ships, threatening hundreds of merchants with ruin.

To make matters worse a rebellion broke out among farmers in western Pennsylvania in the summer of 1794. To produce needed revenue, Congress had placed an excise tax on the distillation of whiskey, which many farm families produced from their surpluses of corn. Throughout rural America, farmers protested that the new tax ran counter to the principles of the Revolution. "Internal taxes upon consumption," declared the citizens of Mingo Creek, in western Pennsylvania, are "most dangerous to the civil rights of freemen, and must in the end destroy the liberties of every country in which they are introduced." Protest turned to riot when the Mingo Creek militia attempted to seize the tax collector, and several of their number were killed in the confrontation.

The "**Whiskey Rebellion**" came at a time when Washington considered the nation to be under siege. The combination of Indian attack, international intrigue, and domestic insurrection, he believed, posed the greatest threat to the nation since the Revolution. He called up a federal army of 13,000 men, approximately the same size as the one he had commanded during the Revolution, and ordered the occupation of western Pennsylvania. Authorities arrested twenty people, and a judge convicted two of treason. The protests gradually died down and Washington pardoned the felons, sparing their lives. The president overreacted, for there was no organized insurrection in western Pennsylvania. Nevertheless, his mobilization of federal military power was a dramatic demonstration of his commitment to the preservation of the Union, the protection of the western boundary, and the supremacy of the national over the local community.

Washington's action was reinforced by an impressive American victory against the western Indian confederacy. Following the disastrous defeat inflicted by Little Turtle, the president directed General Anthony Wayne to lead a greatly strengthened American force to secure the Northwest. At the Battle of Fallen Timbers, fought in northern Ohio on August 20, 1794, Wayne crushed the Indians. This American victory set the stage for the **Treaty of Greenville** in 1795, in which the representatives of twelve Indian nations ceded a huge territory encompassing

The Columbian Tragedy

Broadsides—large sheets printed on one side, suitable for posting—were an important medium of popular communication in the late eighteenth and early nineteenth centuries. This one, lamenting the disastrous defeat of an American expeditionary force at the hands of the Ohio Indian confederacy in 1791, in which more than 900 Americans were killed or wounded was published in Boston and sold throughout New England for the price of six cents. The struggle against the Ohio Indian confederacy was one of the most critical issues during Washington's presidency. Across the top are the names of the officers killed in battle, each accompanied by the icon of a black coffin. On the left is a woodcut of Major-General Richard Butler, the highest-ranking officer to die, and beneath it an Indian warrior alongside a skull and crossbones. On the right is a crude representation of the battleground. As one contemporary critic put it, all the images are "of the commonest description," yet the broadside survives in a number of copies, indicating that it probably sold quite well. The broadside did double duty—as both memorial for the dead and protest against the incompetence of the army's leaders. Most of the broadside is devoted to a mournful ballad that nevertheless concludes that the nation will ultimately prevail because "the *Lord* is on our side." ∎

WHY WOULD Americans purchase this broadside and display it in their homes?

"The Columbian Tragedy" (1791), courtesy Beinecke Rare Book and Manuscript Library, Yale University.

Seeing History

195

In this 1794 painting, President George Washington reviews some 13,000 troops at Fort Cumberland on the Potomac before dispatching them to suppress the Whiskey Rebellion. Washington's mobilization of federal military power dramatically demonstrated the federal commitment to the preservation of the Union and the protection of the western boundary.

Francis Kemmelmeyer, "General George Washington Reviewing the Western Army at Fort Cumberland the 18th of October 1794," after 1794. Oil on paper backed with linen, 18 1/8 × 23 1/8 . Courtesy of Winterthur Museum.

GENERAL GEORGE WASHINGTON.
Reviewing the Western army at Fort Cumberland the 18th of october 1794

most of present-day Ohio, much of Indiana, and other enclaves in the Northwest, including the town of Detroit and the tiny village of Chicago.

SETTLING DISPUTES WITH BRITAIN AND SPAIN

The strengthened American position in the West encouraged the British finally to settle their dispute with the United States so that they might concentrate on defeating republican France. Washington dispatched Chief Justice John Jay to London to arrange a settlement with the British, and in November 1794 Jay and his British counterpart signed an agreement providing for British withdrawal from American soil by 1796, for limited American trade with British colonies, and for "most-favored-nation" status (meaning that each nation would enjoy terms of trade equal to the best terms accorded any other nation). The treaty represented a solid gain for the young republic. With only a small army and no navy to speak of, the United States was in no position to wage war.

Jay's Treaty enshrined Hamilton's conception of American neutrality. Hamilton's opponents, on the other hand, were enraged at what they considered an accommodation with the British at the expense of the French. Moreover, Southerners were alienated by Jay's failure to negotiate compensation for masters whose slaves had fled to the British during the Revolution. Throughout the country opponents of the treaty organized protests and demonstrations. Chief Justice Jay joked he found his way across country by the light of his burning effigies. Nevertheless, the Senate, dominated by supporters of Hamilton, ratified the agreement in June 1795. In the House, a coalition of Southerners, Westerners, and friends of France attempted to stall the treaty by threatening to withhold the necessary appropriations. They demanded they be allowed to examine the diplomatic correspondence regarding the whole affair, but the president refused, establishing the precedent of "executive privilege" in matters of state.

The deadlock continued until late in the year, when word arrived that the Spanish had abandoned their claims to the territory south of the Ohio River.

Jay's Treaty Treaty with Britain negotiated in 1794 in which the United States made major concessions to avert a war over the British seizure of American ships.

Spain had declared war on revolutionary France but quickly suffered a humiliating defeat. Fearing the loss of its American empire, the Spanish found it expedient to come to an agreement with the Americans. In 1795 American envoy Thomas Pinckney negotiated a treaty setting the international boundary at the 31st parallel (the southern boundary of Mississippi and Alabama) and opening the Mississippi to American shipping. This treaty was compatible with the Jeffersonian conception of empire, and congressmen from the South and West were delighted with its terms. Administration supporters, however, demanded that the House agree in the matter of Jay's Treaty before the Senate would approve Pinckney's.

With the ratification of these important treaties, the United States established its sovereignty over the land west of the Appalachians and opened to American commerce a vast market extending from Atlantic ports to the Mississippi Valley. From a political standpoint, however, the events of 1794 and 1795 brought Washington down from his pedestal. Vilified by the opposition press, sick of politics, and longing to return to private life, Washington rejected the idea of a third term.

WASHINGTON'S FAREWELL ADDRESS

During the last months of his term, Washington published a "Farewell Address" to the nation. In the best-remembered portion of the address, he urged that the United States seek commercial connections with all nations but "have with them as little political connection as possible." Why, he asked, "entangle our peace and prosperity in the toils of European ambition, rivalship, interest, humor, or caprice?" Looking forward, he expressed great concern about the growing acrimony between political factions, which, he argued, "agitates the community with ill-founded jealousies and false alarms, . . . and opens the door to foreign influence and corruption."

7–8
George Washington, *Farewell Address* (1746)

FEDERALISTS AND DEMOCRATIC REPUBLICANS

The framers of the Constitution envisioned a one-party state in which partisan distinctions would be muted by patriotism and public virtue. "Among the numerous advantages promised by a well constructed Union," Madison had written, is "its tendency to break and control the violence of faction." Not only did he fail to anticipate the rise of political parties or factions, but also he saw them as potentially harmful to the new nation. Yet it was Madison who took the first steps toward organizing the opposition to the policies of the Washington administration, and it was Hamilton, Madison's coauthor of *The Federalist Papers*, who organized administration supporters into a disciplined political faction. Despite the intentions of the framers, in the twelve years between the ratification of the Constitution and the federal election of 1800, political parties became a fundamental part of the American system of government.

HOW DID American political parties first begin?

 myhistory**lab**
Review Summary

THE RISE OF POLITICAL PARTIES

Evident in the debates and votes of Congress from 1789 to 1795 was a series of shifting coalitions. These coalitions first began to polarize into opposing political factions during the debate over Jay's Treaty in 1795, when agrarians, Westerners, Southerners, and supporters of France came together in opposition. By the time of the election of 1796, the factions had taken names for themselves.

OVERVIEW | The First American Party System

Federalist Party — Organized by figures in the Washington administration who were in favor of a strong federal government, friendship with the British, and opposition to the French Revolution; its power base was among merchants, property owners, and urban workers tied to the commercial economy. A minority party after 1800, it was regionally strong only in New England.

Democratic Republican Party — Arose as the opposition to the Federalists; its adherents were in favor of limiting federal power; they were sympathetic to the French Revolution and hostile to Great Britain; the party drew strength from southern planters and northern farmers and was the majority party after 1800.

myhistorylab

Overview: *The First American Party System*

QUICK REVIEW

Party Politics

- Washington's farewell address denounced partisanship.
- Candidates in presidential election of 1796: John Adams (Federalist), Thomas Jefferson (Republican).
- Adams won despite Hamilton's interference.

XYZ Affair Diplomatic incident in 1798 in which Americans were outraged by the demand of the French for a bribe as a condition for negotiating with American diplomats.

Hamilton's supporters continued to claim the mantle of Federalism. But Jefferson's supporters christened themselves Republicans, suggesting by implication that the Federalists were really monarchists at heart. (Historians use the term "Democratic Republicans" to distinguish them from the modern Republican Party, founded in 1854.)

The two political factions played a fitful role in the presidential election of 1796, which pitted Vice President John Adams against Thomas Jefferson. Partisan organization was strongest in the Middle States, where there was a real contest of political forces, weakest in New England and the South, where sectional loyalty prevailed and organized opposition was weaker. The absence of party discipline was demonstrated when the ballots of the presidential electors, cast in their respective state capitals, were counted in the Senate. Adams was victorious, but in accordance with the Constitution the vice presidency went to the candidate with the second-highest total, and that was Jefferson. The new administration was born divided.

THE ADAMS PRESIDENCY

Adams was put in the difficult situation of facing a political opposition led by his own vice president. On the other hand, Adams benefited from rising tensions between the United States and France. Angered by Jay's Treaty, the French suspended diplomatic relations with the United States at the end of 1796 and inaugurated a tough new policy toward American shipping. Hoping to resolve the crisis, Adams sent an American delegation to France. But in dispatches sent back to the United States, the envoys reported that three agents of the French foreign ministry had demanded a bribe before any negotiations could begin. Skeptical Republicans demanded the release of the dispatches, which Adams agreed to in 1798, substituting the letters X, Y, Z for the names of the French agents. The documents upheld Adams's case and proved a major liability for the Republicans, sparking powerful anti-French sentiment throughout the country. "Millions for defense, but not one cent for tribute!" was the slogan of the day. The **XYZ Affair**, as it became known, sent Adams's popularity soaring.

THE ALIEN AND SEDITION ACTS

During the spring of 1798 Adams and the Federalists prepared the country for war with France. Congress authorized tripling the size of the army, and Washington came out of retirement to command the force. Fears of a French invasion declined

The **presidential election** of 1800 was the first to feature campaign advertising. "T. Jefferson, President of the United States of America; John Adams—no more," reads the streamer on this election banner, illustrated with an American eagle and a portrait of Jefferson. This was mild rhetoric in a campaign characterized by wild charges. The Republicans labeled Adams a warmonger and a monarchist, while the Federalists denounced Jefferson as an atheist, Jacobin, and sexual libertine.

after word arrived of a British naval victory over the French at Aboukir Bay in Egypt in August 1798, but what became known as the "**Quasi-War**" between France and the United States continued.

The Democratic Republicans contested the Federalist war measures and began for the first time to act as a genuine opposition party, complete with caucuses, floor leaders, and partisan discipline. They contested the election of Speaker of the House of Representatives, which henceforth became a partisan office. The more effective the Republicans became as an opposition, the more treasonous they appeared in the eyes of the Federalists.

In the summer of 1798 the Federalist majority in Congress, with the acquiescence of President Adams, passed four acts severely limiting both freedom of speech and the freedom of the press and threatening the liberty of foreigners in the United States. The Naturalization Act extended the period of residence required for citizenship from five to fourteen years. The **Alien Act** and the Alien Enemies Act authorized the president to order the imprisonment or deportation of suspected aliens during wartime. Finally, the **Sedition Act** provided heavy fines and imprisonment for anyone convicted of writing, publishing, or speaking anything of "a false, scandalous and malicious" nature against the government or any of its officers.

The Federalists intended these repressive laws as weapons to defeat the Democratic Republicans. They prosecuted dissent by indicting leading opposition newspaper editors and writers, fining and imprisoning at least twenty-five of them. The most vilified was Congressman Matthew Lyon of Vermont, scorned by Federalists as "Ragged Matt the Democrat." In July 1798 Lyon was convicted of publishing libelous statements about President Adams and thrown into prison. Later that year, he conducted a campaign from his jail cell and was reelected to Congress.

THE REVOLUTION OF 1800

In 1799 the French convinced President Adams that they were willing to settle their dispute with the United States when they released seized American ships and requested negotiations. Adams sensed a public mood running toward peace. But the Hamiltonian wing of the party, always scornful of public sentiment, continued to beat the drums of war. When Federalists in Congress attempted to block

7–9
The Alien and Sedition Acts
(1798)

7–10
Questions of Constitutionality and the Roots of Nullification (1798)

Quasi-War Undeclared naval war of 1797 to 1800 between the United States and France.

Alien Act Act passed by Congress in 1798 that authorized the president to imprison or deport suspected aliens during wartime.

Sedition Act An act passed by Congress in 1798 that provided fines for anyone convicted of writing, publishing, or speaking out against the government or its officers.

States' rights   Favoring the rights of individual states over rights claimed by the national government.

---

the negotiations, Adams threatened to resign and turn the government over to Vice President Jefferson.

The presidential campaign of 1800 was the first to be contested by two disciplined political parties. Caucuses of congressmen nominated respective slates: Adams and Charles Cotesworth Pinckney of South Carolina for the Federalists, Jefferson and Aaron Burr of New York for the Republicans. Both tickets thus represented attempts at sectional balance. The Democratic Republicans presented themselves as the party of traditional agrarian purity, of liberty and **states' rights**, of "government rigorously frugal and simple," in the words of Jefferson. The Federalists, divided and embittered, waged a defensive struggle for strong central government and public order and often resorted to negative campaigning. They denounced Jefferson as an atheist, a Jacobin, and the father of mulatto children.

Adams won in New England but elsewhere was overwhelmed (see Map 8.4). Jefferson called it "the Revolution of 1800." Party discipline was so effective, in fact, that it created a constitutional crisis. By casting all their ballots for Jefferson and Burr, Republican electors thoughtlessly produced a tie vote, thus forcing the election into the lame duck House of Representatives controlled by the Federalists. Eventually the Federalists arranged with their opponents to elect Jefferson without any of them having to vote in his favor. Afterward, Congress passed and the states ratified the Twelfth Amendment, creating separate ballots for president and vice president in time for the next presidential election.

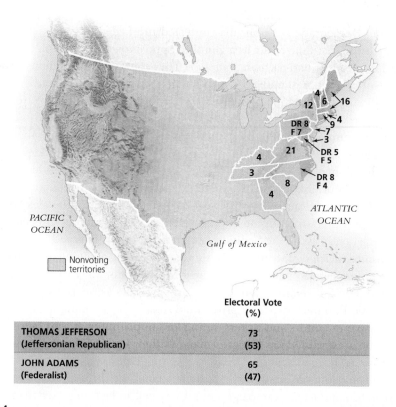

	Electoral Vote (%)
THOMAS JEFFERSON (Jeffersonian Republican)	73 (53)
JOHN ADAMS (Federalist)	65 (47)

MAP 8.4

The Election of 1800   In the presidential election of 1800, Democratic Republican victories in New York and the divided vote in Pennsylvania threw the election to Jefferson. The combination of the South and these crucial Middle States would keep the Democratic Republicans in control of the federal government for the next generation.

WHAT WERE the key issues in the election of 1800?

DEMOCRATIC POLITICAL CULTURE

Accompanying the rise of partisan politics was a transformation in popular political participation. Consider the custom of celebrating Independence Day. At the beginning of the 1790s, in many communities, the day featured demonstrations of military prowess by veteran officers, followed by banquets for leaders. Relatively few Americans played a direct role. But during the political controversies of the decade, a tradition of popular celebration developed. People took to the streets, set off fireworks, erected liberty poles, and listened to readings of the preamble of the Declaration of Independence, which more than any other document encapsulated and symbolized republican ideology.

There was a corresponding increase in the **suffrage**. In 1789 state regulations limited the franchise to a small percentage of the adult population. Women, African Americans, and Indians could not vote, but neither could a third to a half of all free adult males, who were excluded by tax-paying or property-owning requirements. Moreover, even among the eligible, the turnout was generally low.

The situation changed with the increasing competition between Democratic Republicans and Federalists. Popular pressure resulted in the introduction of universal white manhood suffrage in four states by 1800 and the reduction of property requirements in others. Thus was inaugurated a movement that would sweep the nation over the next quarter century. As a consequence voter turnout increased in all the states. The growth of popular interest in politics was a transformation as important as the peaceful transition from Federalists to Democratic Republicans in national government.

"THE RISING GLORY OF AMERICA"

I n 1771, Philip Freneau and Hugh Henry Brackenridge addressed their graduating class at Princeton on "The Rising Glory of America." Thus far American contributions to learning and the arts had been slim, they admitted, but they were boundlessly optimistic about the potential of their country.

THE LIBERTY OF THE PRESS

At the beginning of the Revolution in 1775, there were thirty-seven weekly or semi-weekly newspapers in the thirteen colonies, only seven of which were Loyalist in sentiment. By 1789, the number of papers in the United States had grown to ninety-two, including eight dailies; three papers were being published west of the Appalachians. Relative to population, there were more newspapers in the United States than in any other country in the world—a reflection of the remarkably high literacy rate of the American people. During the political controversy of the 1790s, the press became the principal medium of Federalist and Jeffersonian Republican opinion, and papers came to be identified by their politics.

The prosecutions under the Sedition Act, however, threatened to curb the further development of the media, and in their opposition to these measures Democratic Republicans played an important role in establishing the principle of a free press. In *An Essay on Liberty of the Press* (1799), the Virginia lawyer George Hay, later appointed to the federal bench by President Jefferson, wrote that "a man may say everything which his passions suggest." Were this not true, he argued, the First Amendment would have been "the grossest absurdity that was ever conceived by the human mind." In his first inaugural address, Jefferson echoed this early champion of the freedom of expression. "Error of opinion

Suffrage   The right to vote in a political election.

WHAT WERE the first stirrings of an authentic American national culture?

myhistorylab
Review Summary

CHRONOLOGY

1786	Annapolis Convention
1787	Constitutional Convention
1787–88	*The Federalist Papers* published
1788	Constitution ratified
	First federal elections
1789	President George Washington inaugurated in New York City
	Judiciary Act
	French Revolution begins
1790	Agreement on site on the Potomac River for the nation's capital
	Indian Intercourse Act
	Judith Sargent Murray publishes *On the Equality of the Sexes*
1791	Bill of Rights ratified
	Bank of the United States chartered
	Alexander Hamilton's "Report on Manufactures"
	Ohio Indians defeat General Arthur St. Clair's army
1792	Washington reelected
1793	England and France at war; America reaps trade windfall

	Citizen Genêt affair
	President Washington proclaims American neutrality in Europe
	Supreme Court asserts itself as final authority in *Chisholm* v. *Georgia*
1794	Whiskey Rebellion
	Battle of Fallen Timbers
	Jay's Treaty with the British concluded
1795	Pinckney's Treaty negotiated with the Spanish
	Treaty of Greenville
1796	President Washington's Farewell Address
	John Adams elected president
1797–98	French seize American ships
1798	XYZ Affair
	"Quasi-War" with France
	Alien and Sedition Acts
1800	Convention of 1800
	Thomas Jefferson elected president
	Mason Locke Weems publishes *Life of Washington*

---

myhistorylab

Exploring America: *The Partisan Press*

may be tolerated," he declared, "where reason is left free to combat it." During Jefferson's presidency the Alien and Sedition Acts, which had justified the suppression of political opinion, were repealed or allowed to expire.

BOOKS, BOOKS, BOOKS

During the post-Revolutionary years there was an enormous outpouring of American publications. In the cities the number of bookstores grew in response to the demand for reading matter. Perhaps even more significant was the appearance in the countryside of numerous book peddlers who supplied farm households with Bibles, gazettes, almanacs, sermons, and political pamphlets.

Some of the most interesting American books of the postwar years examined the developing American character. The French emigrant Michel-Guillaume Jean de Crevecoeur, in *Letters from an American Farmer* (1782), proposed that the American, a product of many cultures, was a "new man" with ideas new to the world. John Filson, the author of *The Discovery, Settlement, and Present State of Kentucke* (1784), presented the narrative of one such new man, the Kentucky pioneer Daniel Boone. In doing so, he took an important step toward the creation of that most American of literary genres, the western.

But for Americans, the most important "new man" was George Washington. In 1800, an itinerant bookseller, Mason Locke Weems, published a short biography of the first president that became the new nation's first best seller. Weems's *Life of Washington* introduced a series of popular and completely fabricated anecdotes, including the story of young Washington and the cherry tree. The biography was beloved by ordinary Americans of all political persuasions. Decades later, Abraham Lincoln recalled that he had read Weems "away back in my childhood, the earliest days of my being able to read," and had been profoundly impressed by "the struggles for the liberties of the country." Although Washington had in fact become a partisan leader of the Federalists during his second term, Weems presented him as a unifying figure for the political culture of the new nation, and that was the way he would be remembered.

WOMEN ON THE INTELLECTUAL SCENE

One of the most interesting literary trends of the 1790s was the growing demand for books appealing to women readers. Susanna Haswell Rowson's *Charlotte Temple* (1791), a tale of seduction and abandonment, ran up tremendous sales and remained in print for more than a century. The young republic thus marked the first dramatic appearance of women writers and women readers. Although women's literacy rates continued lower than men's, they rose steadily as girls joined boys in common schools. This increase was one of the most important social legacies of the democratic struggles of the Revolutionary era.

Some writers argued that the new republican order ought to provide new roles for women as well as for men. The first avowed feminist in American history was Judith Sargent Murray. Her essay "On the Equality of the Sexes," written in 1779 and published in 1790, threw down a bold challenge to men. "Yes, ye lordly, ye haughty sex," she wrote, "our souls are by nature equal to yours," and predicted that American women would commence "a new era in female history." Federalists listened to such opinions with horror. "Women of masculine minds," one Boston minister sneered, "have generally masculine manners."

There seemed to be general agreement among all parties, however, that the time had come for women to be better educated. Republican institutions of self-government were widely thought to depend on the wisdom and self-discipline of the American people. Civic virtue, so indispensable for the republic, needed to be taught at home. Thus were women provided the opportunity to be not simply "helpmates" but also people "learned and wise." But they were also expected to be content with a narrow role, not to wish for fuller participation in the American experiment.

Judith Sargent Murray, a portrait by John Singleton Copley, completed in 1771. Born into an elite merchant family, she became a wife and mother but also a poet, essayist, playwright, novelist, and historian.

John Singleton Copley (1738–1815), "Portrait of Mrs. John Stevens (Judith Sargent, later Mrs. John Murray)," 1770–72. Oil on canvas, 50 × 40 in. Daniel J. Terra Art Acquisition Endowment Fund, 2000.6. © Terra Foundation for American Art, Chicago/Art Resource, New York.

 6–12
Molly Wallace, *Valedictory Oration* (1792)

CONCLUSION

During the last years of the eighteenth century, the United States adopted a new constitution and established a new national government. It repaid the debt run up during the Revolution and made peace with adversaries abroad and Indian peoples at home. Americans began to learn how to channel their disagreements into political struggle. The new government,

born in the economic and political crisis that surrounded Shays' Rebellion, had withstood a first decade of stress, but tensions would continue to divide the people. At the beginning of the new century, it remained uncertain whether the new nation would find a way to control and channel the energies of an expanding people.

REVIEW QUESTIONS

1. Discuss the conflicting ideals of local and national authority in the debate over the Constitution.

2. What were the major crises faced by the Washington and Adams administrations?

3. Describe the roles of Madison and Hamilton in the formation of the first American political parties.

4. What did Jefferson mean when he talked of "the Revolution of 1800"?

5. Discuss the contributions of the Revolutionary generation to the construction of a national culture.

KEY TERMS

Flashcard Review

Alien Act (p. 199)	**New Jersey Plan** (p. 185)
Annapolis Convention (p. 184)	**Quasi-War** (p. 199)
Anti-Federalists (p. 186)	**Sedition Act** (p. 199)
Bill of Rights (p. 187)	**States' rights** (p. 200)
Federalists (p. 186)	**Suffrage** (p. 201)
Great Compromise (p. 185)	**Treaty of Greenville** (p. 194)
Intercourse Act (p. 192)	**Virginia Plan** (p. 185)
Jay's Treaty (p. 196)	**Whiskey Rebellion** (p. 194)
Judicial review (p. 189)	**XYZ Affair** (p. 198)
Judiciary Act of 1789 (p. 189)	

RECOMMENDED READING

Akhil Reed Amar, *The Bill of Rights: Creation and Reconstruction* (1998). A legal analysis arguing that the first ten amendments were meant to protect the majority from the potential tyranny of the federal government.

Robert A. Dahl, *How Democratic Is the American Constitution?* (2003). An eminent political scientist examines the antidemocratic character of the nation's defining political document.

Stanley Elkins and Eric McKitrick, *The Age of Federalism* (1993). A massive and informative account of the politics of the 1790s, from the ratification of the Constitution to the election of Jefferson.

Paul Finkelman, *Slavery and the Founders: Race and Liberty in the Age of Jefferson* (2001). A persuasive historical argument that the Constitution legitimated a "slaveholders' republic."

Joanne B. Freeman, *Affairs of Honor: National Politics in the New Republic* (2001). A major reassessment of political culture in the new republic, stressing the importance of the culture of honor.

Reginald Horsman, *The Frontier in the Formative Years, 1783–1815* (1970). A sensitive survey of developments in the West, emphasizing that the "western question" was one of the most important facing the young republic.

Calvin H. Johnson, *Righteous Anger at the Wicked States: The Meaning of the Founders' Constitution* (2005). An argument that the authors of the Constitution were responding to the turmoil of the "wicked states," particularly their economic and fiscal policies.

Jackson Turner Main, *The Antifederalists: Critics of the Constitution, 1781–1788* (1961). A detailed examination of the localist tradition in early American politics. Includes a discussion of the ratification of the Constitution from the point of view of its opponents.

Simon P. Newman, *Parades and the Politics of the Street: Festive Culture in the Early American Republic* (1997). The participation of ordinary Americans in the political culture of the new republic.

Leonard L. Richards, *Shays' Rebellion: The American Revolution's Final Battle* (2002). A new interpretation that significantly broadens the meaning of the uprising of farmers in western Massachusetts.

James M. Smith, *Freedom's Fetters: The Alien and Sedition Laws and American Civil Liberties* (1966). Remains the best overview of the Federalist threat to liberty, as well as the Jeffersonian Republican counterattack.

Bernard A. Weisberger, *America Afire: Jefferson, Adams, and the Revolutionary Election of 1800* (2000). Shows that the election and the transfer of power were victories for popular self-government and that they set a major precedent for all other elections.

Gordon Wood, *The Creation of the American Republic, 1776–1787* (1969). This general survey provides the best overview of the Constitutional Convention.

myhistorylab™

Where it's a good time to connect to the past!

For study resources for this chapter, go to **www.myhistorylab.com** and choose *Out of Many, Teaching and Learning Classroom Edition*. You will find a wealth of study and review material for this chapter, including pretests and posttests, customized study plan, key-term review flash cards, interactive map and document activities, and documents for analysis.

Since I started this letter we have been in a state of continual alarm, and now I have time to write only two or three lines to ask you to tell Papa that we are alive, in good health, and I hope safe from danger . . .

—Rosalie E. Calvert–August 30, 1814

"Burning of the White House" by Leslie Saalburg.

9

AN EMPIRE FOR LIBERTY
1790–1824

WITH WHAT powers did the United States share North America in the decades after independence?

WHAT WERE the most important strengths of the American economy in the early 1800s?

WHAT VALUES were embodied in agrarian republicanism?

WHAT FACTORS led to conflict between the United States and Britain in North America?

WHAT WERE the consequences of the War of 1812?

WHAT WERE the principle provisions of the Missouri Compromise?

1790   1824

AMERICAN COMMUNITIES
Expansion Touches Mandan Villages on the Upper Missouri

IN MID-OCTOBER 1804, NEWS ARRIVED AT THE MANDAN VILLAGES, prominently situated on bluffs overlooking the upper Missouri River, that an American military party led by Meriwether Lewis and William Clark was coming up the river. The principal chiefs, hoping for expanded trade and support against their enemies the Sioux, welcomed these first American visitors. As the expedition's three boats and forty-three men approached the village, Clark wrote, "great numbers on both sides flocked down to the bank to view us." That evening, the Mandans welcomed the Americans with an enthusiastic dance and gifts of food.

Lewis and Clark had been sent by President Thomas Jefferson to survey the Louisiana Purchase and to find an overland route to the Pacific Ocean. They were also instructed to inform the Indians that they now owed loyalty—and trade— to the American government. Meeting with the village chiefs, the Americans offered the Mandans a military and economic alliance. His people would like nothing better, responded Chief Black Cat, for the Mandans had fallen on hard times over the past decade. [Some twenty years earlier], "the smallpox destroyed the greater part of the nation," the chief said. "All the nations before this malady [were] afraid of them, [but] after they were reduced, the Sioux and other Indians waged war, and killed a great many."

The Americans spent the winter with the Mandans, joining in their communal life and establishing firm and friendly relations with them. Lewis and Clark spent many hours acquiring important geographic information from the Mandans. The information provided by the Mandans and other Indian peoples to the west was vital to the success of the expedition. Lewis and Clark's "voyage of discovery" depended largely on the willingness of Indian peoples to share their knowledge of the land with the Americans.

In need of interpreters who could help them communicate with other Indian communities on their way, the Americans hired several multilingual Frenchmen who lived with the Mandans. They also acquired the services of Sacajawea, the fifteen-year-old Lemhi wife of one of the Frenchmen, who became the only woman to join the westward journey.

When the party left the Mandan villages in March, Clark wrote, his men were "generally healthy, except venereal complaints which is very common amongst the natives and the men catch it from them." After an arduous journey across the Rock-

Mandan Villages

ies, the party reached the Pacific Ocean at the mouth of the Columbia River, where they spent the winter. Overdue and feared lost, they returned in triumph to St. Louis in September 1806. Before long the Americans had established Fort Clark at the Mandan villages, giving American traders a base for challenging British dominance of the western fur trade. The permanent American presence brought increased contact, and with it much more disease. In 1837, a terrible smallpox epidemic carried away the vast majority of the Mandans, reducing the population to fewer than 150. Four Bears, a Mandan chief who had been a child at the time of the Lewis and Clark visit, spoke these last words to the remnants of his people:

"I have loved the whites," he declared. "I have lived with them ever since I was a boy." But in return for the kindness of the Mandans, the Americans had brought this plague. "I do not fear death, my friends," he said, "but to die with my face rotten, that even the wolves will shrink with horror at seeing me, and say to themselves, that is Four Bears, the friend of the whites. They have deceived me," he pronounced with his last breath. "Those that I always considered as brothers turned out to be my worst enemies."

In sending Lewis and Clark on their "voyage of discovery" to claim the land and the loyalty of the Mandans and other western Indian communities, President Jefferson was motivated by his vision of an expanding American republic of self-sufficient farmers. During his and succeeding presidencies, expansion became a key element of national policy and pride. Yet, as the experience of the Mandans showed, what Jefferson viewed as enlargement of "the empire for liberty" had a dark side—the destruction, from disease and coerced displacement, of the communities created by America's first peoples.

In the first quarter of the nineteenth century, the young American nation was preoccupied with defining its place on the North American continent and in the larger world of independent nations. At the same time that America found opportunities in world trade and in territorial expansion, it encountered international opposition from Britain and resistance at home from hard-pressed Indian nations. This chapter describes the ways in which, through war and diplomacy, the United States defined and controlled the nation's expanded boundaries, a vital step in building a sense of national identity and community.

NORTH AMERICAN COMMUNITIES FROM COAST TO COAST

In spite of the political turmoil of the 1790s, the young United States entered the new century full of national pride and energy. But the larger issue, America's place in the world, was still uncertain, beginning with its situation on the North American continent (see Map 9.1).

THE NEW NATION

At first glance, the United States of America in 1800 was little different from the scattered colonies of the pre-Revolution era. Two-thirds of the young nation's people still lived in a long thin line of settlement within fifty miles of the Atlantic coast. Most people lived on farms or in small towns. Because they rarely traveled far from home, peoples' horizons were limited and local.

Although only 3 percent of the nation's population lived in cities, the Atlantic ports continued to dominate the nation economically and politically. In 1800, the nation's most important urban centers were all Atlantic seaports: Charleston (population 20,000), Baltimore (26,000), Philadelphia (70,000), New York (60,000), and Boston (25,000).

Nevertheless, the new nation was already transforming itself: between 1790 and 1800, according to the first and second federal censuses, the American population grew from 3.9 million to 5.3 million. Growth by migration was greatest in the trans-Appalachian West, a region that was already home to approximately 100,000 Indians. To the immediate north was the continuing presence of the British in what is now Canada and the growing Russian presence in Alaska. To the west and south loomed the Spanish empire, while closer still was the nearby racial powder keg in the Caribbean.

NORTHERN NEIGHBORS: BRITISH NORTH AMERICA AND RUSSIAN AMERICA

Although Britain had lost its war to keep the American colonies, it kept a firm grasp on British North America, which had once been French Canada (see Chapter 6). Legislative assemblies were established in Upper and Lower Canada and in the Maritimes in 1791, but, learning from their American fiasco, Britain kept the legislatures under strong executive control. British North America dominated the continental fur trade and the great succession of waterways—the St. Lawrence River, the Great Lakes, and the rivers beyond—that made it possible. Britain was on friendly terms with many of the native peoples who were part of the trade. This economic grip was a challenge and frustration to many westward-moving Americans. At the same time, the dispersed nature of the Canadian colonies made them, at least in the eyes of some Americans, ripe for conquest.

Russian settlement of what is now Alaska posed another more remote threat to the United States. Alaska was an extension of the Russian conquest of Siberia, which was driven by the fur trade.

The Russians sometimes took furs by force, holding whole villages hostage and brutalizing the native Inuit and Aleut peoples. After the Aleut Revolt of 1766, the Russian authorities promised to end the abuse, but by 1800, the precontact population of 25,000 Aleuts had been greatly reduced. At the same time, sexual relations and intermarriage between fur trappers and Aleut women created a large group of Russian creoles who assumed an increasingly prominent position in the Alaskan fur trade as navigators, explorers, clerks, and traders.

WITH WHAT powers did the United States share North America in the decades after independence?

myhistory**lab**

Review Summary

IMAGE KEY
for pages 206–207

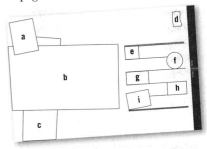

a. Thomas Jefferson (1743–1826), by Rembrandt Peale, c. 1805.

b. "Burning of the White House" by Leslie Saalburg.

c. A map of the Erie Canal.

d. An antique wooden compass used by Lewis and Clark.

e. The clipper ship *Flying Cloud*, which sailed in 1894 from New York to San Francisco in 89 days.

f. A symbol of the Philadelphia Society for Promoting Agriculture.

g. An 1833 portrait of two Sauk Indians by John Wesley Jarvis.

h. The Battle of Lake Erie in the War of 1812.

i. James Monroe and Robert R. Livingstone negotiations with Comte Talleyrand for the Louisiana Purchase.

MAP 9.1

North America in 1800   In 1800, the new United States of America shared the North American continent with territories held by the European powers: British Canada, French Louisiana (secretly ceded that year to France by Spain), Spanish Florida, Spanish Mexico, and Russian Alaska, expanding southward along the Pacific Coast. Few people could have imagined that by 1850, the United States would span the continent. But the American settlers who had crossed the Appalachians to the Ohio River Valley were already convinced that opportunity lay in the West.

WHAT MOTIVATED American settlers to move to the West?

The Russian-American Company, chartered by the tsar in 1799, first set up American headquarters at Kodiak. When overhunting caused a scarcity of furs, the Russians moved their headquarters south to Sitka, in what is now the southeastern panhandle of Alaska, only to have their first fortress destroyed in the Tlingit Revolt of 1802. The Russians reestablished Sitka by force in 1804, and over the next generation, established Russian settlements along the Pacific Coast as far south as Fort Ross, which was just north of San Francisco Bay.

This view shows Sitka, the center of Russian activities in Alaska, in 1827. Russian architectural styles and building techniques are apparent in the Church of St. Michael the Archangel in the right background, contrasting with the Asian and Indian origins of most of Sitka's inhabitants.

THE SPANISH EMPIRE

On paper, Spain posed the greatest threat to the United States because it possessed most of North and South America. Mexico City, with a population of 200,000, was by far the largest and most elegant city on the continent. But Spanish control crumbled rapidly in the 1790s. Tensions mounted between the Spanish-born *peninsulares,* high officials and bureaucrats, and the native-born *criollos* of Spanish descent, who chafed at their subordination, especially after the success of the American Revolution. Furthermore, none of New Spain's northern provinces, created to protect the approaches to Mexico's fabulously wealthy silver mines, thrived.

In 1769, in their last effort to protect their rich colony of Mexico, the Spanish established a chain of twenty-one missions in Alta California that stretched north from San Diego (1769) to Sonoma (1823). Despite Spain's desire to seal its territory from commerce with other nations, a brisk but illegal trade in otter skins, hides, and tallow developed between the United States and California.

American traders were making inroads on Spanish-held territory along the Mississippi River as well. New Orleans, acquired by Spain from France at the end of the Seven Years' War in 1763, was becoming a thriving international port. Every year, a greater proportion of products for the New Orleans trade was supplied by Americans living some distance up the Mississippi River. Pinckney's 1795 treaty with Spain guaranteed Americans free navigation of the Mississippi River and the right to deposit goods at the port of New Orleans. Nevertheless, Americans were uncomfortably aware that the city's crucial location at the mouth of the Mississippi meant that whatever foreign nation possessed New Orleans had the power to choke off the flourishing trade in the vast Mississippi Valley river system.

More than 600 miles north was the small trading town of St. Louis, founded by the New Orleans trader Pierre Laclède in 1763. By 1800, the town had fewer than a thousand residents, three-quarters of whom were involved in the Indian trade of the Missouri River. Spanish officials tried to supervise that trade from their offices in the town, but real control rested in the hands of the Laclèdes and other French traders.

HAITI AND THE CARIBBEAN

The Caribbean posed other challenges. The rich sugar-producing islands, variously colonies of Spain, France, and Britain provided 80 to 90 percent of the European supply of sugar. All the sugar plantations used enslaved Africans as the labor force. Thus, they shared with the slaveholding American South a distinctive Afro–North American society that cut across national boundaries. This world was jolted in 1791 by the revolt of black slaves in Saint-Domingue, France's richest colony. Under the leadership of Toussaint L'Ouverture, the former colony, renamed Haiti, became North America's first independent black nation. Its existence struck fear into the hearts of white slaveowners at the same time that it served as a beacon of hope to the enslaved.

TRANS-APPALACHIA

Within the United States itself, the region of greatest growth was territory west of the Appalachian Mountains, and it was this area that was most affected by fears of continuing British influence on Indian peoples. By 1800, about 500,000 people (the vast majority from Virginia and North Carolina) had found rich and fertile land along the Ohio River system. Soon there was enough population for statehood. Kentucky (1792) and Tennessee (1796) were the first trans-Appalachian states admitted to the Union.

Migration to the west was generally a family affair, with groups of kin moving together to a new area. One observer wrote of a caravan moving across the mountains: "They had prepared baskets made of fine hickory withe or splints, and fastening two of them together with ropes they put a child in each basket and put it across a pack saddle." Once pioneers had managed to struggle by road over the Appalachians, they gladly took to the rivers, especially the Ohio, to move farther west.

Cincinnati, strategically situated 450 miles downstream from Pittsburgh, was a particularly dramatic example of the rapid community growth and development that characterized the trans-Appalachian region. Founded in 1788, Cincinnati began life as a military fort, defending settlers in the fertile Miami River Valley of Ohio from resistance by Shawnee and Miami Indians. After the Battle of Fallen Timbers broke Indian resistance in 1794, Cincinnati became the point of departure for immigrants arriving by the Ohio River on their way to settle the interior of the Old Northwest: Ohio, Indiana, and Illinois.

Cincinnati merchants were soon shipping farm goods from the fertile Miami Valley down the Ohio–Mississippi River system to New Orleans, 1,500 miles away. River traffic increased yearly, and control of New Orleans became a key concern of western farmers and merchants. If New Orleans refused to accept American goods, Cincinnati merchants and many thousands of trans-Appalachian farmers would be ruined.

A NATIONAL ECONOMY

WHAT WERE the most important strengths of the American economy in the early 1800s?

myhistorylab

Review Summary

Concern about New Orleans illustrates the new nation's weak position in international trade. In 1800, the United States was a producer of raw materials. It faced the same challenge that developing nations confront today. At the mercy of fluctuating world commodity prices they cannot control, such countries have great difficulty protecting themselves from economic dominance by stronger, more established nations.

COTTON AND THE ECONOMY OF THE YOUNG REPUBLIC

In 1800, the United States was predominantly rural and agricultural. Farming families followed centuries-old traditions of working with hand tools and draft animals, producing most of their own food and fiber. Crops were grown for subsistence (home use) rather than for sale. Commodities such as whiskey and hogs (both easy to transport) provided small and irregular cash incomes or items for barter.

The situation was very different in the South, where plantation agriculture based on enslaved workers was wholly commercial and international. Cotton, and the slave labor system that produced it, assumed a commanding place in southern life and in the foreign trade of the United States. The essential contribution of cotton to the nation's economy was the most important social and political reality of the early nineteenth century.

In 1790, however, increasing foreign demand for American goods and services hardly seemed likely. Trade with Britain, still the biggest customer for American raw materials, was considerably less than it had been before the Revolution. Britain and France both excluded Americans from their lucrative West Indian trade and taxed American ships with discriminatory duties. It was difficult to be independent in a world dominated by great powers.

The cotton gin, invented in 1793, was a simple device with huge consequences. It transformed the South, condemned millions of African Americans to slavery, and was the single largest source of American economic growth before 1860.

SHIPPING AND THE ECONOMIC BOOM

Despite these restrictions on American commerce, the strong shipping trade begun during the colonial era and centered in the Atlantic ports became a major asset in the 1790s, when events in Europe provided America with extraordinary opportunities. The French Revolution, which began in 1789, initiated nearly twenty-five years of warfare between Britain and France. All along the Atlantic seaboard, urban centers thrived as American ships carried European goods that could no longer be transported on British ships without danger of French attack (and vice versa). Because America was neutral, its merchants had the legal right to import European goods and promptly reexport them to other European countries. In spite of British and French efforts to prevent the practice (see Chapter 8), reexports amounted to half of the profits in the booming shipping trade (see Figure 9.1). The long series of European wars also allowed enterprising Americans to seize such lucrative international opportunities, such as the China trade.

The active American participation in international trade fostered a strong and diversified shipbuilding industry. All the major Atlantic ports boasted expanding shipbuilding enterprises. Demands for speed increased as well, resulting in what many people have regarded as the flower of American shipbuilding, the clipper ship. The narrow-hulled, many-sailed clipper ships of the 1840s and 1850s set records for ships of their size. In 1854, *Flying Cloud,* built in the Boston shipyards of Donald McKay, sailed from New York to San Francisco—a 16,000-mile trip that usually took 150 to 200 days—in a mere 89 days.

Figure 9.1 American Export Trade, 1790–1815
This graph shows how completely the American shipping boom was tied to European events. Exports, half of which were reexports, surged when Britain and France were at war and America could take advantage of its neutral status. Exports slumped in the brief period of European peace from 1803 to 1805 and plunged following the Embargo Act of 1807 and the outbreak of the War of 1812.

WHAT VALUES were embodied in agrarian republicanism?

myhistorylab
Review Summary

8–2
Thomas Jefferson, *First Inaugural Address* (1801)

8–7
Fisher Ames, *The Republican. No. II* (1804)

THE JEFFERSON PRESIDENCY

At noon on March 4, 1801, Thomas Jefferson walked from his modest boardinghouse through the swampy streets of the new federal city of Washington to the unfinished Capitol. George Washington and John Adams had ridden in elaborate carriages to their inaugurals. Jefferson, although accepting a military honor guard, demonstrated by his actions that he rejected the elaborate, quasi-monarchical style of the two Federalist presidents and (to his mind) their autocratic style of government as well.

For all its lack of pretension, Jefferson's inauguration as the third president of the United States was a momentous occasion in American history, for it marked the peaceful transition from one political party, the Federalists, to their hated rivals, the Jeffersonian Republicans. Beginning in an atmosphere of exceptional political bitterness, Jefferson's presidency was to demonstrate that a strongly led party system could shape national policy without leading either to dictatorship or to revolt. Jefferson's own moderation may have been the crucial factor. Setting a tone of conciliation in his inaugural address, he announced, "We are all republicans; we are all federalists" and during his eight years in office he paid close attention to ways to attract moderate Federalists to the Jeffersonian Republican party.

REPUBLICAN AGRARIANISM

Behind all the events of Jefferson's administration (1801–1809) was a clear set of beliefs that embodied his interpretation of the meaning of republicanism for Americans. Jefferson's years as ambassador to France in the 1780s were particularly important in shaping his political thinking. Recoiling from the extremes of wealth and poverty he saw there, he came to believe that it was impossible for Europe to achieve a just society that could guarantee to most of its members the "life, liberty and . . . pursuit of happiness" of which he had written in the Declaration of Independence. Only America, he believed, provided fertile earth for the true citizenship necessary to a republican form of government. What America had, and Europe lacked, was room to grow.

Jefferson envisaged a nation of small family farms clustered together in rural communities—an agrarian republic. He believed that only a nation of roughly equal yeoman farmers, each secure in his own possessions and not dependent on someone else for his livelihood, would exhibit the concern for the community good that was essential in a republic. Indeed, Jefferson said that "those who labor in the earth are the chosen people of God," and so he viewed himself, though his "farm" was the large slave-owning plantation of Monticello.

Jefferson's vision of an expanding agrarian republic remains to this day one of our most compelling ideas about America's uniqueness and special destiny. But expansionism contained some negative aspects. The lure of the western lands fostered constant mobility and dissatisfaction rather than the stable, settled communities Jefferson envisaged. Expansionism caused environmental damage, in particular soil exhaustion—a consequence of abandoning old lands, rather than conserving them, and moving on to new ones. Expansionism encouraged the spread of plantations based on slave labor in the South (see Chapter 10). Finally, it bred a ruthlessness toward Indian peoples, who were pushed out of the way for white settlement or who, like the Mandans, were devastated by the diseases that accompanied European trade and contact. Jefferson's agrarianism thus bred some of the best and some of the worst traits of the developing nation.

QUICK REVIEW

Growth of American Trade: 1793–1807

◆ French Revolution initiated renewed period of warfare between France and Britain.

◆ American merchants wanted to supply both sides.

◆ Expansion of trade led to development of shipbuilding industry and growth of coastal cities.

Tall, ungainly, and diffident in manner, Thomas Jefferson was nonetheless a man of genius: an architect, naturalist, philosopher, and politician. His political philosophy, republican agrarianism, is illustrated by this symbol of the Philadelphia Society for Promoting Agriculture, in which the farmer exemplifies Jefferson's hopes for America. As he said, "those who labor in the earth are the chosen people of God."

JEFFERSON'S GOVERNMENT

Thomas Jefferson came to office determined to reverse the Federalist policies of the 1790s and to ensure an agrarian "republic of virtue." Accordingly, he proposed a program of "simplicity and frugality," promising to cut all internal taxes, to reduce the size of the army, the navy, and the government staff, and to eliminate the entire national debt inherited from the Federalists. He kept all of these promises, even the last, although the Louisiana Purchase of 1803 cost the Treasury $15 million. This diminishment of government was a key matter of republican principle to Jefferson. If his ideal yeoman farmer was to be a truly self-governing citizen, the federal government must not, Jefferson believed, be either large or powerful.

Perhaps one reason for Jefferson's success was that the federal government he headed was small and unimportant by today's standards. The national government's main service to ordinary people was mail delivery, and already in 1800 there were persistent complaints about the slowness, unreliability, and expense of the Postal Service! Everything else—law and order, education, welfare, road maintenance, economic control—rested with state or local governments. Power and political loyalty were still local, not national.

8–3
Margaret Bayard Smith, On *Thomas Jefferson and the Peaceful Transfer of Power from the Federalists to the Jeffersonian Republicans* (1801)

AN INDEPENDENT JUDICIARY

Although determined to reverse Federalist fiscal policies, Jefferson was much more moderate concerning Federalist officeholders. He resisted demands by other Jeffersonian Republicans that "the board should be swept" and all

Federalist officeholders replaced with party loyalists. During his term of office, Jefferson allowed 132 Federalists to remain at their posts, while placing Jeffersonian Republicans in 158 other posts. Jefferson's restraint, however, did not extend to the most notorious Federalist appointees, the so-called midnight judges.

In the last days of the Adams administration, the Federalist-dominated Congress passed several acts that created new judgeships and other positions within the federal judiciary. Jeffersonian Republicans feared that the losing Federalist Party was trying to politicize the judiciary by appointing Federalists who would use their positions to strengthen the powers of the federal government, a policy the Jeffersonians opposed. In one of his last acts in office, President Adams appointed Federalists—quickly dubbed the "midnight judges"—to these new positions. William Marbury, whom President Adams had appointed justice of the peace for Washington, DC, and three other appointees sued James Madison, Jefferson's secretary of state, to receive their commissions for their offices. Before the case came to trial, however, Congress, controlled by Jeffersonian Republicans, repealed the acts. This case, *Marbury* v. *Madison*, provoked a landmark decision from the U.S. Supreme Court.

At issue was a fundamental constitutional point: Was the judiciary independent of politics? In his celebrated 1803 decision in **Marbury v. Madison**, Chief Justice John Marshall, himself a strong Federalist and an Adams appointee, managed to find a way to please both parties. Marshall ruled that Marbury was entitled to his commission but that the Supreme Court did not have the power to force the executive branch to give it to him. At first glance, Jefferson's government appeared to have won the battle. But in the long run, Marshall established the principle that only the federal judiciary could "say what the law is," thus unequivocally defending the independence of the judiciary and the principle of judicial review. This was a vital step in realizing the three-way balance of power among the branches of the federal government—executive (president), legislative (Congress), and judiciary (courts)—envisaged in the Constitution. Equally important, during his long tenure in office (1801–35), Chief Justice Marshall consistently led the Supreme Court in a series of decisions that favored the federal government over state governments (see Chapter 12). Under Marshall's direction, the Supreme Court became a powerful nationalizing force, often to the dismay of defenders of states' rights, Jefferson's Republicans among them.

OPPORTUNITY: THE LOUISIANA PURCHASE

In 1800, the United States was a new and fragile democracy in a world dominated by two contending great powers: Britain and France. In 1799, the young general Napoleon Bonaparte seized control of France and began a career of military conquests. Great Britain promptly went to war against him. If England and France fought in North America, as they had in the Seven Years' War (see Chapter 6), America's national security would be directly threatened. Jefferson, who had once ardently supported the goals of the French Revolution, viewed Napoleon's ambitions with increasing apprehension. He feared a resumption of the political animosity of the 1790s, when Federalists and Jeffersonian Republicans had so bitterly disagreed on policy toward France (see Chapter 8).

As had his predecessors, Napoleon considered North America a potential battleground on which to fight the British. He looked first at the Caribbean, where he planned to reconquer Haiti, the world's first independent black nation, reenslave its people, and use the rich profits from sugar to finance his European wars. As a first step, in 1800, France secretly reacquired the Louisiana Territory, the vast western drainage of the Mississippi and Missouri Rivers, from Spain, which had held the region since 1763.

QUICK REVIEW

Marbury v. Madison (1803)

♦ Case sparked by Jefferson's refusal to recognize Adams's "midnight judges."

♦ Justice Marshall ruled that the duty of the courts was "to say what the law is."

♦ Ruling made the Supreme Court a powerful nationalizing force.

Exploring America: *Continentalism*

Marbury v. Madison Supreme Court decision of 1803 that created the precedent of judicial review by ruling as unconstitutional part of the Judiciary Act of 1789.

In 1801, when President Jefferson first learned of the French–Spanish secret agreement about Louisiana, he was concerned about the threat to American commerce on the Mississippi River. In fact, in 1802, the Spanish commander at New Orleans (the French had not yet taken formal control) closed the port to American shippers, thus disrupting commerce as far away as Cincinnati. As Jefferson feared, Federalists in Congress clamored for military action to reopen the port.

In the summer of 1802, Jefferson instructed Robert Livingston, the American ambassador to France, to negotiate to buy New Orleans and the surrounding area for $2 million (or up to $10 million, if necessary). The initial bargaining was not promising, but suddenly, in early 1803, Napoleon was ready to sell. His effort to reconquer Haiti failed, defeated by yellow fever and by an army of former slaves led by Toussaint L'Ouverture. Expecting the British to declare war against him again, and in need of money for European military campaigns, Napoleon suddenly offered the entire Louisiana Territory, including the crucial port of New Orleans, to the Americans for $15 million. In an age when it took at least two months for messages to cross the Atlantic, special American envoy James Monroe and Ambassador Livingston could not wait to consult Jefferson. They seized the opportunity: they bought the entire Louisiana Territory from Napoleon in Paris in April 1803. Overnight, the size of the United States more than doubled. It was the largest peaceful acquisition of territory in U.S. history.

At home, Jefferson suffered brief qualms. The Constitution did not authorize the president to purchase territory, and Jefferson had always rigidly insisted on a limited interpretation of executive rights. But he had also long held a sense of destiny about the West and had planned the Lewis and Clark expedition before the Louisiana Purchase was a reality. Jefferson now argued that Louisiana was vital to the nation's republican future. "By enlarging the empire of liberty," Jefferson wrote, "we . . . provide new sources of renovation, should its principles, at any time, degenerate, in those portions of our country which gave them birth." In other words, expansion was essential to liberty. But for African American slaves and Native Americans, the Louisiana Purchase simply increased the scope of their enslavement and destruction. By 1850, four of the six states in the Louisiana Purchase had entered the Union as slave states (see Chapter 10), and Indian Territory, envisaged by Jefferson as a distant refuge for beleaguered eastern Indian peoples, was surrounded by new settlements (see Chapter 15). No matter how noble Jefferson's rhetoric, neither African Americans nor American Indians shared in his "empire of liberty" (see Map 9.2).

8–4
Thomas Jefferson,
Constitutionality of the Louisiana Purchase (1803)

INCORPORATING LOUISIANA

In 1803, when the region that is now the state of Louisiana became American property, it had a racially and ethnically diverse population of 43,000 people, of whom only 6,000 were American. French and French-speaking people were numerically and culturally dominant, especially in the city of New Orleans. The city itself had a population of about 8,000, half white and half black. Two-thirds of the black population were slaves; the remainder were "free persons of color," who under French law enjoyed legal rights equal to those of white people. In New Orleans the French community effectively challenged the initial American plan of rapidly supplanting French culture and institutions with American ones. As a result, with Claiborne's full support, Louisiana adopted a legal code in 1808 that was based on French civil law rather than English common law. This was not a small concession. French law differed from English law in many fundamental respects, such as in family property (communal versus male ownership), in inheritance (forced heirship versus free disposal), and even in contracts, which were much more strictly

MAP EXPLORATION

To explore an interactive version of this map, go to **http://www.prenhall.com/faraghertlc/map9.2**

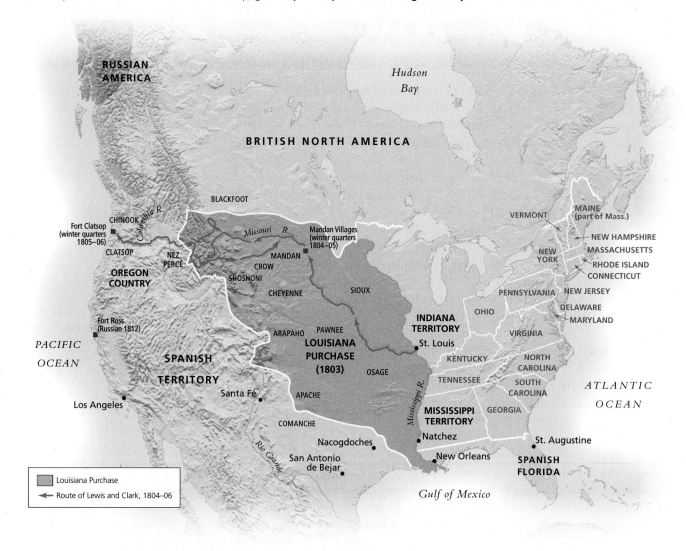

MAP 9.2

Louisiana Purchase   The Louisiana Purchase of 1803, the largest peaceful acquisition of territory in U.S. history, more than doubled the size of the nation. The Lewis and Clark expedition (1804–06) was the first to survey and document the natural and human richness of the area. The American sense of expansiveness and continental destiny owes more to the extraordinary opportunity provided by the Louisiana Purchase than to other factors.

HOW DID the terrain of the Lewis and Clark expedition influence the routes of the journey?

regulated in the French system. In 1812, with the required 60,000 free inhabitants, Louisiana was admitted to the Union. New Orleans remained for years a distinctively French city, illustrating the flexibility possible under a federal system.

TEXAS AND THE STRUGGLE FOR MEXICAN INDEPENDENCE

Spain objected, in vain, to Napoleon's 1803 sale of Louisiana to America. For years, Spain had attempted to seal off its rich colony of Mexico from commerce with other nations. Now, American Louisiana shared a vague and disputed boundary with Mexico's northern province of Texas.

Soon Napoleon brought turmoil to all of Mexico. In 1808, having invaded Spain, he installed his brother Joseph Bonaparte as king, forcing Spain's king, Charles IV, to renounce his throne. For the next six years, as warfare convulsed Spain, the country's long-prized New World empire slipped away. Mexico, divided between royalists loyal to Spain and populists seeking social and economic justice for mestizos and Indians, edged toward independence. Two populist revolts were suppressed by the royalists.

In 1812, a small force, led by Mexican republican Bernardo Gutiérrez but composed mostly of American adventurers, invaded Texas, captured San Antonio, assassinated the provincial governor Manuel Salcedo, and declared Texas independent. A year later, however, the Mexican republicans were defeated by a royalist army, which then killed suspected collaborators and pillaged the province so thoroughly that the local economy was devastated. The Mexican population declined to fewer than 2,000. Under these circumstances, Mexico's difficult path toward independence seemed, at least to some Americans, to offer yet another opportunity for expansion.

RENEWED IMPERIAL RIVALRY IN NORTH AMERICA

Fresh from the triumph of the Louisiana Purchase, Jefferson scored a major victory over the Federalist Charles Cotesworth Pinckney in the presidential election of 1804. Jefferson's shrewd wooing of moderate Federalists had been so successful that the remaining Federalists dwindled to a highly principled but sectional group, unable to attract voters outside of its home base in New England. Jefferson's Louisiana success was not repeated, however, and few other consequences of the ongoing struggle between Britain and France were so easy to solve.

WHAT FACTORS led to conflict between the United States and Britain in North America?

Review Summary

PROBLEMS WITH NEUTRAL RIGHTS

In his first inaugural address in 1801, Jefferson had announced a foreign policy of "peace, commerce, and honest friendship with all nations, entangling alliances with none." This was a difficult policy to pursue after 1803, when the Napoleonic Wars resumed. By 1805, Napoleon had conquered most of Europe, but Britain, the victor at the great naval battle of Trafalgar, controlled the seas. The United States, trying to profit from trade with both countries, was caught in the middle. Beginning in 1805, the British targeted the American reexport trade between the Caribbean and France by seizing American ships that were bringing French West Indian goods to Europe. Angry Americans viewed these seizures as violations of their rights as shippers of a neutral nation.

An even more contentious issue arose from the substantial desertion rate of British sailors. Many deserters promptly signed up on American ships, where they drew better pay and sometimes obtained false naturalization papers as well. As many as a quarter of the 100,000 seamen on American ships were British. Soon the British were stopping American merchant vessels and removing any man they believed to be British, regardless of his papers. The British refusal to recognize genuine naturalization papers (on the principle "once a British subject, always a British subject") was particularly insulting to the new American sense of nationhood. At least 6,000 innocent American citizens suffered forced impressment into the British navy from 1803 to 1812.

THE EMBARGO ACT

Fully aware that commerce was essential to the new nation, Jefferson was determined to insist on America's right as a neutral nation to ship goods to Europe. He first tried diplomatic protests, then negotiations, and finally threats, all to no avail. In 1806, Congress passed the Non-Importation Act, hoping that a boycott of British goods, which had worked so well during the Revolutionary War, would be effective once again. It was not. Finally, in desperation, Jefferson imposed the **Embargo Act** in December 1807. This act forbade American ships from sailing to any foreign port, thereby cutting off all exports as well as imports. The intent of the act was to force both Britain and France to recognize neutral rights by depriving them of American-shipped raw materials.

But the results were a disaster for American trade. The commerce of the new nation, which Jefferson himself had done so much to promote, came to a standstill. Exports fell from $108 million in 1807 to $22 million in 1808, and the nation was driven into a deep depression. There was widespread evasion of the embargo. Pointing out that the American navy's weakness was due largely to the deep cuts Jefferson had inflicted on it, the Federalists sprang to life with a campaign of outspoken opposition to Jefferson's policy.

MADISON AND THE FAILURE OF "PEACEABLE COERCION"

In this troubled atmosphere, Thomas Jefferson despondently ended his second term, acknowledging the failure of what he called "peaceable coercion." He was followed in office by his friend and colleague James Madison of Virginia. Although Madison defeated the Federalist candidate—again Charles Cotesworth Pinckney—Pinckney's share of the votes was three times what it had been in 1804.

Ironically, the Embargo Act had almost no effect on its intended victims. The French used the embargo as a pretext for seizing American ships, claiming they must be British ships in disguise. The British, in the absence of American competition, developed new markets for their goods in South America. In March 1809, Congress admitted failure, and the Embargo Act was repealed. But the struggle to remain neutral in the confrontation between the European giants continued.

A CONTRADICTORY INDIAN POLICY

The United States faced other conflicts besides those with Britain and France over neutral shipping rights. In the West, the powerful Indian nations of the Ohio Valley were determined to resist the wave of expansion that had carried thousands of white settlers onto their lands.

According to the Indian Intercourse Act of 1790, the United States could not simply seize Indian land; it could only acquire it when the Indians ceded it by treaty. But this policy conflicted with the harsh reality of westward expansion. Commonly, settlers pushed ahead of treaty boundaries. When Indian peoples resisted the invasion of their lands, the pioneers fought back and called for military protection. Defeat of an Indian people led to further land cessions. The result for the Indians was a relentless cycle of invasion, resistance, and defeat.

Thomas Jefferson was deeply concerned with the fate of the western Indian peoples. Convinced that Indians had to give up hunting in favor of the yeoman-farmer lifestyle he so favored for all Americans, Jefferson directed the governors of the Northwest Territories to "promote energetically" his vision for civilizing the Indians, which included Christianizing them and teaching them to read.

After the Louisiana Purchase, Jefferson offered traditionalist Indian groups new lands west of the Mississippi River, where they could live undisturbed by white settlers. But he failed to consider the pace of westward expansion. Less than twenty

Embargo Act Act passed by Congress in 1807 prohibiting American ships from leaving for any foreign port.

years later, Missouri, the first trans-Mississippi state, was admitted to the Union. Western Indians like the Mandans, who had seemed so remote, were now threatened by further westward expansion.

In fact, Jefferson's Indian policy, because it did nothing to slow down the ever-accelerating westward expansion, offered little hope to Indian peoples. The alternatives they faced were stark: acculturation, removal, or extinction. Deprived of hunting lands, decimated by disease, increasingly dependent on the white economy for trade goods and annuity payments in exchange for land cessions, many Indian peoples despaired. Nearly every tribe found itself bitterly split between accommodationists and traditionalists. Some, like groups of Cherokees and associated tribes in the South, advocated adapting their traditional agricultural lifestyles and pursuing a pattern of peaceful accommodation. In the Northwest Territory, however, many Indians chose the path of armed resistance.

INDIAN RESISTANCE

The Shawnees, a seminomadic hunting and farming tribe (the men hunted, the women farmed) of the Ohio Valley, had resisted white settlement in Kentucky and Ohio since the 1750s. Anthony Wayne's decisive defeat of the Indian confederacy led by Little Turtle at Fallen Timbers (1794) and the continuing pressure of American settlement, however, had left the Shawnees divided. One group, led by Black Hoof, accepted acculturation. The rest of the tribe tried to maintain traditional ways. Most broke into small bands and tried to eke out a living by hunting. One group of traditional Shawnees, however, led by the warrior Tecumseh, sought refuge farther west.

(left) Tecumseh, a Shawnee military leader, and (right) his brother Tenskwatawa, a religious leader called The Prophet, led a pan-Indian revitalization and resistance movement that posed a serious threat to American westward expansion. Tecumseh traveled widely, attempting to build a military alliance on his brother's spiritual message. He achieved considerable success in the Old Northwest but less in the Old Southwest, where many Indian peoples put their faith in accommodation. Tecumseh's death at the Battle of the Thames (1813) and British abandonment of their Shawnee allies at the end of the War of 1812 brought an end to organized Indian resistance in the Old Northwest.

(right): 1830. Oil on canvas. 29 × 24 in. (73.7 × 60.9 cm) Location: Smithsonian American Art Museum, Washington, DC, U.S.A.

Pan-Indian military resistance movement Movement calling for the political and cultural unification of Indian tribes in the late eighteenth and early nineteenth centuries.

9–2
The Cherokee Treaty of 1817

8–9
Chief Tecumseh, *An "Uncommon Genius" Advocates Indian Unity* (1809)

WHAT WERE the consequences of the War of 1812?

myhistorylab
Review Summary

But there was no escape from white encroachment. Between 1801 and 1809, William Henry Harrison, governor of Indiana Territory, concluded fifteen treaties with the Delawares, Potawatomis, Miamis, and other tribes. These treaties opened eastern Michigan, southern Indiana, and most of Illinois to white settlement and forced the Indians onto ever-smaller reservations. Many of these treaties were obtained by coercion, bribery, and outright trickery, and most Indians did not accept them.

In 1805, Tecumseh's brother, Tenskwatawa, known as The Prophet, began preaching a message of Indian revitalization: a rejection of all contact with the Americans and a return to traditional practices of hunting and farming. He preached an end to quarreling, violence, and sexual promiscuity and to the accumulation of private property.

Tecumseh succeeded in molding his brother's religious following into a powerful **pan-Indian military resistance movement**. With each new treaty that Harrison concluded, Tecumseh gained new followers among the Northwest Confederation tribes. Significantly, he also had the support of the British, who, after 1807, began sending food and guns to him from Canada, and who promised an alliance with the Indians if war broke out between Britain and America.

Tecumseh's pan-Indian strategy was at first primarily defensive, aimed at preventing further westward expansion. But after the Treaty of Fort Wayne in 1809, in which the United States gained 3 million acres of Delaware and Potawatomi land in Indiana, Tecumseh moved from passive to active resistance. He warned that any surveyors or settlers who ventured into the 3 million acres would risk their lives.

Tecumseh took his message of common land ownership and military resistance to all the Indian peoples of the Northwest Confederacy. He was not uniformly successful, even among the Shawnees. Black Hoof, for example, refused to join. Tecumseh also recruited, with mixed success, among the tribes south of the Ohio River (see Map 9.3).

In November 1811, while Tecumseh was still recruiting among the southern tribes, Harrison marched to the pan-Indian village of Tippecanoe with 1,000 soldiers. The 600 to 700 Indian warriors at the town, urged on by Tenskwatawa, attacked Harrison's forces before dawn on November 7, hoping to surprise them. The attack failed, and in the battle that followed, the Americans inflicted about 150 Indian casualties, while sustaining about as many themselves. Although Harrison claimed victory, the truth was far different. Dispersed from Tippecanoe, Tecumseh's angry followers fell on American settlements in Indiana and southern Michigan, killing many pioneers and forcing the rest to flee to fortified towns. Tecumseh himself entered into a formal alliance with the British. For western settlers, the Indian threat was greater than ever.

THE WAR OF 1812

Many Westerners blamed the British for Tecumseh's attacks on pioneer settlements in the Northwest. British support of western Indians and the long-standing difficulties over neutral shipping rights were the two grievances cited by President Madison when he asked Congress for a declaration of war against Britain on June 1, 1812. Congress obliged him on June 18. But the war had other, more general causes as well.

THE WAR HAWKS

A rising young generation of political leaders, first elected to Congress in 1810, strongly resented the continuing influence of Britain, the former mother country, on American affairs. Eager to assert independence from England once and for all, these

MAP 9.3

Indian Resistance, 1790–1816   American westward expansion put relentless pressure on the Indian nations in the trans-Appalachian South and West. The trans-Appalachian region was marked by constant warfare from the time of the earliest settlements in Kentucky in the 1780s to the War of 1812. Tecumseh's Alliance in the Old Northwest (1809–11) and the Creek Rebellion in the Old Southwest (1813–14) were the culminating struggles in Indian resistance to the American invasion of the trans-Appalachian region. Indian resistance was a major reason for the War of 1812.

WHAT HAPPENED to the Indians of the Trans-Appalachian region after 1814?

8–10
Indian Hostilities (1812)

War Hawks Members of Congress, predominantly from the South and West, who aggressively pushed for a war against Britain after their election in 1810.

War of 1812 War fought between the United States and Britain from June 1812 to January 1815 largely over British restrictions on American shipping.

young men saw themselves finishing the job begun by the aging revolutionary generation. They also wanted to occupy Florida to prevent runaway slaves from seeking refuge with the Seminole Indians. Westerners wanted to invade Canada, hoping thereby to end threats from British-backed Indians in the Northwest, such as Tecumseh and his followers. As resentments against England and frustrations over border issues merged, the pressure for war—always a strong force for national unity—mounted.

Unaware that the British, seriously hurt by the American trade embargo, were about to adopt a more conciliatory policy, President James Madison yielded to the **War Hawks'** clamor for action in June 1812, and his declaration of war passed the U.S. Senate by the close vote of 19 to 13, the House by 79 to 49. All the Federalists voted against the war. (The division along party lines continued in the 1812 presidential election, in which Madison garnered 128 electoral votes to 89 for his Federalist opponent, DeWitt Clinton.) The vote was sectional, with New England and the Middle States in opposition and the West and South strongly prowar. Thus, the United States entered the **War of 1812** more deeply divided along sectional lines than during any other foreign war in American history.

As a result of Jefferson's economizing, the American army and navy were small and weak. In contrast, the British, fresh from almost ten years of Napoleonic Wars, were in fighting trim. At sea, the British navy quickly established a strong blockade, harassing coastal shipping along the Atlantic seaboard and attacking coastal settlements at will. In the most humiliating attack, the British burned Washington in the summer of 1814, forcing the president and Congress to flee (see Map 9.4).

THE CAMPAIGNS AGAINST THE NORTHERN AND SOUTHERN INDIANS

The American goal of expansion fared badly as well. Americans envisaged a quick victory over sparsely populated British Canada that would destroy British support for Tecumseh and his Northwest Indian allies, but instead the British–Indian alliance defeated them (see Seeing History).

One reason for the abortive Canadian invasion, aside from failure to appreciate the strength of the British–Indian forces, was that the New England states actively opposed the war. Massachusetts, Rhode Island, and Connecticut refused to provide militia or supplies, and other New England governors turned a blind eye to the flourishing illegal trade across the U.S.–Canadian border. Another reason was the reaction of Canadians themselves, the majority of whom were former Americans. Ironically, the most decisive effect of the American attacks was the formation of a Canadian sense of national identity and a determination never to be invaded or absorbed by the United States.

In the South, warfare similar to that waged against Tecumseh's pan-Indian resistance movement in the Northwest dramatically affected the southern Indian peoples. The first of the Indian peoples to battle the Americans were the Creeks, a trading nation with a long history of contacts with the Spanish and French. When white settlers began to occupy Indian lands in northwestern Georgia and central Alabama early in the nineteenth century, the Creeks, like the Shawnees in the Northwest, were divided in their response. Although many Creek bands argued for accommodation, a group known as the Red Sticks were determined to fight. During the War of 1812, the Red Sticks, allied with the British and Spanish, fought not only the Americans but also other Indian groups.

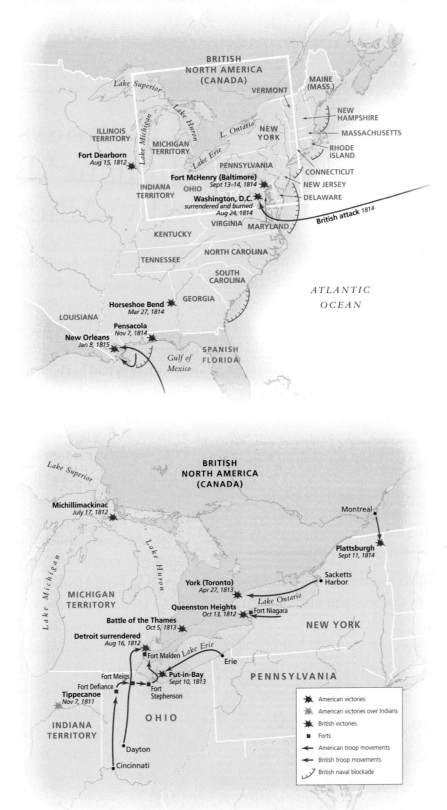

MAP 9.4

The War of 1812 On land, the War of 1812 was fought to define the nation's boundaries. In the North, where military action was most intense, American armies attacked British forts in the Great Lakes region with little success, and several invasions of Canada failed. In the South, the Battle of New Orleans made a national hero of Andrew Jackson, but it occurred after the peace treaty had been signed. On the sea, with the exception of Oliver Perry's victory in the Great Lakes, Britain's dominance was so complete and its blockade so effective that British troops were able to invade the Chesapeake and burn the capital of the United States.

WHAT EVENTS and ambitions led to the outbreak of war in 1812?

"A Scene on the Frontiers as Practiced by the 'Humane' British and their 'Worthy' Allies"

This American cartoon, published during the War of 1812, shows a British officer paying for a scalp from an Indian, while another man is shown in the act of scalping a dead American soldier. The cartoon may have been prompted by an actual event: the offer of bounties for scalps made by British Colonel Proctor at Fort Dearborn (Chicago) in August 1815. In any case, the cartoon evoked horror at Indian barbarity and indignation at the British for using them as pawns in the war. Similar charges had been made against the British and their Indian allies during the American Revolution.

In reality, Indian resistance in the War of 1812 was different from the earlier war. The western Indians were not British pawns. The Shawnee leader Tecumseh and other western Indian groups allied with him claimed that they had been deprived of their lands by fraudulent treaties and stripped of the ability to maintain their traditional culture. Tecumseh began organizing resistance long before the outbreak of war between the United States and Britain. He did accept arms from the British in Canada, and once the war broke out he formally allied with them and became an officer in their army. By allying with the British, the Indians hoped to retain their homelands, but at the peace negotiations the British failed to insist on a buffer state for neutral Indians as they had promised. ■

THIS CARTOON inflamed popular fears of Indians that existed long before the War of 1812. Does it contribute anything to our historical understanding of the reasons for western Indian resistance?

A SCENE ON THE FRONTIERS AS PRACTICED BY THE HUMANE BRITISH AND THEIR WORTHY ALLIES!

In August 1813, the Red Sticks attacked Fort Mims on the Alabama River, killing more than 500 Americans and mixed-race Creeks who had gathered there for safety. Led by Andrew Jackson, troops from the Tennessee and Kentucky militias combined with the Creeks' traditional foes—the Cherokees, Choctaws, and Chickasaws—to exact revenge. Jackson's troops matched the Creeks in ferocity, shooting the Red Sticks "like dogs," one soldier reported.

At the end of the Creek War in 1814, Jackson demanded huge land concessions from the Creeks (including concessions from some Creek bands that had fought on his side): 23 million acres, or more than half the Creek domain. The Treaty of Fort Jackson (1814) confirming these land concessions earned Jackson his Indian name, Sharp Knife. In early 1815 (after the peace treaty had been signed but before news of it arrived in America), Andrew Jackson achieved his best-known victory, an improbable win over veteran British troops in the Battle of New Orleans.

THE HARTFORD CONVENTION

America's occasional successes failed to diminish the angry opposition of New England Federalists to the War of 1812. That opposition culminated in the Hartford Convention of 1814, where Federalist representatives from the five New England states met to discuss their grievances. At first the air was full of talk of secession from the Union, but soon cooler heads prevailed. The convention did insist, however, that a state had the right "to interpose its authority" to protect its citizens against unconstitutional federal laws. This **nullification** doctrine was not new; Madison and Jefferson had proposed it in the Virginia and Kentucky Resolves opposing the Alien and Sedition Acts in 1798 (see Chapter 8). In any event, the nullification threat from Hartford was ignored, for peace with Britain was announced as delegates from the convention made their way to Washington to deliver their message to Congress. There the convention's grievances were treated not as serious business but as an anticlimactic joke.

8–12
Report and Resolutions of the Hartford Convention (1814)

THE TREATY OF GHENT

By 1814, the long Napoleonic Wars in Europe were slowly drawing to a close, and the British decided to end their war with the Americans. The peace treaty, after months of hard negotiation, was signed at Ghent, Belgium, on Christmas Eve in 1814. Like the war itself, the treaty was inconclusive. The major issues of impressment and neutral rights were not mentioned, but the British did agree to evacuate their western posts, and late in the negotiations they abandoned their insistence on a buffer state for neutral Indian peoples in the Northwest.

For all its international inconsequence, the war did have an important effect on national morale. Andrew Jackson's victory at New Orleans allowed Americans to believe that they had defeated the British. It would be more accurate to say that by not losing the war the Americans had ended their own feelings of colonial dependency. Equally important, they convinced the British government to stop thinking of America as its colony.

The only clear losers of the war were the northwestern Indian nations and their southern allies. With the death of Tecumseh at the Battle of the Thames in 1813 and the defeat of the southern Creeks in 1814, the last hope of a united Indian resistance to white expansion perished forever. Britain's abandonment of its Indian allies in the **Treaty of Ghent** sealed their fate. By 1815, American settlers were on their way west again.

Nullification A constitutional doctrine holding that a state has a legal right to declare a national law null and void within its borders.

Treaty of Ghent Treaty signed in December 1814 between the United States and Britain that ended the War of 1812.

WHAT WERE the principle provisions of the Missouri Compromise?

myhistorylab
Review Summary

DEFINING THE BOUNDARIES

With the War of 1812 behind them, Americans turned, more seriously than ever before, to the tasks of expansion and national development. The so-called Era of Good Feelings (1817–23) found politicians largely in agreement on a national agenda, and a string of diplomatic achievements forged by John Quincy Adams gave the nation sharper definition. But the limits to expansion also became clear: the Panic of 1819 showed the dangers in economic growth, and the Missouri Crisis laid bare the sectional split that attended westward expansion.

ANOTHER WESTWARD SURGE

The end of the War of 1812 was followed by a westward surge to the Mississippi River. The extent of the population redistribution was dramatic: in 1790, about 95 percent of the nation's population had lived in states bordering the Atlantic Ocean; by 1820 fully 25 percent of the population lived west of the Appalachians (see Map 9.5).

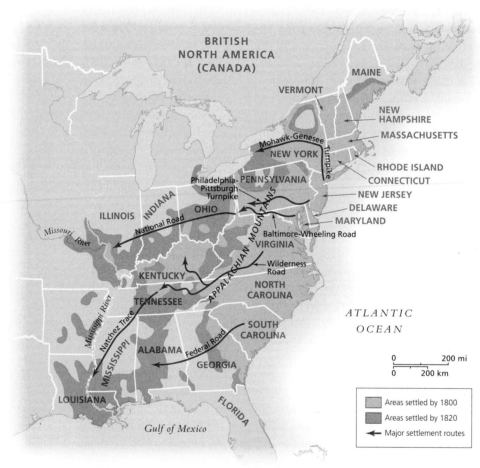

MAP 9.5

Spread of Settlement: Westward Surge, 1800–1820 Within a period of twenty years, a quarter of the nation's population had moved west of the Appalachian Mountains. The westward surge was a dynamic source of American optimism.

HOW DID westward movement vary by region between 1800 and 1820?

What accounted for this extraordinary westward surge? There were both push and pull factors. Between 1800 and 1820, the nation's population almost doubled, increasing from 5.3 million to 9.6 million. Overpopulated farmland in all of the seaboard states pushed farmers off the land, while new land pulled them westward. The defeat and removal of Indians in the War of 1812 was another important pull factor.

The most important pull factor, however, was the attractive price of western land. The Land Ordinance of 1785 priced western lands too high for all but speculators and the wealthy (see Chapter 7), but subsequent realities had slowly forced Congress to enact land laws more favorable to the small farmer. The most sustained challenge came from "squatters," who repeatedly took up land before it was officially open for sale and then claimed a "preemption" right of purchase at a lower price that reflected the value of improvements they had made to the land. Congress sought to suppress this illegal settlement and ordered the expulsion of squatters on several occasions but to no avail.

Finally, in the Land Act of 1820, Congress set the price of land at $1.25 an acre, the minimum purchase at eighty acres (in contrast to the 640-acre minimum in 1785), and a down payment of $100 in cash. This was the most liberal land law yet passed in American history, but the cash requirement still favored speculators, who had more cash than most small farmers (see Figure 9.2). Except in southern Ohio and parts of Kentucky and Tennessee, there was very little contact among regional cultures. New Englanders carried their values and lifestyles directly west and settled largely with their own communities; Southerners did the same. One section of northern Ohio along Lake Erie, for example, had been Connecticut's western land claim since the days of its colonial charter. Rather than give up the land when the Northwest Territory was established in 1787, Connecticut held onto the Western Reserve (as it was known) and encouraged its citizens to move there. Group settlement was common. These New Englanders brought to the Western Reserve their religion (Congregational), their love of learning, and their adamant opposition to slavery.

Western migration in the South was very different. On this frontier, the people clearing the land were African American slaves creating plantations not for themselves but for their owners. Even before the war, plantation owners in the Natchez district of Mississippi had made fortunes growing cotton, which they shipped to Britain from New Orleans. After the war, as cotton growing expanded, hopeful slave owners from older parts of the South (Virginia, North and South Carolina, Georgia) flooded into the region, bringing their slaves with them or, increasingly, purchasing new ones supplied by the internal slave trade. More than half of the migrants to the Old Southwest after 1812 were enslaved African Americans. This involuntary migration of slaves tore African American families apart at the same time that white families viewed migration as a chance to replicate the lifestyle and values of older southern states on this new frontier (see Chapter 10).

The western transplantation of distinctive regional cultures explains why, although by 1820 western states accounted for more than a third of all states (eight out of twenty-three), the West did not form a third, unified political region. Although there were common western issues—in particular, the demand for better roads and other transportation routes—communities in the Old Northwest, in general, shared New England political attitudes, whereas those in the Old Southwest shared southern attitudes.

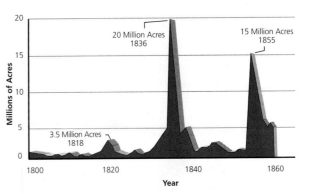

Figure 9.2 Western Land Sales
Surges in western land sales reflect surges in westward expansion. Western land sales following the War of 1812 reached an unprecedented 3.5 million acres, but that was small in comparison with what was to come in the 1830s and 1850s. Not all land sales reflected actual settlement, however, and speculation in western lands was rampant. Collapse of the postwar speculative boom contributed to the Panic of 1819, and the abrupt end to the boom of the 1830s led to the Panic of 1837.

Robert Riegel and Robert Athearn, *America Moves West* (New York: Holt Rinehart 1964).

QUICK REVIEW

Westward Surge, 1800–1820

- By 1820 25 percent of the population lived west of the Appalachians.
- Group settlement was common.
- Lure of new land pulled farmers west.

The hopes of every westward migrant are exemplified in this series of four illustrations imagining inevitable progress from pioneer cabin to prosperous farm. The illustrations, "The Pioneer Settler and His Progress," appeared in a booster history advertising land in western New York.

THE ELECTION OF 1816 AND THE ERA OF GOOD FEELINGS

In 1816, James Monroe, the last of the Virginia Dynasty, was easily elected president over his Federalist opponent Rufus King. This was the last election in which Federalists ran a candidate. Monroe had no opponent in 1820 and was reelected nearly unanimously (231 to 1). The triumph of the Jeffersonian Republicans over the Federalists seemed complete.

Monroe's politics reflected changing times. When he visited Boston, as recently as 1815 the heart of a secession-minded Federalist region, he received an enthusiastic welcome, prompting the Federalist *Columbian Centinel* to proclaim an "**Era of Good Feelings**." The phrase has been applied to Monroe's presidency (1817–25) ever since.

THE AMERICAN SYSTEM

Era of Good Feelings   The period from 1817 to 1823 in which the disappearance of the Federalists enabled the Republicans to govern in a spirit of seemingly nonpartisan harmony.

American System   The program of government subsidies favored by Henry Clay and his followers to promote American economic growth and protect domestic manufacturers from foreign competition.

Monroe sought a government of national unity, and he chose men from North and South, Jeffersonian Republicans and Federalists, for his cabinet. He selected John Quincy Adams, a former Federalist, as his secretary of state, virtually assuring that Adams, like his father, would become president. To balance Adams, Monroe picked John C. Calhoun of South Carolina, a prominent War Hawk, as secretary of war. And Monroe supported the **American System**, a program of national economic development that became identified with westerner Henry Clay, Speaker of the House of Representatives.

In supporting the American System, Monroe was following President Madison, who had proposed the program in his message to Congress in December 1815. Madison and Monroe broke with Jefferson's agrarianism to embrace much of the Federalist program for economic development, including the chartering of a national bank, a tax on imported goods to protect American manufacturers, and a national system of roads and canals. All three of these had first been proposed by Alexander Hamilton in the 1790s (see Chapter 8). At the time, these proposals had met with bitter Jeffersonian Republican opposition. The support that Madison and Monroe gave to Hamilton's ideas following the War of 1812 was a crucial sign of the dynamism of the American commercial economy. Many Republicans now acknowledged that the federal government had a role to play in fostering the economic and commercial conditions in which both yeoman farmer and merchant could succeed.

In 1816, Congress chartered the Second Bank of the United States for twenty years. Because they feared the economic power of rich men, Jeffersonian Republicans had allowed the charter of the original Bank of the United States, founded in 1791, to expire in 1811. The Republican about-face in 1816 was a sign that the strength of commercial interests had grown to rival that of farmers, whose distrust for central banks persisted.

The **Tariff of 1816** was the first substantial protective tariff in American history. In 1815, British manufacturers, who had been excluded for eight years (from the Embargo Act of 1807 to the end of the War of 1812), flooded the U.S. market with their products. American manufacturers complained that the British were dumping goods below cost in order to prevent the growth of American industries. Congress responded with a tariff on imported woolens and cottons, on iron, leather, hats, paper, and sugar. The measure had southern as well as northern support, although in later years, differences over the passage of higher tariffs would become one of the most persistent sources of sectional conflict.

The third item in the American System, funding for roads and canals—internal improvements, as they came to be known—was more controversial. Monroe and Madison both supported genuinely national (that is, interstate) projects such as the National Road from Cumberland, Maryland, to Vandalia, Illinois. Congressmen, however, aware of the urgent need to improve transportation in general, and sensing the political advantages from directing funds to their districts, proposed spending federal money on local projects. Both Madison and Monroe vetoed such local proposals, believing them to be unconstitutional.

The support of Madison and Monroe for measures initially identified with their political opposition was an indicator of their realism. The three aspects of the American System—bank, tariff, roads—were all parts of the basic infrastructure that the American economy needed in order to develop. Briefly, during the Era of Good Feelings, politicians agreed about the need for all three. Later, each would be a source of heated partisan argument.

THE DIPLOMACY OF JOHN QUINCY ADAMS

The diplomatic achievements of the Era of Good Feelings were due almost entirely to the efforts of one man, John Quincy Adams, Monroe's secretary of state. Adams set himself the task of tidying up the borders of the United States. Two accords with Britain—the **Rush-Bagot Treaty of 1817** and the Convention of 1818—fixed the border between the United States and Canada at the 49th parallel and resolved conflicting U.S. and British claims to Oregon with an agreement to occupy it jointly for ten (eventually twenty) years.

Adams's major diplomatic accomplishment was the Adams-Onís or Transcontinental Treaty of 1819, in which he skillfully wrested concessions from the faltering Spanish empire. Adams convinced Spain not only to cede Florida but also to drop all previous claims it had to the Louisiana Territory and Oregon. In return, the United States relinquished claims on Texas and assumed responsibility for the $5 million in claims that U.S. citizens had against Spain.

9–7
Henry Clay, *Defense of the American System* (1832)

Tariff of 1816   A tax imposed by Congress on imported goods.

Rush-Bagot Treaty of 1817   Treaty between the United States and Britain that effectively demilitarized the Great Lakes by sharply limiting the number of ships each power could station on them.

Monroe Doctrine Declaration by President James Monroe in 1823 that the Western Hemisphere was to be closed off to further European colonization and that the United States would not interfere in the internal affairs of European nations.

9–6

The Monroe Doctrine and a Reaction (1823)

Finally, Adams picked his way through the remarkable changes occurring in Latin America, developing the policy that bears his president's name, the **Monroe Doctrine**. The United States was the first country outside Latin America to recognize the independence of Spain's former colonies. When the European powers (France, Austria, Russia, and Prussia) began to talk of a plan to help Spain recover the lost colonies, what was the United States to do? The British, suspicious of the European powers, proposed a British-American declaration against European intervention in the hemisphere. Others might have been flattered by an approach from the British empire, but Adams would have none of it. Showing the national pride that was so characteristic of the era, Adams insisted on an independent American policy. He therefore drafted for the president the hemispheric policy that the United States has followed ever since.

On December 2, 1823, the president presented the Monroe Doctrine to Congress and the world. He called for the end of colonization of the Western Hemisphere by European nations (this was aimed as much at Russia and its Pacific Coast settlements as at other European powers). Intervention by European powers in the affairs of the independent New World nations would be considered by the United States a danger to its own peace and safety. Finally, Monroe pledged that the United States would not interfere in the affairs of European countries or in the affairs of their remaining New World colonies.

All of this was a very loud bark from a very small dog. In 1823, the United States lacked the military and economic force to back up its grand statement. In fact, what kept the European powers out of Latin America was British opposition to European intervention, enforced by the Royal Navy. The Monroe Doctrine was, however, useful in Adams's last diplomatic achievement, the Convention of 1824, in which Russia gave up its claim to the Oregon Territory and accepted 54°40' north latitude as the southern border of Russian America. Thus, Adams had contained another possible threat to American continental expansion (see Map 9.6).

THE PANIC OF 1819

Across this impressive record of political and economic nation building fell the shadow of the Panic of 1819. A delayed reaction to the end of the War of 1812 and the Napoleonic Wars, the panic forced Americans to come to terms with their economic place in a peaceful world. As British merchant ships resumed trade on routes they had abandoned during the wars, the American shipping boom ended. And as European farm production recovered from the wars, the international demand for American foodstuffs declined and American farmers and shippers suffered.

Domestic economic conditions made matters worse. The western land boom that began in 1815 turned into a speculative frenzy. Land sales, which had totaled 1 million acres in 1815, mushroomed to 3.5 million in 1818. Many settlers bought on credit, aided by small "wildcat" state banks that made loans far beyond their resources. This was not the first—or the last—speculative boom in western lands. But it ended like all the rest—with a sharp contraction of credit, begun on this occasion by the Second Bank of the United States, which in 1819 forced state banks to foreclose on many bad loans. Many small farmers were ruined, and they blamed the faraway Bank of the United States for their troubles. In the 1830s, Andrew Jackson would build a political movement on their resentment.

Urban workers lost their jobs as international trade declined and as manufacturers failed because of competition from British imports. As they lobbied for local relief, many workers became deeply involved in urban politics, where they could express their resentment against the merchants and owners who had laid them off. Thus developed another component of Andrew Jackson's new political coalition.

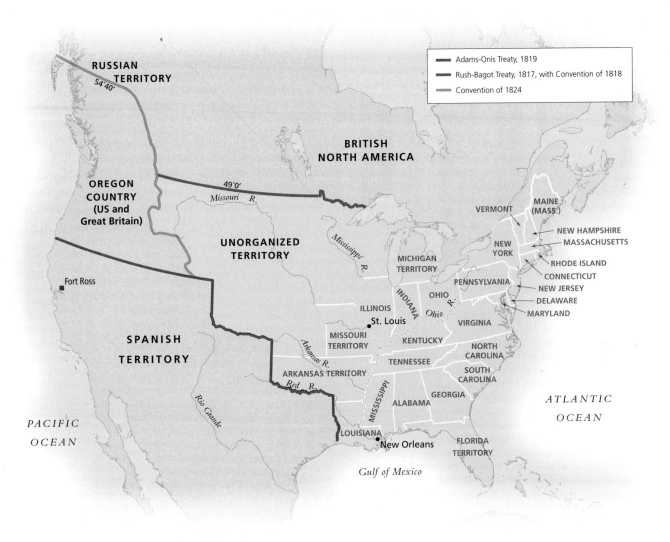

MAP 9.6
John Quincy Adams's Border Treaties   John Quincy Adams, secretary of state in the Monroe administration (1817–25), solidified the nation's boundaries in several treaties with Britain and Spain:
the Rush-Bagot Treaty of 1817 and the Conventions of 1818 and 1824 and the Adams-Onís Treaty
of 1819.

WHAT AGREEMENTS were reached in the treaties signed by John Quincy
Adams to settle U.S. borders?

Another confrontation arose over the tariff. Southern planters, hurt by a
decline in the price of cotton, began to actively protest the protective tariff, which
kept the price of imported goods high even when cotton prices were low. Manufacturers, hurt by British competition, lobbied for even higher rates, which they
achieved in 1824 over southern protests. Southerners then began to express doubts
about the fairness of a political system in which they were always outvoted.

The Panic of 1819 was a symbol of this transitional time. It showed how far
the country had moved since 1800, from Jefferson's republic of yeoman farmers
toward a nation dominated by commerce. And the anger and resentment expressed
by the groups harmed by the depression—farmers, urban workers, and southern
planters—were portents of the politics of the upcoming Jackson era.

9–5
Thomas Jefferson Reacts to the "Missouri Question"
(1820)

THE MISSOURI COMPROMISE

In the Missouri Crisis of 1819–21, the nation confronted the momentous issue that had been buried in the general enthusiasm for expansion: as America moved west, would the largely southern system of slavery expand as well? Until 1819, this question was decided regionally. The Northwest Ordinance of 1787 explicitly banned slavery in the northern section of trans-Appalachia but made no mention of it elsewhere. Because so much of the expansion into the Old Northwest and Southwest was lateral (Northerners stayed in the North, Southerners in the South), there was little conflict over sectional differences. In 1819, however, the sections collided in Missouri, which applied for admission to the Union as a slave state (see Map 9.7).

The northern states, all of which had abolished slavery by 1819, were opposed to the extension of slavery. In addition to the moral issue, the Missouri question raised the political issue of sectional balance. Northern politicians did not want to

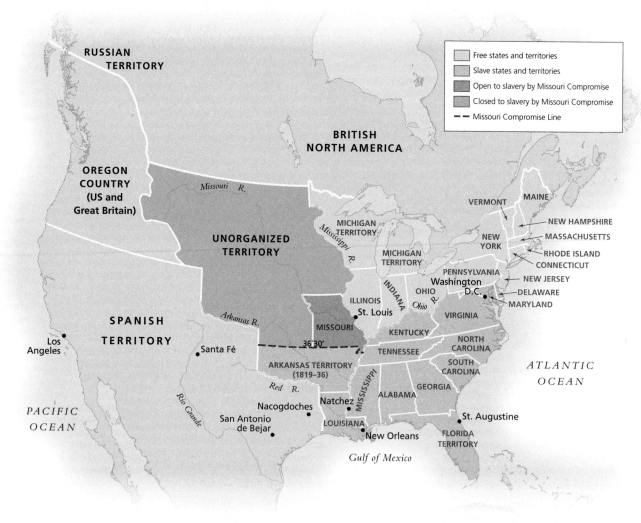

MAP 9.7

The Missouri Compromise Before the Missouri Compromise of 1820, the Ohio River was the dividing line between the free states of the Old Northwest and the slaveholding states of the Old Southwest. The compromise stipulated that Missouri would enter the Union as a slave state (balanced by Maine, a free state), but slavery would be prohibited in the Louisiana Territory north of 36°30' (Missouri's southern boundary). This awkward compromise lasted until 1846, when the Mexican-American War reopened the issue of the expansion of slavery.

HOW DID westward expansion create added pressure to resolve the question of slavery?

CHRONOLOGY

1800	Thomas Jefferson elected president
1802	Russian-American Company headquarters established at Sitka, Alaska
1803	Louisiana Purchase
	Marbury v. *Madison*
	Ohio admitted to the Union
1804	Lewis and Clark expedition leaves St. Louis
	Thomas Jefferson reelected president
1807	*Chesapeake–Leopard* incident
	Embargo Act
1808	James Madison elected president
1809	Tecumseh forms military alliance among Northwest Confederacy peoples
1811	Battle of Tippecanoe
1812	War of 1812 begins
	James Madison reelected president
	Louisiana admitted to the Union
1814	Treaty of Ghent
1815	Battle of New Orleans
1816	James Monroe elected president
	Congress charters Second Bank of the United States
	Indiana admitted to the Union
1817	Mississippi admitted to the Union
1818	Illinois admitted to the Union
1819	Panic of 1819
	Adams-Onís Treaty
	Alabama admitted to the Union
1819–20	Missouri Crisis and Compromise
1820	James Monroe reelected president
	Maine admitted to the Union
1821	Missouri admitted to the Union as a slave state
1823	Monroe Doctrine

admit another slave state. To do so would tip the balance of power in the Senate. For their part, Southerners believed they needed an advantage in the Senate; because of faster population growth in the North, they were already outnumbered (105 to 81) in the House of Representatives. But above all, Southerners did not believe Congress had the power to limit the expansion of slavery. Slavery, in southern eyes, was a question of property and, therefore, a matter for state rather than federal legislation.

In 1819, Representative James Tallmadge Jr. of New York began more than a year of congressional controversy when he demanded that Missouri agree to the gradual end of slavery as the price of entering the Union. At first, the general public paid little attention, but religious reformers (Quakers prominent among them) organized a number of antislavery rallies in northern cities that made politicians take notice. This was the first time that the growing northern reform impulse had intersected with sectional politics. It was also the first time that southern threats of secession were made openly in Congress.

In 1820, Congress achieved compromise over the sectional differences. Henry Clay forged the first of the many agreements that were to earn him the title of "the Great Pacificator" (peacemaker). The **Missouri Compromise** maintained the balance between free and slave states: Maine (which had been part of Massachusetts) was admitted as a free state in 1820 and Missouri as a slave state in the following year. A policy was also enacted with respect to slavery in the rest of the Louisiana Purchase: slavery was prohibited north of 36°30′ north latitude—the southern boundary of Missouri—and permitted south of that line. This meant that the vast majority of the Louisiana Territory would be free. In reality, then, the Missouri Compromise could be only a temporary solution, because it left open the question of how the balance between slave and free states would be maintained.

Missouri Compromise Sectional compromise in Congress in 1820 that admitted Missouri to the Union as a slave state and Maine as a free state and prohibited slavery in the northern Louisiana Purchase territory.

CONCLUSION

In complex ways a developing economy, geographical expansion, and even a minor war helped shape American unity. Local, small, settled, face-to-face communities in both the North and the South began to send their more mobile, expectant members to new occupations in urban centers or west to form new settlements.

The westward population movement dramatically changed the political landscape and Americans' view of themselves. But expansion did not create the "empire for liberty" that Thomas Jefferson had hoped for. While expansion did indeed create economic opportunity, it also displaced and destroyed Indian communities such as the Mandans, the Shawnee, and many others. And it also created an even greater denial of liberty, as we shall see in the next chapter, in a greatly expanded community tied to cotton and to the slave labor that produced it.

REVIEW QUESTIONS

1. What economic and political problems did the United States face as a new nation in a world dominated by war between Britain and France? How successful were the efforts by the Jefferson, Madison, and Monroe administrations to solve these problems?

2. The anti-European cast of Jefferson's republican agrarianism made it appealing to many Americans who wished to believe in their nation's uniqueness, but how realistic was it?

3. Some Federalists opposed the Louisiana Purchase, warning of the dangers of westward expansion. What are arguments for and against expansion?

4. What contradictions in American Indian policy did the confrontations between Tecumseh's alliance and soldiers and settlers in the Old Northwest reveal? Can you suggest solutions to these contradictions?

5. What did the War of 1812 accomplish?

6. What were the issues that made it impossible for the Era of Good Feelings to last?

KEY TERMS

myhistorylab

Flashcard Review

American System (p. 230)
Embargo Act (p. 220)
Era of Good Feelings (p. 230)
Marbury v. *Madison* (p. 216)
Missouri Compromise (p. 235)
Monroe Doctrine (p. 232)
Nullification (p. 227)

Pan-Indian military resistance movement (p. 222)
Rush-Bagot Treaty of 1817 (p. 231)
Tariff of 1816 (p. 231)
Treaty of Ghent (p. 227)
War Hawks (p. 224)
War of 1812 (p. 224)

RECOMMENDED READING

Catharine Allgor, *Parlor Politics: In Which the Ladies of Washington Help Build a City and a Government* (2000). Describes the vital role that women played in the politics of the new capital city.

Stephen E. Ambrose, *Undaunted Courage: Meriwether Lewis, Thomas Jefferson, and the Opening of the American West* (1996). This heroic version of the expedition is told by a master storyteller. It ought, however, to be supplemented by the Ronda version cited below that pays attention to the Indian side of the story.

Walter Borneman, *1812: The War That Forged a Nation* (2004). A very readable account.

R. David Edmunds, *Tecumseh and the Quest for Indian Leadership* (1984). A sympathetic portrait.

Joseph J. Ellis, *American Sphinx: The Character of Thomas Jefferson* (1998). An engaging exploration of Jefferson's many contradictions.

John Mack Faragher, *Sugar Creek* (1987). The fullest examination of the lives of pioneers in the Old Northwest.

Robert Pierce Forbes, *The Missouri Compromise and Its Aftermath: Slavery and the Meaning of America* (2007). Discusses both contemporary debates over the compromise and its impact.

Jon Kukla, *A Wilderness So Immense: The Louisiana Purchase and the Destiny of America* (2003). A personality-filled account of the negotiations and of various hopes and plans for Louisiana.

Glover Moore, *The Missouri Controversy, 1819–1821* (1953). The standard account.

Peter S. Onuf, *Jefferson's Empire* (2000). A thoughtful study of Jefferson's ideas about republicanism, empire, and nationalism.

James Ronda, *Lewis and Clark among the Indians* (1984). An innovative look at the famous explorers through the eyes of the Indian peoples they encountered.

. . . whatever accidents or misfortunes might attend my flight nothing could be worse than what threatened my stay.
— *Hannah Crafts*

A slave auction in Virginia. 1861

10

THE SOUTH AND SLAVERY
1790s–1850s

HOW DID attitudes in the South toward slavery change after the invention of the cotton gin?

WHAT WAS life like for the typical slave in the American South?

SLAVE COLLAR
RICHMOND VIRGINIA
SLAVE MARKET

THIS ANTE-BELLUM SLAVE COLLAR HAS AN OLD TAG ATTACHED FROM AN EARLY HISTORICAL SOCIETY COLLECTION. A RARE AND CHOICE RELIC FROM EARLY VIRGINIA.

WHAT ROLE did religion play in African American slave communities?

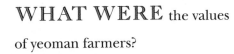

WHAT WERE the values of yeoman farmers?

WHO MADE up the planter elite?

WHAT PROSLAVERY arguments were developed in the first half of the nineteenth century?

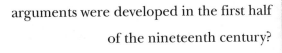

1790s 1850s

AMERICAN COMMUNITIES
Cotton Communities in the Old Southwest

IN 1834, SAMUEL TOWNES OF SOUTH CAROLINA CAUGHT "ALABAMA Fever." Restive under what seemed to him excessive demands from his large and well-connected family, Samuel rebelled by marrying a woman of whom his family disapproved and moving with her and his slaves to Perry County, Alabama, a newly opened part of the Old Southwest suitable for growing cotton. There he practiced law in the village of Marion, bought a plantation on the banks of the Cahaba River, and acquired ten to fifteen more slaves. Almost all of Samuel's new possessions were bought on credit. Samuel's desire for wealth caused him to drive his slaves very hard. Always convinced that they were malingering, he demanded that his overseer "whip them like the devil" to pick more cotton.

The Panic of 1837 devastated Samuel's ambitions. As the price of cotton fell to 7 cents a pound (from 15 cents in 1836), banks demanded repayment of their generous loans. Samuel sold some slaves, and rented out the labor of others, but he was forced to ask for loans from the family he had been so eager to escape. In 1844 his plantation was sold at auction. Three years later, his health failed, and he and his wife, Joanna, had no choice but to return to South Carolina and the charity of kinfolk.

The rapid westward expansion of cotton cultivation exposed the undeveloped state of community formation among the southern elite. The plantation form of agriculture, which had been the rule in the South since its earliest days, meant that cities were few and community institutions like churches and schools were rare. Slave-owning families depended almost entirely on kinship networks for assistance (and the obligations that Samuel Townes wished to avoid) and for sociability. Families who moved west frequently found themselves lost without their customary family connections. Wider community connections and support lagged behind the pursuit of profits to be made from cotton.

What of the slaves that Samuel brought with him? Once part of a larger Townes family group in South Carolina, the slaves that Samuel owned were separated from their kinfolk permanently and had to adjust to living with a number of newly purchased slaves in Alabama. Most of the new slaves were bought as individuals and were usually still in their teens or even younger. Young male slaves were favored for the backbreaking work of cut-

ting trees and clearing land for cultivation. Sometimes owners worked side by side with their workers at this initial stage. But generally, uniformity and strict discipline were the rule on cotton plantations. Owners eager to clear land rapidly and make quick profits often drove the clearing crews at an unmerciful pace. And, as Samuel Townes had, they attempted to impose strict discipline and a rapid pace on the work gangs that planted, hoed, and harvested cotton. Slaves from other parts of the South, used to more individual and less intense work, hated the cotton regime and most of all hated the overseers who enforced it.

Only long-practiced African American community-building strategies saved these young transported slaves—some called it a "Second Middle Passage"—from complete isolation. Beginning in the earliest days of slavery, Africans from many different tribes built their own communities by using the language of kinship (for example, "brother," "sister," "uncle," "aunt," and "child") to encompass everyone in new imagined families. On one hand, the cultivation of cotton required many workers, thus creating the conditions necessary for large slave communities in the Old Southwest. On the other hand, because the price of cotton was unstable, probably many shared the experience of the Townes slaves, who were sold again when the plantation failed.

Thus, the new land in the Old Southwest that appeared to offer so much opportunity for owners bred tensions caused by forcible sale and migration, by the organization and pace of cotton cultivation, and by the owners' often violent efforts to control their slaves in a new region where community bonds were undeveloped. For planters and slaves alike, migration broke long-standing family ties that were the most common form of community throughout the South. The irony is that African Americans, who were the most cruelly affected, knew better how to build new communities than did their privileged owners.

In the first half of the nineteenth century, world demand for cotton transformed the South, promoting rapid expansion and unprecedented prosperity. But it also tied the South to a slave system that was inherently unstable and violent. Although southern slave owners frequently talked about their plantations as communities and their slaves as family, the slave system was not one community but two with the strengths of the slave community largely invisible to the owners.

Marion, AL

KING COTTON AND SOUTHERN EXPANSION

Slavery had long dominated southern life. African American slaves grew the great export crops of the colonial period—tobacco, rice, and indigo—on which slave owners' fortunes were made, and their presence shaped southern society and culture (see Chapter 4). Briefly, in the early days of American independence, the slave system waned, only to be revived by the immense profitability of cotton in a newly industrializing world. Cotton became the dominant crop in a rapidly expanding South that more than doubled in size (see Map 10.1). The overwhelming economic success of cotton and of the slave system on which it depended created a distinctive regional culture quite different from that developing in the North.

COTTON AND EXPANSION INTO THE OLD SOUTHWEST

Short-staple cotton had long been recognized as a crop ideally suited to southern soils and growing conditions. But it had one major drawback: the seeds were so difficult to remove from the lint that it took an entire day to hand-clean a single pound of cotton. The invention in 1793 that made cotton growing profitable was the result of collaboration between a young Northerner named Eli Whitney and Catherine Greene, a South Carolina plantation owner. Whitney built a prototype cotton engine, dubbed "gin" for short, a simple device consisting of a hand-cranked cylinder with teeth that tore the lint away from the seeds. At Greene's suggestion, the teeth were made of wire. With the cotton gin, it was possible to clean more than fifty pounds of cotton a day. Soon large and small planters in the inland regions of Georgia and South Carolina had begun to grow cotton. By 1811, this area was producing 60 million pounds of cotton a year and exporting most of it to England.

Other areas of the South quickly followed South Carolina and Georgia into cotton production. New land was needed because cotton growing rapidly depleted the soil. The profits to be made from cotton growing drew a rush of southern farmers into the so-called black belt—an area stretching through western Georgia, Alabama, and Mississippi that was blessed with exceptionally fertile soil. Following the War of 1812, Southerners were seized by "Alabama Fever." In one of the swiftest migrations in American history, white Southerners and their slaves flooded into western Georgia and the areas that would become Alabama and Mississippi (the Old Southwest). On this frontier, African American pioneers (albeit involuntary ones) cleared the forests, drained the swamps, broke the ground, built houses and barns, and planted the first crops.

Like the simultaneous expansion into the Old Northwest, settlement of the Old Southwest took place at the expense of the region's Indian population (see Chapter 9). Beginning with the defeat of the Creeks at Horseshoe Bend in 1814 and ending with the Cherokee forced migration along the "Trail of Tears" in 1838, the Five Civilized Tribes—the Cherokees, Chickasaws, Choctaws, Creeks, and Seminoles—were forced to give up their lands and move to Indian Territory (see Chapter 11).

Following the "Alabama Fever" of 1816–20, several later surges of southern expansion (1832–38, and again in the mid-1850s) carried cotton planting over the Mississippi River into Louisiana and deep into Texas. In the minds of the mobile, enterprising Southerners who sought their fortunes in the West, cotton profits and expansion went hand in hand. But the expansion of cotton meant the expansion of slavery.

HOW DID attitudes in the South toward slavery change after the invention of the cotton gin?

myhistorylab
Review Summary

IMAGE KEY

for pages 238–239

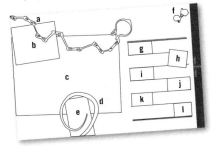

a. A chain used to tie gangs of slaves.
b. "The Shadow" plantation of Louisiana.
c. A slave auction in Virginia, 1861.
d. A whip of coiled rope used on slaves.
e. An auction of eight black slaves.
f. Mature cotton bolls on the stem of a plant.
g. Slaves carry sacks of cotton on their heads on a South Carolina plantation field.
h. A slave collar with an attached tag from the slave market in Richmond, Virginia.
i. African American worshippers in a sketch by Joseph Becker.
j. A log cabin in New Braunfels, Texas in a painting by Carl G. von Iwonski.
k. Colonel and Mrs. James A. Whiteside in a James Cameron painting.
l. A proslavery cartoon, 1841.

MAP EXPLORATION

To explore an interactive version of this map, go to **http://www.prenhall.com/faraghertlc/map10.1**

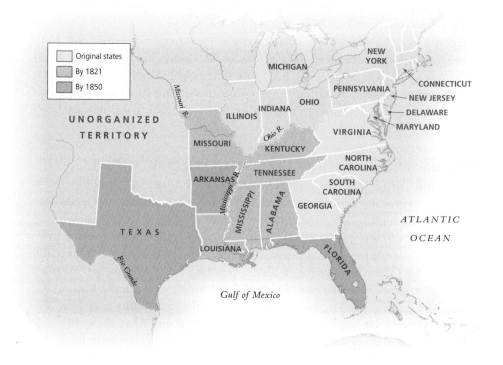

MAP 10.1

The South Expands, 1790–1850   This map shows the dramatic effect cotton production had on southern expansion. From the original six states of 1790, westward expansion, fueled by the search for new cotton lands, added another six states by 1821 and three more by 1850.

WHY WAS cotton production especially suited to slave labor?

SLAVERY THE MAINSPRING—AGAIN

The export of cotton from the South was the dynamic force in the developing American economy in the 1790–1840 period. Just as the international slave trade had been the dynamic force in the Atlantic economy of the eighteenth century (see Chapter 4), southern slavery financed northern industrial development in the nineteenth century.

The rapid growth of cotton production was an international phenomenon. The insatiable demand for cotton was a result of the technological and social changes that we know today as the **Industrial Revolution**. Beginning early in the eighteenth century, a series of inventions resulted in the mechanized spinning and weaving of cloth in the world's first factories in the north of England. The ability of these factories to produce unprecedented amounts of cotton cloth revolutionized the world economy. The invention of the cotton gin came at just the right time. British textile manufacturers were eager to buy all the cotton that the South could produce. By the time of the Civil War, cotton accounted for almost 60 percent of American exports.

The connection between southern slavery and northern industry was very direct. Most mercantile services associated with the cotton trade (insurance,

Industrial Revolution   Revolution in the means and organization of production.

This 1855 illustration of black stevedores loading heavy bales of cotton onto waiting steamboats in New Orleans is an example of the South's dependence on cotton and the slave labor that produced it.

for example) were in northern hands and, significantly, so was shipping. This economic structure was not new. In colonial times, New England ships dominated the African slave trade. Some New England families invested some of their profits in the new technology of textile manufacturing in the 1790s. Other merchants made their money from cotton shipping and brokerage. Thus, as cotton boomed, it provided capital for the new factories of the North (see Chapter 12).

A SLAVE SOCIETY IN A CHANGING WORLD

In the flush of freedom following the American Revolution, all the northern states abolished slavery or passed laws for gradual emancipation, and a number of slave owners in the Upper South freed their slaves (see Chapter 7). On January 1, 1808, the earliest date permitted by the Constitution, a bill to abolish the importation of slaves became law. Nevertheless, southern legislatures were unwilling to write steps toward emancipation into law, preferring to depend on the charity of individual slave owners.

But attitudes toward slavery rapidly changed in the south following the invention of the cotton gin in 1793 and the realization of the riches to be made from cotton. White Southerners believed that only African slaves could be forced to work day after day, year after year, at the rapid and brutal pace required in the cotton fields of large plantations in the steamy southern summer. As the production of cotton climbed higher every year in response to a seemingly inexhaustible international demand, so too did the demand for slaves and the conviction of Southerners that slavery was an economic necessity.

As had been true since colonial times, the centrality of slavery to the economy and the need to keep slaves under firm control required the South to become a slave society, rather than merely a society with slaves, as had been the case in the North. What this meant was that one particular form of social relationship, that of master and slave (one dominant, the other subordinate), became the model for all relationships, including personal interactions between white husbands and wives as well as interactions in politics and at work.

At a time when the North was experiencing the greatest spurt of urban growth in the nation's history (see Chapter 13), most of the South remained rural: less than 3 percent of Mississippi's population lived in cities of more than 2,500 residents, and only 10 percent of Virginia's did. The agrarian ideal, bolstered by

QUICK REVIEW

The Economics of Slavery

♦ Worldwide demand for cotton supported slavery.

♦ Export of cotton a dynamic part of American economy.

♦ Northern industry directly connected to slavery.

 7–6
Benjamin Banneker, *An African American Calls for an End to Slavery* (1791)

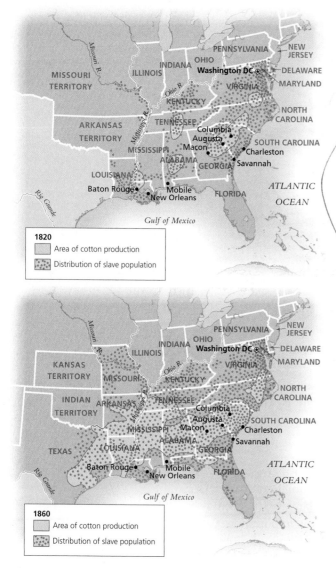

MAP 10.2

Cotton Production and the Slave Population, 1820–60 In the forty years from 1820 to 1860, cotton production grew dramatically in both quantity and extent. Rapid westward expansion meant that by 1860 cotton production was concentrated in the black belt (so called for its rich soils) in the Lower South. As cotton production moved west and south, so did the enslaved African American population that produced it, causing a dramatic rise in the internal slave trade.

Sam Bowers Hilliard, *Atlas of Antebellum Southern Agriculture* (Baton Rouge: Lousiana State University Press, 1984).

WHY WAS the increasing dominance of cotton cultivation in the Lower South accompanied by a growing concentration of slaves in that region?

the cotton boom, encouraged the antiurban and anticommercial sentiments of many white Southerners. The South also lagged behind the North in industrialization and in canals and railroads (see Chapter 12). In 1860, only 15 percent of the nation's factories were located in the South.

Other changes, however, could not be so easily ignored. Nationwide, the slave states were losing their political dominance because their population was not keeping pace with that of the North. Equally alarming, outside the South, antislavery sentiment was growing rapidly. Southerners felt directly threatened by growing abolitionist sentiment in the North and by the 1834 action of the British government eliminating slavery on the sugar plantations of the West Indies. The South felt increasingly hemmed in by northern opposition to the expansion of slavery.

THE INTERNAL SLAVE TRADE

The cotton boom caused a huge increase in the domestic slave trade. Plantation owners in the Upper South (Delaware, Kentucky, Maryland, Virginia, and Tennessee) sold their slaves to meet the demand for labor in the new and expanding cotton-growing regions of the Old Southwest. Cumulatively, between 1820 and 1860, nearly 50 percent of the slave population of the Upper South took part against their will in southern expansion (see Map 10.2). More slaves—an estimated 1 million—were uprooted by this internal slave trade and enforced migration in the early nineteenth century than were brought to North America during the entire time the international slave trade was legal (see Chapter 4).

Purchased by slave traders from owners in the Upper South, slaves were gathered together in notorious "slave pens" in places like Richmond and Charleston and then moved south by train or boat. Often slaves moved on foot, chained together in groups of fifty or more known as "coffles." Chained slaves in coffles were a common sight on southern roads and one difficult to reconcile with the notion of slavery as a benevolent institution. Arriving at a central market in the Lower South like Natchez, New Orleans, or Mobile, the slaves, after being carefully inspected by potential buyers, were sold at auction to the highest bidder (see Map 10.3).

In New Orleans, in the streets outside large slave pens near the French Quarter, thousands of slaves were displayed and sold each year. Dressed in new clothes provided by the traders and exhorted by the traders to walk, run, and otherwise show their stamina, slaves were presented to buyers. For their part, suspicious buyers, unsure that traders and slaves themselves were truthful, poked, prodded, and frequently stripped male and female slaves to be sure they were as healthy as the traders claimed.

Although popular stereotype portrayed slave traders as unscrupulous outsiders who persuaded kind and reluctant masters to sell their slaves, the historical truth is

858-9000
ext 895

MAP 10.3
Internal Slave Trade, 1820–60   Between 1820 and 1860, nearly 50 percent of the slave population of the Upper South was sold to labor on the cotton plantations of the Lower South. This map shows the various routes by which they were "sold down the river," shipped by boat or marched south.
Historical Atlas of the United States (Washington, DC: National Geographic Society, 1988).

WHAT AGRICULTURAL trends help explain the relative decline of slavery in the Upper South?

much harsher. Traders, far from being shunned by slave-owning society, were often respected community members. Similarly, the sheer scale of the slave trade makes it impossible to believe that slave owners only reluctantly parted with their slaves at times of economic distress. Instead, it is clear that many owners sold slaves and separated slave families not out of necessity but to increase their profits. The sheer size and profitability of the internal slave trade made a mockery of southern claims for the benevolence of the slave system.

THE AFRICAN AMERICAN COMMUNITY

Surely no group in American history has faced a harder job of community building than the black people of the antebellum South. Living in intimate, daily contact with their oppressors, African Americans nevertheless created an enduring culture of their own, a culture that had far-reaching and lasting influence on all of southern life and American society as a whole (see Chapter 4).

WHAT WAS life like for the typical slave in the American South?

Review Summary

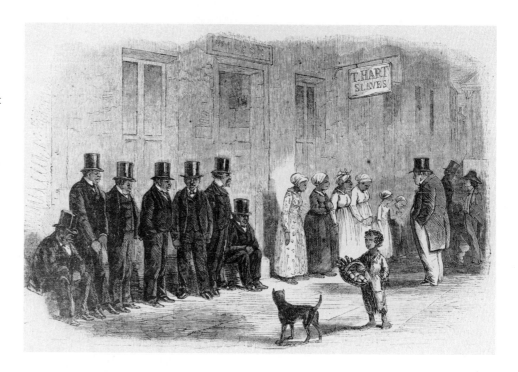

This engraving from *Harper's Weekly* shows slaves, dressed in new clothing, lined up outside a New Orleans slave pen for inspection by potential buyers before the actual auction began. They were often threatened with punishment if they did not present a good appearance and manner that would fetch a high price.

THE MATURE AMERICAN SLAVE SYSTEM

On January 1, 1808, the United States ended its participation in the international slave trade. Although a small number of slaves continued to be smuggled in from Africa, the growth of the slave labor force depended primarily on natural increase—that is, through births within the slave population. The slave population, estimated at 700,000 in 1790, grew to more than 4 million in 1860. A distinctive African American slave community, which had first emerged in the eighteenth century (see Chapter 4), expanded dramatically in the early years of the nineteenth century. This community was as much shaped by King Cotton as was the white South.

Cotton growing concentrated slaves on plantations, in contrast to the more dispersed distribution on smaller farms in earlier generations. The size of cotton plantations fostered the growth of slave communities. Over half of all slaves lived on plantations with twenty or more other slaves, and others, on smaller farms, had links with slaves on nearby properties. Urban slaves were able to make and sustain so many secret contacts with other African Americans in cities or towns that slave owners wondered whether slave discipline could be maintained in urban settings. There can be no question that the bonds among African Americans were what sustained them during the years of slavery.

In law, slaves were property, to be bought, sold, rented, worked, and otherwise used (but not abused or killed) as the owner saw fit. But slaves were also human beings, with feelings, needs, and hopes. Even though most white Southerners believed black people to be members of an inferior, childish race, all but the most brutal masters acknowledged the humanity of their slaves. White masters learned to live with the two key institutions of African American community life: the family and the African American church, and in their turn slaves learned, however painfully, to survive slavery.

THE GROWTH OF THE SLAVE COMMUNITY

Of all the New World slave societies, the one that existed in the American South was the only one that grew by natural increase rather than through the constant importation of captured Africans. This fact alone made the African American community of the South different from the slave societies of Cuba, the Caribbean islands, and Brazil. In order to understand, we must examine the circumstances of survival and growth.

The growth of the African American slave population was not due to better treatment than in other New World slave societies, but to the higher fertility of African American women, who in 1808 (the year the international slave trade ended) had a crude birthrate of 35 to 40, causing a 2.2 percent yearly population growth. This was still below the fertility rate of white women, who had a crude birthrate of 55 and a 2.9 percent annual population growth. But by midcentury, the white rate had dropped to 1.99 percent, while the black rate remained high. African American slave women adopted the white practice of breastfeeding for only one year, and on average gave birth to six or eight children at year-and-a-half intervals. But they also suffered from the contradictory demands of slave owners, who wanted them to work hard while still having children, for every slave baby increased the wealth of the owners.

As a result, because pregnant black women were inadequately nourished, worked too hard, or were too frequently pregnant, mortality rates for slave children under five were twice those for their white counterparts. At the time, owners often accused slave women of smothering their infants by rolling over them when asleep.

Health remained a lifelong issue for slaves. Malaria and infectious diseases such as yellow fever and cholera were endemic in the South. White people as well as black died, as the life expectancy figures for 1850 show: 40 to 43 years for white people and 30 to 33 years for African Americans. Slaves were more at risk because of the circumstances of slave life: poor housing, poor diet, and constant, usually heavy, work. Sickness was chronic: 20 percent or more of the slave labor force on most plantations were sick at any one time.

FROM CRADLE TO GRAVE

Slavery was a lifelong labor system, and the constant and inescapable issue between master and slave was how much work the slave would—or could—be forced to do. Southern white slave owners claimed that by housing, feeding, and clothing their slaves from infancy to death they were acting more humanely than northern industrialists who employed people only during their working years. But in spite of occasional instances of **manumission**—the freeing of a slave—the child born of a slave was destined to remain a slave.

Children lived with their parents (or with their mother if the father was a slave on another farm or plantation) in housing provided by the owner. Husband and wife cooperated in loving and sheltering their children and teaching them survival skills. From birth to about age seven, slave children played with one another and with white children, observing and learning how to survive. They saw the penalties: black adults, perhaps their own parents, whipped for disobedience; black women, perhaps their own sisters, violated by white men. And they might see one or both parents sold away as punishment or for financial gain. They would also see signs of white benevolence: special treats for children at holidays, appeals to loyalty from the master or mistress, perhaps friendship with a white child.

The children would learn slave ways of getting along: apparent acquiescence to white demands; pilfering; malingering, sabotage, and other methods of slowing the relentless work pace. But many white Southerners genuinely believed that their slaves were both less intelligent and more loyal than they really were. Frederick Douglass, whose fearless leadership of the abolitionist movement made him the most famous African American of his time, wryly noted, "As the master studies to keep the slave ignorant, the slave is cunning enough to make the master think he succeeds."

QUICK REVIEW

Life and Death

- Mortality rate of slave children under five was twice that of white counterparts.
- Infectious diseases were endemic in the South.
- Malnutrition and lack of basic sanitation took a high toll on slaves.

Manumission   The freeing of a slave.

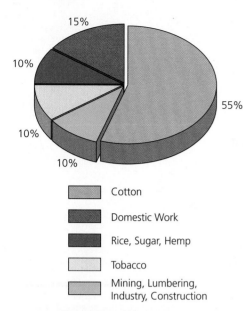

15%

10%

10%

10%

55%

- Cotton
- Domestic Work
- Rice, Sugar, Hemp
- Tobacco
- Mining, Lumbering, Industry, Construction

Figure 10.1 Distribution of Slave Labor, 1850
In 1850, 55 percent of all slaves worked in cotton, 10 percent in tobacco, and another 10 percent in rice, sugar, and hemp. Ten percent worked in mining, lumbering, industry, and construction, and 15 percent worked as domestic servants. Slave labor was not generally used to grow corn, the staple crop of the yeoman farmer.

Gang System   The organization and supervision of slave field hands into working teams on Southern plantations.

Black children had no schooling of any kind: in most of the southern states, it was against the law to teach a slave to read, although indulgent owners often rewarded their "pet" slaves by teaching them in spite of the law. At age twelve, slaves were considered full grown and put to work in the fields or in their designated occupation.

The explosive growth of cotton plantations changed the nature of southern slave labor. In 1850, 55 percent of all slaves were engaged in cotton growing. Another 20 percent labored to produce other crops: tobacco (10 percent), rice, sugar, and hemp. About 15 percent of all slaves were domestic servants, and the remaining 10 percent worked in mining, lumbering, industry, and construction (see Figure 10.1).

FIELD WORK AND THE GANG SYSTEM

The field workers, 75 percent of all slaves, were most directly affected by the gang labor system employed on cotton plantations (as well as in tobacco and sugar). Cotton was a crop that demanded nearly year-round labor: from planting in April, to constant hoeing and cultivation through June, to a picking season that began in August and lasted until December. Owners divided their slaves into gangs of twenty to twenty-five, a communal labor pattern reminiscent of parts of Africa, but with a crucial difference— these workers were supervised by overseers with whips. On most plantations, the bell sounded an hour before sunup, and slaves were expected to be on their way to the fields as soon as it was light. Work continued till noon, and after an hour or so for lunch and rest, the slaves worked until nearly dark. In the evening, the women prepared dinner at the cabins and everyone snatched a few hours of unsupervised socializing before bedtime.

Work was tedious in the hot and humid southern fields, and the overseer's whip was never far away. Cotton growing was hard work: plowing and planting, chopping weeds with a heavy hoe, and picking the ripe cotton from the stiff and scratchy bolls, at the rate of 150 pounds a day.

Slaves aged fast in this regime. Poor diet and heavy labor undermined health. When they were too old to work, they took on other tasks within the black community, such as caring for young children. Honored by the slave community, the elderly were tolerated by white owners, who continued to feed and clothe them until their deaths. Few actions show the hypocrisy of southern paternalism more clearly than the speed with which white owners evicted their elderly slaves in the 1860s when the end of the slave system was in sight.

HOUSE SERVANTS

In the eighteenth century, as profits from slavery grew, slave owners diverted an increasing proportion of slave labor from the fields to the house service necessary to sustain their rich lifestyles. By one calculation, fully one-third of the female slaves in Virginia worked as house servants by 1800, but the figures were much lower in the newly opened cotton lands in the West.

At first glance, working in the big house might seem to have been preferable to working in the fields. Physically, it was much less demanding, and house slaves were often better fed and clothed. They also had much more access to information, for white people, accustomed to servants and generally confident of their loyalty, often forgot their presence and spoke among themselves about matters of interest to the slaves: local gossip, changes in laws or attitudes, or policies toward disobedient or rebellious slaves.

For many white people, one of the worst surprises of the Civil War was the eagerness of their house slaves to flee. Considered by their masters the best treated and the most loyal, these slaves were commonly the first to leave or to organize mass desertions.

From the point of view of the slave, the most unpleasant thing about being a house servant (or the single slave of a small owner) was the constant presence of white people. There was no escape from white supervision. Many slaves who were personal maids and children's nurses were required to live in the big house and rarely saw their own families. Cooks and other house servants were exposed to the tempers and whims of all members of the white family, including the children, who prepared themselves for lives of mastery by practicing giving orders to slaves many times their own age. And house servants, more than any others, were forced to act grateful and ingratiating. At the same time, genuine intimacy was possible, especially between black nurses and white children. But these were bonds that the white children were ultimately forced to reject as the price of joining the master class.

ARTISANS AND SKILLED WORKERS

A small number of slaves were skilled workers: weavers, seamstresses, carpenters, blacksmiths, mechanics. Black people worked as lumberjacks (of the 16,000 lumber workers in the South, almost all were slaves), as miners, as deckhands and stokers on Mississippi riverboats, as stevedores loading cotton on the docks of Charleston, Savannah, and New Orleans, and sometimes as workers in the handful of southern factories. Because slaves were their masters' property, the wages of the slave belonged to the owner, not the slave.

The extent to which slaves made up the laboring class was most apparent in cities. A British visitor to Natchez in 1835 noted slave "mechanics, draymen, hostelers, labourers, hucksters and washwomen and the heterogeneous multitude of every other occupation." In the North, all these jobs were performed by white workers. In part because the South failed to attract as much immigrant labor as the North, southern cities offered both enslaved and free black people opportunities in skilled occupations such as blacksmithing and carpentering that free African Americans in the North were denied.

SLAVE FAMILIES

As had been true in the eighteenth century, families remained essential to African American culture (see Chapter 4). No southern state recognized slave marriages in law. Most owners, though, not only recognized but also encouraged them, sometimes even performing a kind of wedding ceremony for the couple. Masters encouraged marriage among their slaves, believing it made the men less rebellious, and for economic reasons they were eager for the slave women to have children. Whatever marriages meant to the masters, to slaves they were a haven of love and intimacy in a cruel world and the basis of the African American community. Husbands and wives had a chance, in their own cabins, to live their own lives among loved ones. The relationship between slave husband and wife was different from that of the white husband and wife. The master–slave system dictated that the white marriage be unequal, for the man had to be dominant and the woman dependent and submissive. Slave marriages were more equal, for husband and wife were both powerless within the slave system. Both knew that neither could protect the other from abuse at the hands of white people.

Family meant continuity. Parents made great efforts to teach their children the family history and to surround them with a supportive and protective kinship network. The strength of these ties is shown by the many husbands, wives, children,

8–1
Isaac, *Memoirs of a Monticello Slave* (1847)

QUICK REVIEW

Slave Families

- Marriage not legally recognized but encouraged among slaves.
- Parents made great efforts to teach and protect their children.
- The internal slave trade made separation a constant danger.

Slave quarters built by slave owners, like these pictured on a South Carolina plantation, provided more than basic shelter. Slave quarters were the center of the African American community life that developed during slavery.

Collection of The New-York Historical Society. Photograph by G.N. Barnard, Bagoe Collection, ca. 1865, negative number 48169.

WHAT ROLE did religion play in African American slave communities?

myhistorylab

Review Summary

Second Great Awakening Religious revival among black and white Southerners in the 1790s.

and parents who searched for each other after the Civil War when slavery came to an end.

Given the vast size of the internal slave trade, fear of separation was constant—and real. One in every five slave marriages was broken, and one in every three children sold away from their families. These figures clearly show that slave owners' support for slave marriages was secondary to their desire for profits. The scale of the trade was a strong indication of the economic reality that underlay their protestations of paternalism.

In the face of constant separation, slave communities attempted to act like larger families. Following practices developed early in slavery, children were taught to respect and learn from all the elders, to call all adults of a certain age "aunt" or "uncle," and to call children of their own age "brother" or "sister" (see Chapter 4). Thus, in the absence of their own family, separated children could quickly find a place and a source of comfort in the slave community to which they had been sold.

This emphasis on family and on kinship networks had an even more fundamental purpose. The kinship of the entire community, where old people were respected and young ones cared for, represented a conscious rejection of white paternalism. The slaves' ability, in the most difficult of situations, to structure a community that expressed their values, not those of their masters, was extraordinary. Equally remarkable was the way in which African Americans reshaped Christianity to serve their needs.

FREEDOM AND RESISTANCE

Whatever their dreams, most slaves knew they would never escape. Freedom was too far away. Almost all successful escapes in the nineteenth century (approximately a thousand a year) were from the Upper South (Delaware, Maryland, Virginia, Kentucky, and Missouri). A slave in the Lower South or the Southwest simply had too far to go to reach freedom. That meant that ways to endure and to resist became all the more important.

AFRICAN AMERICAN RELIGION

Black Christianity was an enabling religion: it helped slaves to survive, not as passive victims of white tyranny but as active opponents of an oppressive system that they daily protested in small but meaningful ways. In their faith, African Americans expressed a spiritual freedom that white people could not destroy.

African religions managed to survive from the earliest days of slavery in forms that white people considered as "superstition" or "folk belief." In the nineteenth century, these African traditions allowed African Americans to reshape white Christianity into their own distinctive faith that expressed their deep resistance to slavery.

The Great Awakening, which swept the South after the 1760s, introduced many slaves to Christianity, often in mixed congregations with white people (see Chapter 5). The transformation was completed by the **Second Great Awakening**, which took root among black and white Southerners in the 1790s. The number of African American converts, preachers, and lay teachers grew rapidly, and a distinctive form of Christianity took shape. Free African Americans founded their own independent churches and denominations. By the 1830s, free African American ministers like Andrew Marshall of Savannah and many more enslaved black preachers and lay ministers preached, sometimes secretly, to slaves. Their message was one of faith and love, of deliverance, of the coming of the promised land.

African Americans found in Christianity a powerful vehicle to express their longings for freedom and justice. But why did their white masters allow it? Some white people, themselves converted by the revivals, doubtless believed that they should not deny their slaves the same religious experience. But many southern slave owners expected Christianity to make their slaves obedient and peaceful. Forbidding their slaves to hold their own religious gatherings, owners insisted that their slaves attend white church services. On many plantations, slaves attended religious services with their masters every Sunday, sitting quietly in the back of the church or in the balcony, as the minister preached messages justifying slavery and urging obedience. But at night, away from white eyes, they held their own prayer meetings.

In churches and in spontaneous religious expressions, the black community made Christianity its own. Fusing Christian texts with African elements of group activity, such as the circle dance, the call-and-response pattern, and, above all, group singing, black people created a unique community religion full of emotion, enthusiasm, and protest. Nowhere is this spirit more compelling than in the famous spirituals: "Go Down Moses," with its mournful refrain "Let my people go"; the rousing "Didn't My Lord Deliver Daniel . . . and why not every man"; the haunting "Steal Away."

African cultural patterns persisted in the preference for night funerals and for solemn pageantry and song, as depicted in British artist John Antrobus's *Plantation Burial,* ca. 1860. Like other African American customs, the community care of the dead contained an implied rebuke to the masters' care of the living slaves.

John Antrobus, "Negro Burial." Oil painting. The Historic New Orleans Collection. #1960.46.

Harriet Tubman was 40 years old when this photograph (later hand-tinted) was taken. Already famous for her daring rescues, she gained further fame by serving as a scout, spy, and nurse during the Civil War.

This drawing shows the moment, almost two months after the failure of his famous and bloody slave revolt, when Nat Turner was accidentally discovered in the woods near his home plantation. Turner's cool murder of his owner and methodical organization of his revolt deeply frightened many white Southerners.

OTHER KINDS OF RESISTANCE

The rapid geographical spread of cotton introduced a new source of tension and resistance into the slave–master relationship. White Southerners did everything they could to prevent escapes and rebellions. But despite almost certain recapture, slaves continued to flee and to help others do the same. Escaped slave Harriet Tubman of Maryland, who made twelve rescue missions freeing sixty to seventy slaves in all (later inflated to three hundred as Tubman's rescues became legendary), had extraordinary determination and skill. As a female runaway, she was unusual, too: most escapees were young men, for women often had small children they were unable to take and unwilling to leave behind.

Slaves who knew they could not reach freedom still frequently demonstrated their desire for liberty or their discontent over mistreatment by taking unauthorized leave from their plantation. Hidden in nearby forests or swamps, provided with food smuggled by other slaves from the plantation, the runaway might return home after a week or so, often to rather mild punishment. Although in reality, most slaves could have little hope of gaining freedom, even failed attempts at rebellion shook the foundations of the slave system, and thus temporary flight by any slave was a warning sign of discontent that a wise master did not ignore.

SLAVE REVOLTS

The ultimate resistance, however, was the slave revolt. Southern history was dotted with stories of former slave conspiracies and rumors of current plots (see Chapter 4). But when in 1831, Nat Turner actually started a rebellion in which a number of white people were killed, southern fears were greatly magnified.

A literate man, Nat Turner was a lay preacher, but he was also a slave. It was Turner's intelligence and strong religious commitment that made him a leader in the slave community. Turner began plotting his revolt after a religious vision in which he saw "white spirits and black spirits engaged in battle." Turner and five other slaves struck on the night of August 20, 1831. Moving from plantation to plantation and killing a total of fifty-five white people, the rebels numbered sixty by the next morning, when they fled from a group of armed white men. More than forty blacks were executed after the revolt, including Turner, who was captured accidentally after he had hidden for two months in the woods.

Conspiracies and actual or rumored slave resistance began in colonial times (see Chapter 4) and never ceased. These plots exposed the truth white Southerners preferred to ignore: only force kept Africans and African Americans enslaved, and because no system of control could ever be total, white Southerners could never be completely safe from the possibility of revolt. Nat Turner brought white Southerners' fears to the surface. After 1831, the possibility of slave insurrection was never far from their minds.

FREE AFRICAN AMERICANS

Another source of white disquiet was the growing number of free African Americans. By 1860, nearly 250,000 free black people lived in the South. For most, freedom dated from before 1800, when antislavery feeling among slave owners in the Upper South was widespread and cotton cultivation had yet to boom.

Most free black people lived in the countryside of the Upper South, where they worked as tenant farmers or farm laborers. Urban African Americans were much more visible. Life was especially difficult for female-headed families, because only the most menial work—street peddling and laundry work, for example—was available to free black women. The situation for African American males was somewhat better. Although they were discriminated against in employment and in social life, there were opportunities for skilled black craftsmen in trades such as blacksmithing and carpentry. Cities such as Charleston, Savannah, and Natchez were home to flourishing free African American communities that formed their own churches and fraternal orders.

Throughout the South in the 1830s, state legislatures tightened **black codes**—laws concerning free black people. Free African Americans could not carry firearms, could not purchase slaves (unless they were members of their own family), and were liable to the criminal penalties meted out to slaves (that is, whippings and summary judgments without a jury trial). They could not testify against whites, hold office, vote, or serve in the militia. White people increasingly feared the influence free black people might have on slaves, for free African Americans were a living challenge to the slave system. Their very existence disproved the basic southern equations of white equals free, and black equals slave. No one believed more fervently in those equations than the South's largest population group, white people who did not own slaves.

One of the ways Charleston attempted to control its African American population was to require all slaves to wear badges showing their occupation. After 1848, free black people also had to wear badges, which were decorated, ironically, with a liberty cap.

13–3
Nat Turner, *Confession* (1831)

THE WHITE MAJORITY

The pervasive influence of the slave system in the South is reflected in the startling contrast of two facts: two-thirds of all Southerners did not own slaves, yet slave owners dominated the social and political life of the region.

WHAT WERE the values of yeoman farmers?

myhistorylab
Review Summary

POOR WHITE PEOPLE

From 30 to 50 percent of all southern white people were landless, a proportion similar to that in the North. But the existence of slavery limited the opportunities for poor white people. Slaves made up the permanent, stable workforce in agriculture and in many skilled trades. Many poor white people led highly transient lives in search of work, such as farm labor at harvest time, which was only temporary. Others were tenant farmers working under share-tenancy arrangements that kept them in debt to the landowner. Although they farmed poorer land with less equipment than landowning farmers, most tenant farmers grew enough food to sustain their families. Like their landowning neighbors, tenant farmers aspired to independence.

Relationships between poor whites and black slaves were complex. White men and women often worked side by side with black slaves in the fields and were socially and sexually intimate with enslaved and free African Americans. White people engaged in clandestine trade to supply slaves with items like liquor that slave

Black codes Laws passed by states and municipalities denying many rights of citizenship to free black people before the Civil War.

Yeoman Independent farmers of the South, most of whom lived on family-sized farms.

owners prohibited, helped slaves to escape, and even (in an 1835 Mississippi case) were executed for their participation in planning a slave revolt. At the same time, the majority of poor white people insisted, sometimes violently, on their racial superiority over blacks. But the fact was that the difficult lives of poor whites served to blur the crucial racial distinction between independent whites and supposedly inferior, dependent black people on which the system of slavery rested.

SOUTHERN "PLAIN FOLK"

The word "**yeoman**," originally a British term for a farmer who works his own land, is often applied to independent farmers of the South, most of whom lived on family-sized farms. Southerners themselves referred to them as "plain folk," as opposed to the gentry who owned slaves. Although yeoman farmers sometimes owned a few slaves, in general they and their families worked their land by themselves.

Just as elsewhere in the South, family was the mainstay of community. Farm men and women depended on their relatives and neighbors for assistance in large farm tasks such as planting, harvesting, and construction. Projects requiring lots of hands, like logrollings, corn shuckings, and quilting bees, were community events. Farmers repaid this help and obtained needed goods through complex systems of barter with other members of the community.

Where yeomen and large slave owners lived side by side, as in the Georgia black belt where cotton was the major crop, slavery again provided a link between the rich and the "plain folk." Large plantation owners often bought food for their slaves from small local farmers, ground the latter's corn in the plantation mill, ginned their cotton, and transported and marketed it as well. But although planters and much smaller yeomen were part of a larger community network, in the black belt the large slave owners were clearly dominant. Only in their own up-country communities did yeomen feel truly independent.

The goal of yeoman farm families was economic independence. Their mixed farming and grazing enterprises, supported by kinship and community ties, afforded them a self-sufficiency epitomized by Carl G. von Iwonski's painting of this rough but comfortable log cabin in New Braunfels, Texas.

The dominance of the large planters was due at least in part to the ambition of many yeomen, especially those with two or three slaves, to expand their holdings and become rich. These farmers, enthusiastic members of the lively democratic politics of the South, supported the leaders they hoped to join.

But for a larger group of yeomen, independence and not wealth was most important. Many southern yeomen lived apart from large slaveholders in the upcountry regions where plantation agriculture was unsuitable. The very high value southern yeomen placed on freedom grew directly from their own experience as self-sufficient property-owning farmers in small, family-based communities, and from the absolute, patriarchal control they exercised over their own wives and children. This was a way of life that southern "plain folk" were determined to preserve. It made them resistant to the economic opportunities and challenges that capitalism and industrialization posed for northern farmers, which southern yeomen perceived as encroachments on their freedom.

The irony was that the freedom yeomen so prized rested on slavery. White people could count on slaves to perform the hardest and worst labor, and the degradation of slave life was a daily reminder of the freedom they enjoyed in comparison. Slavery meant that all white people, rich and poor, were equal in the sense that they were all free. The democratization of politics in the early nineteenth century and the enactment of nearly universal white manhood suffrage perpetuated the belief in white skin privilege, even though the gap between rich and poor white people was widening.

THE MIDDLING RANKS

In the predominantly rural South, cities provided a home for a small commercial middle class of merchants, bankers, factors (agents), and lawyers on whom the agricultural economy depended to sell its produce to a world market. As in the North, small industrial cities, often including textile mills and heavier industry, clustered along the fall line where the rivers dropped down from the highlands to the coastal plains.

The effort of William Gregg of South Carolina to establish the cotton textile industry illustrates some of the problems facing southern entrepreneurs. Gregg, a successful jeweler from Columbia, South Carolina, became convinced that textile factories were a good way to diversify the southern economy and to provide a living for poor whites who could not find work in the slave-dominated employment system. He enthusiastically publicized the findings of his tour of northern textile mills but found a cool reception. His request to the planter-dominated South Carolina legislature for a charter of incorporation for a textile mill passed by only one vote. In 1846, he built a model mill and a company town in Graniteville, South Carolina, that attracted poor white families as employees. Gregg adapted southern paternalism to industry, providing a school and churches and prohibiting alcohol and dancing, yet paying his workers 20 percent less than northern wages. His experience in the competitive textile industry led him to favor the protective tariff, thus putting him at odds with the general attitude in South Carolina that had solidified at the time of the Nullification Crisis (see Chapter 11).

Another noteworthy exception was the Tredegar Iron Works. Many southern planters scorned members of the commercial middle class like William Gregg because they had to please their suppliers and customers and thus lacked, in planters' eyes, true independence. This was an attitude strikingly different from that in the North, where the commercial acumen of the middle class was increasingly valued (see Chapter 12).

WHO MADE up the planter elite?

myhistorylab

Review Summary

PLANTERS

Remarkably few slave owners fit the popular stereotype of the rich and leisured plantation owner with hundreds of acres of land and hundreds of slaves. Only 36 percent of southern white people owned slaves in 1830, and only 2.5 percent owned fifty slaves or more. Just as yeomen and poor whites were diverse, so, too, were southern slave owners (see Figure 10.2).

SMALL SLAVE OWNERS

The largest group of slave owners were small yeomen taking the step from subsistence agriculture to commercial production. To do this in the South's agricultural economy, they had to own slaves. But upward mobility was difficult. Owning one or two slaves increased farm production only slightly, and it was hard to accumulate the capital to buy more.

Such a slave owner was economically vulnerable: a poor crop or a downturn in cotton prices could wipe out his gains and force him to sell his slaves. When times improved, he might buy a new slave or two and try again, but getting a secure footing on the bottom rung of the slave-owner ladder was very difficult. The roller-coaster economy of the early nineteenth century did not help matters, and the Panic of 1837 was a serious setback to many small farmers.

For a smaller group of slave owners, the economic struggle was not so hard. Middle-class professional men—lawyers, doctors, and merchants—frequently managed to become large slave owners because they already had capital (the pay from their professions) to invest in land and slaves. Sometimes they received payment for their services, not in money, but in slaves. These owners were the most likely to own skilled slaves—carpenters, blacksmiths, and other artisans—and to rent them out for profit. By steady accumulation, the most successful members of this middle class were able to buy their way into the slave-owning elite and to confirm that position by marrying their sons or daughters into the aristocracy.

THE PLANTER ELITE

The slave-owning elite, those 2.5 percent who owned fifty slaves or more, enjoyed the prestige, the political leadership, and the lifestyle to which many white Southerners aspired. Almost all great slave owners inherited their wealth. Increasingly after 1820, as universal manhood suffrage spread, planters had to learn how to appeal to the popular vote, but most never acquired "the common touch." The smaller slave owners, not the great planters, formed a clear majority in every southern state legislature.

The eastern seaboard had first given rise to a class of rich planters in the colonial period. In the nineteenth century, these planters ranged from land rich but labor poor Thomas Chaplin of Tombee Plantation who grew sea-island cotton, to rice planter Nathaniel Heyward, who through wealthy marriages and land purchases amassed 45,000 acres of land and over 2,000 slaves.

As Southerners and slave owning spread westward, membership in the elite broadened to include the new wealth of Alabama, Mississippi, Louisiana, and Texas. Natchez, on the Mississippi River, became so wealthy that its rich planters were popularly called "nabobs" (from a Hindi word for Europeans who had amassed fabulous wealth in India).

The extraordinary concentration of wealth in Natchez—in 1850, it was the richest county in the nation—fostered a self-consciously elite lifestyle that derived not from long tradition but from suddenly acquired riches. Fastidious Northern-

Figure 10.2 Slaveholding and Class Structure in the South, 1830

The great majority of the southern white population were yeoman farmers. In 1830, slave owners made up only 36 percent of the southern white population; owners of more than fifty slaves constituted a tiny 2.5 percent. Yet they and the others who were middling planters dominated politics, retaining the support of yeomen who prized their freedom as white men above class-based politics.

U.S. Bureau of the Census.

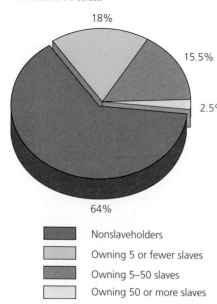

18%

15.5%

2.5%

64%

- Nonslaveholders
- Owning 5 or fewer slaves
- Owning 5–50 slaves
- Owning 50 or more slaves

ers such as Thomas Taylor, a Pennsylvania Quaker who visited Natchez in 1847, noted: "Many of the chivalric gentry whom I have been permitted to see dashing about here on highbred horses, seem to find their greatest enjoyment in recounting their bear hunts, 'great fights,' and occasional exploits with revolvers and Bowie knives—swearing 'terribly' and sucking mint juleps & cherry cobblers with straws."

PLANTATION LIFE

The urban life of the Natchez planters was unusual. Many wealthy planters, especially those on new lands in the Old Southwest, lived in isolation on their plantations with their families and slaves. Through family networks, common boarding school experience, political activity, and frequent visiting, the small new planter elite consciously worked to create and maintain a distinctive lifestyle that was modeled on that of the English aristocracy, as Southerners understood it. This entailed a large estate, a spacious, elegant mansion, and lavish hospitality.

But this gracious image was at odds with the economic reality. Large numbers of black slaves had to be forced to work to produce the wealth that supported the planters' gracious lifestyle. Each plantation, like the yeoman farm but on a larger scale, aimed to be self-sufficient, producing not only the cash crop but also most of the food and clothing for both slaves and family. A large plantation was an enterprise that required many hands, many skills, and a lot of management. Large plantation owners might have overseers or black drivers to supervise field work, but frequently they themselves had direct financial control of daily operations.

The planter elite developed a paternalistic ideology to justify their rigorous insistence on the master–slave relationship. According to this ideology, each plantation was a family composed of both black and white. The master, as head of the plantation, was head of the family, and the mistress was his "helpmate." The master was obligated to provide for all of his family, both black and white, and to treat them with humanity. In return, slaves were to work properly and do as they were told, as children would. Most elite slave owners spoke of their position of privilege as a duty and a burden. John C. Calhoun spoke for many slave owners when he described the plantation as "a little community" in which the master directed all operations so that the abilities and needs of every member, black and white, were "perfectly harmonized." Convinced of their own benevolence, slave owners expected not only obedience but also gratitude from all members of their great "families."

THE PLANTATION MISTRESS

The paternalistic model locked plantation mistresses into positions that bore heavy responsibility but carried no real authority. The difficulties experienced by these privileged women illustrate the way the master–slave relationship of a slave society affected every aspect of the personal life of slave owners.

Plantation mistresses spent most of their lives tending "family" members—including slaves—in illness and in childbirth, and supervising their slaves' performance of such daily tasks as cooking, housecleaning, weaving, and sewing. In addition, the plantation mistress often had to spend hours, even days, of behind-the-scenes preparation for the crowds of guests she was expected to welcome in her role as elegant and gracious hostess.

Despite the reality of the plantation mistress's daily supervision of an often extensive household, she did not rule it: her husband did. The plantation master was the source of authority to whom wife, children, and slaves were expected to look for both rewards and punishments. A wife who challenged her husband or sought

QUICK REVIEW

Plantation Mistresses

- Mistresses ran the household staff.
- Mistresses were responsible for arrangements for visitors.
- Husbands were usually the real authority on the plantation.

more independence from him threatened the entire paternalistic system of control. After all, if she were not dependent and obedient, why should slaves be?

In addition to their strictly defined family roles, many southern women also suffered deeply from their isolation from friends and kin. Sometimes the isolation of life on rural plantations could be overcome by long visits, but women with many small children and extensive responsibilities found it difficult to leave.

Although on every plantation black women served as nursemaids to young white children and as lifelong maids to white women, usually accompanying them when they moved as brides into their own homes, there are few historical examples of genuine sympathy and understanding of black women by white women of the slave-owning class. Few of the latter seemed to understand the sadness, frustration, and despair often experienced by their lifelong maids, who were forced to leave their own husbands and children to serve in their mistresses' new homes.

COERCION AND VIOLENCE

13–1
State v. Boon (1801)

There were generous and benevolent masters, but most large slave owners believed that constant discipline and coercion were necessary to make slaves work hard (see Seeing History). Some slave owners used their slaves with great brutality. Owners who killed slaves were occasionally brought to trial (and usually acquitted), but no legal action was taken in the much more frequent cases of excessive punishment, general abuse, and rape. All southern slave owners, not just those who experienced the special tensions of new and isolated plantations in the Old Southwest, were engaged in a constant battle of wills with their slaves that owners frequently resolved by violence.

One of the most common violations of the paternalistic code of behavior (and of southern law) was the sexual abuse of female slaves by their masters. Usually, masters forcibly raped their women slaves at will, and slave women had little hope of defending themselves from these attacks. Sometimes, however, long-term intimate relationships between masters and slaves developed.

9–12
Harriet Jacobs, *The Trials of a Slave Girl* (1861)

It was rare for slave owners to publicly acknowledge fathering slave children or to free these children, and black women and their families were helpless to protest their treatment. Equally silenced was the master's wife, who for reasons of modesty as well as her subordinate position was not supposed to notice either her husband's infidelity or his flagrant crossing of the color lines.

An owner could do what he chose on his plantation, and his sons grew up expecting to do likewise. Unchecked power is always dangerous, and it is not surprising that it was sometimes misused. Perhaps the most surprising thing about the southern slave system is how much humanity survived despite the intolerable conditions. For that, most of the credit goes not to white paternalism, but to African Americans and the communities they created under slavery.

THE DEFENSE OF SLAVERY

WHAT PROSLAVERY arguments were developed in the first half of the nineteenth century?

myhistorylab
Review Summary

"Slavery informs all our modes of life, all our habits of thought, lies at the basis of our social existence, and of our political faith," announced South Carolina planter William Henry Trescot in 1850, explaining why the South would secede from the Union before giving up slavery. Slavery bound white and black Southerners together in tortuous ways that eventually led, as Trescot had warned, to the Civil War. Population figures tell much of the story of the complex relationship between whites and blacks: of the 12 million people who lived in the South in 1860, 4 million were slaves. These

"Gordon Under Medical Inspection"

This horrifying image of the badly scarred back of a former slave named Gordon appeared in *Harper's Weekly* in July 1863. He was an escaped slave who entered Union lines in Baton Rouge in March 1863, arriving in the bedraggled condition shown on the left. Under medical examination, he revealed the scars from a whipping three months earlier. As the third picture shows, he promptly joined the Union Army.

AFTER VIEWING this image, how seriously would you consider claims that southern slavery was a benign, paternalistic system?

Although abolitionist literature frequently described brutal whippings endured by slaves, few people in the North can have seen such graphic examples before the publication of this article in 1863. Since that time, the picture of Gordon's back has frequently been used to illustrate the violence of the slave system. There is no question that whipping was a frequent punishment in the slaveholding South and that masters, mistresses, and overseers, in fits of temper, whipped harshly. Although we do not know if Gordon's scars were representative, the image makes it impossible to deny the reality of brutality in the slave system. ∎

Illustrations from photographs by McPherson and Oliver, in *Harper's Weekly*, July 4, 1863, p. 429.

sheer numbers of African Americans reinforced white people's perpetual fears of black retaliation for the violence exercised by the slave master. Every rumor of slave revolts, real or imagined, kept those fears alive. The basic question was this: What might slaves do if they were not controlled?

DEVELOPING PROSLAVERY ARGUMENTS

Once the cotton boom began in the 1790s, Southerners increasingly sought to justify slavery. They found justifications for slavery in the Bible and in the histories of Greece and Rome, both slave-owning societies. The strongest defense was a legal one: the Constitution allowed slavery.

The Missouri Crisis of 1819–20 alarmed most Southerners, who were shocked by the evidence of widespread antislavery feeling in the North. South Carolinians viewed **Denmark Vesey's conspiracy**, occurring only two years after the Missouri debate, as an example of the harm that irresponsible northern antislavery talk could cause. In the wake of the Vesey conspiracy, Charlestonians turned their fear and anger outward by attempting to seal off the city from dangerous outside influences. In December 1822, the South Carolina legislature passed a bill requiring that all black seamen be seized and jailed while their ships were in Charleston harbor. Initially most alarmed about free black people from Haiti, Charlestonians soon came to believe that northern free black seamen were spreading antislavery ideas among their slaves.

After **Nat Turner's Revolt** in 1831, Governor John Floyd of Virginia blamed the uprising on "Yankee peddlers and traders" who supposedly told slaves that "all men were born free and equal." Thus, northern antislavery opinion and the fear of slave uprisings were firmly linked in southern minds. This extreme reaction, which Northerners viewed as paranoid, stemmed from the basic nature of a slave society: *anything* that challenged the master–slave relationship was viewed as a basic threat to the entire system.

AFTER NAT TURNER

In 1831, the South began to close ranks in defense of slavery. Several factors contributed to this regional solidarity. Nat Turner's revolt was important, linked as it was in the minds of many Southerners with antislavery agitation from the North. Militant abolitionist William Lloyd Garrison began publishing the *Liberator,* the newspaper that was to become the leading antislavery organ, in 1831. The British gave notice that they would soon abolish slavery on the sugar plantations of the West Indies, an action that seemed to many Southerners much too close to home. Emancipation for West Indian slaves came in 1834. Finally, 1831 was the year before the Nullification Crisis (see Chapter 11) was resolved. Although the other southern states did not support the hotheaded South Carolinians who called for secession, they did sympathize with the argument that the federal government had no right to interfere with a state's special interest (namely, slavery).

By 1835, every southern legislature had tightened its laws concerning control of slaves. For example, they tried to blunt the effect of abolitionist literature by passing laws forbidding slaves to learn how to read. In only three border states—Kentucky, Tennessee, and Maryland—did slave literacy remain legal. Slaves were forbidden to gather for dances, religious services, or any kind of organized social activity without a white person present. They were forbidden to have whiskey because it might encourage them toward revolt. The penalty for plotting insurrection was death. Other laws made manumission illegal and placed even more restrictions on the lives of free black people. In many areas, slave patrols were augmented and became more vigilant in restricting African American movement and communication between plantations.

13–4
Lewis Tappan, *An Abolitionist Defends the* Amistad *Mutineers* (1839)

14–1
William Lloyd Garrison, *The Liberator* (1831)

Denmark Vesey's conspiracy The most carefully devised slave revolt in which rebels planned to seize control of Charleston in 1822 and escape to freedom in Haiti, a free black republic, but they were betrayed by other slaves, and seventy-five conspirators were executed.

Nat Turner's Revolt Uprising of slaves in Southampton County, Virginia, in the summer of 1831 led by Nat Turner that resulted in the death of fifty-five white people.

In 1836, Southerners introduced a "gag rule" in Washington to prevent congressional consideration of abolitionist petitions. Attempts were made to stifle all open debate about slavery within the South; dissenters were pressured to remain silent or to leave.

In addition to fueling fears of slave rebellions, the growing abolitionist sentiment of the 1830s raised the worry that southern opportunities for expansion would be cut off. Southern politicians painted melodramatic pictures of a beleaguered white South hemmed in on all sides by "fanatic" antislavery states. At home, Southerners were forced to contemplate what might happen when they had "to let loose among them, freed from the wholesome restraints of patriarchal authority . . . an idle, worthless, profligate set of free negroes" whom they feared would "prowl the . . . streets at night and [haunt] the woods during the day armed with whatever weapons they could lay their hands on."

Finally, southern apologists moved beyond defensiveness to develop proslavery arguments. One of the first to do this was James Henry Hammond, elected a South Carolina congressman in 1834. In 1836, Hammond delivered a major address to Congress in which he denied that slavery was evil. Rather, he claimed, it had produced "the highest toned, the purest, best organization of society that has ever existed on the face of the earth." In 1854, another southern spokesman, George Fitzhugh, asserted that "the negro slaves of the South are the happiest, and, in some sense, the freest people in the world" because all the responsibility for their care was borne by concerned white masters. Fitzhugh contrasted southern paternalism with the heartless individualism that ruled the lives of northern "wage slaves."

CHANGES IN THE SOUTH

In spite of these defensive and repressive proslavery measures, which made the South seem monolithic in northern eyes, there were some surprising indicators of dissent. One protest occurred in the Virginia state legislature in 1832, when nonslaveholding delegates, alarmed by the Nat Turner rebellion, forced a two-week debate on the merits of gradual abolition. In the final vote, abolition was defeated 73 to 58. Although the subject was never raised again, this debate was a startling indicator of frequently unvoiced doubts about slavery that existed in the South.

But slavery was not a static system. From the 1830s on, financial changes increasingly underlined class differences among southern whites. It was much harder to become a slaveholder: from 1830 to 1860, slave owners declined from 36 to 25 percent of the population. In 1860, the average slaveholder was ten times as wealthy as the average nonslaveholder. A major reason for the shrinking number of slave owners and their increased wealth was the rapidly increasing price of slaves. High prices caused the internal slave trade to flourish: during the 1850s, slave owners from the Upper South sold some 250,000 slaves to the Lower South for handsome profits. By 1850, in the Chesapeake (Virginia, Maryland, and Delaware), where American slavery had its origin, the percentage of slave owners had fallen to 28 percent, while the comparable figures for Louisiana and Mississippi were 45 percent. Such differences in the extent of slaveholding between the Upper and Lower South threatened regional political unity (see Map 10.4).

Another alarming trend was the disintegration of the slave system in southern cities. The number of urban slaves greatly decreased because plantation owners deeply distrusted the effect of cities on the institution of slavery. Urban slaves led much more informed lives than rural ones and were often in daily contact with free blacks and urban poor whites. Many slaves were hired out and a number even hired out their own time, making them nearly indistinguishable from northern

13–2
David Walker, *A Black Abolitionist Speaks Out* (1829)

myhistorylab

Exploring America: *Alexis de Tocqueville*

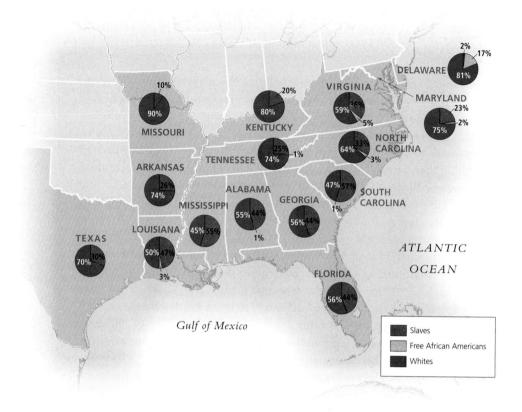

MAP 10.4

Population Patterns in the South, 1850   In South Carolina and Mississippi, the enslaved African American population outnumbered the white population; in four other Lower South states, the percentage was above 40 percent. These ratios frightened many white Southerners. White people also feared the free black population, though only three states in the Upper South and Louisiana had free black populations of over 3 percent. Six states had free black populations that were so small (less than 1 percent) as to be statistically insignificant.

WHERE WERE the greatest concentrations of African Americans? How would you explain the patterns the map reveals?

"free labor." Other urban slaves worked in commercial and industrial enterprises in jobs that were nearly indistinguishable from those of whites.

Economic changes adversely affected poor whites and yeomen as well. Increased commercialization of agriculture (other than cotton) led to higher land prices that made it harder for poor whites to buy or rent land. Extensive railroad building in up-country regions during the boom of the 1850s ended the isolation of many yeomen, exposing them for the first time to the temptations and dangers of the market economy. While slave owners grew increasingly worried about threats from the abolitionist and capitalist North, yeomen worried about local threats to their independence from banks, railroads, and activist state governments.

In spite of these signs of tension and dissent, the main lines of the southern argument were drawn in the 1830s and remained fixed thereafter. The defense of slavery stifled debate within the South, prevented a search for alternative labor systems, and narrowed the possibility of cooperation in national politics. In time, it made compromise impossible.

CHRONOLOGY

1790s   Second Great Awakening

Black Baptist and African Methodist Episcopal churches founded

1793   Cotton gin invented

1800   Gabriel Prosser's revolt discovered in Virginia

1806   Virginia tightens law on manumission of slaves

1808   Congress prohibits U.S. participation in the international slave trade

1816–20   "Alabama Fever": migration to the Old Southwest

1819–20   Missouri Crisis

1822   Denmark Vesey's conspiracy in Charleston

1831   Nat Turner's revolt in Virginia

William Lloyd Garrison begins publishing an antislavery newspaper, the *Liberator*

1832   Nullification Crisis

1832–38   "Flush Times": second wave of westward expansion

1832   Virginia legislature debates and defeats a measure for gradual emancipation

1834   Britain frees slaves throughout the empire, including in its Caribbean colonies

1835   Charleston crowd burns abolitionist literature

Tightening of black codes completed by southern legislatures

1836   Congress passes "gag rule" to prevent discussion of antislavery petitions

James Henry Hammond announces to Congress that slavery is not evil

1846   William Gregg opens model textile mill at Graniteville, South Carolina

1854   George Fitzhugh publishes *Sociology for the South*, a defense of slavery

1857   Hinton Helper publishes *The Impending Crisis*, an attack on slavery

1858   James Henry Hammond's "King Cotton" speech

CONCLUSION

The amazing growth of cotton production after 1793 transformed the South and the nation. Physically, the South expanded explosively westward: in all, seven southern states were admitted to the Union between 1800 and 1845. Cotton production fastened the slave system of labor upon the region. Although the international slave trade was abolished in 1808, the internal slave trade flourished, with devastating effects on African American families. Nationally, the profitable cotton trade fueled economic development and provided much of the original capital for the infant factory system of the North. Cotton production was based on the labor of African American slaves, who built strong communities under extremely difficult circumstances. The cohesion of African American families and the powerful faith of African American Christianity were the key community elements that bred a spirit of endurance and resistance. White Southerners, two-thirds of whom did not own slaves, denied their real dependence on slave labor by claiming equality in white skin privilege, while slave owners boasted of their own paternalism. But the extreme fear generated by a handful of slave revolts and the growing number of free African Americans in many areas gave the lie to white claims of benevolence. In the 1830s, the South defensively closed ranks against real and perceived threats to the slave system. In this sense, the white South was nearly as trapped as the African American slaves they claimed to control. And in its growing concern for the defense of the slave system, the South's role in national politics became more rigid, as we shall see in the next chapter.

REVIEW QUESTIONS

1. How did cotton production after 1793 transform the social and political history of the South? How did the rest of the nation benefit? In what way was it an "international phenomenon"?

2. What were the two key institutions of the African American slave community? How did they function, and what beliefs did they express?

3. The circumstances of two groups—poor whites and free African Americans—put them outside the dominant southern equations of white equals free and black equals slave. Analyze the difficulty each group encountered in the slave-owning South.

4. Who were the yeoman farmers? What was their interest in slavery?

5. Southern slaveholders claimed that their paternalism justified their ownership of slaves, but paternalism implied obligations as well as privileges. How well do you think slaveholders lived up to their paternalistic obligations?

6. How did slave owners justify slavery? How did their defense change over time?

Flashcard Review

KEY TERMS

Black codes (p. 253)
Denmark Vesey's conspiracy (p. 260)
Gang System (p. 248)
Industrial Revolution (p. 242)

Manumission (p. 247)
Nat Turner's Revolt (p. 260)
Second Great Awakening (p. 250)
Yeoman (p. 254)

RECOMMENDED READING

Ira Berlin, *Generations of Captivity* (2003). A compelling survey of the changing nature of American slavery.

Joan E. Cashin, *A Family Venture: Men and Women on the Southern Frontier* (1991). Explores the effects on slave owners of separation from family networks.

Erskine Clarke, *Dwelling Place: A Plantation Epic* (2005). This story of the intertwined lives of a white Christian slaveowning minister and his slaves on a Georgia plantation shows how he failed to reconcile the enslaved to their condition.

Steven Deyle, *Carry Me Back: The Domestic Slave Trade in American Life* (2005). The effects of the trade on American life.

Eugene Genovese, *Roll, Jordan, Roll: The World the Slaves Made* (1974). The landmark book that redirected the attention of historians from slaves as victims to the slave community as an active participant in paternalism.

Anthony E. Kaye, *Joining Places: Slave Neighborhoods in the Old South* (2007). An innovative study about the ways the informal and unnoticed ways of slaves linked plantations into African American neighborhoods.

Peter Kolchin, *American Slavery 1619–1877* (1993). A well-written, comprehensive survey.

Stephanie McCurry, *Masters of Small Worlds: Yeoman Households, Gender Relations, and the Political Culture of the Antebellum South Carolina Low Country* (1995). A study of yeomen that links their prized political and economic independence with their strong patriarchal control over their own families.

Donald P. McNeilly, *The Old South Frontier: Cotton Plantations and the Formation of Arkansas Society, 1819–1861* (2000). Traces slavery and society in Arkansas from frontier to cotton plantations.

Michael O'Brien, *Conjectures of Order: Intellectual Life and the American South* (2004). An outstanding two-volume study of southern life and thought from 1800 to 1865.

Marie Jenkins Schwartz, *Born in Bondage: Growing Up Enslaved in the Antebellum South* (2001). How slave communities sought to protect their children.

For study resources for this chapter, go to **www.myhistorylab.com** and choose *Out of Many, Teaching and Learning Classroom Edition*. You will find a wealth of study and review material for this chapter, including pretests and posttests, customized study plan, key-term review flash cards, interactive map and document activities, and documents for analysis.

I blush for my country when I see such things, and I often tremble with apprehension that our Constitution will not long withstand the current which threatens to overwhelm it . . .

—Benjamin B. French, September 1828

Andrew Jackson speaking to a crowd after his election. Politics in the olden time—General Jackson, President-elect, on his way to Washington.

11

THE GROWTH OF DEMOCRACY
1824–1840

HOW DID suffrage expand between 1800 and 1840?

WHAT STEPS did Andrew Jackson take to strengthen the executive branch of the federal government?

WHO WERE Andrew Jackson's most important opponents and what did they support?

WHAT WERE the main issues of the campaign of 1840?

WHAT ROLE did newspapers and pamphlets play in American popular culture in the first half of the nineteenth century?

AMERICAN COMMUNITIES

A Political Community Replaces Deference with Democracy

PHILADELPHIA HAD LONG BEEN A STRONGHOLD OF CRAFT associations for skilled workers. Their organizations, and their parades and celebrations, were recognized parts of the urban community. Groups of master craftsmen marching in community parades with signs such as "By Hammer and Hand All Arts Do Stand" not only demonstrated pride in their craft but also asserted their importance to the community as a whole. Pennsylvania enfranchised all men who were taxpayers in 1776, enabling many of Philadelphia's skilled workers to vote, but they were willing to follow the leadership of the city's political elite. This was the accepted rule of republican government as understood by leaders such as Thomas Jefferson: an independent and virtuous people willingly deferred to wealthy and enlightened leaders who would govern in the public interest. In reality, most states limited the vote to property owners, and so many ordinary men had little choice but to accept the decisions of the wealthy.

By the 1820s, the lives of workers in Philadelphia had changed. As the Market Revolution transformed the economy, many skilled workers lost their independence and became wage earners in factories owned by others. Members of urban workers' associations realized that their own economic interests were different from those of the owners. In other states, where many men gained the vote for the first time in the 1820s, a similar process of identifying common interests at odds with the traditional political elite was also underway. The spread of universal manhood suffrage marked the transition from traditional deferential politics to democracy.

In 1827, the British-born shoemaker William Heighton urged his fellow workers in Philadelphia to band together under "the banner of equal rights" and form their own political party to press for issues of direct concern to workingmen, including the ten-hour day, free public education for their children, the end of imprisonment for debt, and curbing the powers of banks. "Surely we, the working class, who constitute a vast majority of the nation . . . have a right to expect [that] an improvement in our *individual condition* will be the natural result of legislative proceedings."

Heighton saw in the rising tide of universal manhood suffrage the possibility of reaching his overarching aim of "economic democracy." In response to his new vision of majority

rule, the Philadelphia Working Men's Party was formed in 1828 and elected a slate of local officials as well as voting for Andrew Jackson for president. Andrew Jackson, who was so untraditional that at first national politicians did not take him seriously as a candidate, perfectly personified the new democratic mood and its animosity toward what was often termed "the monied aristocracy."

Thus, when a committee of the Philadelphia Working Men's Party attacked the banking system in 1829, Andrew Jackson paid attention. Their report decried the control by wealthy men of banks and of the paper money each bank issued (there was no national government-controlled currency until 1862), concluding: "If the present system of banking and paper money be perpetuated, the great body of the working people must give over all hopes of ever acquiring any property." This fear of the threat to democracy from a moneyed aristocracy was common among voters in rural areas of the South and West as well as in urban areas. Jackson not only understood this public resentment, but he also shared it. In 1832 he had Philadelphia's workers and others in mind when, speaking for "the humble members of society—the farmers, mechanics and laborers," he refused to renew the charter of the Bank of the United States and thereby instigated the events that we call the **Bank War**.

The Philadelphia Working Men's Party did not last very long. Too small and too narrowly focused to have wide appeal, it was quickly absorbed into Jackson's Democratic Party, with most of its specific demands unmet. Nevertheless, its brief history is significant for marking the end of traditional ideas about a unitary local political community and the transition to the more diverse and contentious community of competing interests that has characterized American democracy ever since. But it also set some limits. Politicians were quick to note that most Americans were uncomfortable with President Jackson's use of the language of class warfare in his veto message. Henceforth, whatever the competing interests might be, appeal to resentment alone was rarely successful. Rather, politicians sought to create national coalitions of voters with similar interests, creating new and more democratic political communities than had existed before.

Philadelphia

Bank War The political struggle between President Andrew Jackson and the supporters of the Second Bank of the United States.

THE NEW DEMOCRATIC POLITICS IN NORTH AMERICA

The early years of the nineteenth century were a time of extraordinary growth and change, not only for the United States but for all the countries of North America as well. Seen in continental perspective, the American embrace of popular democracy was unusual. Elsewhere, crises over popular rights dominated.

STRUGGLES OVER POPULAR RIGHTS: MEXICO, THE CARIBBEAN, CANADA

In 1821, after eleven years of revolts (see Chapter 9), Mexico achieved its independence from Spain. Briefly united under the leadership of Colonel Agustin de Iturbide, Mexico declared itself a constitutional monarchy that promised equality for everyone—peninsulares, criollos, mestizos, and Indians alike. But because Spanish colonial rule had left a legacy of deep social divisions, the initial unity was short-lived. Iturbide reigned as Emperor of Mexico for little more than a year before he was overthrown by a military junta and later executed as a traitor. A series of weak presidents repeatedly invoked emergency powers and relied on the army, as they attempted to revive a faltering economy and reconcile the differences between the centralists—the vested interests of clergy, large landowners, and the military—and the federalists, largely criollos and mestizos, who hoped to create a liberal republic modeled on the American one. The unresolved issue of elite versus popular rule continued to undermine the hope for unity, popular rights, and stable government in an independent Mexico.

The independence of Haiti in 1804 (see Chapter 9) set the pattern for events in many other Caribbean islands in subsequent years. Independence destroyed the sugar industry, for freed slaves asserted their popular rights by refusing to perform the killing labor demanded of them on sugar plantations. The British Caribbean islands were racked with revolts, the largest occurring on Barbados in 1816 and on Jamaica in 1831. In response the British Parliament abolished slavery in all British colonies in 1834. As in Haiti, sugar production then plunged. The economic collapse that followed emancipation destroyed the political authority of local white elites, forcing the British government to impose direct rule.

Still a third crisis of popular rights occurred in British North America. In 1837, both Upper and Lower Canada rebelled against the limited representative government that the British government had imposed in the Constitutional Act of 1791. By far the most serious revolt was in predominantly French Lower Canada, where armed uprisings were brutally suppressed by British troops. In 1840, Britain abolished the local government of Lower Canada and joined it to Upper Canada in a union that most French Canadians opposed and in which they were a minority.

In comparison to these experiences, the rapid spread of suffrage in the United States and the growth of a vibrant but stable democratic political culture seemed all the more extraordinary. But after a brilliant start, in the 1850s the United States, like its neighbors, foundered on a basic sectional difference—slavery—that not even political democracy could reconcile (see Chapter 15).

HOW DID suffrage expand between 1800 and 1840?

myhistorylab
Review Summary

IMAGE KEY
for pages 266–267

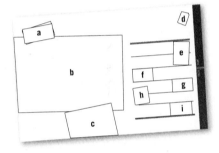

a. A $5 note of the Second Bank of the United States.

b. Andrew Jackson speaking to a crowd after his election.

c. A Cherokee Indian newspaper, *Cherokee Phoenix*.

d. An old, antique Bible bound in leather with a gold cross on the cover.

e. A portrait of Andrew Jackson by Thomas Scully.

f. Political cartoon showing Andrew Jackson destroys the Second Bank of the United States.

g. Americans endured poverty and unemployment by drinking, begging, and rioting in the streets of a city during the 1837 Specie Panic.

h. A banner for William Henry Harrison and John Tyler features political slogans of the Log Cabin campaign above the date of the rally.

i. An 1841 issue of the *Crockett Almanac*.

THE EXPANSION AND LIMITS OF SUFFRAGE

Before 1800, most of the original thirteen states had limited the vote to property owners or taxpayers, thereby excluding about half of the white male population. Westward expansion changed the nature of American politics by undermining the traditional authority structures in the older states and supporting democracy in the newer states (see Map 11.1).

Most of the new states extended the right to vote to all white males over the age of twenty-one. Vermont led the way in 1791, followed by Kentucky in 1792. Tennessee (1796) and Ohio (1803) entered with low taxpayer qualifica-

MAP 11.1

Population Trends: Westward Expansion, 1830 Westward population movement, only a trickle in 1800, had become a flood by 1830. Between 1800 and 1830, the U.S. white and African American population more than doubled (from 5.3 million to 12.9 million), but the trans-Appalachian population grew tenfold (from 370,000 to 3.7 million). By 1830, more than a third of the nation's inhabitants lived west of the original thirteen states.

WHO WERE the western settlers and why did they leave the East?

tions that approached universal suffrage. By 1820, most of the older states had followed suit. The War of 1812 was an important impetus to change in many states, for the propertyless men called up for militia service in that war questioned why they were eligible to fight but not to vote. By 1840, more than 90 percent of adult white males in the nation could vote. And they could vote for more officials: governors and (most important) presidential electors were now elected by direct vote, rather than chosen by small groups of state legislators).

Universal white manhood suffrage, of course, was far from true universal suffrage: the right to vote remained barred to most of the nation's free African American males and to women of any race. Only in five New England states (Maine, New Hampshire, Vermont, Massachusetts, and Rhode Island) could free African American men vote before 1865. In the rest of the northern states, the right of free African American men to vote was restricted to only the most affluent property owners. Free African American men were denied the vote in all of the new western states as well. The constitutions of Illinois, Indiana, Michigan, Iowa, Wisconsin, and (later) Oregon—attempted to solve the "problem" of free African Americans by simply denying them entry into the state at all. Of course, all free black men were prohibited from voting in the slave states of the South.

What accounted for this nearly universal denial of voting rights to free black men? Racism accounted for much of it, an attitude that was strengthened by the backlash against the extremely controversial abolitionist movement of the 1830s and 1840s (see Chapter 13). In addition, as party lines hardened, northern Democrats, the party most closely aligned with the slave South, opposed enfranchising African American men who were almost certain to vote for their opponents. Above all, it was a sign of the growing influence that the southern slave system cast over all of American politics.

In contrast, the reason for the denial of suffrage to white women stemmed from the patriarchal belief that men headed households and represented the interests of all household members. Even wealthy single women who lived alone were considered subordinate to male relatives and denied the right to vote. Although unable to vote, women of the upper classes had long played important informal roles in national politics. At the local level as well, women—often the wives of leading citizens—were accustomed to engaging informally in politics through their benevolent groups. These groups, often church related, had since colonial times not only provided charity to the poor but also raised money to support basic community institutions such as schools, churches, and libraries, in effect setting community priorities in the process.

Although the extension of suffrage to all classes of white men seemed to indicate that women had no role in public affairs, in fact women's informal involvement in politics grew along with the increasing pace of political activity. At the same time, however, as "manhood" rather than property became the qualification for voting, men began to ignore women's customary political activity and to regard their participation as inappropriate, an attitude that politically active women increasingly resented.

THE ELECTION OF 1824

The 1824 election marked a dramatic end to the political truce that James Monroe had established in 1817. Five candidates, all of them members of the Republican Party, ran for president in the elections of 1824: William H. Crawford of Georgia, Secretary of State John Quincy Adams of Massachusetts, Henry Clay of Kentucky, Andrew Jackson of Tennessee, and John C. Calhoun of South Carolina, who withdrew before the election, to run for vice president. Jackson, a

	Electoral Vote (%)	Popular Vote (%)
Andrew Jackson	99 (38)	153,544 (43)
JOHN QUINCY ADAMS	84 (32)	108,740 (31)
William H. Crawford	41 (16)	46,618 (13)
Henry Clay	37 (14)	47,136 (13)

MAP 11.2

The Election of 1824 The presidential vote of 1824 was clearly sectional. John Quincy Adams carried his native New England and little else, Henry Clay carried only his own state of Kentucky and two adjoining states, and Crawford's appeal was limited to Virginia and Georgia. Only Andrew Jackson moved beyond the regional support of the Old Southwest to wider appeal and the greatest number of electoral votes. Because no candidate had a majority, however, the election was thrown into the House of Representatives, which chose Adams.

WHAT ROLE did political parties play in the election of 1824?

10–2

John Quincy Adams, *A "Corrupt Bargain" or Politics as Usual?* (1824)

latecomer to the race, was at first not taken seriously because his record as a legislator was lackluster and his political views unknown. He was not a member of the elite political group that had made up the governing class since 1790. However, owing to his national reputation as a military leader, Jackson won 43 percent of the popular vote and 99 electoral votes—more than any other candidate. The runner-up, John Quincy Adams, won 31 percent of the popular vote and 84 electoral votes. But neither had an electoral majority, leaving it up to the House of Representatives, as in the election of 1800, to pick the winner.

After some political dealing, Henry Clay threw his support to Adams, and the House elected Adams president. This was customary and proper: the Constitution gave the House the power to decide, and Clay had every right to advise his followers how to vote. But when Adams named Clay his secretary of state, the traditional stepping-stone to the highest office, Jackson's supporters promptly accused them of a "corrupt bargain." Popular opinion, the new element in politics, supported Jackson. John Quincy Adams served four miserable years as president, knowing that Jackson would challenge him, and win, in 1828 (see Map 11.2).

THE NEW POPULAR DEMOCRATIC CULTURE

Mass campaigns—huge political rallies, parades, and candidates with wide "name recognition," such as military heroes—were the hallmarks of the new popular democratic culture. So were less savory customs, such as the distribution of lavish food and (especially) drink at polling places, which frequently turned elections into rowdy, brawling occasions. The spirit that motivated the new mass politics was democratic pride in participation. And as the election of 1824 showed, along with the spread of universal male suffrage went a change in popular attitudes that spelled the end of the dominance of small political elites. New national parties that superseded sectional interests were beginning to emerge and to succeed, they had to appeal to the interests of a diverse range of voters.

A print revolution helped to democratize politics by spreading word far beyond the nation's cities about the parades, protests, and celebrations that became a basic part of popular democracy. The print revolution had begun in 1826, when a reform organization, the American Tract Society, installed the country's first steam-powered press and rapidly turned out 300,000 Bibles and 6 million religious tracts. The greatest growth, however, was in newspapers that reached a mass audience. The number of newspapers soared from 376 in 1810 to 1,200 in 1835. This rise paralleled the growth of interest in politics, for most newspapers were published by political parties and were openly partisan. Packed with articles that today would be considered libelous and scandalous, newspapers were entertaining and popular reading, and they rapidly became a key part of democratic popular culture.

This well-known painting by George Caleb Bingham, *Stump Speaking*, shows a group of men (and boys and dogs) of all social classes brought together by their common interest in politics.

George Caleb Bingham (American 1811–1879), "Stump Speaking," 1853–54. Oil on canvas, 42 1/2 × 58 in. Saint Louis Art Museum, Gift of Bank of America.

The new politics placed great emphasis on participation and party loyalty. One way for ordinary citizens to show their loyalty was to turn out for parades, which derived from processions like those of Philadelphia artisans' associations in earlier times. Political processions were huge affairs, marked by the often spontaneous participation of men carrying badges and party regalia, banners and placards, and portraits of the candidates, accompanied by bands, fireworks, and the shouting and singing of party slogans and songs. The political party provided some of the same satisfactions that popular sports offer today: excitement, entertainment, and a sense of belonging. In effect, political parties functioned as giant national men's clubs. They made politics an immediate and engrossing topic of conversation and argument for men of all walks of life. In this sense, the political party was the political manifestation of a wider social impulse toward community (see Figure 11.1).

THE ELECTION OF 1828

The election of 1828 was the first to demonstrate the power and effectiveness of the new popular democratic culture and party system. With the help of Martin Van Buren, his campaign manager, Andrew Jackson rode the wave of the new democratic politics to

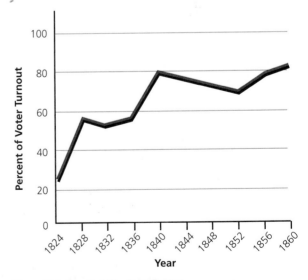

Figure 11.1 Pre–Civil War Voter Turnout

The turnout of voters in presidential elections more than doubled from 1824 to 1828, the year Andrew Jackson was first elected. Turnout surged to 80 percent in 1840, the year the Whigs triumphed. The extension of suffrage to all white men, and heated competition between two political parties with nationwide membership, turned presidential election campaigns into events with great popular appeal.

Politics, abetted by the publication of inexpensive party newspapers, was a great topic of conversation among men in early nineteenth-century America, as Richard Caton Woodville's 1845 painting *Politics in an Oyster House* suggests.

Richard Caton Woodville, "Politics in an Oyster House," 1848. Oil on canvas. The Walters Art Museum, Baltimore.

the presidency. Voter turnout in 1828 was more than twice that of 1824. Jackson's party, the Democratic Republicans (they soon dropped "Republicans" and became simply the **Democrats**), spoke the language of democracy, and they opposed the special privilege personified for them by President John Quincy Adams and his National Republican (as distinguished from the earlier Jeffersonian Republican) Party. Neither Jackson nor Adams campaigned on his own—that was considered undignified. But the supporters of both candidates campaigned vigorously, freely, and negatively. Jackson's supporters, playing on popular resentment of a wealthy political elite, portrayed the campaign as a contest between "the democracy of the country, on the one hand, and a lordly purse-proud aristocracy on the other." In their turn, Adams's supporters depicted Jackson as an illiterate backwoodsman, a murderer (he had ordered the execution of deserters in the Tennessee militia), and an adulterer (apparently unwittingly, he had married Rachel Robards before her divorce was final).

Jackson won 56 percent of the popular vote (well over 80 percent in much of the South and West) and a decisive electoral majority of 178 votes to Adams's 83. The vote was interpreted as a victory for the common man. But the most important thing about Jackson's victory was the coalition that achieved it. The new democratically based political system worked together to elect him. Popular appeal, which Jackson the military hero certainly possessed, was not enough to ensure victory. To be truly national, a party had to create and maintain a coalition of North, South, and West. The Democrats were the first to do this (see Map 11.3).

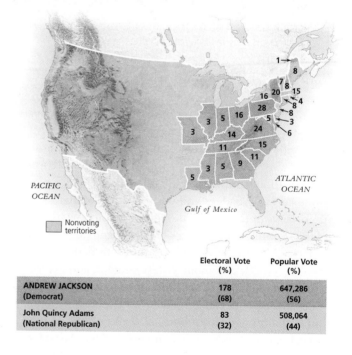

	Electoral Vote (%)	Popular Vote (%)
ANDREW JACKSON (Democrat)	178 (68)	647,286 (56)
John Quincy Adams (National Republican)	83 (32)	508,064 (44)

MAP 11.3

The Election of 1828 Andrew Jackson's victory in 1828 was the first success of the new national party system. The coalition of state parties that elected him was national, not regional. Although his support was strongest in the South and West, his ability to carry Pennsylvania and parts of New York demonstrated his national appeal.

Democrats Political party formed in the 1820s under the leadership of Andrew Jackson; favored states' rights and a limited role for the federal government.

TO WHAT extent was Andrew Jackson a "popular" president?

THE JACKSON PRESIDENCY

Andrew Jackson's election ushered in a new era in American politics, an era that historians have called the "Age of the Common Man." Jackson himself, however, was no common man: he was a military hero, a rich slave owner, and an imperious and decidedly undemocratic personality. "Old Hickory," as Jackson was affectionately called, was tough and unbending, just like hickory itself, one of the hardest of woods. Yet he had a mass appeal to ordinary people, unmatched—and indeed unsought—by earlier presidents. The secret to Jackson's extraordinary appeal lies in the changing nature of American society. Jackson was the first to respond to the ways in which westward expansion and the extension of the suffrage were changing politics at the national as well as the local and state levels.

A POPULAR PRESIDENT

Jackson was born in 1767 and raised in North Carolina. During the American Revolution, he was captured and beaten by the British, an insult he never forgot. As a young man without wealth or family support, he moved west to the frontier station (fort) at Nashville, Tennessee, in 1788. There he made his career as a lawyer and his considerable wealth as a slave-owning planter. He first became a national hero with his underdog win against the British in the Battle of New Orleans in 1815. In the popular mind, his fierce belligerence came to symbolize pioneer independence. The fact that he had little political experience, which would have made his nomination impossible under the traditional system of politics, was not a hindrance in the new age of popular politics.

On March 4, 1829, Andrew Jackson was inaugurated as president of the United States. Jackson himself was still in mourning for his beloved wife Rachel, whose recent death he attributed to the slanders of the campaign. But everyone else was celebrating. The small community of Washington was crowded with strangers, many of them Westerners and common people who had come especially for Jackson's inauguration. Jackson's brief inaugural address was almost drowned out by the cheering of the crowd, and after the ceremony the new president was mobbed by well-wishers. The same unrestrained enthusiasm was evident at a White House reception, where the crowd was large and disorderly (see Seeing History). This was the exuberance of democracy in action. It marked something new in American politics. Indeed, Jackson's administration was different from all those before it.

A STRONG EXECUTIVE

The mob scene that accompanied Jackson's inauguration was more than a reflection of the popular enthusiasm for Old Hickory. It also signaled a higher level of controversy in national politics. Jackson's personal style quickly stripped national politics of the polite and gentlemanly aura of cooperation it had acquired during the Era of Good Feelings. Jackson had played rough all his life, and he relished controversy. His administration (1829–37) had plenty of it. Andrew Jackson dominated his administration. Except for Martin Van Buren, whom he appointed secretary of state, he mostly ignored the heads of government departments

WHAT STEPS did Andrew Jackson take to strengthen the executive branch of the federal government?

myhistorylab
Review Summary

10–4
Andrew Jackson, *The "Commoner" Takes Office* (1828)

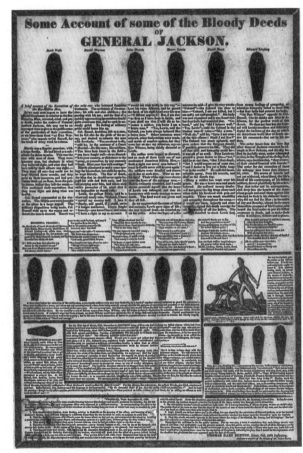

This anti-Jackson "coffin bill" from the election of 1828 accuses Jackson of murder because he ordered three men executed for desertion during the War of 1812.

10–5
Andrew Jackson, *First Annual Message to Congress* (1829)

who made up his official cabinet. Instead he consulted with an informal group, dubbed the "Kitchen Cabinet," made up of Van Buren and old western friends.

Jackson freely used the tools of his office to strengthen the executive branch of government at the expense of the legislature and judiciary. By using the veto more frequently than all previous presidents combined (twelve vetoes compared with nine by the first six presidents), Jackson forced Congress to constantly consider his opinions. Even more important, Jackson's "negative activism" restricted federal activity (see Chapter 9). Only his strong and popular leadership made this sharp change of direction possible.

THE NATION'S LEADER VERSUS SECTIONAL SPOKESMEN

Despite his western origins, Jackson was a genuinely national figure. He was more interested in asserting strong national leadership than in promoting sectional compromise. He believed that the president, who symbolized the popular will of the people, ought to dominate the government. As he put it in his first annual message, "the first principle of our system [is that] the majority is to govern." This was new. Voters were much more accustomed to thinking of politics in sectional terms. Jackson faced a Congress full of strong and immensely popular sectional figures. Three stood out: Southerner John C. Calhoun, Northerner Daniel Webster, and Westerner Henry Clay.

Intense, dogmatic, and uncompromising, John C. Calhoun of South Carolina had begun his political career as an ardent nationalist and expansionist in his early days as a War Hawk before the War of 1812. Since the debate over the Missouri Compromise in 1820, however, Calhoun had wholeheartedly identified with southern interests, first and foremost among which was the preservation and expansion of slavery.

Senator Daniel Webster of Massachusetts was the outstanding orator of the age. Large, dark, and stern, Webster delivered his speeches in a deep, booming voice that, listeners said, "shook the world." Webster became the main spokesman for the new northern commercial interests, supporting a high protective tariff, a national bank, and a strong federal government.

In contrast with the other two, Henry Clay of Kentucky, spokesman of the West, was charming, witty, and always eager to forge political compromises. Clay held the powerful position of Speaker of the House of Representatives from 1811 to 1825 and later served several terms in the Senate. Well known for his ability to make a deal—he was known as "the Great Pacificator" (compromiser)—Clay worked to incorporate western desires for cheap and good transportation into national politics. Clay might well have forged a political alliance between the North and the West if not for the policies of President Jackson, his fellow Westerner and greatest rival. Jackson's preeminence thwarted Clay's own ambition to be president.

The prominence and popularity of these three politicians show that sectional interests remained strong even under a president as determined as Jackson to override them and disrupt "politics as usual" by imposing his own personal style. Nothing showed the power of sectional interests more clearly than the unprecedented confrontation provoked by South Carolina in Jackson's first term, the **Nullification Crisis**.

THE NULLIFICATION CRISIS

The crisis raised the fundamental question concerning national unity in a federal system: What was the correct balance between local interests—the rights of the states—and the powers of the central government? The men who wrote the federal

Nullification Crisis Sectional crisis in the early 1830s in which a states' rights party in South Carolina attempted to nullify federal law.

"President's Levee, or all Creation Going to the White House"

Until 1829, presidential inaugurations had been small, polite, and ceremonial occasions. Andrew Jackson's popularity, however, brought a horde of well-wishers to Washington for his inaugural. "Thousands and thousands of people, without distinction of rank," reported Washington resident Margaret Bayard Smith, "collected in an immense mass round the Capitol, silent, orderly and tranquil," to watch Jackson's swearing-in. But afterwards, when the crowd followed Jackson to an open house at the White House, says Smith, "what a scene did we witness! . . . a rabble, a mob of boys, negros, women, children, scrambling, fighting, romping. What a pity what a pity." Her consternation was echoed by many respectable people who feared that "the reign of King Mob" had begun.

DOES IT matter that the details are not authentic? Why or why not?

This famous illustration of the raucous crowd at the White House reception is by the British caricature artist Robert Cruikshank. It was probably first shown, along with other pictures, in a London printmaker's window display in 1829, with copies sold for two shillings. For the British, amusement came from the fact that American democracy so quickly turned into a rowdy mob, just as the British had always predicted.

Cruikshank was not in Washington at the time of Jackson's inaugural. At best, the details of the illustration are based on accounts provided to him by others or perhaps simply invented. Nevertheless, the illustration captures the mood of the celebrating crowd. ■

Margaret Bayard Smith, *The First Forty Years of Washington Society* (New York: Charles Scribner's Sons, 1906); Robert Cruikshank, *President's Levee, or all Creation Going to the White House,* illustrated in *The Playfair Papers* (London: Saunders and Otley, 1841).

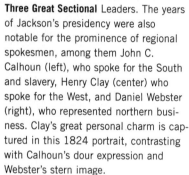

Three Great Sectional Leaders. The years of Jackson's presidency were also notable for the prominence of regional spokesmen, among them John C. Calhoun (left), who spoke for the South and slavery, Henry Clay (center) who spoke for the West, and Daniel Webster (right), who represented northern business. Clay's great personal charm is captured in this 1824 portrait, contrasting with Calhoun's dour expression and Webster's stern image.

(center) Matthew H. Joulett (1788–1827), "Henry Clay," c. 1824. Oil on panel. (attr. to Joulett) © Chicago Historical Society, Chicago, USA.

Constitution in Philadelphia in 1787 had not been able to reach agreement on this question. Because the Constitution deliberately left the federal structure ambiguous, all sectional disagreements automatically became constitutional issues that carried a threat to national unity.

The political issue that came to symbolize the divergent economic interests of North and South was the protective tariff that placed a duty (or surcharge) on imported goods. The first substantial tariff was enacted in 1816 after northern manufacturing interests clamored for protection from the ruthless British competition that followed the War of 1812 (see Chapter 9). As a group, wealthy southern planters were opposed to tariffs, both because duties raised the cost of the luxury goods they imported from Europe and because they feared that American tariffs would cause other countries to retaliate with tariffs against southern cotton. Most southern congressmen, assured that the 1816 tariff was a temporary postwar recovery measure, voted for it. But it was not temporary.

As the North industrialized and new industries demanded protection, tariff bills in 1824 and 1828 raised rates still higher and protected more items. Southerners protested, but they were outvoted in Congress by northern and western representatives. The 1828 tariff imposed especially high tariffs on imported textiles and iron. Southern opponents of the tariff insisted that it was not a truly national measure but rather a sectional one that helped only some groups while harming others. Thus, they claimed, it was unconstitutional because it violated the rights of some of the states.

South Carolina, Calhoun's home state, reacted the most forcefully to the Tariff of 1828. Of the older southern states, South Carolina had been the hardest hit by the opening of the new cotton lands in the Old Southwest, which had drained both population and commerce from the state. To these economic woes were added the first real fears about national attitudes toward slavery. South Carolinians, who had always had close personal ties with slave owners in the Caribbean islands, were shaken by the news that the British Parliament, bowing to popular pressure at home, was planning to emancipate all the slaves in the British West Indies. If Congress had the power to impose tariffs that were harmful to some states, South Carolinians asked, what would prevent it from enacting legislation like Britain's, depriving Southerners of their slaves and, thus, of their livelihood? In this sense, although the Nullification Crisis was about the tariff, it was also about the greatest of all sectional issues, slavery.

The result of these fears was a renewed interest in the doctrine of nullification, a topic that became the subject of widespread discussion in South Carolina. The doctrine upheld the right of a state to declare a federal law null and void and to refuse to enforce it within the state. Calhoun wrote a widely circulated defense of the doctrine, the *Exposition and Protest*, in 1828. Because Calhoun was soon to serve as Andrew Jackson's vice president, he wrote the *Exposition* anonymously. He hoped to use his influence with Jackson, a fellow slave owner, to gain support for nullification, but he was disappointed.

Where Calhoun saw nullification as a safeguard of the rights of the minority, Jackson saw it as a threat to national unity. The president and the vice president were thus in open disagreement on a matter of crucial national importance. The outcome was inevitable: Calhoun lost all influence with Jackson, and two years later, he took the unusual step of resigning the vice presidency. Martin Van Buren was elected to the office for Jackson's second term. Calhoun, his presidential aspirations in ruins, became a senator from South Carolina, and in that capacity, participated in the last act of the nullification drama.

In 1832, the nullification controversy became a full-blown crisis. In passing the Tariff of 1832, Congress (in spite of Jackson's disapproval) retained high taxes on woolens, iron, and hemp, although it reduced duties on other items. South Carolina responded with a special convention and an Ordinance of Nullification, in which it rejected the tariff and refused to collect the taxes it required. The state further issued a call for a volunteer militia and threatened to secede from the Union if Jackson used force against it. Jackson responded vehemently, denouncing the nullifiers and obtaining from Congress a Force Bill authorizing the federal government to collect the tariff in South Carolina at gunpoint if necessary. Intimidated, the other southern states refused to follow South Carolina's lead. More quietly, Jackson also asked Congress to revise the tariff. Henry Clay, the Great Pacificator, swung into action and soon, with Calhoun's support, had crafted the Tariff Act of 1833.

The Nullification Crisis was the most serious threat to national unity that the United States had ever experienced. South Carolinians, by threatening to secede, had forced concessions on a matter they believed to be of vital economic importance. They—and a number of other Southerners—believed that the resolution of the crisis illustrated the success of their uncompromising tactics.

10–8
President Andrew Jackson's Proclamation Regarding Nullification (1832)

10–9
The Force Bill (1833)

CHANGING THE COURSE OF GOVERNMENT

As Martin Van Buren later recalled, Jackson came to the presidency with a clear agenda: "First, the removal of the Indians from the vicinity of the white population and their settlement beyond the Mississippi. Second, to put a stop to the abuses of the Federal government in regard to internal improvements [and] Third, to oppose as well the existing re-incorporation of the existing National Bank." As Jackson enacted his agenda, which he believed expressed the popular will, he changed the course of the federal government as decisively as Jefferson had during his presidency (see Chapter 9). But the opposition that Jackson evoked also revealed the limits of presidential authority in an age of democratic politics.

WHO WERE Andrew Jackson's most important opponents and what did they support?

Review Summary

INDIAN REMOVAL

The official policy of the U.S. government from the time of Jefferson's administration was to promote the assimilation of Indian peoples by encouraging them to adopt white ways. To Indian groups that resisted "civilization" or that needed more time to adapt, Jefferson offered the alternative of removal from settled areas in the East to the new Indian Territory west of the Mississippi River. Following this logic, at the end of the War of 1812, the federal government signed removal treaties with a number of Indian nations of the Old Northwest, thereby opening up large tracts of land for white settlement (see Chapter 9). In the Southwest, however, the Five Civilized Tribes—the Cherokees, Chickasaws, Choctaws, Creeks, and Seminoles—remained.

Of these, the Cherokees took the most extensive steps to adopt white ways. Their tribal lands in northwestern Georgia boasted prosperous farms, businesses, grain and lumber mills, and even plantations with black slaves. Intermarriage with whites and African Americans had produced an influential group of mixed-bloods within the Cherokee nation, some of whom were eager to accept white ways. Schooled by Congregationalist, Presbyterian, and Moravian missionaries, the Cherokees were almost totally literate in English.

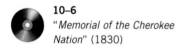
10–6
"*Memorial of the Cherokee Nation*" (1830)

Despite the evidence of the Cherokees' successful adaptation to the dominant white culture, in the 1820s, the legislatures of Georgia, Alabama, and Mississippi, responding to pressures from land-hungry whites, voted to invalidate federal treaties granting special self-governing status to Indian lands. Because the federal government, not the states, bore responsibility for Indian policy, these state actions constituted a sectional challenge to federal authority. In this instance, however, unlike the Nullification Crisis, the resisting states had presidential support. Living up to his reputation as a ruthless Indian fighter, Jackson determined on a federal policy of wholesale removal of the southern Indian tribes.

In 1830, at President Jackson's urging, the U.S. Congress passed the hotly debated **Indian Removal Act**, which appropriated funds for relocation, by force if necessary. When Jackson increased the pressure by sending federal officials to negotiate removal treaties with the southern tribes, most reluctantly signed and prepared to move. The Cherokees, however, fought their removal by using the white man's weapon—the law. At first they seemed to have won: in *Cherokee Nation* v. *Georgia* (1831) and *Worcester* v. *Georgia* (1832), Chief Justice John Marshall ruled that the Cherokees, though not a state or a foreign nation, were a "domestic dependent nation" that could not be forced by the state of Georgia to give up its land against its will. Ignoring the decision, Jackson continued his support for removal.

Although some Seminole bands mounted a successful resistance war in the Florida Everglades, the majority of Seminoles and members of other tribes were much less fortunate: most of the Choctaws moved west in 1830; the last of the Creeks were forcibly moved by the military in 1836, and the Chickasaws a year later. And in 1838, in the last and most infamous removal, resisting Cherokees were driven west to Oklahoma along what came to be known as the "**Trail of Tears**." A 7,000-man army escorting them watched thousands (perhaps a quarter of the 16,000 Cherokees) die along the way (see Map 11.4).

Indian removal was a deeply divisive national issue. President Jackson's sweeping policy undoubtedly expressed the opinion of most Southerners and Westerners. But northern opinion, led by Protestant missionaries and reform groups, was strongly opposed. Among the groups mobilized in protest were members of female benevolent societies who had a direct interest in the issue, for they had long raised money to support missionary activities aimed at assimilating, not removing, American Indians. Now, they joined together to organize the first national female petition drive. A surprised Congress was deluged by women's petitions against removal,

Indian Removal Act President Andrew Jackson's measure that allowed state officials to override federal protection of Native Americans.

Trail of Tears The forced march in 1838 of the Cherokee Indians from their homelands in Georgia to the Indian Territory in the West.

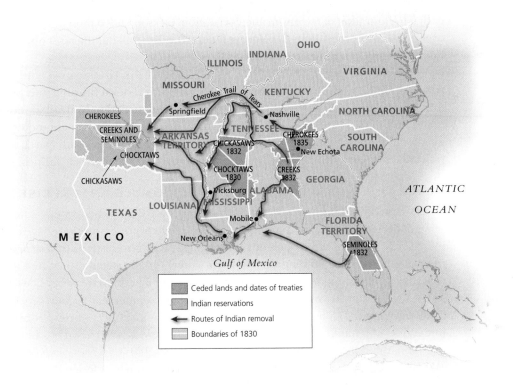

MAP 11.4

Southern Indian Cessions and Removals, 1830s   Pressure on the five major southern Indian peoples—the Cherokees, Chickasaws, Choctaws, Creeks, and Seminoles—that began during the War of 1812 culminated with their removal in the 1830s. Some groups from every tribe ceded their southern homelands peacefully and moved to the newly established Indian Territory west of Arkansas and Missouri. Some, like the Seminoles, resisted by force. Others, like the Cherokees, resisted in the courts, but finally lost when President Andrew Jackson refused to enforce a Supreme Court decision in their favor. The Cherokees, the last to move, were forcibly removed by the U.S. Army along the "Trail of Tears" in 1838.

WHAT GROUPS supported the Indian Removal Act?

many with hundreds of signatures (670 from Pittsburgh alone). In the end, the protest failed, but by the barest of margins: the Indian Removal Act passed the House of Representatives by only 3 votes (out of 200).

INTERNAL IMPROVEMENTS

Because Jackson was a Westerner, his supporters expected him to recognize the nation's urgent need for better transportation and to provide federal funding for internal improvements, especially in the West. Jackson's veto of the Maysville Road Bill of 1830 was, therefore, one of his most unexpected actions. Jackson refused to allow federal funding of a southern spur of the National Road in Kentucky, claiming it should be paid for by the state. Jackson argued that federal funding for extensive and expensive transportation measures was unconstitutional because it infringed on the "reserved powers" the Constitution left to the states.

Internal improvements were a part of Clay's American System (which had been supported by the Monroe and Adams administrations) that envisaged the national government as planner and administrator of a coordinated policy to encourage economic growth and foster the development of a national market. But since 1816, it had proved impossible to propose a nationally funded transportation plan that satisfied everyone. Repeatedly, disappointed claimants for federal funds accused each administration of favoritism and corruption. Jackson ended most of the debate over internal improvements by refusing federal funds for all but the most obviously interstate projects (such as the National Road).

But the country still needed a basic infrastructure of roads, canals, and railroads to tie the national economy together. Without federal funding and planning, the initiative passed to private developers, who turned to individual states. States and towns, especially in newly populated areas of the West, competed in giving land, subsidies, and other forms of encouragement to road, canal, and railroad companies to provide transportation to their particular localities.

FEDERAL AND STATE SUPPORT FOR PRIVATE ENTERPRISE

At the same time that funding for internal improvements passed to the states, a series of decisions by federal courts asserted broad federal powers over interstate commerce. The effect of these decisions, contradictorily, was to vastly encourage commercial enterprise by limiting the regulatory power of the states at the same time that they were putting up most of the money for the new transportation network. By preventing states from interfering with interstate commerce, the courts encouraged development by assuring entrepreneurs the freedom and security to operate in the risky new national market. Two key decisions were handed down by Chief Justice John Marshall (who had been on the bench since 1801). In *Dartmouth College* v. *Woodward* (1819), the Supreme Court prevented states from interfering in contracts, and in *Gibbons* v. *Ogden* (1824), it enjoined the State of New York from giving a monopoly over a steamboat line to Robert Fulton, inventor of the vessel. Although Fulton's invention was protected by a federal patent, its commercial application was not. A decision handed down by Marshall's successor, Roger Taney, *Charles River Bridge* v. *Warren Bridge* (1837), again supported economic opportunity by denying a monopoly.

At the state level, another crucial commercial protection was the passage of laws concerning incorporation of businesses that had grown too large for individual proprietorship, family ownership, or limited partnership. Businesses that needed to raise large amounts of capital by attracting many investors found the contractual protections provided by incorporation to be essential. The protection investors wanted most was limited liability—the assurance that they would lose no more than what they had invested in a corporation if it were sued or went bankrupt. The net effect of state incorporation laws was to encourage large-scale economic activity and to hasten the commercialization of rural areas, both crucial aspects of the Market Revolution (see Chapter 12).

THE BANK WAR

In the case of internal improvements, Jackson rejected, on behalf of popular democracy, the notion of coordinated economic planning by the government. His rejection set up the conditions for a speculative frenzy. Precisely the same result occurred in his epic battle with the Second Bank of the United States.

In 1816, Congress had granted a twenty-year charter to the Second Bank of the United States. The Bank was owned by private investors, with the U.S. government holding only one-fifth of the shares. But its most important function was the control it exercised over state banks. Because state banks tended to issue more paper money than they could back with hard currency, the Bank always demanded repayment of its loans to them in hard currency. This policy forced state banks to maintain adequate reserves and restricted speculative activities. In times of recession, the Bank eased the pressure on state banks, demanding only partial payment in coin. Thus, the Bank acted as a currency stabilizer by helping to control the money supply.

In this political cartoon, Jackson destroys the Second Bank of the United States by withdrawing government deposits. As the Bank crashes, it crushes the director Nicholas Biddle (depicted as the Devil), wealthy investors (with moneybags), and the newspaper editors (surrounded by paper) who opposed Jackson on this issue.

The concept of a strong national bank controlled by wealthy investors, not the federal government, was supported by the majority of the nation's merchants and businessmen. Nevertheless, the Bank had many opponents. Both western farmers and urban workers had bitter memories of the Panic of 1819, which the Bank had caused (at least in part) by sharply cutting back on available credit. Many ordinary people believed that a system based on paper currency would be manipulated by bankers—the "monied aristocracy"—in selfish and dangerous ways.

Early in his administration, Jackson hastened to tell Nicholas Biddle, the director of the Bank: "I do not dislike your Bank any more than all banks." By 1832, Jackson's opinion had changed, and he and Biddle were locked in a personal conflict that harmed not only the national economy but also the reputations of both men. Biddle, urged on by Henry Clay and Daniel Webster, precipitated the conflict by making early application for rechartering the Bank. Congress approved the application in July 1832. Jackson immediately decided on a stinging veto, announcing to Van Buren, "The bank . . . is trying to kill me, but I will kill it!"

And kill it he did that same July, with one of the strongest veto messages in American history. Denouncing the Bank as unconstitutional, harmful to states' rights, and "dangerous to the liberties of the people," Jackson presented himself as the spokesman for the majority of ordinary people and the enemy of special privilege.

Jackson's veto message was a great popular success, and it set the terms for the presidential election of 1832. Henry Clay, the nominee of the anti-Jackson forces, lost the battle for popular opinion. Democrats successfully painted Clay as the defender of the Bank and of privilege. These were accusations with great popular appeal. Clay's defeat was decisive: he drew only 49 electoral votes to Jackson's 219.

10–7
Andrew Jackson, *Veto of the Bank Bill* (1832)

This figurehead of Andrew Jackson, carved in 1834 for the navy frigate *Constitution,* captures the unmovable resolve that made Jackson so popular early in his presidency and so reviled during the Bank War.

Museum of the City of New York (M52.11).

Whigs　The name used by advocates of colonial resistance to British measures during the 1760s and 1770s.

Specie Circular　Proclamation issued by President Andrew Jackson in 1836 stipulating that only gold or silver could be used as payment for public land.

Although the election was a triumph for Jackson, the Bank War continued because Jackson decided to kill the Bank by transferring its $10 million in government deposits to favored state banks ("pet banks," critics called them).

Jackson's refusal to renew the charter of the Second Bank of the United States had lasting economic and political consequences. Economically, it inaugurated the economic policy known as *laissez-faire,* where decision-making power rests with commercial interests, not with government. Politically, it so infuriated Jackson's opponents that they formed a permanent opposition party. It was from the heat of the Bank War that the now characteristic American two-party system emerged.

WHIGS, VAN BUREN, AND THE PANIC OF 1837

In 1833, as the government withdrew its deposits, Nicholas Biddle, the Bank's director, counterattacked by calling in the Bank's commercial loans, thereby causing a sharp panic and recession in the winter of 1833–34. Merchants, businessmen, and southern planters were all furious—at Jackson. His opponents, only a loose coalition up to this time, coalesced into a formal opposition party that called itself the **Whigs**. Just as Jackson's own calls for popular democracy had appealed to voters in all regions, so his opponents overcame their sectional differences to unite in opposition to his economic policies and arbitrary methods.

Vice President Martin Van Buren, Jackson's designated successor, won the presidential election of 1836 because the Whigs ran four sectional candidates, hoping their combined votes would deny Van Buren a majority and force the election into the House of Representatives.

Meanwhile, the consequences of the Bank War continued. The recession of 1833–34 was followed by a wild speculative boom, caused as much by foreign investors as by the expiration of the Bank. Many new state banks were chartered that were eager to give loans, the price of cotton rose rapidly, and speculation in western lands was feverish. A government surplus of $37 million distributed to the states in 1836 made the inflationary pressures worse. Jackson became alarmed at the widespread use of paper money (which he blamed for the inflation), and in July 1836, he issued the **Specie Circular**, announcing that the government would accept payment for public lands only in hard currency. At the same time, foreign investors, especially British banks, affected by a world recession, called in their American loans. The sharp contraction of credit led to the Panic of 1837 and a six-year recession, the worst the American economy had yet known.

In neither 1837 nor 1819 did the federal government take any action to aid victims of economic recession. No banks were bailed out, no bank depositors were saved by federal insurance, no laid-off workers got unemployment payments. Nor did the government undertake any public works projects or pump money into the economy. All of these steps, today seen as essential to prevent economic collapse and to alleviate human suffering, were unheard of then. Soup kitchens and charities were mobilized in major cities, but only by private, volunteer groups, not by local or state governments. As a result, workers, farmers, and members of the new business middle class suddenly realized that participation in America's booming economy was very dangerous.

Martin Van Buren (quickly nicknamed "Van Ruin") spent a dismal four years in the White House presiding over bank failures, bankruptcies, and massive unemployment. Van Buren, who lacked Jackson's compelling personality, could find no remedies to the depression. His misfortune gave the opposition party, the newly formed Whigs, its opportunity.

THE SECOND AMERICAN PARTY SYSTEM

The First American Party System, the confrontation between the Federalists and the Jeffersonian Republicans that began in the 1790s, had been widely viewed at the time as an unfortunate factional squabble that threatened the common good of the republic (see Chapter 8). By the 1830s, with the expansion of suffrage, attitudes had changed. The political struggles of the Jackson era, coupled with the dramatic social changes caused by expansion and economic growth, created the basic pattern of American politics: two major parties, each with at least some appeal among voters of all social classes and in all sections of the country. That pattern, which we call the "**Second American Party System**," continues to this day.

WHIGS AND DEMOCRATS

There were genuine differences between the Whigs and the Democrats, but they were not sectional differences. Instead, the two parties reflected just-emerging class and cultural differences. The Democrats, as they themselves were quick to point out, had inherited Thomas Jefferson's belief in the democratic rights of the small, independent yeoman farmer. They had nationwide appeal, especially in the South and West, the most rural regions. As a result of Jackson's presidency, Democrats came to be identified with independence and a distaste for interference, whether from the government or from economic monopolies such as the Bank of the United States. They favored expansion, Indian removal, and the freedom to do as they chose on the frontier. Most Democratic voters were opposed to the rapid social and economic changes of the 1830s and 1840s.

The Whigs were themselves often the initiators and beneficiaries of economic change and were more receptive to it. They supported Henry Clay's American System: a strong central government, the Bank of the United States, a protective tariff, and internal improvements. Whigs favored government intervention in both economic and social affairs, calling for education and

WHAT WERE the main issues of the campaign of 1840?

myhistörylab
Review Summary

8–13
Davy Crockett, *Advice to Politicians* (1833)

Second American Party System The basic pattern of American politics of two parties, each with appeal among voters of all social voters and in all sections of the country.

This contemporary cartoon bitterly depicts the terrible effects of the Panic of 1837 on ordinary people—bank failures, unemployment, drunkenness, and destitution—which the artist links to the insistence of the rich on payment in specie (as Jackson had required in the Species Circular of 1836). Over the scene waves the American flag, accompanied by the ironic message, "61st Anniversary of Our Independence."

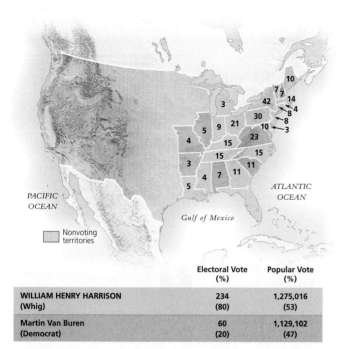

	Electoral Vote (%)	Popular Vote (%)
WILLIAM HENRY HARRISON (Whig)	234 (80)	1,275,016 (53)
Martin Van Buren (Democrat)	60 (20)	1,129,102 (47)

MAP 11.5
The Election of 1840   The Whigs triumphed in the election of 1840 by beating the Democrats at their own game. Whigs could expect to do well in the commercializing areas of New England and the Old Northwest, but their adopted strategy of popular campaigning worked well in the largely rural South and West as well, contributing to Harrison's victory. The Whigs' choice of John Tyler as vice presidential candidate, another strategy designed to appeal to southern voters, backfired when Harrison died and Tyler, who did not share Whig principles, became America's first vice president to succeed to the presidency.

WHAT POLICIES did Tyler promote? Which did he reject?

WHAT ROLE did newspapers and pamphlets play in American popular culture in the first half of the nineteenth century?

Review Summary

social reforms, such as temperance, that aimed to improve the ordinary citizen. Many rich men were Whigs, but so were many poorer men who had a democratic faith in the perfectibility of all Americans. The Whigs' greatest strength was in New England and the northern part of the West (the Old Northwest), the areas most affected by commercial agriculture and factory work (see Chapter 13).

THE CAMPAIGN OF 1840

In 1840, the Whigs set out to beat the Democrats at their own game. Passing over the ever-hopeful Henry Clay, the Whigs nominated a man as much like Andrew Jackson as possible, the aging Indian fighter William Henry Harrison, former governor of the Indiana Territory from 1801 to 1812. The Whigs reached out to ordinary people with torchlight parades, barbecues, songs, coonskin caps, bottomless jugs of hard cider, and claims that Martin Van Buren, Harrison's hapless opponent, was a man of privilege and aristocratic tastes. Nothing could be further from the truth: Van Buren was the son of a tavern keeper.

The Whig campaign tactics, added to the popular anger at Van Buren because of the continuing depression, gave Harrison a sweeping electoral victory (see Map 11.5).

THE WHIG VICTORY TURNS TO LOSS: THE TYLER PRESIDENCY

Although the Whig victory of 1840 was a milestone in American politics, the triumph of Whig principles was short-lived. William Henry Harrison, who was sixty-eight, died of pneumonia a month after his inauguration. For the first time in American history, the vice president stepped up to the presidency. John Tyler of Virginia, quickly nicknamed "His Accidency," was a former Democrat who had left the party because he disagreed with Jackson's autocratic style. The Whigs had sought him primarily for his sectional appeal and had not inquired too closely into his political opinions, which turned out to be anti-Whig as well as anti-Jackson.

President Tyler vetoed a series of bills embodying all the elements of Henry Clay's American System: tariffs, internal improvements, a new Bank of the United States. In exasperation, congressional Whigs forced Tyler out of the party, and his entire cabinet of Whigs resigned. To replace them, Tyler appointed former Democrats like himself.

AMERICAN ARTS AND LETTERS

Jackson's presidency was a defining moment in the development of an American identity. His combination of western belligerency and combative individualism was the strongest statement of American distinctiveness since Thomas Jefferson's agrarianism. Did Jackson speak for all of America? The Whigs did not think so. And the definitions of American identity that were beginning to emerge in popular culture and in intellectual circles were more complex than

OVERVIEW | The Second American Party System

Democrats	First organized to elect Andrew Jackson to the presidency in 1828. The Democratic Party spoke for Jeffersonian democracy, expansion, and the freedom of the "common man" from interference from government or from financial monopolies like the Bank of the United States. It found its power base in the rural South and West and among some northern urban workers. The Democratic Party was the majority party from 1828 to 1860.
Whigs	Organized in opposition to Andrew Jackson in the early 1830s. Heir to Federalism, the Whig Party favored a strong role for the national government in the economy (for example, it promoted Henry Clay's American System) and supported active social reform. Its power base lay in the North and Old Northwest among voters who benefited from increased commercialization and among some southern planters and urban merchants. The Whigs won the elections of 1840 and 1848.

the message coming from the White House. Throughout the nation, however, there was a widespread interest in information and literature of all kinds. The Age of the Common Man would prove to be the period when American writers and painters found the national themes that allowed them to produce the first distinctively American literature and art.

POPULAR CULTURES AND THE SPREAD OF THE WRITTEN WORD

Newspapers and pamphlets fostered a variety of popular cultures. For western readers, the Crockett almanacs offered a mix of humorous stories and tall tales. In New York City, the immensely popular "penny papers" (so called from their price) that began appearing in 1833 fostered a distinctive urban culture. These papers, with lurid headlines such as "Double Suicide" and "Secret Tryst," fed the same popular appetite for scandal as did other popular publications. Throughout the country, religious literature was still most widely read, but a small middle-class audience existed for literary magazines and, among women especially, for sentimental magazines and novels.

Accompanying all these changes in print communication was an invention that outsped them all: telegraph. The impact of this revolutionary invention, the first to separate the message from the speed at which a human messenger could travel, was immediate. The timeliness of information available to the individual, from important national news to the next train's arrival time, vastly increased. Distant events gained new and exciting immediacy. Everyone's horizon and sense of community were widened.

CREATING A NATIONAL AMERICAN CULTURE

In the early years of the nineteenth century, eastern seaboard cities actively built the cultural foundation that would nurture American art and literature. Philadelphia's American Philosophical Society, founded by Benjamin Franklin in 1743, boasted a distinguished roster of scientists. Culturally, Boston ran a close second to Philadelphia. Southern cities were much less successful in supporting culture. Charleston had a Literary and Philosophical Society (founded in 1814), but the widely dispersed residences of the southern elite made urban cultural institutions difficult to sustain. Thus, unwittingly, the South ceded cultural leadership to the North.

myhistorylab

Overview: *The Second American Party System*

QUICK REVIEW

William Henry Harrison of Ohio

- Untainted by association with Bank of the United States, Masonic Order, or slaveholding.
- Hero of War of 1812.
- Selected John Tyler of Virginia as his running mate.

LIBRARY OF THE ATHENÆUM.

The Boston Athenaeum was one of Boston's leading cultural institutions. The library, shown in this engraving, was probably the finest in the country in the early nineteenth century.

9–10
James F. Cooper, *Notions of the Americans* (1840)

10–11
Alexis de Tocqueville, *A French Traveler Reports on American Society* (1835)

QUICK REVIEW

The Print Revolution

♦ 1826: American Tract Society installs first steam-powered press in the United States.

♦ Greatest growth was in newspapers.

♦ Newspapers and pamphlets fostered a variety of popular cultures.

The cultural picture was much spottier in the West. A few cities had civic cultural institutions, and some transplanted New Englanders maintained connections with New England culture. A group of pioneers in Ames, Ohio, for example, founded a "coonskin library" composed of books purchased from Boston and paid for in coonskins. But most pioneers were at best uninterested and at worst actively hostile to traditional literary culture. This was neither from lack of literacy nor from a failure to read. Newspaper and religious journals both had large readerships in the West: the *Methodist Christian Advocate,* for example, reached 25,000 people yearly (compared with the *North American Review*'s 3,000 readers). The frontier emphasis on the practical was hard to distinguish from anti-intellectualism.

Thus, in the early part of the nineteenth century, the gap between the intellectual and cultural horizons of a wealthy Bostonian and a frontier farmer in Michigan widened. Part of the unfinished task of building a national society was the creation of a national culture that could fill this gap. For writers and artists, the challenge was to find distinctively American themes.

Of the eastern cities, New York produced the first widely recognized American writers. In 1819, Washington Irving published *The Sketch Book*, thus immortalizing Rip Van Winkle and the Headless Horseman. Within a few years, James Fenimore Cooper's Leatherstocking novels (of which *The Last of the Mohicans*, published in 1826, is the best known) achieved wide success in both America and Europe. Cooper's novels established the experience of westward expansion, of which the conquest of the Indians was a vital part, as a serious and distinctive American literary theme.

It was New England, however, that claimed to be the forge of American cultural independence from Europe. As Ralph Waldo Emerson proclaimed in "The American Scholar," a lecture he delivered in 1837 to the Harvard faculty, "Our day of dependence, our long apprenticeship to the learning of other lands, draws to a close."

CHRONOLOGY

1819	*Dartmouth College* v. *Woodward*	1834	Whig Party organized
1821	Mexican independence from Spain		British abolish slavery in their Caribbean colonies
1824	*Gibbons* v. *Ogden*	1836	Jackson issues Specie Circular
	John Quincy Adams elected president by the House of Representatives		Martin Van Buren elected president
1826	First American use of the steam-powered printing press	1837	*Charles River Bridge* v. *Warren Bridge*
1828	Congress passes "Tariff of Abominations"		Revolts against Britain in Upper and Lower Canada
	Andrew Jackson elected president		Ralph Waldo Emerson first presents "The American Scholar"
	John C. Calhoun publishes *Exposition and Protest* anonymously		Panic of 1837
1830	Jackson vetoes Maysville Road Bill	1838	Cherokee removal along the "Trail of Tears"
	Congress passes Indian Removal Act	1840	Whig William Henry Harrison elected president
1832	Nullification Crisis begins		Act of Union merges Upper and Lower Canada
	Jackson vetoes renewal of Bank of the United States charter	1841	John Tyler assumes presidency at the death of President Harrison
	Jackson reelected president		
1833	General Antonio Lopez de Santa Anna elected president of Mexico		

ARTISTS AND BUILDERS

Artists were as successful as novelists in finding American themes. Thomas Cole, who came to America from England in 1818, painted American scenes in the style of the British romantic school of landscape painting. Cole founded the Hudson River school of American painting, a style and subject matter frankly nationalistic in tone.

The western painters—realists such as Karl Bodmer and George Catlin as well as the romantics who followed them, like Albert Bierstadt and Thomas Moran—drew on the dramatic western landscape and its peoples. All these painters found much to record and to celebrate in American life.

The haste and transience of American life are nowhere as obvious as in the architectural record of this era, which is sparse. The monumental neoclassical style (complete with columns) that Jefferson had recommended for official buildings in Washington continued to be favored for public buildings elsewhere and by private concerns trying to project an imposing image, such as banks. But in general, Americans were in too much of a hurry to build for the future, and in balloon-frame construction they found the perfect technique for the present. Balloonframe structures—which consist of a basic frame of wooden studs fastened with crosspieces top and bottom—could be put up quickly, cheaply, and without the help of a skilled carpenter. Covering the frame with wooden siding was equally simple, and the resultant dwelling was as strong, although not as well insulated, as a house of solid timber or logs.

myhistorylab

Exploring America: *American Art*

CONCLUSION

Andrew Jackson's presidency witnessed the building of a strong national party system based on nearly universal white manhood suffrage. Sectionalism and localism seemed to have been replaced by a more national consciousness that was clearly expressed in the two national political parties, the Whigs and the Democrats. The Second American Party System created new democratic political communities united by common political opinions and often mobilized by common political resentments.

Culturally, American writers and artists began to establish a distinctive American identity in the arts. But as the key battles of the Jackson presidency—the Nullification Crisis, Indian removal, and the Bank War—showed, the forces of sectionalism resisted the strong nationalizing tendencies of the era. Equally clearly, popular political opinion, once aroused, was not always as controllable as politicians may have wished. As the next chapter will show, economic developments in the North were beginning to create a very different society and electorate from that of the slave South or the rural West.

REVIEW QUESTIONS

1. What reasons might a person of the 1820s and 1830s give for opposing universal white manhood suffrage? Suffrage for free African American men? For women of all races?

2. Opponents believed that Andrew Jackson was unsuited in both political experience and temperament to be president of the United States, yet his presidency is considered one of the most influential in American history. Why?

3. Both the Nullification Crisis and Indian removal raised the constitutional issue of the rights of a minority in a nation governed by majority rule. What rights, in your opinion, does a minority have, and what kinds of laws are necessary to defend those rights?

4. Why was the issue of government support for internal improvements so controversial? What *is* the appropriate role for government in economic development?

5. What were the key differences between Whigs and Democrats? What did each party stand for? Who were their supporters? What were the links between each party's programs and party supporters?

6. What distinctive American themes did the writers, artists, and builders of the 1820s and 1830s express in their works? Are they still considered American themes today?

Flashcard Review

KEY TERMS

Bank War (p. 268)

Democrats (p. 274)

Indian Removal Act (p. 280)

Nullification Crisis (p. 276)

Second American Party System (p. 285)

Specie Circular (p. 284)

Trail of Tears (p. 280)

Whigs (p. 284)

RECOMMENDED READING

Anne M. Boylan, *The Origins of Women's Activism: New York and Boston 1797–1840* (2002). How and why the first women's volunteer associations were formed and their political influence.

Bray Hammond, *Banks and Politics in America* (1957). The classic study of the Bank War and its consequences.

Patrick J. Jung, *The Black Hawk War of 1832* (2007). An up-to-date study of one of the last Indian wars in the eastern United States.

Alexander Keyssar, *The Right to Vote: The Contested History of Democracy in the United States* (2000). A survey that examines the reasons for continual limits on the franchise.

Simon Newman, *Parades and the Politics of the Street* (1997). Examines how festive culture became an expression of popular political culture.

Robert Remini, *Andrew Jackson and the Source of American Freedom* (1981). An account of Jackson's White House years by his major biographer.

Alan Taylor, *William Cooper's Town: Power and Persuasion on the Frontier of the Early American Republic* (1995). An engrossing study of the effects of the democratization of politics.

Harry L. Watson, *Liberty and Power: The Politics of Jacksonian America* (1990). An excellent overview of Jacksonian politics.

Sean Wilentz, *The Rise of American Democracy: Jefferson to Lincoln* (2005). A massive new political study that traces the different histories of "city" and "country" democracy.

For study resources for this chapter, go to **www.myhistorylab.com** and choose *Out of Many, Teaching and Learning Classroom Edition.* You will find a wealth of study and review material for this chapter, including pretests and posttests, customized study plan, key-term review flash cards, interactive map and document activities, and documents for analysis.

Jacksonian Democracy and American Politics

Historians have referred to the years of Jackson's presidency as the Age of the Common Man and the Rise of Democracy. Perhaps this does carry a little too much elaboration with it, but the time of Andrew Jackson was a period of great ferment and change. The Second Great Awakening was stirring the religious and reform values of American citizens. The rise of the second two party system was creating both conflict and confrontation in American politics. The issues of national tariffs and slavery were beginning to divide the states and the slow movement toward civil war was becoming clearly apparent.

John Adams, Andrew Jackson, and Henry Clay and the election of 1824 comprise a turning point in U.S. politics. With a field of four candidates, the election for president was thrown to the U.S. House of Representatives where Henry Clay was the Speaker of the House and had heavy influence upon the vote of the members of that chamber. After Adams was elected over Jackson, who had the largest share of popular votes, Adams appointed Clay as the Secretary of State, then seen as a stepping stone to the presidency. Jackson's supporters immediately screamed "corrupt bargain" and the campaign of 1828 was underway before Adams was even inaugurated. Jackson's people coalesced into the Democratic party. Adams' followers became the National Republicans, later evolving into the Whigs.■

TO WHAT degree was the election of 1824 a turning point in American political history? Considering the role of the common man, changes in party operations and campaign tactics, and the growing influence of political patronage, how did the events initiated in that election change American politics between 1824 and 1840?

 Henry Clay

JOHN QUINCY ADAMS, A "CORRUPT BARGAIN" OR POLITICS AS USUAL? (1824)

9TH. . . . Mr. Clay came at six, and spent the evening with me in a long conversation explanatory of the past and prospective of the future. He said that the time was drawing near when the choice must be made in the House of Representatives of a President from the three candidates presented by the electoral colleges; that he had been much urged and solicited with regard to the part in that transaction that he should take, and had not been five minutes landed at his lodgings before he had been applied to by a friend of Mr. Crawford's, in a manner so gross that it had disgusted him; that some of my friends also, disclaiming, indeed, to have any authority from me, had repeatedly applied to him, directly or indirectly, urging considerations personal to himself as motives to his cause. He had thought it best to reserve for sometime his determination to himself: first, to give a decent time for his own funeral solemnities as a candidate; and, secondly, to prepare and predispose all his friends to a state of neutrality between the three candidates who would be before the House, so that they might be free ultimately to take that course which might be most conducive to the public interest. The time had now come at which he might be explicit in his communication with me, and he had for that purpose asked this confidential interview. He wished me, as far as I might think proper, to satisfy him with regard to some principles of great public importance, but without any personal considerations for himself. In the question to come before the House between General Jackson, Mr. Crawford, and myself, he had no hesitation in saying that his preference would be for me.■

Charles Francis Adams, ed. Memoirs of John Quincy Adams, 12 Volumes (Philadelphia: J. B. Lippincott & Co., 1875)

PRESIDENTIAL CANDIDATES AND POLITICAL PARTIES, 1788–1840

IN THE slightly more than fifty years covered in this list, some parties flourished and some died. Some parties rose up to replace earlier parties and some changed into a new political alliance with a different name and evolved political goals.

1788	George Washington – No Party Designation John Adams – No Party Designation	1816	James Monroe – Democratic-Republican Rufus King – Federalist
1792	George Washington – No Party Designation John Adams – No Party Designation George Clinton – No Party Designation	1820	James Monroe – Democratic-Republican John Q. Adams – Independent Republican
1796	John Adams – Federalist Thomas Jefferson – Democratic-Republican Thomas Pinckney – Federalist Aaron Burr – Democratic-Republican	1824	John Q. Adams – Democratic-Republican Andrew Jackson – Democratic-Republican William H. Crawford – Democratic-Republican Henry Clay – Democratic-Republican
1800	Thomas Jefferson – Democratic-Republican Aaron Burr – Democratic-Republican John Adams – Federalist Charles C. Pinckney – Federalist	1828	Andrew Jackson – Democratic John Q. Adams – National Republican
1804	Thomas Jefferson – Democratic-Republican Charles C. Pinckney – Federalist	1832	Andrew Jackson – Democratic Henry Clay – National Republican William Wirt – Anti-Masonic John Floyd – National Republican
1808	James Madison – Democratic-Republican Charles C. Pinckney – Federalist George Clinton – Democratic-Republican	1836	Martin Van Buren – Democratic William H. Harrison – Whig Hugh L. White – Whig Daniel Webster – Whig W.P. Mangum – Whig
1812	James Madison – Democratic-Republican Dewitt Clinton – Federalist	1840	William H. Harrison – Whig Martin Van Buren – Democratic.■

SENATOR WILLIAM MARCY

SENATOR WILLIAM Marcy gave the name "spoils system" to the practice of awarding political office to the supporters of your own party once you had won control of either state or federal government. His famous statement on the floor of the U.S. Senate: "When they are contending for victory, they avow the intention of enjoying it. If they are defeated, they expect to retire from office. If they are successful, they claim as matter of right the advantages of success. They see nothing wrong in the rule that to the victors belong the spoils of the enemy." This principal had been used heavily in the states of New York and Pennsylvania where Marcy engaged brutally in applying the practice. It was not until Jackson's election in 1828 the spoils system was introduced at the federal level. Previous presidents had been circumspect in removing federal office servers from their jobs. Washington had removed only 9 in two terms; Adams had removed 9 in one term. After the Federalists were defeated in 1800 and the Democratic Republicans took office, Jefferson refused to utilize the spoils system and removed only 39 federal office holders in two terms. Madison then dropped only 5 in two terms, Monroe removed only 9 in two terms, and John Q. Adams fired only 2 in one administration. This changed in 1829 when Jackson removed a total of 734 federal office holders in a single year of his first administration. The age of the spoils system had arrived. The Democrats clearly used the spoils system to their advantage. How did the other political parties respond to this concept?

◄ William Learned Marcy (1786–1857). American political leader. Steel engraving, 19th century.

ANDREW JACKSON, STATE OF THE UNION MESSAGE TO CONGRESS, DECEMBER 8, 1829

…The duties of all public officers are, or at least admit of being made, so plain and simple that men of intelligence may readily qualify themselves for their performance; and I can not but believe that more is lost by the long continuance of men in office than is generally to be gained by their experience. I submit, therefore, to your consideration whether the efficiency of the Government would not be promoted and official industry and integrity better secured by a general extension of the law which limits appointments to four years.■

Now if rights are founded on the nature of moral being, then the mere circumstance of sex does not give to man higher rights and responsibilities, than to woman. To suppose that it does, would be to deny the self-evident truth, that the physical constitution is the mere instrument of the moral nature.

—Angelina Emily Grimké, October 2, 1837

LOWELL OFFERING

November, 1845.

" Is Saul also among the prophets?"

A REPOSITORY
OF ORIGINAL ARTICLES, WRITTEN BY
"FACTORY GIRL."

LOWELL: MISSES CURTIS & FARLEY.
BOSTON: JORDAN & WILEY, 121
Washington street.
1845.

MERRIMACK MILLS AND BOARDING-
(LOWELL.)

12

INDUSTRY AND THE NORTH
1790s–1840s

WHAT WERE the effects of the transportation revolution?

WHAT WAS the market revolution?

WHAT IMPACT did advances in transportation have in the Old Northwest?

HOW DID industrialization affect workers in early factories?

HOW DID the market revolution change the lives of ordinary people?

WHAT VALUES were promoted by the new middle class?

AMERICAN COMMUNITIES

Women Factory Workers Form a Community in Lowell, Massachusetts

IN THE 1820s AND 1830s, YOUNG FARM WOMEN FROM ALL OVER NEW England flocked to Lowell to work a twelve-hour day in one of the first cotton textile factories in America. Living six to eight to a room in nearby boardinghouses, the women of Lowell earned an average of $3 a week. Some also attended inexpensive nighttime lectures or classes. Lowell, considered a model factory town, drew worldwide attention. As one admirer of its educated workers said, Lowell was less a factory than a "philanthropic manufacturing college."

The choice of young women as factory workers seemed shockingly unconventional. In the 1820s and 1830s, young unmarried women simply did not live alone; they lived and worked with their parents until they married. In these years of growth and westward expansion, however, America was chronically short of labor, and the Lowell manufacturers were shrewd enough to realize that young farm women were an untapped labor force. To attract respectable young women, Lowell offered supervision both on the job and at home, with strict rules of conduct, compulsory religious services, cultural opportunities such as concerts and lectures, and cash wages.

When they first arrived in Lowell, the young women were often bewildered by the large numbers of townspeople and embarrassed by their own rural clothing and country ways. It was company policy for senior women to train the newcomers, and often sisters or neighbors who had preceded them to the mill helped them adjust to their new surroundings.

Textile mills ran on a rigid work schedule with fines or penalties imposed on latecomers and slackers. Power-driven machinery operated at a sustained, uniform pace throughout every mill; human workers had to learn to do the same. This precise work schedule represented the single largest change from preindustrial work habits, and it was the hardest adjustment for the workers. Moreover, each mill positioned one or two male overseers on every floor to make sure the pace was maintained.

Why did young farm women come to Lowell? Some worked out of need, but most regarded Lowell as an opportunity: an escape from rural isolation and from parental supervision, a chance to buy the latest fashions and learn "city ways," to attend lectures and concerts, to save for a dowry, or to pay for an education. As writer Lucy Larcom, one of the most famous workers, said, the women who came to Lowell sought "an opening into freer life." Working side by side and living with six to twelve other women, some of whom might be relatives or friends from home, the Lowell women built a close, supportive community for themselves.

The owners of Lowell made large profits and also drew praise for their carefully managed community, with its intelligent and independent workforce. But their success was short-lived. In the 1830s, facing competition and poor economic conditions, the owners imposed wage cuts and work speedups that their model workforce did not take lightly. Despite the system of paternalistic control at the mills, the close bonds the women forged gave them the courage and solidarity to "turn out" in spontaneous protests, which were, however, unsuccessful in reversing the wage cuts. By 1850, the "philanthropic manufacturing college" was no more. The original Lowell workforce of New England farm girls had been largely replaced by poor Irish immigrants of both sexes, who earned much less than their predecessors. Now Lowell was simply another mill town.

The history of Lowell epitomizes the process by which the North (New England and the Middle Atlantic states) industrialized. A society composed largely of self-sufficient farm families (Jefferson's "yeoman farmers") changed to one of urban wage earners. Industrialization did not occur overnight. Once under way, the market revolution changed how people worked, how they thought, and how they lived: the very basis of community. In the early years of the nineteenth century, northern communities led this transformation, fostering attitudes far different from those prevalent in the agrarian South.

Lowell

THE TRANSPORTATION REVOLUTION

Between 1800 and 1840, the United States experienced truly revolutionary improvements in transportation. More than any other development, these improvements encouraged Americans to look beyond their local communities to broader ones and to foster the enterprising commercial spirit for which they became so widely known (see Map 12.1).

ROADS

In 1800, travel by road was difficult for much of the year. Mud in the spring, dust in the summer, and snow in the winter all made travel by horseback or carriage uncomfortable, slow, and sometimes dangerous. Localities and states tried to improve local roads or contracted with private turnpike companies to build, maintain, and collect tolls on important stretches of road. In general, however, local roads remained poor. The federal government demonstrated its commitment to the improvement of interregional transportation by funding the National Road in 1808, at the time the greatest single federal transportation expense. Stretching from Cumberland, Maryland, to Vandalia, Illinois, the National Road tied the East and the West together, strong evidence of the nation's commitment to both expansion and cohesion, and helped to foster a national community.

WHAT WERE the effects of the transportation revolution?

myhistorylab
Review Summary

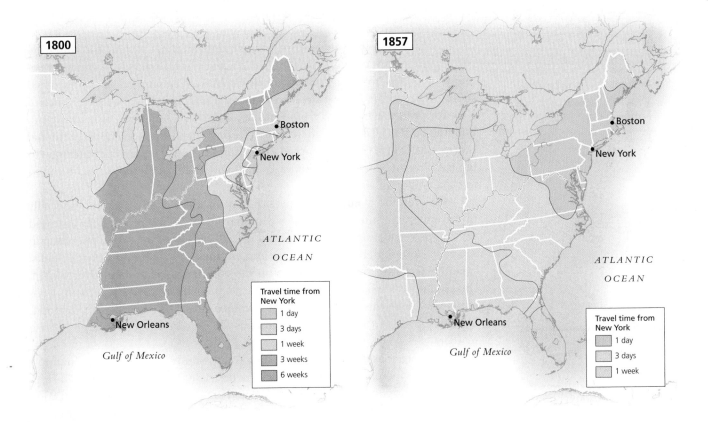

MAP 12.1
Travel Times, 1800 and 1857 The transportation revolution dramatically reduced travel times and vastly expanded everyone's horizons. Improved roads, canals, and the introduction of steamboats and railroads made it easier for Americans to move and made even those who did not move less isolated. Better transportation linked the developing West to the eastern seaboard and fostered a sense of national identity and pride.

HOW DID the federal government's funding of the National Road affect life in the United States?

IMAGE KEY

for pages 294–295

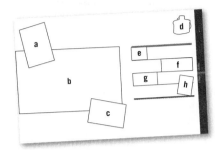

a. A magazine from the Lowell, Massachusetts mills.

b. The Merrimack textile mills with boarding houses Middlesex Company Woolen Mills, Lowell, Massachusetts.

c. Well-dressed nineteenth-century adults enjoy a formal picnic outdoors.

d. A metal lunch pail of a nineteenth-century factory worker.

e. 1849 Currier and Ives print, *The Express Train*.

f. A one dollar banknote from the Manufacturers Bank of Lowell, Massachusetts.

g. Cyrus McCormick demonstrating his reaper to farmers.

h. A nineteenth-century family portrait.

9–3

Jesse Hawley, *The Case for the Erie Canal* (1807)

QUICK REVIEW

The Erie Canal

* Link between New York City and the Great Lakes.

* Built first by local farmers and then by Irish and imigrant labor.

* Completed in 10 years.

CANALS AND STEAMBOATS

However much they helped the movement of people, the National Road and other roads were unsatisfactory in a commercial sense. Shipments of bulky goods like grain were too slow and expensive by road. Waterborne transportation was much cheaper and still the major commercial link among the Atlantic seaboard states and in the Mississippi–Ohio River system. But before the 1820s, most water routes were north–south or coastal (Boston to Charleston, for example); east–west links were urgently needed. Canals turned out to be the answer.

The Erie Canal—the most famous canal of the era—was the brainchild of New York governor DeWitt Clinton, who envisioned a link between New York City and the Great Lakes through the Hudson River, and a 364-mile-long canal stretching from Albany to Buffalo.

DeWitt Clinton had promised, to general disbelief, that the Erie Canal would be completed in less than ten years, and he made good on his promise. The canal was the wonder of the age. The Erie Canal provided easy passage to and from the interior, both for people and for goods. It drew settlers like a magnet from the East and, increasingly, from overseas: by 1830, some 50,000 people a year were moving west on the canal to the rich farmland of Indiana, Illinois, and territory farther west. Earlier settlers now had a national, indeed an international, market for their produce. Moreover, farm families along the canal began purchasing household goods and cloth, formerly made at home. Indeed, one of the most dramatic illustrations of the canal's impact was a rapid decline in the production of homespun cloth in the towns and counties along its route.

Towns along the canal—Utica, Rochester, Buffalo—became instant cities, each an important commercial center in its own right. Perhaps the greatest beneficiary was New York City, which quickly established a commercial and financial supremacy no other American city could match. The Erie Canal decisively turned New York's merchants away from Europe and toward America's own heartland, building both interstate commerce and a feeling of community. The phenomenal success of the Erie Canal prompted other states to construct similar waterways to tap the rich interior market. Between 1820 and 1840, $200 million was invested in canal building.

An even more important improvement in water transportation, especially in the American interior, was the steamboat. Robert Fulton first demonstrated the commercial feasibility of steamboats in 1807, and they were soon operating in the East. Redesigned with more efficient engines and shallower, broader hulls, steamboats transformed commerce on the country's great inland river system: the Ohio, the Mississippi, the Missouri, and their tributaries. Steamboats were extremely dangerous, however; boiler explosions, fires, and sinkings were common, leading to one of the first public demands for regulation of private enterprise in 1838.

Dangerous as they were, steamboats greatly stimulated trade in the nation's interior. The increased river- and canal-borne trade, like the New England shipping boom of a generation earlier, stimulated urban growth and all kinds of commerce. Cities such as Cincinnati, already notable for its rapid growth, experienced a new economic surge. A frontier outpost in 1790, Cincinnati was by the 1830s a center of steamboat manufacture and machine tool production as well as a central shipping point for food for the southern market.

This Currier and Ives print of 1849, *The Express Train*, captures the popular awe at the speed and wonder of the new technology. This "express" probably traveled no more than 30 miles per hour.

RAILROADS

Remarkable as all these transportation changes were, the most remarkable was still to come. Railroads, new in 1830 (when the Baltimore and Ohio Railroad opened with 13 miles of track), grew to an astounding 31,000 miles by 1860. By that date, New England and the Old Northwest had laid a dense network of rails, and several lines had reached west beyond the Mississippi. The South, the least industrialized section of the nation, had fewer railroads.

Early railroads, like the steamboat, had to overcome many technological and supply problems. For example, locomotives, to generate adequate power, had to be heavy. Heavy locomotives, in turn, required iron rather than wooden rails. The resulting demand forced America's iron industry to modernize. Heavy engines also required a solid gravel roadbed and strong wooden ties. Arranging steady supplies of both and the labor to lay them was a construction challenge on a new scale. Finally, there were problems of standardization: because so many early railroads were short and local, builders used any gauge (track width) that served their purposes. It was not until the 1850s that consolidation of local railroads into larger systems began in earnest. But already it was clear that this newest transportation innovation would have far-reaching social consequences.

THE EFFECTS OF THE TRANSPORTATION REVOLUTION

The new ease of transportation fueled economic growth by making distant markets accessible. The startling successes of innovations such as canals and railroads attracted large capital investments, including significant amounts from foreign investors ($500 million between 1790 and 1861), which fueled further growth.

Every east–west road, canal, and railroad helped to reorient Americans away from the Atlantic and toward the heartland. This new focus was decisive in the creation of national pride and identity. The transportation revolution fostered an optimistic, risk-taking mentality in the United States that stimulated invention and innovation. More than anything, the transportation revolution allowed people to move with unaccustomed ease. Transportation improvements such as the Erie Canal and the National Road linked Americans in larger communities of interest, beyond the local communities in which they lived. And improved transportation made possible the larger market on which commercialization and industrialization depended (see Map 12.2).

THE MARKET REVOLUTION

The **market revolution**, the most fundamental change American communities had ever experienced, was the outcome of three interrelated developments: the rapid improvements in transportation just described, commercialization, and industrialization.

THE ACCUMULATION OF CAPITAL

In the northern states, the business community was composed largely of merchants in the seaboard cities: Boston, Providence, New York City, Philadelphia, and Baltimore. Many had made substantial profits in the international shipping boom period from 1790 to 1807 (as discussed in Chapter 9).

When the early years of the nineteenth century posed difficulties for international trade, some of the nation's wealthiest men turned to local investments. In Providence, Rhode Island, Moses Brown and his son-in-law William Almy began to invest some of the profits the Brown family had reaped from a worldwide trade in iron, candles, rum, and African slaves in the new manufacture of cotton textiles. Cincinnati merchants banded together to finance the building of the first steamboats to operate on the Ohio River.

Much of the capital for the new investments came from banks, both those in seaport cities that had been established for the international trade and those, like the Lynn, Massachusetts, Mechanics Bank, founded in 1814 by a group of Lynn's Quaker merchants, that served local clients. An astonishing amount of capital, however, was raised through family connections. In the late eighteenth century, members of the business communities in the seaboard cities had begun to consolidate their position and property by intermarriage.

Southern cotton provided the capital for continuing development. Because Northerners built the nation's ships, controlled the shipping trade, and provided the nation's banking, insurance, and financial services, the astounding growth in southern cotton exports enriched northern merchants almost as much as southern planters. Southerners complained that their combined financial and shipping costs diverted forty cents of every dollar paid for their cotton to Northerners. Although imperfectly understood at the time, the truth is that the development of northern industry was paid for by southern cotton produced by enslaved African American labor. The surprising wealth that cotton brought to southern planters fostered the market revolution.

Finally, the willingness of American merchants to "think big" and risk their money in the development of a large domestic market was caused in part by American nationalism. Their confidence in a future that did not yet exist was not simply a sober economic calculation but an assertion of pride in the potential of this new and expanding nation.

WHAT WAS the market revolution?

myhistorylab
Review Summary

Market revolution The outcome of three interrelated developments: rapid improvements in transportation, commercialization, and industrialization.

MAP EXPLORATION

To explore an interactive version of this map, go to **http://www.prenhall.com/faraghertlc/map12.2**

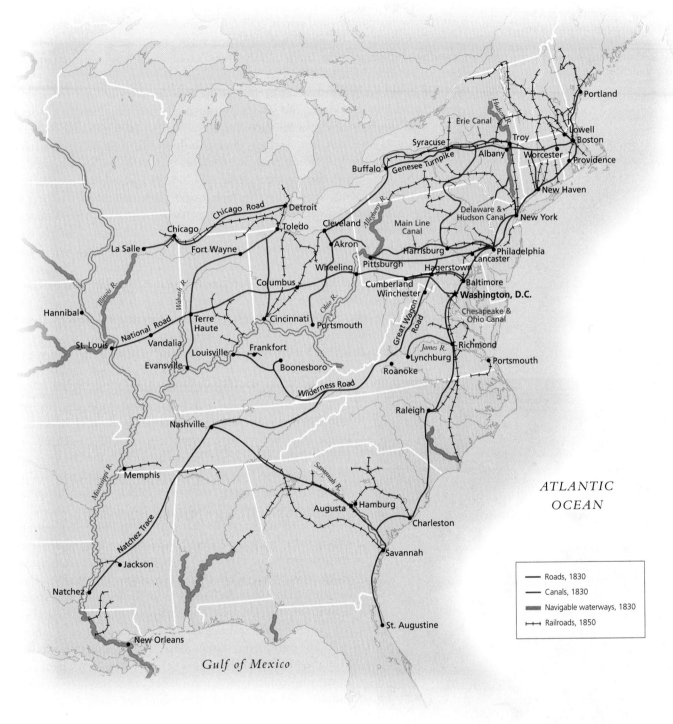

MAP 12.2

Commercial Links: Rivers, Canals, Roads, 1830, and Rail Lines, 1850 By 1830, the United States was tied together by a network of roads, canals, and rivers. This transportation revolution fostered a great burst of commercial activity and economic growth. Transportation improvements accelerated the commercialization of agriculture by getting farmers' products to wider, nonlocal markets. Access to wider markets likewise encouraged new textile and other manufacturers to increase their scale of production. By 1850, another revolutionary mode of transportation, the railroad, had emerged as a vital link to the transportation infrastructure.

HOW DID the transportation revolution of the mid-nineteenth century fuel the American economy?

Putting-out system Production of goods in private homes under the supervision of a merchant who "put out" the raw materials, paid a certain sum per finished piece, and sold the completed item to a distant market.

THE PUTTING-OUT SYSTEM

Initially, the American business community invested not in machinery and factories, but in the "**putting-out system**" of home manufacture, thereby expanding and transforming it. In this significant departure from preindustrial work, people still produced goods at home, but under the direction of a merchant, who "put out" the raw materials to them, paid them a certain sum per finished piece, and sold the completed item to a distant market. A look at the shoe industry in Lynn, Massachusetts, shows how the putting-out system transformed American manufacturing.

Long a major center of the shoe industry, Lynn, in 1800, produced 400,000 pairs of shoes—enough for every fifth person in the country. Skilled craftsmen in Lynn controlled production through the traditional system of apprenticeship. Apprentices lived with the master craftsman and were treated like members of the family. Commonly, apprentices became journeymen craftsmen, working for wages in the shops of master craftsmen until they had enough capital to set up shop for themselves. In Lynn, 200 master artisans and their families, including their journeymen and apprentices, worked together in hundreds of small home workshops called "ten-footers" (from their size, about ten feet square). The artisans and journeymen cut the leather, the artisans' wives and daughters did the binding of the upper parts of the shoe, the men stitched the shoe together, and children and apprentices helped where needed. In the early days, the artisan commonly bartered his shoes for needed products. Sometimes an artisan sold his shoes to a larger retailer in Boston or Salem. Although production of shoes in Lynn increased yearly from 1780 to 1810 as markets widened, shoes continued to be manufactured in traditional ways.

The investment of merchant capital in the shoe business changed everything. In Lynn, a small group of Quaker shopkeepers and merchants, connected by family, religious, and business ties, took the lead in reorganizing the trade. Financed by the bank they founded in 1814, Lynn capitalists like Micajah Pratt built large, two-story central workshops. Pratt employed a few skilled craftsmen to cut leather for shoes, but he put out the rest of the shoemaking to less-skilled workers who were no longer connected by family ties. Putting-out workers were paid on a piecework basis and much less than a master craftsman or a journeyman. This arrangement allowed the capitalist to employ much more labor for the same investment than the traditional artisan workshop. Gradually the putting-out system and central workshops replaced artisans' shops.

The putting-out system moved the control of production from the individual artisan households to the merchant capitalists, who could now control labor costs, production goals, and shoe styles to fit certain markets. For example, the Lynn trade quickly monopolized the market for cheap boots for southern slaves and western farmers, leaving workshops in other cities to produce shoes for wealthier customers. Additionally, and most important from the capitalist's point of view, the owner of the business controlled the workers and could cut back or expand the labor force as economic and marketplace conditions warranted. The unaccustomed severity of economic slumps like the Panics of 1819 and 1837 made this flexibility especially desirable.

This carved and painted figure, designed as a whirligig and trade sign, shows a woman at a spinning wheel. Until the transportation revolution made commercial cloth widely available, spinning was one of the most time-consuming tasks that women and young girls did at home.

Industrialization and Rural Life

George Inness was an American artist of the Hudson River School. Like the better-known Thomas Cole (see Chapter 11), Inness specialized in painting settled and cultivated eastern landscapes. This painting was commissioned by the president of the Delaware Lackawanna and Western Railroad to mark its opening. Inness rose to the challenge of showing both the double tracks (foreground) and the roundhouse (background) in a rural landscape, but the railroad committee was not satisfied, demanding that he show all four company locomotives (three are in the background) and that the letters *D.L.&W* be painted on the side of the locomotive. At first Inness refused on artistic grounds, but being in need of money, he finally agreed. The painting is thus one of the first American examples of a "fine art" advertisement. Even at this early date, there was conflict between the demands of art and those of the advertiser.

WHAT DOES the Inness painting insist that you notice about the impact of industrialization on rural life?

The presence of a locomotive, the symbol of the machine age, in this pastoral setting must have been a real shock to the first viewers, who were familiar with pastoral landscapes but uncomfortable with new inventions like the steam locomotive. Contrast this painting to the Currier and Ives print *The Express Train* on p. 299. ■

LeRoy Ireland, *The Works of George Inness; An Illustrated Catalogue Raisonne* (Austin: University of Texas Press, 1965), p. 28.

George Inness, The Lackawanna Valley Painting, 1825. © 1856. Oil on canvas, 86 × 127.5 cm (33 7/8 × 50 3/16 in.) Gift of Mrs. Huttleston Rogers. Board of Trustees, National Gallery of Art, Washington, D.C.

While the central workshop system prevailed in Lynn and in urban centers like New York City, the putting-out system also fostered a more dispersed form of home production. By 1810, there were an estimated 2,500 so-called outwork weavers in New England, operating handlooms in their own homes. Other crafts that rapidly became organized according to the putting-out system were flax and wool spinning, straw braiding, glove making, and the knitting of stockings.

THE SPREAD OF COMMERCIAL MARKETS

Although the putting-out system meant a loss of independence for artisans such as those in Lynn, Massachusetts, New England farm families liked it. From their point of view, the work could easily be combined with domestic work, and the pay was a new source of income that they could use to purchase mass-produced goods rather than spend the time required to make those things themselves. In this way farm families moved away from the local barter system and into a larger market economy.

Commercialization, or the replacement of barter by a cash economy, did not happen immediately or uniformly throughout the nation. Fixed prices for goods produced by the new principles of specialization and division of labor appeared first along established trade routes. Rural areas in established sections of the country that were remote from trade routes continued in traditional ways (see Seeing History). Strikingly, however, western farming frontiers were commercial from the very start. The existence of a cash market was an important spur to westward expansion.

THE YANKEE WEST

Every advance in transportation—better roads, canals, steamboats, railroads—made it easier for farmers to get their produce to market. Improvements in agricultural machinery increased the amount of acreage a farmer could cultivate. These two developments, added to the availability of rich, inexpensive land in the heartland, dramatically changed the Old Northwest. The sudden change from subsistence to commercial agriculture in the Old Northwest is a particularly vivid example of the impact of transportation changes and commercialization.

NEW ROUTES WEST

The impact of the transportation revolution on the Old Northwest was startling. Settlement of the region, ongoing since the 1790s, vastly accelerated. In the decade of the 1830s, three quarters of a million people migrated to the region, and by 1850 the population of the Old Northwest almost quadrupled.

Migrants of New England origin (Yankees) accounted for at least 40 percent of the population, and they brought with them a distinctive culture that stressed community building. New Englanders immediately established schools, churches, and town government in their new locations. Southern migrants, like their counterparts who migrated to the Old Southwest, were much more likely to rely on kinship ties rather than found community institutions, except for churches. Yankees were different from Southerners in another way: they welcomed commercial agriculture.

COMMERCIAL AGRICULTURE IN THE OLD NORTHWEST

The long period of subsistence farming that had characterized colonial New England and the early Ohio Valley frontier before 1830 was superseded by commercial agriculture stimulated by the transportation revolution.

Cyrus McCormick is shown demonstrating his reaper to skeptical farmers. When they saw that the machine cut four times as much wheat a day as a hand held scythe, farmers flocked to buy McCormick's invention. Agricultural practices, little changed for centuries, were revolutionized by machines such as this.

The very need for cash to purchase land involved western settlers in commercial agriculture from the beginning. Farmers, and the towns and cities that grew up to supply them, needed access to markets for their crops. Local residents clamored for the canals and railroads (often financed by state as well as private money) that tied the individual farm into national and international commercial networks. Commercial agriculture in turn encouraged regional specialization. Because in each new western area wheat yields were higher than in earlier ones, farmers in older regions were forced to shift away from wheat to other crops. The constant opening of new farmland encouraged mobility. Prepared to move on when the price was right, they regarded their farmland not as a permanent investment but as a speculation. This too marked a difference from colonial and southern attitudes in which permanent ownership of farms, with enough to land to endow one's sons, had always been the goal.

New tools made western farmers unusually productive. John Deere's steel plow (invented in 1837) and Cyrus McCormick's reaper (patented in 1834) greatly increased potential production. Western farmers rushed to buy the new machines, confident that increased production would rapidly pay for them. In most years, their confidence was justified. But in bad years, farmers found that their new levels of debt could mean failure and foreclosure.

Thus, within a few short years the Old Northwest became the nation's agricultural heartland. In 1859, the region produced 46 percent of the nation's wheat and 33 percent of its corn. Moreover, a steadily increasing amount was exported to foreign markets: from 12 percent in 1820 to 27 percent in 1840 to 70 percent in 1860. While Southerners boasted in 1858 that "Cotton is King," in fact the Old Northwest, not the South, had become the export heart of the national economy.

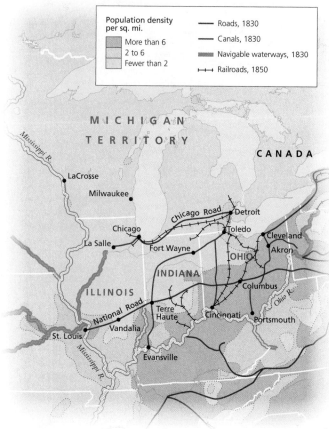

MAP 12.3

Commercial Links: The Old Northwest, 1850 After 1825, the Erie Canal brought streams of migrants to the upper parts of the Old Northwest, where they quickly built the roads, canals and railroads that made their commercial agriculture possible.

WHAT EFFECT did the opening of various canals, including the Erie Canal, have on cities such as St. Louis, Chicago, and New Orleans?

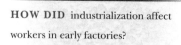

HOW DID industrialization affect workers in early factories?

Review Summary

9–7

Henry Clay, *Defense of the American System* (1832)

TRANSPORTATION CHANGES AFFECT THE CITIES

The changing fortunes of the region's major cities demonstrate the dramatic effects of improvements in transportation. Before 1830, when the easiest way to move goods and people was by water, Ohioans shipped corn and hogs first by flatboat and later by steamboat down the Ohio and Mississippi Rivers to New Orleans. Cincinnati, the center of the Ohio trade, earned the nickname "Porkopolis" because of the importance of its slaughterhouses.

After 1830, with the opening of the Erie Canal and canals in Ohio and Illinois, St. Louis became the distribution point for the flood of goods New York merchants sent westward via the canal system. St. Louis became a magnet for migration: in 1849, the year of the California gold rush (see Chapter 14), 60,000 people passed through the city.

After 1840, with the impact of railroads, the region's distribution system changed again, causing Chicago, barely a dot on the map early in the century, to grow at an incredible rate. By 1860, it had reached a population of 100,000 and, although still smaller than Cincinnati and St. Louis, was clearly destined to become the nation's east–west hub (see Map 12.3).

The loser in this economic redistribution was New Orleans. As early as 1853, only 30 percent of Old Northwest produce was shipped via New Orleans, while 60 percent was exported via the Erie Canal. Railroads increased the disparity, while at the same time they provided easy transportation to New Englanders who wanted to move west. These new transportation links tied the Old Northwest to New York and New England economically and politically, creating, as one Southerner bitterly commented, a "universal Yankee nation" that was a huge factor in the sectional disputes and eventual civil war that were to come (see Chapter 15).

INDUSTRIALIZATION BEGINS

The most dramatic single aspect of the market revolution was industrialization. Even in its earliest stages, industrialization changed the nature of work itself.

BRITISH TECHNOLOGY AND AMERICAN INDUSTRIALIZATION

Begun in Britain in the eighteenth century, industrialization was the result of a series of technological changes in the textile trade. In marked contrast to the putting-out system, in which capitalists had dispersed work into many individual households, industrialization required workers to concentrate in factories and pace themselves to the rhythms of power-driven machinery.

The simplest and quickest way for America to industrialize was to copy the British, but the British, well aware of the value of their machinery, enacted laws forbidding its export and even the emigration of skilled workers. Over the years, however, Americans managed to lure a number of British artisans to the United States.

This photograph shows the much restored Slater Mill, the first cotton textile factory in the United States, and the falls that powered its machinery. Built in 1793, the mill—now a National Historic Landmark—, is an example of the way early entrepreneurs used the power potential of New England's swiftly flowing streams.

In 1789, Samuel Slater, who had just finished an apprenticeship in the most up-to-date cotton spinning factory in England, disguised himself as a farm laborer and slipped out of England without even telling his mother good-bye. In Providence, Rhode Island, he met Moses Brown and William Almy, who had been trying without success to duplicate British industrial technology. Having carefully committed the designs to memory before leaving England, Slater promptly built copies of the latest British machinery for Brown and Almy.

Many other merchants and mechanics followed Slater's lead, and the rivers of New England were soon dotted with mills wherever waterpower could be tapped.

THE LOWELL MILLS

Another way to deal with British competition was to beat the British at their own game. With the intention of designing better machinery, a young Bostonian, Francis Cabot Lowell, made an apparently casual tour of British textile mills in 1810.

When he returned to the United States, he went to work with a Boston mechanic, Paul Moody, to improve on the British models. Lowell and Moody not only made the machinery for spinning cotton more efficient, but they also invented a power loom. This was a great advance, for now all aspects of textile manufacture, from the initial cleaning and carding (combing) to the production of finished lengths of cloth, could be gathered together in the same factory. Such a mill required a much larger capital investment than a small spinning mill such as Slater's, but Lowell's family network gave him access to the needed funds. In 1814, he opened the world's first integrated cotton mill in Waltham, near Boston. It was a great success: in 1815, the Boston Associates (Lowell's partners) made profits of 25 percent, and their efficiency allowed them to survive the intense British competition following the War of 1812. Many smaller New England mills did not survive.

The Boston Associates took the lesson to heart, and when they moved their enterprise to a new location in 1823, they thought big. They built an entire town at the junction of the Concord and Merrimack Rivers where the village of East Chelmsford stood, renaming it Lowell in memory of Francis, who had died, still a young man, in 1817 (see Map 12.4).

FAMILY MILLS

Lowell was unique. Much more common in the early days of industrialization were small rural spinning mills, on the model of Slater's first mill, built on swiftly running streams near existing farm communities. Because the owners of smaller mills often hired entire families, their operations came to be called family mills. Children aged eight to twelve, whose customary job was "doffing" (changing) bobbins on the spinning machines, made up 50 percent of the workforce. Women and men each made up about 25 percent of the workforce, but men had the most skilled and best-paid jobs. (See Figure 12.1.)

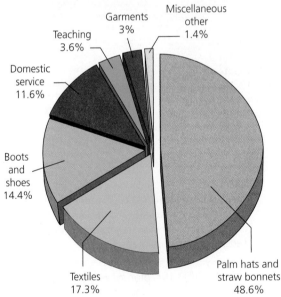

Total women employed
105,977

Figure 12.1 Occupations of Women Wage Earners in Massachusetts, 1837

This chart shows how important piecework was for women workers. Textile work in factories occupied less than 20 percent of women, while piecework making palm-leaf hats, straw bonnets, and boots and shoes accounted for over half of the total workforce. Teaching was a new occupation for women in 1837; the small percentage of 3.6 would grow in the future.

Based on Thomas Dublin, *Transforming Women's Work* (Ithaca, NY: Cornell University Press, 1991), Table 1.1, p. 20.

 **MAP EXPLORATION**

To explore an interactive version of this map, go to **http://www.prenhall.com/faraghertlc/map12.4**

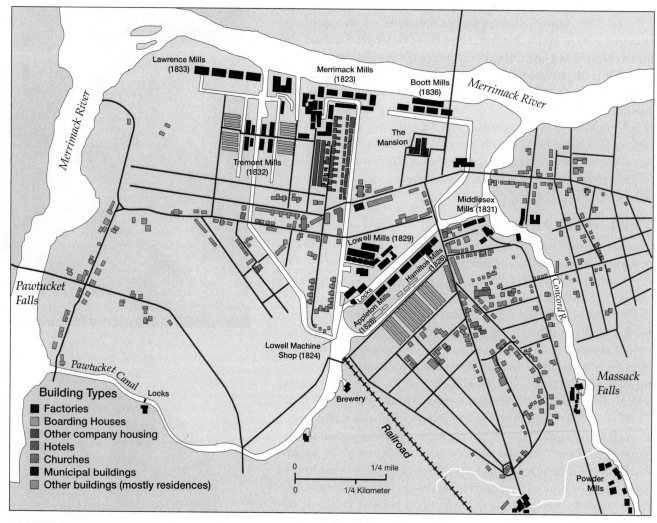

MAP 12.4

Lowell, Massachusetts, 1832 This town plan of Lowell, Massachusetts, in 1832, illustrates the comprehensive relationship the owners envisaged between the factories and the workforce. The mills are located on the Merrimack River, while nearby are the boardinghouses for the single young female workers, row houses for the male mechanics and their families, and houses for the overseers. Somewhat farther away is the mansion of the company agent.

HOW DID the plan of the town of Lowell affect the people who lived there?

Relations between these small rural mill communities and the surrounding farming communities were often difficult, as the history of the towns of Dudley and Oxford, Massachusetts, shows. Samuel Slater, now a millionaire, built three small mill communities near these towns in the early years of the nineteenth century and Slater's mills provided a substantial amount of work for local people. But in spite of this economic link, relations between Slater and his workers on one side and the farmers and shopkeepers of the Dudley and Oxford communities on the other were stormy. They disagreed over the building of mill dams, over taxes, over the upkeep of local roads, and over schools. The residents of Dudley and Oxford became increasingly hostile to Slater's authoritarian control, which they regarded as undemocratic. Their dislike carried over to the workers as well. Disdaining the mill workers for their poverty and transiency, people in the rural communities began referring to them as "operatives," making them somehow different in their work roles from themselves. Industrial work thus led to new social distinctions.

"THE AMERICAN SYSTEM OF MANUFACTURES"

Not all American industrial technology was copied from British inventions, for there were many homegrown inventors. Perhaps the most important invention was the development of standardized parts.

The concept of interchangeable parts, realized first in gun manufacturing, was so unusual that the British soon dubbed it the "**American system**." In this system, a gun was broken down into its component parts and an exact mold was made for each. All pieces made from the same mold (after being hand filed by inexpensive unskilled laborers) matched a uniform standard. As a result, repairing a gun required only installing a replacement for the defective part rather than laboriously making a new part or perhaps an entirely new gun, as had been the customary practice.

America's early lead in interchangeable parts was a substantial source of national pride. Standardized production quickly revolutionized the manufacture of items as simple as nails and as complicated as clocks.

American businesses mass-produced high-quality goods for ordinary people earlier than manufacturers in Britain or any other European country were able to do. The availability of these goods was a practical demonstration of American beliefs in democracy and equality.

> **American system**   A technique of production pioneered in the United States in the first half of the nineteenth century that relied on precision manufacturing with the use of interchangeable parts.

FROM ARTISAN TO WORKER

The changes wrought by the market revolution had major and lasting effects on ordinary Americans. The proportion of wage laborers in the nation's labor force rose from 12 percent in 1800 to 40 percent by 1860. Most of these workers were employed in the North, and almost half were women.

HOW DID the market revolution change the lives of ordinary people?

myhistorylab
Review Summary

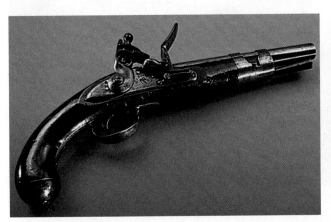
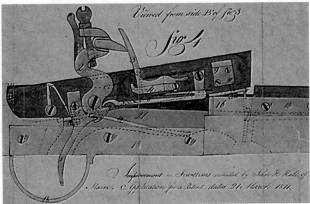

In 1816, Connecticut gunsmith Simeon North did what Eli Whitney had only hoped to do. North produced the first gun with interchangeable parts. North's invention, taken up and improved by the national armories at Springfield and Harpers Ferry, formed the basis of the American system of manufactures.

9–9
The Harbinger, *Female Workers of Lowell* (1836)

11–6
A Lowell Mill Girl Tells Her Story (1836)

PREINDUSTRIAL WAYS OF WORKING

When Lowell began operation, 97 percent of all Americans still lived on farms, and most work was done in or near the home. As had been true in colonial times, the lives of most people were family and community based and depended on local networks of barter and mutual obligation. Work was slow, unscheduled, and task oriented. People did their jobs as they needed to be done, along with the daily household routine. "Home" and "work" were not separate locations or activities but were intermixed. Likewise, in urban areas, skilled craftsmen organized the apprenticeship system in the family-learning model used in farms, training apprentices who became journeymen and skilled workers in turn.

In both rural and urban settings, working families were organized along strictly patriarchal lines. The man had unquestioned authority to direct the lives and work of family members and apprentices and to decide on occupations for his sons and marriages for his daughters. His wife had many crucial responsibilities—feeding, clothing, child rearing, taking care of apprentices, and all the other domestic affairs of the household—but in all these duties she was subject to the direction of her husband. Men were heads of families and bosses of artisanal shops; although entire families were engaged in the enterprise, the husband and father was the trained craftsman, and assistance by the family was informal and generally unrecognized.

MECHANIZATION AND GENDER

The apprenticeship system was destroyed by the immense increase in productivity made possible by the principles of division of labor and specialization applied in shoe production in Lynn and in other trades elsewhere.

In the 1840s, Edward Hicks painted his childhood home, rendering an idealized image of rural harmony that owes more to faith in republican agrarianism than to the artist's accurate memory. The prosperous preindustrial farm had a mixed yield—sheep, cattle, dairy products, and field crops—and had an African American farm worker (perhaps a slave), shown plowing.

"Residence of David Twining," 1787. Oil on canvas. Abby Aldrich Rockefeller Folk Art Museum, Colonial Williamsburg Foundation, Williamsburg, VA.

This illustration of seamstresses at work, from *Sartain's Union Magazine*, January 1851, shows an early abuse created by the market revolution. Women workers were crowded into just a few occupations, thereby allowing owners to offer very low wages for very long hours of work. The women in this illustration appear to be gathered together in a central workshop, where they had each other for company. Many other women sewed alone at home, often for even lower wages.

Industrialization posed a further threat to the status and independence of skilled male workers. In trade after trade, mechanization meant that most tasks could be performed by unskilled labor. In fact, the work in the textile mills was so simple that children came to form a large part of the workforce. By 1850, in New York City, many formerly skilled trades were filled with unskilled, low-paid workers who did one specialized operation or tended machinery. Many former artisans were reduced to performing wage labor for others. Because women were so frequently hired in the putting-out system, male workers began to oppose female participation in the workforce, fearing that it would lower their own wages.

These fears appeared to be confirmed by the experience of women in the new garment industry, which emerged in the 1820s. In New York City, employers began hiring women to sew ready-made clothing, at first rough, unfitted clothing for sailors and southern slaves, but later, overalls and shirts for Westerners, and finer items, such as men's shirts. Most women performed this work at low piecework rates in their homes.

Soon the low pay and seasonal nature of the industry became notorious. Overcrowding of the market—all women could sew—led to low wages. To make matters worse, most people believed that "respectable" women did not do factory work, and this disparagement fostered low pay and poor working conditions.

Manufacturers in the garment trade made their profits not from efficient production but by obtaining intensive labor for very low wages. The lower the piece rate, the more each woman, sewing at home, had to produce to earn enough to live.

myhistorylab

Exploring America: *Machinery*

QUICK REVIEW

Women in the Workforce

- Industrialization threatened skilled male workers.
- Mechanization created opportunities for women to work outside the home.
- The growing garment industry of the 1820s depended on cheap female labor.

TIME TABLE OF THE LOWELL MILLS,
To take effect on and after Oct. 21st, 1851.

The Standard time being that of the meridian of Lowell, as shown by the regulator clock of JOSEPH RAYNES, 43 Central Street.

	From 1st to 10th inclusive.				From 11th to 20th inclusive.				From 21st to last day of month.			
	1st Bell	2d Bell	3d Bell	Eve. Bell	1st Bell	2d Bell	3d Bell	Eve. Bell	1st Bell	2d Bell	3d Bell	Eve. Bell
January,	5.00	6.00	6.50	*7.30	5.00	6.00	6.50	*7.30	5.00	6.00	6.50	*7.30
February,	4.30	5.30	6.40	*7.30	4.30	5.30	6.25	*7.30	4.30	5.30	6.15	*7.30
March,	5.40	6.00		*7.30	5.20	5.40		*7.30	5.05	5.25		6.35
April,	4.45	5.05		6.45	4.30	4.50		6.55	4.30	4.50		7.00
May,	4.30	4.50		7.00	4.30	4.50		7.00	4.30	4.50		7.00
June,	"	"		"	"	"		"	"	"		"
July,	"	"		"	"	"		"	"	"		"
August,	"	"		"	"	"		"	"	"		"
September,	4.40	5.00		6.45	4.50	5.10		6.30	5.00	5.20		*7.30
October,	5.10	5.30		*7.30	5.20	5.40		*7.30	5.35	5.55		*7.30
November,	4.30	5.30	6.10	*7.30	4.30	5.30	6.20	*7.30	5.00	6.00	6.35	*7.30
December,	5.00	6.00	6.45	*7.30	5.00	6.00	6.50	*7.30	5.00	6.00	6.50	*7.30

* Excepting on Saturdays from Sept. 21st to March 20th inclusive, when it is rung at 20 minutes after sunset.

YARD GATES,
Will be opened at ringing of last morning bell, of meal bells, and of evening bells; and kept open Ten minutes.

MILL GATES.
Commence hoisting Mill Gates, Two minutes before commencing work.

WORK COMMENCES,
At Ten minutes after last morning bell, and at Ten minutes after bell which "rings in " from Meals.

BREAKFAST BELLS.
During March "Ring out".........at....7.30 a. m.........."Ring in" at 8.05 a. m.
April 1st to Sept. 20th inclusive.....at....7 00 " " .... " " at 7.35 " "
Sept. 21st to Oct. 31st inclusive.....at....7.30 " " .... " " at 8.05 " "
Remainder of year work commences after Breakfast.

DINNER BELLS.
" Ring out "...... ....12.30 p. m........."Ring in".... 1.05 p. m.

In all cases, the *first* stroke of the bell is considered as marking the time.

This timetable from the Lowell Mills illustrates the elaborate time schedules that the cotton textile mills expected their employees to meet. For workers, it was difficult to adjust to the regimentation imposed by clock time, in contrast to the approximate times common to preindustrial work.

The invention of the sewing machine only made matters worse. Manufacturers dropped their piecework rates still lower, and some women found themselves working fifteen to eighteen hours a day, producing more than they ever had but earning the same pay.

TIME, WORK, AND LEISURE

Preindustrial work had a flexibility that factory work did not, and it took factory workers a while to get accustomed to the constant pace of work. Factory workers gradually adjusted to having their lives regulated by the sound of the factory bell, but they did not necessarily become the docile "hands" the owners wanted. Absenteeism was common and there was much pilfering. Workers were beginning to think of themselves as a separate community whose interests differed from those of owners, and the tyranny of time over their work was certainly one reason for this.

Another adjustment required by the constant pace was that time now had to be divided into two separate activities—work and leisure. In preindustrial times, the place of work—often the home—and the pace made it possible to stop and have a chat or a friendly drink with a visitor. Now, however, the separation of home and workplace and the pace of production not only squeezed the fun out of the long workday but also left a smaller proportion of time for leisure activities.

For many workingmen, the favored spot for after-hours and Sunday leisure became the local tavern. Community-wide celebrations and casual sociability, still common in rural areas, began to be replaced in cities by spectator sports and by popular entertainments, such as plays, operas, minstrel shows, concerts, and circuses. Some of these diversions, such as plays and horse racing, appealed to all social classes, but others, like parades, rowdy dance halls, and tavern games were favored working-class amusements. The effect of these changes was to make working-class amusements more distinct, and visible, than they had been before.

FREE LABOR

Another effect of the market revolution was the transformation of a largely barter system into cash payments. For workers, this change was both unsettling and liberating. On the minus side, workers were no longer part of a settled, orderly, and familiar community. On the plus side, they were now free to labor wherever they could, at whatever wages their skills or their bargaining power could command. That workers took their freedom seriously is evidenced by the very high rate of turnover—50 percent a year—in the New England textile mills.

But if moving on was a sign of increased freedom of opportunity for some workers, for others it was an unwanted consequence of the market revolution. In New England, for example, many quite prosperous artisans and farmers faced disruptive competition from factory goods and western commercial agriculture. They could remain where they were only if they were willing to become factory workers or, in the case of farmers, to move west and try to become successful commercial farmers themselves.

At the heart of this industrializing economy was the notion of free labor. Originally, "free" referred to individual economic choice—that is, to the right of workers to move to another job rather than be held to a position by customary obligation or the formal contract of apprenticeship or journeyman labor. But "free labor" soon came to encompass as well the range of attitudes—hard work, self-discipline, and a striving for economic independence—that were necessary for success in a competitive, industrializing economy.

The spread of the factory system and of the ideology of free labor soon became an issue in the growing political battle between the North and the South over slavery. Southern defenders of slavery compared their cradle-to-grave responsibility to their slaves with northern employers' "heartless" treatment of their "wage slaves." Southerners were right: this was a heartless system. But Northerners were also right: industrialization was certainly freer than the slave system, freer even than the hierarchical craft system, although it sometimes offered only the freedom to starve.

EARLY STRIKES

Rural women workers led some of the first strikes in American labor history. Among the most famous were the strikes led by the women at the model mill at Lowell. The first serious trouble came in 1834, when 800 women participated in a spontaneous turnout to protest a wage cut of 25 percent. The owners were shocked and outraged by the strike, considering it both unfeminine and ungrateful. The workers, however, were bound together by a sense of sisterhood and were protesting not just the attack on their economic independence but also the blow to their position as "daughters of freemen still." Nevertheless, the wage cuts were enforced, as were more cuts in 1836, again in the face of a turnout. Many women simply packed their clothes in disgust and returned home to the family farm. Others who remained formed the New England Female Labor Reform Association in 1845. In 1847, legislators in New Hampshire, responding to a petition from women workers in Nashua, made theirs the first state to enact a ten-hour-day law. For the first time, thanks to women's pioneering role in factory protests, a group of workers had obtained state legislation improving their working conditions.

THE NEW MIDDLE CLASS

The market revolution reached into every aspect of life, down to the most personal family decisions. As just described, it changed working life. The market revolution also fundamentally changed the social order, creating a new middle class with distinctive habits and beliefs.

WHAT VALUES were promoted by the new middle class?

myhistorylab
Review Summary

WEALTH AND RANK

There had always been social divisions in America. Since the early colonial period, planters in the South and merchants in the North had comprised a wealthy elite. Somewhere below the elite but above the mass of people were the "middling sort": a small professional group that included lawyers, ministers, schoolteachers, doctors, public officials, some prosperous farmers, prosperous urban shopkeepers and innkeepers, and a few wealthy artisans. "Mechanics and farmers"—artisans and yeoman farmers—made up another large group, and the laboring poor, consisting of ordinary laborers, servants, and marginal farmers, were below them. At the very bottom were the paupers—those dependent on public charity—and the enslaved. This was the "natural" social order that fixed most people in the social rank to which they were born.

The market revolution ended this stable and hierarchical social order, creating the dynamic and unstable one we recognize today: upper, middle, and working classes, whose members all share the hope of climbing as far up the social ladder as they can. This social mobility was new. The expanding opportunities of the market revolution enriched the already rich. At the other extreme, fully one-third of the population possessed little more than the clothes they wore and some loose change. The major transformation came in the lives of the "middling sort."

The market revolution downgraded many independent artisans. Formerly independent artisans or farmers (or, more frequently, their children) joined the rapidly growing ranks of managers and white-collar workers. These new white-collar workers owed not only their jobs but also their lifestyles to the new structure and organization of industry. The new economic order demanded certain habits and attitudes of workers: sobriety, responsibility, steadiness, and hard work. Inevitably, employers found themselves not only enforcing these new standards but also adopting them themselves.

RELIGION AND PERSONAL LIFE

Religion, which had undergone dramatic changes since the 1790s, played a key role in the emergence of the new attitudes. The Second Great Awakening had supplanted the orderly and intellectual Puritan religion of early New England. The new evangelical religious spirit, which stressed the achievement of salvation through personal faith, was more democratic and more enthusiastic than the earlier faith. Conversion and repentance were no longer private, because they now took place in huge revival meetings in which an entire congregation focused on the sinners about to be saved and where group support actively encouraged individual conversion. The converted bore a heavy personal responsibility to demonstrate their faith in their own daily lives through morally respectable behavior. In this way, the new religious feeling fostered individualism and self-discipline.

The Second Great Awakening had its greatest initial success on the western frontier in the 1790s, but by the 1820s, evangelical religion was reaching a new audience: the people whose lives were being changed by the market revolution and who needed help in adjusting to the demands made by the new economic conditions. In 1825, in Utica, New York, and in other towns along the recently opened Erie Canal, evangelist Charles G. Finney began a series of dramatic revival meetings. His spellbinding message reached both rich and poor, converting members of all classes to the new evangelistic religion.

Middle-class women in particular carried Finney's message by prayer and pleading to the men of their families, who found that evangelism's stress on self-discipline and individual achievement helped them adjust to new business conditions. The enthusiasm and optimism of evangelism aided what was often a profound personal transformation in the face of the market's stringent new demands. Moreover, it gave businessmen a basis for demanding the same behavior from their workers. Businessmen now argued that traditional paternalism had no role in the new business world. Because achievement depended on individual character, each worker was responsible for making his own way.

THE NEW MIDDLE-CLASS FAMILY

The economic changes of the market revolution reshaped family roles, first in the middle class and eventually throughout the entire society. As men increasingly concentrated their energies on their careers and occupations, women assumed major new responsibilities for rearing the children and inculcating in them the new attitudes necessary for success in the business world.

11–1
Joshua and Sally Wilson,
Letters to George Wilson
(1823)

When the master craftsman became a small manufacturer, or the small subsistence farmer began to manage a large-scale commercial operation, production moved away from both the family home and its members. Husbands and fathers became managers of paid workers—or workers themselves—and although they were still considered the heads of their households, they spent most of the day away from their homes and families. Their wives, on the other hand, remained at home, where they were still responsible for cooking, cleaning, and other domestic tasks but no longer contributed directly to what had previously been the family enterprise. Instead, women took on a new responsibility, that of providing a quiet, well-ordered, and relaxing refuge from the pressures of the industrial world.

As the work roles of middle-class men and women diverged, so did social attitudes about appropriate male and female characteristics and behavior. Men were expected to be steady, industrious, responsible, and painstakingly attentive to their business. In contrast, women were expected to be nurturing, gentle, kind, moral, and selflessly devoted to their families. They were expected to operate within the "woman's sphere"—the home.

The maintenance or achievement of a middle-class lifestyle required the joint efforts of husband and wife. More cooperation between them was called for than in the preindustrial, patriarchal family. The nature of the new, companionate marriage that evolved in response to the market revolution was reflected most clearly in decisions concerning children. Middle-class couples had fewer children than did their predecessors. The dramatic fall in the birthrate during the nineteenth century (from an average of seven children per woman in 1800 to five in 1860) is evidence of conscious decisions about family limitation, first by members of the new middle class and later by working-class families.

When mutual efforts at birth control failed, married women often sought a surgical abortion, a new technique that was much more reliable than the folk remedies women had always shared among themselves. Surgical abortions were widely advertised after 1830, and widely used, especially by middle-class married women seeking to limit family size. Some historians estimate that one out of every four pregnancies was aborted in the years from 1840 to 1860 (compared to one in six in 2000). The rising rate of abortion by married women (in other words, its use as birth control) prompted the first legal bans; by 1860, twenty states had outlawed the practice.

Accompanying the interest in family limitation was a redefinition of sexuality. Doctors generally recommended that sexual urges be controlled, but they believed that men would have much more difficulty exercising such control than women, partly because they also believed that women were uninterested in sex. Although it is always difficult to measure the extent to which the suggestions in advice books were applied in actual practice, it seems that many middle-class women accepted this new and limited definition of their sexuality because of the desire to limit the number of their pregnancies.

MIDDLE-CLASS CHILDREN

Child rearing had been shared in the preindustrial household, boys learning farming or craft skills from their fathers while girls learned domestic skills from their mothers. The children of the new middle class, however, needed a new kind of upbringing, one that involved a long period of nurturing in the beliefs and personal habits necessary for success. Mothers assumed primary responsibility for this training, in part because fathers were too busy but also because people believed that women's superior qualities of gentleness, morality, and loving watchfulness were essential to the task.

11–3
The Mother's Magazine, "*Early Habits of Industry*" (1834)

Middle-class status required another sharp break with tradition. As late as 1855, artisanal families expected all children over 15 years to work. Middle-class families, in contrast, sacrificed to keep their sons in school or in training for their chosen professions, and they often housed and fed their sons until the young men had "established" themselves financially and could marry. Mothers took the lead in an important informal activity: making sure their children had friends and contacts that would be useful when they were old enough to consider careers and marriage. Matters such as these, rarely considered by earlier generations living in small communities, now became important in the new middle-class communities of America's towns and cities.

Contrary to the growing myth of the self-made man, middle-class success was not a matter of individual achievement. Instead it was usually based on a family strategy in which fathers provided the money and mothers the nurturance. The reorganization of the family described in this section was successful: from its shelter and support emerged generations of ambitious, responsible, and individualistic middle-class men. But although boys were trained for success, this was not an acceptable goal for their sisters. Women were trained to be the silent "support system" that undergirded male success. And women were also expected to ease the tensions of the transition to new middle-class behavior by acting as models and monitors of traditional values.

SENTIMENTALISM AND TRANSCENDENTALISM

11–8
Ralph Waldo Emerson,
"*Self-Reliance*" (1841)

Just as factory workers were forced by the nature of their work to develop new attitudes, so too the new middle class adopted attitudes that suited their new social roles. Two new "isms" soon emerged: sentimentalism, which appealed particularly to women, and transcendentalism, which encouraged men to a new self-reliance.

The individualistic competitiveness brought by the market revolution caused women of the new middle class to place extraordinary emphasis on sincerity and feeling. So-called sentimentalism sprang from nostalgia for the imagined trust and security of the familiar, face-to-face life of the preindustrial village. Middle-class women were expected to counteract the impersonality and hypocrisy of the business world by the example of their own morality and sincere feeling.

For guidance in this new role, women turned to a new literary form, the sentimental novel. Although denounced by ministers and scholars as frivolous, immoral, and subversive of authority, the novel found a ready audience among American women. By 1850, *Harper's Magazine* estimated, four-fifths of the reading public were women, and they were reading novels written by women.

Sentimental novels concentrated on private life. Religious feeling, antipathy toward the dog-eat-dog world of the commercial economy, and the need to be prepared for unforeseen troubles were common themes. Although the heroines usually married happily at the end of the story, few novels concentrated on romantic love. Most of these domestic novels, as they were known, presented readers with a vision of responsibility and community based on moral and caring family life.

Although sentimentalism originally sprang from genuine fear of the dangers individualism posed to community trust, it rapidly hardened into a rigid code of etiquette for all occasions. Moments of genuine and deep feeling, such as death, were smothered in elaborate rules concerning condolences, expressions of grief, and appropriate clothing. Transformed into a set of rules about genteel manners to cover all occasions, sentimentalism itself became a mark of middle-class status. And it became one of the tasks of the middle-class woman to make sure her family conformed to the social code and associated only with other respectable families. In this way, women forged and enforced the distinctive social behavior of the new middle class.

As the new middle class conformed to the rules of sentimental behavior, it also sought a more general intellectual reassurance. Middle-class men, in particular,

CHRONOLOGY

1790	Samuel Slater's first mill opens in Rhode Island	**1823**	Lowell mills open
1798	Eli Whitney contracts with the federal government for 10,000 rifles, which he undertakes to produce with interchangeable parts	**1824**	John Hall successfully achieves interchangeable parts at Harpers Ferry armory
			Women lead strike at Pawtucket textile mill
1810	Francis Cabot Lowell tours British textile factories	**1825**	Erie Canal opens
	First steamboat on the Ohio River	**1830**	Baltimore and Ohio Railroad opens
1812	Micajah Pratt begins his own shoe business in Lynn, Massachusetts		Charles G. Finney's Rochester revivals
1813	Francis Cabot Lowell raises $300,000 to build his first cotton textile factory at Waltham, Massachusetts	**1833**	National Road completed to Columbus, Ohio
		1834	First strike at Lowell mills
1815	War of 1812 ends; British competition in manufactures resumes		Cyrus McCormick patents the McCormick reaper
1817	Erie Canal construction begins	**1837**	John Deere invents steel plow
1818	National Road completed to Wheeling, Virginia (now West Virginia)	**1841**	Catharine Beecher's *Treatise on Domestic Economy* published
1820s	Large-scale outwork networks develop in New England	**1845**	New England Female Reform Association formed

needed to feel comfortable about their public assertions of individualism and self-interest. One source of reassurance was the philosophy of transcendentalism and its well-known spokesman, Ralph Waldo Emerson. Famous as a writer and lecturer, Emerson popularized transcendentalism, a romantic philosophical theory claiming that there was an ideal, intuitive reality transcending ordinary life. The best place to achieve that individual intuition of the Universal Being, Emerson suggested, was not in church or in society but alone in the natural world. The same assertion of individualism rang through Emerson's stirring polemic "Self-Reliance" (1841). Announcing "Whoso would be a man, must be a nonconformist," Emerson urged that "Nothing is at last sacred but the integrity of your own mind."

Emerson's younger friend, Henry David Thoreau, pushed the implications of individualism further than the more conventional Emerson. Determined to live the transcendental ideal of association with nature, Thoreau lived in solitude in a primitive cabin for two years at Walden Pond, near Concord, Massachusetts, confronting "the essential facts of life." His experience was the basis for *Walden* (1854), a penetrating criticism of the spiritual cost of the market revolution. Margaret Fuller, perhaps the most intellectually gifted of the transcendental circle, was patronized by Emerson because she was a woman. She expressed her sense of women's wasted potential in her pathbreaking work *Woman in the Nineteenth Century* (1845).

Although Thoreau and Fuller were too radical for many readers, Emerson's version of the romantic philosophy of transcendentalism, seemingly so at odds with the competitive and impersonal spirit of the market revolution, was in fact an essential component of it. Individualism, or, as Emerson called it, self-reliance, was at the heart of the personal transformation required by the market revolution. Sentimentalism, transcendentalism, and evangelical religion all helped the new middle class to forge values and beliefs that were appropriate to their social roles.

Emerson's romantic glorification of nature included the notion of himself as a "transparent eyeball," as he wrote in "Nature" in 1836. This caricature of Emerson is from "Illustrations of the New Philosophy" by Christopher Pearce Cranch.

CONCLUSION

The three transformations of the market revolution—improvements in transportation, commercialization, and industrialization—changed the ways people worked, and in time, changed how they thought.

For most people, the changes were gradual. Until midcentury, the lives of rural people were still determined largely by community events, although the spread of democratic politics and the availability of newspapers and other printed material increased their connection to a larger world. Wage earners made up only 40 percent of the working population in 1860, and factory workers made up an even smaller percentage.

The new middle class was most dramatically affected by the market revolution. All aspects of life, including intimate matters of family organization, gender roles, and the number and raising of children, changed. New values—evangelical religion, sentimentalism, and transcendentalism—helped the members of the new middle class in their adjustment. As the next chapter describes, the nation's cities were the first arena where old and new values collided.

REVIEW QUESTIONS

1. What changes in preindustrial life and work were caused by the market revolution?

2. This chapter argues that when people begin doing new kinds of work, their beliefs and attitudes change. Give three examples of such changes described in the chapter. Can you think of other examples?

3. Discuss the opinion offered by historian David Potter that mass production has been an important democratizing force in American politics. Do you agree? Why or why not?

4. Consider the portrait of the nineteenth-century middle-class family offered in this chapter and imagine yourself as a member of such a family. What new aspects of family relations would you welcome? Which would be difficult? Why?

myhistorylab

Flashcard Review

KEY TERMS

American system (p. 309)
Market revolution (p. 300)
Putting-out system (p. 302)

RECOMMENDED READING

Jeffrey S. Adler, *Yankee Merchants and the Making of the Urban West* (1991). The importance of New England entrepreneurs in St. Louis.

Peter L. Bernstein, *Wedding of the Waters: The Erie Canal and the Making of a Great Nation* (2005). The economic consequences of one of the first public works projects.

Christopher Clark, *The Roots of Rural Capitalism: Western Massachusetts, 1780–1860* (1990). The most thorough examination to date of how the commercial spirit changed rural life.

Alan Dawley, *Class and Community: The Industrial Revolution in Lynn* (1976). A pathbreaking study of the shift from artisanal to wage labor.

Susan E. Gray, *The Yankee West* (1996). Demonstrates the Yankee connection between capitalism and community in lower Michigan.

David Houndshell, *From the American System to Mass Production, 1800–1932* (1984). How an entire network of New England "mechanics" contributed to the invention of interchangeable parts.

Paul Johnson, *Sam Patch, the Famous Jumper* (2003). Johnson uses the story of Patch, famous for plunging over Niagara Falls, to explore the bumpy transition from independent artisan to wage worker.

Mary Ryan, *The Making of the Middle Class* (1981). A study of Utica, New York, demonstrating the role of women in the family strategies of the new middle class.

Charles Sellers, *The Market Revolution: Jacksonian America, 1815–1846* (1991). A synthesis of the political, religious, and economic changes of the period.

Carol Sheriff, *The Artificial River: The Erie Canal and the Paradox of Progress, 1817–1862* (1996). Shows how the building of the Erie Canal changed personal lives and fostered religious beliefs in human perfectability.

George Rogers Taylor, *The Transportation Revolution, 1815–1860* (1951). The indispensable book on all aspects of the American economy during this period.

myhistorylab
Where it's a good time to connect to the past!

For study resources for this chapter, go to **www.myhistorylab.com** and choose *Out of Many, Teaching and Learning Classroom Edition.* You will find a wealth of study and review material for this chapter, including pretests and posttests, customized study plan, key-term review flash cards, interactive map and document activities, and documents for analysis.

The Second Great Awakening and Religious Diversity in America

One of the reasons that separation of church and state has worked so well in the United States is the wide diversity of religious affiliations within the American population. From the beginning of English colonial efforts to the time of the American Revolution, this happy scenario was not necessarily present. In the northern colonies the Congregationalist Church was the established state religion among Puritan settlers. In the middle and southern colonies the Anglican Church or Church of England was the established church.

THE SECOND Great Awakening (1800–1830s) led to the creation of many new religious affiliations and an increased diversity within American religious life. How has this growing diversity impacted American society.

In 1801 the Danbury Baptist Association wrote a letter to newly elected President Thomas Jefferson complaining that the dominant Congregationalist sect in Connecticut was threatening to legislate against them and called for religious freedom. Jefferson responded with a letter outlining what we now call the separation of church and state.

Religious diversity grew slowly in the early years of the American colonies and nation. The First Great Awakening of the 1730s and 1740s strengthened the Presbyterian, Baptist, and Methodist churches in their quest to attract the followers of the Congregationalist and Anglican churches and create diversity of American religions. The Second Great Awakening created even greater diversity.■

Rev. Charles G. Finney – 1839

CHARLES GRANDISON FINNEY, *LECTURES ON THE REVIVAL OF RELIGION*, 1835

I WOULD say nothing to undervalue, or lead you to undervalue a thorough education for ministers. But I do not call that a thorough education, which they get in our colleges and seminaries. It does not fit them for their work…. Those fathers who have the training of our young ministers are good men, but they are ancient men, men of another age and different stamp from what is needed in these days of excitement, when the church and world are rising to new thought and action. Those dear fathers will not, I suppose, see this; and will - perhaps think hard of me for saying it; but it is the cause of Christ.■

FROM *AUTOBIOGRAPHY OF PETER CARTWRIGHT, THE BACKWOODS PREACHER*

The revival, or "camp meeting," was the signal event of the Second Great Awakening.
Somewhere between 1800 and 1801, in the upper part of Kentucky, at a memorable place called "Cane Ridge," there was appointed a sacramental meeting by some of the Presbyterian ministers, at which meeting, seemingly unexpected by ministers or people, the mighty power of God was displayed in a very extraordinary manner; many were moved to tears, and bitter and loud crying for mercy. The meeting was protracted for weeks. Ministers of almost all denominations flocked in from far and near. The meeting was kept up by night and day. Thousands heard of the mighty work, and came on foot, on horseback, in carriages and wagons. It was supposed that there were in attendance at times during the meeting from twelve to twenty-five thousand people. Hundreds fell prostrate under the mighty

power of God, as men slain in battle. Stands were erected in the woods from which preachers of different Churches proclaimed repentance toward God and faith in our Lord Jesus Christ, and it was supposed, by eye and ear witnesses, that between one and two thousand souls were happily and powerfully converted to God during the meeting.

SIMPLE GIFTS

'Tis the gift to be simple, 'tis the gift to be free,

'Tis the gift to come down where we ought to be,

And when we find ourselves in the place just right,

'Twill be in the valley of love and delight.

When true simplicity is gain'd,

To bow and to bend we shan't be asham'd,

To turn, turn will be our delight,

Till by turning, turning we come round right.

"*Simple Gifts*" is a Shaker quick dance or dancing song used in worship services. The hymn was written by Elder Joseph Brackett Jr. in 1848. Although they originated much earlier than the Second Great Awakening, the Shakers benefited from the diversity and growth of religious movements during the first decades of the 19th century. Shakers lived a communal, celibate lifestyle. Men and women lived in separate quarters, used separate stairs, and sat on opposite sides of the room during worship. Their devotions included rituals of trembling, shouting, dancing, shaking, singing, and speaking in unknown tongues. By the end of the 19th century the Shakers were practically extinct. ■

CHURCH OF JESUS CHRIST OF LATTER-DAY SAINTS

Founded in 1830 in New York by Joseph Smith, Jr., the Church of Jesus Christ of Latter-day Saints is based upon the Book of Mormon. Smith moved his followers to Missouri in the 1830's where controversy and persecution resulted in the Mormon War of 1838 after which the governor of the state ordered Smith to move his church elsewhere. Smith settled his people in Illinois and built the town of Navuoo. Mormon practices led to more persecution and the murder of Smith in 1844. Leadership of the church was taken over by Brigham Young who led his followers out of Illinois to the Mexican territories in Utah in 1846. The Mormon Church continued to thrive in Utah and the Southwest and in the 20th century has become one of the faster growing denominations in the U.S. ■

Religious camp meeting, ca. 1839

Shaker Dance, Joseph Becker, *Frank Leslie's Illustrated Newspaper*, 1873

Brigham Young, Mormon leader and Second Mormon President

Our duties originate, not from difference of sex,
but from the diversity of the relations of life,
the various gifts and talents committed to our care,
and the different eras in which we live.

—Angelina Emily Grimké, October 2, 1837

An abolitionist freeing a slave from his shackles: A colored woodcut, c. 1840, from an American antislavery almanac.

13

MEETING THE CHALLENGES OF THE NEW AGE

IMMIGRATION, URBANIZATION, SOCIAL REFORM

1820S–1850S

WHO MIGRATED to America

in the first half of the nineteenth century?

WHO WERE the major

proponents of the labor movement?

WHAT ROLE did women play

in the development of American education?

WHO WERE the abolitionists

and what were their racial attitudes?

WHAT CONNECTIONS were there between

the women's rights movement and previous movements

for social reform?

AMERICAN COMMUNITIES

Women Reformers of Seneca Falls Respond to the Market Revolution

IN THE SUMMER OF 1848, CHARLOTTE WOODWARD, A NINETEEN-YEAR-old glove maker who did outwork in her rural home, saw a small advertisement in an upstate New York newspaper announcing a "convention to discuss the social, civil, and religious condition and rights of woman," to be held at Seneca Falls on July 19 and 20. Woodward persuaded six friends to join her in the forty-mile journey to the convention. "At first we travelled quite alone," she recalled. "But before we had gone many miles we came on other wagon-loads of women, bound in the same direction. As we reached different crossroads we saw wagons coming from every part of the country, and long before we reached Seneca Falls we were a procession."

To the surprise of the convention organizers, almost 300 people—men as well as women—attended the two-day meeting, which focused on the **Declaration of Sentiments**, a petition for women's rights modeled on the Declaration of Independence. "We hold these truths to be self-evident," it announced: "That all men and women are created equal." As the Declaration of Independence detailed the oppressions King George III had imposed on the colonists, the Declaration of Sentiments detailed, in a series of resolutions, the oppressions men had imposed on women.

The struggle for women's rights was only one of many reform movements that emerged in the United States in the wake of the economic and social disruptions of the market revolution that deeply affected regions like Seneca Falls. Swamped by newcomers (among them a growing number of poor Irish Catholics), the inhabitants of Seneca Falls struggled to maintain a sense of community. They formed volunteer organizations of all kinds—religious, civic, social, educational, and recreational. And they became active participants in reform movements seeking to counteract the effects of industrialization, rapid growth, and the influx of newcomers.

Many reformers belonged to liberal religious groups with wide social perspectives. Perhaps a third of those attending the women's rights convention, for example, were members of the Wesleyan Methodist Society of Seneca Falls, which had broken with the national Methodist organization because it would not take a strong stand against slavery. Another quarter were Progressive Quakers of the nearby town of Waterloo, who had broken with their national organization for the same reason.

The idea for the women's rights convention emerged during a meeting in early July 1848 between Lucretia Mott, a Philadelphia Quaker and the nation's best-known woman reformer, and Elizabeth Cady Stanton of Seneca Falls, wife of a well-known antislavery orator. Stanton first met Mott in 1840 at the World AntiSlavery Conference in London. In 1848, Stanton renewed her acquaintance with Mott and, in this context of friendship and shared concern for reform, the two began planning the convention.

But what of Charlotte Woodward, a local farm girl, unaware of the national reform community? Why was she there? In this age of hopefulness and change, she wanted a better life for herself. She was motivated, she said, by "all the hours that I sat and sewed gloves for a miserable pittance, which, after it was earned, could never be mine." By law and custom, her father, as head of the household, was entitled to her wages. "I wanted to work," she explained, "but I wanted to choose my task and I wanted to collect my wages." The reforming women of Seneca Falls, grouped together on behalf of social improvement, had found in the first women's rights convention a way to speak for the needs of working women such as Charlotte Woodward.

Seneca Falls

All over the North, in communities like Seneca Falls as well as in cities like New York, Americans gathered together in reform organizations to try to solve the problems that the market revolution posed for work, family life, personal and social values, and urban growth. Through these organizations, local women and men became participants in wider communities of social concern, but in spite of their best efforts, they were rarely able to settle the issues that had brought them together. The aspirations of some, among them women, free blacks, and immigrants, clashed with the social control agendas of other groups. In this fervent atmosphere of reform, many problems were raised but few were resolved.

Declaration of Sentiments The resolutions passed at the Seneca Falls Convention in 1848 calling for full female equality, including the right to vote.

IMMIGRATION AND THE CITY

Although the market revolution affected all aspects of American life, nowhere was its impact so noticeable as in the cities. And it was primarily in cities that the startlingly large number of new immigrants clustered.

THE GROWTH OF CITIES

The market revolution dramatically increased the size of America's cities, with the great seaports leading the way. The proportion of America's population living in cities increased from only 7 percent in 1820 to almost 20 percent in 1860, a rate of growth greater than at any other time in the country's history. The nation's five largest cities in 1850 were the same as in 1800, with one exception. New York, Philadelphia, Baltimore, and Boston still topped the list, but New Orleans had edged out Charleston. The rate of urban growth was extraordinary. All four Atlantic seaports grew at least 25 percent each decade between 1800 and 1860, and often much more. New York, which grew from 60,000 in 1800 to 202,600 in 1830 and to more than 1 million in 1860, emerged as the nation's most populous city, its largest port, and its financial center.

Philadelphia, which had been the nation's largest city in 1800, was half the size of New York in 1850. Nevertheless, its growth was substantial—from 70,000 in 1800 to 389,000 in 1850 and to 565,529 in 1860. Philadelphia became as much an industrial as a commercial city.

Another result of the market revolution was the appearance of "instant" cities at critical points on the new transportation network. Utica, New York, once a frontier trading post, was transformed by the opening of the Erie Canal into a commercial and manufacturing center. Chicago, on the shores of Lake Michigan, was transformed by the coming of the railroad into a major junction for water and rail transport. The city, which emerged as a fur trading center around Fort Dearborn, an army post built in 1803, had become, by the 1850s, a hub of trade boasting grain storage facilities, slaughterhouses, and warehouses of all kinds. Farm implement manufacturers such as Cyrus McCormick built manufacturing plants there to serve the needs of midwestern farmers. By 1860 Chicago had a population of over 100,000, making it the nation's eighth largest city (see Table 13.1).

WHO MIGRATED to America in the first half of the nineteenth century?

myhistorylab
Review Summary

TABLE 13.1

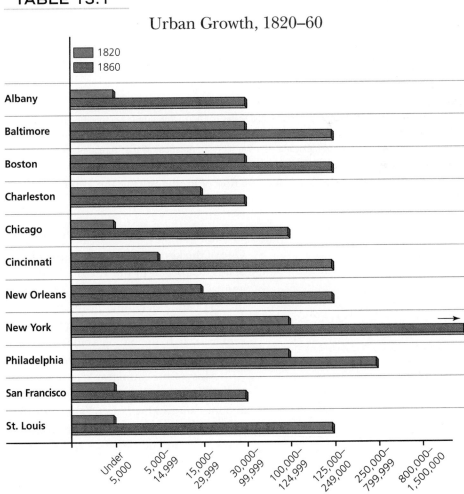

Urban Growth, 1820–60

MAP EXPLORATION

To explore an interactive version of this map, go to **http://www.prenhall.com/faraghertlc/map13.1**

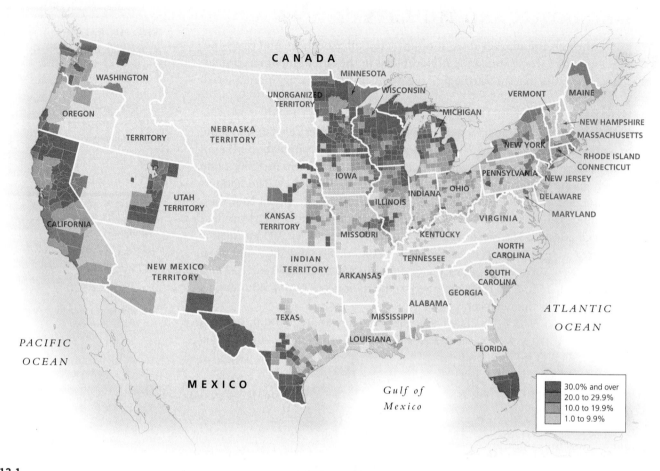

MAP 13.1

Distribution of Foreign-Born Residents of the United States in 1860 The ethnic composition of the American population was increased by Irish and German immigration in the 1840s and 1850s, Chinese attraction to the California gold rush, Mormon recruitment of Scottish and English followers to Utah, and the reclassification of Mexicans after the Mexican-American War as foreigners in what had been their own lands.

HOW DID events in Europe affect the flow of immigrants to the United States in the 1840s and 1850s?

PATTERNS OF IMMIGRATION

One of the key aspects of urban growth was a surge in immigration to the United States that began in the 1820s and accelerated dramatically after 1830. From an annual figure of about 20,000 in 1831, immigration ballooned to a record 430,000 in 1854 before declining in the years prior to the Civil War. The proportion of immigrants in the population jumped from 1.6 percent in the 1820s to 11.2 percent in 1860. In the nation's cities, the proportion was vastly larger: by 1860, nearly half of New York's population (48 percent) was foreign-born (see Map 13.1).

Most of the immigrants to the United States during this period came from Ireland and Germany. Political unrest and poor economic conditions in Germany and the catastrophic Potato Famine of 1845–49 in Ireland were responsible for an enormous surge in immigration from those countries between 1845 and 1854. Between them, the Germans and the Irish represented the largest influx of non-English immigrants the country had known. They were also the poorest: most of the Irish arrived destitute. In addition, most of the Irish and half of the Germans were Catholics, an unwelcome novelty that provoked a nativist backlash among some Protestant Americans, including many leaders of national reform movements (see Chapter 15).

It would be a mistake, however, to think that immigration was unwelcome to everyone. Industries needed willing workers, and western states, among them Wisconsin, Iowa, and Minnesota, actively advertised in Europe for settlers. Many of the changes in industry and transportation that accompanied the market revolution would have been impossible without immigrants.

Few immigrants found life in the United States pleasant or easy. In addition to the psychological difficulties of leaving a home and familiar ways behind, most immigrants endured harsh living and working conditions. America's cities were unprepared for the social problems posed by large numbers of immigrants.

IRISH IMMIGRATION

The first major immigrant wave to test American cities was caused by the catastrophic Irish Potato Famine of 1845–49. Throughout Ireland, many native Irish subsisted on small landholdings and a diet of potatoes while working as laborers on British-owned farms. Young people who knew they could not hope to own land in Ireland had long looked to America for better opportunities. But in 1845, Ireland's green fields of potato plants turned black with blight. The British government could not cope with the scale of the disaster. The Irish had two choices: starve or leave. One million people died, and another 1.5 million emigrated, the majority to the United States. Starving, diseased, and destitute, hundreds of thousands (250,000 in 1851 alone) disembarked in the East Coast ports of New York, Philadelphia, Boston, and Baltimore. Lacking the money to go inland and begin farming, they remained in the cities. Crowded together in miserable housing, desperate for work at any wages, foreign in their religion and pastimes, tenaciously nationalistic and bitterly anti-British, they created ethnic enclaves of a kind new to American cities.

The largest numbers of Irish came to New York, which managed to absorb them. But Boston, a much smaller and more homogeneous city, was overwhelmed by the Irish influx. By 1850, a quarter of Boston's population was Irish, most of them recent immigrants. Boston, the home of Puritanism and the center of American intellectualism, did not welcome illiterate Irish Catholic peasants. All over the city, in places of business and in homes normally eager for domestic servants, the signs went up: "No Irish Need Apply."

GERMAN IMMIGRATION

Germans, like the Irish, had a long history of emigration to America. The nineteenth-century immigration of Germans began somewhat later and more slowly than that of the Irish, but by 1854 it had surpassed the Irish influx. The typical German immigrant was a small farmer or artisan dislodged by the same market forces at work in America: the industrialization of production and consolidation, and the commercialization of farming. There was also a small group of middle-class liberal intellectuals who left the German states (Germany was not yet a unified nation) after 1848 when attempts at revolution had failed.

German migrants were not as poor as the Irish, and they could afford to move out of the East Coast seaports to other locations. Many settled in Pittsburgh, Cincinnati, St. Louis, and Milwaukee and on farms in Ohio, Indiana, Missouri, and Texas. In Texas, the nucleus of a German community began with a Mexican land grant in the 1830s. Few Germans settled either in northeastern cities or in the South.

German agricultural communities took a distinctive form that fostered cultural continuity. Immigrants formed predominantly German towns by clustering, or taking up adjoining land. A small cluster could support German churches, German-language schools, and German customs and thereby attract other Germans, some directly from Europe and some from other parts of the United States.

IMAGE KEY

for pages 322–323

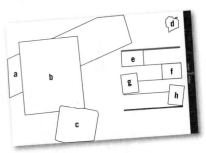

a. A map of western New York State in 1811 including the proposed Erie Canal route, the Finger Lakes, Lake Ontario, and Lake Erie.

b. An abolitionist freeing a slave from his shackles: colored woodcut, c. 1840, from an American antislavery almanac.

c. Pages from an *American Pictorial Primer*, c. 1845.

d. A Cotton gin used to separate cotton from its seeds, stems, etc.

e. New York's most notorious slum, Five Points, is illustrated in this 1859 lithograph.

f. The seal of the General Society of Mechanics and Tradesman.

g. Dorothea Dix, a crusader for mental health reforms.

h. Frederick Douglass (1817?–1895), a portrait attributed to E. Hammond.

Wright's Grove, shown here in an 1868 illustration, was the popular picnic grounds and beer garden for the large German community on Chicago's North Side. Establishments such as this horrified American temperance advocates, who warned about the dangerous foreign notion of mixing alcohol with family fun.

THE CHINESE IN CALIFORNIA

Another area attracting immigrants in the early nineteenth century was Gold Rush California, which drew, among others, numbers of Chinese (see Chapter 14). The Chinese who came to California worked in the mines, mostly as independent prospectors. Other miners disliked their industriousness and their clannishness. By the mid-1860s, Chinese workers made up 90 percent of the laborers building the Central Pacific Railroad, replacing more expensive white laborers and sowing the seeds of the long-lasting hostility of American workers toward Chinese. In the meantime, however, San Francisco's Chinatown, the oldest Chinese ethnic enclave in America, became a well-established, thriving community and a refuge in times of anti-Chinese violence.

ETHNIC NEIGHBORHOODS

Ethnic neighborhoods were not limited to the Chinese. Almost all new immigrants preferred to live in neighborhoods where they could find not only family ties and familiar ways but also community support as they learned how to survive in new surroundings. Isolated partly by their religious beliefs, Irish immigrants created their own communities in Boston and New York, their major destinations. They raised the money to erect Catholic churches with Irish priests. They established parochial schools with Irish nuns as teachers and sent their children to them in preference to the openly anti-Catholic public schools. They formed mutual aid societies based on kinship or town of origin in Ireland. Men and women formed religious and social clubs, lodges, and brotherhoods and their female auxiliaries. Irishmen manned fire and militia companies as well. This dense network of associations served the same purpose that social welfare organizations do today: providing help in time of need and offering companionship in a hostile environment.

Germans who settled in urban areas also built their own ethnic enclaves— "Little Germanies"—in which they sought to duplicate the rich cultural life of their homeland. Like the Irish, the Germans formed church societies, mutual benefit societies, and fire and militia companies to provide mutual support. Partly because their communities were more prosperous than those of the Irish, the Germans also formed a network of leisure organizations: singing societies, debating and political clubs, concert halls like New York's Beethoven Hall, theaters, *turnvereins* (gymnastics associations), and beer gardens. They published German-language newspapers as well.

URBAN PROBLEMS

It was within the new urban environment, with its stimulating and frightening confusion of rapid growth, occupational and ethnic change, and economic competition, that new American political and social forms began to emerge.

NEW LIVING PATTERNS IN THE CITIES

The preindustrial cities of eighteenth-century America had been small and compact "walking cities," in which people, rich and poor, lived near their work in a dense, small-scale housing pattern that fostered neighborliness and the mingling of social classes. The growth caused by immigration changed the character of urban life by sharpening class differences.

Even though per capita income in America is estimated to have doubled between 1800 and 1850, the gap between rich and poor was glaringly apparent in the nation's cities. Differences in income affected every aspect of urban life. Very poor families, including almost all new immigrants, performed unskilled labor in jobs where the future was uncertain at best, lived in cheap rented housing, moved frequently, and depended on more than one income to survive. Artisans and skilled workers with incomes of $500 or more could live adequately, though often in cramped quarters that also served as their shops. A middle-class family with an income of more than $1,000 a year could live comfortably in a house of four to six rooms complete with carpeting, wallpaper, and good furniture. The very rich built mansions and large town houses and staffed them with many servants. In the summer, they left the cities for country estates or homes at seaside resorts such as Newport, Rhode Island, which attracted wealthy families from all over the country.

Early nineteenth-century cities lacked municipal water supplies, sewers, and garbage collection. Every American city suffered epidemics of sanitation-related diseases such as yellow fever, cholera, and typhus. Philadelphia's yellow fever epidemic of 1793 caused 4,000 deaths and stopped all business with the outside world for more than a month. Major cholera epidemics ravaged New York in 1832 and 1849, and New Orleans suffered repeated episodes of cholera and yellow fever.

WHO WERE the major proponents of the labor movement?

Review Summary

Yet the cities were slow to take action. Mostly, this was due to poor understanding of the links between sanitation and disease, but expense was also a factor. Garbage collection remained a private service, and cities charged property owners for the costs of sewers, water mains, and street paving. Poorer areas of the cities could not afford the costs. When disease struck, wealthier people simply left the cities, leaving the poor to suffer.

Lack of municipal services encouraged residential segregation. Richer people clustered in neighborhoods that had the new amenities. By the 1850s, the middle class began to escape cities completely by moving to the new "streetcar suburbs," named for the new mode of urban transportation that connected these nearby areas to the city itself.

As the middle class left the city, the poor clustered in bad neighborhoods that became known as slums. The worst New York slum in the nineteenth century was Five Points, a stone's throw from City Hall. There, immigrants, free black people, and criminals were crammed into rundown buildings known in the slang of the time as "rookeries." Notorious gangs of thieves and pickpockets with names such as the Plug Uglies and the Shirt Tails dominated the district. Starvation and murder were commonplace.

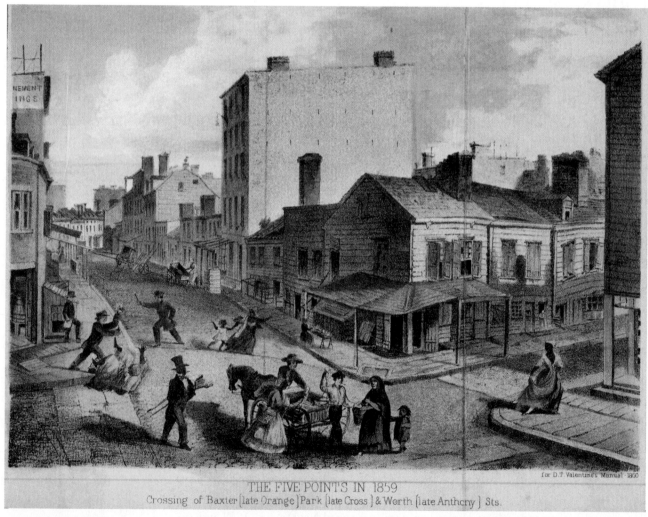

THE FIVE POINTS IN 1859
Crossing of Baxter (late Orange) Park (late Cross) & Worth (late Anthony) Sts.

The Five Points neighborhood in lower Manhattan illustrates the segregated housing patterns that emerged as New York City experienced rapid growth. Immigrants, free African Americans, the poor, and criminals were crowded together in New York's most notorious slum, while wealthier people moved to more prosperous neighborhoods.

With the influx of European immigrants after 1830, middle-class Americans increasingly saw slums as the home of strange and foreign people, who deserved less than American-born citizens did. In this way, residential patterns came to embody larger issues of class and citizenship. Even disease itself was blamed on immigrants. As banker John Pintard reasoned in 1832, the cholera epidemic must be God's judgment on "the lower classes of intemperate dissolute and filthy people huddled together like swine in their polluted habitations."

ETHNICITY IN URBAN POPULAR CULTURE

Immigrants to American cities contributed to a new urban popular culture, with New York, the largest city, leading the way. In the period 1820–60, New York experienced the replacement of artisanal labor by wagework, two serious depressions (1837–43 and 1857), and a vast influx of immigrant labor (see Figure 13.1). In response to these pressures, working-class amusements became rougher and rowdier.

Irish immigrants, in particular, faced not only employment discrimination but also persistent cultural denigration. It was common for newspapers of the time to caricature the Irish as monkeys, similar to the way cartoonists portrayed African Americans. The Irish response, which was to insist on their "whiteness," played itself out in urban popular culture in violence and mockery.

Theaters, which had been frequented by men of all social classes, provided another setting for violence. Few women, except for the prostitutes who met their customers in the third tier of the balcony, attended.

By the 1830s, middle-class and upper-class men withdrew to more respectable theaters to which they could bring their wives and daughters, and workers found new amusements in theaters such as the Lafayette Circus, which featured dancing girls and horseback riders as well as theatrical acts (see Seeing History).

The new working-class culture flourished especially on the Bowery, a New York City street filled with workshops, small factories, shops with cheap goods, dance halls, theaters, ice cream parlors, and oyster bars. Here working-class youth, the "Bowery b'hoys" (slang pronunciation of "boys") and "gals," found Saturday night amusement and provided it for themselves with outrageous clothing and behavior. The deliberately provocative way they dressed was, in effect, a way of thumbing their noses at the more respectable classes.

THE LABOR MOVEMENT AND URBAN POLITICS

By the 1830s, the status of artisans and independent craftsmen in the nation's cities had deteriorated. Members of urban workers' associations, increasingly angry over their declining status in the economic and social order, became active defenders of working-class interests in their cities.

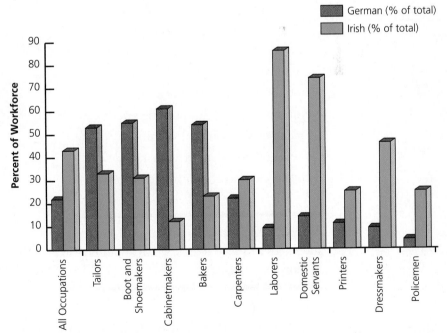

Figure 13.1 Participation of Irish and German Immigrants in the New York City Workforce for Selected Occupations, 1855
This chart shows the impact of the new immigrants on the New York's workforce, and the dramatic difference between groups. German workers predominate in the skilled trades, while the Irish are clustered in low-skilled, low paying occupations.

Robert Ernst, *Immigrant Life in New York City 1825–1863* (Syracuse: Syracuse University Press, 1994).

Thomas "Daddy" Rice, Blackface Minstrel, Dances Jim Crow

In 1832, a young white man in blackface appeared at a variety show at the Bowery Theater where he sang and danced the following:

First, on de heel tap,
Den on the toe
Every time I wheel about
I jump Jim Crow.
Wheel about and turn about
En do j's so
And every time I wheel about,
I jump Jim Crow.

This performance was so wildly popular that Thomas Rice had to repeat it twenty times before the audience would let him go. In this way, the cruel stereotype of the slow-witted slave, Jim Crow, entered American popular culture and Rice himself became one of the best-known blackface minstrels. He was far from alone, for blackface minstrel shows were among the most popular American entertainments. A full evening's performance by a company of minstrels (all white men with faces blackened by cork) consisted of songs, wisecracks, parodies of politicians and other notable figures, comedy scenes of plantation life, dancing, and music. Minstrel shows were a favorite American entertainment for the rest of the nineteenth century.

WHAT EXPLAINS its appeal to white audiences and what does it tell us about popular stereotypes of blacks?

When it first appeared, in the popular culture of the 1830s and 1840s, blackface minstrelsy was a clear indicator of how the issue of slavery permeated all aspects of American life in both the North and South. ■

IRISH EMIGRANT.

Patrick, (just landing.) "BY MY SOWL, YOU'RE BLACK, OLD FELLOW! HOW LONG HAVE YE BIN HERE?"

Nigger, (imitatng the brogue.) "JIST THREE MONTHS, MY HONEY!"

Pat. "BY THE POWERS, I'LL GO BACK TO TIPPERARY IN A JIFFY! I'D NOT BE SO BLACK AS THAT FUR ALL THE WHISKEY IN ROSCREA!"

Between 1833 and 1837, a wave of strikes in New York City cut the remaining ties between master craftsmen and the journeymen who worked for them. In 1833, journeymen carpenters struck for higher wages. Workers in fifteen other trades came to their support, and within a month the strike was won. The same year, representatives from nine different craft groups formed the General Trades Union (GTU) of New York. By 1834, similar groups had sprung up in over a dozen cities. In 1834 also, representatives of several local GTUs met in Baltimore and organized the National Trades Union (NTU). In its founding statement the NTU criticized the "unjustifiable distribution of the wealth of society in the hands of a few individuals," which had created for working people "a humiliating, servile dependency, incompatible with . . . natural equality."

Naturally, employers disagreed with the NTU's criticism of the economic system. In Cincinnati and elsewhere, employers prevailed upon police to arrest strikers even when no violence had occurred. In another case, New York employers took striking journeymen tailors to court in 1836. Judge Ogden Edwards pronounced the strikers guilty of conspiracy and declared unions un-American. The GTU responded with a mass rally at which Judge Edwards was burned in effigy.

A year later, stunned by the effects of the Panic of 1837, the GTU collapsed. The founding of these general unions, a visible sign of a class-based community of interest among workers, is generally considered to mark the beginning of the American labor movement. However, the early unions included only white men in skilled trades, who made up only a small percentage of all workers. The majority of workers—men in unskilled occupations, all free African Americans, and all women—were excluded.

Although workers were unable to create strong unions or stable political parties that spoke for their economic interests, they were a vital factor in urban politics. As America's cities experienced unprecedented growth, the electorate mushroomed. In New York, for example, the number of voters grew from 20,000 in 1825 to 88,900 in 1855. Furthermore, by 1855 half of the voters were foreign-born. Because immigrants clustered in neighborhoods, their impact on politics could be concentrated and manipulated. In New York, for example, the Irish-dominated districts quickly became Democratic Party strongholds. Germans, who were less active politically than the Irish, nevertheless voted heavily for the new Republican Party in the 1850s. Between them, these two new blocs of immigrant voters destroyed the Whig Party that had controlled New York politics before the immigrants arrived.

In New York City, the **Tammany Society**, begun in the 1780s as a fraternal organization of artisans, slowly evolved into the key organization of the new mass politics. Tammany, which was affiliated with the national Democratic Party, reached voters by using many of the techniques of mass appeal made popular earlier by craft organizations—parades, rallies, popular songs, and party newspapers.

CIVIC ORDER

The challenges to middle-class respectability posed by new immigrants and unruly workers were fostered and publicized by the immensely popular "penny papers," which began publication in 1833, and by the rapidly growing number of political papers. This exuberant urban popular culture was unquestionably a part of the same new democratic political spirit that led to the great upsurge in political participation discussed in Chapter 11.

In New York, the prosperous classes were increasingly frightened by the urban poor and by working-class rowdyism. New York City's tradition of New Year's Eve "frolics," in which laborers, apprentices, and other members of the lower classes paraded through the streets playing drums, trumpets, whistles, and other noisemakers, was an example. By 1828, the revelry had been taken over by gangs of young workers from the lower classes, 4,000 strong, who marched through the city, overturning carts, breaking windows, obstructing traffic, and harassing middle-class citizens. In the following year, the city government banned the traditional New Year's Eve parade.

In colonial days, civic disturbances had been handled informally: members of the city watch asked onlookers for whatever assistance was necessary to keep the peace. New York City's first response in the 1820s and 1830s to increasing civic disorder was to hire more city watchmen and to augment them with constables and marshals. When riots occurred, the militia were called, and deaths were increasingly common as they forcibly restrained mobs. Finally, in 1845, the city created a permanent police force with a mandate to keep the poor in order. Southern cities, because of fear of slave disorder, had police forces much earlier.

But even with police forces in place, the pressures of rapid urbanization, immigration, and the market revolution proved to be too much for America's cities. Beginning in the 1830s, a series of urban riots broke out against the two poorest urban groups: Catholics and free black people. As if their miserable living conditions were not enough, Irish immigrants were met with virulent anti-Catholicism.

Tammany Society A fraternal organization of artisans begun in the 1780s that evolved into a key organization of the new mass politics in New York City.

By 1855, half the voters in New York City were foreign-born. This 1858 engraving of an Irish bar in the Five Points area appeared in the influential *Harper's Weekly*. It expressed the temperance reformers' dislike of immigrants and their drinking habits and the dismay of political reformers that immigrant saloons and taverns were such effective organizing centers for urban political machines.

In 1834, rioters burned an Ursuline convent in Charlestown, Massachusetts; in 1844, a Philadelphia mob attacked priests and nuns and vandalized Catholic churches; in 1854, a mob destroyed an Irish neighborhood in Lawrence, Massachusetts. Often the Irish replied in kind—for example, in an 1806 riot in New York, when they counterattacked a mob that disrupted their Christmas Eve mass in a Catholic church on Augustus Street. But the most common targets of urban violence were free African Americans.

FREE AFRICAN AMERICANS IN THE CITIES

By 1860, there were nearly half a million free African Americans in the United States, constituting about 11 percent of the country's total black population. More than half of all free African Americans lived in the North, mostly in cities, where they competed with immigrants and native-born poor white people for jobs as day laborers and domestic servants. Philadelphia and New York had the largest black communities. There were much smaller but still significant black communities in the New England cities of Boston, Providence, and New Haven and in Ohio cities like Cincinnati.

Free African Americans in northern cities faced residential segregation, pervasive job discrimination, segregated public schools, and severe limitations on their civil rights. In addition to these legal restrictions, there were matters of custom: African Americans of all economic classes endured daily affronts, such as exclusion from public concerts, lectures, and libraries, and segregation or exclusion from public transportation. For example, in Massachusetts—which had the reputation

This appealing portrait of a musician, *The Bone Player*, evokes the prevalent stereotype of African Americans as innately musical, but it also clearly portrays a man who is proud of his talent.

William Sidney Morris (American, 1807–1868), "The Bone Player," 1856. Oil on canvas, 91.76 × 73.98 cm (36 1/8 × 29 1/8 in.). Courtesy, Museum of Fine Arts, Boston. Bequest of Martha C. Karolik for the M. and M. Karolik Collection of American Paintings. 48.46 Reproduced with permission. Photograph © 2006 Museum of Fine Arts, Boston. All Rights Reserved.

of being more hospitable to black people than any other northern state—the famed African American abolitionist Frederick Douglass was denied admission to a zoo on Boston Common, a public lecture and revival meeting, a restaurant, and a public omnibus, all within the space of a few days.

In common with Irish and German immigrants, African Americans created defenses against the hostile larger society by building their own community structures. They formed associations for aiding the poorest members of the community, for self-improvement, and for socializing. Tired of being insulted by the white press, African American communities supported their own newspapers. The major community organization was the black Baptist or African Methodist Episcopal (AME) church.

Employment prospects for black men deteriorated from 1820 to 1850. Those who had held jobs as skilled artisans were forced from their positions, and their sons denied apprenticeships, by white mechanics and craftsmen who were themselves suffering from the effects of the market revolution. Limited to day labor, African Americans found themselves in direct competition with the new immigrants, especially the Irish, for jobs. On the waterfront, black men lost their jobs as carters and longshoremen to the Irish. One of the few occupations to remain open to them was that of seaman. More than 20 percent of all American sailors in 1850 were black. Mothers, wives, and daughters worked as domestic servants (in competition with Irishwomen), washerwomen, and seamstresses.

Free African Americans remained committed to their enslaved brethren in the South. In New York, for example, black communities rioted four times—in 1801, 1819, 1826, and 1832—against slave catchers taking escaped slaves back to slavery. But even more frequently, free African Americans were themselves targets of urban violence. Philadelphia, "the City of Brotherly Love," was repeatedly rocked by antiblack riots in the period between 1820 and 1859.

SOCIAL REFORM MOVEMENTS

The passion for reform that had become such an important part of the new middle-class thinking was focused on the problems of the nation's cities. As the opening of this chapter describes, the earliest response to the dislocations caused by the market revolution was community based and voluntary. Middle-class people tried to deal with social changes in their communities by joining organizations devoted to reforms. The reform message was vastly amplified by inventions such as the steam printing press, which made it possible to publish reform literature in great volume. Soon there were national networks of reform groups.

RELIGION, REFORM, AND SOCIAL CONTROL

Evangelical religion was fundamental to social reform. Men and women who had been converted to the enthusiastic new faith assumed personal responsibility for making changes in their own lives. Personal reform quickly led to social reform. Religious converts were encouraged in their social activism by such leading revivalists as Charles G. Finney, who preached a doctrine of "perfectionism," claiming it

WHAT ROLE did women play in the development of American education?

myhist🔍rylab

Review Summary

11–4
Charles Finney, *What a Revival of Religion Is* (1835)

was possible for all Christians to personally understand and live by God's will and thereby become "as perfect as God." This new religious feeling evoked by Finney was intensely hopeful: members of evangelistic religions really did expect to convert the world and create the perfect moral and religious community on earth.

Much of America was swept by this reform-minded religious fervor, and it was the new middle class that set the agenda. Reform efforts arose from the recognition that the traditional methods of small-scale local relief were no longer adequate. Reformers realized that large cities had to make large-scale provisions for social misfits and that institutional rather than private efforts were needed. This thinking was especially true of the institutional reform movements that began in the 1830s, such as the push for insane asylums. At this time, of course, the federal government provided no such relief.

A second characteristic of the reform movements was a belief in the basic goodness of human nature. All reformers believed that the condition of the unfortunate—the poor, the insane, the criminal—would improve in a wholesome environment. Prison reform carried this sentiment to the extreme. On the theory that bad social influences were largely responsible for crime, some "model" prisons completely isolated prisoners from one another, making them eat, sleep, work, and do required Bible reading in their own cells. The failure of these prisons to achieve dramatic changes for the better in their inmates (a number of isolated prisoners went mad, and some committed suicide) or to reduce crime was one of the first indications that reform was not a simple task.

A third characteristic of the reform movements was their moralistic dogmatism. Reformers were certain they knew what was right and were determined to see their improvements enacted. It was a short step from developing individual self-discipline to imposing discipline on others. The reforms that were proposed thus took the form of social controls. Lazy, sinful, intemperate, or unfit members of society were to be reformed for their own good, whether they wanted to be or not. This attitude was bound to cause controversy; by no means did all Americans share the reformers' beliefs, nor did those for whom it was intended always take kindly to being the targets of the reformers' concern.

Indeed, some aspects of the social reform movements were harmful. The evangelical Protestantism of the reformers promoted a dangerous hostility to Catholic immigrants from Ireland and Germany that, as noted earlier, repeatedly led to urban riots. The temperance movement, in particular, targeted immigrants for their free drinking habits. Seeking uniformity of behavior rather than tolerance, the reformers thus helped to promote the virulent nativism that infected American politics between 1840 and 1860 (see Chapter 15).

Regional and national reform organizations quickly grew from local projects to deal with social problems such as drinking, prostitution, mental illness, and crime. In 1828, for example, Congregationalist minister Lyman Beecher joined other ministers in forming a General Union for Promoting the Observance of the Christian Sabbath; the aim was to prevent business on Sundays. To achieve its goals, the General Union adopted the same methods used by political parties: lobbying, petition drives, fundraising, and special publications.

In effect, Beecher and similar reformers engaged in political action but remained aloof from direct electoral politics, stressing their religious mission. In any case, sabbatarianism was controversial. Workingmen (who usually worked six days a week) were angered when the General Union forced the Sunday closure of their favorite taverns and were quick to vote against the Whigs, the party perceived to be most sympathetic to reform thinking. But in many new western cities, **sabbatarianism** divided the business class itself. In Rochester, a city created by the Erie Canal,

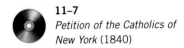

11–7
Petition of the Catholics of New York (1840)

Sabbatarianism   Reform movement that aimed to prevent business on Sundays.

businessmen who wished to observe Sunday only in religious ways were completely unable to stop the traffic of passenger and freight boats owned by other businessmen. Other reforms likewise muddied the distinction between political and social activity. It is not surprising that women, who were barred from electoral politics but not from moral and social activism, were major supporters of reform.

EDUCATION AND WOMEN TEACHERS

Women became deeply involved in reform movements through their churches. It was they who did most of the fundraising for the home missionary societies that were beginning to send the evangelical message worldwide—at first by ministers alone, later by married couples. Nearly every church had a maternal association, where mothers gathered to discuss ways to raise their children as true Christians. These associations reflected a new and more positive definition of childhood. The Puritans had believed that children were born sinful and that their wills had to be broken before they could become godly. Early schools reflected these beliefs: teaching was by rote, and punishment was harsh and physical. Educational reformers, however, tended to believe that children were born innocent and needed gentle nurturing and encouragement if they were to flourish. At home, mothers began to play the central role in child rearing. Outside the home, women helped spread the new public education pioneered by Horace Mann, secretary of the Massachusetts State Board of Education.

Although literacy had long been valued, especially in New England, schooling since colonial times had been a private enterprise and a personal expense. In 1827, Massachusetts pioneered compulsory education by legislating that public schools be supported by public taxes. Soon schooling for white children between the ages of five and nineteen was common, although, especially in rural schools, the term might be only a month or so long. Uniformity in curriculum and teacher training, and the grading of classes by ability—measures pioneered by Horace Mann in the 1830s— quickly caught on in other states. In the North and West (the South lagged far behind), more and more children went to school, and more and more teachers, usually young single women, were hired to teach them.

The spread of public education created the first real career opportunity for women. By 1850, women were dominant in primary school teaching, which had come to be regarded as an acceptable occupation for educated young women during the few years between their own schooling and marriage. For some women, teaching was a great adventure; they enthusiastically volunteered to be "schoolmarms" on the distant western frontiers of Wisconsin and Iowa. Still others thought globally. The young women who attended Mary Lyon's Mount Holyoke Female Seminary in Massachusetts, founded in 1837, hoped to be missionary teachers in distant lands. For others, a few years of teaching was quite enough. Low pay (half of what male schoolteachers earned) and strict community supervision (women teachers had to board with families in the community) were probably sufficient to make almost any marriage proposal look appealing.

TEMPERANCE

Reformers believed not only that children could be molded but also that adults could change. The largest reform organization of the period, the **American Society for the Promotion of Temperance**, founded in 1826, boasted more than 200,000 members by the mid-1830s. Dominated by evangelicals, local chapters used revival methods—lurid **temperance** tracts detailing the evils of alcohol, large prayer and song meetings, and heavy group pressure—to encourage young men to stand up, confess their bad habits, and "take the pledge" not to drink. Here again, women played an important role (see Figure 13.2).

11–11
Horace Mann, *Report No. 12 of the Massachusetts School Board* (1848)

QUICK REVIEW

Women and Reform

◆ Women often became involved in reform through their churches.

◆ Maternal associations focused on raising of children as true Christians.

◆ Women helped spread public education of children.

American Society for the Promotion of Temperance Largest reform organization of its time dedicated to ending the sale and consumption of alcoholic beverages.

Temperance Reform movement originating in the 1820s that sought to eliminate the consumption of alcohol.

Excessive drinking was a national problem, and it appears to have been mostly a masculine one, for respectable women did not drink in public. Men drank hard cider and liquor—whiskey, rum—in abundance. Traditionally, drinking had been a basic part of men's working lives. It concluded occasions as formal as the signing of a contract and accompanied such informal activities as card games. Drink was a staple offering at political speeches, rallies, and elections. In the old artisanal workshops, drinking had been a customary pastime. Much of the drinking was well within the bounds of sociability, but the widespread use must have encouraged drunkenness.

There were many reasons to support temperance. Heavy-drinking men hurt their families economically by spending their wages on drink. Women had no recourse: the laws of the time gave men complete financial control of the household, and divorce was difficult as well as socially unacceptable. Excessive drinking also led to violence and crime, both within the family and in the larger society.

But there were other reasons. The new middle class, preoccupied with respectability, morality, and efficiency, found the old easygoing drinking ways unacceptable. Temperance became a social and political issue. Whigs, who embraced the new morality, favored it; Democrats, who in northern cities consisted increasingly of immigrant workers, were opposed. Both German and Irish immigrants valued the social drinking that occurred in beer gardens and saloons and were hostile to temperance reform.

The Panic of 1837 affected the temperance movement. Whereas most temperance crusaders in the 1820s had been members of the middle class, the long depression of 1837–43 prompted artisans and skilled workers to give up or at least cut down substantially on drinking. Forming associations known as Washington Temperance Societies, these workers spread the word that temperance was the workingman's best chance to survive economically and to maintain his independence. Their wives, gathered together in Martha Washington Societies, were frequently even more committed to temperance than their husbands.

By the mid-1840s, alcohol consumption had been more than halved, to about the level of today. Concern over drinking would remain constant throughout the nineteenth century and into the twentieth.

MORAL REFORM, ASYLUMS, AND PRISONS

Alcohol was not the only "social evil" that reform groups attacked. Another was prostitution, which was common in the nation's port cities. The customary approach of evangelical reformers was to "rescue" prostitutes, offering them the salvation of religion, prayer, and temporary shelter. The success rate was not very high. As an alternative to prostitution, reformers usually offered domestic work, a low-paying and restrictive occupation that many women scorned. Nevertheless, campaigns against prostitution, generally organized by women, continued throughout the nineteenth century.

One of the earliest and most effective antiprostitution groups was the **Female Moral Reform Society**. Founded by evangelical women in New York in 1834 (the first president was Lydia Finney), it boasted 555 affiliates throughout the country by 1840. The societies quickly realized that prostitution was not as much a moral as an economic issue and moved to organize charity and work for poor women and orphans. They also took direct action against the patrons of prostitutes by printing their names in local papers and then successfully lobbied the New York state legislature for criminal penalties against the male clients as well as the women themselves.

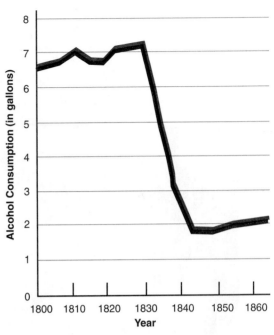

Figure 13.2 Per Capita Consumption of Alcohol, 1800–60
The underlying cause of the dramatic fall in alcohol consumption during the 1830s was the changing nature of work brought about by the market revolution. Contributing factors were the shock of the Panic of 1837 and the untiring efforts of temperance reformers.

W. J. Rorabaugh, *The Alcoholic Republic: An American Tradition* (New York: Oxford University Press, 1979).

11–2
Lyman Beecher, *Six Sermons on Intemperance* (1828)

11–5
Temperance and the Washingtonians (1836)

Female Moral Reform Society
Antiprostitution group founded by evangelical women in New York in 1834.

This **Currier and** Ives lithograph, *The Drunkard's Progress*, dramatically conveys the message that the first glass leads the drinker inevitably to alcoholism and finally to the grave, while his wife and child (shown under the arch) suffer.

Another dramatic example of reform was the asylum movement, spearheaded by the evangelist Dorothea Dix. In 1843, Dix horrified the Massachusetts state legislature with the results of her several years of study of the conditions to which insane women were subjected. She described in lurid detail how the women were incarcerated with ordinary criminals, locked up in "cages, closets, stalls, pens! Chained, naked, beaten with rods, and lashed into obedience!" Dix's efforts led to the establishment of a state asylum for the insane in Massachusetts and to similar institutions in other states.

Other reformers were active in related causes, such as prison reform and the establishment of orphanages, homes of refuge, and hospitals. Model penitentiaries were built in Auburn and Ossining (known as "Sing Sing"), New York, and in Philadelphia and Pittsburgh. Characterized by strict order and discipline, these prisons were supposed to reform rather than simply incarcerate their inmates, but their regimes of silence and isolation caused despair more often than rehabilitation.

UTOPIANISM AND MORMONISM

Amid all the political activism and reform fervor of the 1830s, a few people chose to escape into utopian communities and new religions. The upstate New York area along the Erie Canal was the seedbed for this movement, just as it was for evangelical revivals and reform movements like the **Seneca Falls convention**. The area was so notable for its reform enthusiasm that it has been called "the Burned-Over District," a reference to the waves of reform that swept through like forest fires (see Map 13.2).

Seneca Falls convention The first convention for women's equality in legal rights, held in upstate New York in 1848.

MAP EXPLORATION

To explore an interactive version of this map, go to **http://www.prenhall.com/faraghertlc/map13.2**

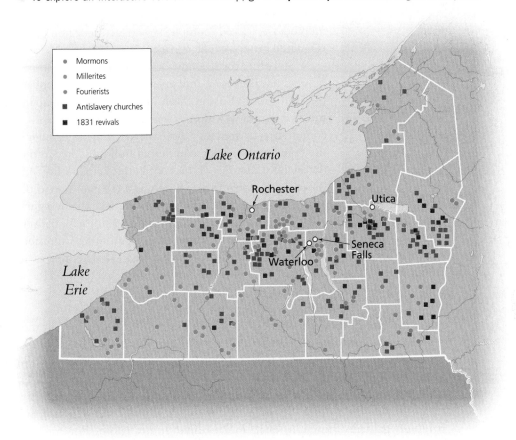

Legend:
- Mormons
- Millerites
- Fourierists
- Antislavery churches
- 1831 revivals

Lake Ontario

Rochester

Utica

Seneca Falls

Waterloo

Lake Erie

MAP 13.2

Reform Movements in the Burned-Over District   The so-called Burned-Over District, the region of New York State most changed by the opening of the Erie Canal, was a seedbed of religious and reform movements. The Mormon Church originated there and utopian groups and sects like the Millerites and the Fourierists thrived. Charles G. Finney held some of his most successful evangelical revivals in the district. Antislavery feeling was common in the region, and the women's rights movement began at Seneca Falls.

Whitney Cross, *The Burned-Over District* (1950; reprint, New York: Hippocrene Books, 1981).

WHY WERE the many religious revivals and reform movements in the Burned-Over District in the 1830s and 1840s strongest in this region of the country?

Apocalyptic religions tend to spring up in places experiencing rapid social change. The Erie Canal region, which experienced the full impact of the market revolution in the early nineteenth century, was such a place. A second catalyst is hard times, and the prolonged depression that began with the Panic of 1837 led some people to embrace a belief in imminent catastrophe.

The **Shakers**, founded by "Mother" Ann Lee in 1774, were the oldest utopian group. An offshoot of the Quakers, the Shakers espoused a radical social philosophy that called for the abolition of the traditional family in favor of a family of brothers and sisters joined in equal fellowship. Despite its insistence on celibacy, the Shaker movement grew between 1820 and 1830, eventually reaching twenty settlements in eight states with a total membership of 6,000. The Shakers' simple and highly structured lifestyle, their isolation from the changing world, and their belief in equality drew new followers, especially among women. In contrast, another

 11–12
John Humphrey Noyes, *Speech to the Convention of Perfectionists* (1845) and *Bible Communism* (1849)

Shakers   The followers of Mother Ann Lee, who preached a religion of strict celibacy and communal living.

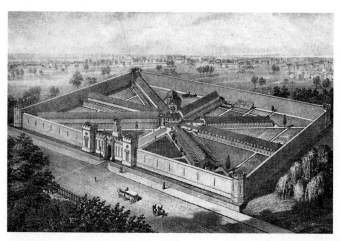

Begun in 1822, the castle-like Eastern State Penitentiary in Philadelphia was intended as a model of rational prison reform. Replacing the crowded mass imprisonment of the past, prisoners were held in isolation from other inmates in separate cells. But instead of the expected repentance and reform, isolation bred despair and attempts at suicide.

The Library Company of Philadelphia.

10–1
Joseph Smith, *The Beginnings of Mormorism* (1823)

14–2
Harriet Beecher Stowe, *Uncle Tom's Cabin* (1852)

Mormonism The doctrines based on the Book of Mormon, taught by Joseph Smith and the succeeding prophets and leaders of the Church.

WHO WERE the abolitionists and what were their racial attitudes?

myhistorylab
Review Summary

utopian community, the Oneida Community, became notorious for its sexual freedom. Founded by John Humphrey Noyes in 1848, the Oneida community, like the Shaker community, viewed itself as one family. But rather than celibacy, members practiced "complex marriage," a system of highly regulated group sexual activity.

Still other forthrightly socialist communities flourished briefly. New Harmony, Indiana, founded by the famous Scottish industrialist Robert Owen in 1825, was to be a manufacturing community without poverty and unemployment. The community survived only three years. Faring little better were the "phalanxes," huge communal buildings structured on the socialist theories of the French thinker Charles Fourier. Based on his belief that there was a rational way to divide work, Fourier suggested, for example, that children would make the best garbage collectors because they didn't mind dirt! The rapid failure of these socialist communities was due largely to inadequate planning and organization. Another reason may have been, as author Louisa May Alcott suggested in her satirical reminiscence, *Transcendental Wild Oats*, that the women were left to do all the work while the men philosophized.

The most successful of the nineteenth-century communitarian movements was also a product of the Burned-Over District. In 1830, a young man named Joseph Smith founded the Church of Jesus Christ of Latter-Day Saints, based on the teachings of the Book of Mormon, which he claimed to have received from an angel in a vision. Initially **Mormonism**, as the new religion became known, seemed little different from the many other new religious groups and utopian communities of the time. But under the benevolent authority of its patriarch, Joseph Smith, it rapidly gained distinction for its extraordinary unity. Close cooperation and hard work made the Mormon community successful, attracting both new followers and the animosity of neighbors.

The Mormons were harassed in New York and driven west to Ohio and then Missouri. Finally they seemed to find an ideal home in Nauvoo, Illinois, where in 1839 they built a model community, achieving almost complete self-government and isolation from non-Mormon neighbors. But in 1844, dissension within the community over Joseph Smith's new doctrine of polygamy (marriage between one man and more than one woman simultaneously) gave outsiders a chance to intervene. Smith and his brother were arrested peacefully but were killed by a mob from which their jailers failed to protect them. The beleaguered Mormon community decided to move beyond reach of harm. Led by Brigham Young, the Mormons migrated in 1846 to the Great Salt Lake in present-day Utah. Their hopes of isolation were dashed, however, by the California Gold Rush of 1849. (See Chapter 14)

ANTISLAVERY AND ABOLITIONISM

The antislavery feeling that was to play such an important role in the politics of the 1840s and 1850s also had its roots in the religious reform movements that began in the 1820s and 1830s. Three groups—free African Americans, Quakers, and militant white reformers—worked to bring an end to slavery, but each in different ways. Their efforts eventually turned a minor reform movement into the dominant political issue of the day.

THE AMERICAN COLONIZATION SOCIETY

The first national attempt to "solve" the problem of slavery was a plan for gradual emancipation of slaves (with compensation to their owners) and their resettlement in Africa. This plan was the work of the **American Colonization Society**, formed in 1817 by northern religious reformers (Quakers prominent among them) and a number of southern slave owners, most from the Upper South and the border states (Kentuckian Henry Clay was a supporter). The American Colonization Society was remarkably ineffective; by 1830, it had managed to send only 1,400 black people to a colony in Liberia, West Africa. Critics pointed out that more slaves were born in a week than the society sent back to Africa in a year.

AFRICAN AMERICANS AGAINST SLAVERY

For free African Americans, the freedom of other black people had always been a goal, but in order to achieve change, they needed white allies. Most free African Americans rejected the efforts of the American Colonization Society, insisting instead on a commitment to the immediate end of slavery and the equal treatment of black people in America. "We are natives of this country," an African American minister in New York pointed out. Then he added bitterly, "We only ask that we be treated as well as foreigners." By 1830, there were at least fifty African American abolitionist societies in the North. The first African American newspaper, founded in 1827 by John Russwurm and Samuel Cornish, announced its antislavery position in its title, *Freedom's Journal.*

In 1829, David Walker, a free African American in Boston, wrote a widely distributed pamphlet, *Appeal to the Colored Citizens of the World*, that encouraged slave rebellion. "We must and shall be free . . . in spite of you," Walker warned whites. "And woe, woe will be it to you if we have to obtain our freedom by fighting." White Southerners blamed pamphlets such as these and the militant articles of African American journalists for stirring up trouble among southern slaves and, in particular, for Nat Turner's revolt in 1831.

ABOLITIONISTS

The third and best-known group of antislavery reformers was headed by William Lloyd Garrison. In 1831, Garrison broke with the gradualist persuaders of the American Colonization Society and began publishing his own paper, the *Liberator.* Garrison's approach was to mount a sweeping crusade condemning slavery as sinful and demanding its immediate abolition. In reality, Garrison did not expect that all slaves would be freed immediately, but he did want and expect everyone to acknowledge the immorality of slavery. On the other hand, Garrison took the truly radical step of demanding full social equality for African Americans, referring to them individually as "a man and a brother" and "a woman and a sister."

Garrison's moral vehemence radicalized northern antislavery religious groups. Theodore Weld, an evangelical minister, joined Garrison in 1833 in forming the American Anti-Slavery Society. The following year, Weld encouraged a group of students at Lane Theological Seminary in Cincinnati to form an antislavery society. When the seminary's president, Lyman Beecher, sought to suppress it, the students moved en masse to Oberlin College in northern Ohio, where they were joined by revivalist Charles Finney, who became president of the college. Oberlin soon became known as the most liberal college in the country, not only for its antislavery stance but for its acceptance of African American students and of women students as well.

The style of abolitionist writings and speeches was similar to the oratorical style of the religious revivalists. Northern abolitionists believed that a full description of the evils of slavery would force southern slave owners to confront their wrongdoing

American Colonization Society Organization founded in 1817 by antislavery reformers, that called for gradual emancipation and the removal of freed blacks to Africa.

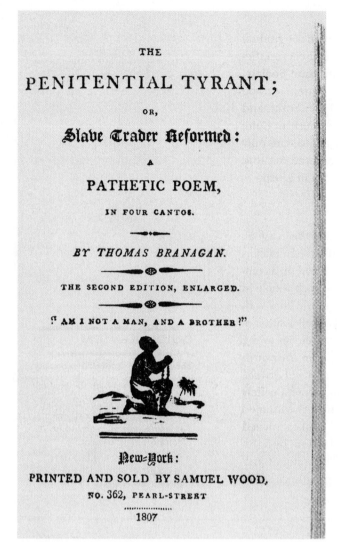

The different dates on these two widely used antislavery images are important. The title page of Thomas Branagan's 1807 book includes an already commonly used image at the time of a male slave. The engraving of a chained female slave was made by Patrick Reason, a black artist, in 1835. The accompanying message saying "Am I Not a Woman and a Sister?" spoke particularly to white female abolitionists in the North, who were just becoming active in antislavery movements in the 1830s.

and lead to a true act of repentance—freeing their slaves. They were confrontational, denunciatory, and personal in their message, much like the evangelical preachers. Southerners, however, regarded abolitionist attacks as libelous and abusive.

Abolitionists adopted another tactic of revivalists and temperance workers when, to enhance their powers of persuasion, they began to publish great numbers of antislavery tracts. In 1835 alone, they mailed more than a million pieces of antislavery literature to southern states. This tactic also drew a backlash: southern legislatures banned abolitionist literature, encouraged the harassment and abuse of anyone distributing it, and looked the other way when (as in South Carolina) proslavery mobs seized and burned it. Most serious, the majority of southern states reacted by toughening laws concerning emancipation, freedom of movement, and all aspects of slave behavior. Hoping to prevent the spread of the abolitionist message, most southern states reinforced laws making it a crime to teach a slave how to read. Ironically, then, the immediate impact of abolitionism in the South was to stifle dissent and make the lives of slaves harder.

Even in the North, controversy over abolitionism was common. Some places were prone to anti-abolitionist violence. The Ohio Valley, settled largely by Southerners, was one such place, as were northern cities experiencing the strains of rapid growth, such as Philadelphia. Immigrant Irish, who found themselves pitted against free black people for jobs, were often violently anti-abolitionist. William Lloyd Garrison was stoned, dragged through the streets, and on one occasion almost hanged by a Boston mob. In a three-day New York riot of 1834, abolitionist Arthur Tappan's home and store were sacked at the same time that black churches and homes were damaged and free blacks attacked. In 1837, antislavery editor Elijah P. Lovejoy of Alton, Illinois, was killed and his press destroyed.

ABOLITIONISM AND POLITICS

Abolitionism began as a social movement but soon intersected with sectional interests and became a national political issue. In the 1830s, massive abolitionist petition drives gathered a total of nearly 700,000 petitions requesting the abolition of slavery and the slave trade in the District of Columbia but were rebuffed by Congress. At southern insistence and with President Andrew Jackson's approval, Congress passed a "gag rule" in 1836 that prohibited discussion of antislavery petitions.

In 1837, white abolitionist Elijah P. Lovejoy had placed the press he used to print his antislavery newspaper in an Alton, Illinois, warehouse in order to protect the press against a mob. This contemporary woodcut depicts the mob's attack on the warehouse. Lovejoy died defending it.

Many Northerners viewed the gag rule and censorship of the mails, which Southerners saw as necessary defenses against abolitionist frenzy, as alarming threats to free speech. First among them was Massachusetts representative John Quincy Adams, the only former president ever to serve in Congress after leaving the executive branch. Adams so publicly and persistently denounced the gag rule as a violation of the constitutional right to petition that it was repealed in 1844. Less well-known Northerners, like the thousands of women who canvassed their neighborhoods with petitions, made personal commitments to abolitionism that they did not intend to abandon.

Although abolitionist groups raised the nation's emotional temperature, they failed to achieve the moral unity they had hoped for, and they began to splinter. Frederick Douglass and William Lloyd Garrison parted ways when Douglass, refusing to be limited to a simple recital of his life as a slave, began to make specific suggestions for improvements in the lives of free African Americans.

Douglass and other free African Americans worked under persistent discrimination, even from antislavery whites; some of the latter refused to hire black people or to meet with them as equals. While many white reformers eagerly pressed for civil equality for African Americans, they did not accept the idea of social equality. On the other hand, black and white "stations" worked closely in the risky enterprise of passing fugitive slaves north over the famous Underground Railroad, as the various routes by which slaves made their way to freedom were called. Contrary to abolitionist legend, however, it was free African Americans, rather than white people, who played the major part in helping the fugitives.

In 1840, the abolitionist movement formally split. The majority moved toward party politics (which Garrison abhorred), founding the **Liberty Party** and choosing James G. Birney (whom Theodore Weld had converted to abolitionism) as their presidential candidate. Thus, the abolitionist movement, which began as an effort at moral reform, took its first major step into politics, and this step in turn led to the formation of the Republican Party in the 1850s and to the Civil War. (See Chapter 15)

For one particular group of antislavery reformers, the abolitionist movement opened up new possibilities for action. Through their participation in antislavery activity, some women came to a vivid realization of the social constraints on their activism.

Liberty Party   The first antislavery political party, formed in 1840.

THE WOMEN'S RIGHTS MOVEMENT

American women, without the vote or a role in party politics, found a field of activity in social reform movements. There was scarcely a reform movement in which women were not actively involved. The majority of women did not participate in these activities, for they were fully occupied with housekeeping and child rearing (families with five children were the average). A few women— mostly members of the new middle class, who could afford servants—had the time and energy to look beyond their immediate tasks. Touched by the religious revival, these women enthusiastically joined reform movements. Led thereby to challenge social restrictions, some, such as the Grimké sisters, found that their commitment carried them beyond the limits of what was considered acceptable activity for women.

THE GRIMKÉ SISTERS

Sarah and Angelina Grimké, members of a prominent South Carolina slaveholding family, rejected slavery out of religious conviction and moved north to join a Quaker community near Philadelphia. In the 1830s, these two sisters found themselves drawn into the growing antislavery agitation in the North. Because they knew about slavery firsthand, they were in great demand as speakers. At first they spoke to "parlor meetings" of women only, as was considered proper. But interested men kept sneaking into the talks, and soon the sisters found themselves speaking to mixed gatherings. The meetings got larger and larger, and the sisters became the first female public speakers in America.

The Grimké sisters were criticized for speaking because they were women. A letter from a group of ministers cited the Bible in reprimanding the sisters for stepping out of "woman's proper sphere" of silence and subordination. Sarah Grimké answered the ministers in her 1838 *Letters on the Equality of the Sexes and the Condition of Women*, claiming that "men and women were CREATED EQUAL. . . . Whatever is right for a man to do, is right for woman."

Not all female assertiveness was as dramatic as Sarah Grimké's, but women in the antislavery movement found it a constant struggle to be heard. Some solved the problem of male dominance by forming their own groups, like the Philadelphia Female Anti-Slavery Society. In the antislavery movement and other reform groups as well, men accorded women a secondary role, even when—as was frequently the case—women constituted a majority of the members.

WOMEN'S RIGHTS

The Seneca Falls Convention of 1848, the first women's rights convention in American history, was an outgrowth of almost twenty years of female activity in social reform. As described in the chapter opener, the long agenda of rights was drawn directly from the discrimination many women had experienced in social reform groups. Every year after 1848, women gathered to hold women's rights conventions and to work for political, legal, and social equality. Over the years, in response to persistent lobbying, states passed property laws more favorable to women, and altered divorce laws to allow women to retain custody of children. Teaching positions in higher education opened up to women, as did jobs in some other occupations, and women gained the vote in some states, beginning with Wyoming Territory in 1869. In 1920, seventy-two years after universal woman suffrage was first proposed at Seneca Falls, a woman's right to vote was at last guaranteed in the Nineteenth Amendment to the Constitution.

Historians have only recently realized how much the reform movements of this "Age of the Common Man" were due to the efforts of the "common woman." Women played a vital role in all the social movements of the day. In doing so, they implicitly

A CONVENTION OF HEMMERS AND STITCHERS HELD AT LYNN, FEB. 28, FOR ADOPTING A LIST OF PRICES; MRS. E. HALL, PRESIDING.—(See page 284.)

Women's gatherings, like the first women's rights convention in Seneca Falls in 1848, and this meeting of strikers in Lynn in 1860, were indicators of widespread female activism.

challenged the popular notion of separate spheres for men and women—the public world for him, home and family for her. The separate spheres argument, although it heaped praise on women for their allegedly superior moral qualities, was meant to exclude them from political life. The reforms discussed in this chapter show clearly that women reformers believed they had a right and a duty to propose solutions for the moral and social problems of the day. Empowered by their own religious beliefs and activism, the Seneca Falls reformers spoke for all American women when they demanded an end to the unfair restrictions they suffered as women.

QUICK REVIEW

Seneca Falls Convention

◆ 1848: First women's rights convention in American history.

◆ Every year after 1848 conventions gathered to work for equality.

◆ Efforts resulted in political and legal advances.

CONCLUSION

Beginning in the 1820s, the market revolution changed the size and social order of America's preindustrial cities and towns. Immigration, dramatically rapid population growth, and changes in working life and class structure created a host of new urban problems ranging from sanitation to civic order. These changes occurred so rapidly that they seemed overwhelming. Former face-to-face methods of social control no longer worked. To fill the gap, new kinds of associations—the political party, the religious crusade, the reform cause, the union movement—sprang up. These associations were new manifestations of the deep human desire for social connection, for continuity, and—especially in the growing cities—for social order. A striking aspect of these associations was the uncompromising nature of the attitudes and beliefs on which they were based. Most groups were formed of like-minded people who wanted to impose their will on others. Such intolerance boded ill for the future. If political parties, religious bodies, and reform groups were to splinter along sectional lines (as happened in the 1850s), political compromise would be very difficult. In the meantime, however, Americans came to terms with the market revolution by engaging in a passion for improvement. As a perceptive foreign observer, Francis Grund noted, "Americans love their country not as it is but as it will be."

CHRONOLOGY

1817	American Colonization Society founded
1820s	Shaker colonies grow
1825	New Harmony founded, fails three years later
1826	American Society for the Promotion of Temperance founded
1827	Workingmen's Party founded in Philadelphia
	Freedom's Journal begins publication
	Public school movement begins in Massachusetts
1829	David Walker's *Appeal to the Colored Citizens of the World* is published
1830	Joseph Smith founds Church of Jesus Christ of Latter-Day Saints (Mormon Church)
	Charles G. Finney's revivals in Rochester
1831	William Lloyd Garrison begins publishing antislavery newspaper, the *Liberator*
1832	Immigration begins to increase
1833	American Anti-Slavery Society founded by William Lloyd Garrison and Theodore Weld
1834	First Female Moral Reform Society founded in New York
	National Trades Union formed
1836	Congress passes "gag rule" to prevent discussion of antislavery petitions
1837	Antislavery editor Elijah P. Lovejoy killed
	Angelina Grimké addresses Massachusetts legislature
	Sarah Grimké writes *Letters on the Equality of the Sexes and the Condition of Women*
	Panic begins seven-year depression
1839	Theodore Weld publishes *American Slavery As It Is*
1840s	New York and Boston complete public water systems
1840	Liberty Party founded
1843	Millerites await the end of the world
	Dorothea Dix spearheads asylum reform movement
1844	Mormon leader Joseph Smith killed by mob
1845	New York creates city police force
	Beginning of Irish Potato Famine and mass Irish immigration into the United States
1846	Mormons begin migration to the Great Salt Lake
1848	Women's Rights Convention at Seneca Falls
	John Noyes founds Oneida Community

REVIEW QUESTIONS

1. What impact did the new immigration of the 1840s and 1850s have on American cities?
2. Why did urbanization produce so many problems?
3. What motivated the social reformers of the period? Were they benevolent helpers or dictatorial social controllers? Study several reform causes and discuss similarities and differences among them.
4. Abolitionism differed little from other reforms in its tactics, but the effects of antislavery activism were politically explosive. Why was this so?
5. Women were active members of almost every reform group. What reasons might women have given for their unusual degree of participation?

KEY TERMS

American Colonization Society (p. 343)
**American Society for the Promotion of
   Temperance** (p. 338)
Declaration of Sentiments (p. 324)
Female Moral Reform Society (p. 339)
Liberty Party (p. 345)

Mormonism (p. 342)
Sabbatarianism (p. 337)
Seneca Falls convention (p. 340)
Shakers (p. 341)
Tammany Society (p. 334)
Temperance (p. 338)

Flashcard Review

RECOMMENDED READING

Tyler Anbinder, *Five Points* (2001). A social history of New York's most notorious slum.

Paul Boyer, *Urban Masses and the Moral Order in America, 1820–1920* (1978). Interprets reform as an effort to reestablish the moral order of the preindustrial community.

Kathleen Neils Conzen, *Immigrant Milwaukee, 1836–1860: Accommodation and Community in a Frontier City* (1976). Milwaukee rapidly became the most German city in the nation. This book explains how and why.

David Grimsted, *American Mobbing, 1828–1865: Toward Civil War* (1998). A national perspective on mob violence, North and South, including political violence.

James Oliver Horton and Lois E. Horton, *In Hope of Liberty: Culture, Community and Protest Among Northern Free Blacks, 1700–1860* (1997). A fine portrait that adds the perspective of change over time to earlier studies.

Mary Kelley, *Learning to Stand and Speak: Women, Education, and Public Life in America's Republic* (2006). The centrality of education to women's growing role in civic life.

Bruce Laurie, *Beyond Garrison: Antislavery and Social Reform* (2005). Focus on reformers in Massachusetts shows how antislavery and other social reforms were interconnected.

Steven Mintz, *Moralists and Modernizers: America's Pre–Civil War Reformers* (1995). A brief but inclusive study of reforms and reformers.

David Roediger, *The Wages of Whiteness* (1991). Explores the links between artisanal republicanism, labor organization, and white racism.

Mary Ryan, *Civic Wars: Democracy and Public Life in the American City During the Nineteenth Century* (1997). A study of New York, New Orleans, and San Francisco that argues that urban popular culture was "meeting-place democracy" in action.

Deborah Van Broekhoven, *The Devotion of These Women: Rhode Island in the Antislavery Network* (2002). Shows how informal women's activities sustained antislavery protest at the local level.

For study resources for this chapter, go to **www.myhistorylab.com** and choose *Out of Many, Teaching and Learning Classroom Edition.* You will find a wealth of study and review material for this chapter, including pretests and posttests, customized study plan, key-term review flash cards, interactive map and document activities, and documents for analysis.

*They immigrate constantly, hardly no one
to prevent them, and take possession of
the location that best suits them without either
asking leave or going through any formality
other than that of building their homes.*
—José Maria Sánchez

Albert Bierstadt (1830–1902), "The Oregon Trail" (oil on canvas).

Private Collection/Bridgeman Art Library International Ltd., New York

Butler Institute of American Art, Youngstown, OH, USA/Gift of Joseph G. Butler III
1946/Bridgeman Art Library.

14

THE TERRITORIAL EXPANSION OF THE UNITED STATES
1830s–1850s

WHAT ROLE did the federal government play in the exploration of the West?

WHAT WERE the major differences between the Oregon, Texas, and California frontiers?

WHAT WERE the most important consequences of the Mexican-American War?

WHAT KINDS of people participated in the California Gold Rush?

WHAT KEY factors explain the outcome of the election of 1848?

AMERICAN COMMUNITIES
Texans and Tejanos "Remember the Alamo!"

FOR THIRTEEN DAYS IN FEBRUARY AND MARCH 1836, A FORCE OF 187 Texans held the mission fortress known as the Alamo against a siege by 5,000 Mexican troops under General Antonio López de Santa Anna, president of Mexico. Santa Anna had come north to subdue rebellious Texas, the northernmost part of the Mexican province of Coahuila y Tejas, and to place it under central authority. On March 6 he ordered a final assault, and in brutal fighting that claimed over 1,500 Mexican lives, his army took the mission. All the defenders were killed, including Commander William Travis and the well-known frontiersmen Jim Bowie and Davy Crockett. It was a crushing defeat for the Texans. But the cry "Remember the Alamo!" rallied their remaining forces, which, less than two months later, routed the Mexican army and forced Santa Anna to grant Texas independence from Mexico. Today, the Alamo is one of the most cherished historic sites in the United States.

But memory is selective: within a generation of the uprising, few remembered that many Tejanos, Spanish-speaking people born in Texas, had joined with American settlers fighting for Texas independence.

The Tejano community, descended from eighteenth-century Spanish and Mexican settlers, included wealthy rancheros who raised cattle on the shortgrass prairies of southern Texas, as well as the cowboys known as *vaqueros* and the *peónes*, or poor tenant farmers. The Tejano elite, enthusiastic about American plans for the economic development of Texas, welcomed the American immigrants. Many Americans married into elite Tejano families, who hoped that by thus assimilating and sharing power with the Americans, they could not only maintain but also strengthen their community.

The Mexican state, however, was politically and socially unstable during these first years after its successful revolt against Spain in 1821. When, in 1828, the conservative centralists came to power in Mexico City and decided the Americans had too much influence in Texas, many Tejanos rose up with the Americans in opposition. In 1832, the Tejano elite of San Antonio and many prominent rancheros favored provincial autonomy and a strong role for the Americans.

As Santa Anna's army approached from the south, the wealthy ranchero Juan Nepomuceno Seguín recruited a company of Tejano volunteers and joined the American force inside the walls of the Alamo. In April, Seguín led a regiment of Tejanos in the decisive battle of San Jacinto that won independence for Texas.

Pleased with independence, Tejanos played an important political role in the new Republic of Texas at first. The liberal Lorenzo de Zavala was chosen vice president, and Seguín became the mayor of San Antonio. But soon things began to change. Illustrating a recurring pattern in the American occupation of new lands—a striking shift in the relations between different cultures in frontier areas. Most commonly, in the initial stage newcomers blended with native Peoples, creating a "frontier of inclusion." The first hunters, trappers, and traders on every American frontier—west of the Appalachians, in the Southwest, and in the Far West—married into the local community and tried to learn native ways. Outnumbered American settlers—initially invited in by Mexicans and Tejanos—developed an anti-Mexican passion, regarding all Spanish speakers as their Mexican enemies rather than their Tejano allies. Tejanos were attacked and forced from their homes; some of their villages were burned to the ground. "On the pretext that they were Mexicans," Seguín wrote, Americans treated Tejanos "worse than brutes. . . . My countrymen ran to me for protection against the assaults or exactions of these adventurers." But even in his capacity as mayor, Seguín could do little, and in 1842, he and his family, like hundreds of other Tejano families, fled south to Mexico in fear for their lives.

Spanish-speaking communities in Texas, and later in New Mexico and California, like the communities of Indians throughout the West, became conquered peoples. "White folks and Mexicans were never made to live together," a Texas woman told a traveler a few years after the revolution. "The Mexicans had no business here," she said, and the Americans might "just have to get together and drive them all out of the country." The descendants of the first European settlers of the American Southwest had become foreigners in the land their people had lived in for two centuries.

San Antonio

EXPLORING THE WEST

There seemed to be no stopping the expansion of the American people. By 1840, they had occupied all of the land east of the Mississippi River and had organized all of it (except for Florida and Wisconsin) into states. The speed and success of this expansion were a source of deep national pride that whetted appetites for further expansion. Many Americans looked eagerly westward to the vast unsettled reaches of the Louisiana Purchase: to Texas, Santa Fé, to trade with Mexico, and even to the Far West, where New England sea captains had been trading for furs since the 1780s. By 1848, the United States had gained all of these coveted western lands. This chapter examines the way the United States became a continental nation, forming many frontier communities in the process. Exploring the vast continent of North America and gaining an understanding of its geography took several centuries and the efforts of many people.

THE FUR TRADE

The fur trade, which flourished from the 1670s to the 1840s, was an important spur to exploration on the North American continent. In the 1670s, the British Hudson's Bay Company and its French Canadian rival, Montreal's North West Company, began exploring beyond the Great Lakes in the Canadian West in search of beaver pelts. Indeed, Alexander Mackenzie of the North West Company reached the Pacific Ocean in 1793, becoming the first European to make a transcontinental crossing of North America. Traders and trappers for both companies depended on the goodwill and cooperation of the native peoples of the region. From the marriages of European men with native women arose a distinctive mixed-race group, the "métis" (French for "mixed").

WHAT ROLE did the federal government play in the exploration of the West?

myhistorylab
Review Summary

IMAGE KEY

for pages 350–351

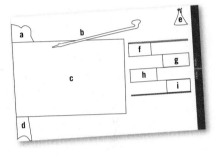

a. A tanned buffalo skin.

b. A long wooden pipe of the Mandan tribe.

c. Albert Bierstadt (1830–1902), "The Oregon Trail."

d. Cactus with a large pink flower.

e. A model of a Plains Indian tepee.

f. John Gast's "American Progress," c. 1872, depicting America heading westward.

g. "The Interior of Fort Laramie," 1858–1860, by Alfred Jacob Miller.

h. "General Winfield Scott at the Siege of Vera Cruz, March 1847" by Nathaniel Currier.

i. A drawing of an 1855 San Francisco gambling saloon.

The artist Alfred Jacob Miller, a careful observer of the western fur trade, shows a mountain man and his Indian wife in his 1837 *Bourgeois Walker and His Wife.* Walker and his wife worked together to trap and prepare beaver pelts for market, as did other European men and their Indian wives.

Alfred Jacob Miller, "Bourgeois Walker and His Wife," 1837. Watercolor. 37.1940.78. The Walters Art Museum, Baltimore.

Most American trappers, like the British and French before them, sought accommodation and friendship with Indian peoples: nearly half of them contracted long-lasting marriages with Indian women, who not only helped in the trapping and curing of furs but also acted as vital diplomatic links between the white and Indian worlds. One legendary trapper adapted so well that he became a Crow chief: the African American Jim Beckwourth, who married a Crow woman and was accepted into her tribe.

For all its adventure, the American fur trade was short-lived. By the 1840s, the population of beaver in western streams was virtually destroyed, and the day of the mountain man was over. But with daring journeys like that of Jedediah Smith, the first American to enter California over the Sierra Nevada Mountains, the mountain men had helped forge a clear picture of western geography. Soon permanent settlers would follow the trails they had blazed.

GOVERNMENT-SPONSORED EXPLORATION

Following the lead of fur trade explorers like Alexander Mackenzie, David Thompson and others', the federal government played a major role in the exploration and development of the U.S. West. The exploratory and scientific aspects of the Lewis and Clark expedition in 1804–06 set a precedent for many government-financed quasi-military expeditions. In 1806 and 1807, Lieutenant Zebulon Pike led an expedition to the Rocky Mountains in Colorado. Major Stephen Long's exploration and mapping of the Great Plains in the years 1819–20 was part of a show of force meant to frighten British fur trappers out of the West. Then, in 1843 and 1844, another military explorer, John C. Frémont, mapped the overland trails to Oregon and California. In the 1850s, the Pacific Railroad surveys explored possible transcontinental railroad routes (see Map 14.1).

In the wake of the pathfinders came hundreds of government geologists and botanists as well as the surveyors who mapped and plotted the West for settlement according to the Land Ordinance of 1785. The basic pattern of land survey and sale established by these measures (see Chapter 7) was followed all the way to the Pacific Ocean. The federal government sold the western public lands at low prices. The federal government also shouldered the expense of Indian removal by making long-term commitments to compensate the Indian people themselves and supporting the forts and soldiers whose task was to maintain peace between settlers and Indian peoples in newly opened areas.

EXPANSION AND INDIAN POLICY

While American artists were painting the way of life of western Indian peoples, eastern Indian tribes were being removed from their homelands to Indian Territory (present-day Oklahoma, Kansas, and Nebraska), a region west of Arkansas, Missouri, and Iowa on the eastern edge of the Great Plains, widely regarded as unfarmable and popularly known as the Great American Desert.

Encroachment on Indian Territory was not long in coming (see Map 14.2). The territory was crossed by the **Santa Fé Trail**, established in 1821; in the 1840s, the northern part was crossed by the heavily traveled Overland Trails to California, Oregon, and the Mormon community in Utah. In 1854, the government abolished the northern half of Indian Territory, establishing the Kansas and Nebraska Territories in its place and opening them to immediate white settlement. The tribes of the area—the Potawatomis, Wyandots, Kickapoos, Sauks, Foxes, Delawares, Shawnees, Kaskaskias, Peorias, Piankashaws, Weas, Miamis, Omahas, Otos, and Missouris—signed treaties accepting either vastly reduced reservations or allotments. Those who accepted allotments—sections of private land—

Santa Fé Trail The 900-mile trail opened by American merchants for trading purposes following Mexico's liberalization of the formerly restrictive trading policies of Spain.

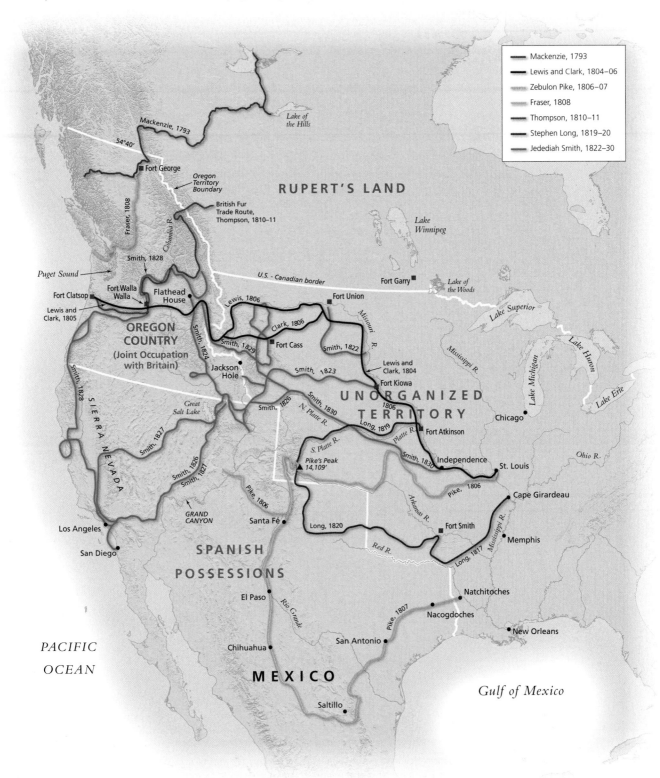

MAP 14.1

Exploration of the Continent, 1804–30 Members of British fur trading companies like Alexander Mackenzie and David Thompson led the way. Lewis and Clark's "voyage of discovery" of 1804–06 was the first of many U.S. government-sponsored western military expeditions. Lieutenant Zebulon Pike crossed the Great Plains in 1806, followed by Major Stephen Long in 1819–20. Meanwhile, American fur trappers, among them the much-traveled Jedediah Smith, became well acquainted with the Far West as they hunted beaver for their pelts.

WHAT ROLE did the routes taken by major expeditions westward between 1804 and 1830 play in shaping United States policy in the West?

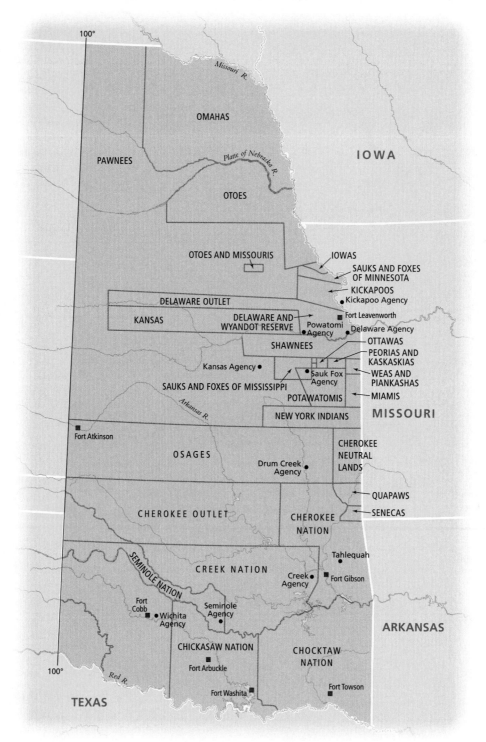

MAP 14.2

Indian Territory Before the Kansas-Nebraska Act of 1854   Indian Territory lay west of Arkansas, Missouri, and Iowa and east of Mexican Territory. Most of the Indian peoples who lived there in the 1830s and the 1840s had been "removed" from east of the Mississippi River. The southern part (now Oklahoma) was inhabited by peoples from the Old Southwest: the Cherokees, Chickasaws, Choctaws, Creeks, and Seminoles. North of that (in what is now Kansas and Nebraska) lived peoples who had been removed from the Old Northwest. All these Indian peoples had trouble adjusting not only to a new climate and a new way of life but also to the close proximity of some Indian tribes who were their traditional enemies.

DISCUSS THE effect of the Kansas-Nebraska Act on Indian tribes and territories.

often sold them, under pressure, to white people. Thus, many of the Indian people who had hoped for independence and escape from white pressures in Indian Territory lost both their autonomy and their tribal identity.

The people in the southern part of Indian Territory, in what is now Oklahoma, fared somewhat better. Those members of the southern tribes—the Cherokees, Chickasaws, Choctaws, Creeks, and Seminoles—who had survived the trauma of forcible removal from the Southeast in the 1830s, quickly created impressive new communities. Until after the Civil War, these southern tribes were able to withstand outside pressures and remain the self-governing communities that treaties had assured them they would be.

The Politics of Expansion

America's rapid expansion had many consequences, but perhaps the most significant was that it reinforced Americans' sense of themselves as pioneering people. Ever since the time of Daniel Boone, venturing into the wilderness has held a special place in the American imagination and been seen almost as a right.

Manifest Destiny, an Expansionist Ideology

How did Americans justify their restless expansionism? After all, the United States was already a very large country with much undeveloped land. In 1845, newspaperman John O'Sullivan provided such a justification. It was, he wrote, "our **manifest destiny** to overspread the continent allotted by Providence for the free development of our yearly multiplying millions." Sullivan argued that Americans had a God-given right to bring the benefits of American democracy to other, more backward peoples—meaning Mexicans and Indians—by force, if necessary. The notion of manifest destiny summed up the powerful combination of pride in what America had achieved and missionary zeal and racist attitudes toward other peoples that lay behind the thinking of many expansionists. Americans were proud of their rapid development: the surge in population, the remarkable canals and railroads, the grand scale of the American enterprise. Why shouldn't America be even bigger?

Expansionism was deeply tied to national politics. O'Sullivan, whose "manifest destiny" became the expansionist watchword, was not a neutral observer: he was the editor of the *Democratic Review*, a party newspaper. Most Democrats were wholehearted supporters of expansion, whereas many Whigs (especially in the North) opposed it. Whigs welcomed most of the changes brought by industrialization but advocated strong government policies that would guide growth and development within the country's existing boundaries. They feared (correctly, as it turned out) that expansion would raise the contentious issue of the extension of slavery to new territories.

On the other hand, many Democrats feared the industrialization that the Whigs welcomed. Where the Whigs saw economic progress, Democrats saw economic depression, uncontrolled urban growth, and growing social unrest. For many Democrats, the answer to the nation's social ills was to continue to follow Thomas Jefferson's vision of establishing agriculture in the new territories in order to counterbalance industrialization. Another factor in the political struggle over expansion in the 1840s was that many Democrats were Southerners, for whom the continual expansion of cotton-growing lands was a matter of social faith as well as economic necessity.

WHAT WERE the major differences between the Oregon, Texas, and California frontiers?

Review Summary

12–4
John L. O'Sullivan, *The Great Nation of Futurity* (1845)

Manifest destiny Doctrine, first expressed in 1845, that the expansion of white Americans across the continent was inevitable and ordained by God.

MAP 14.3
The Overland Trails, 1840 All the great trails west started at the Missouri River. The Oregon, California, and Mormon Trails followed the Platte River into Wyoming, crossed South Pass, and divided in western Wyoming. The much harsher Santa Fé Trail stretched 900 miles southwest across the Great Plains. All of the trails crossed Indian Territory and, to greater or lesser extent, Mexican possessions as well.

WHAT DANGERS did settlers face as they followed the overland trails?

These were politicians' reasons. The average farmer moved west for many other reasons: land hunger, national pride, plain and simple curiosity, and a sense of adventure.

THE OVERLAND TRAILS

The 2,000-mile trip on the Overland Trails from the banks of the Missouri River to Oregon and California usually took seven months, sometimes more. Travel was slow, dangerous, tedious, and exhausting. Yet despite the risks, settlers streamed west: 5,000 to Oregon by 1845 and about 3,000 to California by 1848 (before the discovery of gold) (see Map 14.3).

Pioneers had many motives for making the trip. Glowing reports from Oregon's Willamette Valley, for example, seemed to promise economic opportunity and healthy surroundings, an alluring combination to farmers in the malaria-prone Midwest who had been hard hit by the Panic of 1837. But rational motives do not tell the whole story. Many men were motivated by a sense of adventure, by a desire to experience the unknown.

12–3
Across the Plains with Catherine Sager Pringle (1844)

17–2
Lydia Allen Rudd, Diary of Westward Travel (1852)

Few pioneers traveled alone, partly because they feared Indian attack (which was rare) but largely because they needed help fording rivers or crossing mountains with heavy wagons. Most Oregon pioneers traveled with their families but usually also joined a larger group, forming a "train." In the earliest years, when the route was still uncertain, trains hired "pilots," generally former fur trappers.

Wagon trains started westward as soon as the prairies were green (thus ensuring feed for the livestock). The daily routine was quickly established. Men took care of the moving equipment and the animals, while the women cooked and kept track of the children. Slowly, at a rate of about fifteen miles a day, the wagon trains moved west. In addition to tedium and exhaustion, wagon trains were beset by such trail hazards as illness and accident. Danger from Indian attack, which all pioneers feared, was actually very small. It appears that unprovoked white attacks on Indians were more common than the reverse.

In contrast, cholera killed at least a thousand people a year in 1849 and in the early 1850s, when it was common along sections of the trail along the Platte River. Drownings were not uncommon, nor were accidental ax wounds or shootings, and children sometimes fell out of wagons and were run over. The members of the wagon train community provided support for survivors: men helped widows drive their wagons onward, women nursed and tended babies whose mothers were dead, and at least one parentless family, the seven Sager children, were brought to Oregon in safety.

By 1860, almost 300,000 people had traveled the Overland Trails to Oregon or California. Ruts from the wagon wheels can be seen in a number of places along the route even today. In 1869, the completion of the transcontinental railroad marked the end of the wagon train era (see Figure 14.1).

This painting by William Henry Jackson shows the wagon of westward migrants waiting at Council Bluffs, Iowa, to cross the Missouri River on the ferry established by the Mormons. At the height of the migration this was a major bottleneck: some people waited as long as ten days for their turn to cross.

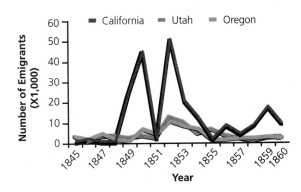

Figure 14.1 Overland Emigration to Oregon, California, and Utah, 1840–60

Before 1849, the westward migration consisted primarily of family groups going to Oregon or Utah. The discovery of gold in California dramatically changed the migration: through 1854, most migrants were single men "rushing" to California, which remained the favored destination up until 1860. Over the twenty-year period from 1840 to 1860, the Overland Trails were transformed from difficult and dangerous routes to well-marked and well-served thoroughfares.

John Unruh Jr., *The Plains Across* (Champaign-Urbana: University of Illinois Press, 1979), pp. 119–20.

OREGON

The American settlement of Oregon provides a capsule example of the stages of frontier development. The first contacts between the region's Indian peoples and Europeans were commercial. Spanish, British, Russian, and American ships traded for sea otter skins from the 1780s to about 1810. Subsequently, land-based groups scoured the region for beaver skins as well. In this first "frontier of inclusion" there were frequent contacts, many of them sexual, between Indians and Europeans.

Both Great Britain and the United States claimed the Oregon Country by right of discovery, but in the Convention of 1818, the two nations agreed to occupy it jointly, postponing a final decision on its disposition. In reality, the British clearly dominated the region. In 1824, the Hudson's Bay Company consolidated Britain's position by establishing a major fur trading post at Fort Vancouver, on the banks of the Columbia River. Like all fur-trading ventures, the post exemplified the racial mixing of a "frontier of inclusion." Fort Vancouver housed a polyglot population of eastern Indians (Delawares and Iroquois), local Chinook Indians, French and métis from Canada, British traders, and Hawaiians. But the effect of the fur trade on native tribes in Oregon was catastrophic; suffering the fate of all Indian peoples after their initial contact with Europeans, they were decimated by European diseases.

The first permanent European settlers in Oregon were retired fur trappers and their Indian wives and families. The next to arrive were Protestant and Catholic. None of these missionaries was very successful. Epidemics had taken the lives of many of the region's peoples, and those who were left were disinclined to give up their nomadic life and settle down as the missionaries wanted them to do.

Finally, in the 1840s, came the Midwest farmers who would make up the majority of Oregon's permanent settlers, carried on the wave of enthusiasm known as "Oregon fever" and lured by free land and patriotism. By 1845, Oregon boasted 5,000 American settlers, most of them living in the Willamette Valley and laying claim to lands to which they had as yet no legal right. Their arrival signaled Oregon's transition away from a "frontier of inclusion."

In June 1846, Britain and the United States concluded a treaty establishing the 49th parallel as the U.S.–Canada border but leaving the island of Vancouver in British hands. The British then quietly wound up their declining fur trade in the region. In 1849, the Hudson's Bay Company closed Fort Vancouver and moved its operations to Victoria, thus ending the Pacific Northwest's largely successful experience with joint occupancy. Oregon's Donation Land Claim Act of 1850 codified the practice of giving 320 acres to each white male age eighteen or over and 640 acres to each married couple to settle in the territory (African Americans, Hawaiians, and American Indians were excluded).

The white settlers realized that they had to forge strong community bonds if they hoped to survive on their distant frontier. Cooperation and mutual aid were the rule. Until well into the 1850s, residents organized yearly parties that traveled back along the last stretches of the **Oregon Trail** to help straggling parties making their way to the territory. Kinship networks were strong and vital: many pioneers came to join family who had migrated before them. Food sharing and mutual labor were essential in the early years when crop and livestock loss to weather or natural predators was common. Help, even to total strangers, was customary in times of illness or death.

Relations with the small and unthreatening disease-thinned local Indian tribes were generally peaceful until 1847, when Cayuse Indians killed the missionaries Marcus and Narcissa Whitman. Their deaths triggered a series of "wars" against the remaining native people. A "frontier of exclusion" had been achieved.

Oregon Trail   Overland trail of more than two thousand miles that carried American settlers from the Midwest to new settlements in Oregon, California, and Utah.

This view of Fort Vancouver on the Columbia River shows established agriculture and thriving commerce, indicated by the large sailing ship on the river, which is probably the Hudson's Bay Company yearly supply ship from England. It was a scene like this that led Narcissa Whitman to call Fort Vancouver "the New York of the Pacific."

Nonetheless, the process by which Oregon became part of the United States (it was admitted as a state in 1859) was relatively peaceful, especially when compared with American expansion into the Spanish provinces of New Mexico and Texas.

THE SANTA FÉ TRADE

Commerce with Santa Fé, first settled by colonists from Mexico in 1609, and the center of the Spanish frontier province of New Mexico, had long been desired by American traders. But Spain had forcefully resisted American penetration.

When Mexico gained its independence from Spain in 1821, this exclusionary policy changed. American traders were now welcome in Santa Fé, but the trip over the legendary Santa Fé Trail from Independence, Missouri, was a forbidding 900 miles of arid plains, deserts, and mountains. The number of people venturing west in the trading caravans increased yearly because the profits were so great. By the 1840s, a few hundred American trappers and traders (called *extranjeros*, or "foreigners") lived permanently in New Mexico. In Santa Fé, some American merchants married daughters of important local families, suggesting the start of the inclusive stage of frontier contact.

Tejanos Persons of Spanish or Mexican descent born in Texas.

Settlements and trading posts soon grew up along the long Santa Fé Trail. One of the most famous was Bent's Fort, on the Arkansas River in what is now eastern Colorado, which did a brisk trade in beaver skins and buffalo robes. Like most trading posts, it had a multiethnic population. This racially and economically mixed existence was characteristic of all early trading frontiers, but another western frontier, the American agricultural settlement in Texas, was different from the start.

MEXICAN TEXAS

In 1821, when Mexico gained its independence from Spain, there were 2,240 Tejano (Spanish-speaking) residents of Texas. As was customary throughout New Spain, communities were organized around three centers: missions and *presidios* (forts), which formed the nuclei of towns, and the large cattle-raising *ranchos* on which rural living depended. As elsewhere in New Spain, society was divided into two classes: the *ricos* (rich), who claimed Spanish descent, and the mixed-blood *pobres* (poor). Most **Tejanos** were neither ricos nor vaqueros but small farmers or common laborers who led hardscrabble frontier lives. But all Tejanos, rich and poor, faced the constant threat of raids by Comanche Indians.

Legendary warriors, the Comanches raided the small Texas settlements at will and even struck deep into Mexico itself. The nomadic Comanches followed the immense buffalo herds on which they depended for food and clothing. Their relentless raids on the Texas settlements rose from a determination to hold onto this rich buffalo territory, for the buffalo provided all that they wanted. They had no interest in being converted by mission priests or incorporated into mixed-race trading communities.

AMERICANS IN TEXAS

In 1821, seeking to increase the strength of its buffer zone between the heart of Mexico and the marauding Comanches, the Mexican government granted Moses Austin of Missouri an area of 18,000 square miles within the territory of Texas. Moses died shortly thereafter, and the grant was taken up by his son Stephen F. Austin, who became the first American empresario (land agent). From the beginning, the American settlement of Texas differed markedly from that of other frontiers. Elsewhere, Americans frequently settled on land to which Indian peoples still held title, or, as in the case of Oregon, they occupied lands to which other

Painted by George Catlin in about 1834, this scene, *Commanche Village Life*, shows how the everyday life of the Comanches was tied to buffalo. The women in the foreground are scraping buffalo hide, and buffalo meat can be seen drying on racks. The men and boys may be planning their next buffalo hunt.

countries also made claim. In contrast, the Texas settlement was fully legal: Austin and other **empresarios** owned their lands as a result of formal contracts with the Mexican government.

Insisting that "no frontiersman who has no other occupation than that of hunter will be received—no drunkard, no gambler, no profane swearer, no idler," Austin chose instead prosperous southern slave owners eager to expand the lands devoted to cotton. Soon Americans (including African American slaves, to whose presence the Mexican government turned a blind eye) outnumbered Tejanos by nearly two to one.

The Austin settlement of 1821 was followed by others, twenty-six in all, concentrating in the fertile river bottoms of eastern Texas (along the Sabine River) and south central Texas (the Brazos and the Colorado Rivers). These large settlements were highly organized farming enterprises whose principal crop was cotton, grown by African American slave labor and sold in the international market.

Austin's colonists and those who settled later were predominantly Southerners who viewed Texas as a natural extension of the cotton frontier in Mississippi and Louisiana. These settlers created "**enclaves**" (self-contained communities) that had little contact with Tejanos or Indian peoples. In fact, although they lived in Mexican territory, most Americans never bothered to learn Spanish. Yet, because of the nature of agreements made by the empresarios, the Americans could not set up local American-style governments like the one created by settlers in Oregon. Like the immigrants who flooded into East Coast cities (see Chapter 13), the Americans in Texas were immigrants to another country—but one to which they did not intend to adapt.

For a brief period, Texas was big enough to hold three communities: Comanche, Tejano, and American. Each group would fight to hold its land: the Comanches, their rich hunting grounds; the Mexicans, their towns and ranchos; and the newcomers, the Americans, their rich land grants.

The balance among the three communities in Texas was broken in 1828, when centrists gained control of the government in Mexico City and, in a dramatic shift of policy, decided to exercise firm control over the northern province. As the Mexican government restricted American immigration, outlawed slavery, levied customs duties and taxes, and planned other measures, Americans seethed and talked of rebellion. Bolstering their cause were as many as 20,000 additional Americans, many of them openly expansionist, who flooded into Texas after 1830.

Many of the post-1830 immigrants were vehemently anti-Mexican. Statements of racial superiority were commonplace, and even Stephen Austin wrote in 1836 that he saw the Texas conflict as one of barbarism on the part of "a mongrel Spanish-Indian and negro race, against civilization and the Anglo-American race."

Between 1830 and 1836, in spite of the mediation efforts of Austin, the mood on both the Mexican and the American-Texan sides became more belligerent. In the fall of 1835, war finally broke out, and a volunteer American and Tejano army assembled. After the disastrous defeat at the **Alamo** described in the chapter opener, Mexican general and president Antonio López de Santa Anna led his army in pursuit of the remaining army of American and Tejano volunteers commanded by General Sam Houston.

On April 21, 1836, at the San Jacinto River in eastern Texas, Santa Anna thought he had Houston trapped at last. Confident of victory against the exhausted Texans, Santa Anna's army rested in the afternoon, failing even to post sentries. Although Houston advised against it, Houston's men voted to attack immediately rather than wait till the next morning. Shouting "Remember the Alamo!" for the first time, the Texans completely surprised their opponents and won an overwhelming victory. On May 14, 1836, Santa Anna signed a treaty fixing the southern boundary of the newly independent Republic of Texas at the Rio Grande. The

Empresarios Agents who received a land grant from the Spanish or Mexican government in return for organizing settlements.

Enclave Self-contained community.

Alamo Franciscan mission at San Antonio, Texas that was the site in 1836 of a siege and massacre of Texans by Mexican troops.

MAP 14.4

Texas: From Mexican Province to U.S. State In the space of twenty years, Texas changed shape three times. Initially part of the Mexican province of Coahuila y Tejas, it became the Republic of Texas in 1836, following the Texas Revolt, and was annexed to the United States in that form in 1845. Finally, in the Compromise of 1850 following the Mexican-American War, it took its present shape.

WHO SUPPORTED the formation of the Republic of Texas? What were the forces that resulted in eventual statehood?

Mexican Congress, however, repudiated the treaty and refused to recognize Texan independence (see Map 14.4).

THE REPUBLIC OF TEXAS

The Republic of Texas was unexpectedly rebuffed in another quarter as well. The U.S. Congress refused to grant it statehood when, in 1837, Texas applied for admission to the Union. Petitions opposing the admission of a fourteenth slave state (there were then thirteen free states) poured into Congress. Congressman (and former president) John Quincy Adams of Massachusetts led the opposition to the admission of Texas. Congress debated and ultimately dropped the Texas application.

The unresolved conflict with Mexico put heavy stress on American–Tejano relations. As before, ambitious Anglos married into the Tejano elite, which made it easier for those Tejano families to adjust to the changes in law and commerce that the Americans quickly enacted. But following a temporary recapture of San Antonio by Mexican forces in 1842, positions hardened. Many more of the Tejano elite fled to Mexico, and Americans discussed banishing or imprisoning all Tejanos until the border issue was settled. This was, of course, impossible. Culturally, San Antonio remained a Mexican city long after the Americans had declared independence.

American control over the other Texas residents, the Indians, was also slow in coming. The Comanches still rode the high plains of northern and western Texas. West of the Rio Grande, equally fierce Apache bands were in control. Both groups soon learned to distrust American promises to stay out of their territory, and they did not hesitate to raid settlements and to kill trespassers. Not until after the Civil War and major campaigns by the U.S. Army were these fierce Indian tribes conquered.

Texans continued to press for annexation to the United States, while at the same time seeking recognition and support from Great Britain. The idea of an independent and expansionist republic on its southern border that might gain the support of America's traditional enemy alarmed many Americans. Annexation thus became an urgent matter of national politics. This issue also added to the troubles of a governing Whig Party that was already deeply divided by the policies of John Tyler, who had become president by default when William Harrison died in office (see Chapter 11). Tyler raised the issue of annexation in 1844, hoping thereby to ensure his reelection, but the strategy backfired. Presenting the annexation treaty to Congress, Secretary of State John Calhoun awakened sectional fears by connecting Texas with the urgent need of southern slave owners to extend slavery.

In a storm of antislavery protest, Whigs rejected the treaty proposed by their own president and ejected Tyler himself from the party. In his place, they chose Henry Clay, the party's longtime standard-bearer, as their presidential candidate. Clay took a noncommittal stance on Texas, favoring annexation, but only if Mexico approved. Since Mexico's emphatic disapproval was well known, Clay's position was widely interpreted as a politician's effort not to alienate voters on either side of the fence.

In contrast, in the Democratic Party, wholehearted and outspoken expansionists seized control. The Democrats nominated their first "dark horse" candidate, James K. Polk of Tennessee. Democrats enthusiastically endorsed Polk's platform, which called for "the re-occupation of Oregon and the re-annexation of Texas at the earliest practicable period."

Polk won the 1844 election by a narrow margin. The 1844 election was widely interpreted as a mandate for expansion. Thereupon, John Tyler, in one of his last actions as president, pushed through Congress a joint resolution (which did not require the two-thirds approval by the Senate necessary for treaties) for the annexation of Texas. When Texas entered the Union in December 1845, it was the twenty-eighth state and the fifteenth slave state.

THE MEXICAN-AMERICAN WAR

James K. Polk lived up to his campaign promises. In 1846, he peacefully added Oregon south of the 49th parallel to the United States; in 1848, following the **Mexican-American War**, he acquired Mexico's northern provinces of California and New Mexico as well. Thus, with the annexation of Texas, the United States, in the short space of three years, had added 1.5 million square miles of territory, an increase of nearly 70 percent. Polk was indeed the "manifest destiny" president.

ORIGINS OF THE WAR

In the spring of 1846, just as the controversy over Oregon was drawing to a peaceful conclusion, tensions with Mexico grew more serious. Because the United States supported the Texas claim of all land north of the Rio Grande, it became embroiled

WHAT WERE the most important consequences of the Mexican-American War?

myhistorylab
Review Summary

Mexican-American War   War fought between Mexico and the United States between 1846 and 1848 over control of territory in southwest North America.

in a border dispute with Mexico. In June 1845, Polk sent General Zachary Taylor to Texas, and by October a force of 3,500 Americans were on the Nueces River with orders to defend Texas in the event of a Mexican invasion.

Polk had something bigger than border protection in mind. He coveted the continent clear to the Pacific Ocean. At the same time that he sent Taylor to Texas, Polk secretly instructed the Pacific naval squadron to seize the California ports if Mexico declared war. He also wrote the American consul in Monterey, Thomas Larkin, that a peaceful takeover of California by its residents—Spanish Mexicans and Americans alike—would not be unwelcome.

In April 1846, a brief skirmish between American and Mexican soldiers broke out in the disputed zone. Polk seized on the event, sending a war message to Congress: "Mexico has passed the boundary of the United States, has invaded our territory and shed American blood upon American soil. . . . War exists, and, notwithstanding all our efforts to avoid it, exists by the act of Mexico herself." This claim of President Polk's was, of course, contrary to fact. On May 13, 1846, Congress declared war on Mexico (see Map 14.5).

MR. POLK'S WAR

From the beginning, the Mexican-American War was politically divisive. Whig critics in Congress, among them a gawky young congressman from Illinois named Abraham Lincoln, questioned Polk's account of the border incident. They accused the president of misleading Congress and of maneuvering the country into an unnecessary war. As the Mexican-American War dragged on and casualties and costs mounted, opposition increased, especially among northern antislavery Whigs. Many Northerners asked why Polk had been willing to settle for only a part of Oregon but was so eager to pursue a war for slave territory. Thus, expansionist dreams served to fuel sectional antagonisms.

Whigs termed the war with Mexico "Mr. Polk's War," but the charge was not just a Whig jibe. Although he lacked a military background, Polk assumed the overall planning of the war's strategy. By his personal attention to the coordination of civilian political goals and military requirements, Polk gave a new and expanded definition to the

---

QUICK REVIEW

War with Mexico

- Polk sought a war that would give United States control of California.
- Mexico fought hard but could not match American military.
- Treaty of Guadalupe Hidalgo (1848): Mexico gave up claim to Texas north of Rio Grande, Alta California, and New Mexico.

General Winfield Scott's amphibious attack on the Mexican coastal city of Veracruz in March 1847 was greeted with wide popular acclaim in the United States. It was the first successful amphibious attack in U.S. military history. Popular interest in the battles of the Mexican-American War was fed by illustrations such as this in newspapers and magazines.

LANDING OF THE AMERICAN FORCES UNDER GENL SCOTT
AT VERA CRUZ MARCH 9th 1847

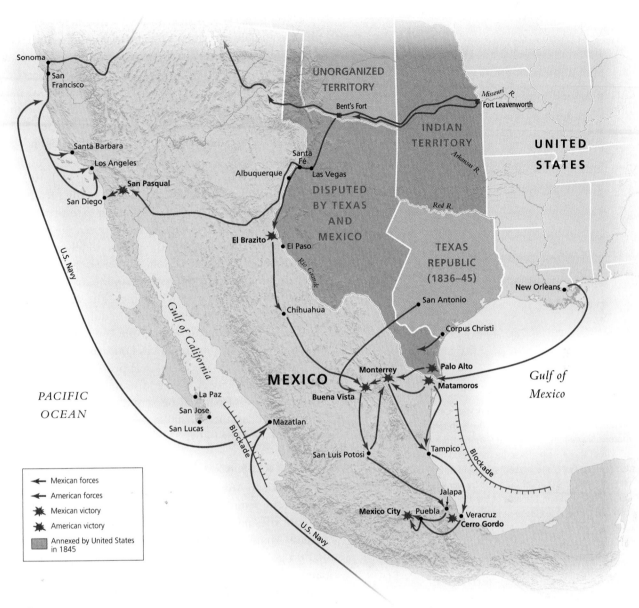

MAP 14.5
The Mexican-American War, 1846–48   The Mexican-American War began with an advance by U.S. forces into the disputed area between the Nueces River and the Rio Grande in Texas. The war's major battles were fought by General Zachary Taylor in northern Mexico and General Winfield Scott in Veracruz and Mexico City. Meanwhile Colonel Stephen Kearny secured New Mexico and, with the help of the U.S. Navy and John C. Frémont's troops, California.

WHY WAS the United States more successful than Mexico in achieving its goals?

role of the president as commander in chief during wartime. By the end of 1846, the northern provinces that Polk had coveted were secured, but contrary to his expectations, Mexico refused to negotiate. In March 1847, General Winfield Scott launched an amphibious attack on the coastal city of Veracruz and rapidly captured it. Americans celebrated these twin victories joyously, but they were to be the last easy victories of the war. It took Scott six months of brutal fighting against stubborn Mexican resistance on the battlefield and harassing guerrilla raids to force his way to Mexico City. American troops reacted bitterly to their high casualty rates, retaliating against Mexican citizens with acts of murder, robbery, and rape. In September, Scott took Mexico City, and Mexican resistance came to an end.

MAP 14.6

Territory Added, 1845–53 James K. Polk was elected president in 1844 on an expansionist platform. He lived up to most of his campaign rhetoric by gaining the Oregon Country (to the 49th parallel) peacefully from the British, Texas by the presidential action of his predecessor John Tyler, and present-day California, Arizona, Nevada, Utah, New Mexico, and part of Colorado by war with Mexico. In the short space of three years, the size of the United States grew by 70 percent. In 1853, the Gadsden Purchase added another 30,000 square miles.

WHAT CHALLENGES did the United States face as it absorbed substantial new territories?

12–5
Thomas Corwin, *Against the Mexican War* (1847)

WHAT KINDS of people participated in the California Gold Rush?

myhistorylab

Review Summary

Californios Californians of Spanish descent.

With the American army went a special envoy, Nicholas Trist, who delivered Polk's terms for peace. In the Treaty of Guadalupe Hidalgo, signed February 2, 1848, Mexico ceded its northern provinces of California and New Mexico (which included present-day Arizona, Utah, Nevada, and part of Colorado) and accepted the Rio Grande as the boundary of Texas. The United States agreed to pay Mexico $15 million and assume about $2 million in individual claims against that nation.

When Trist returned to Washington with the treaty, however, Polk was furious. He had actually recalled Trist after Scott's sweeping victory, intending to send a new envoy with greater demands, but Trist had ignored the recall order. "All Mexico!" had become the phrase widely used by those in favor of further expansion, Polk among them. But two very different groups opposed further expansion. The first group, composed of northern Whigs. The second group was composed of Southerners who realized that Mexicans could not be kept as conquered people but would have to be offered territorial government as Louisiana had been offered in 1804. Bowing to these political protests, Polk reluctantly accepted the treaty. A later addition, the $10 million Gadsden Purchase of parts of present-day New Mexico and Arizona, added another 30,000 square miles to the United States in 1853 (see Map 14.6).

THE PRESS AND POPULAR WAR ENTHUSIASM

The Mexican-American War was the first war in which regular, on-the-scene reporting by representatives of the press caught the mass of ordinary citizens up in the war's daily events. Thanks to the recently invented telegraph, newspapers could get the latest news from their reporters, who were among the world's first war correspondents. The "penny press," with more than a decade's experience of reporting urban crime and scandals, was quick to realize that the public's appetite for sensational war news was apparently insatiable. For the first time in American history, accounts by journalists, and not the opinions of politicians, became the major shapers of popular attitudes toward a war. From beginning to end, news of the war stirred unprecedented popular excitement (see Seeing History).

Exciting, sobering, and terrible, war news had a deep hold on the popular imagination. It was a lesson newspaper publishers never forgot.

CALIFORNIA AND THE GOLD RUSH

In the early 1840s, California was inhabited by many seminomadic Indian tribes whose people numbered approximately 50,000. There were also some 7,000 **Californios**, descendants of the Spanish-Mexican pioneers who had begun to settle in 1769. Even American annexation at the end of the Mexican-American War changed little for the handful of Americans on this remote frontier. But then came the gold rush of 1849, which changed California permanently.

War News from Mexico

The unprecedented immediacy of the news reporting from the battlefields of the Mexican-American War, transmitted for the first time by telegraph, is captured in this painting by the American artist Richard Caton Woodville, painted in 1848 (the year the war ended). Woodville was one of a number of genre painters who enlivened their depictions of everyday life and ordinary people by focusing on political debates or dramatic moments like the one shown here.

Almost every aspect of this painting is political commentary. The central figure in the painting is standing on the porch of the American Hotel reading the latest war news to the crowd of men gathered around him from a cheap "penny paper" full of sensational stories, war news, and lithographs of battle scenes from the war. Although the audience seems deeply engaged, the range of expressions reminds the viewer that the war was very divisive, with many antislavery Northerners in outright opposition. The placement of the African American man at a lower level on the step is a clear statement of his exclusion from political participation. Don't overlook the woman leaning out of the window on the right side of the painting. She too is excluded from politics but is obviously just as interested and concerned as the men. Woodville's inclusion of the black child in a white smock seems to be an ambiguous statement about the impact of the Mexican-American War on slavery. ■

ARE YOU surprised at the extent of political commentary in this painting? Are paintings an appropriate media for political opinion?

Richard Caton Woodville, "War News from Mexico," Oil on canvas. Manovgian Foundation on loan to the National Gallery of Art, Washington, DC. © Board of Trustees, National Gallery of Art, Washington.

RUSSIAN–CALIFORNIOS TRADE

The first outsiders to penetrate the isolation of Spanish California were not Americans but Russians. A mutually beneficial barter of California food for iron tools and woven cloth from Russia was established in 1806. This arrangement became even brisker after the Russians settled Fort Ross (near present-day Mendocino) in 1812 and led in time to regular trade with Mission San Rafael and Mission Sonoma. That the Russians in Alaska, so far from their own capital, were better supplied with manufactured goods than the Californios is an index of the latter's isolation.

When Mexico became independent in 1821, the California trade was thrown open to ships of all nations. Nevertheless, Californios continued their special relationship with the Russians, exempting them from the taxes and inspections that they required of Americans. However, agricultural productivity declined after 1832, when the Mexican government ordered the secularization of the California missions, and the Russians regretfully turned to the rich farms of the Hudson's Bay Company in the Pacific Northwest for their food supply. In 1841, they sold Fort Ross, and the Russian–Californio connection came to an end.

EARLY AMERICAN SETTLEMENT

It was Johann Augustus Sutter, a Swiss who had settled in California in 1839, becoming a Mexican citizen, who served as a focal point for American settlement in the 1840s. In the 1840s, Sutter offered valuable support to the handful of American overlanders who chose California over Oregon, the destination preferred by most pioneers. Most of these Americans, keenly aware that they were interlopers in Mexican territory, settled near Sutter in California's Central Valley, away from the Californios clustered along the coast.

The 1840s' immigrants made no effort to intermarry with the Californios or to conform to Spanish ways. They were bent on taking over the territory. In June 1846, these Americans banded together at Sonoma in the Bear Flag Revolt (so called because their flag bore a bear emblem), declaring independence from Mexico. The American takeover of California was not confirmed until the Treaty of Guadalupe Hidalgo in 1848.

GOLD!

In January 1848, carpenter James Marshall noticed small flakes of gold in the millrace at Sutter's Mill (present-day Coloma). Soon he and all the rest of John Sutter's employees were panning for gold in California's streams. But not until the autumn of 1848 did the East Coast hear the first rumors about the discovery of gold in California. The spirit of excitement and adventure so recently aroused by the Mexican-American War was now directed toward California, the new El Dorado. Thousands left farms and jobs and headed west, by land and by sea, to make their fortune. Later known as "forty-niners" for the year the gold rush began in earnest, these people came from all parts of the United States—and indeed, from all over the world. They transformed what had been a quiet ranching paradise into a teeming and tumultuous community in search of wealth in California's rivers and streams.

Eighty percent of the forty-niners were Americans. The second largest group of migrants was from nearby Mexico and the western coast of Latin America (13 percent). The remainder came from Europe and Asia (see Figure 14.2).

The presence of Chinese miners surprised many Americans. Several hundred Chinese arrived in California in 1849 and 1850, and in 1852 more than 20,000 landed in San Francisco hoping to share in the wealth of "Gum Sam"

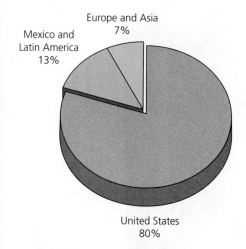

Europe and Asia
7%

Mexico and
Latin America
13%

United States
80%

Figure 14.2 Where the Forty-Niners Came From
Americans drawn to the California gold rush of 1849 encountered a more diverse population than most had previously known. Nearly as novel to them as the 20 percent from foreign countries was the regional variety from within the United States itself.

This drawing of the bar of a gambling saloon in San Francisco in 1855 shows the effects of the gold rush on California. Men from all parts of the world are gathered at this elegant bar in the large cosmopolitan city of San Francisco, which had been only a small trading post before gold was discovered in 1849.

Frank Marryat, "The Bar of a Gambling Saloon," published 1855. Lithograph. Collection of the New-York Historical Society, New York City.

(Golden Mountain). Most came, like the Americans, as temporary sojourners, intending to return home as soon as they made some money. Again, like most of the American miners, the majority of Chinese were men who left their wives at home. The distinctive appearance of the Chinese, added to the threat of economic competition that they posed, quickly aroused American hostility. A special tax was imposed on foreign miners in 1852, and in the 1870s, Chinese immigration was sharply curtailed.

In 1849, as the gold rush began in earnest, San Francisco, the major entry port and supply point, sprang to life. From a settlement of 1,000 in 1848, it grew

Chinese first came to California in 1849 attracted by the gold rush. Frequently, however, they were forced off their claims by intolerant whites. Rather than enjoy an equal chance in the goldfields, they were often forced to work as servants or in other menial occupations.

QUICK REVIEW

Discovery of Gold

♦ Gold discovered at Sutter's Mill in 1848.

♦ Most forty-niners were Americans.

♦ Gold rush led rapid growth of San Francisco.

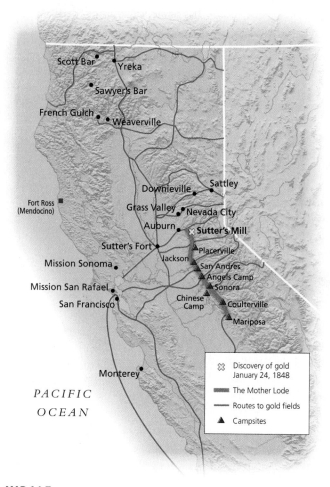

MAP 14.7

California in the Gold Rush This map shows the major gold camps along the mother lode in the western foothills of the Sierra Nevada Mountains. Gold seekers reached the camps by crossing the Sierra Nevada near Placerville on the Overland Trail or by sea via San Francisco. The main area of Spanish-Mexican settlement, the coastal region between Monterey and Los Angeles, was remote from the goldfields.

Warren A. Beck and Ynez D. Haase, *Historical Atlas of California* (Norman: University of Oklahoma Press, 1974), map 50.

WHAT WAS life like in the California gold camps during the gold rush?

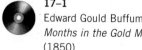

Exploring America:
The Unwelcome Mat

17-1
Edward Gould Buffum, *Six Months in the Gold Mines* (1850)

to a city of 35,000 in 1850. This surge suggested that the real money to be made in California was not in panning for gold but in feeding, clothing, housing, provisioning, and entertaining the miners. The white population of California jumped from an estimated pre–gold rush figure of 11,000 to more than 100,000 by 1852. California was admitted into the Union as a state in 1850.

MINING CAMPS

As had occurred in San Francisco, most mining camps boomed almost instantly to life, but unlike San Francisco, they were empty again within a few years. Most miners lived in tents or hovels, unwilling to take time from mining to build themselves decent quarters. They cooked monotonous meals of beans, bread, and bacon or, if they had money, bought meals at expensive restaurants and boardinghouses. They led a cheerless, uncomfortable, and unhealthy existence, especially during the long, rainy winter months, with few distractions apart from the saloon, the gambling hall, and the prostitute's bed (see Map 14.7).

Most miners were young, unmarried, and unsuccessful. Only a small percentage ever struck it rich in California. Gold deposits that were accessible with pick and shovel were soon exhausted, and the deeper deposits required capital and machinery. Increasingly, those who stayed on in California had to give up the status of independent miners and become wage earners for large mining concerns.

Every mining community had its saloonkeepers, gamblers, prostitutes, merchants, and restauranteurs. Like the miners themselves, these people were transients, always ready to pick up and move at the word of a new gold strike. The majority of women in the early mining camps were prostitutes. Most of the other women were hardworking wives of miners, and in this predominantly male society, they made good money doing domestic work by keeping boardinghouses, cooking, and doing laundry.

Partly because few people put any effort into building communities violence was endemic in mining areas, and much of it was racial. Discrimination, especially against Chinese, Mexicans, and African Americans, was common.

By the mid-1850s, the immediate effects of the gold rush had passed. California had a booming population, a thriving agriculture, and a corporate mining industry. The gold rush also left California with a population that was larger, more affluent, and (in urban San Francisco) more culturally sophisticated than that in other newly settled territories. And it was significantly more multicultural than the rest of the nation, for many of the Chinese and Mexicans, as well as immigrants from many European countries, remained in California after the gold rush subsided. But the gold rush left some permanent scars, and not just on the foothills landscape: the virtual extermination of the California Indian peoples, the dispossession of many Californios who were legally deprived of their land grants, and the growth of racial animosity toward the Chinese in particular.

THE POLITICS OF MANIFEST DESTINY

In three short years, from 1845 to 1848, the territory of the United States grew an incredible 70 percent, and a continental nation took shape. This expansion, pushed by economic desires and feelings of American cultural superiority, led directly to the emergence of the divisive issue of slavery as the dominant issue in national politics.

THE WILMOT PROVISO

In 1846, almost all the northern members of the Whig Party opposed Democratic president James Polk's belligerent expansionism on antislavery grounds. Northern Whigs correctly feared that expansion would reopen the issue of slavery in the territories. But the outpouring of popular enthusiasm for the Mexican-American War convinced most Whig congressmen that they needed to vote military appropriations for the war in spite of their misgivings.

Ironically, it was not the Whigs but a freshman Democratic congressman from Pennsylvania, David Wilmot, who opened the door to sectional controversy over expansion. In August 1846, only a few short months after the beginning of the Mexican-American War, Wilmot proposed, in an amendment to a military appropriations bill, that slavery be banned in all the territories acquired from Mexico. In the debate and voting that followed, something new and ominous occurred: southern Whigs joined southern Democrats to vote against the measure, while Northerners of both parties supported it. Sectional interest had triumphed over party loyalty.

The **Wilmot Proviso** was so controversial that it was deleted from the necessary military appropriations bills during the Mexican-American War. But in 1848, following the Treaty of Guadalupe Hidalgo, the question of the expansion of slavery could no longer be avoided or postponed. Antislavery advocates from the North argued with proslavery Southerners in a debate that was much more prolonged and bitter than in the Missouri Crisis debate of 1819. The Wilmot Proviso posed a fundamental challenge to both parties. Neither the Democrats nor the Whigs could

WHAT KEY factors explain the outcome of the election of 1848?

Review Summary

myhistorylab
Overview: *Expansion Causes the First Splits in the Second American Party System*

Wilmot Proviso   The amendment offered by Pennsylvania Democrat David Wilmot in 1846 which stipulated that "as an express and fundamental condition to the acquisition of any territory from the Republic of Mexico ... neither slavery nor involuntary servitude shall ever exist in any part of said territory."

OVERVIEW	Expansion Causes the First Splits in the Second American Party System

1844	Whigs reject President John Tyler's move to annex Texas and expel him from the Whig Party.
	Southern Democrats choose expansionist James K. Polk as their presidential candidate, passing over Martin Van Buren, who is against expansion.
	Liberty Party runs abolitionist James Birney for president, attracting northern antislavery Whigs.
1846	The Wilmot Proviso, proposing to ban slavery in the territories that might be gained in the Mexican-American War, splits both parties: southern Whigs and Democrats oppose the measure; northern Whigs and Democrats support it.
1848	The new Free-Soil Party runs northern Democrat Martin Van Buren for president, gaining 10 percent of the vote from abolitionists, antislavery Whigs, and some northern Democrats. This strong showing by a third party causes Democrat Lewis Cass to lose the electoral votes of New York and Pennsylvania, allowing the Whig Zachary Taylor to win.

In 1848, the Whigs nominated a hero of the Mexican-American War, General Zachary Taylor, who ran on his military exploits. In this campaign poster, every letter of Taylor's name is decorated with scenes from the recent war, which had seized the popular imagination in a way no previous conflict had done.

QUICK REVIEW

Slavery and the Election of 1848

◆ Democratic candidate Lewis Cass argued that territorial residents should decide issue of slavery.

◆ Whig nominee Zachary Taylor remained silent on slavery issue.

◆ Taylor's election gave country first president from Lower South.

Liberty Party The first antislavery political party, formed in 1840.

Popular sovereignty A solution to the slavery crisis suggested by Michigan senator Lewis Cass by which territorial residents, not Congress, would decide slavery's fate.

take a strong stand on the amendment because neither party could get its northern and southern wings to agree.

THE FREE-SOIL MOVEMENT

Why did David Wilmot propose this controversial measure? Wilmot, a northern Democrat, was propelled not by ideology but by the pressure of practical politics. The dramatic rise of the **Liberty Party**, founded in 1840 by abolitionists, threatened to take votes away from both the Whig and the Democratic parties.

The Liberty Party took an uncompromising stance against slavery. The party proposed to prohibit the admission of slave states to the Union, end slavery in the District of Columbia, and abolish the interstate slave trade that was vital to the expansion of cotton growing into the Old Southwest. Liberty Party doctrine was too uncompromising for the mass of northern voters, who immediately realized that the southern states would leave the Union before accepting it. Still, many Northerners opposed slavery. From this sentiment, the Free-Soil Party was born.

The free-soil argument was a calculated adjustment of abolitionist principles to practical politics. It shifted the focus from the question of the morality of slavery to the ways in which slavery posed a threat to northern expansion. The free-soil doctrine thus established a direct link between expansion, which most Americans supported, and sectional politics.

Free-soilers were willing to allow slavery to continue in the existing slave states because they supported the Union, not because they approved of slavery. They were unwilling, however, to allow the extension of slavery to new and unorganized territory. If the South were successful in extending slavery, they argued, northern farmers who moved west would find themselves competing at an economic disadvantage with large planters using slave labor. Free-soilers also insisted that the northern values of freedom and individualism would be destroyed if the slave-based southern labor system were allowed to spread.

Many free-soilers really meant "anti-black" when they said "antislavery." They proposed to ban all African American people from the new territories, Most Northerners were unwilling to consider social equality for African Americans, free or slave. Banning all black people from the western territories seemed a simple solution.

THE ELECTION OF 1848

A swirl of emotions—pride, expansionism, sectionalism, abolitionism, free-soil sentiment—surrounded the election of 1848. Lewis Cass of Michigan, the Democratic nominee for president (Polk, in poor health, declined to run for a second term), proposed to apply the doctrine of popular sovereignty to the crucial slave–free issue. **Popular sovereignty** was based on the accepted constitutional principle that decisions about slavery should be made at the state rather than the national level. In reality, popular sovereignty was an admission of the national failure to resolve sectional differences.

For their part, the Whigs passed over perennial candidate Henry Clay and turned to a war hero, General Zachary Taylor. Taylor, a Louisiana slaveholder, refused to take a position on the Wilmot Proviso, allowing both northern and southern voters to hope that he agreed with them.

The deliberate vagueness of the two major candidates displeased many northern voters. An uneasy mixture of disaffected Democrats (among them David Wilmot) and Whigs joined former Liberty Party voters to support the candidate

CHRONOLOGY

1609	First Spanish settlement in New Mexico
1670s	British and French Canadians begin fur trade in western Canada
1716	First Spanish settlements in Texas
1769	First Spanish settlement in California
1780s	New England ships begin sea otter trade in Pacific Northwest
1793	Alexander Mackenzie of the North West Company reaches the Pacific Ocean
1803	Louisiana Purchase
1804–06	Lewis and Clark expedition
1806	Russian–Californio trade begins
1806–07	Zebulon Pike's expedition across the Great Plains to the Rocky Mountains
1819–20	Stephen Long's expedition across the Great Plains
1821	Hudson's Bay Company gains dominance of western fur trade
	Mexico seizes independence from Spain
	Santa Fé Trail opens, soon protected by U.S. military
	Stephen F. Austin becomes first American empresario in Texas
1824	First fur rendezvous sponsored by Rocky Mountain Fur Company
	Hudson's Bay Company establishes Fort Vancouver in Oregon Country
1830	Indian Removal Act moves eastern Indians to Indian Territory

1833–34	Prince Maximilian and Karl Bodmer visit Plains Indians
1834	Jason Lee establishes first mission in Oregon Country
1835	Texas revolts against Mexico
1836	Battles of the Alamo and San Jacinto
	Republic of Texas formed
1843–44	John C. Frémont maps trails to Oregon and California
1844	Democrat James K. Polk elected president on an expansionist platform
1845	Texas annexed to the United States as a slave state
	John O'Sullivan coins the phrase "manifest destiny"
1846	Oregon question settled peacefully with Britain
	Mexican-American War begins
	Bear Flag Revolt in California
	Wilmot Proviso
1847	Cayuse War begins in Oregon
	Americans win battles of Buena Vista, Veracruz, and Mexico City
1848	Treaty of Guadalupe Hidalgo
	Free-Soil Party captures 10 percent of the popular vote in the North
	General Zachary Taylor, a Whig, elected president
1849	California gold rush

of the Free-Soil Party, former president Martin Van Buren. In the end, Van Buren garnered 10 percent of the vote (all in the North). The vote for the Free-Soil Party cost Cass the electoral votes of New York and Pennsylvania, and General Zachary Taylor won the election with only 47 percent of the popular vote. This was the second election after 1840 that the Whigs had won by running a war hero who could duck hard questions by claiming to be above politics. Uncannily, history was to repeat itself: Taylor, like William Henry Harrison, died before his term was completed, and the chance he offered to maintain national unity—if ever it existed—was lost.

CONCLUSION

In the decade of the 1840s, westward expansion took many forms, from relatively peaceful settlement in Oregon, to war with Mexico over Texas, to the overwhelming numbers of gold rushers who changed California forever. Most of these frontiers—in Oregon, New Mexico, and California—began as frontiers of inclusion, in which small numbers of Americans were eager for trade, accommodation, and intermarriage with the original inhabitants. Texas, with its agricultural enclaves, was the exception to this pattern. Yet on every frontier, as the number of American settlers increased, so did the sentiment for exclusion, so that by 1850, whatever their origins, the far-flung American continental settlements were more similar than different, and the success of manifest destiny seemed overwhelming.

The amazing expansion achieved by the Mexican-American War—America's manifest destiny—made the United States a continental nation but stirred up the issue that was to tear it apart. Sectional rivalries and fears now dominated every aspect of politics. Expansion, once a force for unity, now divided the nation into Northerners and Southerners, who could not agree on the community they shared—the federal Union.

REVIEW QUESTIONS

1. Define and discuss the concept of manifest destiny.

2. Trace the different ways in which the frontiers in Oregon, Texas, and California moved from frontiers of inclusion to frontiers of exclusion.

3. Take different sides (Whig and Democrat) and debate the issues raised by the Mexican-American War.

4. The California gold rush was an unprecedented scramble for riches. What were its effects on its participants, on California, and on the nation as a whole?

5. Referring to Chapter 13, compare the positions of the Liberty Party and the Free-Soil Party. Examine the factors that made the free-soil doctrine politically so acceptable and abolitionism so controversial.

KEY TERMS

myhistorylab
Flashcard Review

Alamo (p. 363)
Californios (p. 368)
Empresarios (p. 363)
Enclave (p. 363)
Liberty Party (p. 374)
Manifest destiny (p. 357)

Mexican-American War (p. 365)
Oregon Trail (p. 360)
Popular sovereignty (p. 374)
Santa Fé Trail (p. 354)
Tejanos (p. 362)
Wilmot Proviso (p. 373)

RECOMMENDED READING

Sucheng Chan, *This Bittersweet Soil: The Chinese in California Agriculture 1860–1910* (1987). The Chinese in California after the gold rush.

John Mack Faragher, *Women and Men on the Overland Trail* (1979). One of the first books to consider the experience of women on the journey west.

Paul Foos, *A Short, Offhand, Killing Affair: Soldiers and Social Conflict During the Mexican-American War* (2002). The lives and attitudes of ordinary American soldiers.

Robert W. Johannsen, *To the Halls of the Montezumas: The Mexican War in the American Imagination* (1985). A lively book that explores the impact of the Mexican-American War on public opinion.

Susan Johnson, *Roaring Camp: The Social World of the California Gold Rush* (2000). A beautifully written study of the varieties of mining camp experience.

Paul D. Lack, *The Texas Revolutionary Experience: A Political and Social History, 1835–1836* (1992). A political and social history that stresses the chaotic and discordant nature of the Texas Revolt.

Andrés Reséndez, *Changing National Identities at the Frontier: Texas and New Mexico, 1800–1850* (2004). The choices faced by Latinos, American Indians, and Anglos.

Randy Roberts and James S. Olson, *A Line in the Sand: The Alamo in Blood and Memory* (2001). How the battle became a symbol.

Malcolm Rohrbough, *Days of Gold: The California Gold Rush and the American Nation* (1997). A lively history that emphasizes the effects of this "great American epic" on the national self-image.

David J. Weber, *The Mexican Frontier, 1821–1846: The American Southwest under Mexico* (1982). A fine study of the history of the Southwest before American conquest by a leading borderlands historian.

Where it's a good time to connect to the past!

This horror, this nightmare abomination!
Can it be in my country! It lies like lead on
my heart, it shadows my life with sorrow . . .
— Harriet Beecher Stowe, December 16, 1852

Republican night-time parade.

15

THE COMING CRISIS
THE 1850S

WHY DID people in the North and the South tend to see the issue of slavery differently?

WHAT WAS the intent of the Compromise of 1850?

WHAT EXPLAINS the end of the Second American Party System and the rise of the Republican Party?

WHAT WAS the outcome of the *Dred Scott* decision?

WHY DID the South secede following the Republican Party victory in the election of 1860?

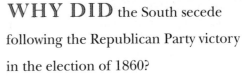

AMERICAN COMMUNITIES
Illinois Communities Debate Slavery

"THE PRAIRIES ARE ON FIRE," ANNOUNCED THE *NEW YORK EVENING POST* correspondent who covered the debates. "It is astonishing how deep an interest in politics these people take." The reason was clear: by 1858, the American nation was in political crisis. The decade-long effort to solve the problem of the future of slavery had failed. For most of this time, Washington politicians trying to build broad national parties with policies acceptable to voters in both the North and the South had done their best not to talk about slavery. That the **Lincoln–Douglas debates** were devoted to one issue alone—slavery and the future of the Union—showed how serious matters had become.

Democratic Senator Stephen A. Douglas of Illinois and his Republican challenger, Springfield lawyer Abraham Lincoln, presented their views in three hours of closely reasoned argument. But they did not speak alone. Cheers, boos, groans, and shouted questions from active, engaged listeners punctuated all seven of the now famous confrontations between the two men. Thus, the Lincoln–Douglas debates were community events in which Illinois citizens—who, as did Americans everywhere, held varying political beliefs—took part.

Stephen Douglas was the leading Democratic contender for the 1860 presidential nomination, but before he could mount a campaign for national office, he had first to win reelection to the Illinois seat he had held in the U.S. Senate for twelve years. His vote against allowing slavery in Kansas had alienated him from the strong southern wing of his own party and had put him in direct conflict with its top leader, President James Buchanan. Because the crisis of the Union was so severe and Douglas's role so pivotal, his reelection campaign clearly previewed the 1860 presidential election.

Lincoln had represented Illinois in the House of Representatives in the 1840s but had lost political support in 1848 because he had opposed the Mexican-American War. Developing a prosperous Springfield law practice, he had been an influential member of the Illinois Republican Party since its founding in 1856. Lincoln was radicalized by the issue of the extension of slavery. Even though his wife's family were Kentucky slave owners, Lincoln's commitment to freedom and

his resistance to the spread of slavery had now become absolute: for him, freedom and the Union were inseparable.

The first of the seven debates, held in Ottawa, in northern Illinois, on Saturday, August 21, 1858, showed not only the seriousness but also the exuberance of the democratic politics of the time. By early morning, the town was jammed with people. The clouds of dust raised by carriages driving to Ottawa, one observer complained, turned the town into "a vast smoke house." By one o'clock, the town square was filled to overflowing, and the debate enthralled an estimated 12,000 people. Ottawa in northern Illinois, was pro-Republican, and the audience heckled Douglas unmercifully. But as the debates moved south in the state, where Democrats predominated, the tables were turned, and Lincoln sometimes had to plead for a chance to be heard.

Although Douglas won the 1858 senatorial election in Illinois, the acclaim that Lincoln gained in the famous debates helped establish the Republicans' claim to be the only party capable of stopping the spread of slavery and made Lincoln himself a strong contender for the Republican presidential nomination in 1860. But the true winners of the Lincoln–Douglas debates were the people of Illinois who gathered peacefully to discuss the most serious issue of their time. The young German immigrant Carl Schurz, who attended the Quincy debate, was deeply impressed by its democratic character. He noted, "There was no end of cheering and shouting and jostling on the streets of Quincy that day. But in spite of the excitement created by the political contest, the crowds remained very good-natured, and the occasional jibes flung from one side to the other were uniformly received with a laugh."

The Lincoln–Douglas debates are famous for their demonstration of the widespread public belief in commonality and community to resolve disagreements. Unfortunately, differences that could be resolved through conversation and friendship in the local community were less easy to resolve at the national level. In the highly charged and highly public political atmosphere of Congress, politicians struggled in vain to find compromises to hold the national community together.

Illinois

Lincoln-Douglas debates Series of debates in the 1858 Illinois senatorial campaign during which Douglas and Lincoln staked out their differing opinions on the issue of slavery.

AMERICA IN 1850

The America of 1850 was a very different nation from the republic of 1800. Geographic expansion, population increase, economic development, and the changes wrought by the market revolution had transformed the struggling new nation. Economically, culturally, and politically Americans had forged a strong sense of national identity.

EXPANSION AND GROWTH

America was now a much larger nation than it had been in 1800. Through war and diplomacy, the country had grown to continental dimensions, more than tripling in size from 890,000 to 3 million square miles. Its population had increased enormously from 5.3 million in 1800 to more than 23 million, 4 million of whom were African American slaves and 2 million new immigrants, largely from Germany and Ireland. Comprising just sixteen states in 1800, America in 1850 had thirty-one states, and more than half of the population lived west of the Appalachians. America's cities had undergone the most rapid half century of growth they were ever to experience (see Map 15.1).

America was also much richer: it is estimated that real per capita income doubled between 1800 and 1850 Southern cotton was no longer the major influence on the domestic economy. The growth of manufacturing in the Northeast and the rapid opening up of rich farmlands in the Midwest had serious domestic implications. As the South's share of responsibility for economic growth waned, so did its political importance—at least in the eyes of many Northerners. Thus, the very success of the United States both in geographic expansion and in economic development served to undermine the role of the South in national politics and to hasten the day of open conflict between the slave South and the free-labor North and Midwest.

POLITICS, CULTURE, AND NATIONAL IDENTITY

Pride in democracy was one unifying theme in a growing sense of national identity and the new middle-class values, institutions, and culture that supported it. Since the turn of the century, American writers had struggled to find distinctive American themes, and these efforts bore fruit in the 1850s in the burst of creative activity termed the "American Renaissance." Newspapers, magazines, and communication improvements of all kinds created a national audience for the American scholars and writers who emerged during this decade.

During the American Renaissance, American writers pioneered new literary forms. Nathaniel Hawthorne, in works like "Young Goodman Brown" (1835), raised the short story to a distinctive American literary form. Poets like Walt Whitman and Emily Dickinson experimented with unrhymed and "off-rhyme" verse. Henry David Thoreau published *Walden* in 1854. A pastoral celebration of his life at Walden Pond, in Concord, Massachusetts, the essay was also a searching meditation on the cost to the individual of the loss of contact with nature that was a consequence of the market revolution.

Indeed, although the midcentury popular mood was one of self-congratulation, most of the writers of the American Renaissance were social critics. In *The Scarlet Letter* (1850) and *The House of the Seven Gables* (1851), Nathaniel Hawthorne brilliantly exposed the repressive and hypocritical aspects of Puritan New England in the colonial period and the often impossible moral choices faced by individuals. Hawthorne's friend Herman Melville, in his great work *Moby Dick* (1851), used the story of Captain Ahab's obsessive search for the white whale to write a profound study of the nature of good and evil and a critique of American society in the 1850s. The strongest social critique, however, was Frederick Douglass's starkly simple autobiography, *Narrative of the Life of Frederick Douglass* (1845), which told of his brutal life as a slave.

WHY DID people in the North and the South tend to see the issue of slavery differently?

myhistorylab
Review Summary

IMAGE KEY

for pages 378–379

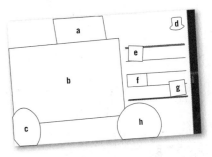

a. Dred Scott and his family, c. 1857.

b. Republican night-time parade.

c. A portrait photo of John Brown (1800–1859).

d. An old fashioned black stovepipe hat with a narrow brim like the one worn by Abe Lincoln.

e. A poster of *Uncle Tom's Cabin* with an illustration of a slave woman standing in the doorway of a log cabin. The copy describes various editions of the book for sale.

f. Robert Marshall Root's painting of the Lincoln-Douglas debate.

g. A contemporary colored engraving of the inside of the Armory at Harper's Ferry, Virginia, where John Brown and his men were trapped by the fire of the U.S. Marines under the command of Col. Robert E. Lee, October 18, 1859.

h. Gold ore and gravel in a shallow pan like those used by '49ers.

MAP EXPLORATION

To explore an interactive version of this map, go to **http://www.prenhall.com/faraghertlc/map15.1**

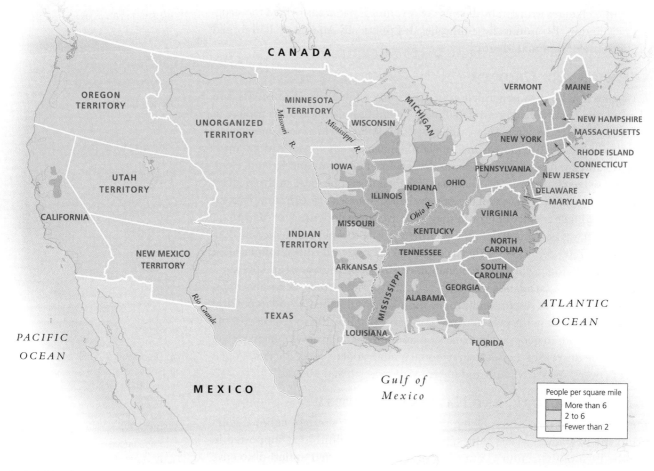

MAP 15.1

U.S. Population and Settlement, 1850 By 1850, the United States was a continental nation. Its people, whom Thomas Jefferson had once thought would not reach the Mississippi River for forty generations, had not only passed the river but also leapfrogged to the West Coast. In comparison to the America of 1800 (see Map 9.1 on p. 210), the growth was astounding.

WHAT WERE the reasons behind these growth patterns?

14–2

Harriet Beecher Stowe, *Uncle Tom's Cabin* (1852)

The most successful American novel of the mid-nineteenth century was also about the great issue of the day—slavery. In writing *Uncle Tom's Cabin*, Harriet Beecher Stowe combined the literary style of the popular women's domestic novels of the time (discussed in Chapter 12) with vivid details of slavery culled from firsthand accounts by northern abolitionists and escaped slaves. Published in 1851, it was a runaway best seller. More than 300,000 copies were sold in the first year, and within ten years, the book had sold more than 2 million copies, becoming the all-time American best seller in proportion to population. Turned into a play that remained popular throughout the nineteenth century, *Uncle Tom's Cabin* reached an even wider audience. *Uncle Tom's Cabin* was more than a heart-tugging story: it was a call to action. In 1863, when Harriet Beecher Stowe was introduced to Abraham Lincoln, the president is said to have remarked, "So you're the little woman who wrote the book that made this great war!"

CRACKS IN NATIONAL UNITY

Stowe's novel clearly spoke to the growing concern of the American people. The year 1850 opened to the most serious political crisis the United States had ever known. The issue raised by the 1846 Wilmot Proviso—whether slavery should be extended to the new territories—could no longer be ignored (see Chapter 14). Furthermore, California, made rich and populous by the gold rush, applied for statehood in 1850, thereby reopening the issue of the balance between slave and free states.

THE COMPROMISE OF 1850

The **Compromise of 1850** was actually five separate bills embodying three separate compromises.

First, California was admitted as a free state, but the status of the remaining former Mexican possessions was left to be decided by **popular sovereignty** (a vote of the territory's inhabitants) when they applied for statehood. The result was, for the time being, fifteen slave states and sixteen free states. Second, Texas (a slave state) was required to cede land to New Mexico Territory (free or slave status undecided). Finally, the slave trade, but not slavery itself, was ended in the District of Columbia, but a stronger fugitive slave law, to be enforced in all states, was enacted (see Map 15.2).

Jubilation and relief greeted the news that compromise had been achieved, but analysis of the votes on the five bills that made up the compromise revealed no consistent majority. The sectional splits within each party that had existed before the compromise remained. Antislavery northern Whigs and proslavery southern Democrats, each the larger wing of their party, were the least willing to compromise.

POLITICAL PARTIES SPLIT OVER SLAVERY

The Second American Party System, forged in the great controversies of Andrew Jackson's presidency (see Chapter 11), was a national party system. At a time when the ordinary person still had very strong sectional loyalties, the mass political party created a national community of like-minded voters. Yet, by the election of 1848, sectional interests were eroding the political "glue" in both parties. Although each party still appeared united, sectional fissures ran deep.

Political splits were preceded by divisions in other social institutions. Disagreements about slavery had already split the country's great religious organizations into northern and southern groups: the Presbyterians in 1837, the Methodists in 1844, and the Baptists in 1845. Theodore Weld, the abolitionist leader, saw these splits as inevitable: "Events . . . have for years been silently but without a moment's pause, settling the basis of two great parties, the nucleus of one slavery, of the other, freedom."

CONGRESSIONAL DIVISIONS

But was freedom national and slavery sectional, or was it the other way around? In the midst of the debate that preceded the Compromise of 1850, President Zachary Taylor died. A bluff military man, Taylor had been prepared to follow Andrew Jackson's precedent during the Nullification Crisis of 1832 and simply demand that southern dissidents compromise. Vice President Millard Fillmore, who assumed the presidency, was a much weaker man who did not seize the opportunity for presidential action.

135,000 SETS, 270,000 VOLUMES SOLD.

UNCLE TOM'S CABIN

FOR SALE HERE.

AN EDITION FOR THE MILLION, COMPLETE IN 1 Vol., PRICE 37 1-2 CENTS.
"   "   IN GERMAN, IN 1 Vol., PRICE 50 CENTS.
"   "   IN 2 Vols., CLOTH, 6 PLATES, PRICE $1.50.
SUPERB ILLUSTRATED EDITION, IN 1 Vol., WITH 153 ENGRAVINGS,
PRICES FROM $2.50 TO $5.00.

The Greatest Book of the Age.

This poster advertises *Uncle Tom's Cabin*, the best-selling novel by Harriet Beecher Stowe. The poignant story of long-suffering African American slaves had an immense impact on northern popular opinion, swaying it decisively against slavery. In that respect, the poster's boast, "The Greatest Book of the Age," was correct.

WHAT WAS the intent of the Compromise of 1850?

myhistorylab
Review Summary

Compromise of 1850   The four-step compromise which admitted California as a free state, allowed the residents of the New Mexico and Utah territories to decide the slavery issue for themselves, ended the slave trade in the District of Columbia, and passed a new fugitive slave law to enforce the constitutional provision stating that a slave escaping into a free state shall be delivered back to the owner.

Popular sovereignty   A solution to the slavery crisis suggested by Michigan senator Lewis Cass by which territorial residents, not Congress, would decide slavery's fate.

OVERVIEW | The Great Sectional Compromises

1820	**Missouri Compromise**	Admits Missouri to the Union as a slave state and Maine as a free state; prohibits slavery in the rest of the Louisiana Purchase Territory north of 36°30′.
		Territory Covered: The entire territory of the Louisiana Purchase, exclusive of the state of Louisiana, which had been admitted to the Union in 1812.
1850	**Compromise of 1850**	Admits California to the Union as a free state, settles the borders of Texas (a slave state); sets no conditions concerning slavery for the rest of the territory acquired from Mexico. Enacts national Fugitive Slave Law.
		Territory Covered: The territory that had been part of Mexico before the end of the Mexican-American War and the Treaty of Guadalupe Hidalgo (1848): part of Texas, California, Utah Territory (now Utah, Nevada, and part of Colorado), and New Mexico Territory (now New Mexico and Arizona).

myhistorylab

Overview: *The Great Sectional Compromises*

14–7
Hinton Rowan Helper, *A White Southerner Speaks Out Against Slavery* (1857)

14–4
John C. Calhoun, *A Dying Statesman Speaks Out Against the Compromise of 1850*

And southerners, personified by John C. Calhoun, were unwilling to compromise. Calhoun, who had uncompromisingly spoken for the slave South since the Nullification Crisis in 1828 (see Chapter 11) insisted that the states rights' doctrine was necessary to protect the legitimate rights of a minority in a democratic system governed by majority rule. Now in 1850 Calhoun broadened his argument to insist that Congress did not have a constitutional right to prohibit slavery in the territories. The territories, he said, were the common property of all the states, North and South, and slave owners had a constitutional right to the protection of their property wherever they moved. Calhon's position on the territories quickly became southern dogma: anything less than full access to the territories was unconstitutional. As Congressman Robert Toombs of Georgia put the case in 1850, the choice was stark: "Give us our just rights and we are ready to stand by the Union. Refuse [them] and for one, I will strike for independence."

Calhoun's failing health served to make his ultimatum all the more ominous. He brought an aura of death with him as he sat on the Senate floor for the last time, listening to the speech that he was too ill to read for himself. He died less than a month later, still insisting on the right of the South to secede if necessary, to preserve its way of life.

The southern threat to secede confirmed for many Northerners the warnings of antislavery leaders that they were endangered by a menacing "slave power." Liberty Party leader James Birney, in a speech in 1844, was the first to add this phrase to the nation's political vocabulary. "The slave power," Birney explained, was a group of aristocratic slave owners who not only dominated the political and social life of the South but conspired to control the federal government as well, posing a danger to free speech and free institutions throughout the nation.

Birney's warning about the "slave power" in 1844 had seemed merely the overheated rhetoric of an extremist group of abolitionists. But the defensive southern political strategies of the 1850s convinced an increasing number of northern voters that "the slave power" did in fact exist. The long-standing proslavery strategy of maintaining supremacy in the Senate by having at least as many slave as free states admitted to the Union (a plan that required slavery expansion) now looked like a conspiracy by sectional interests to control national politics. In northern eyes, the South became a demonic monolith that threatened the national government.

TWO COMMUNITIES, TWO PERSPECTIVES

Ironically, it was their common commitment to expansion that made the argument between Northerners and Southerners so irreconcilable. Basically, both North and South believed in manifest destiny, but each on its own terms.

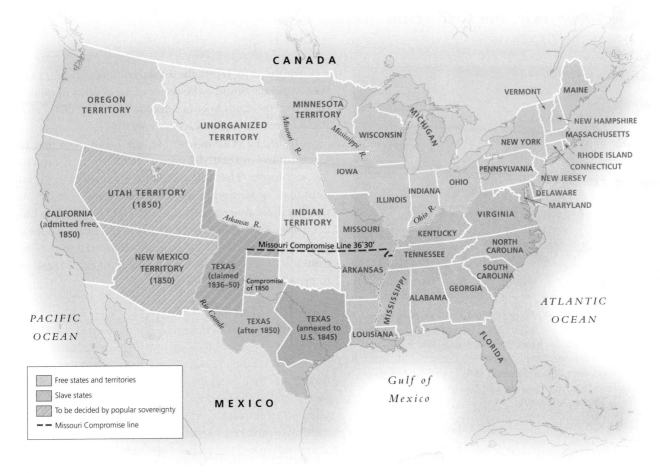

MAP 15.2

The Compromise of 1850 The Compromise of 1850, messier and more awkward than the Missouri Compromise of 1820, reflected heightened sectional tensions. California was admitted as a free state, the borders of Texas were settled, and the status of the rest of the former Mexican territory was left to be decided later by popular sovereignty. No consistent majority voted for the five separate bills that made up the compromise.

WHAT GROUPS opposed the Compromise of 1850? Why?

Similarly, both North and South used the language of basic rights and liberties in the debate over expansion. But free-soilers were speaking of personal liberty, whereas Southerners meant their right to own a particular kind of property (slaves) and to maintain a way of life based on the possession of that property. In defending its own rights, each side had taken measures that infringed on the rights of the other.

By 1850, North and South had created fixed stereotypes of the other. To antislavery Northerners, the South was an economic backwater dominated by a small slave-owning aristocracy that lived off the profits of forced labor and deprived poor whites of their democratic rights and the fruits of honest work. The slave system was not only immoral but also a drag on the entire nation, for, in the words of Senator William Seward of New York, it subverted the "intelligence, vigor and energy" that were essential for national growth. In contrast, the dynamic and enterprising commercial North boasted a free-labor ideology that offered economic opportunity to the common man and ensured his democratic rights.

Things looked very different through southern eyes. Far from being economically backward, the South, through its export of cotton, was, according to Southerners, the great engine of national economic growth from which the North benefited. Slavery was not only a blessing to an inferior race but also the cornerstone of democracy, for it ensured the freedom and independence of all white men without entailing the bitter class divisions that marked the North. Slave owners accused northern manufacturers of hypocrisy for practicing "wage slavery" without the paternal benevolence they claimed to bestow on their slaves.

In 1850, the three men who had long represented America's three major regions attempted to resolve the political crisis brought on by the application of California for statehood. Henry Clay is speaking; John C. Calhoun stands second from right; and Daniel Webster is seated at the left, with his head in his hand. Both Clay and Webster were ill, and Calhoun died before the Compromise of 1850 was arranged by a younger group of politicians led by Stephen A. Douglas.

13–5
De Bow's Review, *"The Stability of the Union,"* (1850)

myhistorylab

Exploring America: *Anthony Burns*

Fugitive Slave Law Part of the Compromise of 1850 that required the authorities in the North to assist Southern slave catchers and return runaway slaves to their owners.

By the early 1850s, these vastly different visions of the North and the South—the result of many years of political controversy—had become fixed, and the chances of national reconciliation increasingly slim.

In the country as a whole, the feeling was that the Compromise of 1850 had solved the question of slavery in the territories. The *Philadelphia Pennsylvanian* was confident that "peace and tranquillity" had been ensured, and the *Louisville Journal* said that a weight seemed to have been lifted from the heart of America. But many Southerners felt that their only real gain in the contested compromise was the Fugitive Slave Law, which quickly turned out to be an inflammatory measure.

THE FUGITIVE SLAVE LAW

From the early days of their movement, northern abolitionists had urged slaves to escape, promising assistance and support when they reached the North. Some free African Americans had given far more than verbal support, and most escaped slaves found their most reliable help within northern free black communities. Northerners had long been appalled by professional slave catchers, who zealously seized African Americans in the North and took them south into slavery again. Most abhorrent in northern eyes was that captured black people were at the mercy of slave catchers because they had no legal right to defend themselves. In more than one case, a free African American was captured in his own community and helplessly shipped into slavery.

As a result of stories like this, nine northern states passed personal liberty laws between 1842 and 1850, serving notice that they would not cooperate with federal recapture efforts. These laws enraged Southerners, who had long been convinced that all Northerners, not just abolitionists, were actively hindering efforts to reclaim their escaped slaves. At issue were two distinct definitions of "rights": Northerners were upset at the denial of legal and personal rights to escaped slaves.

The **Fugitive Slave Law**, enacted in 1850, dramatically increased the power of slave owners to capture escaped slaves. The full authority of the federal government now supported slave owners, and although fugitives were guaranteed a hearing before a federal commissioner, they were not allowed to testify on their own behalf. Furthermore, the new law imposed federal penalties on citizens who protected or assisted fugitives or who did not cooperate in their return. A number of free northern blacks, estimated at 30,000 to 40,000, emigrated to Canada to avoid the possibility of capture.

In Boston, the center of the American abolitionist movement, reaction to the Fugitive Slave Law was fierce. In the most famous Boston case, a biracial group of armed abolitionists led by Unitarian clergyman Thomas Wentworth Higginson stormed the federal courthouse in 1854 in an attempt to save escaped slave Anthony Burns. The rescue effort failed, and a federal deputy marshal was killed. President Pierce sent marines, cavalry, and artillery to Boston to reinforce the guard over Burns and ordered a federal ship to be ready to deliver the fugitive back into slavery. When the effort by defense lawyers to argue for Burns's freedom failed, Bostonians raised money to buy his freedom. But the U.S. attorney, ordered by the president to enforce the Fugitive Slave Law in all circumstances, blocked the purchase. The case was lost, and Burns was marched to the docks through streets lined with sorrowing abolitionists. Buildings were shrouded in black and draped with American flags hanging upside down, while bells tolled as if for a funeral.

In this volatile atmosphere, escaped African Americans wrote and lectured bravely on behalf of freedom. Frederick Douglass, the most famous and eloquent of the fugitive slaves, spoke out fearlessly in support of armed resistance. Openly active in the underground network that helped slaves reach safety in Canada, Douglass himself had been constantly in danger of capture until his friends bought his freedom in 1847. Harriet Jacobs, who escaped to the North after seven years in hiding in the South, wrote bitterly in her *Incidents in the Life of a Slave Girl* (1861) that "I was, in fact, a slave in New York, as subject to slave laws as I had been in a slave state . . . I had been chased during half my life, and it seemed as if the chase was never to end." Threatened by owners who came north for her, Jacobs was forced into hiding while northern white friends arranged her purchase. "A gentleman near me said, 'It's true; I have seen the bill of sale.' 'The bill of sale!' Those words struck me like a blow. So I was sold at last! A human being sold in the free city of New York!"

The Fugitive Slave Law made slavery national and forced northern communities to confront the full meaning of slavery. Although most people were still unwilling to grant social equality to the free African Americans who lived in the northern states, more and more had come to believe that the institution of slavery was wrong. The strong northern reaction against the Fugitive Slave Law also had consequences in the South. Northern protests against the Fugitive Slave Law bred suspicion in the South and encouraged secessionist thinking. These new currents of public opinion were reflected in the election of 1852.

13–7
George Fitzhugh, *"The Blessings of Slavery"* (1857)

13–6
Benjamin Drew, *Narratives of Escaped Slaves* (1855)

14–5
Frederick Douglass, *Independence Day Speech* (1852)

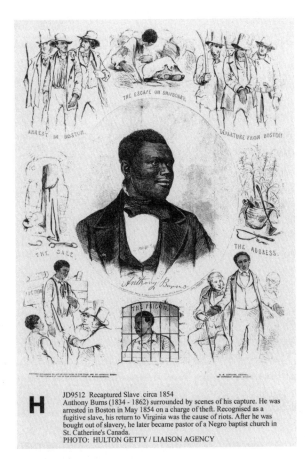

Escaped slave Anthony Burns, shown here surrounded by scenes of his capture in 1854, was the cause of Boston's greatest protest against the Fugitive Slave Law. The injustice of his trial and shipment back to the South converted many Bostonians to the antislavery cause.

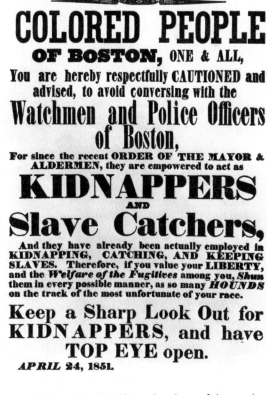

This handbill warning free African Americans of danger circulated in Boston following the first of the infamous recaptures under the Fugitive Slave Law, that of Thomas Sims in 1851.

THE ELECTION OF 1852

The first sign of the weakening of the national party system in 1852 was the difficulty both parties experienced at their nominating conventions. After fifty-two ballots General Winfield Scott (a military hero like two of the party's previous three candidates), rather than the sitting President Fillmore, was nominated. Many southern Whigs were permanently alienated by the choice; although Whigs were still elected to Congress from the South, their loyalty to the national party was strained to the breaking point.

The Democrats had a wider variety of candidates. Lewis Cass, Stephen Douglas, and James Buchanan competed for forty-nine ballots, each strong enough to block the others but not strong enough to win. Finally, the party turned to Franklin Pierce of New Hampshire, who was thought to have southern sympathies. Uniting on a platform pledging "faithful execution" of all parts of the Compromise of 1850, including the Fugitive Slave Law, Democrats polled well in the South and in the North. Most Democrats who had voted for the Free-Soil Party in 1848 voted for Pierce. So, in record numbers, did immigrant Irish and German voters, who were eligible for citizenship after three years' residence. The strong immigrant vote for Pierce was a sign of the strength of Democratic Party organizations in northern cities. Pierce easily won the 1852 election, 254 electoral votes to 42.

"YOUNG AMERICA": THE POLITICS OF EXPANSION

Pierce entered the White House in 1853 on a wave of good feeling. This goodwill was soon strained by Pierce's support for the expansionist adventures of the "Young America" movement.

The "Young America" movement began as a group of writers and politicians in the New York Democratic Party who believed in the democratic and nationalistic promise of "manifest destiny." By the 1850s, however, their lofty goals had shrunk to a desire to conquer Central America and Cuba. During the Pierce administration, several private "filibusters" (from the Spanish *filibustero*, meaning an "adventurer" or "pirate") invaded Caribbean and Central American countries, usually with the declared intention of extending slave territory.

The Pierce administration, not directly involved in the filibustering, *was* deeply involved in an effort to obtain Cuba. In 1854, Pierce authorized his minister to Spain, Pierre Soulé, to try to force the unwilling Spanish to sell Cuba for $130 million. Soulé met in Ostend, Belgium, with the American ministers to France and England, John Mason and James Buchanan, to compose the offer. At first appealing to Spain to recognize the deep affinities between the Cubans and American Southerners that made them "one people with one destiny," the document went on to threaten to "wrest" Cuba from Spain if necessary. This amazing document, which became known as the Ostend Manifesto, was supposed to be secret but was soon leaked to the press. Deeply embarrassed, the Pierce administration was forced to repudiate it.

In another expansionist gesture in another direction, President Franklin Pierce dispatched Commodore Matthew Perry across the Pacific to Japan, a nation famous for its insularity and hostility to outsiders. The mission resulted in 1854 in a commercial treaty that opened Japan to American trade.

Overall, however, the complicity between the Pierce administration and proslavery expansionists was foolhardy and lost it the northern goodwill with which it had begun. The sectional crisis that preceded the Compromise of 1850 had made obvious the danger of reopening the territorial issue. Ironically, it was not the Young America expansionists but the prime mover of the Compromise of 1850, Stephen A. Douglas, who reignited the sectional struggle over slavery expansion.

THE CRISIS OF THE NATIONAL PARTY SYSTEM

In 1854, Douglas introduced the **Kansas-Nebraska Act**, proposing to open those lands that had been the northern part of Indian Territory to American settlers under the principle of popular sovereignty. He thereby reopened the question of slavery in the territories. Douglas knew he was taking a political risk, but he believed he could satisfy both his expansionist aims and his presidential ambitions. He was wrong: he pushed the national party system into crisis, first killing the Whigs and then destroying the Democrats.

WHAT EXPLAINS the end of the Second American Party System and the rise of the Republican Party?

myhistorylab
Review Summary

THE KANSAS-NEBRASKA ACT

In a stunning example of the expansionist pressures generated by the market revolution, Stephen Douglas introduced the Kansas-Nebraska Act to further the construction of a transcontinental railroad across what was still considered the "Great American Desert" to California. Douglas wanted the rail line to terminate in Chicago, in his own state of Illinois, rather than in the rival St. Louis, but for that to happen, the land west of Iowa and Missouri had to be organized into territories (the first step toward statehood). To get Congress to agree to the organization of the territories, however, Douglas needed the votes of southern Democrats, who were unwilling to support him unless the territories were open to slavery (see Map 15.3).

The Kansas-Nebraska bill passed, but it badly strained the major political parties. Southern Whigs voted with southern Democrats in favor of the measure; northern Whigs rejected it absolutely, creating an irreconcilable split that left Whigs unable to field a presidential candidate in 1856. The damage to the Democratic Party was almost as great. In the congressional elections of 1854, northern Democrats lost two-thirds of their seats (a drop from ninety-one to twenty-five), giving the southern Democrats (who were solidly in favor of slavery extension) the dominant voice both in Congress and within the party.

Douglas had committed one of the greatest miscalculations in American political history. A storm of protest arose throughout the North. Douglas, who confidently

Kansas-Nebraska Act Law passed in 1854 creating the Kansas and Nebraska Territories but leaving the question of slavery open to residents, thereby repealing the Missouri Compromise.

A Japanese painting shows Commodore Matthew Perry landing in Japan in 1853. The commercial treaty Perry signed with the Japanese government, which opened a formerly closed country to American trade, was viewed in the United States as another fruit of manifest destiny.

"The Landing of Commodore Perry in Japan in 1853." (Detail) Japanese, Edo period, 19th century. Handscroll; ink and color on paper, 10 7/8 × 211 1/8 in. (27.6 × 536.3 cm). Museum of Fine Arts, Boston. William Sturgis Bigelow Collection, RES.11.6054. Photograph © 2006 Museum of Fine Arts, Boston.

This engraving shows "Border Ruffians" from Missouri lining up to vote for slavery in the Kickapoo, Kansas Territory, election of 1855. The widespread practice of illegal voting and of open violence earned Kansas the dreadful nickname of "Bleeding Kansas."

QUICK REVIEW

The Kansas-Nebraska Act

♦ Passed in 1854.

♦ Made the status of slavery in new territories subject to the principal of popular sovereignty.

♦ Act aroused storm of protest in the North.

14–6
Kansas Begins to Bleed
(1856)

believed that "the people of the North will sustain the measure when they come to understand it," found himself shouted down more than once at public rallies when he tried to explain the bill.

The Kansas-Nebraska bill shifted a crucial sector of northern opinion: the wealthy merchants, bankers, and manufacturers, called the "Cotton Whigs," who had economic ties with southern slave owners and had always disapproved of abolitionist activity. Convinced that the bill would encourage antislavery feeling in the North, Cotton Whigs urged southern politicians to vote against it, only to be ignored. Passage of the Kansas-Nebraska Act convinced many northern Whigs that compromise with the South was impossible.

In Kansas in 1854, hasty treaties were concluded with the Indian tribes who owned the land. Some, such as the Kickapoos, Shawnees, Sauks, and Foxes, agreed to relocate to small reservations. Others, like the Delawares, Weas, and Iowas, agreed to sell their lands to whites. Once the treaties were signed, both proslavery and antislavery white settlers began to pour in, and the battle was on.

"BLEEDING KANSAS"

The first to claim land in Kansas were residents of nearby Missouri, itself a slave state. Missourians took up land claims, established proslavery strongholds such as the towns of Leavenworth, Kickapoo, and Atchison, and repeatedly and blatantly swamped Kansas elections with Missouri votes. In 1855, in the second of several notoriously fraudulent elections, 6,307 ballots were cast in a territory that had fewer than 3,000 eligible voters. Most of the proslavery votes were cast by "border ruffians," as they proudly called themselves, from Missouri.

Northerners quickly responded. The first party of New Englanders arrived in the summer of 1854 and established the free-soil town of Lawrence, named for former "Cotton Whig" Amos Lawrence, who financed them. More than a thousand others had joined them by the following summer. Many northern migrants were Free-Soilers, and many were religious reformers as well. The contrast of values between them and the border ruffians was almost total.

Kansas soon became a bloody battleground as the two factions struggled to secure the mandate of "popular sovereignty." Free-Soilers in Lawrence received shipments of heavy crates, innocuously marked "BOOKS" but actually containing Sharps repeating rifles, sent by eastern supporters. For their part, the border ruffians called for reinforcements.

In the summer of 1856, these lethal preparations exploded into open warfare. First, proslavery forces burned and looted the town of Lawrence. In retaliation, a grim old man named John Brown led his sons in a raid on the proslavery settlers of Pottawatomie Creek, killing five unarmed people. A wave of violence ensued. Armed bands roamed the countryside, and burnings and killings became commonplace.

The rest of the nation watched in horror as the residents of Kansas slaughtered each other in the pursuit of sectional goals. Americans' pride in their nation's great achievements was threatened by the endless violence in one small part—but a part that increasingly seemed to represent the divisions of the whole.

THE POLITICS OF NATIVISM

The violence in Kansas was echoed by increasing violence in the nation's cities. Serious violence marred the elections of 1854 and 1856 in New York. In New Orleans, anger over corrupt elections caused a self-appointed vigilance committee to erect barricades in Jackson Square in the heart of the city, where they skirmished for five

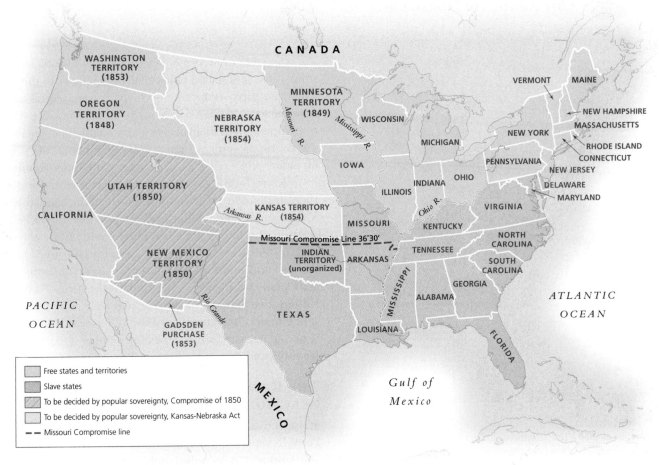

MAP 15.3

The Kansas-Nebraska Act, 1854   The Kansas-Nebraska Act, proposed by Steven A. Douglas in 1854, opened the central and northern Great Plains to settlement. The act had two major faults: it robbed Indian peoples of half the territory guaranteed to them by treaty and, because it repealed the Missouri Compromise line, it opened up the lands to warring proslavery and antislavery factions.

WHY DID the act provoke such a passionate response from antislavery activists?

days with an opposing force composed largely of Catholics and immigrants. In Chicago, riots started in 1855, when the mayor attempted to close the saloons on Sunday. German workingmen joined by Irishmen and Swedes paraded in protest and were met by 200 men of the National Guard, militia, and special police. The ensuing "Lager Beer Riots" ended with the imposition of martial law on the entire city.

This urban violence, like that in Kansas, was caused by the breakdown of the two-party system. The breakup of the Whig Party left a political vacuum that was filled by one of the strongest bursts of nativism, or anti-immigrant feeling, in American history, and by the rapid growth of the new American Party, which formed in 1850 to give political expression to nativism. The new party was in part a reaction to the Democratic Party's success in capturing the support of the rapidly growing population of mostly Catholic foreign-born voters. Irish immigrants in particular voted Democratic, both in reaction to Whig hostility (as in Boston) and because of their own antiblack prejudices.

The reformist and individualistic attitudes of many Whigs inclined them toward nativism. Many Whigs disapproved of the new immigrants because they were poor, Catholic, and often disdainful of the temperance movement. Moreover nativist Whigs held immigration to be solely responsible for the increases in crime and the rising cost of relief for the poor that accompanied the astoundingly rapid urban growth of the 1830s and 1840s (see Chapter 13).

myhistorylab

Exploring America: *The Unwelcome Mat*

	Electoral Vote (%)	Popular Vote (%)
JAMES BUCHANAN (Democrat)	174 (59)	1,832,955 (45)
John C. Frémont (Republican)	114 (39)	1,339,932 (33)
Millard Fillmore (American)	8 (3)	871,731 (22)

MAP 15.4

The Election of 1856 Because three parties contested the 1856 election, Democrat James Buchanan was a minority president. Although Buchanan alone had national support, Republican John Frémont won most of the free states, and Millard Fillmore of the American Party gained 40 percent of the vote in most of the slave states.

WHAT GROUPS constituted Buchanan's political base?

This nighttime meeting of supporters of the Know-Nothing Party in New York City was dramatically spotlighted by a new device borrowed from the theater, an incandescent calcium light, popularly called a limelight.

Nativism drew former Whigs, especially young men in white-collar and skilled blue-collar occupations, to the new American Party. At the core of the party were several secret fraternal societies open only to native-born Protestants. When questioned about their beliefs, party members maintained secrecy by answering, "I know nothing"—hence, the popular name for American Party members, the **Know-Nothings**.

Know-Nothings scored startling victories in northern state elections in 1854, winning control of the legislature in Massachusetts and polling 40 percent of the vote in Pennsylvania. But in the 1850s, no party could ignore slavery, and in 1855, the American Party split into northern (antislavery) and southern (proslavery) wings. Soon after this split, many people who had voted for the Know-Nothings shifted their support to another new party, one that combined many characteristics of the Whigs with a westward-looking, expansionist, free-soil policy. This was the **Republican Party**, founded in 1854.

THE REPUBLICAN PARTY AND THE ELECTION OF 1856

Many constituencies found room in the new Republican Party. Its supporters included many former northern Whigs who opposed slavery absolutely, many Free-Soil Party supporters who opposed the expansion of slavery but were willing to tolerate it in the South, and many northern reformers concerned about temperance and Catholicism. The Republicans also attracted the economic core of the old Whig Party—the merchants and industrialists who wanted a strong national government to promote economic growth by supporting a protective tariff, transportation improvements, and cheap land for western farmers.

The immediate question facing the nation in 1856 was which new party, the Know-Nothings or the Republicans, would emerge the stronger. But the more important question was whether the Democratic Party could hold together. The two strongest contenders for the Democratic nomination were President Pierce and Stephen A. Douglas. Douglas had proposed the Kansas-Nebraska Act and Pierce had actively supported it. But it was precisely their support of this act that made Northerners oppose both of them. The Kansas-Nebraska Act's divisive effect on the Democratic Party now became clear: no one who had voted on the bill, either for or against, could satisfy both wings of the party. A compromise candidate was found in James Buchanan of Pennsylvania, the "northern man with southern principles." Luckily for him, he had been ambassador to Great Britain at the time of the Kansas-Nebraska Act and, thus, had not had to commit himself.

The election of 1856 appeared to be a three-way contest that pitted Buchanan against explorer John C. Frémont of the Republican Party and the American (Know-Nothing) Party's candidate, former president Millard Fillmore (see Map 15.4). In fact, the election was two separate contests, one in the North and one in the South. The northern race was between Buchanan and Frémont, the southern

Brooks Beats Sumner

In a violent episode on the floor of the U.S. Senate in 1856, Senator Charles Sumner of Massachusetts suffered permanent injury in a vicious attack by Congressman Preston Brooks of South Carolina. Trapped at his desk, Sumner was helpless as Brooks beat him so hard with his cane that it broke. A few days earlier, Sumner had given an insulting antislavery speech. Using the abusive, accusatory style favored by abolitionists, he had singled out for ridicule Senator Andrew Butler of South Carolina, charging him with choosing "the harlot, slavery" as his mistress. Senator Butler was Preston Brooks's uncle; in Brooks's mind, he was simply avenging an intolerable affront to his uncle's honor.

So far had the behavioral codes of North and South diverged that each man found his own action perfectly justifiable and the action of the other outrageous. Their attitudes were mirrored in their respective sections. Protest rallies were held in most northern cities; Sumner himself received sympathy letters from hundreds of strangers, all expressing indignation, as one writer put it, over "the most foul, most damnable and dastardly attack," and sympathetic illustrations like this one appeared in northern papers. In contrast, southern newspapers almost unanimously supported Brooks, regarding it as a well-deserved whipping for an intolerable insult. A group of Charleston merchants even bought Brooks a new cane inscribed: "Hit him again." ■

WHAT WOULD a southern version of this episode look like? Which version is "true"?

SOUTHERN CHIVALRY — ARGUMENT versus CLUB'S.

Know-Nothings Name given to the antiimmigrant party formed from the wreckage of the Whig Party and some disaffected Northern democrats in 1854.

Republican Party Party that emerged in the 1850s in the aftermath of the bitter controversy over the Kansas-Nebraska Act, consisting of former Whigs, some Northern Democrats, and many Know-Nothings.

WHAT WAS the outcome of the *Dred Scott* decision?

myhistorylab
Review Summary

These sympathetic portraits of Harriet and Dred Scott and their daughters in 1857 helped to shape the northern reaction to the Supreme Court's decision that denied the Scotts' claim to freedom. The infamous *Dred Scott* decision was intended to resolve the issue of slavery expansion but instead heightened angry feelings in both North and South.

one between Buchanan and Fillmore. Buchanan won the election with only 45 percent of the popular vote, because he was the only national candidate. But the Republicans, after studying the election returns, claimed "victorious defeat," for they realized that in 1860, the addition of just two more northern states to their total would mean victory. Furthermore, the Republican Party had clearly defeated the American Party in the battle to win designation as a major party. These were grounds for great optimism—and great concern—for the Republican Party was a sectional, rather than a national, party; it drew almost all its support from the North. Southerners viewed its very existence as an attack on their vital interests. Thus, the rapid rise of the Republicans posed a growing threat to national unity.

THE DIFFERENCES DEEPEN

Although James Buchanan firmly believed that he alone could hold together a nation so split by hatred and violence, his self-confidence outran his abilities. He was so deeply indebted to the strong southern wing of the Democratic Party that he could not take the impartial actions necessary to heal "**Bleeding Kansas**." And his support for a momentous pro-southern decision by the Supreme Court further aggravated sectional differences.

THE *DRED SCOTT* DECISION

In *Dred Scott* v. *Sandford*, decided on March 6, 1857, two days after James Buchanan was sworn in, a southern-dominated Supreme Court attempted—and failed—to solve the political controversy over slavery. Dred Scott had been a slave all his life. His owner, army surgeon John Emerson, had taken Scott on his military assignments during the 1830s to Illinois (a free state) and Wisconsin Territory (a free territory, north of the Missouri Compromise line). During that time, Scott married another slave, Harriet, and their daughter Eliza was born in free territory. Emerson and the Scotts then returned to Missouri (a slave state) and there, in 1846, Dred Scott sued for his freedom and that of his wife and his daughter born in Wisconsin Territory (who as women had no legal standing of their own) on the grounds that residence in free lands had made them free. It took eleven years for the case to reach the Supreme Court, and by then its importance was obvious to everyone.

Declaring the Missouri Compromise unconstitutional Chief Justice Roger B. Taney asserted that the federal government had no right to interfere with the free movement of property throughout the territories. He then dismissed the *Dred Scott* case on the grounds that only citizens could bring suits before federal courts and that black people—slave or free—were not citizens. With this bold judicial intervention into the most heated issue of the day, Taney intended to settle the controversy over the expansion of slavery once and for all. Instead, he inflamed the conflict.

The five southern members of the Supreme Court concurred in Taney's decision, as did one Northerner, Robert C. Grier. Historians have found that President-elect Buchanan had pressured Grier, a fellow Pennsylvanian, to support the majority. Two of the three other Northerners vigorously dissented, and the last voiced other objections. This was clearly a sectional decision, and the response to it was sectional. Southerners expressed great satisfaction and strong support for the Court.

Northerners disagreed. Many were so troubled by the *Dred Scott* **decision** that, for the first time, they found themselves seriously questioning the power of the Supreme Court to establish the "law of the land." The

New York legislature passed a resolution declaring that the Supreme Court had lost the confidence and respect of the people of that state and another resolution refusing to allow slavery within its borders "in any form or under any pretense, or for any time, however short."

THE LECOMPTON CONSTITUTION

In Kansas, the doctrine of popular sovereignty led to continuing civil strife and the political travesty of two territorial governments. The first election of officers to a territorial government in 1855 produced a lopsided proslavery outcome that was clearly the result of illegal voting by Missouri border ruffians. Free-Soilers protested by forming their own government, giving Kansas both a proslavery territorial legislature in Lecompton and a Free-Soil government in Topeka.

Free-Soil voters boycotted a June 1857 election of representatives to a convention called to write a constitution for the territory once it reached statehood. As a result, the convention had a proslavery majority that wrote the proslavery **Lecompton constitution** and then applied to Congress for admission to the Union under its terms. In the meantime, in October, Free-Soil voters had participated in relatively honest elections for the territorial legislature, elections that returned a clear Free-Soil majority. Nevertheless, Buchanan, in the single most disastrous mistake of his administration, endorsed the proslavery constitution, because he feared the loss of the support of southern Democrats. It seemed that Kansas would enter the Union as a sixteenth slave state, making the number of slave and free states equal.

Unexpected congressional opposition came from none other than Stephen Douglas, author of the legislation that had begun the Kansas troubles in 1854. Now, in 1857, in what was surely the bravest step of his political career, Douglas opposed the Lecompton constitution on the grounds that it violated the principle of popular sovereignty. He insisted that the Lecompton constitution must be voted on by Kansas voters in honest elections. Defying James Buchanan, the president of his own party, Douglas voted with the majority in Congress in April 1858 to refuse admission to Kansas under the Lecompton constitution. In a new referendum, the people of Kansas also rejected the Lecompton constitution, 11,300 to 1,788. Kansas was finally admitted as a free state in January 1861.

THE PANIC OF 1857

Adding to the growing political tensions was the short, but sharp, depression of 1857 and 1858. Technology played a part. In August 1857, the failure of an Ohio investment house—the kind of event that had formerly taken weeks to be widely known—was the subject of a news story flashed immediately over telegraph wires to Wall Street and other financial markets. A wave of panic selling ensued, leading to business failures and slowdowns that threw thousands out of work. The major cause of the panic was a sharp, but temporary, downturn in agricultural exports to Britain, and recovery was well under way by early 1859.

Because it affected cotton exports less than northern exports, the **Panic of 1857** was less harmful to the South than to the North. Southerners took this as proof of the superiority of their economic system to the free-labor system of the North.

It seemed that all matters of political discussion were being drawn into the sectional dispute. The next step toward disunion was an act of violence perpetrated by the grim abolitionist from Kansas, John Brown.

JOHN BROWN'S RAID

In the heated political mood of the late 1850s, some improbable people became heroes. None was more improbable than John Brown, the self-appointed avenger who had slaughtered unarmed proslavery men in Kansas in 1856. In 1859, Brown

---

14–8
Dred Scott v. Sandford (1857)

QUICK REVIEW

The *Dred Scott* Decision

♦ 1857 attempt by Supreme Court to solve the political controversy over slavery.

♦ Court ruled that slaves were property and government could not restrain free movement of property.

♦ Decision invalidated the Missouri Compromise.

Bleeding Kansas Violence between pro- and antislavery forces in Kansas Territory after the passage of the Kansas-Nebraska Act in 1854.

***Dred Scott* decision** Supreme Court ruling, in a lawsuit brought by Dred Scott, a slave demanding his freedom based on his residence in a free state, that slaves could not be U.S. citizens and that Congress had no jurisdiction over slavery in the territories.

Lecompton constitution Proslavery draft written in 1857 by Kansas territorial delegates elected under questionable circumstances; it was rejected by two governors, supported by President Buchanan, and decisively defeated by Congress.

Panic of 1857 Banking crisis that caused a credit crunch in the North; it was less severe in the South, where high cotton prices spurred a quick recovery.

OVERVIEW | Political Parties Split and Realign

Whig Party	Ran its last presidential candidate in 1852. The candidate, General Winfield Scott, alienated many southern Whigs, and the party was so split it could not field a candidate in 1856.
Democratic Party	Remained a national party through 1856, but Buchanan's actions as president made southern domination of the party so clear that many northern Democrats were alienated. Stephen Douglas, running as a northern Democrat in 1860, won 29 percent of the popular vote; John Breckinridge, running as a southern Democrat, won 18 percent.
Liberty Party	Antislavery party; ran James G. Birney for president in 1844. He won 62,000 votes, largely from northern antislavery Whigs.
Free-Soil Party	Ran Martin Van Buren, former Democratic president, in 1848. Gained 10 percent of the popular vote, largely from Whigs but also from some northern Democrats.
American (Know-Nothing) Party	Nativist party made striking gains in 1854 congressional elections, attracting both northern and southern Whigs. In 1856, its presidential candidate, Millard Fillmore, won 21 percent of the popular vote.
Republican Party	Founded in 1854. Attracted many northern Whigs and northern Democrats. Presidential candidate John C. Frémont won 33 percent of the popular vote in 1856; in 1860, Abraham Lincoln won 40 percent and was elected in a four-way race.

myhistorylab

Overview: *Political Parties Split and Realign*

proposed a wild scheme to raid the South and start a general slave uprising. He believed that discontent among southern slaves was so great that such an uprising needed only a spark to get going. On October 16, 1859, Brown led a group of twenty-two white and African American men against the arsenal. In less than a day, the raid was over. Eight of Brown's men (including two of his sons) were dead, no slaves had joined the fight, and Brown himself was captured. Moving quickly to prevent a lynching by local mobs, the state of Virginia tried and convicted Brown (while he was still weak from the wounds of battle) of treason, murder, and fomenting insurrection.

Brown's death by hanging on December 2, 1859, was marked throughout northern communities with public rites of mourning not seen since the death of George Washington. Church bells tolled, buildings were draped in black, ministers preached sermons, prayer meetings were held, abolitionists issued eulogies. Naturally, not all Northerners supported Brown's action. But many people, while rejecting Brown's raid, increasingly supported the antislavery cause that he represented.

Brown's raid shocked the South because it aroused the fear of slave rebellion. Southerners believed that northern abolitionists were provoking slave revolts, a suspicion apparently confirmed when documents captured at Harpers Ferry revealed that Brown had the financial support of half a dozen members of the northern elite.

Even more shocking to Southerners than the raid itself was the extent of northern mourning for Brown's death. Although the Republican Party disavowed Brown's actions, Southerners simply did not believe the party's statements. Senator Robert Toombs of Georgia warned that the South would "never permit this Federal government to pass into the traitorous hands of the Black Republican party." Talk of secession as the only possible response became common throughout the South.

WHY DID the South secede following the Republican Party victory in the election of 1860?

THE SOUTH SECEDES

By 1860, sectional differences had caused one national party, the Whigs, to collapse. The second national party, the Democrats, stood on the brink of dissolution. Not only the politicians but also ordinary people in both the North and the South were coming to believe there was no way to avoid what in 1858 William Seward (once a Whig, now a Republican) had called an "irrepressible conflict."

myhistorylab

Review Summary

THE ELECTION OF 1860

The split of the Democratic Party into northern and southern wings that had occurred during President Buchanan's tenure became official at the Democratic nominating conventions in 1860. The party convened first in Charleston, South Carolina. Although Stephen Douglas had the support of the plurality of delegates, he did not have the two-thirds majority necessary for nomination. As the price of their support, Southerners insisted that Douglas support a federal slave code—a guarantee that slavery would be protected in the territories. Douglas could not agree without violating his own belief in popular sovereignty and losing his northern support.

After ten days, the convention ended where it had begun: deadlocked. Northern supporters of Douglas were angry and bitter: "I never heard Abolitionists talk more uncharitably and rancorously of the people of the South than the Douglas men," one reporter wrote. "They say they do not care a damn where the South goes."

In June, the Democrats met again in Baltimore. The Douglasites, recognizing the need for a united party, were eager to compromise wherever they could, but most southern Democrats were not. More than a third of the delegates bolted. Later, holding a convention of their own, they nominated Buchanan's vice president, John C. Breckinridge of Kentucky. The remaining two-thirds of the Democrats nominated Douglas, but everyone knew that a Republican victory was inevitable. To make matters worse, some southern Whigs joined with some border-state nativists to form the **Constitutional Union Party**, which nominated John Bell of Tennessee.

Republican strategy was built on the lessons of the 1856 "victorious defeat." The Republicans planned to carry all the states Frémont had won, plus Pennsylvania, Illinois, and Indiana. The two leading Republican contenders were Senator William H. Seward of New York and Abraham Lincoln of Illinois. Seward, the party's best-known figure, had enemies among party moderates, who thought he was too radical, and among nativists with whom he had clashed in the New York Whig Party. Lincoln, on the other hand, appeared new, impressive, more moderate than Seward, and certain to carry Illinois. Lincoln won the nomination on the third ballot.

The election of 1860 presented voters with one of the clearest choices in American history. On the key issue of slavery, Breckinridge supported its extension to the territories; Lincoln stood firmly for its exclusion. Douglas attempted to hold the middle ground with his principle of popular sovereignty; Bell vaguely favored compromise as well. Although they spoke clearly against the extension of slavery, Republicans sought to dispel their radical abolitionist image. The Republican platform condemned John Brown's raid as "the gravest of crimes," repeatedly denied that Republicans favored the social equality of black people, and strenuously affirmed that they sought to preserve the Union. In reality, Republicans simply did not believe the South would secede if Lincoln won.

The only candidate who spoke urgently and openly about the impending threat of secession was Douglas. Breaking with convention, Douglas campaigned personally, in both the North and, bravely, in the hostile South. Realizing his own chances for election were slight, he told his private secretary, "Mr. Lincoln is the next President. We must try to save the Union. I will go South."

In accordance with tradition, Lincoln did not campaign for himself, but many other Republicans spoke for him. The Republicans did not campaign in the South; Breckinridge did not campaign in the North. Each side was, therefore, free to believe the worst about the other.

The mood in the Deep South was close to mass hysteria. Rumors of slave revolts swept the region, and vigilance committees sprang up to counter the

In a contemporary engraving, John Brown and his followers are shown trapped inside the armory at Harpers Ferry in October 1859. Captured, tried, and executed, Brown was regarded as a martyr in the North and a terrorist in the South.

Constitutional Union Party National party formed in 1860, mainly by former Whigs, that emphasized allegiance to the Union and strict enforcement of all national legislation.

	Electoral Vote (%)	Popular Vote (%)
ABRAHAM LINCOLN (Republican)	180 (59)	1,865,593 (40)
John C. Breckinridge (Southern Democrat)	72 (24)	848,356 (18)
John Bell (Constitutional Union)	39 (13)	592,906 (13)
Stephen A. Douglas (Northern Democrat)	12 (4)	1,382,713 (29)
States that Republicans lost in 1856, won in 1860		

MAP 15.5

The Election of 1860   The election of 1860 was a sectional election. Lincoln won no votes in the South, Breckinridge none in the North. The contest in the North was between Lincoln and Douglas, and although Lincoln swept the electoral vote, Douglas's popular vote was uncomfortably close. The large number of northern Democratic voters opposed to Lincoln was a source of political trouble for him during the Civil War.

WHAT DO the results of the election of 1860 tell us about support for Lincoln in the North on the eve of the Civil War?

supposed threat. In the South Carolina up-country, the question of secession dominated races for the state legislature. Candidates such as A. S. Wallace of York, who advocated "patriotic forbearance" if Lincoln won, were soundly defeated. The very passion and excitement of the election campaign moved Southerners toward extremism.

The election of 1860 produced the second highest voter turnout in U.S. history. The election turned out to be two regional contests: Breckinridge versus Bell in the South, Lincoln versus Douglas in the North. Lincoln won all eighteen of the free states (he split New Jersey with Douglas) and almost 40 percent of the popular vote. Douglas carried only Missouri but gained nearly 30 percent of the popular vote. Lincoln's electoral vote total was overwhelming: 180 to a combined 123 for the other three candidates. But although Lincoln had won 54 percent of the vote in the northern states, his name had not even appeared on the ballot in ten southern states. The true winner of the 1860 election was sectionalism (see Map 15.5).

THE SOUTH LEAVES THE UNION

The results of the election shocked Southerners. They were humiliated and frightened by the prospect of becoming a permanent minority in a political system dominated by a party pledged to the elimination of slavery. In southern eyes, the Republican triumph meant they would become unequal partners in the federal enterprise, their way of life (the slave system) existing on borrowed time. Mary Boykin Chesnut, member of a well-connected South Carolina family, confided to her diary, "The die is cast—no more vain regrets—sad forebodings are useless. The stake is life or death."

The governors of South Carolina, Alabama, and Mississippi, each of whom had committed his state to secession if Lincoln were elected, immediately issued calls for special state conventions. At the same time, calls went out to southern communities to form vigilance committees and volunteer militia companies. Cooperationists (the term used for those opposed to immediate secession) were either intimidated into silence or simply left behind by the speed of events.

On December 20, 1860, a state convention in South Carolina, accompanied by all the hoopla and excitement of bands, fireworks displays, and huge rallies, voted unanimously to secede from the Union. In the weeks that followed, conventions in six other southern states (Mississippi, Florida, Alabama, Georgia, Louisiana, and Texas) followed suit, with the support, on average, of 80 percent of their delegates. There was genuine division of opinion in the Deep South, especially in Georgia and Alabama, along customary up-country–low-country lines. Yeoman farmers who did not own slaves and workers in the cities of the South were most likely to favor compromise with the North. But secessionists constantly reminded both groups that the Republican victory would lead to the emancipation of the slaves and the end of white privilege. And all Southerners, most of whom were deeply loyal to their state and region, believed that Northerners threatened their way of life. Throughout the South, secession occurred because Southerners no longer believed they had a choice.

In every state that seceded, the joyous scenes of South Carolina were repeated as the decisiveness of action replaced the long years of anxiety and tension. People danced in the streets, most believing the North had no choice but to accept secession peacefully. They ignored the fact that eight other slave states—Delaware, Maryland, Kentucky, Missouri, Virginia, North Carolina, Tennessee, and Arkansas—had not acted, though the latter four states did secede after war broke out (see Map 15.6). Just as Republicans had miscalculated in thinking southern threats a mere bluff, so secessionists now miscalculated in believing they would be able to leave the Union in peace.

THE NORTH'S POLITICAL OPTIONS

What should the North do? Buchanan, indecisive as always, did nothing. The decision thus rested with Abraham Lincoln, even before he officially became president. One possibility was compromise, and many proposals were suggested, ranging from full adoption of the Breckinridge campaign platform to reinstatement of the Missouri Compromise line. Lincoln cautiously refused them all, making it clear that he would not compromise on the extension of slavery, which was the South's key demand. He hoped, by appearing firm but moderate, to discourage additional southern states from seceding, while giving pro-Union Southerners time to organize. He succeeded in his first aim but not in the second. Lincoln and most of the Republican Party had seriously overestimated the strength of pro-Union sentiment in the South.

A second possibility, suggested by Horace Greeley of the *New York Tribune*, was to let the seven seceding states "go in peace." This is what many secessionists expected, but too many Northerners—including Lincoln himself—believed in the Union for this to happen. As Lincoln said, what was at stake was "the necessity of proving that popular government is not an absurdity. We must settle this question now, whether in a free government the minority have the right to break up the government whenever they choose."

The third possibility was force, and this was the crux of the dilemma. Although he believed their action was wrong, Lincoln was loath to go to war to force the seceding states back into the Union. On the other hand, he refused to give up federal powers over military forts and customs posts in the South. These were precisely the powers the seceding states had to command if they were to function as an independent nation. A confrontation was bound to come.

ESTABLISHMENT OF THE CONFEDERACY

In February, delegates from the seven seceding states met in Montgomery, Alabama, and created the **Confederate States of America**. They wrote a constitution that was identical to the Constitution of the United States, with a few crucial exceptions: it strongly supported states' rights and made the abolition of slavery practically impossible. These two clauses did much to define the Confederate enterprise. L. W. Spratt of South Carolina confessed as much in 1859: "We stand committed to the South, but we stand more vitally committed to the cause of slavery. It is, indeed, to be doubted whether the South [has] any cause apart from the institution which affects her."

The Montgomery convention chose Jefferson Davis of Mississippi as president and Alexander Stephens of Georgia as vice president of the new nation. Both men were known as moderates. The choice of moderates was deliberate, for the strategy of the new Confederate state was to argue that secession was a normal, responsible, and expectable course of action, and nothing for the North to get upset about. This was the theme that President Jefferson Davis of the Confederate States of America struck in his Inaugural Address, delivered to a crowd of 10,000 from the steps of the State Capitol at Montgomery, Alabama, on February 18, 1861. Secession was a legal and peaceful step that, Davis said, quoting from the Declaration of Independence, "illustrates the American idea that governments rest on the consent

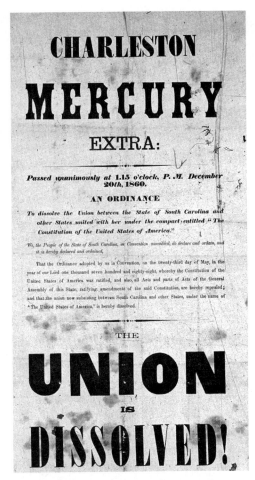

This special edition of the *Charleston Mercury* was issued on December 20, 1860, the day South Carolina voted to secede from the Union.

 14–9
Abraham Lincoln, *A House Divided* (1858)

Confederate States of America
Nation proclaimed in Montgomery, Alabama, in February 1861, after the seven states of the Lower South seceded from the United States.

OVERVIEW | The Irrepressible Conflict

1776	**Declaration of Independence**	Thomas Jefferson's denunciation of slavery deleted from the final version.
1787	**Northwest Ordinance**	Slavery prohibited in the Northwest Territory (north of the Ohio River).
1787	**Constitution**	Slavery unmentioned but acknowledged in Article I, Section 2, counting three-fifths of all African Americans, slave and free, in a state's population; and in Article I, Section 9, which barred Congress from prohibiting the international slave trade for twenty years.
1803	**Louisiana Purchase**	Louisiana admitted as a slave state in 1812; no decision about the rest of Louisiana Purchase.
1820	**Missouri Compromise**	Missouri admitted as a slave state, but slavery prohibited in Louisiana Purchase north of 36°30'.
1846	**Wilmot Proviso**	Proposal to prohibit slavery in territory that might be gained in Mexican-American War causes splits in national parties.
1850	**Compromise of 1850**	California admitted as free state; Texas (already admitted in 1845) is a slave state; the rest of Mexican Cession to be decided by popular sovereignty. Ends the slave trade in the District of Columbia, but a stronger Fugitive Slave Law, leading to a number of violent recaptures, arouses northern antislavery opinion.
1854	**Kansas-Nebraska Act**	At the urging of Stephen A. Douglas, Congress opens Kansas and Nebraska Territories for settlement under popular sovereignty. Open warfare between proslavery and antislavery factions breaks out in Kansas.
1857	**Lecompton Constitution**	President James Buchanan's decision to admit Kansas to the Union with a proslavery constitution is defeated in Congress.
1857	**Dred Scott Decision**	The Supreme Court's denial of Dred Scott's case for freedom is welcomed in the South, condemned in the North.
1859	**John Brown's Raid and Execution**	Northern support for John Brown shocks the South.
1860	**Democratic Party Nominating Conventions**	The Democrats are unable to agree on a candidate; two candidates, one northern (Stephen A. Douglas) and one southern (John C. Breckinridge) split the party and the vote, thus allowing Republican Abraham Lincoln to win.

myhistorylab

Overview: *The Irrepressible Conflict*

QUICK REVIEW

Northern Response to Secession

- Buchanan did nothing in response to secession.

- Lincoln refused calls to compromise on the question of slavery.

- Lincoln also rejected proposals to let the seven seceding states leave the Union.

of the governed . . . and that it is the right of the people to alter or abolish them at will whenever they become destructive of the ends for which they were established."

LINCOLN'S INAUGURATION

The country as a whole waited to see what Abraham Lincoln would do, which at first appeared to be very little. In Springfield, Lincoln refused to issue public statements before his inaugural for fear of making a delicate situation worse. Similarly, during a twelve-day whistle-stopping railroad trip east from Springfield, he was careful to say nothing controversial. Eastern intellectuals, already suspicious of a mere "prairie lawyer," were not impressed. These signs of moderation and caution did not appeal to an American public with a penchant for electing military heroes. Americans wanted leadership and action.

Lincoln continued, however, to offer nonbelligerent firmness and moderation. And at the end of his Inaugural Address on March 4, 1861, as he stood ringed by federal troops called out in case of a Confederate attack, the new president offered unexpected eloquence:

> I am loath to close. We are not enemies, but friends. We must not be enemies. Though passion may have strained, it must not break our bonds of affection. The mystic chords of memory, stretching from every battlefield, and patriot grave, to every living heart and hearthstone, all over this broad land, will yet swell the chorus of the Union, when again touched, as surely they will be, by the better angels of our nature.

MAP EXPLORATION

To explore an interactive version of this map, go to **http://www.prenhall.com/faraghertlc/map15.6**

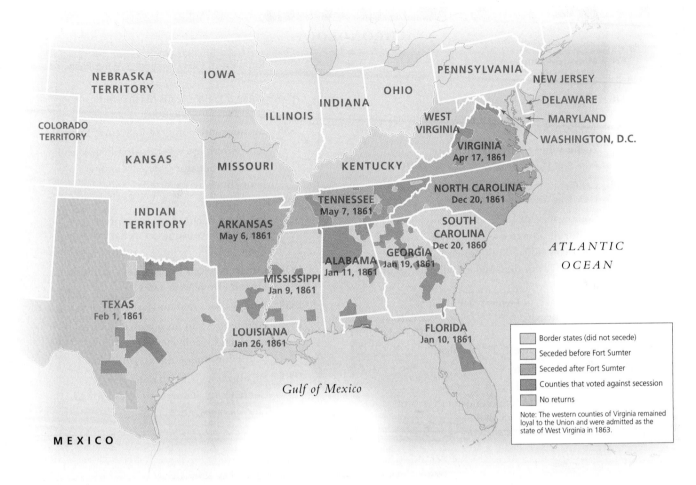

Border states (did not secede)

Seceded before Fort Sumter

Seceded after Fort Sumter

Counties that voted against secession

No returns

Note: The western counties of Virginia remained loyal to the Union and were admitted as the state of West Virginia in 1863.

MAP 15.6

The South Secedes The southern states that would constitute the Confederacy seceded in two stages. The states of the Lower South seceded before Lincoln took office. Arkansas and three states of the Upper South—Virginia, North Carolina, and Tennessee—waited until after the South fired on Fort Sumter. And four border slave states—Delaware, Maryland, Kentucky, and Missouri—chose not to secede. Every southern state (except South Carolina) was divided on the issue of secession, generally along up-country–low-country lines. In Virginia, this division was so extreme that West Virginia split off to become a separate nonslave state admitted to the Union in 1863.

WHY WERE some states quicker to secede than others?

CONCLUSION

Americans had much to boast about in 1850. Their nation was vastly larger, richer, and more powerful than it had been in 1800. But the issue of slavery was slowly dividing the North and the South, two communities with similar origins and many common bonds. The following decade was marked by frantic efforts at political compromise, beginning with the Compromise of 1850, continuing with the Kansas-Nebraska Act of 1854, and culminating in the Supreme Court's 1859 decision in the *Dred Scott* case. Increasingly, the ordinary people of the two regions demanded resolution of the crisis. The two great parties of the Second American Party System, the Democrats and the Whigs, unable to find a solution, were destroyed. Two new sectional parties—the Republican Party and a southern party devoted to the defense of slavery—fought the 1860 election, but Southerners refused to accept the national verdict. Politics had failed: the issue of slavery was irreconcilable. The only remaining recourse was war. But although Americans were divided, they were still one people. That made the war, when it came, all the more terrible.

401

CHRONOLOGY

1820	Missouri Compromise
1828–32	Nullification Crisis
1846	Wilmot Proviso
1848	Treaty of Guadalupe Hidalgo ends Mexican-American War
	Zachary Taylor elected president
	Free-Soil Party formed
1849	California and Utah seek admission to the Union as free states
1850	Compromise of 1850
	California admitted as a free state
	American (Know-Nothing) Party formed
	Zachary Taylor dies; Millard Fillmore becomes president
1851	North reacts to Fugitive Slave Law
	Harriet Beecher Stowe's *Uncle Tom's Cabin* published
1852	Franklin Pierce elected president
1854	Ostend Manifesto
	Kansas-Nebraska Act
	Treaties with Indians in northern part of Indian Territory renegotiated

	Republican Party formed as Whig Party dissolves
1855	William Walker leads his first filibustering expedition to Nicaragua
1856	Burning and looting of Lawrence, Kansas
	John Brown leads Pottawatomie massacre
	Attack on Senator Charles Sumner
	James Buchanan elected president
1857	*Dred Scott* decision
	President Buchanan accepts proslavery Lecompton constitution in Kansas
	Panic of 1857
1858	Congress rejects Lecompton constitution
	Lincoln–Douglas debates
1859	John Brown's raid on Harpers Ferry
1860	Four parties run presidential candidates
	Abraham Lincoln elected president
	South Carolina secedes from Union
1861	Six other Deep South states secede
	Confederate States of America formed
	Lincoln takes office

REVIEW QUESTIONS

1. What aspects of the remarkable economic development of the United States in the first half of the nineteenth century contributed to the sectional crisis of the 1850s?

2. How might the violent efforts by abolitionists to free escaped slaves who had been recaptured and the federal armed enforcement of the Fugitive Slave Law have been viewed differently by northern merchants (the so-called Cotton Whigs), Irish immigrants, and abolitionists?

3. Consider the course of events in "Bloody Kansas" from Douglas's Kansas-Nebraska Act to the congressional rejection of the Lecompton constitution. Were these events the inevitable result of the political impasse in Washington, or could other decisions have been made that would have changed the outcome?

4. The nativism of the 1850s that surfaced so strongly in the Know-Nothing Party was eclipsed by the crisis over slavery. But nativist sentiment has been a recurring theme in American politics. Discuss why it was strong in the 1850s and why it has emerged periodically since then.

5. Evaluate the character and actions of John Brown. Was he the hero proclaimed by northern supporters or the terrorist condemned by the South?

6. Imagine that you lived in Illinois, home state to both Douglas and Lincoln, in 1860. How would you have voted in the presidential election, and why?

KEY TERMS

Bleeding Kansas (p. 395)

Compromise of 1850 (p. 383)

Confederate States of America
   (p. 399)

Constitutional Union Party (p. 397)

Dred Scott decision (p. 395)

Fugitive Slave Law (p. 386)

Kansas-Nebraska Act (p. 389)

Know-Nothings (p. 394)

Lecompton constitution (p. 395)

Lincoln-Douglas debates (p. 380)

Panic of 1857 (p. 395)

Popular sovereignty (p. 383)

Republican Party (p. 394)

Flashcard Review

RECOMMENDED READING

William L. Barney, *The Secessionist Impulse: Alabama and Mississippi in 1860*
   (1974). Covers the election of 1860 and the subsequent conventions that
   led to secession.

Nicole Etcheson, *Bleeding Kansas: Contested Liberty in the Civil War Era* (2004).
   A look at the Kansas issue from the perspective of white settlers.

Don E. Fehrenbacher, *The* Dred Scott *Case: Its Significance in American Law and
   Politics* (1978). A major study by the leading historian on this controversial
   decision.

Eric Foner, *Free Soil, Free Labor, Free Men: The Ideology of the Republican Party before
   the Civil War* (1970). One of the first studies to focus on the free labor ideology of the North and its importance in the political disputes of the 1850s.

William A. Link, *Roots of Secession: Slavery and Politics in Antebellum Virginia* (2003).
   Draws connections between the changing circumstances of slavery and politics in the 1850s.

Robert E. May, *Manifest Destiny's Underworld: Filibustering in Antebellum America*
   (2002). A study of the activities and attitudes toward the adventurers.

David S. Reynolds, *John Brown, Abolitionist* (2005). Argues that Brown's extremism became the Civil War norm.

Kenneth M. Stampp, *America in 1857: A Nation on the Brink* (1990). A study of
   the "crucial" year by a leading southern historian.

John Stauffer, *The Black Hearts of Men: Radical Abolitionists and the Transformation
   of Race* (2001). Argues that radical abolitionists rejected the gender and
   racial conventions of their day.

For study resources for this chapter, go to **www.myhistorylab.com** and choose *Out of Many,
Teaching and Learning Classroom Edition.* You will find a wealth of study and review material
for this chapter, including pretests and posttests, customized study plan, key-term review
flash cards, interactive map and document activities, and documents for analysis.

*If it is necessary that I should
fall on the battle-field
for my Country I am ready.*
—Sullivan Ballou

Awaiting combat, 1861: Union Soldiers from New York relax
at camp awaiting orders to move to the front. The young men
show great confidence and determination for their coming
engagements, though one fellow to the left of the tent,
perhaps a teenager far from home, seems to long for something
as he stares beyond the camera. Note also the young
African American with a broom sitting apart from the soldiers.

16

THE CIVIL WAR
1861–1865

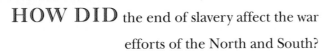

WHAT ADVANTAGES did the North possess at the outset of the Civil War?

HOW DID the power of the federal government expand as the war progressed?

WHAT SUCCESSES did the South enjoy in the early years of the war and how were they achieved?

HOW DID the end of slavery affect the war efforts of the North and South?

WHAT IMPACT did the war have on northern political, economic, and social life? and on the same aspects of southern life?

HOW DID Grant and Sherman turn the tide of the war?

AMERICAN COMMUNITIES
Mother Bickerdyke Connects Northern Communities to Their Boys at War

IN MAY 1861, THE REVEREND EDWARD BEECHER INTERRUPTED HIS customary Sunday service at Brick Congregational Church in Galesburg, Illinois, to read a disturbing letter to the congregation. Two months earlier, Galesburg had proudly sent 500 of its young men off to join the Union army. They had not yet been in battle. Yet, the letter reported, an alarming number were dying of diseases caused by inadequate food, medical care, and sanitation at the crowded military camp in Cairo, Illinois. Most army doctors were surgeons trained to operate and amputate on the battlefield. The letter writer, appalled by the squalor and misery he saw around him, complained of abuses by the army. The Union army, however, was overwhelmed with the task of readying recruits for battle and had made few provisions for their health when they were not in combat.

The shocked and grieving members of Beecher's congregation quickly decided to send not only supplies but also one of their number to inspect the conditions at the Cairo camp and to take action. In spite of warnings that army regulations excluded women from encampments, the congregation voted to send their most qualified member, Mary Ann Bickerdyke, a middle-aged widow who made her living as a "botanic physician."

"Mother" Bickerdyke, as she was called, let nothing stand in the way of helping her "boys." When she arrived in Cairo, she immediately set to work cleaning the hospital tents and the soldiers themselves, and finding and cooking nourishing food for them. The hospital director, who resented her interference, ordered her to leave, but she blandly continued her work. When he reported her to the commanding officer, General Benjamin Prentiss, she quickly convinced the general to let her stay.

A plain spoken, hardworking woman, totally unfazed by rank or tender masculine egos, Mother Bickerdyke single-mindedly devoted herself to what she called "the Lord's work." Once, when an indignant officer's wife complained about Bickerdyke's rudeness, General William Tecumseh Sherman joked, "You've picked the one person around here who outranks me. If you want to lodge a complaint against her, you'll have to take it to President Lincoln."

Other communities all over the North rallied to make up for the Army's shortcomings with supplies and assistance. By their actions, Mother Bickerdyke and others like her exposed the War Department's inability to meet the needs of the nation's first mass army. The efforts of women on the local level quickly took on national dimensions. The Women's Central Association of Relief (WCAR) eventually had 7,000 chapters throughout the North. Its volunteers raised funds, made and collected food, clothes, medicine, bandages, and more than 250,000 quilts and comforters, and sent them to army camps and hospitals. All told, association chapters supplied an estimated $15 million worth of goods to the Union troops.

In June 1861, responding to requests by officials of the WCAR for formal recognition of the organization, President Abraham Lincoln created the United States Sanitary Commission and gave it the power to investigate and advise the Medical Bureau.

Although at first she worked independently and remained suspicious of all organizations (and even of many other relief workers), in 1862 Mother Bickerdyke was persuaded to become an official agent of "the Sanitary," as it was known. The advantage to her was access to the commission's warehouses and the ability to order from them precisely what she needed. The advantage to the Sanitary was that Mother Bickerdyke was an unequaled fundraiser. With the help of Bickerdyke's blunt appeals, the Sanitary raised $50 million for the Union war effort.

The Civil War was a national tragedy, ripping apart the political fabric of the country and causing more casualties than any other war in the nation's history. The death toll of approximately 620,000 exceeded the number of dead in all the other wars from the Revolution through the Vietnam War. Yet in another sense, it was a community triumph. Local communities directly supported and sustained their soldiers on a massive scale in unprecedented ways. As national unity failed, the strength of local communities, symbolized by Mother Bickerdyke, endured.

Illinois

COMMUNITIES MOBILIZE FOR WAR

A neutral observer in March 1861 might have seen ominous similarities. Two nations—the United States of America (shorn of seven states in the Deep South) and the Confederate States of America—each blamed the other for the breakup of the Union. Two new presidents—Abraham Lincoln and Jefferson Davis—each faced the challenging task of building and maintaining national unity. Two regions—North and South—scorned each other and boasted of their own superiority. But the most important similarity was not yet apparent: both sides were unprepared for the ordeal that lay ahead.

FORT SUMTER: THE WAR BEGINS

Fort Sumter, a federal military installation, sat on a granite island at the entrance to Charleston harbor. So long as it remained in Union hands, Charleston, the center of secessionist sentiment, would be immobilized. Thus, it was hardly surprising that Fort Sumter would provide President Lincoln with his first crisis.

With the fort dangerously low on supplies, Lincoln had to decide whether to abandon it or risk the fight that might ensue if he ordered it resupplied. On April 6, 1861, Lincoln took cautious and careful action, notifying the governor of South Carolina that he was sending a relief force to the fort carrying only food and no military supplies. Now the decision rested with Jefferson Davis. On April 10, he ordered General P. G. T. Beauregard to demand the surrender of Fort Sumter and to attack it if the garrison did not comply. On April 12, Beauregard opened fire. Two days later, the defenders surrendered.

Even before the attack on Fort Sumter, the Confederate Congress had authorized a volunteer army of 100,000 men to serve for twelve months. Men flocked to enlist, and their communities sent them off in ceremonies featuring bands, bonfires, and belligerent oratory.

The "thunderclap of Sumter" startled the North into an angry response. The apathy and uncertainty that had prevailed since Lincoln's election disappeared, to be replaced by strong feelings of patriotism. On April 15, Lincoln issued a proclamation calling for 75,000 state militiamen to serve in the federal army for ninety days. Enlistment offices were swamped with so many enthusiastic volunteers that men were sent home. Free African Americans, among the most eager to serve, were turned away: this was not yet a war for or by black people.

WHAT ADVANTAGES did the North possess at the outset of the Civil War?

Review Summary

15–1
Jefferson Davis, *Address to the Provisional Congress of the Confederate States of America* (1861)

15–2
Alexander Hamilton Stephens, *The "Cornerstone Speech"* (1861)

15–4
Why They Fought (1861)

This Currier and Ives lithograph shows the opening moment of the Civil War. On April 12, 1861, Confederate General P.G.T. Beauregard ordered the shelling of Fort Sumter in Charleston harbor. Two days later, Union Major Robert Anderson surrendered, and mobilization began for what turned out to be the most devastating war in American history.

IMAGE KEY

for pages 404–405

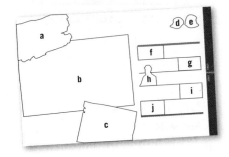

a. A federal flag that flew over Fort Sumter.

b. A photo of engineers of the 8th New York State Militia, 1861.

c. The battle flag of the Second Battalion Hilliard's Alabama Legion. This flag was pierced 83 times during the charge up Snod Grass Hill at Chickamauga, Georgia.

d. The gray cap of a Confederate soldier from the American Civil War.

e. A blue Union soldier's hat with a bugle emblem embroidered on the front.

f. The opening moment of the Civil War, April 12, 1861, at Fort Sumter in Charleston harbor.

g. A painting by William C. Washington, *Jackson Entering the City of Winchester*, shows General "Stonewall" Jackson saving the Virginia town from Union capture in 1862.

h. Robert E. Lee (1807–1870), commander-in-chief of the Confederate armies during the Civil War.

i. American President Abraham Lincoln presents the Emancipation Proclamation to grateful black slaves and white peasants in a political cartoon about education, freedom, and equality.

j. A black family runs through a vacant lot while being chased by white hooligans during the 1863 race riots in New York City.

The mobilization in Chester, Pennsylvania, was typical of the northern response to the outbreak of war. As volunteers marched off to Washington (the gathering place for the Union army), companies of home guards were organized by the men who remained behind. Within a month, the women of Chester had organized a countywide system of war relief. Such relief organizations, some formally organized, some informal, emerged in every community, North and South, that sent soldiers off to the Civil War. These organizations not only played a vital role in supplying the troops, but they also maintained the human, local link on which so many soldiers depended. In this sense, every American community accompanied its young men to war.

THE BORDER STATES

The first secession, between December 20, 1860, and February 1, 1861, had taken seven Deep South states out of the Union. Now, in April, the firing on Fort Sumter and Lincoln's call for state militias forced the other southern states to take sides. Courted—and pressured—by both North and South, four states of the Upper South (Virginia, Arkansas, Tennessee, and North Carolina) joined the original seven in April and May 1861. Virginia's secession tipped the other three toward the Confederacy. The capital of the Confederacy was now moved to Richmond.

Still undecided was the loyalty of the northernmost tier of slave-owning states: Missouri, Kentucky, Maryland, and Delaware. Each controlled vital strategic assets. Missouri not only bordered the Mississippi River but also controlled the routes to the west. Kentucky controlled the Ohio River. The main railroad link with the West ran through Maryland and the hill region of western Virginia. Delaware controlled access to Philadelphia. Finally, were Maryland to secede, the nation's capital would be completely surrounded by Confederate territory.

Delaware was loyal to the Union (less than 2 percent of its population were slaves), but Maryland's loyalty was divided, as an ugly incident on April 19 showed. When the Sixth Massachusetts Regiment marched through Baltimore, a hostile crowd of 10,000 southern sympathizers, carrying Confederate flags, pelted the troops with bricks, paving stones, and bullets. Finally, in desperation, the troops fired on the crowd, killing twelve people and wounding others. In retaliation, southern sympathizers burned the railroad bridges to the North and destroyed the telegraph line to Washington, cutting off communication between the capital and the rest of the Union for six days.

Lincoln's response was swift and stern. He stationed Union troops along Maryland's crucial railroads, declared martial law in Baltimore, and arrested the suspected ringleaders of the pro-Confederate mob and held them without trial. The arrests in Maryland were the first of a number of violations of basic civil rights during the war, all of which the president justified on the basis of national security.

An even bloodier division occurred in Missouri, where old foes from "Bleeding Kansas" faced off. The proslavery governor and most of the legislature fled to Arkansas, where they declared a Confederate state government in exile, while Unionists remained in control in St. Louis. Consequently, Missouri was plagued by guerrilla battles throughout the war. In Kentucky, division took the form of a huge illegal trade with the Confederacy through neighboring Tennessee.

That Delaware, Maryland, Missouri, and Kentucky chose to stay in the Union was a severe blow to the Confederacy. Among them, the four states could have added 45 percent to the white population and military manpower of the Confederacy and 80 percent to its manufacturing capacity.

THE BATTLE OF BULL RUN

Once sides had been chosen and the initial flush of enthusiasm had passed, the nature of the war, and the mistaken notions about it, soon became clear. The event that shattered the illusions was the First Battle of Bull Run, at Bull Run Creek near Manassas in Virginia in July 1861. Confident of a quick victory, a Union army of 35,000 men marched south. The troops were accompanied not only by journalists but also by a crowd of politicians and sightseers. At first the Union troops held their ground against the 25,000 Confederate troops. But when 2,300 fresh Confederate troops arrived as reinforcements, the untrained northern troops broke ranks in an uncontrolled retreat that swept up the frightened sightseers as well.

THE RELATIVE STRENGTHS OF NORTH AND SOUTH

Bull Run was sobering—and prophetic. The Civil War was the most lethal military conflict in American history, leaving a legacy of devastation on the battlefield and desolation at home. It claimed the lives of nearly 620,000 soldiers, more than the First and Second World Wars combined. One out of every four soldiers who fought in the war never returned home.

Overall, in terms of both population and productive capacity, the Union seemed to have a commanding edge over the Confederacy. The North had two and a half times the South's population and enjoyed an even greater advantage in industrial capacity (nine times that of the South). These advantages were ultimately to prove decisive: by the end of the war, the Union had managed to field and equip more than 2 million soldiers as compared to the Confederacy's 800,000. The Confederacy's problems of supply, however, were due mostly to a poor railroad system. But in the short term, the South had important assets to counter the advantage of the North (see Figure 16.1).

The first was the nature of the struggle. For the South, this was a defensive war, in which the basic principle of the defense of home and community united almost all white citizens, regardless of their views about slavery. The North would have to invade the South and then control it against guerrilla opposition in order to win.

Second, the military disparity was less extreme than it appeared. Although the North had manpower, its troops were mostly untrained. Moreover, the South appeared to have an advantage in military leaders, the most notable of which was Robert E. Lee.

Finally, it was widely believed that slavery would work to the South's advantage, for slaves could continue to do the vital plantation work while their masters

15–3
Mary Boykin Chesnut,
A Confederate Lady's Diary
(1861)

15–5
*A Confederate General
Assesses First Bull Run*
(1861)

QUICK REVIEW

The First Battle of Bull Run

◆ July 1861: Beauregard (Confederacy) and McDowell (Union) meet at Manassas.

◆ Confederate troops repulse a strong Union attack.

◆ Battle foreshadowed war to come.

QUICK REVIEW

Northern Advantages

◆ Two and a half times the South's population.

◆ North controlled much of nation's industrial capacity.

◆ Could field a much larger army.

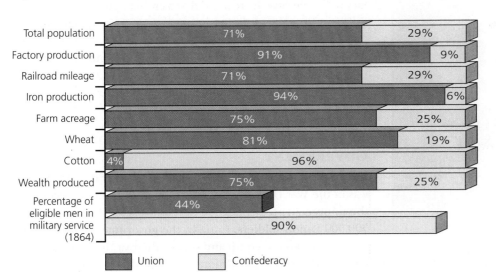

	Union	Confederacy
Total population	71%	29%
Factory production	91%	9%
Railroad mileage	71%	29%
Iron production	94%	6%
Farm acreage	75%	25%
Wheat	81%	19%
Cotton	4%	96%
Wealth produced	75%	25%
Percentage of eligible men in military service (1864)	44%	90%

Figure 16.1
As this chart shows, the North far surpassed the South in the resources necessary to support a large, long war. Initially, however, these strengths made little difference in a struggle that began as a traditional war of maneuver in which the South held the difensive advantage. Only slowly did the Civil War become a modern war in which all the resources of society, including the property and lives of civilians, were mobilized for battle.

The Times Atlas of World History (Maplewood, New Jersey: Hammond, 1978).

went off to war. But above all, the South had the weapon of cotton. Because of the crucial role of cotton in industrialization, Southerners were confident that the British and French need for southern cotton would soon bring those countries to recognize the Confederacy as a separate nation.

THE GOVERNMENTS ORGANIZE FOR WAR

HOW DID the power of the federal government expand as the war progressed?

myhistorylab

Review Summary

The Civil War forced the federal government to assume powers unimaginable just a few years before. Abraham Lincoln took as his primary task leading and unifying the nation in his role as commander in chief. He found the challenge almost insurmountable. Jefferson Davis's challenge was even greater. He had to create a Confederate nation out of a loose grouping of eleven states, each believing strongly in states' rights. Yet in the Confederacy, as in the Union, the conduct of the war required central direction.

LINCOLN TAKES CHARGE

Lincoln's first task as president was to assert control over his own cabinet. Because he had few national contacts outside the Republican Party, Lincoln chose to staff his cabinet with other Republicans, including, most unusually, several who had been his rivals for the presidential nomination. That the Republican Party was a not-quite-jelled mix of former Whigs, abolitionists, moderate Free-Soilers, and even some prowar Democrats made Lincoln's task as party leader much more difficult than it might otherwise have been.

After the fall of Fort Sumter, military necessity prompted Lincoln to call up the state militias, order a naval blockade of the South, and vastly expand the military budget. Breaking with precedent, he took these actions without congressional sanction because Congress was not in session. Military necessity—the need to hold the border states—likewise prompted other early actions, such as the suspension of habeas corpus and the acceptance of Kentucky's ambiguous neutrality. The president also repudiated an unauthorized declaration issued by General John C. Frémont, military commander in Missouri, in August 1861 that would have freed Missouri's slaves. Lincoln feared that such an action would lead to the secession of Kentucky and Maryland.

Lincoln was the first president to act as commander in chief in both a practical and a symbolic way. He actively directed military policy, because he realized that a civil war presented problems different from those of a foreign war of conquest. Lincoln wanted above all to persuade the South to rejoin the Union, and his every military order was dictated by the hope of eventual reconciliation—hence, his caution and his acute sense of the role of public opinion. At the same time, he presided over a vast expansion of the powers of the federal government.

EXPANDING THE POWER OF THE FEDERAL GOVERNMENT

The greatest expansion in government power during the war was in the War Department, which by early 1862 was faced with the unprecedented challenge of feeding, clothing, and arming 700,000 Union soldiers. Initially, the government relied on the individual states to equip and supply their vastly expanded militias. But the size of the Union army and the complexity of fully

This photograph, taken a month before his inauguration, shows Lincoln looking presidential. It was clearly intended to reassure a public still doubtful about his abilities.

supplying it demanded constant efforts at all levels—government, state, and community—throughout the war. Thus, in the matter of procurement and supply, as in mobilization, the battlefront was related to the home front on a scale that Americans had not previously experienced.

The need for money for the vast war effort was pressing. Treasury Secretary Salmon P. Chase worked closely with Congress to develop ways to finance the war. With the help of Philadelphia financier Jay Cooke, the Treasury used patriotic appeals to sell war bonds to ordinary people in amounts as small as $50. By the war's end, the United States had borrowed $2.6 billion for the war effort, the first example in American history of the mass financing of war.

Most radical of all was Chase's decision to print and distribute Treasury notes (paper money). Until then, the money in circulation had been a mixture of coins and state bank notes issued by 1,500 different state banks. The **Legal Tender Act** of February 1862 created a national currency. In 1863, Congress passed the **National Bank Act**, which prohibited state banks from issuing their own notes and forced them to apply for federal charters. The switch to a national currency was widely recognized as a major step toward centralization of economic power in the hands of the federal government.

Although the outbreak of war overshadowed everything else, the Republican Party in Congress was determined to fulfill its campaign pledge of a comprehensive program of economic development. Republicans quickly passed the **Morrill Tariff Act** (1861). In 1862 and 1864, Congress created two federally chartered corporations to build a transcontinental railroad thus fulfilling the dreams of the many expansionists who believed America's economic future lay in trade with Asia across the Pacific Ocean. The **Homestead Act** (1862) gave 160 acres of public land to any citizen who agreed to live on the land for five years, improve it by building a house and cultivating some of the land, and pay a small fee. The **Morrill Land Grant Act** (1862) gave states public land that would allow them to finance land-grant colleges offering education to ordinary citizens in practical skills such as agriculture, engineering, and military science. Coupled with this act, the establishment of a federal Department of Agriculture in 1862 gave American farmers a big push toward modern commercial agriculture.

The enactment of the Republican program increased the role of the federal government in national life. Although many of the executive war powers lapsed when the battles ended, the accumulation of strength by the federal government was never reversed.

DIPLOMATIC OBJECTIVES

To Secretary of State William Seward fell the job of making sure that Britain and France did not extend diplomatic recognition to the Confederacy. Although Southerners had been certain that King Cotton would gain them European support, they were wrong. British public opinion would not countenance the recognition of a new nation based on slavery. British cotton manufacturers found economic alternatives to southern cotton. In spite of Union protests, however, both Britain and France did allow Confederate vessels to use their ports, and British shipyards sold six ships to the Confederacy. But in 1863, when the Confederacy commissioned Britain's Laird shipyard to build two ironclad ships, the Union threatened war, and the British government made sure that the Laird ironclads were never delivered.

JEFFERSON DAVIS TRIES TO UNIFY THE CONFEDERACY

Although Jefferson Davis had held national cabinet rank (as secretary of war under President Franklin Pierce), had experience as an administrator, and was a former military man, he was unable to hold the Confederacy together.

Legal Tender Act Act creating a national currency in February 1862.

National Bank Act Act prohibiting state banks from issuing their own notes and forcing them to apply for federal charters.

Morrill Tariff Act Act that raised tariffs to more than double their prewar rate.

Homestead Act Law passed by Congress in May 1862 providing homesteads with 160 acres of free land in exchange for improving the land within five years of the grant.

Morrill Land Grant Act Law passed by Congress in July 1862 awarding proceeds from the sale of public lands to the states for the establishment of agricultural and mechanical colleges.

15–6

Charles Harvey Brewster, *Three Letters from the Civil War Front* (1862)

Davis's first cabinet of six men, appointed in February 1861, included a representative from each of the states of the first secession except Mississippi, which was represented by Davis himself. This careful attention to the equality of the states pointed to the fundamental problem Davis was unable to overcome. A shared belief in states' rights—that is, in their own autonomy—was a poor basis on which to build a unified nation. Although Davis saw the need for unity, he was unable to impose it. Soon his style of leadership—micromanagement—angered his generals, alienated cabinet members, and gave southern governors reason to resist his orders. After the first flush of patriotism had passed, the Confederacy never lived up to its hope of becoming a unified nation.

CONTRADICTIONS OF SOUTHERN NATIONALISM

The failure of "cotton diplomacy" was a crushing blow. White Southerners were stunned that Britain and France would not recognize their claim to independence. Well into 1863, the South hoped that a decisive battlefield victory would change the minds of cautious Europeans.

Perhaps the greatest southern failure was in the area of finances. At first, the Confederate government tried to raise money from the states, but governors refused to impose new taxes. By the time uniform taxes were levied in 1863, it was too late. Heavy borrowing and the printing of great sums of paper money produced runaway inflation (a ruinous rate of 9,000 percent by 1865, compared with 80 percent in the North). Inflation, in turn, caused incalculable damage to morale and prospects for unity.

After the initial surge of volunteers, enlistment in the military fell off, as it did in the North also. In April 1862, the Confederate Congress passed the first draft law in American history, and the Union Congress followed suit in March 1863. The southern law declared that all able-bodied men between eighteen and thirty-five were eligible for three years of military service. Purchase of substitutes was allowed, as in the North. The most disliked part of the draft law was a provision exempting one white man on each plantation with twenty or more slaves. This provision not only seemed to disprove the earlier claim that slavery freed white men to fight, but also it aroused class resentments.

In the early days of the war, Jefferson Davis successfully mobilized feelings of regional identity and patriotism. Many Southerners felt part of a beleaguered region that had been forced to resist northern tyranny. But most felt loyalty to their own state and local communities, not to a Confederate nation. The strong belief in states' rights and aristocratic privilege undermined the Confederate cause. Some southern governors resisted potentially unifying actions such as moving militias outside their home states. Broader measures, such as general taxation, were widely evaded by rich and poor alike.

The inequitable draft was only one of many things that convinced the ordinary people of the South that this was a war for privileged slave owners, not for them. With its leaders and

This painting by William C. Washington, *Jackson Entering the City of Winchester,* shows the dashing Confederate General "Stonewall" Jackson saving the Virginia town from Union capture in 1862. Jackson and other Confederate generals evoked fierce loyalty to the Confederacy. Unfortunately, by the time this victory was commemorated, Jackson himself was dead from wounds caused by friendly fire at the Battle of Chancellorsville in May of 1863.

William Washington, "Stonewall Jackson Entering the City of Winchester, Virginia." Oil painting. Valentine Museum Library, Richmond, Virginia.

The contrast between the hope and valor of these young southern volunteer soldiers, photographed shortly before the First Battle of Bull Run, and the later advertisements for substitutes (at right), is marked. Southern exemptions for slave owners and lavish payment for substitutes increasingly bred resentment among the ordinary people of the South.

(above) Cook Collection. Valentine Museum Library/Richmond History Center.

SUBSTITUTE NOTICES.

WANTED—A SUBSTITUTE for a conscript, to serve during the war. Any good man over the age of 35 years, not a resident of Virginia, or a foreigner, may hear of a good situation by calling at Mr. GEORGE BAGBY'S office, Shockoe Slip, to-day, between the hours of 9 and 11 A. M.   [jy 9—1t*]   A COUNTRYMAN.

WANTED—Two SUBSTITUTES—one for artillery, the other for infantry or cavalry service. Also, to sell, a trained, thoroughbred cavalry HORSE. Apply to   DR. BROOCKS,
Corner Main and 12th streets, or to
T. T. BROOCKS,
jy 9—3t*   Petersburg, Va.

WANTED—Immediately, a SUBSTITUTE. A man over 35 years old, or under 18, can get a good price by making immediate application to Room No. 50, Monument Hotel, or by addressing "J. W.," through Richmond P. O.   jy 9—1t*

WANTED—A SUBSTITUTE, to go into the 24th North Carolina State troops, for which a liberal price will be paid. Apply to me at Dispatch office this evening at 4 o'clock P. M.
jy 9—1t*   R. R. MOORE.

WANTED—A SUBSTITUTE, to go in a first-rate Georgia company of infantry, under the heroic Jackson. A gentleman whose health is impaired, will give a fair price for a substitute. Apply immediately at ROOM, No. 13, Post-Office Department, third story, between the hours of 10 and 3 o'clock.   jy 9—6t*

WANTED—Two SUBSTITUTES for the war. A good bonus will be given. None need apply except those exempt from Conscript. Apply to-day at   GEORGE I. HERRING'S,
jy 9—1t*   Grocery store, No. 56 Main st.

citizens fearing (perhaps correctly) that centralization would destroy what was distinctively southern, the Confederacy was unable to mobilize the resources—financial, human, and otherwise—that might have prevented its destruction by northern armies.

THE FIGHTING THROUGH 1862

Just as political decisions were often driven by military necessity, the basic northern and southern military strategies were affected by political considerations as much as by military ones. The initial policy of limited war, thought to be the best route to ultimate reconciliation, ran into difficulties because of the public's impatience for victories. But victories, as the mounting slaughter made clear, were not easy to achieve.

THE WAR IN NORTHERN VIRGINIA

The initial northern strategy, dubbed by critics the Anaconda Plan (after the constrictor snake), envisaged slowly squeezing the South with a blockade at sea and on the Mississippi River. The plan avoided invasion and conquest in the hope that a strained South would recognize the inevitability of defeat and thus surrender. Lincoln accepted the basics of the plan, but public clamor for a fight pushed him to agree to the disastrous Battle of Bull Run and then to a major buildup of Union troops in northern Virginia under General George B. McClellan (see Map 16.1).

WHAT SUCCESSES did the South enjoy in the early years of the war and how were they achieved?

Review Summary

MAP EXPLORATION

To explore an interactive version of this map, go to **http://www.prenhall.com/faraghertlc/map16.1**

1861–62

	Area controlled by Union	←	Union advance
	Area gained by Union	✹	Union victory
	Area controlled by Confederacy	✶	Confederate victory

1863

1864–65

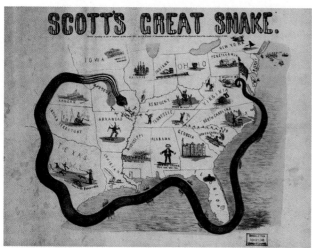

SCOTT'S GREAT SNAKE.

MAP 16.1

Overall Strategy of the Civil War   The initial northern strategy for subduing the South, the so-called Anaconda Plan (see cartoon above), entailed strangling it by a blockade at sea and obtaining control of the Mississippi River. But at the end of 1862, it was clear that the South's defensive strategy could only be broken by the invasion of southern territory. In 1864, Sherman's "March to the Sea" and Grant's hammering tactics in northern Virginia brought the war home to the South. Lee's surrender to Grant at Appomattox Courthouse on April 9, 1865, ended the bloodiest war in the nation's history.

HOW DID the military strategies of the North and the South reflect each side's larger goals?

In March 1862, after almost a year spent drilling the raw Union recruits and after repeated exhortations by an impatient Lincoln, McClellan committed 120,000 troops to what became known as the **Peninsular campaign**. The objective was to capture Richmond, the Confederate capital. Inching up the James Peninsula, he tried to avoid battle, hoping his overwhelming numbers would convince the South to surrender. In a series of battles known as the Seven Days, Robert E. Lee boldly counterattacked, repeatedly catching McClellan off guard. Taking heavy losses as well as inflicting them, Lee drove McClellan back. In August, Lee routed another Union army, commanded by General John Pope, at the Second Battle of Bull Rull (Second Manassas).

Lincoln, alarmed at the threat to Washington and disappointed by McClellan's inaction, ordered him to abandon the Peninsular campaign and return to the capital.

Jefferson Davis, like Abraham Lincoln, was an active commander in chief. And like Lincoln, he responded to a public that clamored for more action than a strictly defensive war entailed. After the Seven Days victories, Davis supported a Confederate march into Maryland. At the same time, he issued a proclamation urging the people of Maryland to make a separate peace. But in the brutal battle of Antietam on September 17, 1862, which claimed more than 5,000 dead and 19,000 wounded, McClellan's army checked Lee's advance. Lee retreated to Virginia, inflicting terrible losses on northern troops at Fredricksburg when they again made a thrust toward Richmond in December 1862. The war in northern Virginia was stalemated: neither side was strong enough to win, but each was too strong to be defeated (see Map 16.2).

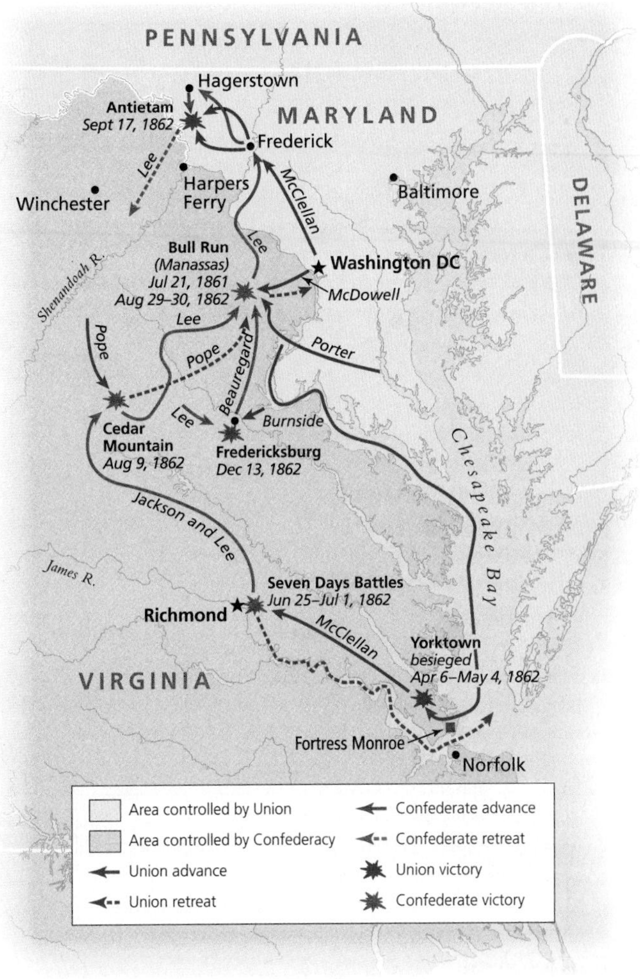

SHILOH AND THE WAR FOR THE MISSISSIPPI

Although most public attention was focused on the fighting in Virginia, battles in Tennessee and along the Mississippi River proved to be the key to eventual Union victory. In February 1862, General Ulysses S. Grant captured Fort Henry and Fort Donelson, on the Tennessee and Cumberland Rivers, establishing Union control of much of Tennessee and forcing Confederate troops to retreat into northern Mississippi.

Moving south with 28,000 men, Grant met a 40,000-man Confederate force at Shiloh Church in April 1862. Seriously outnumbered on the first day, Grant's forces were reinforced by the arrival of 35,000 troops. After two days of bitter and bloody fighting in the rain, the Confederates withdrew. The losses on both sides were enormous: the North lost 3,000 men, the South 11,000. Nevertheless, Union forces kept moving, capturing Memphis in June and beginning a campaign to eventually capture Vicksburg. Grant and other Union generals faced strong Confederate resistance, and progress was slow. Earlier that year, naval forces under Admiral David Farragut had captured New Orleans and then continued up the Mississippi River. By the end of 1862, it was clearly only a matter of time before the entire river would be in Union hands. Arkansas, Louisiana, and Texas would then be cut off from the rest of the Confederacy (see Map 16.3).

THE WAR IN THE TRANS–MISSISSIPPI WEST

Although only one western state, Texas, seceded from the Union, the Civil War was fought in small ways in many parts of the West. A Confederate force led by General Henry H. Sibley occupied Santa Fé and Albuquerque early in 1862 without resistance, thus posing a serious threat to the entire Southwest. Confederate hopes were dashed,

MAP 16.2

Major Battles in the East, 1861–62   Northern Virginia was the most crucial and the most constant theater of battle. The prizes were the two opposing capitals, Washington and Richmond, only 70 miles apart. By the summer of 1862, George B. McClellan, famously cautious, had achieved only stalemate in the Peninsular campaign. He did, however, turn back Robert E. Lee at Antietam in September.

WHAT WAS the Anaconda Plan? Why did it fail?

Peninsular campaign   Union offensive led by McClellan with the objective of capturing Richmond.

MAP 16.3

Major Battles in the Interior, 1862–63 Ulysses S. Grant waged a mobile war, winning at Fort Henry and Fort Donelson in Tennessee in February 1862, at Shiloh in April, and capturing Memphis in June. He then laid siege to Vicksburg, as Admiral David Farragut captured New Orleans and began to advance up the Mississippi River.

WHAT ROLE did Indians Play in the Fighting in the West?

however, by a ragtag group of 950 miners and adventurers organized into the first Colorado Volunteer Infantry Regiment. After an epic march of 400 miles from Denver, which was completed in thirteen days despite snow and high winds, the Colorado militia stopped the unsuspecting Confederate troops in the Battle of Glorieta Pass on March 26–28, 1862. This dashing action, coupled with the efforts of California militias to safeguard Arizona and Utah from seizure by Confederate sympathizers, secured the Far West for the Union.

Another civil war took place in Indian Territory, south of Kansas. The southern Indian tribes who had been removed there from the Old Southwest in the 1830s included many who were still bitter over the horrors of their removal by federal troops, and they sympathized with the Confederacy. The Confederacy actively sought Indian support by offering Indian people representation in the Confederate Congress. Consequently, many Indians fought for the South. Union victories at Pea Ridge (in northwestern Arkansas) in 1862 and near Fort Gibson (in Indian Territory) in 1863 secured the area for the Union but did little to stop dissension among the Indian groups themselves. After the Civil War, the victorious federal government used the tribes' wartime support for the Confederacy as a justification for demanding further land cessions.

Elsewhere in the West, other groups of Indians found themselves caught up in the wider war. An uprising by the Santee Sioux in Minnesota occurred in August 1862, just as McClellan conceded defeat in the Peninsular campaign in Virginia. Alarmed whites, certain that the uprising was a Confederate plot, ignored legitimate Sioux grievances and responded in kind to Sioux ferocity. In little more than a month, 500 to 800 white settlers and an even greater number of Sioux were killed. Thirty-eight Indians were hanged in a mass execution in Mankato on December 26, 1862, and subsequently all Sioux were expelled from Minnesota. In 1863, U.S. Army Colonel Kit Carson invaded Navajo country in Arizona in retaliation for Indian raids on U.S. troops. Eight thousand Navajos were forced on the brutal "Long Walk" to Bosque Redondo on the Pecos River in New Mexico, where they were held prisoner until a treaty between the United States and the Navajos was signed in 1868.

THE NAVAL WAR

The Union's naval blockade of the South, intended to cut off commerce between the Confederacy and the rest of the world, was initially unsuccessful. The U.S. Navy had only thirty-three ships with which to blockade 189 ports along 3,500 miles of coastline. Beginning in 1863, however, as the Union navy became larger, the blockade began to take effect. As a result, fewer and fewer supplies reached the South.

North and South also engaged in a brief duel featuring the revolutionary new technology of ironcladding. The Confederacy refitted a scuttled Union vessel, the *Merrimac*, with iron plating and renamed it the *Virginia*. On March 8, 1862, the *Virginia* steamed out of Norfolk harbor to challenge the Union blockade. The iron plating protected the *Virginia* from the fire of the Union ships, which found themselves defenseless against its ram and its powerful guns. Two Union ships went down, and the blockade seemed about to be broken. But the North had an experimental ironclad of its own, the *Monitor*, which was waiting for the *Virginia* when it emerged from port on March 9. The historic duel between these first two ironclads was inconclusive. But this brief duel prefigured the naval and land battles of the world wars of the twentieth century as much as did the massing of huge armies on the battlefield.

For the Union, the most successful naval operation in the first two years of the war was not the blockade but the seizing of exposed coastal areas. The Sea Islands of South Carolina were taken, as were some of the North Carolina islands and Fort Pulaski, which commanded the harbor of Savannah, Georgia. Most damaging to the South was the capture of New Orleans.

THE BLACK RESPONSE

The capture of Port Royal in the South Carolina Sea Islands in 1861 was important for another reason. Whites fled at the Union advance, but 10,000 slaves greeted the troops with jubilation and shouts of gratitude. Union troops had unwittingly freed these slaves in advance of any official Union policy on the status of slaves in captured territory.

Early in the war, an irate Southerner who saw three of his slaves disappear behind Union lines at Fortress Monroe, Virginia, demanded the return of his property, citing the Fugitive Slave Law. The Union commander, Benjamin Butler, replied that the Fugitive Slave Law no longer applied and that the escaped slaves were "contraband of war." Two days later, eight runaway slaves appeared; the next day, fifty-nine black men and women arrived at the fort. Union commanders had found an effective way to rob the South of its basic workforce. The "contrabands," as they were known, were put to work building fortifications and doing other useful work in northern camps.

THE DEATH OF SLAVERY

As Union troops drove deeper into the South, the black response grew. When Union General William Tecumseh Sherman marched his army through Georgia in 1864, 18,000 slaves—entire families, people of all ages—flocked to the Union lines. By the war's end, nearly a million black people, fully a quarter of all the slaves in the South, had "voted with their feet" for the Union. The overwhelming response of black slaves to the Union advance changed the nature of the war. As increasing numbers of slaves flocked to Union lines, the conclusion that the South refused to face was unmistakable: the southern war to defend the slave system did not have the support of the slaves themselves. Any northern policy that ignored the issue of slavery and the wishes of the slaves themselves was unrealistic.

THE POLITICS OF EMANCIPATION

In 1862, as the issue of slavery loomed ever larger, Abraham Lincoln, acutely aware of divided northern opinion, inched his way toward a declaration of emancipation. Lincoln was correct to be worried about opinion in the North. Before the war, within the Republican Party, only a small group of abolitionists had favored freeing the slaves. There was also the question of what would become of slaves who were freed. Northern Democrats effectively played on racial fears in the 1862 congressional elections, warning that freed slaves would pour into northern cities and take jobs from white laborers.

QUICK REVIEW

The War at Sea

◆ Union naval blockade strengthened over time.

◆ Confederate ships had limited success running the blockade.

◆ Restriction of trade hurt the Southern cause.

HOW DID the end of slavery affect the war efforts of the North and South?

myhistorylab

Review Summary

Nevertheless, the necessities of war demanded that Lincoln adopt a policy to end slavery. Even as Radical Republicans chafed at Lincoln's slow pace, he was edging toward a new position. Following the Union victory at Antietam in September 1862, Lincoln issued a preliminary decree: unless the rebellious states returned to the Union by January 1, 1863, he would declare their slaves "forever free." Although Lincoln did not expect the Confederate States to surrender because of his proclamation, the decree increased the pressure on the South by directly linking the slave system to the war effort.

On January 1, 1863, Lincoln duly issued the final **Emancipation Proclamation**, which turned out to be less than sweeping. The proclamation freed the slaves in the areas of rebellion—the areas the Union did not control—but specifically exempted slaves in the border states and in former Confederate areas conquered by the Union. Lincoln's purpose was to meet the abolitionist demand for a war against slavery while not losing the support of conservatives, especially in the border states.

One group greeted the Emancipation Proclamation with open celebration. On New Year's Day, hundreds of African Americans gathered outside the White House and cheered the president. Free African Americans predicted that the news would encourage southern slaves either to flee to Union lines or refuse to work for their masters. Both of these things were already happening as African Americans seized on wartime changes to reshape white–black relations in the South. In one sense, then, the Emancipation Proclamation simply gave a name to a process already in motion.

Abolitionists set about moving Lincoln beyond his careful stance in the Emancipation Proclamation. Reformers such as Elizabeth Cady Stanton and Susan B. Anthony lobbied and petitioned for a constitutional amendment outlawing slavery. Congress, at Lincoln's urging, approved and sent to the states a statement banning slavery throughout the United States. Quickly ratified by the Union states in 1865, the statement became the **Thirteenth Amendment** to the Constitution. (The southern states, being in a state of rebellion, could not vote.) Lincoln's firm support for this amendment is a good indicator of his true feelings about slavery when he was freed of the kinds of military and political considerations necessarily taken into account in the Emancipation Proclamation.

BLACK FIGHTING MEN

As part of the Emancipation Proclamation, Lincoln gave his support for the first time to the recruitment of black soldiers. Early in the war, eager black volunteers had been bitterly disappointed at being turned away. Many, like Robert Fitzgerald, a free African American from Pennsylvania, found other ways to serve the Union cause. Fitzgerald first drove a wagon and mule for the Quartermaster Corps, and later, in spite of persistent seasickness, he served in the Union navy. After the Emancipation Proclamation, however, Fitzgerald was able to do what he had wanted to do all along: be a soldier. He enlisted in the Fifth Massachusetts Cavalry, a regiment that, like all the units in which black soldiers served, was 100 percent African American but commanded by white officers (see Seeing History).

In Fitzgerald's company of eighty-three men, half came from slave states and had run away to enlist. Other regiments had volunteers from Africa. The proportion of volunteers from the loyal border states (where slavery was still legal) was upwards of 25 percent—a lethal blow to the slave system in those states.

Black volunteers, eager and willing to fight, made up 10 percent of the Union army. Nearly 200,000 African Americans (one out of every five black males in the nation) served in the Union army or navy. A fifth of them—37,000—died defending their own freedom and the Union.

Emancipation Proclamation   Decree announced by President Abraham Lincoln in September 1862 and formally issued on January 1, 1863, freeing slaves in all Confederate states still in rebellion.

Thirteenth Amendment
Constitutional amendment ratified in 1865 that freed all slaves throughout the United States.

Come and Join Us Brothers

This is a recruitment poster for the Massachusetts 54th Infantry regiment, one of the first official black regiments in the U.S. Army. Organized in March 1863, the 600-man unit led the charge against Fort Wagner, South Carolina, in July, resulting in 116 deaths, including that of the white commanding officer, Colonel Robert Gould Shaw, and many casualties. The bravery of the recruits at Fort Wagner and in other battles changed the minds of many Union officers, who had previously disparaged the fighting abilities of African Americans.

COMPARE THE portraits of the men in this recruiting poster with the caricatures of African Americans shown in Chapter 13. What has changed? Frederick Douglass said, "Once let the black man get upon his person the brass letters, U.S., let him get an eagle on his button and a musket on his shoulder and bullets in his pocket," Douglass continued, and "there is no power on earth that can deny that he has earned the right to citizenship." Was Douglass right?

A general belief in African American inferiority was rampant in the North, but the army service of black men made a dent in white racism. Massachusetts enacted the first law forbidding discrimination against African Americans in public facilities. Some major cities, among them San Francisco, Cincinnati, Cleveland, and New York, desegregated their streetcars. Some states—Ohio, California, Illinois—repealed statutes that had barred black people from testifying in court or serving on juries. ■

PUBLISHED BY THE SUPERVISORY COMMITTEE FOR RECRUITING COLORED REGIMENTS
1210 CHESTNUT ST. PHILADELPHIA.

E. Sachse and Company, "The Shackle Broken by the Genius of Freedom", Baltimore, Md.; 1874, Chicago Historical Society.

Military service was something no black man could take lightly. African American soldiers faced prejudice within the army and had to prove themselves in battle. Moreover, the Confederates hated and feared African American troops and threatened to treat any captured black soldier as an escaped slave subject to execution. In 1864, Confederate soldiers massacred 262 black soldiers at Fort Pillow, Tennessee, after they had surrendered. Although large-scale episodes such as this were rare (especially after President Lincoln threatened retaliation), smaller ones were not.

Another extraordinary part of the story of the African American soldiers was their reception by black people in the South, who were overjoyed at the sight of armed black men, many of them former slaves themselves, wearing the uniform of the Union army. As his regiment entered Wilmington, North Carolina, one soldier wrote, "Men and women, old and young, were running throughout the streets, shouting and praising God. We could then truly see what we have been fighting for."

African American soldiers were not treated equally by the Union army. They were segregated in camp, given the worst jobs, and paid less than white soldiers ($10 a month rather than $13). Although they might not be able to do much about the other kinds of discrimination, the men of the Fifty-fourth Massachusetts found an unusual way to protest their unequal pay: they refused to accept it, preferring to serve the army for free until it decided to treat them as free men. The protest was effective; in June 1864, the War Department equalized the wages of black and white soldiers.

THE FRONT LINES AND THE HOME FRONT

Civil War soldiers wrote millions of letters home, more proportionately than in any American war. Their letters and the ones they received in return were links between the front lines and the home front, between the soldiers and their home communities. They are a testament to the patriotism of both Union and Confederate troops, for the story they tell is frequently one of slaughter and horror.

THE TOLL OF WAR

In spite of early hopes for what one might call a "brotherly" war, one that avoided excessive brutality, Civil War battles were appallingly deadly (see Figure 16.2). One reason was technology: improved weapons, particularly modern rifles, had much greater range and accuracy than the muskets they replaced.

Civil War generals, however, were slow to adjust to this new reality. Almost all Union and Confederate generals remained committed to the conventional military doctrine of massed infantry offensives. Part of this strategy had been to "soften up" a defensive line with artillery before an infantry assault, but now the range of the new rifles made artillery itself vulnerable to attack. As a result, generals relied less on "softening up" than on immense numbers of infantrymen, hoping that enough of them would survive the withering rifle fire to overwhelm the enemy line.

Medical ignorance was another factor in the casualty rate. Because the use of antiseptic procedures was in its infancy, men often died because minor wounds became infected. Disease was an even more frequent killer, taking twice as many men as were lost in battle.

Both North and South were completely unprepared to handle the supply and health needs of their large armies. Nor were the combatants prepared to deal with masses of war prisoners, as the shocking example of the Confederate prison camp at Andersonville in northern Georgia demonstrated. Andersonville was an open stockade with no shade or shelter, erected early in 1864 to hold 10,000 northern prisoners. But by midsummer, it held 33,000.

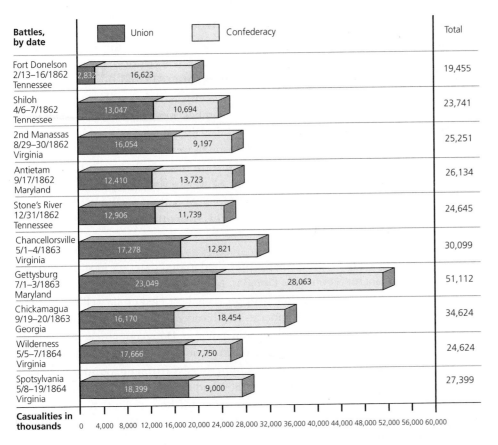

Battles, by date	Union	Confederacy	Total
Fort Donelson 2/13–16/1862 Tennessee	2,832	16,623	19,455
Shiloh 4/6–7/1862 Tennessee	13,047	10,694	23,741
2nd Manassas 8/29–30/1862 Virginia	16,054	9,197	25,251
Antietam 9/17/1862 Maryland	12,410	13,723	26,134
Stone's River 12/31/1862 Tennessee	12,906	11,739	24,645
Chancellorsville 5/1–4/1863 Virginia	17,278	12,821	30,099
Gettysburg 7/1–3/1863 Maryland	23,049	28,063	51,112
Chickamagua 9/19–20/1863 Georgia	16,170	18,454	34,624
Wilderness 5/5–7/1864 Virginia	17,666	7,750	24,624
Spotsylvania 5/8–19/1864 Virginia	18,399	9,000	27,399

Casualities in thousands 0 4,000 8,000 12,000 16,000 20,000 24,000 28,000 32,000 36,000 40,000 44,000 48,000 52,000 56,000 60,000

ARMY NURSES

There was an urgent need for skilled nurses to care for wounded and convalescent soldiers. Under the pressure of wartime necessity, and over the objections of most army doctors, women became army nurses. Hospital nursing, previously considered a job only disreputable women would undertake, now became a suitable vocation for middle-class women. By the war's end more than 3,000 northern women had worked as paid army nurses and many more as volunteers.

15–7
Clara Barton, *Medical Life at the Battlefield* (1862)

Southern women were also active in nursing and otherwise aiding soldiers, though the South never boasted a single large-scale organization like the Sanitary Commission. As in the North, middle-class women at first faced strong resistance from army doctors and even their own families, who believed that a field hospital was "no place for a refined lady." Kate Cumming of Mobile, who nursed in Corinth, Mississippi, after the Battle of Shiloh, faced down such reproofs, though she confided to her diary that nursing wounded men was very difficult: "Nothing that I had ever heard or read had given me the faintest idea of the horrors witnessed here." She and her companion nurses persisted and became an important part of the Confederate medical services. For southern women, who had been much less active in the public life of their communities than their northern reforming sisters, this Civil War activity marked an important break with prewar tradition.

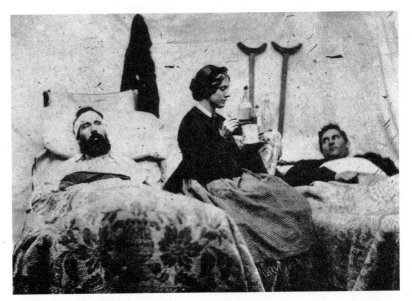

Nurse Ann Bell shown preparing medicine for a wounded soldier. Prompted by the medical crisis of the war, women such as Bell and "Mother" Bickerdyke actively participated in the war effort as nurses.

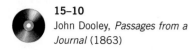

15–10
John Dooley, *Passages from a Journal* (1863)

THE LIFE OF THE COMMON SOLDIER

The conditions experienced by the eager young volunteers of the Union and Confederate armies included massive, terrifying, and bloody battles, apparently unending, with no sign of victory in sight. Soldiers suffered from the uncertainty of supply, which left troops, especially in the South, without uniforms, tents, and sometimes even food. They endured long marches over muddy, rutted roads while carrying packs weighing fifty or sixty pounds. Disease was rampant in their dirty, verminous, and unsanitary camps, and hospitals were so dreadful that more men left them dead than alive. As a result, desertion was common: an estimated one of every nine Confederate soldiers and one of every seven Union soldiers deserted. Unauthorized absence was another problem. At Antietam, Robert E. Lee estimated that unauthorized absence reduced his strength by a third to a half.

WARTIME POLITICS

In the earliest days of the war, Northerners had joined together in support of the war effort. Democrat Stephen A. Douglas, Lincoln's defeated rival, paid a visit to the White House to offer Lincoln his support, then traveled home to Illinois, where he addressed a huge rally of Democrats in Chicago: "There can be no neutrals in this war, only patriots—or traitors!" Within a month, Douglas was dead at age forty-eight. By 1862, Democrats had split into two factions: the War Democrats and the Peace Democrats, derogatorily called "**Copperheads**" (from the poisonous snake).

Despite the split in the party in 1860 and the secession of the South, the Democratic Party remained a powerful force in northern politics. It had received 44 percent of the popular vote in the North in the 1860 election, and its united opposition to the emancipation of slaves explains much of Lincoln's equivocal action on this issue.

The leader of the Copperheads, Clement Vallandigham, a former Ohio congressman, advocated an armistice and a negotiated peace that would "look only to the welfare, peace and safety of the white race, without reference to the effect that settlement may have on the African." Western Democrats, he threatened, might form their own union with the South, excluding New England with its radical abolitionists and high-tariff industrialists. Indeed, in the fall and winter of 1862–63 rumors swirled that the Northwest was ready to secede. Lincoln could not afford to take these threats and rumors lightly. In 1862, Lincoln proclaimed that all people who discouraged enlistments in the army or otherwise engaged in disloyal practices would be subject to martial law. More than 13,000 people, most of them deserters and war profiteers, were arrested, tried in military courts, and imprisoned. Some, however, were convicted in military courts on charges of "declaring sympathy for the enemy." Lincoln rejected all protests, claiming that his arbitrary actions were necessary for national security.

Lincoln also faced challenges from the radical faction of his own party. As the war continued, the Radicals gained strength: it was they who pushed for emancipation in the early days of the war and for harsh treatment of the defeated South after it ended. The most troublesome Radical was Salmon P. Chase, who in December 1862 caused a cabinet crisis when he encouraged Senate Republicans to complain that Secretary of State William Seward was "lukewarm" in his support for emancipation. This Radical challenge was a portent of the party's difficulties after the war, which Lincoln did not live to see—or prevent.

ECONOMIC AND SOCIAL STRAINS ON THE NORTH

Wartime needs caused a surge in northern economic growth, but the gains were unequally distributed. Early in the war, some industries suffered: textile manufacturers could not get cotton, and shoe factories that had made cheap shoes for

Copperheads A term Republicans applied to Northern war dissenters and those suspected of aiding the Confederate cause during the Civil War.

slaves were without a market. But other industries boomed—boot making, ship-building, and the manufacture of woolen goods such as blankets and uniforms, to give just three examples. Coal mining expanded, as did ironmaking, especially the manufacture of iron rails for railroads. Agricultural goods were in great demand, promoting further mechanization of farming. Women, left to tend the family farm while the men went to war, found that with mechanized equipment, they could manage the demanding task of harvesting.

Meeting wartime needs enriched some people honestly, but speculators and profiteers also flourished, as they have in every war. By the end of the war, government contracts had exceeded $1 billion. Not all of this business was free from corruption. New wealth was evident in every northern city.

For most people, however, the war brought the day-to-day hardship of inflation. During the four years of the war, the North suffered an inflation rate of 80 percent, or nearly 15 percent a year. Wages rose only half as much as prices, and workers responded by joining unions and striking. Manufacturers, bitterly opposed to unions, freely hired strikebreakers (many of whom were African Americans, women, or immigrants) and formed organizations of their own to prevent further unionization and to blacklist union organizers. Thus, both capital and labor moved far beyond the small, localized confrontations of the early industrial period. The formation of large-scale organizations, fostered by wartime demand, laid the groundwork for the national battle between workers and manufacturers that would dominate the last part of the nineteenth century.

Another major source of social tension was conscription. The Union introduced a draft in March 1863. Especially unpopular was a provision in the draft law that allowed the hiring of substitutes or the payment of a commutation fee of $300. Substitutes were mostly recent immigrants who had not yet filed for citizenship and were thus not yet eligible to be drafted. It is estimated that immigrants (some of whom were citizens) made up 20 percent of the Union army.

As practiced in the local communities, conscription was indeed often marred by favoritism and prejudice. Local officials called up many more poor than rich men and selected a higher proportion of immigrants than nonimmigrants. In reality, however, only 7 percent of all men called to serve actually did so. About 25 percent hired a substitute, another 45 percent were exempted for "cause" (usually health reasons), and another 20 to 25 percent simply failed to report to the community draft office. Nevertheless, by 1863, many northern urban workers believed that the slogan "a rich man's war but a poor man's fight," though coined in the South, applied to them as well.

The New York City Draft Riots

In the spring of 1863, there were protests against the draft throughout the North. Riots and disturbances broke out in many cities, and several federal enrollment officers were killed. The greatest trouble occurred in New York City between July 13 and July 16, 1863, where a wave of working-class looting, fighting, and lynching claimed the lives of 105 people, many of them African American. The rioting, the worst up to that time in American history, was quelled only when five units of the U.S. Army were rushed from the battlefield at Gettysburg, where they had been fighting Confederates the week before.

The riots had several causes. Anger at the draft and racial prejudice were what most contemporaries saw. From a historical perspective, however, the riots were at least as much about the urban growth and tensions described in Chapter 13. The Civil War made urban problems worse and heightened the visible contrast between the lives of the rich and those of the poor. These tensions exploded, but were not solved, during those hot days in the summer of 1863.

QUICK REVIEW

Sources of Social and Economic Tension in the North

◆ Uneven economic growth.

◆ Runaway inflation.

◆ Conscription.

15–11
A Firsthand Account of the New York Draft Riots (1863)

Ironically, African American men, a favorite target of the rioters' anger, were a major force in easing the national crisis over the draft. Though they had been barred from service until 1863, in the later stages of the war African American volunteers filled much of the manpower gap that the controversial draft was meant to address.

THE FAILURE OF SOUTHERN NATIONALISM

The war brought even greater changes to the South. As in the North, war needs led to expansion and centralization of government control over the economy. The expansion of government brought sudden urbanization, a new experience for the predominantly rural South. The population of Richmond, the Confederate capital, almost tripled, in large part because the Confederate bureaucracy grew to 70,000 people. Because of the need for military manpower, a good part of the Confederate bureaucracy consisted of women, who were referred to as "government girls." All of this—government control, urban growth, women in the paid workforce—was new to Southerners, and not all of it was welcomed.

Even more than in the North, the voracious need for soldiers fostered class antagonisms. When small yeoman farmers went off to war, their wives and families struggled to farm on their own, without the help of mechanization, which they could not afford, and without the help of slaves, which they had never owned. But wealthy men could be exempted from the draft if they had more than twenty slaves. Furthermore, many upper-class Southerners—at least 50,000—avoided military service by paying liberally ($5,000 and more) for substitutes. Worst of all was the starvation. The North's blockade and the breakdown of the South's transportation system restricted the availability of food in the South, and these problems were vastly magnified by runaway inflation. Prices in the South rose by an unbelievable 9,000 percent from 1861 to 1865. Speculation and hoarding by the rich made matters even worse. In the spring of 1863, food riots broke out in four Georgia cities (Atlanta among them) and in North Carolina. In Richmond, more than a thousand people, mostly women, broke into bakeries and snatched loaves of bread, crying "Bread! Bread! Our children are starving while the rich roll in wealth!"

Increasingly, the ordinary people of the South, preoccupied with staying alive, refused to pay taxes, to provide food, or to serve in the army. Soldiers were drawn home by the desperation of their families as well as by the discouraging course of the war. By January 1865, the desertion rate had climbed to 8 percent a month.

At the same time, the life of the southern ruling class was irrevocably altered by the changing nature of slavery. By the end of the war, one-quarter of all slaves had fled to the Union lines, and those who remained often stood in a different relationship to their owners. As white masters and overseers left to join the army, white women were left behind on the plantation to cope with shortages, grow crops, and manage the labor of slaves. Lacking the patriarchal authority of their husbands, white women found that white–black relationships shifted, sometimes drastically (as when slaves fled) and sometimes more subtly. Slaves increasingly made their own decisions about when and how they would work. One black woman, implored by her mistress not to reveal the location of a trunk of money and silver plate when the invading Yankees arrived, looked her in the eye and said, "Mistress, I can't lie over that; you bought that silver plate when you sold my three children."

Peace movements in the South were motivated by a confused mixture of realism, war weariness, and the animosity of those who supported states' rights and opposed Jefferson Davis. The anti-Davis faction was led by his own vice president, Alexander Stephens, who early in 1864 suggested a negotiated peace. Peace sentiment was especially strong in North Carolina, where more than a hundred public meetings in support of negotiations were held in the summer of 1863. Davis would have none of it, and he commanded enough votes in the Confederate Congress to enforce his will and to suggest that peace sentiment was traitorous.

THE TIDE TURNS

As Lincoln's timing of the Emancipation Proclamation showed, by 1863 the nature of the war was changing. The proclamation freeing the slaves struck directly at the southern home front and the civilian workforce. That same year, the nature of the battlefield war changed as well. The Civil War became the first total war.

THE TURNING POINT OF 1863

In the summer of 1863, the moment finally arrived when the North could begin to hope for victory. But for the Union army, the year opened with stalemate in the East and slow and costly progress in the West. For the South, 1863 represented its highest hopes for military success and for diplomatic recognition by Britain or France.

Attempting to break the stalemate in northern Virginia, General Joseph "Fighting Joe" Hooker and a Union army of 130,000 men attacked a Confederate army half that size at Chancellorsville in May. In response, Robert E. Lee daringly divided his forces, sending General Thomas "Stonewall" Jackson and 30,000 men on a day-long flanking movement that caught the Union troops by surprise. Chancellorsville was a great Confederate victory; there were 17,000 Union losses. However, Confederate losses were also great: 13,000 men, representing more than 20 percent of Lee's army.

Though weakened, Lee moved to the attack. In June, in his second and most dangerous single thrust into Union territory, he moved north into Maryland and Pennsylvania. His purpose was as much political as military: he hoped that a great Confederate victory would lead Britain and France to intervene in the war and demand a negotiated peace. The ensuing Battle of Gettysburg, July 1–3, 1863, was another horrible slaughter.

Lee retreated from the field, leaving more than one-third of his army behind—28,000 men killed, wounded, or missing. Union general George Meade elected not to pursue with his battered Union army (see Map 16.4).

The next day, July 4, 1863, Ulysses S. Grant took Vicksburg, Mississippi, after a costly siege. The combined news of Gettysburg and Vicksburg dissuaded Britain and France from recognizing the Confederacy and checked the northern peace movement. It also tightened the North's grip on the South, for the Union now controlled the entire Mississippi River. In November, Generals Grant and Sherman broke the Confederate hold on Chattanooga, Tennessee, thereby opening the way to Atlanta.

HOW DID Grant and Sherman turn the tide of the war?

MAP EXPLORATION

To explore an interactive version of this map, go to
http://www.prenhall.com/faraghertlc/map16.4

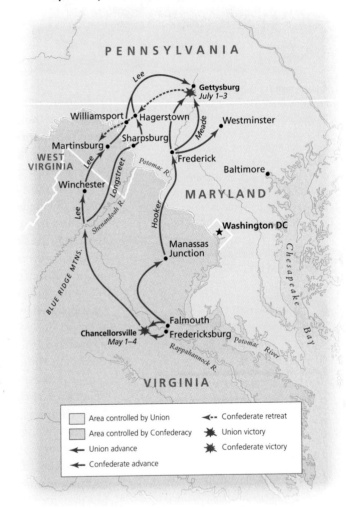

MAP 16.4

The Turning Point, 1863   In June, Lee boldly struck north into Maryland and Pennsylvania, hoping for a victory that would cause Britain and France to demand a negotiated peace on Confederate terms. Instead, he lost the hard-fought battle of Gettysburg, July 1–3. The very next day, Grant's long siege of Vicksburg succeeded. These two great Fourth of July victories turned the tide in favor of the Union. The Confederates never again mounted a major offensive. Total Union control of the Mississippi now exposed the Lower South to attack.

WHAT WAS Lee hoping to achieve with his campaign northward and why was his defeat at Gettysburg the war's turning point?

A black man is lynched during the New York City Draft Riots in July 1863. Free black people and their institutions were major victims of the worst rioting in American history until then. The riots were more than a protest against the draft; they were also an outburst of frustration over urban problems that had been festering for decades.

15–9
Abraham Lincoln, *Gettysburg Address* (1863)

15–13
General William Tecumseh Sherman on War (1864)

QUICK REVIEW

Grant's Strategy

◆ Better coordination of Union effort and the application of steady pressure.

◆ The waging of nonstop warfare.

◆ Grant's plan worked in the long run, but at a high cost.

GRANT AND SHERMAN

In March 1864, President Lincoln called Grant east and appointed him general-in-chief of all the Union forces. Grant devised a plan of strangulation and annihilation. While he took on Lee in northern Virginia, he sent General William Tecumseh Sherman to defeat Confederate general Joe Johnston's Army of Tennessee, which was defending the approach to Atlanta. Both Grant and Sherman exemplified the new kind of warfare. They aimed to inflict maximum damage on the fabric of southern life, hoping that the South would choose to surrender rather than face total destruction. This decision to broaden the war so that it directly affected civilians was new in American military history and prefigured the total wars of the twentieth century.

In northern Virginia, Grant pursued a policy of destroying civilian supplies. He said he "regarded it as humane to both sides to protect the persons of those found at their homes, but to consume everything that could be used to support or supply armies." One of those supports was slaves. Grant welcomed fleeing slaves to Union lines and encouraged army efforts to put them to work or enlist them as soldiers.

The most famous example of the new strategy of total war was General Sherman's 1864 march through Georgia. Sherman captured Atlanta on September 2, 1864, and the rest of Georgia now lay open to him. In November, Sherman set out to march the 285 miles to the coastal city of Savannah, living off the land and destroying everything in his path. His military purpose was to tighten the noose around Robert E. Lee's army in northern Virginia by cutting off Mississippi, Alabama, and Georgia from the rest of the Confederacy. But his second purpose, openly stated, was to "make war so terrible" to the people of the South, to "make them so sick of war that generations would pass away before they would again appeal to it." Accordingly, he told his men to seize, burn, or destroy everything in their path (but, significantly, not to harm civilians).

It was estimated that Sherman's army did $100 million worth of damage. "They say no living thing is found in Sherman's track," Mary Boykin Chesnut wrote, "only chimneys, like telegraph poles, to carry the news of [his] attack backwards."

Terrifying to white southern civilians, Sherman was initially hostile to black Southerners as well. In the interests of speed and efficiency, his army turned away many of the 18,000 slaves who flocked to it in Georgia, causing a number to be recaptured and reenslaved. This callous action caused such a scandal in Washington that Secretary of War Edwin Stanton arranged a special meeting in Georgia with Sherman and twenty African American ministers who spoke for the freed slaves. This meeting in itself was extraordinary: no one had ever before asked slaves what they wanted. Equally extraordinary was Sherman's response in Special Field Order 15, issued in January 1865: he set aside more than 400,000 acres of Confederate land to be given to the freed slaves in forty-acre parcels. This was war of a kind that white Southerners had never imagined.

THE 1864 ELECTION

The war complicated the 1864 presidential election. Lincoln was renominated during a period when the war was going badly. Opposed by the Radicals, who thought he was too conciliatory toward the South, and by Republican conservatives, who disapproved of the Emancipation Proclamation, Lincoln had little support within his own party.

In contrast, the Democrats had an appealing candidate: General George McClellan, a war hero (always a favorite with American voters) who was known to be sympathetic to the South. Democrats played shamelessly on the racist fears of the urban working class, accusing Republicans of being "negro-lovers" and warning that racial mixing lay ahead.

A deeply depressed Lincoln fully expected to lose the election. "I am going to be beaten," he told an army officer in August 1864, "and unless some great change takes place badly beaten." A great change did take place: Sherman captured Atlanta on September 2. Lincoln won the election with 55 percent of the popular vote. The vote probably saved the Republican Party from extinction. Ordinary people and war-weary soldiers had voted to continue a difficult and divisive conflict. The election was important evidence of northern support for Lincoln's policy of unconditional surrender for the South. There would be no negotiated peace; the war would continue.

NEARING THE END

As Sherman devastated the lower South, Grant was locked in struggle with Lee in northern Virginia. Grant did not favor subtle strategies. He bluntly said, "The art of war is simple enough. Find out where your enemy is. Get at him as soon as you can. Strike at him as hard as you can, and keep moving on." Following this plan, Grant eventually hammered Lee into submission but at enormous cost. Lee inflicted heavy losses on the Union army in a succession of bloody encounters in the spring and summer of 1864: almost 18,000 at the battle of the Wilderness, more than 8,000 at Spotsylvania, and 12,000 at Cold Harbor. At Cold Harbor, Union troops wrote their names and addresses on scraps of paper and pinned them to their backs, so certain were they of being killed or wounded in battle.

Grim and terrible as Grant's strategy was, it proved effective. Rather than pulling back after his failed assaults, he kept moving South, finally settling in for a prolonged siege of Lee's forces at Petersburg. The North's great advantage in population finally began to tell. There were more Union soldiers to replace those lost in battle, but there were no more white Confederates (see Map 16.5).

In desperation, the South turned to what had hitherto been unthinkable: arming slaves to serve as soldiers in the Confederate army. But—and this was the bitter irony—the African American soldiers and their families would have to be promised freedom or they would desert to the Union at the first chance they had. The Confederate Congress balked at first. As one member said, the idea was "revolting to Southern sentiment, Southern pride, and Southern honor." Another candidly admitted, "If slaves make good soldiers our whole theory of slavery is wrong." Finally, on March 13, the Confederate Congress authorized a draft of black soldiers—without mentioning freedom.

This striking photograph by Thomas C. Roche shows a dead Confederate soldier, killed at Petersburg on April 3, 1865, only six days before the surrender at Appomattox. The new medium of photography conveyed the horror of the war with a gruesome reality to the American public.

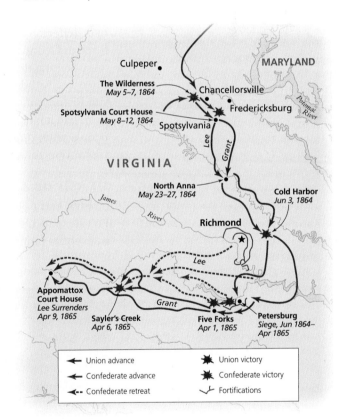

MAP 16.5

The Final Battles in Virginia, 1864–65 In the war's final phase early in 1865, Sherman closed one arm of a pincers by marching north from Savannah, while Grant attacked Lee's last defensive positions in Petersburg and Richmond. Lee retreated from them on April 2 and surrendered at Appomattox Court House on April 9, 1865.

WHAT DESPERATE measures did the South resort to as the war came to an end?

By the spring of 1865, public support for the war simply disintegrated in the South. Starvation, inflation, dissension, and the prospect of military defeat were too much. In February, Jefferson Davis sent his vice president, Alexander Stephens, to negotiate terms at a peace conference at Hampton Roads. Lincoln would not countenance anything less than full surrender, although he did offer gradual emancipation with compensation for slave owners. Davis, however, insisted on southern independence at all costs. Consequently, the Hampton Roads conference failed and southern resistance faded away. In March 1865, Mary Boykin Chesnut recorded in her diary: "I am sure our army is silently dispersing. Men are going the wrong way all the time. They slip by now with no songs nor shouts. They have given the thing up."

APPOMATTOX

In the spring of 1865, Lee and his remaining troops, outnumbered two to one, still held Petersburg and Richmond. Starving, short of ammunition, and losing men in battle or to desertion every day, Lee retreated from Petersburg on April 2. The Confederate government fled Richmond, stripping and burning the city. Seven days later, Lee and his 25,000 troops surrendered to Grant at Appomattox Court House. Grant treated Lee with great respect and set a historic precedent by giving the Confederate troops parole. This meant they could not subsequently be prosecuted for treason. Grant then sent the starving army on its way with three days' rations for every man. Jefferson Davis, who had hoped to set up a new government in Texas, was captured in Georgia on May 10. The war was finally over.

Sensing that the war was near its end, Abraham Lincoln visited Grant's troops when Lee withdrew from Petersburg on April 2. Thus it was that Lincoln came to visit Richmond, and to sit briefly in Jefferson Davis's presidential office, soon after Davis had left it. As Lincoln walked the streets of the burned and pillaged city, black people poured out to see him and surround him, shouting "Glory to God! Glory! Glory! Glory!"

DEATH OF A PRESIDENT

Lincoln had only the briefest time to savor the victory. On the night of April 14, President and Mrs. Lincoln went to Ford's Theater in Washington. There Lincoln was shot at point-blank range by John Wilkes Booth, a Confederate sympathizer.

The 55th Massachusetts Colored Regiment is shown entering Charleston, February 21, 1865, greeted by happy crowds of African Americans. For white Charlestonians, the sight of victorious black troops in the cockpit of the Confederacy must have been devastating.

Harper's Weekly, March 18, 1865. Courtesy of William C. Hine.

CHRONOLOGY

1861 March: Morrill Tariff Act

April: Fort Sumter falls; war begins

April: Mobilization begins

April–May: Virginia, Arkansas, Tennessee, and North Carolina secede

June: United States Sanitary Commission established

July: First Battle of Bull Run

December: French troops arrive in Mexico, followed by British and Spanish forces in January

1862 February: Legal Tender Act

February: Battles of Fort Henry and Fort Donelson

March: Battle of Pea Ridge

March: Battle of the *Monitor* and the *Merrimack* (renamed the *Virginia*)

March–August: George B. McClellan's Peninsular campaign

March: Battle of Glorieta Pass

April: Battle of Shiloh

April: Confederate Conscription Act

April: David Farragut captures New Orleans

May: *El Cinqo de Mayo:* Mexican troops repel French invaders

May: Homestead Act

June–July: Seven Days Battles

July: Pacific Railway Act

July: Morrill Land Grant Act

August: Santee Sioux Uprising, Minnesota

September: Battle of Antietam

December: Battle of Fredericksburg

1863 January: Emancipation Proclamation

February: National Bank Act

March: Draft introduced in the North

March: Colonel Kit Carson sends 8,000 Navajos on the "Long Walk" to Bosque Redondo, New Mexico Territory

April: Richmond bread riot

May: Battle of Chancellorsville

June: French occupy Mexico City

July: Battle of Gettysburg

July: Surrender of Vicksburg

July: New York City Draft Riots

November: Battle of Chattanooga

November: Union troops capture Brownsville, Texas

1864 March: Ulysses S. Grant becomes general-in-chief of Union forces

April: Fort Pillow massacre

May: Battle of the Wilderness

May: Battle of Spotsylvania

June: Battle of Cold Harbor

June: Maximilian becomes Emperor of Mexico

September: Atlanta falls

October: St. Albans incident

November: Abraham Lincoln reelected president

November–December: William Tecumseh Sherman's march to the sea

1865 April: Richmond falls

April: Robert E. Lee surrenders at Appomattox

April: Lincoln assassinated

December: Thirteenth Amendment to the Constitution becomes law

He died the next day. After a week of observances in Washington, Lincoln's coffin was loaded on a funeral train that slowly carried him back to Springfield. All along the railroad route, day and night, in small towns and large, people gathered to see the train pass and to pay their last respects. At that moment, the Washington community and the larger Union community were one and the same.

The nation as a whole was left with Lincoln's vision for the coming peace, expressed in the unforgettable words of his Second Inaugural Address:

With malice toward none, with charity for all, with firmness in the right as God gives us to see the right, let us strive on to finish the work we are in, to bind up the nation's wounds, to care for him who shall have borne the battle and for his widow and his orphan, to do all which may achieve and cherish a just and lasting peace among ourselves and with all nations.

CONCLUSION

In 1865, a divided people were forcibly reunited by battle. Their nation, the United States of America, had been permanently changed by civil war. Devastating losses among the young men of the country—the greatest such losses the nation was ever to suffer—would affect not only their families but also all of postwar society. Politically, the deepest irony of the Civil War was that only by fighting it had America become completely a nation. For it was the war that broke down local isolation. Ordinary citizens in local communities, North and South, developed a national perspective as they sent their sons and brothers to be soldiers, their daughters to be nurses and teachers. Then, too, the federal government, vastly strengthened by wartime necessity, reached the lives of ordinary citizens more than ever before. The question now was whether this strengthened but divided national community, forged in battle, could create a just peace.

REVIEW QUESTIONS

1. At the outset of the Civil War, what were the relative advantages of the North and the South, and how did they affect the final outcome?

2. In the absence of the southern Democrats, in the early 1860s, the new Republican Congress was able to pass a number of party measures with little opposition. What do these measures tell you about the historical roots of the Republican Party? More generally, how do you think we should view legislation passed in the absence of the customary opposition, debate, and compromise?

3. The greatest problem facing Jefferson Davis and the Confederacy was the need to develop a true feeling of nationalism. Can the failure of this effort be blamed on Davis's weakness as a leader alone, or are there other causes?

4. In what ways can it be said that the actions of African Americans, both slave and free, came to determine the course of the Civil War?

5. Wars always have unexpected consequences. List some of those consequences both for soldiers and for civilians in the North and in the South.

6. Today Abraham Lincoln is considered one of our greatest presidents, but he did not enjoy such approval at the time. List and evaluate some of the contemporary criticisms of Lincoln.

KEY TERMS

myhistorylab
Flashcard Review

Copperheads (p. 422)
Emancipation Proclamation (p. 418)
Homestead Act (p. 411)
Legal Tender Act (p. 411)
Morrill Land Grant Act (p. 411)

Morrill Tariff Act (p. 411)
National Bank Act (p. 411)
Peninsular campaign (p. 415)
Thirteenth Amendment (p. 418)

RECOMMENDED READING

Edward Ayers, *In the Presence of Mine Enemies: War in the Heart of America, 1859–1863* (2003). A study of two counties, one Confederate, one Union, in the war.

Paul A. Cimbala and Randall M. Miller, *Union Soldiers and the Northern Home Front: Wartime Experiences, Postwar Adjustments* (2002). The effects of the Civil War on ordinary people.

Paul Escott, *After Secession: Jefferson Davis and the Failure of Confederate Nationalism* (1978). A thoughtful study of Davis's record as president of the Confederacy.

Drew Gilpin Faust, *Mothers of Invention: Women of the Slaveholding South in the American Civil War* (1996). A major study that considers the importance of gender at the white South's "moment of truth."

James M. Mc Pherson, *Battle Cry of Freedom: The Civil War Era* (1988). An acclaimed, highly readable synthesis of much scholarship on the war.

—, *The Atlas of the Civil War* (1994). Detailed battle diagrams with clear descriptions.

Pauli Murray, *Proud Shoes: The Story of an American Family* (1956). Murray tells the proud story of her African American family and her grandfather, Robert Fitzgerald.

Nina Silbar, *Daughters of the Union: Northern Women Fight the Civil War* (2005). Argues that women found a new sense of self and citizenship in wartime.

Keith P. Wilson, *Campfires of Freedom: The Camp Life of Black Soliders During the Civil War* (2002). Camp life examined to show the soldiers' personal transition from slavery to freedom.

myhistorylab
Where it's a good time to connect to the past!

For study resources for this chapter, go to **www.myhistorylab.com** and choose *Out of Many, Teaching and Learning Classroom Edition.* You will find a wealth of study and review material for this chapter, including pretests and posttests, customized study plan, key-term review flash cards, interactive map and document activities, and documents for analysis.

*The war passed from words to stones which
the white children began to hurl at the colored.
Several colored children were hurt and, as they
had not resented the rock throwing . . . , the white
children became more aggressive and abusive.*

— *T. Thomas Fortune, from* Norfolk Journal and Guide, *1866*

Women and children escaping slavery.

Theo. Kaufmann, "On to Liberty," 1867, Oil on canvas. The Metropolitan Museum of Art. Gift of Erving and Joyce Wolf, 1982 (1982.443.3) Photograph © 1982 The Metropolitan Museum of Art.

17

RECONSTRUCTION
1863–1877

WHAT WERE the competing political plans for reconstructing the defeated Confederacy?

WHAT WERE the most important changes in the lives of African Americans in the years immediately following the war?

WHAT MAJOR groups made up the Southern Republicans?

WHAT PRECIPITATED the electoral crisis of 1876?

1863   1877

AMERICAN COMMUNITIES

Hale County, Alabama: From Slavery to Freedom in a Black Belt Community

ON A BRIGHT SATURDAY MORNING IN MAY 1867, 4,000 FORMER SLAVES streamed into the town of Greensboro to hear speeches from two delegates to a recent freedmen's convention in Mobile and to find out about the political status of black people under the Reconstruction Act just passed by Congress. Tensions mounted in the days following this unprecedented gathering, as military authorities began supervising voter registration for elections to the upcoming constitutional convention that would rewrite the laws of Alabama. On June 13, John Orrick, a local white, confronted Alex Webb, a politically active freedman, on the streets of Greensboro and shot Webb dead. Hundreds of armed and angry freedmen formed a posse to search for Orrick but failed to find him. Galvanized by Webb's murder, 500 local freedmen formed a chapter of the Union League, the Republican Party's organizational arm in the South. The chapter functioned as both a militia company and a forum to agitate for political rights.

West-central Alabama had emerged as a fertile center of cotton production just two decades before the Civil War. There African Americans, as throughout the South's black belt, constituted more than three-quarters of the population. With the arrival of federal troops in the spring of 1865, African Americans in Hale County, like their counterparts elsewhere, began to challenge the traditional organization of plantation labor.

Above all, freed people wanted more autonomy. Overseers and owners grudgingly allowed them to work the land "in families," letting them choose their own supervisors and find their own provisions. The result was a shift from the gang labor characteristic of the antebellum period, in which large groups of slaves worked under the harsh and constant supervision of white overseers, to the sharecropping system, in which African American families worked small plots of land in exchange for a small share of the crop. This shift represented less of a victory for newly freed African Americans than a defeat for plantation owners, who resented even the limited economic independence it forced them to concede to their black workforce.

Local African Americans also organized politically. In 1866, Congress had passed the Civil Rights Act and sent the Fourteenth Amendment to the Constitution to the states for ratification; both promised full citizenship rights to former

slaves. Hale County freedmen joined the Republican Party and local Union League chapters. They used their new political power to press for better labor contracts, demand greater autonomy for the black workforce, and agitate for the more radical goal of land confiscation and redistribution. "The colored people are very anxious to get land of their own to live upon independently; and they want money to buy stock to make crops," reported one black Union League organizer. "The only way to get these necessaries is to give our votes to the [Republican] party." Two Hale County former slaves, Brister Reese and James K. Green, won election to the Alabama state legislature in 1869.

It was not long before these economic and political gains prompted a white counterattack. In the spring of 1868, the Ku Klux Klan came to Hale County. Disguised in white sheets, armed with guns and whips, and making nighttime raids on horseback, Klansmen flogged, beat, and murdered freed people. They intimidated voters and silenced political activists. Planters used Klan terror to dissuade former slaves from leaving plantations or organizing for higher wages.

With the passage of the Ku Klux Klan Act in 1871, the federal government cracked down on the Klan, breaking its power temporarily in parts of the former Confederacy. But no serious effort was made to stop Klan terror in the west Alabama black belt, and planters there succeeded in reestablishing much of their social and political control.

The events in Hale County illustrate the struggles that beset communities throughout the South during the Reconstruction era after the Civil War. The destruction of slavery and the Confederacy forced African Americans and white people to renegotiate their old roles. These community battles both shaped and were shaped by the victorious and newly expansive federal government in Washington. But the new arrangements of both political power sharing and the organization of labor had to be worked out within local communities. In the end, Reconstruction was only partially successful. Not until the "Second Reconstruction" of the twentieth-century civil rights movement would the descendants of Hale County's African Americans begin to enjoy the full fruits of freedom—and even then not without challenge.

Greensboro

THE POLITICS OF RECONSTRUCTION

Although President Abraham Lincoln insisted early on that the purpose of the war was to preserve the Union, by 1863 it had evolved as well into a struggle for African American liberation. Indeed, the political, economic, and moral issues posed by slavery were the root cause of the Civil War, and the war ultimately destroyed slavery, although not racism, once and for all.

The Civil War also settled the Constitutional crisis provoked by the secession of the Confederacy and its justification in appeals to states' rights. The old notion of the United States as a voluntary union of sovereign states gave way to the new reality of a single nation, in which the federal government took precedence over the individual states. The key historical developments of the Reconstruction era revolved around precisely how the newly strengthened national government would define its relationship with the defeated Confederate states and the 4 million newly freed slaves.

THE DEFEATED SOUTH

The white South paid an extremely high price for secession, war, and defeat. In addition to the battlefield casualties, the Confederate states sustained deep material and psychological wounds. Much of the best agricultural land lay waste. Many towns and cities were in ruins. By 1865, the South's most precious commodities, cotton and African American slaves, no longer were measures of wealth and prestige.

Emancipation proved the most bitter pill for white Southerners to swallow, especially the planter elite. Conquered and degraded, and in their view robbed of their slave property, white people responded by regarding African Americans, more than ever, as inferior to themselves. In the antebellum South, white skin had defined a social bond that transcended economic class. It gave even the lowliest poor white a badge of superiority over even the most skilled slave or prosperous free African American. Emancipation, however, forced white people to redefine their world. The specter of political power and social equality for African Americans made racial order the consuming passion of most white Southerners during the Reconstruction years. In fact, racism can be seen as one of the major forces driving Reconstruction and, ultimately, undermining it.

WHAT WERE the competing political plans for reconstructing the defeated Confederacy?

myhistorylab
Review Summary

16–2
Carl Schurz, *Report on the Condition of the South* (1865)

16–9
The Nation, *"The State of the South"* (1872)

"Decorating the Graves of Rebel Soldiers," *Harper's Weekly,* August 17, 1867. After the Civil War, both Southerners and Northerners created public mourning ceremonies honoring fallen soldiers. Women led the memorial movement in the South that, by establishing cemeteries and erecting monuments, offered the first cultural expression of the Confederate tradition. This engraving depicts citizens of Richmond, Virginia, decorating thousands of Confederate graves with flowers at the Hollywood Memorial Cemetery on the James River. A local women's group raised enough funds to transfer over 16,000 Confederate dead from northern cemeteries for reburial in Richmond.

Photography pioneer Timothy O'Sullivan took this portrait of a multi-generational African American family on the J. J. Smith plantation in Beaufort, South Carolina, in 1862. Many white plantation owners in the area had fled, allowing slaves like these to begin an early transition to freedom before the end of the Civil War.

16–1

"Address from the Colored Citizens of Norfolk, Virginia, to the People of the United States" (1865)

Radical Republicans A shifting group of Republican congressmen, usually a substantial minority, who favored the abolition of slavery from the beginning of the Civil War and later advocated harsh treatment of the defeated South.

Field Order 15 Order by General William T. Sherman in January 1865 to set aside abandoned land along the southern Atlantic coast for forty-acre grants to freedmen; rescinded by President Andrew Johnson later that year.

Abraham Lincoln's Plan

By late 1863, Union military victories had convinced President Lincoln of the need to fashion a plan for the reconstruction of the South (see Chapter 16). Lincoln based his reconstruction program on bringing the seceded states back into the Union as quickly as possible. His Proclamation of Amnesty and Reconstruction of December 1863 offered "full pardon" and the restoration of property, not including slaves, to white Southerners willing to swear an oath of allegiance to the United States and its laws, including the Emancipation Proclamation. Prominent Confederate military and civil leaders were excluded from Lincoln's offer, though he indicated that he would freely pardon them.

The president also proposed that when the number of any Confederate state's voters who took the oath of allegiance reached 10 percent of the number who had voted in the election of 1860, this group could establish a state government that Lincoln would recognize as legitimate. Fundamental to this Ten Percent Plan was acceptance by the reconstructed governments of the abolition of slavery. Lincoln's plan was designed less as a blueprint for reconstruction than as a way to shorten the war and gain white people's support for emancipation.

Lincoln's amnesty proclamation angered those Republicans—known as **Radical Republicans**—who advocated not only equal rights for the freedmen but also a tougher stance toward the white South. In July 1864, Senator Benjamin F. Wade of Ohio and Congressman Henry W. Davis of Maryland, both Radicals, proposed a harsher alternative to the Ten Percent Plan. The Wade–Davis bill required 50 percent of a seceding state's white male citizens to take a loyalty oath before elections could be held for a convention to rewrite the state's constitution. Lincoln wanted to weaken the Confederacy by creating new state governments that could win broad support from southern white people. The Wade–Davis bill threatened his efforts to build political consensus within the southern states. Lincoln, therefore, pocket-vetoed the bill by refusing to sign it within ten days of the adjournment of Congress.

As Union armies occupied parts of the South, commanders improvised a variety of arrangements involving confiscated plantations and the African American labor force. For example, in 1862 General Benjamin F. Butler began a policy of transforming slaves on Louisiana sugar plantations into wage laborers under the close supervision of occupying federal troops.

In January 1865, General William T. Sherman issued Special **Field Order 15**, setting aside the Sea Islands off the Georgia coast and a portion of the South Carolina low-country rice fields for the exclusive settlement of freed people. Each family would receive forty acres of land and the loan of mules from the army. By the summer of 1865 some 40,000 freed people, eager to take advantage of the general's order, had been settled on 400,000 acres of "Sherman land."

Conflicts within the Republican Party prevented the development of a systematic land distribution program. Still, Lincoln and the Republican Congress supported other measures to aid the emancipated slaves. In March 1865 Congress established the **Freedmen's Bureau**. Along with providing food, clothing, and fuel to destitute former slaves, the bureau was charged with supervising and managing "all the abandoned lands in the South and the control of all subjects relating to refugees and freedmen." The act that established the bureau also stated that forty acres of abandoned or confiscated land could be leased to freed slaves or white Unionists, who would have an option to purchase after three years.

On the evening of April 14, 1865, while attending the theater in Washington, President Lincoln was shot by John Wilkes Booth and died of his wounds several hours later. At the time of his assassination, Lincoln's reconstruction policy remained unsettled and incomplete. In its broad outlines the president's plans had seemed to favor a speedy restoration of the southern states to the Union and a minimum of federal intervention in their affairs. But with his death the specifics of postwar Reconstruction had to be hammered out by a new president, Andrew Johnson of Tennessee, a man whose personality, political background, and racist leanings put him at odds with the Republican-controlled Congress.

ANDREW JOHNSON AND PRESIDENTIAL RECONSTRUCTION

Throughout his career, Andrew Johnson had championed yeoman farmers and viewed the South's plantation aristocrats with contempt. He was the only southern member of the U.S. Senate to remain loyal to the Union, and he held the planter elite responsible for secession and defeat. In 1862, Lincoln appointed Johnson to the difficult post of military governor of Tennessee. There he successfully began wartime Reconstruction and cultivated Unionist support in the mountainous eastern districts of that state.

In 1864, the Republicans, in an appeal to northern and border state "**War Democrats,**" nominated Johnson for vice president. But despite Johnson's success in Tennessee and in the 1864 campaign, many Radical Republicans distrusted him. In the immediate aftermath of Lincoln's murder, however, Johnson appeared to side with those Radical Republicans who sought to treat the South as a conquered province. But support for Johnson quickly faded as the new president's policies unfolded. Johnson defined Reconstruction as the province of the executive, not the legislative branch, and he planned to restore the Union as quickly as possible. He blamed individual Southerners—the planter elite—rather than entire states for leading the South down the disastrous road to secession. In line with this philosophy, Johnson outlined mild terms for reentry to the Union.

In the spring of 1865, Johnson granted amnesty and pardon, including restoration of property rights except slaves, to all Confederates who pledged loyalty to the Union and support for emancipation. Fourteen classes of Southerners, mostly major Confederate officials and wealthy landowners, were excluded. But these men could apply individually for presidential pardons. (During his tenure Johnson pardoned roughly 90 percent of those who applied.) Significantly, Johnson instituted this plan while Congress was not in session.

By the fall of 1865, ten of the eleven Confederate states claimed to have met Johnson's requirements to reenter the Union. But a serious division within the federal government was taking shape, for the Congress was not about to allow the president free rein in determining the conditions of southern readmission. Johnson's open sympathy for his fellow white Southerners, his antiblack bias, and his determination to control the course of Reconstruction placed him on a collision course with the powerful Radical wing of the Republican Party.

FREE LABOR AND THE RADICAL REPUBLICAN VISION

Most Radicals were men whose careers had been shaped by the slavery controversy. One of the most effective rhetorical weapons used against slavery and its

IMAGE KEY

for pages 432–433

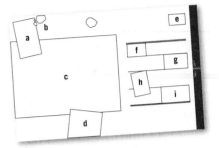

a. A young African American boy with new clothes and a book provided by the Freedmen's Bureau.

b. Rocks and stones like those used to hurl at slaves.

c. Women and children escaping slavery.

d. Two members of the Ku Klux Klan holding guns and wearing hoods and long robes, pictured in *Harper's Weekly*.

e. Pages 44 and 45 from the New England primer show the religious content of the work.

f. The dead at Gettysburg were strewn across the battlefield.

g. Freedmen (freed black slaves) vote in 1867 while standing in line. The Stars and Stripes hang overhead.

h. Three white men decry the Reconstruction Acts of Congress as "usurpations and unconstitutional, revolutionary, and void" while clasping hands above the fallen body of a black man.

i. The "tramp" became a symbol of the misery caused by industrial depression as seen in this *Harper's Weekly* illustration, "The Tramp," September 2, 1876.

Freedmen's Bureau Agency established by Congress in March 1865 to provide social, educational, and economic services, advice, and protection to former slaves and destitute whites; lasted seven years.

War Democrats Those from the North and the border states who broke with the Democratic Party and supported the Abraham Lincoln's military policies during the Civil War.

Black codes   Laws passed by states and municipalities denying many rights of citizenship to free black people before the Civil War.

Civil Rights Bill   1866 act that gave full citizenship to African Americans.

16–3
Clinton B. Fisk, *Plain Counsels for Freedmen* (1865)

16–4
Mississippi Black Codes (1865)

16–7
The Fourteenth Amendment (1868)

spread had been the ideal of a society based upon free labor. The model of free individuals, competing equally in the labor market and enjoying equal political rights, formed the core of this worldview.

Radicals now looked to reconstruct southern society along these same lines, backed by the power of the national government. They argued that once free labor, universal education, and equal rights were implanted in the South, that region would be able to share in the North's material wealth, progress, and social mobility. In the Radicals' view, the power of the federal government would be central to the remaking of southern society, especially in guaranteeing civil rights and suffrage for freedmen.

Northern Republicans were especially outraged by the stringent "**black codes**" passed by South Carolina, Mississippi, Louisiana, and other states. These were designed to restrict the freedom of the black labor force and keep freed people as close to slave status as possible. Laborers who left their jobs before contracts expired would forfeit wages already earned and be subject to arrest by any white citizen. Vagrancy, very broadly defined, was punishable by fines and involuntary plantation labor. Apprenticeship clauses obliged black children to work without pay for employers. Some states attempted to bar African Americans from land ownership. Other laws specifically denied African Americans equality with white people in civil rights, excluding them from juries and prohibiting interracial marriages.

The Radicals, although not a majority of their party, were joined by moderate Republicans as growing numbers of Northerners grew suspicious of white southern intransigence and the denial of political rights to freedmen. When the Thirty-ninth Congress convened in December 1865, the large Republican majority prevented the seating of the white Southerners elected to Congress under President Johnson's provisional state governments.

In the spring of 1866, Congress passed two important bills designed to aid African Americans. The landmark **Civil Rights Bill**, which bestowed full citizenship on African Americans, overturned the 1857 *Dred Scott* decision and the black codes. It defined all persons born in the United States (except Indian peoples) as national citizens, and it enumerated various rights, including the rights to make and enforce contracts, to sue, to give evidence, and to buy and sell property. Under this bill,

"Office of the Freedmen's Bureau, Memphis, Tennessee," *Harper's Weekly*, June 2, 1866. Established by Congress in 1865, the Freedmen's Bureau provided economic, educational, and legal assistance to former slaves in the post–Civil War years. Bureau agents were often called on to settle disputes between black and white Southerners over wages, labor contracts, political rights, and violence. Although most southern whites only grudgingly acknowledged the bureau's legitimacy, freed people gained important legal and psychological support through testimony at public hearings like this one.

African Americans acquired "full and equal benefit of all laws and proceedings for the security of person and property as is enjoyed by white citizens."

Congress also voted to enlarge the scope of the Freedmen's Bureau, empowering it to build schools and pay teachers, and also to establish courts to prosecute those charged with depriving African Americans of their civil rights. The bureau achieved important, if limited, success in aiding African Americans. Bureau-run schools helped lay the foundation for southern public education. The bureau's network of courts allowed freed people to bring suits against white people in disputes involving violence, nonpayment of wages, or unfair division of crops. The very existence of courts hearing public testimony by African Americans provided an important psychological challenge to traditional notions of white racial domination.

An angry President Johnson vetoed both of these bills. But Johnson's intemperate attacks on the Radicals—he damned them as traitors unwilling to restore the Union—united moderate and Radical Republicans and they succeeded in overriding the vetoes. Congressional Republicans, led by the Radical faction, were now unified in challenging the president's power to direct Reconstruction and in using national authority to define and protect the rights of citizens.

In June 1866, fearful that the Civil Rights Act might be declared unconstitutional, and eager to settle the basis for the seating of southern representatives, Congress passed the Fourteenth Amendment. The amendment defined national citizenship to include former slaves and prohibited the states from violating the privileges of citizens without due process of law. It also empowered Congress to reduce the representation of any state that denied the suffrage to males over twenty-one. Republicans adopted the Fourteenth Amendment as their platform for the 1866 congressional elections and suggested that southern states would have to ratify it as a condition of readmission.

For their part, the Republicans skillfully portrayed Johnson and northern Democrats as disloyal and white Southerners as unregenerate. Republicans began an effective campaign tradition known as "waving the bloody shirt"—reminding northern voters of the hundreds of thousands of Yankee soldiers left dead or maimed by the war. In the November 1866 elections, the Republicans increased their majority in both the House and the Senate and gained control of all the northern states. The stage was now set for a battle between the president and Congress. Was it to be Johnson's "restoration" or **Congressional Reconstruction**?

CONGRESSIONAL RECONSTRUCTION AND THE IMPEACHMENT CRISIS

In March 1867, Congress passed the **First Reconstruction Act** over Johnson's veto. This act divided the South into five military districts subject to martial law. To achieve restoration, southern states were first required to call new constitutional conventions, elected by universal manhood suffrage. Once these states had drafted new constitutions, guaranteed African American voting rights, and ratified the Fourteenth Amendment, they were eligible for readmission to the Union. Supplementary legislation, also passed over the president's veto, invalidated the provisional governments established by Johnson, empowered the military to administer voter registration, and required an oath of loyalty to the United States (see Map 17.1).

Congress also passed several laws aimed at limiting Johnson's power. One of these, the **Tenure of Office Act**, stipulated that any officeholder appointed by the president with the Senate's advice and consent could not be removed until the Senate had approved a successor. In August 1867, with Congress

Congressional Reconstruction Name given to the period 1867–1870 when the Republican-dominated Congress controlled Reconstruction-era policy.

First Reconstruction Act 1877 act that divided the South into five military districts subject to martial law.

Tenure of Office Act Act stipulating that any officeholder appointed by the president with the Senate's advice and consent could not be removed until the Senate had approved a successor.

QUICK REVIEW

Key Components of the Radical Agenda

◆ Free labor.
◆ Universal education.
◆ Equal rights.

QUICK REVIEW

The Tenure of Office Act and Johnson's Impeachment

◆ Act prohibited the president from removing certain officeholders without the Senate's approval of a successor.
◆ Johnson deliberately violated the act in February 1868.
◆ Johnson escaped impeachment by one vote.

MAP EXPLORATION

To explore an interactive version of this map, go to
http://www.prenhall.com/faraghertlc/map17.1

- — Five military districts est. 1867
- ▨ Border states
- **1868** Date of readmission to Union
- *(1874)* Date of reestablishment of Democratic Party control

MAP 17.1

Reconstruction of the South, 1866–77   Dates for the readmission of former Confederate states to the Union and the return of Democrats to power varied according to the specific political situations in those states.

WHAT WERE the competing plans for reconstructing the Southern states?

adjourned, Johnson suspended Stanton and appointed General Ulysses S. Grant interim secretary of war. This move enabled the president to remove generals in the field that he judged to be too radical and replace them with men who were sympathetic to his own views. It also served as a challenge to the Tenure of Office Act. In January 1868, when the Senate overruled Stanton's suspension, Grant broke openly with Johnson and vacated the office. Stanton resumed his position and barricaded himself in his office when Johnson attempted to remove him once again.

Outraged by Johnson's relentless obstructionism, and seizing upon his violation of the Tenure of Office Act as a pretext, moderate and Radical Republicans in the House of Representatives again joined forces and voted to impeach the president by a vote of 126 to 47 on February 24, 1868, charging him with eleven counts of high crimes and misdemeanors. To ensure the support of moderate Republicans, the articles of impeachment focused on violations of the Tenure of Office Act.

An influential group of moderate Senate Republicans feared the damage a conviction might do to the constitutional separation of powers. They also worried about the political and economic policies that might be pursued by Benjamin Wade, the president pro tem of the Senate and a leader of the Radical Republicans, who, because there was no vice president, would succeed to the presidency if Johnson were removed from office. Behind the scenes during his Senate trial, Johnson agreed to abide by the Reconstruction Acts. In May, the Senate

The Fifteenth Amendment, ratified in 1870, stipulated that the right to vote could not be denied "on account of race, color, or previous condition of servitude." This illustration expressed the optimism and hopes of African Americans generated by this consitutional landmark aimed at protecting black political rights. Note the various political figures (Abraham Lincoln, John Brown, Frederick Douglass) and movements (abolitionism, black education) invoked here, providing a sense of how the amendment ended a long historical struggle.

voted 35 for conviction, 19 for acquittal—one vote shy of the two-thirds necessary for removal from office. Johnson's narrow acquittal established the precedent that only criminal actions by a president—not political disagreements—warranted removal from office.

THE ELECTION OF 1868

By the summer of 1868, seven former Confederate states (Alabama, Arkansas, Florida, Louisiana, North Carolina, South Carolina, and Tennessee) had ratified the revised constitutions, elected Republican governments, and ratified the Fourteenth Amendment. They had thereby earned readmission to the Union. In 1868 Republicans nominated Ulysses S. Grant, the North's foremost military hero, as their nominee for President. Grant enjoyed tremendous popularity after the war, especially when he broke with Johnson. Totally lacking in political experience, Grant admitted, after receiving the nomination, that he had been forced into it in spite of himself.

Significantly, at the very moment that the South was being forced to enfranchise former slaves as a prerequisite for readmission to the Union, the Republicans rejected a campaign plank endorsing black suffrage in the North. State referendums calling for black suffrage failed in eight northern states between 1865 and 1868, succeeding only in Iowa and Minnesota. The Democrats, determined to reverse Congressional Reconstruction, nominated Horatio Seymour, former governor of New York and a longtime foe of emancipation and supporter of states' rights.

The **Ku Klux Klan** emerged as a potent instrument of terror (see the opening of this chapter). In Louisiana, Arkansas, Georgia, and South Carolina, the Klan threatened, whipped, and murdered black and white Republicans to prevent them from voting. This terrorism enabled the Democrats to carry Georgia and Louisiana, but it ultimately cost the Democrats votes in the North. In the final tally, Grant carried twenty-six of the thirty-four states for an electoral college victory of 214 to 80. Significantly, more than 500,000 African American voters cast their ballots for Grant, demonstrating their overwhelming support for the Republican Party. The Republicans also retained large majorities in both houses of Congress.

In February 1869, Congress passed the **Fifteenth Amendment**, providing that "the right of citizens of the United States to vote shall not be denied or abridged on account of race, color, or previous condition of servitude." To enhance the chances of ratification, Congress required the four remaining unreconstructed states—Mississippi, Georgia, Texas, and Virginia—to ratify both the Fourteenth and Fifteenth Amendments before readmission. They did so and rejoined the Union in early 1870. The Fifteenth Amendment was ratified in February 1870. In the narrow sense of simply readmitting the former Confederate states to the Union, Reconstruction was complete.

WOMAN SUFFRAGE AND RECONSTRUCTION

Many women's rights advocates had long been active in the abolitionist movement. The Fourteenth and Fifteenth Amendments, which granted citizenship and the vote to freedmen, both inspired and frustrated these activists. Insisting that the causes of the African American vote and the women's vote were linked, Elizabeth Cady Stanton, Susan B. Anthony, and Lucy Stone founded the American Equal Rights Association in 1866. The group launched a series of lobbying and petition campaigns to remove racial and sexual restrictions on voting from state constitutions. Throughout the nation, the old abolitionist organizations and the Republican Party

Ku Klux Klan Perhaps the most prominent of the vigilante groups that terrorized black people in the South during Reconstruction era, founded by the Confederate veterans in 1866.

Fifteenth Amendment Passed by Congress in 1869, guaranteed the right of American men to vote, regardless of race.

 16–8
Albion W. Tourgee, *Letter on Ku Klux Klan Activities* (1870)

Susan B. Anthony (1820–1906) and Elizabeth Cady Stanton (1815–1902), the two most influential leaders of the woman suffrage movement. As founders of the militant National Woman Suffrage Association, Stanton and Anthony established an independent woman suffrage movement with a broader spectrum of goals for women's rights and drew millions of women into public life during the late nineteenth century.

OVERVIEW | Reconstruction Amendments to the Constitution, 1865–1870

Amendment and Date Passed by Congress	Main Provisions	Ratification Process (3/4 of all States Including Ex-Confederate States Required)
13 (January 1865)	• Prohibited slavery in the United States	December 1865 (27 states, including 8 southern states)
14 (June 1866)	• Conferred national citizenship on all persons born or naturalized in the United States • Reduced state representation in Congress proportionally for any state disfranchising male citizens • Denied former Confederates the right to hold state or national office • Repudiated Confederate debt	July 1868 (after Congress made ratification a prerequisite for readmission of ex-Confederate states to the Union)
15 (February 1869)	• Prohibited denial of suffrage because of race, color, or previous condition of servitude	March 1870 (ratification required for readmission of Virginia, Texas, Mississippi, and Georgia)

myhistorylab

Overview: *Reconstruction Amendments to the Constitution, 1865–1870*

16–10
Susan B. Anthony and the "New Departure" for Women (1873)

WHAT WERE the most important changes in the lives of African Americans in the years immediately following the war?

myhistorylab

Review Summary

emphasized passage of the Fourteenth and Fifteenth Amendments and withdrew funds and support from the cause of woman suffrage. Disagreements over these amendments divided suffragists for decades and by 1869 woman suffragists had split into two competing organizations: the moderate American Woman Suffrage Association (AWSA), which sought the support of men, and the more radical all-female National Woman Suffrage Association (NWSA).

Although women did not win the vote in this period, they did establish an independent suffrage movement that eventually drew millions of women into political life. The NWSA in particular demonstrated that self-government and democratic participation in the public sphere were crucial for women's emancipation. The failure of woman suffrage after the Civil War was less a result of factional fighting than of the larger defeat of Radical Reconstruction and the ideal of expanded citizenship.

THE MEANING OF FREEDOM

For nearly 4 million slaves, freedom arrived in various ways in different parts of the South. In many areas, slavery had collapsed long before Lee's surrender at Appomattox. In regions far removed from the presence of federal troops, African Americans did not learn of slavery's end until the spring of 1865. But regardless of specific regional circumstances, the meaning of "freedom" would be contested for years to come. The deep desire for independence from white control formed the underlying aspiration of newly freed slaves. For their part, most southern white people sought to restrict the boundaries of that independence.

MOVING ABOUT

The first impulse of many emancipated slaves was to test their freedom. The simplest, most obvious way to do this involved leaving home. Throughout the summer and fall of 1865, observers in the South noted enormous numbers of freed

People on the move. When urged to stay on with the South Carolina family she had served for years as a cook, a slave woman replied firmly: "No, Miss, I must go. If I stay here I'll never know I am free."

Yet many who left their old neighborhoods returned soon afterward to seek work in the general vicinity or even on the plantation they had left. Many wanted to separate themselves from former owners, but not from familial ties and friendships. Others moved away altogether, seeking jobs in nearby towns and cities. Many former slaves left predominantly white counties, where they felt more vulnerable and isolated, for new lives in the relative comfort of predominantly black communities. In most southern states, there was a significant population shift toward black belt plantation counties and towns after the war. Many African Americans, attracted by schools, churches, and fraternal societies as well as the army, preferred the city.

Disgruntled planters had difficulty accepting African American independence. The deference and humility white people expected from African Americans could no longer be taken for granted. Indeed, many freed people went out of their way to reject the old subservience. Moving about freely was one way of doing this, as was refusing to tip one's hat to white people, ignoring former masters or mistresses in the streets, and refusing to step aside on sidewalks.

The African American Family

Emancipation allowed freed people to strengthen family ties. For many former slaves, freedom meant the opportunity to find long-lost family members. To track down these relatives, freed people trekked to faraway places, put ads in newspapers, sought the help of Freedmen's Bureau agents, and questioned anyone who might have information about loved ones. Many thousands of family reunions, each with its own story, took place after the war. One North Carolina slave, who had seen his parents separated by sale, recalled many years later what for him had been the most significant aspect of freedom. "I has got thirteen great-gran' chilluns an' I know whar dey ever'one am. In slavery times dey'd have been on de block long time ago." Thousands of African American couples who had lived together under slavery streamed to military and civilian authorities and demanded to be legally married. By 1870, the two-parent household was the norm for a large majority of African Americans.

Emancipation brought changes to gender roles within the African American family as well. By serving in the Union army, African American men played a more direct role than women in the fight for freedom. In the political sphere, black men could now serve on juries, vote, and hold office; black women, like their white counterparts, could not. Freedmen's Bureau agents designated the husband as household head and established lower wage scales for women laborers.

African American men asserted their male authority, denied under slavery, by insisting their wives work at home instead of in the fields. African American women generally wanted to devote more time than they had under slavery to caring for their children and to performing such domestic chores as cooking, sewing, gardening, and laundering. Yet African American women continued to work outside the home, engaging in seasonal field labor for wages or working a family's rented plot. The key difference from slave times was that African American families themselves, not white masters and overseers, decided when and where women and children worked.

African American Churches and Schools

The creation of separate African American churches proved the most lasting and important element of the energetic institution building that went on in post-emancipation years. Before the Civil War, southern Protestant churches had

An overflow congregation crowds into Richmond's First African Baptist Church in 1874. Despite their poverty, freed people struggled to save money, buy land, and erect new buildings as they organized hundreds of new black churches during Reconstruction. As the most important African American institution outside the family, the black church, in addition to tending to spiritual needs, played a key role in the educational and political life of the community.

relegated slaves and free African Americans to second-class membership. Black worshipers were required to sit in the back during services, they were denied any role in church governance, and they were excluded from Sunday schools. Even in larger cities, where all-black congregations sometimes built their own churches, the law required white pastors.

In communities around the South, African Americans now pooled their resources to buy land and build their own churches. Churches became the center not only for religious life but also for many other activities that defined the African American community: schools, picnics, festivals, and political meetings. The church became the first social institution fully controlled by African Americans. In nearly every community, ministers, respected for their speaking and organizational skills, were among the most influential leaders. By 1877, the great majority of black Southerners had withdrawn from white-dominated churches.

The rapid spread of schools reflected African Americans' thirst for self-improvement. Southern states had prohibited education for slaves. But many free black people managed to attend school, and a few slaves had been able to educate themselves. Still, over 90 percent of the South's adult African American population was illiterate in 1860. Access to education thus became a central part of the meaning of freedom. Freedmen's Bureau agents repeatedly expressed amazement at the number of makeshift classrooms organized by African Americans in rural areas.

African American communities received important educational aid from outside organizations. By 1869, the Freedmen's Bureau was supervising nearly 3,000 schools serving over 150,000 students throughout the South. Over half of the roughly 3,300 teachers in these schools were African Americans, many of whom had been free before the Civil War. Other teachers included dedicated northern white women, volunteers sponsored by the American Missionary Association (AMA). The bureau and the AMA also assisted in the founding of several black colleges, including Tougaloo, Hampton, and Fisk, designed to train black teachers. Black self-help proved crucial to the education effort. Throughout the South in 1865 and 1866, African Americans raised money to build schoolhouses, buy supplies, and pay teachers. Black artisans donated labor for construction, and black families offered room and board to teachers.

LAND AND LABOR AFTER SLAVERY

Most newly emancipated African Americans aspired to quit the plantations and to make new lives for themselves. Some freed people did find jobs in railroad building, mining, ranching, or construction work. Others raised subsistence crops and tended vegetable gardens as squatters. White planters, however, tried to retain African Americans as permanent agricultural laborers. Restricting the employment of former slaves was an important goal of the black codes.

The majority of African Americans hoped to become self-sufficient farmers. Many former slaves believed they were entitled to the land they had worked throughout their lives. This perception was not merely a wishful fantasy. Frequent reference in the Congress and the press to the question of land distribution made the idea of "forty acres and a mule" not just a pipe dream but a matter of serious public debate. But by 1866, the federal government had already pulled back from the various wartime experiments involving the breaking up of large plantations and the leasing of small plots to individual families. President Johnson directed General Oliver O. Howard of the Freedmen's Bureau to evict tens of thousands of freed people settled on confiscated and abandoned land in southeastern Virginia, southern Louisiana, and the Georgia and South Carolina low country.

In communities throughout the South, freed people and their former masters negotiated new arrangements for organizing agricultural labor (see Map 17.2). By the late 1860s, **sharecropping** and tenant farming had emerged as the dominant form of working the land. Sharecropping represented a compromise between planters and former slaves. Under sharecropping arrangements that were usually very detailed, individual families contracted with landowners to be responsible for a specific plot. Large plantations were thus broken into family-sized farms. Generally, sharecropper families received one-third of the year's crop if the owner furnished implements, seed, and draft animals or one-half if they provided their own supplies. African Americans preferred sharecropping to gang labor, as it allowed families to set their own hours and tasks and offered freedom from white supervision and control. For planters, the system stabilized the workforce by requiring sharecroppers to remain until the harvest and to employ all family members. It also offered a way around the chronic shortage of cash and credit that plagued the postwar South. Freed people did not aspire to sharecropping. Owning land outright or tenant farming (renting land) were both more desirable. But though black sharecroppers clearly enjoyed more autonomy than in the past, the vast majority never achieved economic independence or land ownership. They remained a largely subordinate agricultural labor force.

THE ORIGINS OF AFRICAN AMERICAN POLITICS

Inclusion, rather than separation, was the objective of early African American political activity. The greatest political activity by African Americans occurred in areas occupied by Union forces during the war. In 1865 and 1866, African Americans throughout the South organized scores of mass meetings, parades, and petitions that demanded civil equality and the right to vote. In the cities, the growing web of churches and fraternal societies helped bolster early efforts at political organization.

Hundreds of African American delegates, selected by local meetings or churches, attended statewide political conventions held

16–5
James C. Beecher, *Report on Land Reform in the South Carolina Islands* (1865, 1866)

16–11
James T. Rapier, *Testimony Before U.S. Senate Regarding the Agricultural Labor Force in the South* (1880)

A Sharecrop Contract (1882)

Sharecropping Labor system that evolved during and after Reconstruction whereby landowners furnished laborers with a house, farm animals, and tools and advanced credit in exchange for a share of the laborers' crop.

"The First Vote," *Harper's Weekly*, November 16, 1867, reflected the optimism felt by much of the northern public as former slaves began to vote for the first time. The caption noted that freedmen went to the ballot box "not with expressions of exultation or of defiance of their old masters and present opponents depicted on their countenances, but looking serious and solemn and determined."

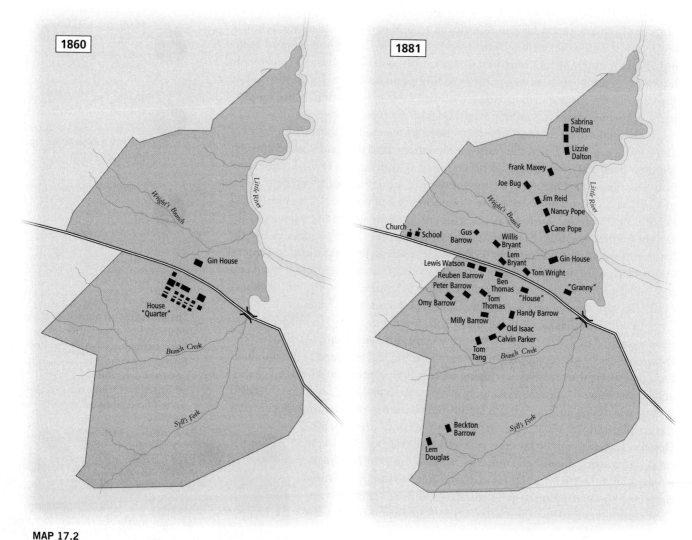

MAP 17.2
The Barrow Plantation, Oglethorpe County, Georgia, 1860 and 1881 (approx. 2,000 acres)   These two maps, based on drawings from *Scribner's Monthly*, April 1881, show some of the changes brought by emancipation. In 1860, the plantation's entire black population lived in the communal slave quarters, right next to the white master's house. In 1881, black sharecropper and tenant families lived on individual plots, spread out across the land. The former slaves had also built their own school and church.

WHAT CHANGES in the lives of Black Southerners are reflected in the two maps of the Barrow Plantation?

throughout the South in 1865 and 1866. Previously free African Americans, as well as black ministers, artisans, and veterans of the Union army, tended to dominate these proceedings, setting a pattern that would hold throughout Reconstruction. Convention debates sometimes reflected the tensions within African American communities, such as friction between poorer former slaves and better-off free black people, or between lighter- and darker-skinned African Americans. But most of these state gatherings concentrated on passing resolutions on issues that united all African Americans. The central concerns were suffrage and equality before the law.

The passage of the First Reconstruction Act in 1867 encouraged even more political activity among African Americans. The military started registering the South's electorate, ultimately enrolling approximately 735,000 black and 635,000 white voters in the ten unreconstructed states. Five states—Alabama, Florida, Louisiana, Mississippi, and South Carolina—had black electoral majorities. Four-fifths of the

Changing Images of Reconstruction

After the Civil War, northern journalists and illustrators went south to describe Reconstruction in action. They took a keen interest in how the newly freed slaves were reshaping local and national politics. A drawing by *Harper's Weekly* illustrator William L. Sheppard titled "Electioneering in the South" clearly approved of the freedmen's exercise of their new citizenship rights. "Does any man seriously

HOW DOES the portrayal of the larger African American community in "Electioneering in the South" reflect the political point being made? What do the caricatures in "The Ignorant Vote" suggest about Reconstruction era ideas about the meaning of "whiteness"?

doubt," the caption asked, "whether it is better for this vast population to be sinking deeper and deeper in ignorance and servility, or rising into general intelligence and self-respect? They can not be pariahs; they can not be peons; they must be slaves or citizens."

Thomas Nast was the nation's best-known political cartoonist during the 1860s and 1870s. During the Civil War he strongly supported the Union cause and the aspirations of the newly freed slaves. But by 1876, like many Northerners originally sympathetic to guaranteeing blacks full political and civil rights, Nast had turned away from the early ideals of Reconstruction. Nast used grotesque racial caricature to depict southern African Americans and northern Irish

immigrants as undeserving of the right to vote. The aftermath of the disputed 1876 presidential election included charges of widespread vote fraud from both Republicans and Democrats. Nast's view—published in *Harper's Weekly* in December 1876, while the election's outcome was still in doubt—reflected concerns among many middle-class Northerners that the nation's political system was tainted by the manipulation of "ignorant" voters in both the South and the North. ∎

registered black voters cast ballots in these elections. Much of this new African American political activism was channeled through local **Union League** chapters throughout the South.

Begun during the war as a northern, largely white middle-class patriotic club, the Union League now became the political voice of the former slaves. Union League chapters brought together local African Americans, soldiers, and Freedmen's Bureau agents to demand the vote and an end to legal discrimination against African Americans. It brought out African American voters, instructed freedmen in the rights and duties of citizenship, and promoted Republican candidates. Not surprisingly, newly enfranchised freedmen voted Republican and formed the core of the Republican Party in the South. For most ordinary African Americans, politics was inseparable from economic issues, especially the land question. Grassroots political organizations frequently intervened in local disputes with planters over the terms of labor contracts. African American political groups closely followed the congressional debates over Reconstruction policy and agitated for land confiscation and distribution. Perhaps most important, politics was the only arena where black and white Southerners might engage each other on an equal basis.

SOUTHERN POLITICS AND SOCIETY

By the summer of 1868, when the South had returned to the Union, the majority of Republicans believed the task of Reconstruction to be finished. Ultimately, they put their faith in a political solution to the problems facing the vanquished South. Most Republican congressmen were moderates, conceiving Reconstruction in limited terms. They rejected radical calls for confiscation and redistribution of land, as well as permanent military rule of the South. The Reconstruction Acts of 1867 and 1868 laid out the requirements for the readmission of southern states, along with the procedures for forming and electing new governments.

Yet over the next decade, the political structure created in the southern states proved too restricted and fragile to sustain itself. To most southern whites, the active participation of African Americans in politics seemed extremely dangerous. Federal troops were needed to protect Republican governments and their supporters from violent opposition. Congressional action to monitor southern elections and protect black voting rights became routine. Despite initial successes, southern Republicanism proved an unstable coalition of often conflicting elements, unable to sustain effective power for very long. By 1877, Democrats had regained political control of all the former Confederate states.

SOUTHERN REPUBLICANS

Three major groups composed the fledgling Republican coalition in the postwar South. African American voters made up a large majority of southern Republicans throughout the Reconstruction era. Yet African Americans outnumbered whites in only three southern states; Republicans would have to attract white support to win elections and sustain power.

A second group consisted of white Northerners, derisively called "**carpetbaggers**" by native white Southerners. Most were veterans of the Union army who stayed in the South after the war. Others included Freedmen's Bureau agents and businessmen who had invested capital in cotton plantations and other enterprises. Although they made up a tiny percentage of the population, carpetbaggers played

---

WHAT MAJOR groups made up the Southern Republicans?

myhistorylab

Review Summary

Union League Republican party organizations in Northern cities that became an important organizing device among freedmen in Southern cities after 1865.

Carpetbaggers Northern transplants to the South, many of whom were Union soldiers who stayed in the South after the war.

a disproportionately large role in southern politics. They won a large share of Reconstruction offices, particularly in Florida, South Carolina, and Louisiana and in areas with large African American constituencies.

The third major group of southern Republicans were the native whites pejoratively termed "**scalawags**." They had even more diverse backgrounds and motives than the northern-born Republicans. Some were prominent prewar Whigs who saw the Republican Party as their best chance to regain political influence. Others viewed the party as an agent of modernization and economic expansion. Loyalists during the war and traditional enemies of the planter elite (most were small farmers), these white Southerners looked to the Republican Party for help in settling old scores and relief from debt and wartime devastation.

Southern Republicanism also reflected prewar political divisions. Its influence was greatest in those regions that had long resisted the political and economic power of the plantation elite. Yet few white Southerners identified with the political and economic aspirations of African Americans. Moderate elements more concerned with maintaining white control of the party, and encouraging economic investment in the region, outnumbered and defeated "confiscation radicals" who focused on obtaining land for African Americans.

Scalawags Southern whites, mainly small landowning farmers and well-off merchants and planters, who supported the Southern Republican party during Reconstruction.

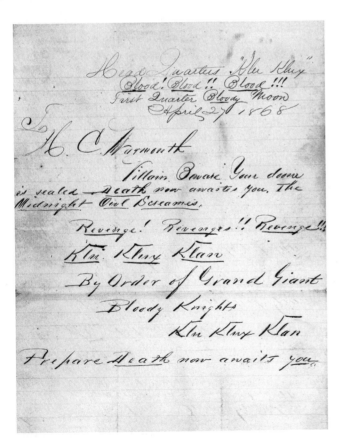

The Ku Klux Klan emerged as a potent political and social force during Reconstruction, terrorizing freed people and their white allies. An 1868 Klan warning threatens Louisiana governor Henry C. Warmoth with death. Warmoth, an Illinois-born "carpetbagger," was the state's first Republican governor. Two Alabama Klansmen, photographed in 1868, wear white hoods to hide their identities.

myhistorylab

Exploring America: *Did Reconstruction Work for the Freed People?*

RECONSTRUCTING THE STATES: A MIXED RECORD

With the old Confederate leaders barred from political participation, and with carpetbaggers and newly enfranchised African Americans representing many of the plantation districts, Republicans managed to dominate the ten southern constitutional conventions from 1867 to 1869. Most of these conventions produced constitutions that expanded democracy and the public role of the state. The new documents guaranteed the political and civil rights of African Americans, and they abolished property qualifications for officeholding and jury service as well as imprisonment for debt. They created the first state-funded systems of education in the South to be administered by state commissioners. The new constitutions also mandated establishment of orphanages, penitentiaries, and homes for the insane. In 1868, only three years after the end of the war, Republicans came to power in most of the southern states. By 1869, new constitutions had been ratified in all the old Confederate states.

Republican governments in the South faced a continual crisis of legitimacy that limited their ability to legislate change. They had to balance reform against the need to gain acceptance, especially by white Southerners. Their achievements were thus mixed. In the realm of race relations there was a clear thrust toward equal rights and against discrimination. Republican legislatures followed up the federal Civil Rights Act of 1866 with various antidiscrimination clauses in new constitutions and laws prescribing harsh penalties for civil rights violations.

Segregation, though, became the norm in public school systems. African American leaders often accepted segregation because they feared that insistence on integrated education would jeopardize funding for the new school systems. Segregation in railroad cars and other public places was more objectionable. By the early 1870s, as black influence and assertiveness grew, laws guaranteeing equal access to transportation and public accommodation were passed in many states. By and large, though, such civil rights laws were difficult to enforce in local communities.

In economic matters, Republican governments failed to fulfill African Americans' hopes of obtaining land. Few former slaves possessed the cash to buy land in the open market, and they looked to the state for help. Republicans tried to weaken the plantation system and promote black ownership by raising taxes on land. Yet even when state governments seized land for nonpayment of taxes, the property was never used to help create black homesteads.

Republican leaders envisioned promoting northern-style capitalist development—factories, large towns, and diversified agriculture—through state aid. Much Republican state lawmaking was devoted to encouraging railroad construction. But in spite of all the new laws, it proved impossible to attract significant amounts of northern and European investment capital. The obsession with railroads withdrew resources from education and other programs. As in the North, it also opened the doors to widespread corruption and bribery of public officials. Railroad failures eroded public confidence in the Republicans' ability to govern.

WHITE RESISTANCE AND "REDEMPTION"

The emergence of a Republican Party in the reconstructed South brought two parties, but not a two-party system, to the region. The opponents of Reconstruction, the Democrats, refused to acknowledge Republicans' right to participate in southern political life. Republicans were split between those who urged conciliation in an effort to gain white acceptance and those who emphasized consolidating the party under the protection of the military.

From its founding in 1868 through the early 1870s, the Ku Klux Klan fought an ongoing terrorist campaign against Reconstruction governments and local leaders. Just as the institution of slavery had depended on violence and the threat of violence, the Klan acted as a kind of guerrilla military force in the service of the Democratic Party, the planter class, and all those who sought the restoration of white supremacy. It employed a wide array of terror tactics: destroying ballot boxes, issuing death threats, the beating and murdering of politically active blacks and their white allies. Freedmen and their allies sometimes resisted the Klan. In Hale County, Alabama, Union Leaguers set up a warning system using buglers to signal the activities of Klan raiders. But violence and intimidation decimated Union League leadership in the countryside by 1869.

In October 1870, after Republicans carried Laurens County in South Carolina, bands of white people drove 150 African Americans from their homes and murdered thirteen white and black Republican activists. In March 1871, three African Americans were arrested in Meridian, Mississippi, for giving "incendiary" speeches. At their court hearing, Klansmen killed two of the defendants and the Republican judge, and thirty more African Americans were murdered in a day of rioting. The single bloodiest episode of Reconstruction era violence took place in Colfax, Louisiana, on Easter Sunday 1873. Nearly 100 African Americans were murdered after they failed to hold a besieged courthouse during a contested election.

Southern Republicans looked to Washington for help. In 1870 and 1871, Congress passed three Enforcement Acts designed to counter racial terrorism. These declared that interference with voting was a federal offense. The acts provided for federal supervision of voting and authorized the president to send the army and to suspend the writ of habeas corpus in districts declared to be in a state of insurrection. The most sweeping measure was the Ku Klux Klan Act of April 1871, which made the violent infringement of civil and political rights a federal crime punishable by the national government. By the election of 1872, the federal government's intervention had helped break the Klan and restore a semblance of law and order.

The Civil Rights Act of 1875 outlawed racial discrimination in theaters, hotels, railroads, and other public places. But the law proved more an assertion of principle than a direct federal intervention in southern affairs. Enforcement required African Americans to take their cases to the federal courts, a costly and time-consuming procedure.

As wartime idealism faded, northern Republicans became less inclined toward direct intervention in southern affairs. They had enough trouble retaining political control in the North. In 1874, the Democrats gained a majority in the House of Representatives for the first time since 1856. Key northern states also began to fall to the Democrats. Northern Republicans slowly abandoned the freedmen and their white allies in the South. Southern Democrats were also able to exploit a deepening fiscal crisis by blaming Republicans for excessive extension of public credit and the sharp increase in tax rates.

Gradually, conservative Democrats "redeemed" one state after another. Virginia and Tennessee led the way in 1869, North Carolina in 1870, Georgia in 1871, Texas in 1873, and Alabama and Arkansas in 1874. In Mississippi, white conservatives employed violence and intimidation to wrest control in 1875 and "redeemed" the state the following year. Republican infighting in Louisiana in 1873 and 1874 led to a series of contested election results, including bloody clashes between black militia and armed whites, and finally to "redemption" by the Democrats in 1877.

Several Supreme Court rulings involving the Fourteenth and Fifteenth Amendments effectively constrained federal protection of African American civil rights. In

Slaughterhouse cases Group of cases resulting in one sweeping decision by the U.S. Supreme Court in 1873 that contradicted the intent of the Fourteenth Amendment by decreeing that most citizenship rights remained under state, not federal, control.

the so-called **Slaughterhouse cases** of 1873, the Court issued its first ruling on the Fourteenth Amendment. The cases involved a Louisiana charter that gave a New Orleans meatpacking company a monopoly over the city's butchering business on the grounds of protecting public health. A rival group of butchers had sued, claiming the law violated the Fourteenth Amendment, which prohibited states from depriving any person of life, liberty, or property without due process of law. The Court held that the Fourteenth Amendment protected only the former slaves, not butchers, and that it protected only national citizenship rights, not the regulatory powers of states. It separated national citizenship from state citizenship and declared that most of the rights that Americans enjoyed on a daily basis—freedom of speech, fair trials, the right to sit on juries, protection from unreasonable searches, and the right to vote—were under the control of state law. The ruling in effect denied the original intent of the Fourteenth Amendment—to protect against state infringement of national citizenship rights as spelled out in the Bill of Rights.

Three other decisions curtailed federal protection of black civil rights. In *United States* v. *Reese* (1876) and *United States* v. *Cruikshank* (1876), the Court restricted congressional power to enforce the Ku Klux Klan Act. Future prosecution would depend on the states rather than on federal authorities. In these rulings, the Court held that the Fourteenth Amendment extended the federal power to protect civil rights only in cases involving discrimination by states; discrimination by individuals or groups was not covered. The Court also ruled that the Fifteenth Amendment did not guarantee a citizen's right to vote; it only barred certain specific grounds for denying suffrage—"race, color, or previous condition of servitude." This interpretation opened the door for southern states to disenfranchise African Americans for allegedly nonracial reasons. States back under Democratic control began to limit African American voting by passing laws restricting voter eligibility through poll taxes and property requirements.

Finally, in the 1883 Civil Rights Cases decision, the Court declared the Civil Rights Act of 1875 unconstitutional, holding that the Fourteenth Amendment gave Congress the power to outlaw discrimination by states but not by private individuals. The majority opinion held that black people must no longer "be the special favorite of the laws." Together, these Supreme Court decisions marked the end of federal attempts to protect African American rights until well into the next century.

QUICK REVIEW

The End of Federal Intervention: Key Supreme Court Cases

- Slaughterhouse cases (1873).
- *United States* v. *Reese* (1876).
- *United States* v. *Cruikshank* (1876).
- Civil Rights Cases (1883).

KING COTTON: SHARECROPPERS, TENANTS, AND THE SOUTHERN ENVIRONMENT

The Republicans' vision of a "New South" remade along the lines of the northern economy failed to materialize. In the post–Civil War years, "King Cotton" expanded its realm, as greater numbers of small white farmers found themselves forced to switch from subsistence crops to growing cotton for the market (see Map 17.3).

A chronic shortage of capital and banking institutions made local merchants and planters the sole source of credit. They advanced loans and supplies to small owners, tenant farmers, and sharecroppers in exchange for a lien, or claim, on the year's cotton crop. At the end of the year, sharecroppers and tenants found themselves deep in debt to stores for seed, supplies, and clothing. The spread of the "crop lien" system as the South's main form of agricultural credit forced more and more farmers into cotton growing.

As the "crop lien" system spread, and as more and more farmers turned to cotton growing as the only way to obtain credit, expanding production depressed cotton prices. Competition from new cotton centers in the world market, such as Egypt and India, accelerated the downward spiral. As cotton prices declined, per

MAP EXPLORATION

To explore an interactive version of this map, go to **http://www.prenhall.com/faraghertlc/map17.3**

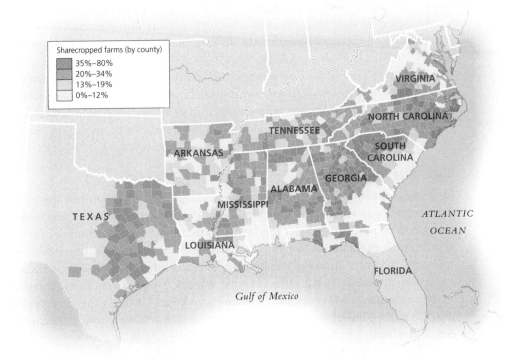

Sharecropped farms (by county)
- 35%–80%
- 20%–34%
- 13%–19%
- 0%–12%

MAP 17.3

Southern Sharecropping and the Cotton Belt, 1880   The economic depression of the 1870s forced increasing numbers of southern farmers, both white and black, into sharecropping arrangements. Sharecropping was most pervasive in the cotton belt regions of South Carolina, Georgia, Alabama, Mississippi, and eastern Texas.

HOW DID this new form of labor affect the lives of former slaves?

capita wealth in the South fell steadily, equaling only one-third that of the East, Midwest, or West by the 1890s. Small farmers caught up in a vicious cycle of low cotton prices, debt, and dwindling food crops found their old ideal of independence sacrificed to the cruel logic of the cotton market.

To obtain precious credit, most southern farmers, both black and white, found themselves forced to produce cotton for market and, thus, became enmeshed in the debt-ridden crop lien system. In traditional cotton producing areas, especially the black belt, landless farmers growing cotton had replaced slaves growing cotton. In the up-country and newer areas of cultivation, cotton-dominated commercial agriculture, with landless tenants and sharecroppers as the main workforce, had replaced the more diversified subsistence economy of the antebellum era. By 1900, over roughly half of the South's 2,620,000 farms were operated by tenants, who rented land, or sharecroppers, who pledged a portion of the crop to owners in exchange for some combination of work animals, seed, and tools. Over one-third of the white farmers and nearly three-quarters of the African American farmers in the cotton states were tenants or sharecroppers. Large parts of the southern landscape would remain defined by this system well into the twentieth century: small farms operated by families who did not own their land, mired in desperate poverty and debt.

WHAT PRECIPITATED the

electoral crisis of 1876?

Review Summary

RECONSTRUCTING THE NORTH

The triumph of the North brought with it fundamental changes in the economy, labor relations, and politics. The spread of the factory system, the growth of large and powerful corporations, and the rapid expansion of capitalist enterprise all hastened the development of a large unskilled and routinized workforce.

The old Republican ideal of a society bound by a harmony of interests had become overshadowed by a grimmer reality of class conflict. A violent national railroad strike in 1877 was broken only with the direct intervention of federal troops. That conflict struck many Americans as a turning point. Northern society, like the society of the South, appeared more hierarchical than equal.

THE AGE OF CAPITAL

In the decade following Appomattox, the North's economy continued the industrial boom begun during the Civil War. By 1873, America's industrial production had grown 75 percent over the 1865 level. By that time, too, the number of nonagricultural workers in the North had surpassed the number of farmers. Between 1860 and 1880, the number of wage earners in manufacturing and construction more than doubled, from 2 million to over 4 million. Only Great Britain boasted a larger manufacturing economy than the United States. During the same period, nearly 3 million immigrants arrived in America, almost all of whom settled in the North and West.

The railroad business both symbolized and advanced the new industrial order. Shortly before the Civil War, enthusiasm mounted for a transcontinental line. Private companies took on the huge and expensive job of construction, but the federal government funded the project, providing the largest subsidy in American history. The Pacific Railway Act of 1862 granted the Union Pacific and the

Chinese immigrants, like these section gang workers, provided labor and skills critical to the successful completion of the first transcontinental railroad. This photo was taken in Promontory Point, Utah Territory, in 1869.

Central Pacific rights to a broad swath of land extending from Omaha, Nebraska, to Sacramento, California. An 1864 act bestowed a subsidy of $15,000 per mile of track laid over smooth plains country and varying larger amounts up to $48,000 per mile in the foothills and mountains of the Far West. The Union Pacific employed gangs of Irish American and African American workers to lay track heading west from Omaha.

Meanwhile the Central Pacific, pushing east from California, had a tougher time finding workers, and began recruiting thousands of men from China. Some 12,000 Chinese laborers (about 90 percent of the workforce) bore the brunt of the difficult conditions in the Sierra Nevada where blizzards, landslides, and steep rock faces took an awful toll. But after completion of the transcontinental line threw thousands of Chinese railroad workers onto the California labor market, these workers faced a virulent tide of anti-Chinese agitation among western politicians and labor unions. In 1882, Congress passed the Chinese Exclusion Act, suspending any further Chinese immigration for ten years.

Railroad corporations became America's first big businesses. Railroads required huge outlays of investment capital, and their growth increased the economic power of banks and investment houses centered in Wall Street. Bankers often gained seats on the boards of directors of railroad companies, and their access to capital sometimes gave them the real control of the corporations. By the early 1870s the Pennsylvania Railroad was the nation's largest single company with more than 20,000 employees. A new breed of aggressive entrepreneur sought to ease cutthroat competition by absorbing smaller companies and forming "pools" that set rates and divided the market.

Some of the nation's most prominent politicians routinely accepted railroad largesse. Republican senator William M. Stewart of Nevada, a member of the Committee on Pacific Railroads, received a gift of 50,000 acres of land from the Central Pacific for his services. The worst scandal of the Grant administration grew out of corruption involving railroad promotion. When the scandal broke in 1872, it politically ruined Vice President Schuyler Colfax and led to the censure of two congressmen.

Other industries also boomed in this period, especially those engaged in extracting minerals and processing natural resources. Railroad growth stimulated expansion in the production of coal, iron, stone, and lumber, and these also received significant government aid. For example, under the National Mineral Act of 1866, mining companies received millions of acres of free public land. Oil refining enjoyed a huge expansion in the 1860s and 1870s. As with railroads, an early period of fierce competition soon gave way to concentration.

LIBERAL REPUBLICANS AND THE ELECTION OF 1872

With the rapid growth of large-scale, capital-intensive enterprises, Republicans increasingly identified with the interests of business rather than the rights of freedmen or the antebellum ideology of "free labor." State Republican parties now organized themselves around the spoils of federal patronage rather than grand causes such as preserving the Union or ending slavery. Republicans had no monopoly on political scandal. In 1871 New York City newspapers reported the shocking story of how Democratic Party boss William M. Tweed and his friends had systematically stolen tens of millions from the city treasury. But to many, the scandal represented only the most extreme case of the routine corruption that now plagued American political life.

"The Tramp," *Harper's* *Weekly*, September 2, 1876. The depression that began in 1873 forced many thousands of unemployed workers to go "on the tramp" in search of jobs. Men wandered from town to town, walking or riding railroad cars, desperate for a chance to work for wages or simply for room and board. The "tramp" became a powerful symbol of the misery caused by industrial depression and, as in this drawing, an image that evoked fear and nervousness among the nation's middle class.

By the end of President Grant's first term, a large number of disaffected Republicans sought an alternative. The **Liberal Republicans**, as they called themselves, emphasized the doctrines of classical economics. They called for a return to limited government, arguing that bribery, scandal, and high taxes all flowed from excessive state interference in the economy.

Liberal Republicans were also suspicious of expanding democracy. They believed that politics ought to be the province of "the best men"—educated and well-to-do men like themselves, devoted to the "science of government." They proposed civil service reform as the best way to break the hold of party machines on patronage.

Although most Liberal Republicans had enthusiastically supported abolition, the Union cause, and equal rights for freedmen, they now opposed continued federal intervention in the South. The national government had done all it could for the former slaves; they must now take care of themselves. In the spring of 1872 a diverse collection of Liberal Republicans nominated Horace Greeley to run for president. A longtime foe of the Democratic Party, Greeley nonetheless won that party's presidential nomination as well. All Americans, Greeley urged, must put the Civil War behind them and "clasp hands across the bloody chasm."

Grant easily defeated Greeley, carrying every state in the North and winning 56 percent of the popular vote. But the 1872 election accelerated the trend toward federal abandonment of African American citizenship rights. The Liberal Republicans quickly faded as an organized political force. But their ideas helped define a growing conservative consciousness among the northern public. Their agenda included retreat from the ideal of racial justice, hostility toward trade unions, suspicion of immigrant and working-class political power, celebration of competitive individualism, and opposition to government intervention in economic affairs.

THE DEPRESSION OF 1873

In the fall of 1873 the postwar boom came to an abrupt halt as a severe financial panic triggered a deep economic depression. The collapse resulted from commercial overexpansion, especially speculative investing in the nation's rail-

Liberal Republicans Disaffected Republicans that emphasized the doctrines of classical economics.

road system. By 1876 half the nation's railroads had defaulted on their bonds. Over the next two years more than 100 banks folded and 18,000 businesses shut their doors. The depression that began in 1873 lasted sixty-five months—the longest economic contraction in the nation's history until then.

The human toll was enormous. As factories began to close across the nation, the unemployment rate soared to about 15 percent. In many cities the jobless rate was much higher. The Pennsylvania Bureau of Labor Statistics noted that never before had "so many of the working classes, skilled and unskilled, been moving from place to place seeking employment that was not to be had." Farmers were also hard hit by the depression. Agricultural output continued to grow, but prices and land values fell sharply.

Mass meetings of workers in New York and other cities issued calls to government officials to create jobs through public works. But these appeals were rejected. Indeed, many business leaders and political figures denounced even meager efforts at charity. They saw the depression as a natural, if painful, part of the business cycle, one that would allow only the strongest enterprises (and workers) to survive.

The depression of the 1870s prompted workers and farmers to question the old free-labor ideology that celebrated a harmony of interests in northern society. More people voiced anger at and distrust of large corporations that exercised great economic power from outside their communities.

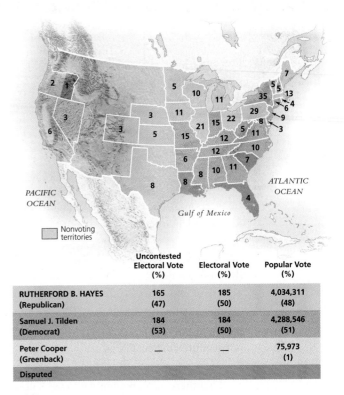

	Uncontested Electoral Vote (%)	Electoral Vote (%)	Popular Vote (%)
RUTHERFORD B. HAYES (Republican)	165 (47)	185 (50)	4,034,311 (48)
Samuel J. Tilden (Democrat)	184 (53)	184 (50)	4,288,546 (51)
Peter Cooper (Greenback)	—	—	75,973 (1)
Disputed			

MAP 17.4
The Election of 1876 The presidential election of 1876 left the nation without a clear-cut winner.

WHAT LED to the electoral crisis of 1876?

THE ELECTORAL CRISIS OF 1876

With the economy mired in depression, Democrats looked forward to capturing the White House in 1876. Democrats nominated Governor Samuel J. Tilden of New York, who brought impeccable reform credentials to his candidacy. In 1871 he had helped expose and prosecute the "Tweed Ring" in New York City. As governor he had toppled the "Canal Ring," a graft-ridden scheme involving inflated contracts for repairs on the Erie Canal. In their platform, the Democrats linked the issue of corruption to an attack on Reconstruction policies.

Republican nominee Rutherford B. Hayes, governor of Ohio, also sought the high ground. As a lawyer in Cincinnati he had defended runaway slaves. Later he had distinguished himself as a general in the Union army. Hayes promised, if elected, to support an efficient civil service system, to vigorously prosecute officials who betrayed the public trust, and to introduce a system of free universal education.

On an election day marred by widespread vote fraud and violent intimidation, Tilden received 250,000 more popular votes than Hayes. But Republicans refused to concede victory, challenging the vote totals in the electoral college. Tilden garnered 184 uncontested electoral votes, one shy of the majority required to win, while Hayes received 165 (see Map 17.4). The problem centered on twenty disputed votes from Florida, Louisiana, South Carolina, and Oregon.

The crisis was unprecedented. In January 1877 Congress moved to settle the deadlock, establishing an Electoral Commission composed of five senators, five representatives, and five Supreme Court justices; eight were Republicans and seven

QUICK REVIEW

The Depression of 1873

- End of postwar boom brought depression.
- Collapse resulted from commercial overexpansion.
- Longest economic contraction in the nation's history until then.

CHRONOLOGY

1865 Freedmen's Bureau established

Abraham Lincoln assassinated

Andrew Johnson begins Presidential Reconstruction

Black codes begin to be enacted in southern states

Thirteenth Amendment ratified

1866 Civil Rights Act passed

Congress approves Fourteenth Amendment

Ku Klux Klan founded

1867 Reconstruction Acts, passed over President Johnson's veto, begin Congressional Reconstruction

Tenure of Office Act

Southern states call constitutional conventions

1868 President Johnson impeached by the House but acquitted in Senate trial

Fourteenth Amendment ratified

Most Southern states readmitted to the Union

Ulysses S. Grant elected president

1869 Congress approves Fifteenth Amendment

Union Pacific and Central Pacific tracks meet at Promontory Point in Utah Territory

Suffragists split into National Woman Suffrage Association and American Woman Suffrage Association

1870 Fifteenth Amendment ratified

1871 Ku Klux Klan Act passed

"Tweed Ring" in New York City exposed

1872 Liberal Republicans break with Grant and Radicals, nominate Horace Greeley for president

Crédit Mobilier scandal

Grant reelected president

1873 Financial panic and beginning of economic depression

Slaughterhouse cases

1874 Democrats gain control of House for first time since 1856

1875 Civil Rights Act

1876 Disputed election between Samuel Tilden and Rutherford B. Hayes

1877 Electoral Commission elects Hayes president

President Hayes dispatches federal troops to break Great Railroad Strike and withdraws last remaining federal troops from the South

---

Compromise of 1877 The Congressional settling of the 1876 election which installed Republican Rutherford B. Hayes in the White House and gave Democrats control of all state governments in the South.

were Democrats. The commission voted along strict partisan lines to award all the contested electoral votes to Hayes. Outraged by this decision, Democratic congressmen threatened a filibuster to block Hayes's inauguration. Violence and stalemate were avoided when Democrats and Republicans struck a compromise in February. In return for Hayes's ascendance to the presidency, the Republicans promised to appropriate more money for southern internal improvements, to appoint a Southerner to Hayes's cabinet, and to pursue a policy of noninterference ("home rule") in southern affairs.

Shortly after assuming office, Hayes ordered removal of the remaining federal troops in Louisiana and South Carolina. Without this military presence to sustain them, the Republican governors of those two states quickly lost power to Democrats. "Home rule" meant Republican abandonment of freed people, Radicals, carpetbaggers, and scalawags. It also effectively nullified the Fourteenth and Fifteenth Amendments and the Civil Rights Act of 1866. The **Compromise of 1877** completed repudiation of the idea, born during the Civil War and pursued during Congressional Reconstruction, of a powerful federal government protecting the rights of all American citizens.

CONCLUSION

Reconstruction succeeded in the limited political sense of reuniting a nation torn apart by the Civil War. The Radical Republican vision, emphasizing racial justice, equal civil and political rights guaranteed by the Fourteenth and Fifteenth Amendments, and a new southern economy organized around independent small farmers, never enjoyed the support of the majority of its party or the northern public. By 1877, the political force of these ideals was spent and the national retreat from them nearly complete.

The end of Reconstruction left the way open for the return of white domination in the South. The freed people's political and civil equality proved only temporary. It would take a "Second Reconstruction," the civil rights movement of the next century, to establish full black citizenship rights once and for all. Yet the newly autonomous black family, along with black-controlled churches, schools, and other social institutions, provided the foundations for the modern African American community. If the federal government was not yet fully committed to protecting equal rights in local communities, the Reconstruction era at least pointed to how that goal might be achieved. Even as the federal government retreated from the defense of equal rights for black people, it took a more aggressive stance as the protector of business interests. In the aftermath of Reconstruction, the struggle between capital and labor had clearly replaced "the southern question" as the number one political issue of the day.

REVIEW QUESTIONS

1. How did various visions of a "reconstructed" South differ? How did these visions reflect the old political and social divisions that had led to the Civil War?

2. What key changes did emancipation make in the political and economic status of African Americans? Discuss the expansion of citizenship rights in the post–Civil War years. To what extent did women share in the gains made by African Americans?

3. What role did such institutions as the family, the church, the schools, and the political parties play in the African American transition to freedom?

4. How did white Southerners attempt to limit the freedom of former slaves? How did these efforts succeed, and how did they fail?

5. Evaluate the achievements and failures of Reconstruction governments in the southern states.

6. What were the crucial economic changes occurring in the North and South during the Reconstruction era?

KEY TERMS

Black codes (p. 438)

Carpetbaggers (p. 448)

Civil Rights Bill (p. 438)

Congressional Reconstruction (p. 439)

Compromise of 1877 (p. 458)

Field Order 15 (p. 436)

Fifteenth Amendment (p. 441)

First Reconstruction Act (p. 439)

Freedmen's Bureau (p. 437)

Ku Klux Klan (p. 441)

Liberal Republicans (p. 456)

Radical Republicans (p. 436)

Scalawags (p. 449)

Sharecropping (p. 445)

Slaughterhouse cases (p. 452)

Tenure of Office Act (p. 439)

Union League (p. 448)

War Democrats (p. 437)

RECOMMENDED READING

David W. Blight, *Race and Reunion: The Civil War in American Memory* (2001). An elegantly written and deeply researched inquiry into how Americans "remembered" the Civil War in the half century after Appomattox, arguing that sectional reconciliation came at the cost of racial division.

Thomas J. Brown, ed., *Reconstructions: New Perspectives on the Postbellum United States* (2006). A wide-ranging collection of essays that explores Reconstruction from a broadly national perspective, including economic, political, and cultural impacts.

Jane Dailey, *Before Jim Crow: The Politics of Race in Postemancipation Virginia* (2000). A fine study that focuses on the tension between the drive to establish white supremacy and the struggle for biracial coalitions in post–Civil War Virginia politics.

Laura F. Edwards, *Gendered Strife & Confusion: The Political Culture of Reconstruction* (1997). An ambitious analysis of how gender ideologies played a key role in shaping the party politics and social relations of the Reconstruction era south.

Michael W. Fitzgerald, *The Union League Movement in the Deep South* (1989). Uses the Union League as a lens through which to examine race relations and the close connections between politics and economic change in the post–Civil War South.

Eric Foner, *Forever Free: The Story of Emancipation and Reconstruction* (2005). An excellent brief one-volume overview that condenses Foner's more comprehensive work on Reconstruction. It also includes several striking "visual essays" by Joshua Brown, documenting the changes in visual representations of African Americans in popular media of the era.

Eric Foner, *Reconstruction: America's Unfinished Revolution, 1863–1877* (1988). The most comprehensive and thoroughly researched overview of the Reconstruction era.

Steven Hahn, *A Nation Under Our Feet: Black Political Struggles in the Rural South from Slavery to the Great Migration* (2003). This Pulitzer Prize–winning history includes excellent chapters detailing the political activism of recently freed slaves and the violent resistance they encountered throughout the rural South.

Elizabeth Regosin, *Freedom's Promise: Ex-Slave Families and Citizenship in the Age of Emancipation* (2002). A thoughtful analysis of how freedmen and freedwomen asserted familial relationships as a means to claiming citizenship rights after emancipation, based on research into federal pension applications made by dependent survivors of Civil War soldiers.

Scott Reynolds Nelson, *Iron Confederacies: Southern Railways, Klan Violence, and Reconstruction* (1999). Pathbreaking analysis of how conservative southern and northern business interests rebuilt the South's railroad system and also achieved enormous political power within individual states.

Heather Cox Richardson, *West From Appomattox: The Reconstruction of America After the Civil War* (2007). A new interpretation of the era that both emphasizes post–Civil War change in the nation's West and large cities and locates the origins of current political divisions in the Reconstruction period.

myhistorylab™
Where it's a good time to connect to the past!

For study resources for this chapter, go to **www.myhistorylab.com** and choose *Out of Many, Teaching and Learning Classroom Edition.* You will find a wealth of study and review material for this chapter, including pretests and posttests, customized study plan, key-term review flash cards, interactive map and document activities, and documents for analysis.

Realities of Freedom

The Freedmen's Bureau established in 1865 by Congress provided freedmen with clothing, temporary shelter, food, and series of freedmen's schools across the South. Southern response was to fall into the use of terror to deter blacks from becoming economically independent using the agencies of groups like the Ku Klux Klan. Sharecropping, tenant farming, and peonage were insidious economic arrangements that placed whites and blacks in a form of economic slavery to large land holders in the South of the post-Civil War era.

FOLLOWING EMANCIPATION, what economic and social opportunities existed for African Americans in the United States? How did these opportunities change the lives of freedmen after the official end to slavery?

The story of African Americans after the end of slavery is complex and varied. Some blacks attempted to seek out better places to establish their new lives while others remained in the security of the only home they had known as slaves.■

African-American family working together in the cotton fields.

AN ACT TO ESTABLISH A BUREAU FOR THE RELIEF OF FREEDMEN AND REFUGEES, 1865

BE IT enacted, That there is hereby established in the War Department, to continue during the present war of rebellion, and for one year thereafter, a bureau of refugees, freedmen, and abandoned lands, to which shall be committed, as hereinafter provided, the supervision and management of all abandoned lands, and the control of all subjects relating to refugees and freedmen from rebel states, or from any district of country within the territory embraced in the operations of the army, under such rules and regulations as may be prescribed by the head of the bureau and approved by the President. The said bureau shall be under the management and control of a commissioner to be appointed by the President, by and with the advice and consent of the Senate. . .■

WHEN WE WORKED ON SHARES, WE COULDN'T MAKE NOTHING

AFTER SLAVERY we had to get in before night too. If you didn't, Ku Klux would drive you in. They would come and visit you anyway. . . . When he got you good and scared he would drive on away. They would whip you if they would catch you out in the night time. . . .

I've forgot who it is that that told us that we was free. Somebody come and told us we're free now. I done forgot who it was.

After freedom, we worked on shares a while. Then we rented. When we worked on shares, we couldn't make nothing, just overalls and something to eat. Half went to the other man and you would destroy your half if you weren't careful. A man that didn't know how to count would always lose. He might lose anyhow. They didn't give no itemized statement. No, you just had to take their word. They never give you no details. They just say you owe so much. No matter how good account you kept, you had to go by their account and now, Brother, I'm tellin' you the truth about this. It's been that way for a long time. You had to take the white man's work on note, and everything. Anything you wanted, you could git if you were a good hand. You could git anything you wanted as long as you worked. If you didn't make no money, that's all right; they would advance you more. But

Share croppers and their families were evicted from the plantation they were working after being convicted of engaging in a conspiracy to retain their homes. This picture was taken just after the evictions before the families were moved into a tent colony.

you better not leave him, you better not try to leave and get caught. They'd keep you in debt. They were sharp. Christmas come, you could take up twenty dollar, in somethin' to eat and much as you wanted in whiskey. You could buy a gallon of whiskey. . . . Anything that kept you a slave because he was always right and you were always wrong it there was difference. If there was an argument, he would get mad and there would be a shooting take place. . . .■

SHARE CROPPER CONTRACT, 1882

TO EVERY one applying to rent land upon shares, the following conditions must be read, and agreed to.

To every 30 or 35 acres, I agree to furnish the team, plow, and farming implements, except cotton planters, and I do not agree to furnish a cart to every cropper. The croppers are to have half of the cotton, corn and fodder (and peas and pumpkins and potatoes if any are planted. . .

Croppers are to have no part or interest in the cotton seed raised from the crop planted and worked by them. No vine crops of any description, that is, no watermelons, muskmelons,…squashes or anything of that kind, except peas and pumpkins, and potatoes, are to be planted in the cotton or corn. All must work under my direction. All plantation work to be done by the croppers. . . .

For every mule or horse furnished by me there must be 1000 good sized rails…hauled, and the fence repaired as far as they will go, the fence to be torn down and put up from the bottom if I so direct. All croppers to haul rails and work on fence whenever I may order. Rails to be split when I may say. . . .

Each cropper must keep in good repair all bridges in his crop or over ditches that he has to clean out and when a bridge needs repairing that is outside of all their crops, then any one that I call on must repair it. . . .

No cropper to work off the plantation when there is any work to be done on the land he has rented, or when his work is needed by me or other croppers. Trees to be cut down on Orchard, House field & Evanson fences, leaving such as I may designate. . . .■

THE DECLARATION OF INDEPENDENCE

When in the course of human events it becomes necessary for one people to dissolve the political bands which have connected them with another and to assume, among the powers of the earth, the separate and equal station to which the laws of nature and of nature's God entitle them, a decent respect to the opinions of mankind requires that they should declare the causes which impel them to the separation.

We hold these truths to be self-evident, that all men are created equal; that they are endowed by their Creator with certain unalienable rights; that among these are life, liberty, and the pursuit of happiness. That, to secure these rights, governments are instituted among men, deriving their just powers from the consent of the governed; that, whenever any form of government becomes destructive of these ends, it is the right of the people to alter or to abolish it, and to institute a new government, laying its foundation on such principles, and organizing its powers in such form, as to them shall seem most likely to effect their safety and happiness. Prudence, indeed, will dictate that governments long established should not be changed for light and transient causes; and, accordingly, all experience hath shown that mankind are more disposed to suffer, while evils are sufferable, than to right themselves by abolishing the forms to which they are accustomed. But when a long train of abuses and usurpations, pursuing invariably the same object, evinces a design to reduce them under absolute despotism, it is their right, it is their duty, to throw off such government and to provide new guards for their future security. Such has been the patient sufferance of these colonies, and such is now the necessity which constrains them to alter their former systems of government. The history of the present King of Great Britain is a history of repeated injuries and usurpations, all having, in direct object, the establishment of an absolute tyranny over these States. To prove this, let facts be submitted to a candid world:

He has refused his assent to laws the most wholesome and necessary for the public good.

He has forbidden his governors to pass laws of immediate and pressing importance, unless suspended in their operation till his assent should be obtained; and, when so suspended, he has utterly neglected to attend to them.

He has refused to pass other laws for the accommodation of large districts of people, unless those people would relinquish the right of representation in the legislature, a right inestimable to them and formidable to tyrants only.

He has called together legislative bodies at places unusual, uncomfortable, and distant from the depository of their public records, for the sole purpose of fatiguing them into compliance with his measures.

He has dissolved representative houses, repeatedly for opposing, with manly firmness, his invasions on the rights of the people.

He has refused, for a long time after such dissolutions, to cause others to be elected; whereby the legislative powers, incapable of annihilation, have returned to the people at large for their exercise; the state remaining, in the mean-time, exposed to all the danger of invasion from without and convulsions within.

He has endeavored to prevent the population of these States; for that purpose, obstructing the laws for naturalization of foreigners, refusing to pass others to encourage their migration hither, and raising the conditions of new appropriations of lands.

He has obstructed the administration of justice by refusing his assent to laws for establishing judiciary powers.

He has made judges dependent on his will alone for the tenure of their offices and the amount and payment of their salaries.

He has erected a multitude of new offices and sent hither swarms of officers to harass our people and eat out their substance.

He has kept among us, in time of peace, standing armies, without the consent of our legislatures.

He has affected to render the military independent of, and superior to, the civil power.

He has combined with others to subject us to a jurisdiction foreign to our Constitution and unacknowledged by our laws, giving his assent to their acts of pretended legislation—

For quartering large bodies of armed troops among us;

For protecting them by mock trial, from punishment for any murders which they should commit on the inhabitants of these States;

For cutting off our trade with all parts of the world;

For imposing taxes on us without our consent;

For depriving us, in many cases, of the benefit of trial by jury;

For transporting us beyond seas to be tried for pretended offences;

For abolishing the free system of English laws in a neighboring province, establishing therein an arbitrary government, and enlarging its boundaries, so as to render it at once an example and fit instrument for introducing the same absolute rule into these colonies;

For taking away our charters, abolishing our most valuable laws, and altering, fundamentally, the powers of our governments.

For suspending our own legislatures and declaring themselves invested with power to legislate for us in all cases whatsoever.

He has abdicated government here by declaring us out of his protection and waging war against us.

He has plundered our seas, ravaged our coasts, burnt our towns, and destroyed the lives of our people.

He is, at this time, transporting large armies of foreign mercenaries to complete the works of death, desolation, and tyranny already begun with circumstances of cruelty and perfidy scarcely paralleled in the most barbarous ages, and totally unworthy the head of a civilized nation.

He has constrained our fellow citizens, taken captive on the high seas, to bear arms against their country, to become the executioners of their friends and brethren, or to fall themselves by their hands.

He has excited domestic insurrections amongst us and has endeavored to bring on the inhabitants of our frontiers, the merciless Indian savages, whose known rule of warfare is an undistinguished destruction of all ages, sexes, and conditions.

In every stage of these oppressions, we have petitioned for redress in the most humble terms; our repeated petitions have been answered only by repeated injury. A prince whose character is thus marked by every act which may define a tyrant is unfit to be the ruler of a free people.

Nor have we been wanting in attention to our British brethren. We have warned them, from time to time, of attempts made by their legislature to extend an unwarrantable jurisdiction over us. We have reminded them of the circumstances of our emigration and settlement here. We have appealed to their native justice and magnanimity, and we have conjured them, by the ties of our common kindred, to disavow these usurpations, which would inevitably interrupt our connections and correspondence. They, too, have been deaf to the voice of justice and consanguinity.

We must, therefore, acquiesce in the necessity which denounces our separation, and hold them, as we hold the rest of mankind, enemies in war, in peace, friends.

We, therefore, the representatives of the United States of America, in general Congress assembled, appealing to the Supreme Judge of the world for the rectitude of our intentions, do, in the name and by the authority of the good people of these colonies, solemnly publish and declare, that these united colonies are, and of right ought to be, free and independent states: that they are absolved from all allegiance to the British Crown, and that all political connection between them and the state of Great Britain is, and ought to be, totally dissolved; and that, as free and independent states, they have full power to levy war, conclude peace, contract alliances, establish commerce, and to do all other acts and things which independent states may of right do. And, for the support of this declaration, with a firm reliance on the protection of Divine Providence, we mutually pledge to each other our lives, our fortunes, and our sacred honor.

The Constitution of the United States of America

We the people of the United States, in order to form a more perfect union, establish justice, insure domestic tranquillity, provide for the common defense, promote the general welfare, and secure the blessings of liberty to ourselves and our posterity, do ordain and establish this Constitution for the United States of America.

Article I

Section 1.   All legislative powers herein granted shall be vested in a Congress of the United States, which shall consist of a Senate and House of Representatives.

Section 2.   1. The House of Representatives shall be composed of members chosen every second year by the people of the several States, and the electors in each State shall have the qualifications requisite for electors of the most numerous branch of the State legislature.

2. No person shall be a representative who shall not have attained to the age of twenty-five years, and been seven years a citizen of the United States, and who shall not, when elected, be an inhabitant of that State in which he shall be chosen.

3. Representatives and direct taxes[1] shall be apportioned among the several States which may be included within this Union, according to their respective numbers, which shall be determined by adding to the whole number of free persons, including those bound to service for a term of years, and excluding Indians not taxed, three fifths of all other persons.[2] The actual enumeration shall be made within three years after the first meeting of the Congress of the United States, and within every subsequent term of ten years, in such manner as they shall by law direct. The num-

ber of representatives shall not exceed one for every thirty thousand, but each State shall have at least one representative; and until such enumeration shall be made, the State of New Hampshire shall be entitled to choose three, Massachusetts eight, Rhode Island and Providence Plantations one, Connecticut five, New York six, New Jersey four, Pennsylvania eight, Delaware one, Maryland six, Virginia ten, North Carolina five, South Carolina five, and Georgia three.

4. When vacancies happen in the representation from any State, the executive authority thereof shall issue writs of election to fill such vacancies.

5. The House of Representatives shall choose their speaker and other officers; and shall have the sole power of impeachment.

Section 3.   1. The Senate of the United States shall be composed of two senators from each State, chosen by the legislature thereof,[3] for six years; and each senator shall have one vote.

2. Immediately after they shall be assembled in consequence of the first election, they shall be divided as equally as may be into three classes. The seats of the senators of the first class shall be vacated at the expiration of the second year, of the second class at the expiration of the fourth year, and of the third class at the expiration of the sixth year, so that one third may be chosen every second year; and if vacancies happen by resignation, or otherwise, during the recess of the legislature of any State, the executive thereof may make temporary appointments until the next meeting of the legislature, which shall then fill such vacancies.[4]

3. No person shall be a senator who shall not have attained to the age of thirty years, and been nine years a cit-

---

[1]See the Sixteenth Amendment.
[2]See the Fourteenth Amendment.

[3]See the Seventeenth Amendment.
[4]See the Seventeenth Amendment.

izen of the United States, and who shall not, when elected, be an inhabitant of that State for which he shall be chosen.

4. The Vice President of the United States shall be President of the Senate, but shall have no vote, unless they be equally divided.

5. The Senate shall choose their other officers, and also a president pro tempore, in the absence of the Vice President, or when he shall exercise the office of the President of the United States.

6. The Senate shall have the sole power to try all impeachments. When sitting for that purpose, they shall be on oath or affirmation. When the President of the United States is tried, the chief justice shall preside: and no person shall be convicted without the concurrence of two thirds of the members present.

7. Judgment in cases of impeachment shall not extend further than to removal from office, and disqualification to hold and enjoy any office of honor, trust or profit under the United States: but the party convicted shall nevertheless be liable and subject to indictment, trial, judgment and punishment, according to law.

Section 4. 1. The times, places, and manner of holding elections for senators and representatives, shall be prescribed in each State by the legislature thereof; but the Congress may at any time by law make or alter such regulations, except as to the places of choosing senators.

2. The Congress shall assemble at least once in every year, and such meeting shall be on the first Monday in December, unless they shall by law appoint a different day.

Section 5. 1. Each House shall be the judge of the elections, returns and qualifications of its own members, and a majority of each shall constitute a quorum to do business; but a smaller number may adjourn from day to day, and may be authorized to compel the attendance of absent members, in such manner, and under such penalties as each House may provide.

2. Each House may determine the rules of its proceedings, punish its members for disorderly behavior, and, with the concurrence of two thirds, expel a member.

3. Each House shall keep a journal of its proceedings, and from time to time publish the same, excepting such parts as may in their judgment require secrecy; and the yeas and nays of the members of either House on any question shall, at the desire of one fifth of those present, be entered on the journal.

4. Neither House, during the session of Congress, shall, without the consent of the other, adjourn for more than three days, nor to any other place than that in which the two Houses shall be sitting.

Section 6. 1. The senators and representatives shall receive a compensation for their services, to be ascertained by law, and paid out of the Treasury of the United States. They shall in all cases, except treason, felony, and breach of the peace, be privileged from arrest during their attendance at the session of their respective Houses, and in going to and returning from the same; and for any speech or debate in either House, they shall not be questioned in any other place.

2. No senator or representative shall, during the time for which he was elected, be appointed to any civil office under the authority of the United States, which shall have been created, or the emoluments whereof shall have been increased, during such time; and no person holding any office under the United States shall be a member of either House during his continuance in office.

Section 7. 1. All bills for raising revenue shall originate in the House of Representatives; but the Senate may propose or concur with amendments as on other bills.

2. Every bill which shall have passed the House of Representatives and the Senate, shall, before it become a law, be presented to the President of the United States; If he approves he shall sign it, but if not he shall return it, with his objections, to that House in which it shall have originated, who shall enter the objections at large on their journal, and proceed to reconsider it. If after such reconsideration two thirds of that House shall agree to pass the bill, it shall be sent, together with the objections, to the other House, by which it shall likewise be reconsidered, and if approved by two thirds of that House, it shall become a law. But in all such cases the votes of both Houses shall be determined by yeas and nays, and the names of the persons voting for and against the bill shall be entered on the journal of each House respectively. If any bill shall not be returned by the President within ten days (Sundays excepted) after it shall have been presented to him, the same shall be a law, in like manner as if he had signed it, unless the Congress by their adjournment prevent its return, in which case it shall not be a law.

3. Every order, resolution, or vote to which the concurrence of the Senate and the House of Representatives may be necessary (except on a question of adjournment) shall be presented to the President of the United States; and before the same shall take effect, shall be approved by him, or being disapproved by him, shall be repassed by two thirds of the Senate and House of Representatives, according to the rules and limitations prescribed in the case of a bill.

Section 8. 1. The Congress shall have the power

1. To lay and collect taxes, duties, imposts, and excises, to pay the debts and provide for the common defense and general welfare of the United States; but all duties, imposts, and excises shall be uniform throughout the United States.

2. To borrow money on the credit of the United States;

3. To regulate commerce with foreign nations, and among the several States, and with the Indian tribes;

4. To establish a uniform rule of naturalization, and uniform laws on the subject of bankruptcies throughout the United States;

5. To coin money, regulate the value thereof, and of foreign coin, and fix the standard of weights and measures;

6. To provide for the punishment of counterfeiting the securities and current coin of the United States;

7. To establish post offices and post roads;

8. To promote the progress of science and useful arts, by securing for limited times to authors and inventors the exclusive right to their respective writings and discoveries;

9. To constitute tribunals inferior to the Supreme Court;

10. To define and punish piracies and felonies committed on the high seas, and offenses against the law of nations;

11. To declare war, grant letters of marque and reprisal, and make rules concerning captures on land and water;

12. To raise and support armies, but no appropriation of money to that use shall be for a longer term than two years;

13. To provide and maintain a navy;

14. To make rules for the government and regulation of the land and naval forces;

15. To provide for calling forth the militia to execute the laws of the Union, suppress insurrections and repel invasions;

16. To provide for organizing, arming, and disciplining the militia, and for governing such part of them as may be employed in the service of the United States, reserving to the States respectively, the appointment of the officers, and the authority of training the militia according to the discipline prescribed by Congress;

17. To exercise exclusive legislation in all cases whatsoever, over such district (not exceeding ten miles square) as may, by cession of particular States, and the acceptance of Congress, become the seat of the government of the United States, and to exercise like authority over all places purchased by the consent of the legislature of the State in which the same shall be, for the erection of forts, magazines, arsenals, dockyards, and other needful buildings; and

18. To make all laws which shall be necessary and proper for carrying into execution the foregoing powers, and all other powers vested by this Constitution in the government of the United States, or any department or officer thereof.

SECTION 9.   1. The migration or importation of such persons as any of the States now existing shall think proper to admit, shall not be prohibited by the Congress prior to the year one thousand eight hundred and eight, but a tax or duty may be imposed on such importation, not exceeding ten dollars for each person.

2. The privilege of the writ of habeas corpus shall not be suspended, unless when in cases of rebellion or invasion the public safety may require it.

3. No bill of attainder or ex post facto law shall be passed.

4. No capitation, or other direct, tax shall be laid, unless in proportion to the census or enumeration hereinbefore directed to be taken.[5]

5. No tax or duty shall be laid on articles exported from any State.

6. No preference shall be given by any regulation of commerce or revenue to the ports of one State over those of another: nor shall vessels bound to, or from, one State be obliged to enter, clear, or pay duties in another.

7. No money shall be drawn from the treasury, but in consequence of appropriations made by law; and a regular statement and account of the receipts and expenditures of all public money shall be published from time to time.

8. No title of nobility shall be granted by the United States: and no person holding any office of profit or trust under them, shall, without the consent of the Congress, accept of any present, emolument, office, or title, of any kind whatever, from any king, prince, or foreign State.

SECTION 10.   1. No State shall enter into any treaty, alliance, or confederation; grant letters of marque and reprisal; coin money; emit bills of credit; make any thing but gold and silver coin a tender in payment of debts; pass any bill of attainder, ex post facto law, or law impairing the obligation of contracts, or grant, any title of nobility.

2. No State shall, without the consent of the Congress, lay any imposts or duties on imports or exports, except what may be absolutely necessary for executing its inspection laws: and the net produce of all duties and imposts laid by any State on imports or exports, shall be for the use of the treasury of the United States; and all such laws shall be subject to the revision and control of the Congress.

3. No State shall, without the consent of the Congress, lay any duty of tonnage, keep troops, or ships of war in time of peace, enter into any agreement or compact with another State, or with a foreign power, or engage in war, unless actually invaded, or in such imminent danger as will not admit of delay.

ARTICLE II

SECTION 1.   1. The executive power shall be vested in a President of the United States of America. He shall hold his office during the term of four years, and, together with the Vice President, chosen for the same term, be elected, as follows:

2. Each State shall appoint, in such manner as the legislature thereof may direct, a number of electors, equal to the whole number of senators and representatives to which the State may be entitled in the Congress: but no senator or representative, or person holding any office of trust or profit under the United States, shall be appointed an elector.

The electors shall meet in their respective States, and vote by ballot for two persons, of whom one at least shall not be an inhabitant of the same State with themselves. And they shall make a list of all the persons voted for, and of the number of votes for each; which list they shall sign and certify, and transmit sealed to the seat of the government of the United States, directed to the president of the Senate. The president of the Senate shall, in the presence of the Senate and House of Representatives, open all the certificates, and the votes shall then be counted. The person having the greatest number of votes shall be the President, if such number be a majority of the whole number of electors appointed; and if there be more than one who have such majority, and have an equal number of votes, then the House of Representatives shall immediately choose by ballot one of them for President; and if no person have a majority, then from the five highest on the list the said House shall in like manner choose the President. But in choosing the President, the votes shall be taken by

---

[5]See the Sixteenth Amendment.

States, the representation from each State having one vote; a quorum for this purpose shall consist of a member or members from two thirds of the States, and a majority of all the States shall be necessary to a choice. In every case after the choice of the President, the person having the greatest number of votes of the electors shall be the Vice President. But if there should remain two or more who have equal votes, the Senate shall choose from them by ballot the Vice President.[6]

3. The Congress may determine the time of choosing the electors, and the day on which they shall give their votes; which day shall be the same throughout the United States.

4. No person except a natural born citizen, or a citizen of the United States, at the time of the adoption of this Constitution, shall be eligible to the office of President; neither shall any person be eligible to the office who shall not have attained to the age of thirty-five years, and been fourteen years a resident within the United States.

5. In case of the removal of the President from office, or of his death, resignation, or inability to discharge the powers and duties of the said office, the same shall devolve on the Vice President, and the congress may by law provide for the case of removal, death, resignation or inability, both of the President and Vice President, declaring what officer shall then act as President, and such officer shall act accordingly until the disability be removed, or a President shall be elected.

6. The President shall, at stated times, receive for his services a compensation which shall neither be increased nor diminished during the period for which he shall have been elected, and he shall not receive within that period any other emolument from the United States, or any of them.

7. Before he enter on the execution of his office, he shall take the following oath or affirmation:—"I do solemnly swear (or affirm) that I will faithfully execute the office of President of the United States, and will to the best of my ability, preserve, protect and defend the Constitution of the United States."

SECTION 2.   1. The President shall be commander in chief of the army and navy of the United States, and of the militia of the several States, when called into the actual service of the United States; he may require the opinion in writing, of the principal officer in each of the executive departments, upon any subject relating to the duties of their respective offices, and he shall have power to grant reprieves and pardons for offenses against the United States, except in cases of impeachment.

2. He shall have power, by and with the advice and consent of the Senate, to make treaties, provided two thirds of the senators present concur; and he shall nominate, and by and with the advice and consent of the Senate, shall appoint ambassadors, other public ministers and consuls, judges of the Supreme Court, and all other officers of the United States, whose appointments are not herein otherwise provided for, and which shall be established by law; but the Congress may by law vest the appointment of such infe-

rior officers, as they think proper, in the President alone, in the courts of laws, or in the heads of departments.

3. The President shall have power to fill up all vacancies that may happen during the recess of the Senate, by granting commissions which shall expire at the end of their next session.

SECTION 3.   He shall from time to time give to the Congress information of the state of the Union, and recommend to their consideration such measures as he shall judge necessary and expedient; he may, on extraordinary occasions, convene both Houses, or either of them, and in case of disagreement between them with respect to the time of adjournment, he may adjourn them to such time as he shall think proper; he shall receive ambassadors and other public ministers; he shall take care that the laws be faithfully executed, and shall commission all the officers of the United States.

SECTION 4.   The President, Vice President, and all civil officers of the United States, shall be removed from office on impeachment for, and conviction of, treason, bribery, or other high crimes and misdemeanors.

ARTICLE III

SECTION 1. The judicial power of the United States shall be vested in one Supreme Court, and in such inferior courts as the Congress may from time to time ordain and establish. The judges, both of the Supreme and inferior courts, shall hold their offices during good behavior, and shall, at stated times, receive for their services, a compensation, which shall not be diminished during their continuance in office.

SECTION 2.   1. The judicial power shall extend to all cases, in law and equity, arising under this Constitution, the laws of the United States, and treaties made, or which shall be made, under their authority;—to all cases of admiralty and maritime jurisdiction;—to controversies to which the United States shall be a party;[7]—to controversies between two or more States;—between a State and citizens of another State;—between citizens of different States;—between citizens of the same State claiming lands under grants of different States, and between a State, or the citizens thereof, and foreign States, citizens or subjects.

2. In all cases affecting ambassadors, other public ministers and consuls, and those in which a State shall be party, the Supreme Court shall have original jurisdiction. In all the other cases before mentioned, the Supreme Court shall have appellate jurisdiction, both as to law and fact, with such exceptions, and under such regulations as the Congress shall make.

3. The trial of all crimes, except in cases of impeachment, shall be by jury; and such trial shall be held in the State where the said crimes shall have been committed; but when not committed within any State, the trial shall be such place or places as the congress may by law have directed.

[6]Superseded by the Twelfth Amendment.

[7]See the Eleventh Amendment.

SECTION 3. 1. Treason against the United States shall consist only in levying war against them, or in adhering to their enemies, giving them aid and comfort. No person shall be convicted of treason unless on the testimony of two witnesses to the same overt act, or on confession in open court.

2. The Congress shall have power to declare the punishment of treason, but no attainder of treason shall work corruption of blood, or forfeiture except during the life of the person attained.

ARTICLE IV

SECTION 1. Full faith and credit shall be given in each State to the public acts, records, and judicial proceedings of every other State. And the Congress may by general laws prescribe the manner in which such acts, records and proceedings shall be proved, and the effect thereof.

SECTION 2. 1. The citizens of each State shall be entitled to all privileges and immunities of citizens in the several States.[8]

2. A person charged in any State with treason, felony, or other crime, who shall flee from justice, and be found in another State, shall on demand of the executive authority of the State from which he fled, be delivered up to be removed to the State having jurisdiction of the crime.

3. No person held to service or labor in one State under the laws thereof, escaping into another, shall, in consequence of any law or regulation therein, be discharged from such service or labor, but shall be delivered up on claim of the party to whom such service or labor may be due.[9]

SECTION 3. 1. New States may be admitted by the Congress into this Union; but no new State shall be formed or erected within the jurisdiction of any other State, nor any State be formed by the junction of two or more States, or parts of States, without the consent of the legislatures of the States concerned as well as of the Congress.

2. The Congress shall have power to dispose of and make all needful rules and regulations respecting the territory or other property belonging to the United States; and nothing in this Constitution shall be so construed as to prejudice any claims of the United States, or of any particular State.

SECTION 4. The United States shall guarantee to every State in this Union a republican form of government, and shall protect each of them against invasion; and on application of the legislature, or of the executive (when the legislature cannot be convened) against domestic violence.

ARTICLE V

The Congress, whenever two thirds of both Houses shall deem it necessary, shall propose amendments to this Constitution, or, on the application of the legislatures of two thirds of the several States, shall call a convention for proposing amendments, which in either case shall be valid to all intents and purposes, as part of this Constitution, when ratified by the legislatures of three fourths of the several States, or by conventions in three fourths thereof, as the one or the other mode of ratification may be proposed by the Congress; Provided that no amendment which may be made prior to the year one thousand eight hundred and eight shall in any manner affect the first and fourth clauses in the ninth section of the first article; and that no State, without its consent, shall be deprived of its equal suffrage in the Senate.

ARTICLE VI

1. All debts contracted and engagements entered into, before the adoption of this Constitution, shall be as valid against the United States under this Constitution, as under the Confederation.[10]

2. This Constitution, and the laws of the United States which shall be made in pursuance thereof; and all treaties made, or which shall be made, under the authority of the United States, shall be the supreme law of the land; and the judges in every State shall be bound thereby, any thing in the Constitution or laws of any State to the contrary notwithstanding.

3. The senators and representatives before mentioned, and the members of the several State legislatures, and all executive and judicial officers, both of the United States and of the several States, shall be bound by oath or affirmation to support this Constitution; but no religious test shall ever be required as a qualification to any office or public trust under the United States.

ARTICLE VII

The ratification of the conventions of nine States shall be sufficient for the establishment of this Constitution between the States so ratifying the same.

Done in Convention by the unanimous consent of the States present the seventeenth day of September in the year of our Lord one thousand seven hundred and eighty-seven, and of the independence of the United States of America the twelfth. In witness whereof we have hereunto subscribed our names.

[Signatories' names omitted]

Articles in addition to, and amendment of, the Constitution of the United States of America, proposed by Congress, and ratified by the legislatures of the several States, pursuant to the fifth article of the original Constitution.

Amendment I
[First ten amendments ratified December 15, 1791]

Congress shall make no law respecting an establishment of religion, or prohibiting the free exercise thereof; or abridging the freedom of speech, or of the press; or the right of the people peaceably to assemble, and to petition the government for a redress of grievances.

---

[8]See the Fourteenth Amendment, Sec. 1.

[9]See the Thirteenth Amendment.

[10]See the Fourteenth Amendment, Sec. 4.

Amendment II

A well regulated militia, being necessary to the security of a free State, the right of the people to keep and bear arms, shall not be infringed.

Amendment III

No soldier shall, in time of peace be quartered in any house, without the consent of the owner, nor in time of war, but in a manner to be prescribed by law.

Amendment IV

The right of the people to be secure in their persons, houses, papers, and effects, against unreasonable searches and seizures, shall not be violated, and no warrants shall issue, but upon probable cause, supported by oath or affirmation, and particularly describing the place to be searched, and the persons or things to be seized.

Amendment V

No person shall be held to answer for a capital or otherwise infamous crime, unless on a presentment or indictment of a grand jury, except in cases arising in the land or naval forces, or in the militia, when in actual service in time of war or public danger; nor shall any person be subject for the same offense to be twice put in jeopardy of life or limb; nor shall be compelled in any criminal case to be a witness against himself, nor be deprived of life, liberty, or property, without due process of law; nor shall private property be taken for public use, without just compensation.

Amendment VI

In all criminal prosecutions, the accused shall enjoy the right to a speedy and public trial, by an impartial jury of the State and district wherein the crime shall have been committed, which district shall have been previously ascertained by law, and to be informed of the nature and cause of the accusation; to be confronted with the witnesses against him; to have compulsory process for obtaining witnesses in his favor, and to have the assistance of counsel for his defense.

Amendment VII

In suits at common law, where the value in controversy shall exceed twenty dollars, the right of trial by jury shall be preserved, and no fact tried by a jury shall be otherwise reexamined in any court of the United States, than according to the rules of the common law.

Amendment VIII

Excessive bail shall not be required, nor excessive fines imposed, nor cruel and unusual punishments inflicted.

Amendment IX

The enumeration in the Constitution of certain rights shall not be construed to deny or disparage others retained by the people.

Amendment X

The powers not delegated to the United States by the Constitution, nor prohibited by it to the States, are reserved to the States respectively, or to the people.

Amendment XI [January 8, 1798]

The judicial power of the United States shall not be construed to extend to any suit in law or equity, commended or prosecuted against one of the United States by citizens of another State, or by citizens or subjects of any foreign State.

Amendment XII [September 25, 1804]

The electors shall meet in their respective States, and vote by ballot for President and Vice President, one of whom, at least, shall not be an inhabitant of the same State with themselves; they shall name in their ballots the person voted for as President, and in distinct ballots, the person voted for as Vice President, and they shall make distinct lists of all persons voted for as President and of all persons voted for as Vice President, and of the number of votes for each, which lists they shall sign and certify, and transmit sealed to the seat of the government of the United States, directed to the President of the Senate;—The President of the Senate shall, in the presence of the Senate and House of Representatives, open all the certificates and the votes shall then be counted;—The person having the greatest number of votes for President, shall be the President, if such number be a majority of the whole number of electors appointed; and if no person have such majority, then from the persons having the highest numbers not exceeding three on the list of those voted for as President, the House of Representatives shall choose immediately, by ballot, the President. But in choosing the President, the votes shall be taken by States, the representation from each State having one vote; a quorum for this purpose shall consist of a member or members from two thirds of the States, and a majority of all the States shall be necessary to a choice. And if the House of Representatives shall not choose a President whenever the right of choice shall devolve upon them, before the fourth day of March next following, then the Vice President shall act as President, as in the case of the death or other constitutional disability of the President. The person having the greatest number of votes as Vice President shall be the Vice President, if such number be a majority of the whole number of electors appointed, and if no person have a majority, then from the two highest numbers on the list, the Senate shall choose the Vice President; a quorum for the purpose shall consist of two thirds of the whole number of Senators, and a majority of the whole number shall be necessary to a choice. But no person constitutionally ineligible to the office of President shall be eligible to that of Vice President of the United States.

Amendment XIII [December 18, 1865]

SECTION 1. Neither slavery nor involuntary servitude, except as a punishment for crime whereof the party shall have been duly convicted, shall exist within the United States, or any place subject to their jurisdiction.

SECTION 2.   Congress shall have power to enforce this article by appropriate legislation.

Amendment XIV [July 28, 1868]

SECTION 1.   All persons born or naturalized in the United States, and subject to the jurisdiction thereof, are citizens of the United States and of the State wherein they reside. No State shall make or enforce any law which shall abridge the privileges or immunities of citizens of the United States; nor shall any State deprive any person of life, liberty, or property, without due process of law; nor deny to any person within its jurisdiction the equal protection of the laws.

SECTION 2.   Representatives shall be apportioned among the several States according to their respective numbers, counting the whole number of persons in each State, excluding Indians not taxed. But when the right to vote at any election for the choice of electors for President and Vice President of the United States, representatives in Congress, the executive and judicial officers of a State, or the members of the legislature thereof, is denied to any of the male inhabitants of such State, being twenty-one years of age, and citizens of the United States, or in any way abridged, except for participating in rebellion, or other crime, the basis of representation there shall be reduced in the proportion which the number of such male citizens shall bear to the whole number of male citizens twenty-one years of age in such State.

SECTION 3.   No person shall be a senator or representative in Congress, or elector of President and Vice President, or hold any office, civil or military, under the United States, or under any State, who having previously taken an oath, as a member of Congress, or as an officer of the United States, or as a member of any State legislature, or as an executive or judicial officer of any State, to support the Constitution of the United States, shall have engaged in insurrection or rebellion against the same, or given aid or comfort to the enemies thereof. But Congress may by a vote of two thirds of each House, remove such disability.

SECTION 4.   The validity of the public debt of the United States, authorized by law, including debts incurred for payment of pensions and bounties for services in suppressing insurrection or rebellion; shall not be questioned. But neither the United States nor any State shall assume or pay any debt or obligation incurred in aid of insurrection or rebellion against the United States, or any claim for the loss or emancipation of any slave; but all such debts, obligations, and claims shall be held illegal and void.

SECTION 5.   The Congress shall have the power to enforce, by appropriate legislation, the provisions of this article.

Amendment XV [March 30, 1870]

SECTION 1.   The right of citizens of the United States to vote shall not be denied or abridged by the United States or by any State on account of race, color, or previous condition of servitude.

SECTION 2.   The Congress shall have power to enforce this article by appropriate legislation.

Amendment XVI [February 25, 1913]

The Congress shall have power to lay and collect taxes on incomes, from whatever source derived, without apportionment among the several States, and without regard to any census or enumeration.

Amendment XVII [May 31, 1913]

The Senate of the United States shall be composed of two senators from each State, elected by the people thereof, for six years; and each senator shall have one vote. The electors in each State shall have the qualifications requisite for electors of the most numerous branch of the State legislature.

When vacancies happen in the representation of any State in the Senate, the executive authority of such State shall issue writs of election to fill such vacancies: Provided, That the legislature of any State may empower the executive thereof to make temporary appointments until the people fill the vacancies by election as the legislature may direct.

This amendment shall not be so construed as to affect the election or term of any senator chosen before it becomes valid as part of the Constitution.

Amendment XVIII[11] [January 29, 1919]

After one year from the ratification of this article, the manufacture, sale, or transportation of intoxicating liquors within, the importation thereof into, or the exportation thereof from the United States and all territory subject to the jurisdiction thereof for beverage purposes is thereby prohibited.

The Congress and the several States shall have concurrent power to enforce this article by appropriate legislation.

This article shall be inoperative unless it shall have been ratified as an amendment to the Constitution by the legislatures of the several States, as provided in the constitution, within seven years from the date of the submission hereof to the States by Congress.

Amendment XIX [August 26, 1920]

The right of citizens of the United States to vote shall not be denied or abridged by the United States or by any State on account of sex.

Congress shall have the power to enforce this article by appropriate legislation.

Amendment XX [January 23, 1933]

SECTION 1.   The terms of the President and Vice President shall end at noon on the 20th day of January and the terms of Senators and Representatives at noon on the 3d day of January, of the years in which such terms would have ended if this article had not been ratified; and the terms of their successors shall then begin.

SECTION 2.   The Congress shall assemble at least once in every year, and such meeting shall begin at noon on the 3d day of January, unless they shall by law appoint a different day.

---

[11]Repealed by the Twenty-first Amendment.

SECTION 3. If, at the time fixed for the beginning of the term of President, the President-elect shall have died, the Vice President-elect shall become President. If a President shall not have been chosen before the time fixed for the beginning of his term, or if the President-elect shall have failed to qualify, then the Vice President-elect shall act as President until a President shall have qualified; and the Congress may by law provide for the case wherein neither a President-elect nor a Vice President-elect shall have qualified, declaring who shall then act as President, or the manner in which one who is to act shall be selected, and such person shall act accordingly until a President or Vice President shall have qualified.

SECTION 4. The Congress may by law provide for the case of the death of any of the persons from whom, the House of Representatives may choose a President whenever the right of choice shall have devolved upon them, and for the case of the death of any of the persons from whom the Senate may choose a Vice President whenever the right of choice shall have devolved upon them.

SECTION 5. Sections 1 and 2 shall take effect on the 15th day of October following the ratification of this article.

SECTION 6. This article shall be inoperative unless it shall have been ratified as an amendment to the Constitution by the legislatures of three-fourths of the several States within seven years from the date of its submission.

Amendment XXI [December 5, 1933]

SECTION 1. The Eighteenth Article of amendment to the Constitution of the United States is hereby repealed.

SECTION 2. The transportation or importation into any State, Territory, or possession of the United States for delivery or use therein of intoxicating liquors in violation of the laws thereof, is hereby prohibited.

SECTION 3. This article shall be inoperative unless it shall have been ratified as an amendment to the Constitution by conventions in the several States, as provided in the Constitution, within seven years from the date of the submission thereof to the States by the Congress.

Amendment XXII [March 1, 1951]

No person shall be elected to the office of the President more than twice, and no person who has held the office of President, or acted as President, for more than two years of a term to which some other person was elected President shall be elected to the office of the President more than once.

But this article shall not apply to any person holding the office of President when this article was proposed by the Congress, and shall not prevent any person who may be holding the office of President, or acting as President, during the term within which this article becomes operative from holding the office of President or acting as President during the remainder of such term.

This article shall be inoperative unless it shall have been ratified as an amendment to the Constitution by the legislatures of three-fourths of the several States within

seven years from the date of its submission to the States by the Congress.

Amendment XXIII [March 29, 1961]

SECTION 1. The District constituting the seat of Government of the United States shall appoint in such manner as the Congress may direct.

A number of electors of President and Vice President equal to the whole number of Senators and Representatives in Congress to which the District would be entitled if it were a State, but in no event more than the least populous State; they shall be in addition to those appointed by the States, but they shall be considered, for the purposes of the election of President and Vice President, to be electors appointed by a State; and they shall meet in the District and perform such duties as provided by the twelfth article of amendment.

SECTION 2. The Congress shall have power to enforce this article by appropriate legislation.

Amendment XXIV [January 23, 1964]

SECTION 1. The right of citizens of the United States to vote in any primary or other election for President or Vice President, for electors for President or Vice President, or for Senator or Representative in Congress, shall not be denied or abridged by the United States or any State by reason of failure to pay any poll tax or other tax.

SECTION 2. The Congress shall have power to enforce this article by appropriate legislation.

Amendment XXV [February 10, 1967]

SECTION 1. In case of the removal of the President from office or of his death or resignation, the Vice President shall become President.

SECTION 2. Whenever there is a vacancy in the office of the Vice President, the President shall nominate a Vice President who shall take office upon confirmation by a majority of both Houses of Congress.

SECTION 3. Whenever the President transmits to the President pro tempore of the Senate and the Speaker of the House of Representatives his written declaration that he is unable to discharge the powers and duties of his office, and until he transmits to them a written declaration to the contrary, such powers and duties shall be discharged by the Vice President as Acting President.

SECTION 4. Whenever the Vice President and a majority of either the principal officers of the executive departments or of such other body as Congress may by law provide, transmit to the President pro tempore of the Senate and the Speaker of the House of Representatives their written declaration that the President is unable to discharge the powers and duties of his office, the Vice President shall immediately assume the powers and duties of the office as Acting President.

Thereafter, when the President transmits to the President pro tempore of the Senate and the Speaker of the House of Representatives his written declaration that no inability exists, he shall resume the powers and duties of his office unless the Vice President and a majority of either the principal officers of the executive departments or of such other body as Congress may by law provide, transmit within four days to the President pro tempore of the Senate and the Speaker of the House of Representatives their written declaration that the President is unable to discharge the powers and duties of his office. Thereupon Congress shall decide the issue, assembling within forty-eight hours for that purpose if not in session. If the Congress, within twenty-one days after receipt of the latter written declaration, or, if Congress is not in session, within twenty-one days after Congress is required to assemble, determines by two-thirds vote of both Houses that the President is unable to discharge the powers and duties of his office, the Vice President shall continue to discharge the same as Acting President; otherwise, the President shall resume the powers and duties of his office.

Amendment XXVI [June 30, 1971]

SECTION 1.   The right of citizens of the United States who are eighteen years of age or older to vote shall not be denied or abridged by the United States or by any State on account of age.

SECTION 2.   The Congress shall have power to enforce this article by appropriate legislation.

Amendment XXVII[12] [May 7, 1992]

No law, varying the compensation for services of the Senators and Representatives, shall take effect until an election of Representatives shall have intervened.

---

[12]James Madison proposed this amendment in 1789 together with the ten amendments that were adopted as the Bill of Rights, but it failed to win ratification at the time. Congress, however, had set no deadline for its ratification, and over the years—particularly in the 1980s and 1990s—many states voted to add it to the Constitution. With the ratification of Michigan in 1992 it passed the threshold of 3/4ths of the states required for adoption, but because the process took more than 200 years, its validity remains in doubt.

PRESIDENT AND VICE PRESIDENT

1. George Washington (1789)
   John Adams (1789)

2. John Adams (1797)
   Thomas Jefferson (1797)

3. Thomas Jefferson (1801)
   Aaron Burr (1801)
   George Clinton (1805)

4. James Madison (1809)
   George Clinton (1809)
   Elbridge Gerry (1813)

5. James Monroe (1817)
   Daniel D. Thompkins (1817)

6. John Quincy Adams (1825)
   John C. Calhoun (1825)

7. Andrew Jackson (1829)
   John C. Calhoun (1829)
   Martin Van Buren (1833)

8. Martin Van Buren (1837)
   Richard M. Johnson (1837)

9. William H. Harrison (1841)
   John Tyler (1841)

10. John Tyler (1841)

11. James K. Polk (1845)
    George M. Dallas (1845)

12. Zachary Taylor (1849)
    Millard Fillmore (1849)

13. Millard Fillmore (1850)

14. Franklin Pierce (1853)
    William R. King (1853)

15. James Buchanan (1857)
    John C. Breckinridge (1857)

16. Abraham Lincoln (1861)
    Hannibal Hamlin (1861)
    Andrew Johnson (1865)

17. Andrew Johnson (1865)

18. Ulysses S. Grant (1869)
    Schuyler Colfax (1869)
    Henry Wilson (1873)

19. Rutherford B. Hayes (1877)
    William A. Wheeler (1877)

20. James A. Garfield (1881)
    Chester A. Arthur (1881)

21. Chester A. Arthur (1881)

22. Grover Cleveland (1885)
    T. A. Hendricks (1885)

23. Benjamin Harrison (1889)
    Levi P. Morgan (1889)

24. Grover Cleveland (1893)
    Adlai E. Stevenson (1893)

25. William McKinley (1897)
    Garret A. Hobart (1897)
    Theodore Roosevelt (1901)

26. Theodore Roosevelt (1901)
    Charles Fairbanks (1905)

27. William H. Taft (1909)
    James S. Sherman (1909)

28. Woodrow Wilson (1913)
    Thomas R. Marshall (1913)

29. Warren G. Harding (1921)
    Calvin Coolidge (1921)

30. Calvin Coolidge (1923)
    Charles G. Dawes (1925)

31. Herbert C. Hoover (1929)
    Charles Curtis (1929)

32. Franklin D. Roosevelt (1933)
    John Nance Garner (1933)
    Henry A. Wallace (1941)
    Harry S. Truman (1945)

33. Harry S. Truman (1945)
    Alben W. Barkley (1949)

34. Dwight D. Eisenhower (1953)
    Richard M. Nixon (1953)

35. John F. Kennedy (1961)
    Lyndon B. Johnson (1961)

36. Lyndon B. Johnson (1963)
    Hubert H. Humphrey (1965)

37. Richard M. Nixon (1969)
    Spiro T. Agnew (1969)
    Gerald R. Ford (1973)

38. Gerald R. Ford (1974)
    Nelson A. Rockefeller (1974)

39. James E. Carter Jr. (1977)
    Walter F. Mondale (1977)

40. Ronald W. Reagan (1981)
    George H. Bush (1981)

41. George H. Bush (1989)
    James D. Quayle III (1989)

42. William J. Clinton (1993)
    Albert Gore (1993)

43. George W. Bush (2001)
    Richard Cheney (2001)

PRESIDENTIAL ELECTIONS

Year	Number of States	Candidates	Party	Popular Vote*	Electoral Vote[†]	Percentage of Popular Vote
1789	11	GEORGE WASHINGTON	No party designations		69	
		John Adams			34	
		Other Candidates			35	
1792	15	GEORGE WASHINGTON	No party designations		132	
		John Adams			77	
		George Clinton			50	
		Other Candidates			5	
1796	16	JOHN ADAMS	Federalist		71	
		Thomas Jefferson	Democratic-Republican		68	
		Thomas Pinckney	Federalist		59	
		Aaron Burr	Democratic-Republican		30	
		Other Candidates			48	
1800	16	THOMAS JEFFERSON	Democratic-Republican		73	
		Aaron Burr	Democratic-Republican		73	
		John Adams	Federalist		65	
		Charles C. Pinckney	Federalist		64	
		John Jay	Federalist		1	
1804	17	THOMAS JEFFERSON	Democratic-Republican		162	
		Charles C. Pinckney	Federalist		14	
1808	17	JAMES MADISON	Democratic-Republican		122	
		Charles C. Pinckney	Federalist		47	
		George Clinton	Democratic-Republican		6	
1812	18	JAMES MADISON	Democratic-Republican		128	
		DeWitt Clinton	Federalist		89	
1816	19	JAMES MONROE	Democratic-Republican		183	
		Rufus King	Federalist		34	
1820	24	JAMES MONROE	Democratic-Republican		231	
		John Quincy Adams	Independent-Republican		1	
1824	24	JOHN QUINCY ADAMS	Democratic-Republican	108,740	84	30.5
		Andrew Jackson	Democratic-Republican	153,544	99	43.1
		William H. Crawford	Democratic-Republican	46,618	41	13.1
		Henry Clay	Democratic-Republican	47,136	37	13.2
1828	24	ANDREW JACKSON	Democrat	647,286	178	56.0
		John Quincy Adams	National Republican	508,064	83	44.0
1832	24	ANDREW JACKSON	Democrat	687,502	219	55.0
		Henry Clay	National Republican	530,189	49	42.4
		William Wirt	Anti-Masonic	33,108	7	2.6
		John Floyd	National Republican		11	

* Percentage of popular vote given for any election year may not total 100 percent because candidates receiving less than 1 percent of the popular vote have been omitted.

[†] Prior to the passage of the Twelfth Amendment in 1904, the electoral college voted for two presidential candidates; the runner-up became Vice-President. Data from Historical Statistics of the United States, Colonial Times to 1957 (1961), pp. 682–683, and The World Almanac.

Presidential Elections (continued)

Year	Number of States	Candidates	Party	Popular Vote	Electoral Vote	Percentage of Popular Vote
1836	26	MARTIN VAN BUREN	Democrat	765,483	170	50.9
		William H. Harrison	Whig		73	
		Hugh L. White	Whig		26	
		Daniel Webster	Whig	739,795	14	49.1
		W. P. Mangum	Whig		11	
1840	26	WILLIAM H. HARRISON	Whig	1,274,624	234	53.1
		Martin Van Buren	Democrat	1,127,781	60	46.9
1844	26	JAMES K. POLK	Democrat	1,338,464	170	49.6
		Henry Clay	Whig	1,300,097	105	48.1
		James G. Birney	Liberty	62,300		2.3
1848	30	ZACHARY TAYLOR	Whig	1,360,967	163	47.4
		Lewis Cass	Democrat	1,222,342	127	42.5
		Martin Van Buren	Free Soil	291,263		10.1
1852	31	FRANKLIN PIERCE	Democrat	1,601,117	254	50.9
		Winfield Scott	Whig	1,385,453	42	44.1
		John P. Hale	Free Soil	155,825		5.0
1856	31	JAMES BUCHANAN	Democrat	1,832,955	174	45.3
		John C. Frémont	Republican	1,339,932	114	33.1
		Millard Fillmore	American ("Know Nothing")	871,731	8	21.6
1860	33	ABRAHAM LINCOLN	Republican	1,865,593	180	39.8
		Stephen A. Douglas	Democrat	1,382,713	12	29.5
		John C. Breckinridge	Democrat	848,356	72	18.1
		John Bell	Constitutional Union	592,906	39	12.6
1864	36	ABRAHAM LINCOLN	Republican	2,206,938	212	55.0
		George B. McClellan	Democrat	1,803,787	21	45.0
1868	37	ULYSSES S. GRANT	Republican	3,013,421	214	52.7
		Horatio Seymour	Democrat	2,706,829	80	47.3
1872	37	ULYSSES S. GRANT	Republican	3,596,745	286	55.6
		Horace Greeley	Democrat	2,843,446	*	43.9
1876	38	RUTHERFORD B. HAYES	Republican	4,036,572	185	48.0
		Samuel J. Tilden	Democrat	4,284,020	184	51.0
1880	38	JAMES A. GARFIELD	Republican	4,453,295	214	48.5
		Winfield S. Hancock	Democrat	4,414,082	155	48.1
		James B. Weaver	Greenback-Labor	308,578		3.4
1884	38	GROVER CLEVELAND	Democrat	4,879,507	219	48.5
		James G. Blaine	Republican	4,850,293	182	48.2
		Benjamin F. Butler	Greenback-Labor	175,370		1.8
		John P. St. John	Prohibition	150,369		1.5
1888	38	BENJAMIN HARRISON	Republican	5,447,129	233	47.9
		Grover Cleveland	Democrat	5,537,857	168	48.6
		Clinton B. Fisk	Prohibition	249,506		2.2
		Anson J. Streeter	Union Labor	146,935		1.3

Because of the death of Greeley, Democratic electors scattered their votes.

PRESIDENTIAL ELECTIONS (CONTINUED)

Year	Number of States	Candidates	Party	Popular Vote	Electoral Vote	Percentage of Popular Vote
1892	44	GROVER CLEVELAND	Democrat	5,555,426	277	46.1
		Benjamin Harrison	Republican	5,182,690	145	43.0
		James B. Weaver	People's	1,029,846	22	8.5
		John Bidwell	Prohibition	264,133		2.2
1896	45	WILLIAM MCKINLEY	Republican	7,102,246	271	51.1
		William J. Bryan	Democrat	6,492,559	176	47.7
1900	45	WILLIAM MCKINLEY	Republican	7,218,491	292	51.7
		William J. Bryan	Democrat; Populist	6,356,734	155	45.5
		John C. Woolley	Prohibition	208,914		1.5
1904	45	THEODORE ROOSEVELT	Republican	7,628,461	336	57.4
		Alton B. Parker	Democrat	5,084,223	140	37.6
		Eugene V. Debs	Socialist	402,283		3.0
		Silas C. Swallow	Prohibition	258,536		1.9
1908	46	WILLIAM H. TAFT	Republican	7,675,320	321	51.6
		William J. Bryan	Democrat	6,412,294	162	43.1
		Eugene V. Debs	Socialist	420,793		2.8
		Eugene W. Chafin	Prohibition	253,840		1.7
1912	48	WOODROW WILSON	Democrat	6,296,547	435	41.9
		Theodore Roosevelt	Progressive	4,118,571	88	27.4
		William H. Taft	Republican	3,486,720	8	23.2
		Eugene V. Debs	Socialist	900,672		6.0
		Eugene W. Chafin	Prohibition	206,275		1.4
1916	48	WOODROW WILSON	Democrat	9,127,695	277	49.4
		Charles E. Hughes	Republican	8,533,507	254	46.2
		A. L. Benson	Socialist	585,113		3.2
		J. Frank Hanly	Prohibition	220,506		1.2
1920	48	WARREN G. HARDING	Republican	16,143,407	404	60.4
		James M. Cox	Democrat	9,130,328	127	34.2
		Eugene V. Debs	Socialist	919,799		3.4
		P. P. Christensen	Farmer-Labor	265,411		1.0
1924	48	CALVIN COOLIDGE	Republican	15,718,211	382	54.0
		John W. Davis	Democrat	8,385,283	136	28.8
		Robert M. La Follette	Progressive	4,831,289	13	16.6
1928	48	HERBERT C. HOOVER	Republican	21,391,993	444	58.2
		Alfred E. Smith	Democrat	15,016,169	87	40.9
1932	48	FRANKLIN D. ROOSEVELT	Democrat	22,809,638	472	57.4
		Herbert C. Hoover	Republican	15,758,901	59	39.7
		Norman Thomas	Socialist	881,951		2.2
1936	48	FRANKLIN D. ROOSEVELT	Democrat	27,752,869	523	60.8
		Alfred M. Landon	Republican	16,674,665	8	36.5
		William Lemke	Union	882,479		1.9
1940	48	FRANKLIN D. ROOSEVELT	Democrat	27,307,819	449	54.8
		Wendell L. Willkie	Republican	22,321,018	82	44.8

PRESIDENTIAL ELECTIONS (CONTINUED)

Year	Number of States	Candidates	Party	Popular Vote	Electoral Vote	Percentage of Popular Vote
1944	48	FRANKLIN D. ROOSEVELT	Democrat	25,606,585	432	53.5
		Thomas E. Dewey	Republican	22,014,745	99	46.0
1948	48	HARRY S. TRUMAN	Democrat	24,105,812	303	49.5
		Thomas E. Dewey	Republican	21,970,065	189	45.1
		J. Strom Thurmond	States' Rights	1,169,063	39	2.4
		Henry A. Wallace	Progressive	1,157,172		2.4
1952	48	DWIGHT D. EISENHOWER	Republican	33,936,234	442	55.1
		Adlai E. Stevenson	Democrat	27,314,992	89	44.4
1956	48	DWIGHT D. EISENHOWER	Republican	35,590,472	457*	57.6
		Adlai E. Stevenson	Democrat	26,022,752	73	42.1
1960	50	JOHN F. KENNEDY	Democrat	34,227,096	303†	49.9
		Richard M. Nixon	Republican	34,108,546	219	49.6
1964	50	LYNDON B. JOHNSON	Democrat	42,676,220	486	61.3
		Barry M. Goldwater	Republican	26,860,314	52	38.5
1968	50	RICHARD M. NIXON	Republican	31,785,480	301	43.4
		Hubert H. Humphrey	Democrat	31,275,165	191	42.7
		George C. Wallace	American Independent	9,906,473	46	13.5
1972	50	RICHARD M. NIXON‡	Republican	47,165,234	520	60.6
		George S. McGovern	Democrat	29,168,110	17	37.5
1976	50	JIMMY CARTER	Democrat	40,828,929	297	50.1
		Gerald R. Ford	Republican	39,148,940	240	47.9
		Eugene McCarthy	Independent	739,256		
1980	50	RONALD REAGAN	Republican	43,201,220	489	50.9
		Jimmy Carter	Democrat	34,913,332	49	41.2
		John B. Anderson	Independent	5,581,379		
1984	50	RONALD REAGAN	Republican	53,428,357	525	59.0
		Walter F. Mondale	Democrat	36,930,923	13	41.0
1988	50	GEORGE BUSH	Republican	48,901,046	426	53.4
		Michael Dukakis	Democrat	41,809,030	111	45.6
1992	50	BILL CLINTON	Democrat	43,728,275	370	43.2
		George Bush	Republican	38,167,416	168	37.7
		H. Ross Perot	United We Stand, America	19,237,247		19.0
1996	50	BILL CLINTON	Democrat	45,590,703	379	49.0
		Robert Dole	Republican	37,816,307	159	41.0
		H. Ross Perot	Reform	7,866,284		8.0
2000	50	GEORGE W. BUSH	Republican	50,459,624	271	47.9
		Albert Gore, Jr.	Democrat	51,003,328	266	49.4
		Ralph Nader	Green	2,882,985	0	2.7
2004	50	GEORGE W. BUSH	Republican	59,117,523	286	51.1
		John Kerry	Democrat	55,557,584	252	48.0
		Ralph Nader	Green	405,623	0	0.3

* *Walter B. Jones received 1 electoral vote.*

† *Harry F. Byrd received 15 electoral votes.*

‡ *Resigned August 9, 1974: Vice President Gerald R. Ford became President.*

ADMISSION OF STATES INTO THE UNION

State	Date of Admission	State	Date of Admission
1. Delaware	December 7, 1787	26. Michigan	January 26, 1837
2. Pennsylvania	December 12, 1787	27. Florida	March 3, 1845
3. New Jersey	December 18, 1787	28. Texas	December 29, 1845
4. Georgia	January 2, 1788	29. Iowa	December 28, 1846
5. Connecticut	January 9, 1788	30. Wisconsin	May 29, 1848
6. Massachusetts	February 6, 1788	31. California	September 9, 1850
7. Maryland	April 28, 1788	32. Minnesota	May 11, 1858
8. South Carolina	May 23, 1788	33. Oregon	February 14, 1859
9. New Hampshire	June 21, 1788	34. Kansas	January 29, 1861
10. Virginia	June 25, 1788	35. West Virginia	June 20, 1863
11. New York	July 26, 1788	36. Nevada	October 31, 1864
12. North Carolina	November 21, 1789	37. Nebraska	March 1, 1867
13. Rhode Island	May 29, 1790	38. Colorado	August 1, 1876
14. Vermont	March 4, 1791	39. North Dakota	November 2, 1889
15. Kentucky	June 1, 1792	40. South Dakota	November 2, 1889
16. Tennessee	June 1, 1796	41. Montana	November 8, 1889
17. Ohio	March 1, 1803	42. Washington	November 11, 1889
18. Louisiana	April 30, 1812	43. Idaho	July 3, 1890
19. Indiana	December 11, 1816	44. Wyoming	July 10, 1890
20. Mississippi	December 10, 1817	45. Utah	January 4, 1896
21. Illinois	December 3, 1818	46. Oklahoma	November 16, 1907
22. Alabama	December 14, 1819	47. New Mexico	January 6, 1912
23. Maine	March 15, 1820	48. Arizona	February 14, 1912
24. Missouri	August 10, 1821	49. Alaska	January 3, 1959
25. Arkansas	June 15, 1836	50. Hawaii	August 21, 1959

DEMOGRAPHICS OF THE UNITED STATES

POPULATION GROWTH

Year	Population	Percent Increase
1630	4,600	
1640	26,600	478.3
1650	50,400	90.8
1660	75,100	49.0
1670	111,900	49.0
1680	151,500	35.4
1690	210,400	38.9
1700	250,900	19.2
1710	331,700	32.2
1720	466,200	40.5
1730	629,400	35.0
1740	905,600	43.9
1750	1,170,800	29.3
1760	1,593,600	36.1
1770	2,148,100	34.8
1780	2,780,400	29.4
1790	3,929,214	41.3
1800	5,308,483	35.1
1810	7,239,881	36.4
1820	9,638,453	33.1
1830	12,866,020	33.5
1840	17,069,453	32.7
1850	23,191,876	35.9
1860	31,443,321	35.6
1870	39,818,449	26.6
1880	50,155,783	26.0
1890	62,947,714	25.5
1900	75,994,575	20.7
1910	91,972,266	21.0
1920	105,710,620	14.9
1930	122,775,046	16.1
1940	131,669,275	7.2
1950	151,325,798	14.5
1960	179,323,175	18.5
1970	203,302,031	13.4
1980	226,542,199	11.4
1990	248,718,301	9.8
2000	281,421,906	13.1

Source: *Historical Statistics of the United States* (1975); *Statistical Abstract by the United States* (2001).
Note: Figures for 1630–1780 include British colonies within limits of present United States only; Native American population included only in 1930 and thereafter.

WORK FORCE

Year	Total Number Workers (1000s)	Farmers as % of Total	Women as % of Total	% Workers in Unions
1810	2,330	84	(NA)	(NA)
1840	5,660	75	(NA)	(NA)
1860	11,110	53	(NA)	(NA)
1870	12,506	53	15	(NA)
1880	17,392	52	15	(NA)
1890	23,318	43	17	(NA)
1900	29,073	40	18	3
1910	38,167	31	21	6
1920	41,614	26	21	12
1930	48,830	22	22	7
1940	53,011	17	24	27
1950	59,643	12	28	25
1960	69,877	8	32	26
1970	82,049	4	37	25
1980	106,940	3	43	23
1990	125,840	3	45	16
2000	140,863	2	47	12

Source: *Historical Statistics of the United States* (1975); *Statistical Abstract of the United States* (2001).

VITAL STATISTICS (IN THOUSANDS)

Year	Births	Deaths	Marriages	Divorces
1800	55	(NA)	(NA)	(NA)
1810	54.3	(NA)	(NA)	(NA)
1820	55.2	(NA)	(NA)	(NA)
1830	51.4	(NA)	(NA)	(NA)
1840	51.8	(NA)	(NA)	(NA)
1850	43.3	(NA)	(NA)	(NA)
1860	44.3	(NA)	(NA)	(NA)
1870	38.3	(NA)	9.6 (1867)	0.3 (1867)
1880	39.8	(NA)	9.1 (1875)	0.3 (1875)
1890	31.5	(NA)	9.0	0.5
1900	32.3	17.2	9.3	0.7
1910	30.1	14.7	10.3	0.9
1920	27.7	13.0	12.0	1.6
1930	21.3	11.3	9.2	1.6
1940	19.4	10.8	12.1	2.0
1950	24.1	9.6	11.1	2.6
1960	23.7	9.5	8.5	2.2
1970	18.4	9.5	10.6	3.5
1980	15.9	8.8	10.6	5.2
1990	16.7	8.6	9.8	4.7
1997	14.6	8.6	8.9	4.3

Source: *Historical Statistics of the United States* (1975); *Statistical Abstract of the United States* (1999).

RACIAL COMPOSITION OF THE POPULATION

(IN THOUSANDS)

Year	White	Black	Indian	Hispanic	Asian/Pacific Islander
1790	3,172	757	(NA)	(NA)	(NA)
1800	4,306	1,002	(NA)	(NA)	(NA)
1820	7,867	1,772	(NA)	(NA)	(NA)
1840	14,196	2,874	(NA)	(NA)	(NA)
1860	26,923	4,442	(NA)	(NA)	(NA)
1880	43,403	6,581	(NA)	(NA)	(NA)
1900	66,809	8,834	(NA)	(NA)	(NA)
1910	81,732	9,828	(NA)	(NA)	(NA)
1920	94,821	10,463	(NA)	(NA)	(NA)
1930	110,287	11,891	(NA)	(NA)	(NA)
1940	118,215	12,866	(NA)	(NA)	(NA)
1950	134,942	15,042	(NA)	(NA)	(NA)
1960	158,832	18,872	(NA)	(NA)	(NA)
1970	178,098	22,581	(NA)	(NA)	(NA)
1980	194,713	26,683	1,420	14,609	3,729
1990	208,727	30,511	2,065	22,372	2,462
2000	211,461	34,658	2,476	35,306	10,642

Source: U.S. Bureau of the Census, U.S. *Census of Population: 1940*, vol. II, part 1, and vol. IV, part 1; *1950*, vol. II, part 1; *1960*, vol. I, part 1; *1970*, vol. I, part B; and *Current Population Reports*, P25-1095 and P25-1104; *Statistical Abstract of the United States* (2001).

IMMIGRATION BY THE ORIGIN

(IN THOUSANDS)

Period	Europe	Americas	Asia
1820–30	106	12	—
1831–40	496	33	—
1841–50	1,597	62	—
1851–60	2,453	75	42
1861–70	2,065	167	65
1871–80	2,272	404	70
1881–90	4,735	427	70
1891–1900	3,555	39	75
1901–10	8,065	362	324
1911–20	4,322	1,144	247
1921–30	2,463	1,517	112
1931–40	348	160	16
1941–50	621	355	32
1951–60	1,326	997	150
1961–70	1,123	1,716	590
1971–80	800	1,983	1,588
1981–90	762	3,616	2,738
1991–2000	1,100	3,800	2,200

Source: Historical Statistics of the United States (1975); *Statistical Abstract of the United States* (1991); Population Estimates Program, Population Division, U.S. Census Bureau, April 2001.

Acquired Immune Deficiency Syndrome (AIDS) A complex of deadly pathologies resulting from infection with the human immunodeficiency virus (HIV).

Act of Toleration Act passed in 1661 by King Charles II ordering a stop to religious persecution in Massachusetts.

Affirmative action A set of policies to open opportunities in business and education for members of minority groups and women by allowing race and sex to be factors included in decisions to hire, award contracts, or admit students to higher education programs.

Alamo Franciscan mission at San Antonio, Texas that was the site in 1836 of a siege and massacre of Texans by Mexican troops.

Albany Conference A 1754 meeting, held in Albany, NY, between the British and leaders of the Iroquois Confederacy.

Albany Movement Coalition formed in 1961 in Albany, a small city in southwest Georgia, of activists from SNCC, the NAACP, and other local groups.

Alien Act Act passed by Congress in 1798 that authorized the president to imprison or deport suspected aliens during wartime.

Alliance for Progress Program of economic aid to Latin America during the Kennedy administration.

Allies In World War I, Britain, France, Russia, and other belligerent nations fighting against the Central Powers but not including the United States.

Almanac A combination calendar, astrological guide, and sourcebook of medical advice and farming tips.

American Colonization Society Organization founded in 1817 by antislavery reformers, that called for gradual emancipation and the removal of freed blacks to Africa.

American Federation of Labor (AFL) Union formed in 1886 that organized skilled workers along craft lines and emphasized a few workplace issues rather than a broad social program.

American Indian Movement (AIM) Group of Native-American political activists who used confrontations with the federal government to publicize their case for Indian rights.

American Society for the Promotion of Temperance Largest reform organization of its time dedicated to ending the sale and consumption of alcoholic beverages.

American System The program of government subsidies favored by Henry Clay and his followers to promote American economic growth and protect domestic manufacturers from foreign competition.

Americans with Disabilities Act An act that required employers to provide access to their facilities for qualified employees with disabilities.

Annapolis Convention Conference of state delegates at Annapolis, Maryland, that issued a call in September 1786 for a convention to meet at Philadelphia to consider fundamental changes.

Anti-Federalists Opponents of the Constitution in the debate over its ratification.

Archaic period The period roughly 10,000 to 2,500 years ago marked by the retreat of glaciers.

Articles of Confederation Written document setting up the loose confederation of states that comprised the first national government of the United States.

Athapascan A people that began to settle the forests in the northwestern area of North America around 5000 B.C.E.

Atlantic Charter Statement of common principles and war aims developed by President Franklin Roosevelt and British Prime Minister Winston Churchill at a meeting in August 1941.

Axis powers The opponents of the United States and its allies in World War II.

Aztecs A warrior people who dominated the Valley of Mexico from 1100–1521.

Bank War The political struggle between President Andrew Jackson and the supporters of the Second Bank of the United States.

Battle of the Bulge German offensive in December 1944 that penetrated deep into Belgium (creating a "bulge"). Allied forces, while outnumbered, attacked from the north and south. By January, 1945, the German forces were destroyed or routed, but not without some 77,000 Allied casualties.

Bay of Pigs Site in Cuba of an unsuccessful landing by fourteen hundred anti-Castro Cuban refugees in April 1961.

Beatnik Term used to designate members of the Beats.

Beats A group of writers from the 50s whose writings challenged American culture.

Beaver Wars Series of bloody conflicts, occurring between 1640s and 1680s, during which the Iroquois fought the French for control of the fur trade in the east and the Great Lakes region.

Beringia A subcontinent bridging Asia and North America, named after the Bering Straits.

Berlin blockade Three-hundred-day Soviet blockade of land access to United States, British, and French occupation zones in Berlin, 1948–1949.

Bill for Establishing Religious Freedom A bill authored by Thomas Jefferson establishing religious freedom in Virginia.

Bill of Rights A written summary of inalienable rights and liberties.

Black codes Laws passed by states and municipalities denying many rights of citizenship to free black people before the Civil War.

Black Panther Party Political and social movement among black Americans, founded in Oakland, California, in 1966 and emphasizing black economic and political power.

Black Power Philosophy emerging after 1965 that real economic and political gains for African Americans could come only through self-help, self-determination, and organizing for direct political influence.

Bleeding Kansas Violence between pro- and antislavery forces in Kansas Territory after the passage of the Kansas-Nebraska Act in 1854.

Blitzkrieg German war tactic in World War II ("lightning war") involving the concentration of air and armored firepower to punch and exploit holes in opposing defensive lines.

Bohemian Artistic individual who lives with disregard for the conventional rules of behavior.

Bolsheviks Members of the Communist movement in Russia that established the Soviet government after the 1917 Russian Revolution.

Bonus Army Unemployed veterans of World War I gathering in Washington in 1932 demanding payment of service bonuses not due until 1945.

Bosnia A nation in southeast Europe that split off from Yugoslavia and became the site of bitter civil and religious war, requiring NATO and U.S. intervention in the 1990s.

Boston Massacre After months of increasing friction between townspeople and the British troops stationed in the city, on March 5, 1770, British troops fired on American civilians in Boston.

Boston Tea Party Incident that occurred on December 16, 1773, in which Bostonians, disguised as Indians, destroyed £18,000 worth of tea belonging to the British East India Company in order to prevent payment of the duty on it.

Brown v. Board of Education Supreme Court decision in 1954 that declared that "separate but equal" schools for children of different races violated the Constitution.

Cahokia One of the largest urban centers created by Mississippian peoples, containing 30,000 residents in 1250.

Californios Californians of Spanish descent.

Calvinist theology of election Belief that salvation was the result of God's sovereign decree and that few people would receive God's grace.

Caminetti Act 1893 act giving the state the power to regulate the mines.

Camp David Accords Agreement signed by Israel and Egypt in 1978 that set the formal terms for peace in the Middle East.

Carpetbaggers Northern transplants to the South, many of whom were Union soldiers who stayed in the South after the war.

Central Intelligence Agency (CIA) Agency established in 1947 that coordinates the gathering and evaluation of military and economic information on other nations.

Central Powers Germany and its World War I allies in Austria, Italy, Turkey, and Bulgaria.

Chinese Exclusion Act Act which suspended Chinese immigration, limited the civil rights of resident Chinese, and forbade their naturalization.

Civil Rights Act of 1964 Federal legislation that outlawed discrimination in public accommodations and employment on the basis of race, skin color, sex, religion, or national origin.

Civil Rights Bill 1866 act that gave full citizenship to African Americans.

Clayton Antitrust Act Replaced the old Sherman Act of 1890 as the nation's basic antitrust law. It exempted unions from being construed as illegal combinations in restraint of trade, and it forbade federal courts from issuing injunctions against strikers.

Coercive Acts Legislation passed by Parliament in 1774; included the Boston Port Act, the Massachusetts Government Act, the Administration of Justice Act, and the Quartering Act of 1774.

Cold war The political and economic confrontation between the Soviet Union and the United States that dominated world affairs from 1946 to 1989.

Committee on Public Information (CPI) Government agency during World War I that sought to shape public opinion in support of the war effort through newspapers, pamphlets, speeches, films, and other media.

Compromise of 1850 The four-step compromise which admitted California as a free state, allowed the residents of the New Mexico and Utah territories to decide the slavery issue for themselves, ended the slave trade in the District of Columbia, and passed a new fugitive slave law to enforce the constitutional provision stating that a slave escaping into a free state shall be delivered back to the owner.

Compromise of 1877 The Congressional settling of the 1876 election which installed Republican Rutherford B. Hayes in the White House and gave Democrats control of all state governments in the South.

Confederate States of America Nation proclaimed in Montgomery, Alabama, in February 1861, after the seven states of the Lower South seceded from the United States.

Congress of Industrial Organizations An alliance of industrial unions that spurred the 1930s organizational drive among the mass-production industries.

Congress of Racial Equality (CORE) Civil rights group formed in 1942 and committed to nonviolent civil disobedience.

Congressional Reconstruction Name given to the period 1867–1870 when the Republican-dominated Congress controlled Reconstruction-era policy.

Conspicuous consumption Highly visible displays of wealth and consumption.

Constitution The written document providing for a new central government of the United States.

Constitutional Convention Convention of delegates from the colonies that first met to organize resistance to the Intolerable Acts.

Constitutional Union Party National party formed in 1860, mainly by former Whigs, that emphasized allegiance to the Union and strict enforcement of all national legislation.

Continental Army The regular or professional army authorized by the Second Continental Congress and commanded by General George Washington during the Revolutionary War.

Contract with America Platform proposing a sweeping reduction in the role and activities of the federal government on which many Republican candidates ran for Congress in 1994.

Contras Nicaraguan exiles armed and organized by the CIA to fight the Sandinista government of Nicaragua.

Copperheads A term Republicans applied to Northern war dissenters and those suspected of aiding the Confederate cause during the Civil War.

Council of Economic Advisers Board of three professional economists established in 1946 to advise the president on economic policy.

Counterculture Various alternatives to mainstream values and behaviors that became popular in the 1960s, including experimentation with psychedelic drugs, communal living, a return to the land, Asian religions, and experimental art.

Coureurs de bois French for "woods runner," an independent fur trader in New France.

Covenant Chain An alliance between the Iroquois Confederacy and the colony of New York which sought to establish Iroquois dominance over all other tribes.

Coxey's Army A protest march of unemployed workers, led by Populist businessman Jacob Coxey, demanding inflation and a public works program during the depression of the 1890s.

Cuban missile crisis Crisis between the Soviet Union and the United States over the placement of Soviet nuclear missiles in Cuba.

Culpeper's Rebellion The overthrow of the established government in the Albermarle region of North Carolina by backcountry men in 1677.

Dawes Severalty Act An 1887 law terminating tribal ownership of land and allotting some parcels of land to individual Indians with the remainder opened for white settlement.

Declaration of Sentiments The resolutions passed at the Seneca Falls Convention in 1848 calling for full female equality, including the right to vote.

D-Day June 6, 1944, the day of the first paratroop drops and amphibious landings on the coast of Normandy, France, in the first stage of Operation Overlord during World War II.

Declaratory Act Law passed in 1776 to accompany repeal of the Stamp Act that stated that Parliament had the authority to legislate for the colonies "in all cases whatsoever."

Democrats Political party formed in the 1820s under the leadership of Andrew Jackson; favored states' rights and a limited role for the federal government.

Denmark Vesey's conspiracy The most carefully devised slave revolt in which rebels planned to seize control of Charleston in 1822 and escape to freedom in Haiti, a free black republic, but they were betrayed by other slaves, and seventy-five conspirators were executed.

Department of Homeland Security (DHS) Cabinet-level department created by George Bush to manage U.S. security.

Deregulation Reduction or removal of government regulations and encouragement of direct competition in many important industries and economic sectors.

Desert culture A way of life based on hunting small game and the foraging of plant foods.

Détente (French for "easing of tension") Used to describe the new U.S. relations with China and the Soviet Union in 1972.

Dixiecrat States' Rights Democrats.

Doughboys Nickname for soldiers during the Civil War era who joined the army for money.

***Dred Scott* decision** Supreme Court ruling, in a lawsuit brought by Dred Scott, a slave demanding his freedom based on his residence in a free state, that slaves could not be U.S. citizens and that Congress had no jurisdiction over slavery in the territories.

Economic Recovery Tax Act of 1981 A major revision of the federal income tax system.

Edmunds Act 1882 act that effectively disenfranchised those who believed in or practiced polygamy and threatened them with fines and imprisonment.

Edmunds-Tucker Act 1887 act which destroyed the temporal power of the Mormon Church by confiscating all assets over $50,000 and establishing a federal commission to oversee all elections in the Utah territory.

Emancipation Proclamation Decree announced by President Abraham Lincoln in September 1862 and formally issued on January 1, 1863, freeing slaves in all Confederate states still in rebellion.

Embargo Act Act passed by Congress in 1807 prohibiting American ships from leaving for any foreign port.

Emergency Banking Act 1933 act which gave the president broad discretionary powers over all banking transactions and foreign exchange.

Empresarios Agents who received a land grant from the Spanish or Mexican government in return for organizing settlements.

Enclave Self-contained community.

Encomienda In the Spanish colonies, the grant to a Spanish settler of a certain number of Indian subjects, who would pay him tribute in goods and labor.

Engagés Catholic immigrants to New France.

Enlightenment Intellectual movement stressing the importance of reason and the existence of discoverable natural laws.

Enumerated goods Items produced in the colonies and enumerated in acts of Parliament that could be legally shipped from the colony of origin only to specified locations.

Environmental Protection Agency (EPA) Federal agency created in 1970 to oversee environmental monitoring and cleanup programs.

Equal Pay Act of 1963 Act that made it illegal for employers to pay men and women different wages for the same job.

Era of Good Feelings The period from 1817 to 1823 in which the disappearance of the Federalists enabled the Republicans to govern in a spirit of seemingly nonpartisan harmony.

Espionage Act Law whose vague prohibition against obstructing the nation's war effort was used to crush dissent and criticism during World War I.

Executive Order 9835 Signed by Harry Truman in 1947 to establish a loyalty program requiring federal employees to sign loyalty oaths and undergo security checks.

Federal Emergency Management Agency (FEMA) Agency charged with providing assistance to communities hit by natural disasters.

Federal Reserve Act The 1913 law that revised banking and currency by extending limited government regulation through the creation of the Federal Reserve System.

Federal Trade Commission (FTC) Government agency established in 1914 to provide regulatory oversight of business activity.

Federalists Supporters of the Constitution who favored its ratification.

Female Moral Reform Society Antiprostitution group founded by evangelical women in New York in 1834.

Field Order 15 Order by General William T. Sherman in January 1865 to set aside abandoned land along the southern Atlantic coast for forty-acre grants to freedmen; rescinded by President Andrew Johnson later that year.

Fifteenth Amendment Passed by Congress in 1869, guaranteed the right of American men to vote, regardless of race.

Fireside chat Speeches broadcast nationally over the radio in which President Franklin D. Roosevelt explained complex issues and programs in plain language, as though his listeners were gathered around the fireside with him.

First Continental Congress Meeting of delegates from most of the colonies held in 1774 in response to the Coercive Acts.

First Reconstruction Act 1877 act that divided the South into five military districts subject to martial law.

Forest Efficiency Creation of a comfortable life through the development of a sophisticated knowledge of available resources.

Forest Management Act 1897 act which, along with the National Reclamation Act, set the federal government on the path of large-scale regulatory activities.

Fourteen Points Goals outlined by Woodrow Wilson for war.

Frame of Government William Penn's constitution for Pennsylvania which included a provision allowing for religious freedom.

Free silver Philosophy that the government should expand the money supply by purchasing and coining all the silver offered to it.

Free speech movement Student movement at the University of California, Berkeley, formed in 1964 to protest limitations on political activities on campus.

Freedmen's Bureau Agency established by Congress in March 1865 to provide social, educational, and economic services, advice, and protection to former slaves and destitute whites; lasted seven years.

Freedom Summer Voter registration effort in rural Mississippi organized by black and white civil rights workers in 1964.

French and Indian War The last of the Anglo-French colonial wars (1754–1763) and the first in which fighting began in North America. The war ended with France's defeat. Also known as the **Seven Years' War**.

Fugitive Slave Law Part of the Compromise of 1850 that required the authorities in the North to assist Southern slave catchers and return runaway slaves to their owners.

Gang System The organization and supervision of slave field hands into working teams on Southern plantations.

General Land Revision Act of 1891 Act which gave the president the power to establish forest reserves to protect watersheds against the threats posed by lumbering, overgrazing, and forest fires.

G.I. Bill Legislation in June 1944 that eased the return of veterans into American society by providing educational and employment benefits.

Gilded Age Term applied to late nineteenth-century America that refers to the shallow display and worship of wealth characteristic of that period.

Gospel of wealth Thesis that hard work and perseverance lead to wealth, implying that poverty is a character flaw.

Grandfather clauses Rules that required potential voters to demonstrate that their grandfathers had been eligible to vote; used in some Southern states after 1890 to limit the black electorate.

Grange The National Grange of the Patrons of Husbandry, a national organization of farm owners formed after the Civil War.

Granger laws State laws enacted in the Midwest in the 1870s that regulated rates charged by railroads, grain elevator operators, and other middlemen.

Great Awakening Tremendous religious revival in colonial America striking first in the Middle Colonies and New England in the 1740s and then spreading to the southern colonies.

Great Compromise Plan proposed at the 1787 Constitutional Convention for creating a national bicameral legislature in which all states would be equally represented in the Senate and proportionally represented in the House.

Great Depression The nation's worst economic crisis, extending through the 1930s, producing unprecedented bank failures, unemployment, and industrial and agricultural collapse.

Great Migration The mass movement of African Americans from the rural South to the urban North, spurred especially by new job opportunities during World War I and the 1920s.

Great Sioux War From 1865 to 1867 the Oglala Sioux warrior Red Cloud waged war against the U.S. Army, forcing the U.S. to abandon its forts built on land relinquished to the government by the Sioux.

Great Society Theme of Lyndon Johnson's administration, focusing on poverty, education, and civil rights.

Great Uprising of 1877 Unsuccessful railroad strike to protest wage cuts and the use of federal troops against strikers; the first nationwide work stoppage in American history.

Gulf of Tonkin resolution Request to Congress from President Lyndon Johnson in response to North Vietnamese torpedo boat attacks in which he sought authorization for "all necessary measures" to protect American forces and stop further aggression.

Harlem Renaissance A new African American cultural awareness that flourished in literature, art, and music in the 1920s.

Hepburn Act Act that strengthened the Interstate Commerce Commission (ICC) by authorizing it to set maximum railroad rates and inspect financial records.

Hispanic-American Alliance Organization formed to protect and fight for the rights of Spanish Americans.

Holocaust The systematic murder of millions of European Jews and others deemed undesirable by Nazi Germany.

Homestead Act Law passed by Congress in May 1862 providing homesteads with 160 acres of free land in exchange for improving the land within five years of the grant.

Homestead Act of 1862 1862 act which granted a quarter section (160 acres) of the public domain free to any settler who lived on the land for at least five years and improved it.

Horizontal combination The merger of competitors in the same industry.

House Concurrent Resolution 108 Resolution passed in 1953 that allowed Congress to pass legislation to terminate a specific tribe as a political entity.

House of Burgesses The legislature of colonial Virginia. First organized in 1619, it was the first institution of representative government in the English colonies.

House Un-American Activities Committee (HUAC)   Originally intended to ferret out pro-Fascists, it later investigated "un-American propaganda" that attacked constitutional government.

Huguenots   French Protestant religious dissenters who planted the first French colonies in North America.

Immigration Act   1921 act setting a maximum of 357,000 new immigrants each year.

Immigration and Nationality Act   Act passed in 1965 that abolished national origin quotas and established overall hemisphere quotas.

Imperialism   The policy and practice of exploiting nations and peoples for the benefit of an imperial power either directly through military occupation and colonial rule or indirectly through economic domination of resources and markets.

Indentured Servants   Individuals who contracted to serve a master for a period of four to seven years in return for payment of the servant's passage to America.

Indian Removal Act   President Andrew Jackson's measure that allowed state officials to override federal protection of Native Americans.

Indios   Name first used by Christopher Columbus for the Taino people of the Caribbean.

Industrial Revolution   Revolution in the means and organization of production.

Intercourse Act   Passed in 1790, this law regulated trade and intercourse with the Indian tribes and declared public treaties between the U.S. and Indian nations the only means of obtaining Indian lands.

International Monetary Fund (IMF)   International organization established in 1945 to assist nations in maintaining stable currencies.

Internet   The system of interconnected computers and servers that allows the exchange of email, posting of Web sites, and other means of instant communication.

Interstate Commerce Commission (ICC)   The 1887 law that expanded federal power over business by prohibiting pooling and discriminatory rates by railroads and establishing the first federal regulatory agency, the Interstate Commerce Commission.

Intolerable Acts   American term for the Coercive Acts and the Quebec Act.

Irreconcilables   Group of U.S. senators adamantly opposed to ratification of the Treaty of Versailles after World War I.

Island-hop   The Pacific campaigns of 1944 that were the American naval versions of the Blitzkrieg.

Jay's Treaty   Treaty with Britain negotiated in 1794 in which the United States made major concessions to avert a war over the British seizure of American ships.

Jim Crow laws   Segregation laws that became widespread in the South during the 1890s.

Judicial review   A power implied in the Constitution that gives federal courts the right to review and determine the constitutionality of acts passed by Congress and state legislatures.

Judiciary Act of 1789   Act of Congress that implemented the judiciary clause of the Constitution by establishing the Supreme Court and a system of lower federal courts.

Kansas-Nebraska Act   Law passed in 1854 creating the Kansas and Nebraska Territories but leaving the question of slavery open to residents, thereby repealing the Missouri Compromise.

King George's War   The third Anglo-French war in North America (1744–1748), part of the European conflict known as the War of the Austrian Succession.

King Philip's War   Conflict in New England (1675–1676) between Wampanoags, Narragansetts, and other Indian peoples against English settlers; sparked by English encroachments on native lands.

King William's War   The first of a series of colonial struggles between England and France, these conflicts occur principally on the frontiers of northern New England and New York between 1689 and 1697.

Knights of Labor   Labor union founded in 1869 that included skilled and unskilled workers irrespective of race or gender.

Know-Nothings   Name given to the antiimmigrant party formed from the wreckage of the Whig Party and some disaffected Northern Democrats in 1854.

Kosovo   Province of Yugoslavia where the United States and NATO intervened militarily in 1999 to protect ethnic Albanians from expulsion.

Ku Klux Klan   Perhaps the most prominent of the vigilante groups that terrorized black people in the South during Reconstruction era, founded by the Confederate veterans in 1866.

Land Ordinance of 1785   Act passed by Congress under the Articles of Confederation that created the grid system of surveys by which all subsequent public land was made available for sale.

Landrum-Griffin Act   1959 act that widened government control over union affairs and further restricted union use of picketing and secondary boycotts during strikes.

League of Nations   International organization created by the Versailles Treaty after World War I to ensure world stability.

League of Women Voters   League formed in 1920 advocating for women's rights, among them the right for women to serve on juries and equal pay laws.

Lecompton constitution   Proslavery draft written in 1857 by Kansas territorial delegates elected under questionable circumstances; it was rejected by two governors, supported by President Buchanan, and decisively defeated by Congress.

Legal Tender Act   Act creating a national currency in February 1862.

Lend-Lease Act   An arrangement for the transfer of war supplies, including food, machinery, and services to nations whose defense was considered vital to the defense of the United States in Word War II.

Liberal Republicans   Disaffected Republicans that emphasized the doctrines of classical economics.

Liberty Bonds   Interest-bearing certificates sold by the U.S. government to finance the American World War I effort.

Liberty Party   The first antislavery political party, formed in 1840.

Limited Nuclear Test-Ban Treaty   Treaty, signed by the United States, Britain, and the Soviet Union, outlawing nuclear testing in the atmosphere, in outer space, and under water.

Lincoln-Douglas debates Series of debates in the 1858 Illinois senatorial campaign during which Douglas and Lincoln staked out their differing opinions on the issue of slavery.

Loyalists British colonists who opposed independence from Britain.

Manhattan Project Scientific research project during World War II specifically devoted to developing the atomic bomb.

Manifest Destiny Doctrine, first expressed in 1845, that the expansion of white Americans across the continent was inevitable and ordained by God.

Manumission The freeing of a slave.

Marbury v. *Madison* Supreme Court decision of 1803 that created the precedent of judicial review by ruling as unconstitutional part of the Judiciary Act of 1789.

March on Washington Historic gathering of over 250,000 people in Washington D.C. in 1963 marching for jobs and freedom.

Market revolution The outcome of three interrelated developments: rapid improvements in transportation, commercialization, and industrialization.

Marshall Plan Secretary of State George C. Marshall's European Recovery Plan of June 5, 1947, committing the United States to help in the rebuilding of post–World War II Europe.

Massachusetts Bay Company A group of wealthy Puritans who were granted a royal charter in 1629 to settle in Massachusetts Bay.

Mayflower Compact The first document of self-government in North America.

McCarthyism Anti-Communist attitudes and actions associated with Senator Joe McCarthy in the early 1950s, including smear tactics and innuendo.

Medicare Basic medical insurance for the elderly, financed through the federal government; program created in 1965.

Mercantilism Economic system whereby the government intervenes in the economy for the purpose of increasing national wealth.

Mesoamerica The region stretching from central Mexico to Central America.

Mexican-American War War fought between Mexico and the United States between 1846 and 1848 over control of territory in southwest North America.

Middle Passage The voyage between West Africa and the New World slave colonies.

Militarism The tendency to see military might as the most important and best tool for the expansion of a nation's power and prestige.

Missouri Compromise Sectional compromise in Congress in 1820 that admitted Missouri to the Union as a slave state and Maine as a free state and prohibited slavery in the northern Louisiana Purchase territory.

Monroe Doctrine Declaration by President James Monroe in 1823 that the Western Hemisphere was to be closed off to further European colonization and that the United States would not interfere in the internal affairs of European nations.

Mormonism The doctrines based on the Book of Mormon, taught by Joseph Smith and the succeeding prophets and leaders of the Church.

Morrill Act of 1862 Act by which "land-grant" colleges acquired space for campuses in return for promising to institute agricultural programs. Also known as Morrill Land Grant Act.

Morrill Land Grant Act Law passed by Congress in July 1862 awarding proceeds from the sale of public lands to the states for the establishment of agricultural and mechanical colleges.

Morrill Tariff Act Act that raised tariffs to more than double their prewar rate.

Muckraking Journalism exposing economic, social, and political evils, so named by Theodore Roosevelt for its "raking the muck" of American society.

Multiculturalism Movement that emphasized the unique attributes and achievements of formerly marginal groups and recent immigrants.

My Lai Massacre Killing of twenty-two Vietnamese civilians by U.S. forces during a 1968 search-and-destroy mission.

Nat Turner's Revolt Uprising of slaves in Southampton County, Virginia, in the summer of 1831 led by Nat Turner that resulted in the death of fifty-five white people.

National Aeronautics and Space Administration (NASA) Federal agency created in 1958 to manage American space flights and exploration.

National American Woman Suffrage Association (NAWSA) The organization, formed in 1890, that coordinated the ultimately successful campaign to achieve women's right to vote.

National Association for the Advancement of Colored People Interracial organization co-founded by W. E. B. Du Bois in 1910 dedicated to restoring African American political and social rights.

National Bank Act Act prohibiting state banks from issuing their own notes and forcing them to apply for federal charters.

National Industrial Recovery Act 1933 act which was meant to be a systematic plan for economic recovery.

National Labor Relations Act Act establishing Federal guarantee of right to organize trade unions and collective bargaining.

National Organization for Women (NOW) Organization founded to campaign for the enforcement of laws related to women's issues.

National Reclamation Act 1902 act which added 1 million acres of irrigated land to the United States.

National Security Council (NSC) The formal policymaking body for national defense and foreign relations, created in 1947 and consisting of the president, the secretary of defense, the secretary of state, and others appointed by the president.

National Security Council Paper 68 (NSC-68) Policy statement that committed the United States to a military approach to the Cold War.

Nation of Islam (NOI) Religious movement among black Americans that emphasizes self-sufficiency, self-help, and separation from white society.

Nativism Favoring the interests and culture of native-born inhabitants over those of immigrants.

Neutrality Act of 1939 Permitted the sale of arms to Britain, France, and China.

New Deal The economic and political policies of the Roosevelt administration in the 1930s.

New Deal coalition Coalition that included traditional-minded white Southern Democrats, big-city political machines, industrial workers of all races, trade unionists, and many Depression-hit farmers.

New Freedom Woodrow Wilson's 1912 program for limited government intervention in the economy to restore competition by curtailing the restrictive influences of trusts and protective tariffs, thereby providing opportunities for individual achievement.

New Frontier John F. Kennedy's domestic and foreign policy initiatives, designed to reinvigorate sense of national purpose and energy.

New Jersey Plan Proposal of the New Jersey delegation for a strengthened national government in which all states would have an equal representation in a unicameral legislature.

New Lights People who experienced conversion during the revivals of the Great Awakening.

Niagara movement African American group organized in 1905 to promote racial integration, civil and political rights, and equal access to economic opportunity.

Nisei U.S. citizens born of immigrant Japanese parents.

Nonimportation movement A tactical means of putting economic pressure on Britain by refusing to buy its exports to the colonies.

North American Free Trade Agreement (NAFTA) Agreement reached in 1993 by Canada, Mexico, and the United States to substantially reduce barriers to trade.

North Atlantic Treaty Organization (NATO) Organization of ten European countries, Canada, and the United States whom together formed a mutual defense pact in April 1949.

Northwest Ordinance of 1787 Legislation that prohibited slavery in the Northwest Territories and provided the model for the incorporation of future territories into the union as co-equal states.

Nullification A constitutional doctrine holding that a state has a legal right to declare a national law null and void within its borders.

Nullification Crisis Sectional crisis in the early 1830s in which a states' rights party in South Carolina attempted to nullify federal law.

Office of Economic Opportunity (OEO) Federal agency that coordinated many programs of the War on Poverty between 1964 and 1975.

Old Lights Religious faction that condemned emotional enthusiasm as part of the heresy of believing in a personal and direct relationship with God outside the order of the church.

Omaha Act of 1882 Act which allowed the establishment of individual title to tribal lands.

Open Door American policy of seeking equal trade and investment opportunities in foreign nations or regions.

Open shop Factory of business employing workers whether or not they are union members; in practice, such a business usually refuses to hire union members and follows antiunion policies.

Operation Desert Storm U.S. military campaign to force Iraqi forces out of Kuwait.

Operation Overlord United States and British invasion of France in June 1944 during World War II.

Operation Torch The Allied invasion of Axis-held North Africa in 1942.

Oregon Trail Overland trail of more than two thousand miles that carried American settlers from the Midwest to new settlements in Oregon, California, and Utah.

Organization of Petroleum Exporting Countries (OPEC) Cartel of oil-producing nations in Asia, Africa, and Latin America that gained substantial power over the world economy in the mid- to late- 1970s by controlling the production and price of oil.

Panic of 1857 Banking crisis that caused a credit crunch in the North; it was less severe in the South, where high cotton prices spurred a quick recovery.

Pan-Indian military resistance movement Movement calling for the political and cultural unification of Indian tribes in the late eighteenth and early nineteenth centuries.

Patriots British colonists who favored independence from Britain.

Pendleton Civil Service Reform Act A law of 1883 that reformed the spoils system by prohibiting government workers from making political contributions and creating the Civil Service Commission to oversee their appointment on the basis of merit rather than politics.

Peninsular campaign Union offensive led by McClellan with the objective of capturing Richmond.

Pentagon Papers Classified Defense Department documents on the history of the United States' involvement in Vietnam, prepared in 1968 and leaked to the press in 1971.

Pequot War Conflict between English settlers and Pequot Indians over control of land and trade in eastern Connecticut.

Persian Gulf War War initiated by President Bush in response to Iraq's invasion of Kuwait.

Pilgrims Settlers of Plymouth Colony, who viewed themselves as spiritual wanderers.

Plan of Union Plan put forward by Benjamin Franklin in 1754 calling for an intercolonial union to manage defense and Indian affairs. The plan was rejected by participants at the Albany Congress.

Plessy* v. *Ferguson Supreme Court decision holding that Louisiana's railroad segregation law did not violate the Constitution as long as the railroads or the state provided equal accommodations.

Popular sovereignty A solution to the slavery crisis suggested by Michigan senator Lewis Cass by which territorial residents, not Congress, would decide slavery's fate.

Populism A mass movement of the 1890s formed on the basis of the Southern Farmers' Alliance and other reform organizations.

Powhatan Confederacy A village of communities of the Chesapeake united under Chief Wahunsonacook, who was called King Powhatan by the colonists.

Preparedness Military buildup in preparation for possible U.S. participation in World War I.

Progressivism A national movement focused on a variety of reform initiatives, including ending corruption, a more business like approach to government, and legislative responses to industrial excess.

Prohibition A ban on the production, sale, and consumption of liquor, achieved temporarily through state laws and the Eighteenth Amendment.

Proposition 187 California legislation adopted by popular vote in California in 1994, which cuts off state-funded health and education benefits to undocumented or illegal immigrants.

Proprietary colony A colony created when the English monarch granted a huge tract of land to an individual or group of individuals, who became "lords proprietor."

Protective association Organizations formed by mine owners in response to the formation of labor unions.

Protestant Reformation Martin Luther's challenge to the Catholic Church, initiated in 1517, calling for a return to what he understood to be the purer practices and beliefs of the early church.

Protestants All European supporters of religious reform under Charles V's Holy Roman Empire.

Pueblo Revolt Rebellion in 1680 of Pueblo Indians in New Mexico against their Spanish overlords.

Pure Food and Drug Act Act that established the Food and Drug Administration (FDA), which tested and approved drugs before they went on the market.

Puritanism Movement to purify and reform the English Church.

Puritans Individuals who believed that Queen Elizabeth's reforms of the Church of England had not gone far enough in improving the church. Puritans led the settlement of Massachusetts Bay Colony.

Putting-out system Production of goods in private homes under the supervision of a merchant who "put out" the raw materials, paid a certain sum per finished piece, and sold the completed item to a distant market.

Quakers Members of the Society of Friends, a radical religious group that arose in the mid-seventeenth century. Quakers rejected formal theology, focusing instead on the Holy Spirit that dwelt within them.

Quartering Act Acts of Parliament requiring colonial legislatures to provide supplies and quarters for the troops stationed in America.

Quasi-War Undeclared naval war of 1797 to 1800 between the United States and France.

Quebec Act Law passed by Parliament in 1774 that provided an appointed government for Canada, enlarged the boundaries of Quebec, and confirmed the privileges of the Catholic Church.

Queen Anne's War American phase (1702–1713) of Europe's War of the Spanish Succession.

Radical Republicans A shifting group of Republican congressmen, usually a substantial minority, who favored the abolition of slavery from the beginning of the Civil War and later advocated harsh treatment of the defeated South.

Rancherias Dispersed settlements of Indian farmers in the Southwest.

Reconquista The long struggle (ending in 1492) during which Spanish Christians reconquered the Iberian peninsula from Muslim occupiers.

Red Power Term for pan-Indian identity.

Red Scare Post–World War I public hysteria over Bolshevik influence in the United States directed against labor activism, radical dissenters, and some ethnic groups.

Referendum Submission of a law, proposed or already in effect, to a direct popular vote for approval or rejection.

Renaissance The intellectual and artistic flowering in Europe during the fourteenth, fifteenth, and sixteenth centuries sparked by a revival of interest in classical antiquity.

Republican Party Party that emerged in the 1850s in the aftermath of the bitter controversy over the Kansas-Nebraska Act, consisting of former Whigs, some Northern Democrats, and many Know-Nothings.

Republicanism A complex, changing body of ideas, values, and assumptions that influenced American political behavior during the eighteenth and nineteenth centuries.

Roe v. Wade U.S. Supreme Court decision (1973) that disallowed state laws prohibiting abortion during the first three months (trimester) of pregnancy and established guidelines for abortion in the second and third trimesters.

Roosevelt Corollary President Theodore Roosevelt's policy asserting U.S. authority to intervene in the affairs of Latin American nations; an expansion of the Monroe Doctrine.

Royal Proclamation of 1763 Royal proclamation declaring the trans-Appalachian region to be "Indian Country."

Rush-Bagot Treaty of 1817 Treaty between the United States and Britain that effectively demilitarized the Great Lakes by sharply limiting the number of ships each power could station on them.

Sabbatarianism Reform movement that aimed to prevent business on Sundays.

Sand Creek Massacre The near annihilation in 1864 of Black Kettle's Cheyenne band by Colorado troops under Colonel John Chivington's orders to "kill and scalp all, big and little."

Santa Fé Trail The 900-mile trail opened by American merchants for trading purposes following Mexico's liberalization of the formerly restrictive trading policies of Spain.

Scalawags Southern whites, mainly small landowning farmers and well-off merchants and planters, who supported the Southern Republican party during Reconstruction.

Second American Party System The basic pattern of American politics of two parties, each with appeal among voters of all social voters and in all sections of the country.

Second Great Awakening Religious revival among black and white Southerners in the 1790s.

Sedition Act An act passed by Congress in 1798 that provided fines for anyone convicted writing, publishing, or speaking out against the government or its officers.

Segregation A system of racial control that separated the races, initially by custom but increasingly by law during and after Reconstruction.

Selective Service Act The law establishing the military draft for World War I.

Self-determination The right of a people or a nation to decide on its own political allegiance or form of government without external influence.

Seneca Falls Convention The first convention for women's equality in legal rights, held in upstate New York in 1848.

Separatists Members of an offshoot branch of Puritanism. Separatists believed that the Church of England was too corrupt to be reformed and hence were convinced they must "separate" from it to save their souls.

Seven Years' War War fought in Europe, North America, and India between 1756 and 1753, pitting France and its allies against Great Britain and its allies.

Shakers The followers of Mother Ann Lee, who preached a religion of strict celibacy and communal living.

Sharecropping Labor system that evolved during and after Reconstruction whereby landowners furnished laborers with a house, farm animals, and tools and advanced credit in exchange for a share of the laborers' crop.

Sheppard-Towner Act The first federal social welfare law, passed in 1921, providing federal funds for infant and maternity care.

Sherman Antitrust Act The first federal antitrust measure, passed in 1890; sought to promote economic competition by prohibiting business combinations in restraint of trade or commerce.

Sherman Silver Purchase Act 1890 act which directed the Treasury to increase the amount of currency coined from silver mined in the West and also permitted the U.S. government to print paper currency backed by the silver.

Silicon Valley The region of California including San Jose and San Francisco that holds the nation's greatest concentration of electronics firms.

Sixteenth Amendment Authorized a federal income tax.

Slaughterhouse cases Group of cases resulting in one sweeping decision by the U.S. Supreme Court in 1873 that contradicted the intent of the Fourteenth Amendment by decreeing that most citizenship rights remained under state, not federal, control.

Slave codes A series of laws passed mainly in the Southern colonies in the late seventeenth and early eighteenth centuries to defend the status of slaves and codify the denial of basic civil rights to them.

Social Darwinism The application of Charles Darwin's theory of biological evolution to society, holding that the fittest and wealthiest survive, the weak and the poor perish, and government action is unable to alter this "natural" process.

Social Security Act of 1935 Act establishing federal old-age pensions and unemployment insurance.

Sons of Liberty Secret organizations in the colonies formed to oppose the Stamp Act.

Southern Christian Leadership Conference (SCLC) Black civil rights organization founded in 1957 by Martin Luther King Jr., and other clergy.

Southern Farmers' Alliance The largest of several organizations that formed in the post-Reconstruction South to advance the interests of beleaguered small farmers.

Southern Manifesto A document signed by 101 members of Congress from Southern states in 1956 that argued that the Supreme Court's decision in *Brown* v. *Board of Education of Topeka* itself contradicted the Constitution.

Specie Circular Proclamation issued by President Andrew Jackson in 1836 stipulating that only gold or silver could be used as payment for public land.

Stamp Act Law passed by Parliament in 1765 to raise revenue in America by requiring taxed, stamped paper for legal documents, publications, and playing cards.

States' Rights Favoring the rights of individual states over rights claimed by the national government.

Stono Rebellion One of the largest and most violent slave uprisings during the Colonial Period that occurred in Stono, South Carolina.

Strategic Arms Limitation Treaty Treaty signed in 1972 by the United States and the Soviet Union to slow the nuclear arms race.

Strategic Defense Initiative (SDI) President Reagan's program, announced in 1983, to defend the United States against nuclear missile attack with untested weapons systems and sophisticated technologies.

Student Nonviolent Coordinating Committee (SNCC) Black civil rights organization founded in 1960 and drawing heavily on younger activists and college students.

Students for a Democratic Society (SDS) The leading student organization of the New Left of the early and mid-1960s.

Suffrage The right to vote in a political election.

Sugar Act Law passed in 1764 to raise revenue in the American colonies. It lowered the duty from 6 pence to 3 pence per gallon on foreign molasses imported into the colonies and increased the restrictions on colonial commerce.

Sunbelt The states of the American South and Southwest.

Taft-Hartley Act Federal legislation of 1947 that substantially limited the tools available to labor unions in labor-management disputes.

Tammany Society A fraternal organization of artisans begun in the 1780s that evolved into a key organization of the new mass politics in New York City.

Tariff of 1816 A tax imposed by Congress on imported goods.

Tea Act Act of Parliament that permitted the East India Company to sell through agents in America without paying the duty customarily collected in Britain, thus reducing the retail price.

Tejanos Persons of Spanish or Mexican descent born in Texas.

Temperance Reform movement originating in the 1820s that sought to eliminate the consumption of alcohol.

Temperance groups Groups dedicated to reducing the sale and consumption of alcohol.

Tenements Four- to six-story residential dwellings, once common in New York, built on tiny lots without regard to providing ventilation or light.

Tennessee Valley Authority (TVA) Federal regional planning agency established to promote conservation, produce electric power, and encourage economic development in seven Southern states.

Tenure of Office Act Act stipulating that any officeholder appointed by the president with the Senate's advice and consent could not be removed until the Senate had approved a successor.

Thirteenth Amendment Constitutional amendment ratified in 1865 that freed all slaves throughout the United States.

Tories A derisive term applied to Loyalists in America who supported the king and Parliament just before and during the American Revolution.

Townshend Revenue Acts   Act of Parliament, passed in 1767, imposing duties on colonial tea, lead, paint, paper, and glass.

Trail of Broken Treaties   1972 event staged by the American Indian Movement (AIM) that culminated in a week-long occupation of the Bureau of Indian Affairs in Washington, D.C.

Trail of Tears   The forced march in 1838 of the Cherokee Indians from their homelands in Georgia to the Indian Territory in the West.

Treaty of Fort Laramie   The treaty acknowledging U.S. defeat in the Great Sioux War in 1868 and supposedly guaranteeing the Sioux perpetual land and hunting rights in South Dakota, Wyoming, and Montana.

Treaty of Ghent   Treaty signed in December 1814 between the United States and Britain that ended the War of 1812.

Treaty of Greenville   Treaty of 1795 in which Native Americans in the Old Northwest were forced to cede most of the present state of Ohio to the United States.

Treaty of Paris   The formal end to British hostilities against France and Spain in February 1763.

Truman Doctrine   President Harry Truman's statement in 1947 that the United States should assist other nations that were facing external pressure or internal revolution.

Underwood-Simmons Act of 1913   Reform law that lowered tariff rates and levied the first regular federal income tax.

Union League   Republican party organizations in Northern cities that became an important organizing device among freedmen in Southern cities after 1865.

USA Patriot Act   Federal legislation adopted in 2001 in response to the terrorist attacks on September 11 to facilitate anti-terror actions by federal law enforcement and intelligence agencies.

Versailles Treaty   The treaty ending World War I and creating the League of Nations.

Vertical integration   The consolidation of numerous production functions, from the extraction of the raw materials to the distribution and marketing of the finished products, under the direction of one firm.

Virginia Company   A group of London investors who sent ships to Chesapeake Bay in 1607.

Virginia Plan   Proposal calling for a national legislature in which the states would be represented according to population.

Virtual representation   The notion that parliamentary members represented the interests of the nation as a whole, not those of the particular district that elected them.

Volstead Act   The 1920 law defining the liquor forbidden under the Eighteenth Amendment and giving enforcement responsibilities to the Prohibition Bureau of the Department of the Treasury.

Voting Rights Act   Legislation in 1965 that overturned a variety of practices by which states systematically denied voter registration to minorities.

War Democrats   Those from the North and the border states who broke with the Democratic Party and supported the Abraham Lincoln's military policies during the Civil War.

War Hawks   Members of Congress, predominantly from the South and West, who aggressively pushed for a war against Britain after their election in 1810.

War Industries Board (WIB)   The federal agency that reorganized industry for maximum efficiency and productivity during World War I.

War of 1812   War fought between the United States and Britain from June 1812 to January 1815 largely over British restrictions on American shipping.

War on Drugs   A paramilitary operation to halt drug trafficking in the United States.

War on Poverty   Set of programs introduced by Lyndon Johnson between 1963 and 1966 designed to break the cycle of poverty by providing funds for job training, community development, nutrition, and supplementary education.

War Powers Act   Gave the U.S. president the power to reorganize the federal government and create new agencies; to establish programs censoring news, information, and abridging civil liberties; to seize foreign-owned property; and award government contracts without bidding.

Watergate   A complex scandal involving attempts to cover up illegal actions taken by administration officials and leading to the resignation of President Richard Nixon in 1974.

Welfare capitalism   A paternalistic system of labor relations emphasizing management responsibility for employee well-being.

Welfare Reform Act   Act passed by Congress in 1996 that abolished the Aids to Families with Dependent Children (AFDC) welfare program.

Whigs   The name used by advocates of colonial resistance to British measures during the 1760s and 1770s.

Whiskey Rebellion   Armed uprising in 1794 by farmers in western Pennsylvania who attempted to prevent the collection of the excise tax on whiskey.

Wilmot Proviso   The amendment offered by Pennsylvania Democrat David Wilmot in 1846 which stipulated that "as an express and fundamental condition to the acquisition of any territory from the Republic of Mexico ... neither slavery nor involuntary servitude shall ever exist in any part of said territory."

Wobblies   Popular name for the members of the Industrial Workers of the World (IWW).

Woman's Christian Temperance Union (WCTU)   Women's organization whose members visited schools to educate children about the evils of alcohol, addressed prisoners, and blanketed men's meetings with literature.

Women's Educational and Industrial Union   Boston organization offering classes to wage-earning women.

World Trade Organization (WTO)   International organization that sets standards and practices for global trade, and the focus of international protests over world economic policy in the late 1990s.

XYZ Affair   Diplomatic incident in 1798 in which Americans were outraged by the demand of the French for a bribe as a condition for negotiating with American diplomats.

Yalta Conference   Meeting of U.S. President Franklin Roosevelt, British Prime Minister Winston Churchill, and Soviet Premier Joseph Stalin held in February 1945 to plan the final stages of World War II and postwar arrangements.

Yeoman   Independent farmers of the South, most of whom lived on family-sized farms.

Text, Tables, Maps and Figures

Chapter 4   Figure 4.1: Reproduced from *The American Colonies: From Settlement to Independence.* Copyright © R.C. Simmons 1976 by permission of PFD (www.pfd.co.uk) on behalf of Professor Richard Simmons. **Figure 4.2:** from TIME ON THE CROSS: THE ECONOMICS OF AMERICAN NEGRO SLAVERY by Robert William Fogel and Stanley L. Engerman. Copyright © 1974 by Robert William Fogel and Stanley L. Engerman. Used by permission of W.W. Norton & Company, Inc.

Chapter 8   Figure 8.1: Used by permission of American Antiquarian Society.

Chapter 9   Figure 9.2: from AMERICA MOVES WEST 5/E by Riegel R. 1971. Reprinted with permission of Wadsworth, a division of Thomson Learning: www.thomsonrights.com. Fax 800 730-2215.

Chapter 11   Figure 11.1: From RIGHT TO VOTE by ALEXANDER KEYSSAR. Reprinted by permission of BASIC BOOKS, a member of Perseus Books Group.

Chapter 12   Figure 12.1: Reprinted from Thomas Dublin: *Transforming Women's Work: New England Lives in the Industrial Revolution.* Copyright © 1994 by Thomas Dublin. Used by permission of the publisher, Cornell University Press.

Chapter 13   Figure 13.1: Reprinted by permission of the estate of Robert Ernst. **Figure 13.2:** From THE ALCOHOLIC REPUBLIC: AN AMERICAN TRADITION by W.J. Rarabaugh, copyright © 1979 by Oxford University Press, Inc. Used by permission of Oxford University Press, Inc. **Map 13.2:** Reprinted from Whitney R. Cross, *The Burned-Over District: The Social and Intellectual History of Enthusiastic Religion in Western New York 1800–1850.* Copyright © 1950 by Cornell University. Used with permission of the publisher, Cornell University Press.

Chapter 14   Figure 14.1: From *The Plains Across: The Overland Emigrants and the Trans-Mississippi West, 1840–60.* Copyright 1979 by the Board of Trustees of the University of Illinois. Used with permission of the University of Illinois Press. **Map 14.7:** From *Historical Atlas of California*, by Warren A. Beck and Ynez D. Haase. Copyright © 1974 by The University of Oklahoma Press, Norman. Reprinted by permission of the publisher. All rights reserved.

Chapter 18   Map 18.1: From *Historical Atlas of Oklahoma, 3rd edition*, by John W. Morris, Charles R. Goins and Edwin C. McReynolds. Copyright © 1965, 1976, 1986 by the University of Oklahoma Press, Norman. Reprinted by permission of the publisher. All rights reserved. **Map 18.4:** "The Geography of the American West, 1847–1964", Donald W. Meinig from *ANNA: Annals of the Association of American Geographers*, vol. 55, issue 2. Reprinted by permission of Blackwell Publishers. www.blackwell-synergy.com

Chapter 19   Table 19.1: From THE GILDED AGE edited by Charles W. Calhoun. © 1996. Reprinted by permission of Rowman & Littlefield. **Map 19.2:** From *Historical Atlas of the United States*, 1st edition by LORD. © 1962. Reprinted with permission of Wadsworth, a division of Thomson Learning: www.thomsonrights.com. Fax: 800 730-2215.

Chapter 22   Map 22.3: From *ATLAS OF AMERICAN WOMEN*, by Barbara C. Shortridge. © 1987. Reprinted by permission of Thomson Learning: www.thomsonrights.com. Fax 800 730-2215.

Chapter 28   Page 821: Reprinted by arrangement with the Estate of Martin Luther King Jr., c/o Writers House for the proprietor New York, NY. *Copyright 1963 Martin Luther King, Jr., copyright renewed 1991 Coretta Scott King.*

Chapter 29   Figure 29.4: From THE GALLUP POLL, 1835–1971 by George Gallup, Copyright © 1972 by the American Institute of Public Opinion. Used by permission of Random House.

Chapter 1 Image Key: **Page xlviii:** A. Cahokia Mounds State Historic Site, painting by Michael Hampshire; **Page 1:** B. Service Historique de la Marine, Vincennes, France/Lauros/Giraudon/Bridgeman Art Library; C. Service Historique de la Marine, Vincennes, France/Lauros/Giraudon/Bridgeman Art Library; D. Courtesy of the Denver Museum of Nature and Science; E. David Hiser/David Hiser Photography; F. Rota/Neg. No. 324281, Photographed by Rota, Engraving by DeBry. American Museum of Natural History Library; **Page xlviii:** G. © Warren Morgan/CORBIS; **Page 3:** James Chatters/James Chatters/Agence France Presse/Getty Images; **Page 5:** © Warren Morgan/CORBIS; **Page 11:** David Muench/CORBIS-NY; **Page 12:** Tony Linck/SuperStock, Inc; George Gerster/Photo Researchers, Inc.; **Page 15:** Bayerische Staatsbibliothek Munchen. Rar. 5k; **Page 20:** Courtesy of the Library of Congress.

Chapter 2 Image Key: **Page 24:** A. © Hulton-Deutsch Collection/CORBIS; Image in lower left; Stapleton Collection/© Stapleton Collection/CORBIS; **Page 25:** C. Robert Frerck/© Robert Frerck/Odyssey/Chicago; D. Getty Images Inc. - Hulton Archive Photos; E. Library of Congress; F. The Granger Collection; Image in lower right; Stapleton Collection/© Stapleton Collection/CORBIS; **Page 28:** October, from Tres Riches Heures du Duc de Berry. Musee Conde, Chantilly/Bridgeman-Giraudon, Art Resource, NY; **Page 31:** Beinecke Rare Book and Manuscript Library, Yale University; **Page 33:** Photo Courtesy of the Edward E. Ayer Collection, The Newberry Library, Chicago; **Page 34:** The Granger Collection; **Page 41:** John White (1570–93), "Woman and Child of Pomeiooc." Watercolor. British Museum, London. The Bridgeman Art Library International Ltd.

Chapter 3 Image Key: **Page 46:** A. Dorling Kindersley/© Dorling Kindersley; B. Beinecke Rare Book and Manuscript Library, Yale University; C. Getty Images, Inc. - Photodisc; **Page 47:** D. Bettmann/© Bettmann/CORBIS; E. Courtesy of Pilgrim Hall Museum, Plymouth, Massachusetts; F. © Bettmann/CORBIS; G. Jonathan Carver, A TREATISE ON THE CULTURE OF THE TOBACCO PLANT (London, 1779), Manuscripts and Rare Book Division, Swem Library, College of William and Mary; H. Courtesy, American Antiquarian Society; I. New Amsterdam, 1650-53. The Hague Facsimile. Museum of the City of New York. The J. Clarence Davies Collection 34.100.29; J. Courtesy of the John Carter Brown Library at Brown University; **Page 49:** Kevin Fleming/Corbis/Bettmann; **Page 51:** Courtesy of the Library of Congress; **Page 52:** From Samuel de Champlain, Les Voyages, Paris, 1613. Illustration opp. pg. 232. Rare Books Division, The New York Public Library, Astor Lenox and Tilden Foundations. The New York Public Library/Art Resource, NY; **Page 53:** Getty Images Inc. - Hulton Archive Photos; **Page 55:** The Granger Collection; **Page 58:** Courtesy, American Antiquarian Society; **Page 60:** Courtesy of The John Carter Brown Library, at Brown University; **Page 63:** Courtesy of The Historical Society of Pennsylvania Collection, Atwater Kent Museum of Philadelphia; **Page 65:** Courtesy of the John Carter Brown Library at Brown University; **Page 70:** Courtesy of the Pilgrim Hall Museum, Plymouth, Massachusetts; **Page 71:** Eliot Elisofon/Getty Images/Time Life Pictures.

Chapter 4 Image Key: **Page 72:** A. Courtesy of The John Carter Brown Library, at Brown University; B. Courtesy of the Library of Congress; **Page 73:** C. Dorling Kindersley/© Dorling Kindersley, Courtesy of the Wilberforce House Museum, Hull; D. British Library; E. Courtesy, American Antiquarian Society; F. John F. Watson, "Annals of Philadelphia," being a collection of memoirs, anecdotes, & incidents of Philadelphia. The London Coffee House. The Library Company of Philadelphia; G. Abby Aldrich Rockefeller Folk Art Museum, Colonial Williamsburg Foundation, VA; H. Samuel Scott (c. 1702–1772) "Old East India Wharf at London Bridge" (CT2825) © Victoria & Albert Museum, London/Art Resource, NY; **Page 75:** Library of Congress; **Page 76:** Beinecke Rare Book and Manuscript Library, Yale University; **Page 80:** Bibliotheque de L'Arsenal, Paris, France/The Bridgeman Art Library; **Page 81:** (top left) The Granger Collection, New York; (bottom right) The Granger Collection, New York; **Page 87:** Courtesy of the Massachusetts Historical Society, Boston. **Page 97:** Virginia Historical Society, Richmond, Virginia.

Chapter 5 Image Key: **Page 100:** A. Liz McAulay/Liz McAulay © Dorling Kindersley, Courtesy of the Worthing Museum and Art Gallery; B. MARK SEXTON/The Granger Collection; C. David Murray/David Murray © Dorling Kindersley; D. Frank Greenaway/Frank Greenaway © Dorling Kindersley, Courtesy of the Natural History Museum, London; E. © Judith Miller/Dorling Kindersley/Sara Covelli; **Page 101:** G. © National Maritime Museum, London; H. Library of Congress; I. North Wind Picture Archives; J. John Wollaston, "George Whitefield," ca. 1770. National Portrait Gallery, London; **Page 106:** Laurie Platt Winfrey, Inc.; **Page 107:** Jack W. Dykinga/Jack Dykinga Photography; **Page 109:** EROS Data Center, U.S. Geological Survey; **Page 111:** Beinecke Rare Book and Manuscript Library, Yale University; **Page 114:** (left) The Granger Collection; (right) The Granger Collection; **Page 118:** "Human Races (Las Castas)", 18th century, oil on canvas, 1.04 × 1.48 m. Museo Nacional del Virreinato, Tepotzotlan, Mexico. Schalkwijk/Art Resource, NY.

Chapter 6 Image Key: **Page 126:** A. (top/bottom left) Getty Images, Inc.; B. Steve Gorton/Steve Gorton © Dorling Kindersley; **Page 127:** A. (top/bottom right) Dave King/Dave King © Dorling Kindersley; C. The Granger Collection, New York; **Page 127:** D. Colonial Williamsburg Foundation; E. © Judith Miller/Dorling Kindersley/Sloan's; F. Library of Congress; G. © Christie's Images Inc. 2004; H. © Bettmann/CORBIS; I. Joseph Sohm/© Joseph Sohm; Visions of America/CORBIS; **Page 134:** National Museum of the American Indian/Smithsonian Institution; **Page 136:** Art Resource/The New York Public Library; **Page 141:** Library of Congress; **Page 143:** © Christie's Images Inc. 2004; **Page 145:** National Archives and Records Administration; **Page 147:** The New York Public Library, Prints Division, Stokes Collection; **Page 149:** The Granger Collection; **Page 150:** The Granger Collection.

Chapter 7 Image Key: **Page 154:** A. Courtesy of the Library of Congress; B. Getty Images Inc. - Hulton Archive Photos; C. © CORBIS; **Page 155:** D. DAVID BOHL/Photograph courtesy of the Concord Museum, Concord, MA and the archives of the Lexington Historical Society, Lexington, MA Photograph by David Bohl; E. Anne S.K. Brown Military Collection, John Hay Library, Brown University; F. Benjamin West, 1783 "American Commissioners of Preliminary Negotiations". Courtesy, Winterthur Museum; G. Corbis/Bettmann; **Page 154:** H. Art Resource/Yale University Art Gallery/John Trumbull (American 1756–1843), "The Surrender of Lord Cornwallis at Yorktown, 19 October 1781", 1787-c. 1828. Oil on canvas, 53.3 × 77.8 × 1.9 cm (21 × 30 5/8 × 3/4 in.) Art Resource; **Page 157:** Anne S.K. Brown Military Collection, John Hay Library, Brown University; **Page 158:** The Granger Collection; **Page 162:** Gilbert Stuart, "The Mohawk Chief Joseph Brant," 1786. Oil on canvas, 30 × 25 in. Fenimore Art Museum, Cooperstown, New York; **Page 167:** The Granger Collection, New York; **Page 169:** Library of Congress; **Page 172:** © CORBIS; **Page 176:** Corbis/Bettmann; **Page 177:** © Bettmann/CORBIS.

Chapter 8 Image Key: **Page 180:** A. Library of Congress; B. Courtesy of The Historical Society of Pennsylvania Collection, Atwater Kent Museum of Philadelphia; C. © Bettmann/CORBIS; **Page 181:** D. Gallery of the Republic; E. Getty Images Inc. - Hulton Archive Photos; F. Francis Kemmelmeyer, "General George Washington Reviewing the Western Army at Fort Cumberland the 18th of October 1794," after 1794. Oil on paper backed with linen, 18 1/8 × 23 1/8. Courtesy of Winterthur Museum; G. "White House Historical Association (White House Collection)" (25); H. The Library Company of Philadelphia; **Page 185:** Print and Picture Collection, The Free Library of Philadelphia; **Page 189:** (left) Smithsonian Institution, NNC, Douglas Mudd; (right) Smithsonian Institution, NNC, Douglas